INDIVIDUAL EMPLOYMENT LAW

SECOND EDITION

$50.00

grwrn Law

20 August 2009

Other books in the *Essentials of Canadian Law Series*

Intellectual Property Law

Income Tax Law

Immigration Law

International Trade Law

Family Law

Copyright Law

The Law of Equitable Remedies

Administrative Law

Ethics and Canadian Criminal Law

Public International Law

Environmental Law 2/e

Securities Law

Youth Criminal Justice Law

Computer Law 2/e

The Law of Partnerships and Corporations 2/e

Media Law 2/e

Maritime Law

Criminal Law 3/e

Insurance Law

International Human Rights Law

Legal Research and Writing 2/e

The Law of Trusts 2/e

Franchise Law

The Charter of Rights and Freedoms 3/e

Personal Property Security Law

The Law of Contracts

Pension Law

Constitutional Law 3/e

Legal Ethics and Professional Responsibility 2/e

Refugee Law

Mergers, Acquisitions, and Other Changes of Corporate Control

Bank and Customer Law in Canada

Statutory Interpretation 2/e

The Law of Torts 3/e

National Security Law: Canadian Practice in International Perspective

Remedies: The Law of Damages 2/e

Public International Law 2/e

The Law of Evidence 5/e

Criminal Procedure

ESSENTIALS OF
CANADIAN LAW

INDIVIDUAL EMPLOYMENT LAW

SECOND EDITION

GEOFFREY ENGLAND

Professor of Labour Law and Industrial Relations,
Edwards School of Business, and
College of Law, University of Saskatchewan

Individual Employment Law, second edition
© Irwin Law Inc., 2008

Published in 2008 by

Irwin Law Inc.
14 Duncan Street
Suite 206
Toronto, ON
M5H 3G8

www.irwinlaw.com

ISBN: 978-1-55221-155-7

Library and Archives Canada Cataloguing in Publication

England, Geoff
   Individual employment law — 2nd ed.

(Essentials of Canadian Law)
Includes bibliographical references and index.
ISBN 978-1-55221-155-7

1. Labour laws and legislation — Canada. 2. Employment rights — Canada.
I. Title II. Series

KE3247.E53 2008   344.71-01   C2008-904952-7
KF3457.E53 2008

The publisher acknowledges the financial support of the Government of Canada through the Book Publishing Industry Development Program (BPIDP) for its publishing activities.

We acknowledge the assistance of the OMDC Book Fund, an initiative of Ontario Media Development Corporation.

Printed and bound in Canada.

1 2 3 4 5   12 11 10 09 08

SUMMARY
TABLE OF CONTENTS

DETAILED
TABLE OF CONTENTS

CHAPTER 7:

HUMAN RIGHTS LEGISLATION IN THE WORKPLACE 213

PREFACE

The writing for this edition was completed in late May 2008. At the end of the editorial process — and, regrettably, too late to incorporate into this edition — the Supreme Court of Canada handed down its ruling in *Honda Canada Inc. v. Keays*.[1] This case is important in two respects. First, it holds that if an employee is dismissed in bad faith and suffers consequential psychological harm, compensation for such harm must be awarded under the usual principles of contract law regarding the award of damages, namely that such harm must be in the reasonable contemplation of the parties at the date the contract was made. Previously, the courts generally extended the period of reasonable notice of termination to account for bad faith dismissal under the *Wallace* doctrine, examined in Chapter 9 of this book. The Supreme Court's new ruling means that *Wallace* extensions can no longer be given in these circumstances. Second, the Supreme Court quashed the award of $100,000 in punitive damages ordered by the Ontario Court of Appeal. In so doing, the Supreme Court signalled that punitive damages should only be awarded in exceptional circumstances where the employer's conduct is flagrantly egregious. The reader is alerted, therefore, that the *Keays* decision significantly modifies Chapter 9 of this book in relation to *Wallace* extensions and compensation for wrongful dismissal.

---

1   2008 SCC 39.

This book is dedicated to Innis Christie

INTRODUCTION

Employment law is concerned with rules that govern the relations between employers and employees: Who creates the rules that govern
the job? How are such rules administered and enforced? And what is
the content of the rules? Clearly, this definition is extremely broad.
A worker's terms and conditions of employment are determined by a
combination of processes:

- negotiations with the employer that are incorporated as express
  terms of the employment contract;
- unilateral decisions by the employer that are given effect through the
  express or implied terms of the employment contract;
- customs and practices in the firm or industry that are given effect
  through the implied terms of the employment contract;
- court precedents on the meaning of standardized terms in the employment contract, such as "reasonable" notice of termination and
  "just cause" for summary dismissal; and
- legislation that fixes minimum labour standards. These standards
  include
  - substantive terms and conditions of employment (e.g., minimum
    wages, maximum hours of work, and minimum leaves of absence
    for designated purposes, such as childbirth or bereavement);
  - safeguards against arbitrary abuse by the employer of its man-
    agerial prerogatives (e.g., banning discrimination in hiring, pro-
    motion, and firing on proscribed grounds such as sex, race, and
    disability, and requiring discharge to be for just cause);

- means of providing employees with the right to participate with their employer as a group in determining designated issues (e.g., joint employer–employee labour adjustment committees in layoffs, and joint employer–employee health and safety committees);
- a safe physical environment in which to work (e.g., minimum health and safety standards) and compensation if the employee is injured at work (e.g., workers' compensation acts); and
- special administrative machinery for cheaply and expeditiously enforcing the statutory rights in question.

Employment law, however, is generally understood as excluding the process of negotiating and enforcing terms and conditions of employment under a collective agreement between an employer and a trade union. The latter process is generally regarded as being within the exclusive domain of "collective labour law" rather than "individual employment law."[1]

Indeed, the courts have held that the individual contract of employment disappears once a collective agreement comes into effect and the collective agreement becomes the sole source of the employee's terms and conditions of employment during its currency (save for legislation).[2]

Nevertheless, it must not be thought that all of the topics covered in this book are irrelevant to unionized organizations—far from it. The protective employment legislation examined in this book—labour standards acts, human rights statutes, and occupational health and safety acts—applies to the unionized as well as to the non-unionized sectors. Occasionally, trade unions will enforce claims under the statutory machinery because private arbitration is either unavailable or too slow and expensive in comparison. However, this occurs relatively infrequently, since the statutory enforcement machinery is sometimes much slower than private arbitration under a collective agreement (the human rights legislation is probably the worst offender in this regard). Moreover, in many provinces the authorities charged with enforcing statutory rights will defer to private arbitration under a collective agreement. In addition, trade unions may lobby governments to pass more generous employment legislation, partly out of social conscience and partly to free up more bargaining capital to be used to win concessions in other areas of the collective agreement. Of course, trade unions often temper their lobbying zeal because they know that the incentive for employees to

---

1   The leading text is G.W. Adams, *Canadian Labour Law*, 2d ed., looseleaf (Aurora, ON: Canada Law Book, 1993) [Adams].
2   Examples: *St. Anne Nackawic Pulp & Paper Co. Ltd. v. C.P.U. Local 219*, [1986] 1 S.C.R. 704; *C.A.I.M.A.W. v. Paccar of Canada Ltd.*, [1989] 2 S.C.R. 983.

become unionized diminishes as the scope of their legislated rights enlarges. Furthermore, the contract of employment remains the gateway into the collective agreement, for in our system of relatively free labour markets, even a unionized employer and its employees must voluntarily agree to create an employment relationship.[3]

This book, therefore, deals with the twin pillars of the employment law regime governing the non-unionized sector: the common law contract of employment and the protective employment legislation. Regarding the employment contract, the critical features of the law are as follows. The first is the application of the general principles of contract law to the contract of employment. These principles are designed to facilitate the operation of relatively free markets as the preferred means for distributing goods and services; hence the principle of "freedom of contract." While free contracting accurately describes the purchase of a used car, it does not accurately describe the nature of the employment relationship for the employer usually has vastly superior bargaining power in relation to most (but not all) employees. Consequently, there exists a chasm between the theory of employment contract law, namely that freedom of contract is being effectuated, and the reality of the law, namely that the employment contract provides employers with a vehicle to effectuate their real-world dominance over the employee. The *raison d'être* of the protective legislation examined in this book—and, indeed, of all employment law[4]—is to redress this imbalance of power. Moreover, we shall see that since the Second World War, many courts have attempted to ameliorate the worst effects of this power imbalance in their application of traditional contract law rules to the employment relationship.

The second critical feature of employment contract law is that even such rights as the employee does enjoy under the employment contract are frequently unobtainable in practice because the high cost of civil litigation is beyond the pocket of many low- and middle-level employees. This explains why most of the reported cases on wrongful dismissal involve relatively senior managers, professionals, and technicians. For employees in less lofty positions, the protective legislation provides the only means for securing their employment rights.

---

3   For example, the rules of forming an employment contract were critically important to the collective agreement dispute before arbitrator Innis Christie in *Saint John Fire Fighters' Assn., Local Union No. 771 v. Saint John (City) [Davidson Grievance]*, [2003] N.B.L.A.A. No. 4 at 23–26.

4   See the seminal analysis by O. Kahn-Freund, *Labour and the Law*, 2d ed. (London: Stevens and Sons, 1977), especially c. 1: "Some Reflections on Law and Power."

The third key feature of employment contract law is that the courts are continually refashioning the rules in order to reflect changing economic and political conditions. This phenomenon is well known in all areas of the common law, and the employment contract is no exception. The crucial point with employment law, however, is that the economic and political environment is changing in dramatic ways and at breakneck speed. Between 1945 and the early 1980s, the economic climate for Canada's major industries was extremely favourable. Canadian manufacturers of textiles, foodstuffs, and relatively unsophisticated machinery and equipment faced relatively little competition from countries with a comparative advantage in labour costs, and could therefore operate profitably while paying their employees relatively generous wages and benefits. These conditions made possible the seemingly endless (at the time) conferral of greater rights on employees under legislation and by judicial reformulations of contract law doctrines, such as reasonable notice of termination. Simultaneously, this period saw an upswing in the popularity of the "rights" movement in all walks of life, especially in employment. The *Canadian Charter of Rights and Freedoms*[5] and the provincial human rights legislation represent the apogee of this movement.

The growth of the emerging economies in the last fifteen or so years, however, has changed this picture, and increasingly intense competition is now pressuring Canadian employers to minimize their labour costs. Other factors contributing to the quest for increasing economic efficiency are the globalization of trade in machinery, services, capital, and (to a lesser extent) labour; technological advances; and the spread of free trade as symbolized in the *North American Free Trade Agreement* between Canada, Mexico, and the United States.[6] Few would regard these developments as undesirable—only an intellectual ostrich would assume that the state of world development either can or should be frozen in time as of the 1945–75 period; it simply means that the law of the employment contract, along with employment protection legislation, must readjust to suit the new conditions.

---

5   Part I of the *Constitution Act, 1982*, being Schedule B to the *Canada Act 1982* (U.K.), 1982, c. 11 [*Charter*].

6   For an overview of these factors, see H.W. Arthurs, *The New Economy and the Demise of Industrial Citizenship* (Kingston, ON: IRC Press, 1997). See also Canada, Commission on the Review of Federal Labour Standards, *Fairness at Work: Federal Labour Standards for the 21st Century* by H.W. Arthurs (Ottawa: Commission on the Review of Federal Labour Standards, 2006) cc. 2, 10, and 11 [*Arthurs Report*].

We shall see how the pressure on Canadian employers to become more competitive has occasioned some courts to reformulate many of the rules of the employment contract in order to reduce employers' labour costs, not to advance employee rights. One of the best examples is the practice of some courts (as yet a minority) to reduce the period of reasonable notice of termination that an employer must give when laying off its employees.[7] Moreover, the federal and provincial governments do not appear to be as aggressive today as they previously were in legislating expanded employment rights for employees. As yet, there has been no widespread movement to rescind existing statutory benefits, but this trend could change. The burning question in contemporary employment law is to what extent the familiar trend in favour of enlarging employee rights will be reversed.

In addressing this issue, the courts and legislators must remain cognizant of the risks associated with unduly curtailing employee rights. First, it is widely recognized that providing employees with a relatively generous "floor of rights" increases their productivity by enhancing their job satisfaction and degree of commitment to the firm. The central problem for the employer in any employment relationship is to induce the employee to commit voluntarily to going the extra mile in pursuit of the firm's interests. Disciplinary sanctions are a poor second best to voluntary cooperation when it comes to getting the most out of an employee's labours.[8] Second, at the societal level, it is a truism that the high degree of social cohesion and stability that results from relatively generous employment rights is a necessary foundation for a productive economy.[9] The pursuit of profitability and the advancement of rights, therefore, are not necessarily contradictory. Clearly, the courts and legislators must find a delicate point of balance between employee rights and employer profitability.

Regarding the protective employment legislation, there is an expansive body of statutory rights for employees in all Canadian jurisdictions. These statutes are commonly referred to as establishing the employee's floor of rights because the benefits they provide cannot be reduced by private bargaining in the individual employment contract,

---

7   This matter is examined in Chapter 5.

8   See generally P. Blyton & P. Turnbull, *The Dynamics of Employee Relations* (Basingstoke, UK: Macmillan Press, 1998) at 85–95.

9   See, for example, F. Wilkinson, "Equality, Efficiency and Economic Progress: The Case for Universally Applied Equitable Standards for Wages and Conditions of Work" in W. Sengenberger & D.C. Campbell, eds., *Creating Economic Opportunities: The Role of Labour Standards in Industrial Restructuring* (Geneva: International Institute for Labour Studies, 1994) 422.

but can only be enlarged upon.[10] Although an enormous number of statutes comprise this floor of rights, in this introductory book attention is focused on the following particularly important ones: labour standards acts, industrial standards acts, human rights acts, privacy acts, pay equity acts, occupational health and safety acts, and workers' compensation acts. This legislation is designed to redress to some degree the disequilibrium of bargaining power between the employer and the employee, and to provide the employee with an expeditious and affordable means of enforcing his or her rights. Unfortunately, we shall see that non-compliance with the protective legislation on the part of employers remains a pervasive problem. Also, the forces of the "new economy" described above will continue to pressure governments to refrain from expanding, and possibly even to rescind, the statutory floor of rights. Again, it remains uncertain how legislators will respond to this pressure. The fact that jurisdiction over employment relations in Canada rests with the provincial governments[11] may facilitate the process of cutting back on legislated rights. This devolution of authority permitted individual provinces to experiment with innovative expansions of the statutory floor in the halcyon days of post-war prosperity. Nova Scotia, for instance, was the trailblazer in legislating protection against "unjust dismissal" for non-unionized workers in 1975.[12] Yet, by the same token, it permits individual provinces to experiment with rescinding particular protections in order to help employers reduce their labour costs.[13]

Chapter 2 of this book examines the threshold definitional question of what constitutes an "employment" relationship, as distinct from a "commercial" relationship in which a "non-employee" sells his or her labour to a client. This question is of critical importance, since

---

10 The employment standards acts commonly contain express provisions to this effect, for example, Alberta *Employment Standards Code*, R.S.A. 2000, c. E-9, ss. 3(1) & 4.

11 *Toronto Electric Commissioners v. Snider*, [1925] A.C. 396 (P.C.). In order to leave more space for the examination of the substance employment law, this book does not deal with the constitutional division of authority over employment relations. See generally, on the constitutional issue in the context of labour relations, Adams, above note 1, c. 3.

12 Nova Scotia *Labour Standards Code*, R.S.N.S. 1989, c. 246, s. 71, introduced by S.N.S. 1975, c. 50, s. 4, and subsequently adopted in the federal jurisdiction and Quebec. See Chapter 9, Section E.

13 Indeed, the Conservative government of Mike Harris in Ontario in the late 1990s initiated this process with its collective bargaining legislation. See H.C. Jain & S. Muthu, "Ontario Labour Law Reforms: A Comparative Study of Bill 40 and Bill 7" (1996) 4 Can. Lab. & Emp. L.J. 311.

"employee" status is the gateway into most protective employment statutes, as well as into the protections available under the contract of employment, such as the entitlement to reasonable notice of termination and just cause in summary dismissal. Today, many employers are attempting to restructure their relationship with their workers from "employee" to "independent contractor" status, as well as outsourcing their operations to non-employee outsiders, in order to avoid the costs of providing these protections.[14]

Chapter 3 examines the process by which an employment contract is formed and modified. The general principles of contract law play an important role in this regard, but legislation also safeguards the employee against abuse—in the case of children's employment contracts, for example. The human rights legislation is especially important in preventing discrimination at the hiring stage. However, because this legislation is critically important throughout the employment relationship, it is dealt with in a chapter of its own, Chapter 7. This latter chapter also examines the safeguards against sexual harassment in the workplace.

In Chapters 4 and 5, we examine the express and implied obligations of, respectively, the employee and the employer under the common law of the employment contract. The first main point here is that the courts have developed a standardized set of obligations that are implied into all employment contracts across the board, based largely on the judges' perception of what an "ideal" employment relationship should resemble. These implied obligations can be regarded as a form of "status" for employees, in the sense that they are created by a third party rather than derived from the party's own bargaining. Second, the implied obligations owed by the employee to the employer are considerably more extensive than those owed by the employer to its employees. The courts have provided employers with a comprehensive body of legal rights to secure employees' compliance with the employer's rule-making power in the workplace.

Chapter 6 analyzes the legislated floor of rights, with particular attention to employment standards acts, equal pay acts, privacy acts, industrial standards acts, occupational health and safety acts, and workers' compensation acts. Attention is focused not only on the substantive benefits provided by the legislation, but also on the legal and practical difficulties of enforcing it.

As noted above, the crucially important human rights legislation is examined in Chapter 7. The duty of reasonable accommodation im-

---

14   See generally Arthurs Report, above note 6, cc. 4 and 10.

posed under the human rights acts is particularly significant because it empowers human rights tribunals to evaluate whether or not an employer has made reasonable attempts to accommodate an employee's interests up to the point of causing the firm "undue hardship." This power takes the tribunal to the very heart of traditional managerial prerogatives in a way that the common law has never done. The effects of this breakthrough will almost certainly spill over into other areas of employment law, but it is not yet fully clear where this will occur.

Chapter 8 examines the difficulties that can arise from the multiplicity of forums when it comes to enforcing employment rights conferred by the various protective statutes and by the common law. For example, can an employee who wishes to sue for wrongful dismissal at common law claim as part of his or her action benefits allegedly due under an employment standards act, or must the employee file a separate claim for such benefits under the machinery provided in the act itself? And if an employee does commence proceedings in one forum, will that preclude him or her from subsequently launching a complaint in another forum? Many of these difficulties could be avoided if each province had a single labour court charged with enforcing claims under all protective statutes and the common law.

Finally, Chapter 9 deals with the massive topic of termination of employment. The common law is examined as it relates to how much notice of termination must be given; when summary dismissal for misconduct or incompetence is justifiable; when an employee can quit in response to objectionable conduct on the employer's part and sue for damages (the "constructive dismissal" situation); when an employment contract is brought to an end by operation of the doctrine of frustration of contract; and what remedies are available for wrongful dismissal. In addition, this chapter examines statutory interventions on the employer's power to dismiss, including the obligation to give minimum notice and severance pay; the obligation to consult with joint management–employee committees in mass layoff situations; and the "unjust discharge" schemes in the federal jurisdiction, Quebec, and Nova Scotia. This area of employment law, too, is in the balance. The dominant trend since the 1950s of expanding the rights of employees in termination situations is now being challenged by the need to reduce the costs to employers of terminating employees. In particular, it is often argued that providing overly generous severance entitlements discourages employers from hiring new employees, which is unfair to persons who are currently unemployed.

How, then, can we evaluate this huge body of employment law? Answering this question is unavoidably coloured by the ideological perspective of the inquirer. For those with a "unitary" perspective of the employment relationship, in which the interests of employees are deemed irrelevant and primacy is accorded to the goal of maximizing the firm's productive efficiency and profitability, legal intervention that puts employee interests first is always problematic. For those with Marxist or radical feminist perspectives, legal protections of employee rights can also be problematic since they are often regarded as mere window dressing designed to cloak underlying class or gender oppression by employers, thereby preserving the latter's dominance. To those with a pluralistic perspective, balancing conflicting interests so that everyone gets a decent share of the pie is not problematic; however, pluralists often disagree on the size of each party's proper share and on how shares are determined.[15] Nevertheless, there seem to be nine useful yardsticks for measuring the success or failure of our system of employment law.

1) *Ensuring that the employee is treated fairly and decently in all aspects of the employment relationship:* This right can be regarded as intrinsically valuable, in the sense that protecting the employee's personal autonomy and dignity is a fundamental human right,[16] or it can be regarded as instrumentally valuable, in the sense that a satisfied workforce is likely to be more productive and stable than a dissatisfied one. Although the specific content of the right is debatable, at the least it includes providing sufficient economic benefits to enable the employee to enjoy the fruits of civic life, providing a fair balance between leisure and working time, respecting the employee's physical and psychological integrity, and making decisions that significantly affect the employee in a procedurally fair manner.

2) *Ensuring that the productive efficiency and profitability of employers is not unduly impaired by legal interventions:* As we saw earlier, there comes a point at which extending employee rights will impair pro-

---

15 The variants of these three basic ideologies are examined in J. Godard, *Industrial Relations, the Economy and Society*, 2d ed. (Concord, ON: Captus Press, 2003) at 11–19.

16 Various sources of this right have been expostulated. See, for example, J. Rawls, *Theory of Justice* (Cambridge: Belknap Press of Harvard University Press, 1971); "Encyclical Laborem Exercens addressed by the Supreme Pontiff John Paul II to the Sons and Daughters of the Church, and to all Men of Goodwill on Human Work on the Nineteenth Anniversary of Rerum Novarum" (Ottawa: Canadian Conference of Catholic Bishops, 1981); H. Collins, *Justice in Dismissal* (Oxford: Clarendon Press, 1992) at 16–20, who draws extensively from J. Raz, *The Morality of Freedom* (Oxford: Clarendon Press, 1986) at 369–73 and 417.

ductive efficiency and profitability, even though a satisfied workforce is likely to be more productive and stable than an unhappy one. The "new economy" has also intensified the competitive pressure on Canadian employers to increase their productive efficiency. Therefore, before extending employee rights, courts and legislators should be careful to understand the economic consequences.[17] The most controversial question, however, is who wins when the employer's right to enhance productive efficiency and profitability clashes with the employee's right to decency?[18] Answering this question puts to the acid test the inquirer's fundamental ideological perspective on employment relations.

3) *Respect for international labour standards:* Canada has ratified thirty International Labor Organization (ILO) conventions and under the 1998 ILO *Declaration on Fundamental Principles and Rights at Work* is obliged "to respect, to promote and to realize in good faith" even those Conventions that it has not formally ratified.[19] Canada has also committed itself to advancing eleven designated employee rights under the Labour Side Agreement of the *North America Free Trade Agreement*[20] (along with Mexico and the United States), and the United Nations *International Covenant on Civil and Political Rights* and *International Covenant on Economic, Social and Cultural Rights.* Although these obligations bind only the federal government—employment relations is within the jurisidction of the provinces, subject to some exceptions—the provinces clearly have a moral obligation to match the standards in question where it is economically feasible to do so. Moreover, ambigous provisions in employment protection acts are normally construed so as to comply with international law standards.

4) *Compliance with the* Charter of Rights and Freedoms *and respect for* Charter *values:*[21] The *Charter* applies directly to protective employ-

---

17   Thus, one of Canada's leading labour economists, Prof. Morley Gunderson, has recommended a cautious approach when considering extending new employment rights because of the potential damage to productive efficiency and profitability: M. Gunderson, *Social and Economic Impact of Labour Standards,* Executive Summary of a Report to the Federal Labour Standards Review Commission (Ottawa: Human Resources and Social Development Canada, 2005).

18   The answer to this question offered in the Arthurs Report is that the employee's right trumps: above note 6 at 47.

19   These Conventions are listed in the Arthurs Report, *ibid.* at 283–84.

20   *North American Free Trade Agreement Between the Government of Canada, the Government of Mexico and the Government of the United States,* 17 December 1992, Can. T.S. 1994 No. 2, 32 I.L.M. 289 (entered into force 1 January 1994) [NAFTA].

21   G. England, "The Impact of the Charter on Individual Employment Law in Canada: Rewriting an Old Story" (2006) 13 C.L.E.L.J. 1.

ment statutes. Thus, if the employment standards act violates a specific *Charter* right, such as the right to equality under section 15, the government would have to prove that the abridgement is justifiable in a free and democratic society under section 1 of the *Charter*. As we shall see in Chapter 6, there have been several important cases in which the courts have struck down offending provisions, and there may well be more to come. The *Charter* does not apply directly to the terms and conditions of an employment contract between a private sector employer and its employees, being concerned with relations between the state and its citizens. Nevertheless, it has had a significant indirect impact on private employment contracts, in that *Charter* values have helped form a climate favourable to employee interests, and many modern judges have refashioned the common law rules of employment to give increasing weight to those interests. Here, the term "*Charter* values" connotes general notions of fairness, equality, and proportionality in the treatment of vulnerable employees by their more powerful employers. The golden thread in the evolution of the common law of the employment contract is that judges are constantly remodelling the rules to reflect changes in standards of personnel management practice and in society's moral and economic vision of work relations. Nowhere is this more apparent than in the judicial refashioning of the standardized implied terms that delineate the default rights and obligations of the employer and the employee.[22] The main impetus to this development is the dissenting remarks of Dickson C.J. in the 1987 *Alberta Reference* case:[23] "Work is one of the most fundamental aspects in a person's life, providing the individual with a means of financial support and, as importantly, a contributory role in society. A person's employment is an essential component of his or her sense of identity, self-worth and emotional well-being."

The learned judge added that since the employee is usually vulnerable to the employer's superior bargaining power, employment protections are necessary to ensure the employee's fundamental human right to economic security, dignity, and respect. Chief Justice Dickson's remarks have profoundly influenced the way modern courts have applied the common law of the employment contract to provide employees with increasingly generous protections, and are

---

22   These are examined in Chapters 4 and 5 of this book.
23   *Reference Re Public Service Employee Relations Act (Alberta)*, [1987] 1 S.C.R. 313 at 368 [*Alberta Reference*].

now regularly cited by the Supreme Court of Canada as authoritative in this regard.[24]

5) *Nation-wide equality for all Canadian workers:* Even though employment relations is within the jurisdiction of the provinces — subject to relatively limited areas reserved for the federal government, such as banking, telecommunications, interprovincial transport, airlines, and railways[25] — every Canadian worker should be guaranteed certain fundamental employment rights, regardless of where he or she works. Accordingly, it should come as no surprise that the employment protection legislation is roughly similar in all jurisdictions of Canada. This does not mean that variances are illegitimate — far from it. Differing economic conditions in particular provinces clearly justify differences in the legislation, and it is desirable that one province should experiment with novel innovations so that other provinces can subsequently adopt them if they succeed, or disregard them if they fail. The most glaring gap in the current nation-wide safety net is that, despite the fact that no employment right can be more fundamental than not to be fired for misconduct or incompetence without just cause, only three jurisdictions have unjust discharge legislation.[26]

6) *Transparency of legal rights and obligations:* It is an axiom of the rule of law that employers and employees should know and understand their rights and obligations under the contract of employment and the protective legislation. Yet, we shall see that no province requires the employee to be given a written statement of the terms of his or her employment contract; the protective employment legislation is often incomprehensibly vague; the legislation is often poorly explained and communicated to the general public; and the legislation frequently gives government officials broad discretion to create exemptions and variances to general standards without any formal criteria delineating the scope of such discretion.

7) *Efficient enforcement mechanisms:* A body of substantive rights, no matter how generous, is only as good as the procedures for enforcing it. Because the costs of civil litigation to enforce rights under

---

24 Examples: *Slaight Communications Inc. v. Davidson* (1989), 59 D.L.R. (4d) 416 (S.C.C.); *Machtinger v. HOJ Industries Ltd.*, [1992] 1 S.C.R. 96; *Wallace v. United Grain Growers Ltd.* (1997), 97 C.L.L.C. ¶210-029 at 141,215 (S.C.C.); *Re Rizzo and Rizzo Shoes Ltd.*, [1998] 1 S.C.R. 27 at 35–36; *McKinley v. B.C. Tel*, [2001] C.L.L.C. ¶210-027 at 141,206 (S.C.C.).

25 *Toronto Electrical Commissioners v. Snider*, [1925] A.C. 396 (P.C.).

26 These are Quebec, Nova Scotia, and the federal jurisdiction, examined in Chapter 9, Section E(1).

the employment contract are beyond the reach of all but the richest employees, the protective employment legislation commonly establishes fast-track, cheap, and informal administrative machinery for enforcing statutory entitlements. Unfortunately, we shall see that these mechanisms too often do not operate efficiently, rendering the legislation of little practical use. Arguably, the worst culprit in this regard is the human rights legislation, with the equal pay acts coming in a close second. Furthermore, the multiplicity of statutes dealing with employment relations, alongside the contract of employment, creates a veritable patchwork quilt of overlapping legal forums that complicates and often impedes the efficient enforcement of employee rights.

8) *Compliance with the rule of law:* Employment law should strive for the best elements of "legalism" and against the worst. Among the best are judicial and administrative decision-making that is unbiased, procedurally fair, and in accordance with the laws of the land, and making laws that are certain and clear enough to enable the parties to know in advance the scope of their rights and obligations, but that are flexible enough to accommodate social and economic changes. Among the worst are nit-picking objections over procedural and other technical obscurities, tardiness in scheduling hearings, constant requests for adjournments, puffed-up formalism and legal jingoism during hearings, and a predilection for unnecesary appeals to the courts.

9) *Widespread acceptability:* Canada's employment laws should be acceptable to a substantial majority of employers, employees, and the general public. The level of acceptability of employment laws depends on the extent to which they measure up to the previously mentioned yardsticks.

When asked why people should bother to read history, the great English historian A.J.P. Taylor replied, "Because it is fun." The same goes for employment law; it is an area where the disciplines of law, economics, history, sociology, politics, and philosophy collide. If this does not titillate the reader's intellectual fancy, it is difficult to imagine what would.

FURTHER READINGS

ARTHURS, H.W., *The New Economy and the Demise of Industrial Citizenship* (Kingston, ON: IRC Press, 1997)

BROOK, P., *Freedom at Work: The Case for Reforming Labour Law in New Zealand* (Oxford: Oxford University Press, 1990)

CANADA, COMMISSION ON THE REVIEW OF FEDERAL LABOUR STANDARDS, *Fairness at Work: Federal Labour Standards for the 21st Century* by H.W. Arthurs (Ottawa: Commission on the Review of Federal Labour Standards, 2006)

COMPA, L., & S. DIAMOND, eds., *Human Rights, Labour Rights and International Trade* (Philadelphia: University of Pennsylvania Press, 1996)

DEAKIN, S., & F. WILLIAMSON, "Rights versus Efficiency? The Economic Case for Transnational Labour Standards" (1994) 23 Indus. L.J. 289

ENGLAND, G., "Recent Developments in the Law of the Employment Contract: Continuing Tension between the Rights Paradigm and the Efficiency Paradigm" (1995) 20 Queen's L.J. 557

ENGLAND, G., "The Impact of the Charter on Individual Employment Law in Canada: Rewriting an Old Story" (2006) 13 C.L.E.L.J. 1

ENGLAND, G., R. WOOD, & I. CHRISTIE, *Employment Law in Canada*, 4th ed., looseleaf (Markham, ON: LexisNexis Canada, 2005–) c. 1

EPSTEIN, R.A., "In Defence of the Contract at Will" (1984) 51 U. Chi. L. Rev. 947

FREEDLAND, M.R., The Personal Contract of Employment (Oxford: Oxford University Press, 2003)

GUNDERSON, M., "Harmonization of Labour Policies under Trade Liberalization" (1998) 53 Rel. Indus. 24

GUNDERSON, M., *Social and Economic Impact of Labour Standards, Executive Summary of a Report to the Federal Labour Standards Review Panel* (Ottawa: Human Resources and Social Development Canada, 2005)

GUNDERSON, M., & A. VERMA, "Canadian Labour Policies and Global Competition" (1992) 20 Can. Bus. L.J. 63

GUNDERSON, M., & C. RIDDELL, "Jobs, Labour Standards and Promoting Competitive Advantage: Canada's Policy Challenge" (1995) Labour 125

INTERNATIONAL LABOUR OFFICE, *The I.L.O. Standard Setting and Globalization: Report of the Director General* (Geneva: International Labour Office, 1997)

KAHN-FREUND, O., "Blackstone's Neglected Child: The Contract of Employment" (1977) 93 L.Q. Rev. 508

KAHN-FREUND, O., *Labour and the Law*, 2d ed. (London: Stevens, 1977) c. 1

KUHN, P., "Employment Protection Laws" (1993) 19 Can. Pub. Pol. 279

POSNER, R.A., "Some Economics of Labour Law" (1984) 51 U. Chi. L. Rev. 988

SENGENBERGER, W., & D.C. CAMPBELL, eds., *Creating Economic Opportunities: The Role of Labour Standards in Industrial Restructuring* (Geneva: International Institute for Labour Studies, 1994), especially WILKINSON, F., "Equality, Economic Efficiency and Economic Progress: The Case for Universally Applied Equitable Standards for Wages and Conditions of Work" 422

STENSLAND, J., "Internationalizing the North American Agreement on Labor Cooperation" (1995) 4 Minn. J. Global Trade 141

VETTEN, L., *International Labour Law: Selected Issues* (Deventer, Neth.: Kluwer, 1993)

IDENTIFYING A CONTRACT OF EMPLOYMENT: WHO IS AN "EMPLOYEE" AND WHO IS THE "EMPLOYER"?

This chapter first analyzes the definition of an "employment" relationship and then the determination of who the "employer" of an employee is.

A. STATUS AS AN "EMPLOYEE"

It is critically important to distinguish between working relationships based on an employment contract in which the worker is an "employee" and those based on a contract for services in which the worker is an "independent contractor."[1] The vast majority of protective employment statutes, including the labour standards legislation and important common-law–implied rights and obligations—such as the duty to give reasonable notice of termination—only apply to contracts of employment *stricto sensu*. Exceptionally, protective legislation may apply to workers who are not employees—for example, the human rights acts and the occupational health and safety acts. Moreover, the courts have implied into contracts for services some of the rights and duties that are usually found in employment contracts, such as the right not to be summarily fired without just cause. Generally speaking, however, the assumption

---

1   For detailed elaboration of this topic, see G. England, R. Wood, & I. Christie, *Employment Law in Canada*, 4th ed., looseleaf (Markham, ON: LexisNexis Canada, 2005–) c. 2 [*Employment Law in Canada*].

is that workers who are not employees must look to market forces to further their interests, rather than to legislation or the common law.

The legal status of employee is also important in other contexts not dealt with in this book. For example, under the *Income Tax Act*, workers who are employees are taxed on a higher scale than independent contractors who are running their own businesses. Under various social welfare statutes, such as the *Employment Insurance Act* and the *Canada Pension Plan*, employers of employees are required to keep records pertaining to them and to periodically remit contributions to the applicable bureaucracies. The common law actions available to a master to protect its employees against third-party interference, such as the action *per quod servitium amisit*[2] or the action for inducing breach of a contract of employment, only apply if the workers concerned are employees.[3] And under the common law doctrine of vicarious liability, an employer is liable for torts committed by its employees during the course of their employment. The caselaw arising in these contexts is clearly relevant in litigation concerning employee status under employment standards acts and in common law wrongful dismissal suits. However, it cannot be overemphasized that the term "employee" is normally interpreted in the "mischief"[4] sense to advance the policy goals of the particular statute or common law action in question.[5] Consequently, cases decided in other legal contexts with their own policy considerations are accorded relatively little weight outside that context.

---

2   *Genereux v. Peterson Howell & Heather (Canada) Ltd.* (1972), 34 D.L.R. (3d) 614 (Ont. C.A.).

3   Example: *Lumley v. Gye* (1853), 2 E. & B. 216, 118 E.R. 749 (Q.B.).

4   The "mischief rule" of interpretation is that the words of an instrument must be interpreted so as to achieve the purpose or objective that the instrument seeks to achieve. See R. Sullivan, *Sullivan and Driedger on the Construction of Statutes*, 4th ed. (Markham, ON: Butterworths, 2002) at 4 and 460.

5   Examples: *Ontario 671122 Ltd. v. Sagaz Industries Canada Inc.*, [2002] C.L.L.C. ¶210-013, especially at 141, 148–50 (S.C.C.), involving the common law doctrine of vicarious liability; *Pointe-Claire (City of) v. Quebec (Labour Court)*, [1997] 1 S.C.R. 1015 at 1047 [*Pointe-Claire*], involving the collective bargaining legislation; *Hokanson v. S.M.W., Local 280* (1985), 12 C.C.E.L. 231 at 234 (B.C.S.C.) [*Hokanson*], involving a wrongful dismissal action; *Hutchison v. Imperial Taxi Brandon (1983) Ltd.* (1987), 46 D.L.R. (4th) 310 at 313 (Man. C.A.) [*Hutchison*], involving the wage protection legislation; *Re Kaszuba and Salvation Army Sheltered Workshop* (10 December 1981), unreported decision of Referee Burkett pursuant to s. 15 of the Ontario *Employment Standards Act*, S.O. 1974, c. 112 (now R.S.O. 1990, c. E.14) [*Ont. ESA*] at paras. 29–32 and 37, aff'd (1983), 83 C.L.L.C. ¶14,032 (Ont. Div. Ct.); *Fenton v. British Columbia (Forensic Psychiatric Services Commission)* (1991), 91 C.L.L.C. ¶14,030 at 12,320 (B.C.C.A.), rev'g in part (1989), 29 C.C.E.L. 168 (B.C.S.C.), leave to appeal to S.C.C. refused, [1992] 1 S.C.R. vii, involving the employment standards statute.

Indeed, the extremely vague definitions of the term employee in most protective employment standards acts[6] and at common law invite such mischief interpretations. Accordingly, a worker may simultaneously be an "employee" under the employment standards legislation yet be an independent contractor under the *Income Tax Act*.[7]

The determination of employee status is also coloured by the prevailing systems of work organization. For example, the traditional common law test for employee status, developed during the early nineteenth century, required that the employer exercise a substantial degree of control over the manner in which the employee performs the job. Of course, work relations in that era were generally highly personalized in nature, and most employers would be expected to exercise hands-on supervision over how the job was done. However, the proliferation of high-trust, high-discretion occupations during the twentieth century ill fits the traditional control test, for the occupants of such positions exercise much independence over how they perform their work. Accordingly, the control test has been reformulated to require that the employer exercise a significant degree of control over the residual organization of the job — the "where and when" of employment.[8] This reflects the contemporary reality that employers typically reserve broad prerogatives to manage the overall framework of the labour process, while frequently delegating considerable discretion to employees on how to do their jobs within that framework.

Today, the major challenge facing the traditional methods for determining employee status is the proliferation of self-employment.[9] Due to the increasing pressure from overseas competitors to reduce their labour costs, many Canadian employers are substituting self-employed labour for employees, escaping the burden of compliance with protective employent legislation and with common law severance pay requirements. It is true that many employees are happy to become self-employed due to the income tax advantages and because they will not

---

6   Example: Nova Scotia *Labour Standards Code*, R.S.N.S. 1989, c. 246, s. 2(d), [*N.S. LSC*] states that an "employee . . . means a person employed to do work."

7   *Dynamex Canada Inc. v. Mamona*, 2003 FCA 248 [*Dynamex*].

8   Example: *Zuijs v. Wirth Brothers Pty. Ltd.* (1955), 93 C.L.R. 561 (H.C.A.) [*Zuijs*].

9   See Canada, Commission on the Review of Federal Labour Standards, *Fairness at Work: Federal Labour Standards for the 21st Century* by H.W. Arthurs (Ottawa: Commission on the Review of Federal Labour Standards, 2006) at 27–28, 61–66 [Arthurs Report]; J. Fudge, E. Tucker, & L. Vosko, "Employee or Independent Contractor? Charting the Legal Significance of the Distinction in Canada" (2003) 10 C.L.E.L.J. 193 at 195–98; H. Collins, "Independent Contractors and the Challenge of Vertical Disintegration to Employment Protection Laws" (1990) 10 Oxford J. Legal Stud. 331.

have deductions made from their wages under social welfare statutes, such as the *Employment Insurance Act*. Nevertheless, many of these self-employed persons do not fit the mould of business entrepreneurs, and they frequently face as much—if not more—economic hardship in the labour market as they did when they were employees *stricto sensu*. Hence, they are often referred to as "precarious" workers.[10] Even though the Supreme Court of Canada has ruled that protective employment legislation must be interpreted broadly and generously in order to expand the rights of vulnerable employees,[11] the difficulty facing courts and tribunals is how far the employee status test can be pushed in order to extend safeguards to these individuals without doing violence to legal principle. Moreover, the salutary lesson of economics is that if the costs of hiring the self-employed increase as a result of broadening the definition of employee status, employers will transfer the increased costs to customers (in the form of price increases) and to other employees (in the form of reduced compensation and benefits), or simply seek a cheaper substitute, such as installing labour-saving technology.[12]

Canadian courts and administrative tribunals use various formulations of the test for determining employee status, but three elements are common: (1) the employer must exercise a relatively high degree of bureaucratic control over the where and when of employment;[13] (2) the worker must be economically dependent on the employer; and (3) the worker must not be an entrepreneur operating a business as a going concern, but must form part of the employer's business.[14] The control element makes sense since the hallmark of the employment relationship is the subordination of the employee to the authority of the employer. The economic dependence element also makes sense since it reflects the main policy of protective employment legislation, namely, to protect the vulnerable worker. As well, requiring the worker to be integrated into the employer's business as opposed to running a business independently makes sense: the purpose of protective employment statutes and common law severance requirements is not to shield entrepreneurs from the risks of the marketplace, but to safeguard employees against the potential abuse by employers of their superior bargaining power.

---

10 Example: Arthurs Report, *ibid.* at 27.

11 *Rizzo and Rizzo Shoes Ltd.*, [1998] 1 S.C.R. 27 at 36 [*Rizzo*].

12 R. Gomez & M. Gunderson,"Non-Standard and Vulnerable Employees: A Case of Mistaken Identity?" (2005) 12 C.L.E.L.J. 177 at 194–96.

13 Examples: *Hokanson*, above note 4 at 235; *Zuijs*, above note 7 and accompanying text.

14 Example: *R. v. Pereira* (1988), 20 C.C.E.L. 187 at 202 (Alta. Q.B.) [*Pereira*], where the court said that it all boils down to the question, "whose business is it?"

The most famous formulation is probably Lord Wright's so-called fourfold test:

> In earlier cases a single test, such as the presence or absence of control, was often relied on to determine whether the case was one of master and servant, mostly in order to decide issues of tortious liability on the part of the master or superior. In the more complex conditions of modern industry, more complicated tests have often to be applied. It has been suggested that a fourfold test would in some cases be more appropriate, a complex involving (1) control; (2) ownership of the tools; (3) chance of profit; (4) risk of loss. Control in itself is not always conclusive. . . . In many cases the question can only be settled by examining the whole of the various elements which constitute the relationship between the parties. . . . In this way it is in some cases possible to decide the issue by raising as the crucial question whose business is it, or in other words by asking whether the party is carrying on the business, in the sense of carrying it on for himself or on his own behalf and not merely for a superior.[15]

Another widely cited formulation is Lord Denning's so-called business integration test:

> It is often easy to recognize a contract of service when you see it, but difficult to say wherein the difference lies. A ship's master, a chauffeur and a reporter on the staff of a newspaper are all employed under a contract of service; but a ship's pilot, a taxi man and newspaper contributor are employed under a contract for services. One feature which seems to run through the instances is that, under a contract of service, a man is employed as part of the business, and his work is done as an integral part of the business; whereas under a contract for services, his work, although done for the business is not integrated into it, but is only accessory to it.[16]

A wide variety of factors are relevant in answering this question:[17]

- *Ownership of tools and equipment:* Normally, ownership suggests independent contractor status only if the worker makes a substantial

---

15   *Montreal (City of) v. Montreal Locomotive Works Ltd.* (1946), [1947] 1 D.L.R. 161 at 169 (P.C.).

16   *Stevenson Jordon & Harrison Ltd. v. MacDonald and Evans,* [1952] 1 T.L.R. 101 at 111 (C.A.).

17   A useful checklist of the relevant factors is provided by Wood J. in *Doyle v. London Life Insurance Co.,* [1984] B.C.J. No. 1119 (S.C.). See also *Wiebe Door Services Ltd. v. M.N.R.,* [1986] 5 W.W.R. 450 at 459 (F.C.A.), arising in the context of the *Unemployment Insurance Act.*

capital investment in tools and equipment, such as purchasing a vehicle for work-related use.[18] However, if the capital investment is relatively small, the worker will likely be an employee, as with many cobblers, carpenters, meatcutters, and motor mechanics who own their own tools. Making a substantial capital investment will not preclude a finding of employee status, though, if the employer significantly limits the worker's freedom to use his or her equipment or tools in order to make a profit in the marketplace from other clients and customers.[19]

- *The risk of economic gains and losses:* This risk does not mean that a person who is remunerated on an incentive basis is automatically self-employed; many employees are paid by commission or "by the piece." Rather, it means that a person who has a substantial financial investment in the business over and above providing labour is likely to be self-employed.

- *The regularity of employment:* If a person works exclusively for one employer (either because of the terms of the parties' contractual arrangement or as a matter of fact) it indicates employee status;[20] a person who regularly provides services for many different employers more closely resembles an independent contractor. Typically, an independent contractor has a business address, business cards, stationery, invoices, and advertising material. However, the fact that a person works for more than one employer does not necessarily make that person an independent contractor: there is no rule of common law that an "employee" cannot simultaneously hold multiple jobs.[21]

- *The right to delegate performance of the work:* Usually, an employee will perform the work personally, while an independent contractor may delegate the work to employees or even to outside subcontractors.[22] This factor is not necessarily determinative, however. For example, some store "owners" operating under franchise agreements

18 Examples: *Lycar v. Lonnie W. Orcutt Farms Ltd.* (2002), 23 C.C.E.L. (3d) 240 at 247 (Alta. Q.B.); *Innis v. Dicom Express Ltd.*(March 1998) at 15–17 (Baum), unreported adjudication decision under *Canada Labour Code*, s. 240.

19 Example: *Racz v. Southern Trucking Ltd.* (May 2002) (Bourassa), unreported adjudication decision arising under *Canada Labour Code*, s. 240.

20 Examples: *Belton v. Liberty Insurance Company of Canada*, [2003] C.L.L.C. 210-006 (Ont. S.C.J.) [*Belton*]; *Truong v. British Columbia* (1999), 47 C.C.E.L. (2d) 307 (B.C.C.A.).

21 *Groat Road Bingo Association v. Schmidt*, unreported decision of Alberta Employment Standards Umpire (3 June 1992), Edmonton file no. CEDM 9879, Hope J.; *Hivac Ltd. v. Park Royal Scientific Instruments Ltd.*, [1946] Ch. 169 (C.A.).

22 *Poiron v. Ritchot (Rural Municipality)* (1988), 53 Man. R. (2d) 25 at 29 (Q.B.).

have been held to be employees of the franchisor even though they can hire their own employees to help run the shop.[23]

- *Legal status of the worker:* If the worker has incorporated his or her own company and performs the contract in the corporate name, the scale will tip in favour of self-employment. But this factor is not determinative. An employee can perform an employment contract in his or her corporate name. Moreover, the courts may look behind the corporate name and find employee status if the parties' relationship is one of subordination and economic exploitation.[24]
- *Public image:* The relationship will resemble employee status if the worker's image to his or her workmates and the general public is that of a regular employee—for example, if he or she wears the company uniform and uses other company facilities on the same basis as regular employees.
- *No rule of law in Canada that working part time, casually, at home, or for an employment agency automatically disqualifies the worker from being an employee:* Rather, the test for employee status is applied to such workers in the usual way.
- *Formal contractual descriptions of the nature of the relationship:* Little weight is given to how the parties describe their relationship in the express terms of the contract, since this is clearly self-serving. Rather, the courts examine the "economic realities" of the relationship in practice.[25]

Clearly, the employer will have the power to decide on many of the factors that are key to the determination of employee status. How employers structure their operations will be governed by the prevailing business climate. Today, many employers facing stiffening overseas competition are trying to increase their productivity by placing the risks associated with their business on their workers—for example, by transforming them into self-employed casuals who report for duty only when required.[26]

Some commentators argue that the current test for employee status is inadequate because it fails to encompass many such workers who need the protection of the legislation on account of their vulnerability and subordination to the employer. They argue that a broader test that

23   Example: *Head v. Inter Tan Canada Inc.* (1991), 38 C.C.E.L. 159 (Ont. Gen. Div.).
24   Example: *Mann v. Northern B.C. Enterprises Ltd.* (2003), 35 C.C.E.L. (3d) 19 at 42 (B.C.S.C.), quashed on a different ground (2005), 46 C.C.E.L. (3d) 253 (B.C.C.A.).
25   Examples: *Belton,* above note 19; *Dynamex,* above note 6.
26   See the important studies at above note 8 and accompanying text.

asks whether the particular worker needs the protection of the legislation because of economic dependence on and subordination to an employer be adopted.[27] They argue that such an approach is long overdue in light of the ILO's 1998 *Declaration of Fundamental Principles and Rights at Work* which advocates extending equal rights to all forms of work in order to safeguard the worker's economic security and personal dignity and autonomy. Nevertheless, the new test appears to ask the same questions now asked under the current test, only in a different form. Indeed, the current test adopts a purposive, broad, and generous interpretation that can potentially capture most relationships of clear vulnerability and subordination that would be caught by the new test. These critics also argue that the current test is too vague to enable the parties to predict the worker's status with any certainty, yet the new test seems just as uncertain. It is true that the current test is vague, but some degree of flexibility is desirable and unavoidable, whatever the test, in order to encompass new methods of work organization that employers may introduce in the future. The current level of uncertainty could be reduced if the recommendation in the Arthurs Report that would require employers to provide workers with a written statement describing their legal status at the date of hiring is legislated.[28] Interestingly, Arthurs noted that failing to provide such a statement would result in the worker being presumed to be an employee, something that would likely provide a potent incentive to employers to obey the law. Therefore, the case for abandoning the current test in dubious.[29] Rather, an arguably more fruitful approach would be to complement the existing test with a new category of "dependent contractor" and specify which statutory and common law entitlements are suitable for extending to them and which are not.[30] Indeed, the collective bargaining statutes in several jurisdictions include "dependent contractor" provisions that extend the basic right to bargain collectively to such

27 Examples: J. Fudge, "New Wine into Old Bottles? Updating Legal Forms to Reflect Changing Employment Norms" (1999) 33 U.B.C. L. Rev. 129; Fudge, Tucker, & Vosko, "Employee or Independent Contractor? Charting the Legal Significance of the Distinction in Canada," above note 8 at 229–30; K.V.W. Stone, "Rethinking Labour Law: Employment Protection for Boundaryless Workers" in G. Davidov & B. Langille, eds., *Boundaries and Frontiers of Labour Law* (Oxford: Hart, 2006) 157 at 176.

28 Arthurs Report, above note 8 at 65.

29 See G. Davidov, "The Reports of My Death Are Greatly Exaggerated: 'Employee' as a Viable (Though Over-Used) Legal Concept," in Davidov & Langille, eds., *Boundaries and Frontiers of Labour Law*, above note 26 at 133.

30 This is recommended by the Arthurs Report, above note 8 at 64, where the term "autonomous" worker is preferred.

workers, subject to specific limitations reflecting their differences from employees *stricto sensu.*

Significantly, the courts have followed a similar path by recognizing a special "intermediate" status for workers whose contracts place them at, or even beyond, the normal boundaries of employee status.[31] In order to protect such workers, the courts have ruled that their employer must give them reasonable notice of termination and must prove just cause for summary dismissal.[32] In return, the workers are bound by a rigorous duty of fidelity to their employer.[33] Arguably, "intermediate" status would be available only for common law purposes since the protective employment legislation expressly applies to "employees" *stricto sensu.* It remains to be seen whether the term "employee" will be given a special statutory meaning that encompasses common law "intermediate" relationships. In light of the Supreme Court of Canada's ruling that provisions in employment protection statutes must be interpreted broadly and generously in order to further the remedial goal of the legislation,[34] this possibility cannot be discounted. Of course, the term "intermediate" status invites the same problem of uncertainty and unpredictability that has plagued the traditional test for "employee" status.

B. IDENTIFYING WHO THE "EMPLOYER" IS

The legal incidents attached to employee status at common law and under protective legislation only apply to the employer.[35] Ordinarily, determining the employer is easy. Difficulties may arise, however, in the following circumstances: (1) where an employee is temporarily transferred to another company, possibly within the same corporate family as his or her usual employer; (2) where the employer's business is sold, taken over, or otherwise transferred to a successor company; and (3) where the employer contracts with an outsider, for example an

---

31   The leading authority is *Carter v. Bell & Sons (Can.) Ltd.*, [1936] 2 D.L.R. 438 at 440 (Ont. C.A.), Middleton J.A.

32   Examples: *Fasslane v. Purolator Courier Ltd.*, [2007] B.C.J. No. 2758 (S.C.); *JKC Enterprises Ltd. v. Woolworth Canada Inc.*, [2002] C.L.L.C. ¶210-015, especially at 141,170 (Alta. Q.B.); *Aqwa v. Centennial Home Renovations Ltd. (c.o.b. Centennial Windows)*, [2001] O.J. No. 3699 (S.C.J.).

33   *Professional Court Reporters v. Carter* (1993), 46 C.C.E.L. 281, especially at 293 (Ont. Gen. Div.).

34   *Rizzo*, above note 10 at 36.

35   For detailed elaboration of this topic, see *Employment Law in Canada*, above note 1, c. 3.

employment agency, to have job functions within the enterprise performed by workers supplied by the outsider. Complications can arise in all of these situations as a result of applying the principle that a contract of employment cannot be transferred from one employer to another unless the existing contract is terminated and replaced by a new contract with the successor employer.[36] In order to avoid the risk of slavery, the courts have traditionally required strong evidence that an employee agrees to enter into an employment contract with a successor employer in the three situations outlined above. The downside of the principle for the employee is that every time there is a technical change in the legal identity of the employer, he or she loses any seniority accrued under the previous contract vis-à-vis the new employer and must commence to rebuild it. Accordingly, the employee may be unable to acquire valuable benefits under the employment contract or under labour standards statutes that depend on accrued seniority.

The reluctance of courts to find that an employee has consented to ending an employment contract and has agreed to become the employee of another employer is demonstrated in the vicarious liability cases involving "borrowed" employees. This scenario occurs where employer A contracts with company B to assign an employee to perform work for company B, and the borrowed employee tortiously injures a third party in the course of performing the work. The question arises: which company is vicariously liable for the employee's tort—company A or company B? The courts have held that company A remains the employer for vicarious liability purposes unless it can clearly be shown that the employee unequivocally agreed to enter into an employment contract with company B, which will rarely be the case.[37] This outcome also makes sense from an insurance perspective, since company A will normally be in the best position to assess the risk of its workers causing injuries and to take out an appropriate amount of insurance coverage.[38] Furthermore, if two employers share a significant degree of control over the worker, the courts can treat them both as the employer for vicarious liability purposes.[39]

---

36 The leading authority is *Nokes v. Doncaster Amalgamated Collieries Ltd.*, [1940] A.C. 1014 (H.L.). In Canada, see *Canada (A.G.) v. Standard Trust Co.* (1994), 8 C.C.E.L. (2d) 58 at 64–65 (Ont. Gen. Div., Commercial List).

37 *Mersey Docks and Harbour Board v. Coggins and Griffiths (Liverpool) Ltd.* (1946), [1947] A.C. 1 (H.L.). See also *Denham v. Midland Employers Mutual Assurance Ltd.*, [1955] 2 Q.B. 437.

38 See J.D. Hynes, "Chaos and the Law of the Borrowed Servant: An Argument for Consistency" (1994) J.L. & Com. 1.

39 *Teskey v. Toronto Transit Commission* (2003), 29 C.C.E.L. (3d) 217 at 221 (Ont. S.C.J.).

The situation where an employee is transferred between different companies within the same corporate family is commonplace today.[40] In order to safeguard the accrued seniority of the employee, the employment standards legislation in several provinces includes "common employer" provisions.[41] For example, section 4 of the Ontario *Employment Standards Act, 2000* reads:

    (1) Subsection (2) applies if,
        (a) associated or related activities or businesses are or were carried on by or through an employer and one or more other persons; and
        (b) the intent or effect of their doing so is or has been to directly or indirectly defeat the intent and purpose of this Act.
    (2) The employer and the other person or persons described in subsection (1) shall all be treated as one employer for the purposes of this Act . . .
    (3) Persons who are treated as one employer under this section are jointly and severally liable for any contravention of this Act and the regulations made under it for any wages owing to an employee of any of them.[42]

Significantly, this provision protects seniority only for the purpose of statutory benefits, such as the minimum notice of termination of employment; it does not safeguard the employee in respect to private benefits in an employment contract. In response, rights-inspired courts have developed a common law equivalence to these provisions that protects an employee's rights under the employment contract. Several recent decisions have held that the parent company and the other companies within the family are jointly and severally liable for all employment benefits owed to the transferred employee, and for preserving his or her accrued seniority when a reassignment takes place.[43]

The situation where one company is taken over in one form or another and its employees continue to work for the successor employer is

---

40 See generally J. Fudge & K. Zavitz, "Vertical Disintegration and Related Employers: Attributing Employment Related Obligations in Ontario" (2006) 13 C.L.E.L.J. 107.

41 Examples: *Canada Labour Code*, R.S.C. 1985, c. L-2, s. 255; Alberta *Employment Standards Code*, R.S.A. 2000, c. E-9, s. 80; British Columbia, *Employment Standards Act*, R.S.B.C. 1996, c. 113, s. 95; Manitoba *Employment Standards Code*, C.C.S.M. c. E110, s. 134; *N.S. LSC*, above note 5, s. 11.

42 S.O. 2000, c. 41, s. 4.

43 Examples: *Downtown Eatery (1993) Ltd. v. Ontario* (2001), 8 C.C.E.L. (3d) 186, especially at 196 (Ont.C.A.); *Sinclair v. Dover Engineering Services Ltd.* (1987), 11 B.C.L.R. (2d) 176 (S.C.), aff'd (1988), 49 D.L.R. (4th) 297 (B.C.C.A.).

commonplace today. Again, the employment standards acts of several provinces attempt to safeguard the employee's accrued seniority with provisions similar to section 5 of the Alberta *Employment Standards Code*:

> For the purposes of this Act, the employment of any employee is deemed to be continuous and uninterrupted when a business, undertaking or other activity or part of it is sold, leased, transferred or merged or if it continues to operate under a receiver or receiver manager.[44]

This provision protects seniority only for the purpose of statutory benefits, such as the minimum notice of termination of employment; it does not safeguard the employee in respect to private benefits in her employment contract.

The courts, however, have somewhat tempered the common law position in two ways. First, courts will take account of any previous employment with a successor company in determining the length of reasonable notice of termination at common law.[45] Second, a successor employer is seen as agreeing to honour the employee's previous seniority under the new employment contract, unless the successor clearly and unequivocally notifies the employee to the contrary.[46]

Today, many employers contract with outside companies, such as an employment agency, to have job functions within the enterprise performed by workers who are supplied by the outside company.[47] In 2000, of the 2.8 million temporary workers in Canada (representing almost 19 percent of the Canadian workforce), between 20 and 25 percent of those temporary workers were assigned to user firms through temporary work agencies.[48] Assuming that these workers are "employees," the question then arises, who is the employer—the outside company or the user company? The answer depends on examining the various indicia of employee status reviewed earlier in this chapter and determining which employer they best fit: the supplier or the user. Here,

---

44 Above note 40.

45 Examples: *Radwan v. Arteif Furniture Manufacturing* (2002), 23 C.C.E.L. (3d) 52 at 62–63 (Alta. Q.B.); *Lingelbach v. James Tire Centres Ltd.* (1994), 7 C.C.E.L. (2d) 297 at 308 (Sask. C.A.).

46 Example: *Szwez v. Allied Van Lines Ltd.* (1993), 45 C.C.E.L. 39 at 45 (Ont. Gen. Div.).

47 J. Fudge, "The Legal Boundaries of the Employer, Precarious Workers and Labour Protection" in Davidov & Langille, eds., *Boundaries and Frontiers of Labour Law*, above note 26 at 295; J. Fudge, "Fragmenting Work and Fragmenting Organizations: The Contract of Employment and the Scope of Labour Regulations" (2006) 44 Osgoode Hall L.J. 609.

48 T. Newton, "Report on the 2000 Survey of Employment Services" (2000) at 7, online: www.statcan.ca/english/sdds/document/4718_D3_T9_V1_E.pdf.

some earlier court decisions, including one Supreme Court of Canada authority, accorded decisive weight to she who signs the paycheque. Thus, if the paycheque was signed in the name of the agency, that fact alone would make it the employer.[49] However, other courts have taken a broader—and, it is submitted, a more realistic—view that what counts is not who signs the paycheque, but who carries the ultimate economic burden of ensuring that the funds are there to honour the cheque.[50] If wages are paid from funds directed to the agency by the user, the user would appear to be the employer. The Supreme Court of Canada has endorsed this broader approach in *Pointe-Claire*,[51] where workers supplied to the city by an employment agency were ruled to be employees of the city so as to bring them within the coverage of a collective agreement, even though their paycheques were signed by the agency. Other relevant factors include who exercises daily control over the employees and who has the real-world responsibility for hiring, disciplining, and dismissing the employees.

Again, the policy context is vital.[52] When this question arises in the context of collective bargaining rights, labour relations boards and arbitrators tend to find the user to be the employer in order to protect the incumbent union's bargaining rights from erosion by this form of contracting-in.[53] However, when the question arises under the employment standards statute or a contract of employment, it will normally make more sense from the employee's viewpoint to define the organization supplying the labour as the employer in order to maximize his or her seniority accrual, at least where the employee is assigned for relatively short times to many different users. However, if the employee is assigned to one user for a substantial time so as to make that person resemble a permanent employee of the user, it makes sense to treat him or her as an employee of the user for seniority accrual purposes. This approach is fine for the purpose of seniority accrual, but argu-

---

49   *Yellow Cab Ltd. v. Alberta (Industrial Relations Board)*, [1980] 2 S.C.R. 761, involving the collective bargaining legislation; *Re Liquid Carbonic Inc. and E.C.W.U., Local 666* (1986), 25 L.A.C. (3d) 309 (Melnyk), involving a collective agreement grievance.

50   *Hutchison*, above note 4; *Pereira*, above note 13.

51   Above note 4, especially at 1050, where the Court emphasized that what counts is the ultimate source of remuneration, not who signs the paycheque. See generally G. Trudeau, "Temporary Employees Hired through a Personnel Agency: Who Is the Real Employer?" (1997) C.L.E.L.J. 359.

52   See the comments to this effect in *Pointe-Claire*, *ibid.* at 1047, where the Court wanted to ensure that the agency workers enjoyed the fruits of coverage by the city's collective agreement.

53   Example: *Stewart v. I.B.T., Local 419* (1983), 83 C.L.L.C. ¶16,060 (O.L.R.B.).

ably, it makes sense for the worker to be treated as an employee of the user for job tolerability protections, such as safeguards against personal harassment, intimidation, and bullying, even though he or she may be assigned to the user for relatively short time. As well, it can be argued that a worker who is contracted-in to perform the same job functions as those done by the user's regular employees should be entitled to no less compensation than the latter, even if the assignment is relatively short—at least where the purpose of the contracting is a "colourable device to avoid normal contracts of employment" as opposed to a legitimate attempt to meet the user's short-term needs.[54] The notion that different employment responsibilities may have to be shared between two simultaneous employers ill fits the traditional model of a bilateral employment contract between one employer and its employees, and may be impossible for courts to achieve under traditional contract law doctrine. Therefore, legislation may be needed to impose on the user and the supplier those employment obligations that are best suited for each of them to bear.[55]

FURTHER READINGS

ATIYAH, P.S., *Vicarious Liability in the Law of Tort* (London: Butterworths, 1967) 31–99

CANADA, COMMISSION ON THE REVIEW OF FEDERAL LABOUR STANDARDS, *Fairness at Work: Federal Labour Standards for the 21st Century* by H.W. Arthurs (Ottawa: Commission on the Review of Federal Labour Standards, 2006)

COLLINS, H., "Independent Contractors and the Challenge of Vertical Disintegration to Employment Protection Laws" (1990) 10 Oxford J. Legal Stud. 331

DAVIDOV, G., "The Reports of My Death Are Greatly Exaggerated: 'Employee' as a Viable (Though Over-Used) Legal Concept," in G. Davidov & B. Langille, eds., *Boundaries and Frontiers of Labour Law* (Oxford: Hart, 2006) 133

---

54   Arthurs Report, above note 8 at 236.
55   *Ibid.* at at 233–37; G. Davidov, "Joint Employer Status in Triangular Employment Relationships" (2004) 42 B.J.I.R. 727; S. Deakin, "Commentary: The Changing Concept of 'Employer' in Labour Law" (2001) 30 Indus. L.J. 72.

DAVIDOV, G., "Joint Employer Status in Triangular Employment Relationships" (2004) 42 B.J.I.R. 727

DEAKIN, S., "The Comparative Evolution of the Employment Relationship" in G. Davidov & B. Langille, eds., *Boundaries and Frontiers of Labour Law* (Oxford: Hart, 2006) 89

ENGLAND, G., R. WOOD, & I. CHRISTIE, *Employment Law in Canada*, 4th ed., looseleaf (Markham, ON: LexisNexis Butterworths, 2005–) cc. 2 & 3

FUDGE, J., E. TUCKER, & L. VOSKO, "Employee or Independent Contractor? Charting the Legal Significance of the Distinction in Canada" (2003) 10 C.L.E.L.J. 193

FUDGE, J., "The Legal Boundaries of the Employer, Precarious Workers, and Labour Protection" in G. Davidov & B. Langille, eds., *Boundaries and Frontiers of Labour Law* (Oxford: Hart, 2006) 296

FUDGE, J., "Beyond Vulnerable Workers: Towards a New Standard Employment Relationship" (2005) 12 C.L.E.L.J. 152

FUDGE, J., "Fragmenting Work and Fragmenting Organizations: The Contract of Employment and the Scope of Labour Regulations" (2006) 44 Osgoode Hall L.J. 609

GOMEZ, R., & M. GUNDERSON, "Non-standard and Vulnerable Workers: A Case of Mistaken Identity?" (2005) 12 C.L.E.L.J. 177

KAHN-FREUND, O., "Servants and Independent Contractors" (1951) 14 Mod. L. Rev. 504

MCKENDRICK, E., "Vicarious Liability and Independent Contractors: A Reexamination" (1990) 53 Mod.L. Rev. 770

TRUDEAU, G., "Temporary Employees Hired through a Personnel Agency: Who Is the Real Employer?" (1997) 5 C.L.E.L.J. 359

CREATION AND MODIFICATION OF THE EMPLOYMENT RELATIONSHIP

This chapter examines the law governing the formation and modification of the employment contract.[1]

First, we analyze who has the "legal capacity" to enter into an employment contract. We shall see that there are restrictions at common law and under legislation on the employment of mental incompetents and children. As well, special legislation sets minimum qualifications for employment in defined trades, professions, and occupations (e.g., nursing and electrical maintenance); immigration laws restrict employment by non-Canadians; and apprenticeship legislation restricts the conditions under which persons can be engaged as apprentices in designated trades and professions.

Second, we examine legislated restrictions on how employers conduct recruitment. Here, we analyze the operation of the general principles of contract formation and modification in the context of the employment relationship, namely,

- offer and acceptance, including the *Statute of Frauds*;
- the requirement of certainty and the sources of contractual terms;
- enforcement of representations by means of the torts of negligent and fraudulent misstatement;

---

1   For further detailed elaboration on this topic, see G. England, R. Wood, & I. Christie, *Employment Law in Canada*, 4th ed., looseleaf (Markham, ON: LexisNexis Canada, 2005–) c. 7.

- the application of the doctrine of consideration to the creation and modification of the contract; and
- factors that will vitiate an employment contract, such as misrepresentation; mistake; duress, unconscionability, and undue influence; and supervening illegality.

Third, we outline the prohibitions against discriminatory hiring contained in human rights and collective bargaining legislation, the statutory restrictions on the activities of private employment agencies, and the statutory prohibitions in Manitoba against conducting personal investigations of job applicants.

A. LEGAL CAPACITY TO ENTER INTO AN EMPLOYMENT CONTRACT

Any person recognized as having legal capacity according to the regular laws of the land is eligible to enter into an employment contract, subject to the statutory limitations reviewed below.

At common law, the term "legal capacity" means that a person must have sufficient mental competency to understand the legal significance of his or her actions. Lack of mental capacity renders the employment contract voidable at the option of the incapacitated party.[2] In addition, if an individual's mental incapacity results in being declared incompetent under provincial incompetent persons legislation, that individual cannot become or remain a party to an employment contract on his or her own behalf, but must act through a guardian.[3] Of course, in deciding whether or not to hire or fire an employee who is mentally incompetent, employers must be mindful that such incompetency constitutes a protected "disability" under the human rights legislation in all jurisdictions.[4] The latter legislation prohibits the employer from refusing to hire a person by reason of mental competence unless the employer can show that the person will be unable to perform the job, and the employer has tried to accommodate the employee up to the point of causing the firm an "undue hardship."

At common law, an "infant"—defined as a person below the age of eighteen—is eligible to enter into an employment contract, but it will only be legally binding during infancy if the contract as a whole

---

2   *Hardman v. Falk* (1955), 15 W.W.R. (N.S.) 337 (B.C.C.A.).

3   Examples.: Alberta *Dependant Adults Act*, R.S.A. 2000, c. D-11; Ontario *Mental Incompetency Act*, R.S.O. 1990, c. M.9.

4   See Chapter 7.

is judged to be in that person's best interests. If not, the entire employment contract will be declared void.[5] In determining whether the contract is for the overall benefit of the infant, the courts examine the degree to which the employee gains educational and career development opportunities from the employment, as well as the relative values of the economic benefits to each party. If the employment contract is declared void, the infant can nonetheless recover compensation for services previously performed under a *quantum meruit*.

The statutory restrictions on an individual's capacity to enter into an employment contract are more extensive than at common law. Especially important is the plethora of legislation governing the employment of children. Here, a balance must be struck between allowing children to gain experience of working life and ensuring that they have enough time and energy to devote to their school and leisure activities. Typically,[6] provincial employment standards acts make the employment of younger children—usually defined as persons aged between 12 and 15—subject to the written consent of their parents/guardians and the director of employment standards. The legislation typically fixes maximum permissible hours of work for these children and designates the industries or occupations in which they can and cannot be engaged. Older teenagers, usually those between 15 and 17, are permitted to work somewhat longer hours, but again, they cannot work in designated industries or occupations, they may have to obtain the consent of their parents/guardians and the director of employment standards, and they are often required to work under the supervision of an adult. In 2003, British Columbia departed from the traditional model by permitting persons aged between 12 and 14 to be employed on the basis of parental/guardian consent alone, without obtaining the approval of the director of employment standards.[7] This amendment, which coincided with a reduction in the statutory minimum wage for persons aged 14 and below, was part of the provincial government's strategy of deregulating the labour market, and it ignited great public controversy.[8] Other

---

5   Example: *Toronto Marlboro Major Junior "A" Hockey Club v. Tonelli* (1978), 18 O.R. (2d) 21 (H.C.J.), aff'd (1979) 23 O.R. (2d) 193 (C.A.).
6   Examples: Alberta *Employment Standards Code*, R.S.A. 2000, c. E-9, ss. 65 & 66. [*Alta. ESC*], and Employment Standards Regulation, Alta. Reg. 14/1997, ss. 51–53.
7   British Columbia *Employment Standards Act*, R.S.B.C. 1996, c. 113, s. 9, as amended by S.B.C. 2003, c. 65, s. 3.
8   Example: J. Irwin, S. McBride, & T. Strubin, *Child and Youth Employment Standards: The Example of Young Workers under British Columbia's New Policy Regime* (Vancouver: Canadian Centre for Policy Alternatives, 2005).

legislation frequently comes into play, such as mandatory school attendance acts, which specify when a child must be present at school,[9]
or occupational health and safety acts, which establish minimum ages
for work in designated industries, such as mining.[10] Beyond that, the
elimination of child labour is one of the eleven principles that the signatories of the *North American Free Trade Agreement* have committed
themselves to promote.[11]

Furthermore, each province has extensive legislation specifying
the qualifications that a person must have in order to work in designated "high-skill" industries and occupations, such as nursing and
health care, law, engineering, electrical installation, heavy equipment
operations, and dentistry. These statutes and regulations are commonly
justified as necessary to guarantee standards of competence and quality, but occasionally they carry the whiff of protectionism. They may
be susceptible to challenge under section 15 of the *Charter*[12] insofar as
they act as barriers to foreign-trained workers, or under section 6(2)(b)
of the *Charter* insofar as they abridge the right to labour mobility within Canada, in which case the government would have to justify them
under section 1.[13]

Regard must also be paid to the *Immigration Act*, which provides
that no person other than a Canadian citizen or a permanent resident of
Canada can be employed without an employment visa.[14] Breach of the
Act is a criminal offence. There are, however, exceptions provided under
the *Immigration Act*. These should be consulted, along with the list of
about sixty designated professionals who are allowed to work in Canada
under chapter 16 of the *North American Free Trade Agreement*.[15]

An employment contract that offends one of the above-mentioned
statutes is void *ab initio*. Arguably, the result is to disentitle the employee from recovering wages for services performed under such a contract.[16]

---

9   Example: Ontario *Child Welfare Act*, R.S.O. 1980, c. 66, s. 53 (replaced by *Child and Family Services Act*, R.S.O. 1990, c. C.11).
10 Example: British Columbia *Mines Act*, R.S.B.C. 1996, c. 293.
11 For further elaboration, see Chapter 6.
12 *Canadian Charter of Rights and Freedoms*, Part 1 of the *Constitution Act, 1982*, being Schedule B to the *Canada Act 1982* (U.K.), 1982, c. 11 [*Charter*].
13 M. Cornish, E. McIntyre, & A. Pask, "Strategies for Challenging Discriminatory Barriers to Foreign Credential Recognition" (2000) 8 C.L.E.L.J. 17.
14 *Immigration Regulations*, C.R.C., c. 940, s. 6.
15 *North American Free Trade Agreement Between the Government of Canada, the Government of Mexico and the Government of the United States*, 17 December 1992, Can. T.S. 1994 No. 2, 32 I.L.M. 289 (entered into force 1 January 1994).
16 Example: *Turner v. Rose-Alberta Construction Ltd.*, [1984] 2 W.W.R. 556 at 560–61 (Sask. Q.B.).

However, this view seems unfair to the employee who is innocent of the illegality; the better view, it is submitted, is that such a person can recover on a *quantum meruit* for the fair value of services rendered.[17] The case for a *quantum meruit* is weakened, however, if the employee willingly and voluntarily engages in the illegal work.

B. THE GENERAL PRINCIPLES OF CONTRACT LAW GOVERNING THE FORMATION AND MODIFICATION OF EMPLOYMENT CONTRACTS

The general contract law rules of offer and acceptance apply to the formation of an employment contract. Thus, one party—usually the employer—must communicate to the other party a firm and unequivocal commitment to enter into an employment relationship. The offer may be made verbally, or it may take the form of a letter of appointment. In either scenario, an employment contract will not be created until the acceptor has communicated to the offeror unequivocal and unconditional assent to all the terms in the offer.[18] Once an acceptance has been communicated, an employment contract comes into existence, even though the parties may postpone the date when work will commence. Accordingly, neither party can back out of such a contract without giving the other party due notice of termination, or wages in lieu thereof.[19] Similarly, an employee can be summarily dismissed for "just cause" if he or she commits serious misconduct before the work commences.[20] An offer and an acceptance of employment may also be inferred from the actual conduct of the parties. If the employer of a seasonal worker consistently recalls someone every season without interruption for a lengthy time under substantially the same terms and conditions of employment, the parties may be held to have intended to create a contract of employment for an indefinite term, by inference from their conduct, rather than a series of separate seasonal con-

---

17 English courts have taken this view, for example, *Hewcastle Catering Ltd. v. Ahmed and Elkamah*, [1991] I.R.L.R. 473 (C.A.).

18 If the parties are still negotiating outstanding conditions of their agreement even after the employee has begun working, an employment contract will not have been formed until those conditions have been agreed upon. See, for example, *Hill v. Develcon Electronics Ltd.* (1991), 37 C.C.E.L. 19 (Sask. Q.B.).

19 *Horvath v. Joytec Ltd.* (1989), 27 C.C.E.L. 269 (Sask. Q.B.).

20 *Levi v. Chartersoft Canada Inc.* (1995), 8 C.C.E.L. (2d) 10 (Man. Q.B.).

tracts.[21] The parties can also make their employment contract subject
to a condition precedent, for example, that the employer will have the
requisite funding in place by the date scheduled for work to begin; that
the board of directors must ratify the contract by a certain date;[22] or
that a formal document embodying the terms of their agreement will
be executed by a certain date.[23] In the latter cases, the employer will not
be liable if the condition is unfulfilled. If the employment contract is
made subject to a condition precedent, however, both sides are bound
to act in good faith and make reasonable efforts to fulfill it.[24]

At common law, an employment contract need not be in writing in
order to be valid. However, special legislation may require that certain
types of employment contracts, such as apprenticeship agreements,[25] be
in writing. Moreover, in provinces having a statute of frauds,[26] an employment contract for a fixed term of at least one year must be evidenced
in writing in order to be legally enforceable. Nevertheless, even though
a contract may be unenforceable for non-compliance with the statute of
frauds, the courts will hold that the employee can recover fair wages
for work performed under a *quantum meruit*.[27] In Ontario, section 2 of
the *Employers and Employees Act* states that a fixed-term employment
contract of longer than nine years' duration is not legally binding. The
Ontario courts have held, however, that if such a contract includes a
provision entitling either party to terminate the relationship before the
nine-year deadline, the contract will be enforceable for its full term.[28]

The major area of uncertainty is not deciding whether the parties
intend to create an employment contract, but rather determining the
exact terms and conditions of their relationship. Most employment
contracts contain relatively few express terms and conditions, except

---

21 Example: *Gray v. Manvers (Township)* (1993), 93 C.L.L.C. ¶14,023, especially at
    12,139 (Ont. Gen. Div.). Compare *Lawton v. Peter Bowden Drilling Ltd.* (1990), 33
    C.C.E.L. 99, especially at 101 (Alta. Q.B.).
22 Example: *Bowen v. Canadian Tire Corp.* (1991), 35 C.C.E.L. 113 at 124 (Ont.
    Gen. Div.).
23 Example: *Ross v. Christian and Timbers Inc.* (2002), 18 C.C.E.L. (3d) 165 at 171
    (Ont. S.C.J.).
24 *Dawson v. Helicopter Exploration Co.*, [1955] 5 S.C.R. 868, especially Rand J., ap-
    plied in the employment context in *Leacock v. Whalen, Bekiveau and Associates
    Inc.* (1996), 22 C.C.E.L. (2d) 249 at 268 (B.C.S.C.).
25 Example: *Ontario Apprenticeship and Certification Act, 1998*, S.O. 1998, c. 22, ss.
    2 "apprentice" and 6(1).
26 Statutes of fraud are in place in New Brunswick, Nova Scotia, and Ontario. In
    other provinces, the old English *Statute of Frauds* is in force as "received law,"
    except in British Columbia.
27 Example: *Graves v. Okanagan Trust Co.* (1956), 6 D.L.R. (2d) 54 (B.C.S.C.).
28 *Hine v. Susan Shoe Industries Ltd.* (1994), 3 C.C.E.L. (2d) 119 at 121 (Ont. C.A.).

in the case of senior executives, professionals, and entertainment stars. A leading economics textbook provides the following explanation:

> The employment contract is typically quite imprecise. The employee agrees that—within limits that are rarely completely described and only partly understood—they will use their minds and muscles to undertake the tasks that their employer directs them to do, perhaps using the methods that the employer specifies. The employer agrees to pay the employees. The range of actions that might be requested or required is unclear. Future compensation and even the criteria used to determine future pay and promotions are unspecified. The mechanisms to be used in case of disputes are not stated, nor the penalties for most possible violations of the contract. Yet these are among the most important contracts that any of us enter throughout our lives . . . .
>
> The incompleteness, the implicit nature and the shape of the employment contract are all responses to the impossibility of complete contracting . . . . Briefly, they involve the difficulties of foreseeing all the events that might possibly arise over time and appropriate actions to take, the difficulties of unambiguously describing these events and actions even if they could be foreseen, and the costs of negotiating acceptable explicit agreements over these many terms even if they could be described . . . . The usual employment contract . . . is much more of a relational contract. It frames the relationship, specifying broad terms and objectives and putting in place some mechanisms for decision making when unforeseen events arise . . . . The decision making mechanism in the employment contract is basically that the boss can order the employee to do anything that is not explicitly forbidden by the contract's terms or by law.[29]

These insights are critically important in understanding the nature of employment contracts. Express terms will rarely cover matters beyond the job title, basic wage rates, basic hours of work, and possibly vacations and holidays. Occasionally, the parties will expressly incorporate into their employment contract terms and conditions contained in some ancillary documentation, such as a works rule book, a personnel manual, or a benefits handbook. The flesh and blood of the employment contract, however, normally consists of implied terms.

The process of implying terms into an employment contract is supposed to be that courts will give effect only to the unexpressed inten-

---

29 P.R. Milgrom & J. Roberts, *Economics, Organization, and Management* (Englewood Cliffs, NJ: Prentice-Hall, 1992) at 329–30.

tions of the parties regarding the matter in issue. Doing this is supposed
to ensure that freedom of contract is respected. Thus, a long-standing
and certain past practice known to both parties may be implied into
the employment contract as reflecting their common unstated intention.[30] Similarly, a recognized "custom" in a particular industry, trade,
or occupation may be implied into the contract, provided that it is "reasonable, certain and notorious."[31] Clearly, if one side either does not
know of the custom or practice[32] or expressly objects to its being applied,[33] the custom or practice cannot be impliedly incorporated as a
term of the contract.

Nevertheless, the process of implying terms into employment
contracts is strongly influenced by judicial policy-making. Indeed,
the golden thread in the evolution of employment contract law is that
courts are continually refashioning the legal rules in order to facilitate
the operation of the prevailing standards of personnel management
practice; they also strive to reflect society's changing vision of what
an employment relationship ought to resemble. The implied term is
one of the main tools used by the courts for this purpose. The factual
intention of the parties test is frequently recited as a mantra — a "fictive formality," so to speak — to cloak the courts' policy preferences as
to what the parties' rights and obligations ought to be. Occasionally,
courts will admit openly that a particular term should be implied into
the contract as a "matter of law" because it reflects sound public policy.
The standardized set of rights and obligations of employers and employees that are implied into all employment contracts across the board
falls into this category. Perhaps the best example of the policy-driven
nature of these standardized implied terms is the employer's implied
duty to give its employees "reasonable" notice of termination, now a
veritable catch-all for an enormous range of policy considerations.[34] In
this sense, it can fairly be said that the courts have fashioned a common
law "status" for employees. But the status point must not be exaggerated: the parties can always expressly contract-out of any standardized

---

30   Examples: *Adams v. Comark Inc.* (1992), 42 C.C.E.L. 15 (Man. C.A.); *Olympic
     Industries Inc. v. McNeill*, [1994] 3 W.W.R. 268, especially at 275 (B.C.C.A.).

31   Example: *Emslie v. Kensington Homes Ltd.* (1992), 43 C.C.E.L. 268, especially at
     271 (Man. C.A.) where it was the recognized custom for real-estate sellers to be
     engaged on a "hiring at will" basis.

32   See *Collins v. Jim Pattison Industries Ltd.* (1995), 11 C.C.E.L. (2d) 74, especially
     at 83 (B.C.S.C.); *Heslop v. Cooper's Crane Rental Ltd.* (1994), 6 C.C.E.L. (2d) 252
     (Ont. Gen. Div.).

33   See *Kennedy v. HMT Realty Corp.* (1986), 14 C.C.E.L. 113 (Ont. Dist. Ct.).

34   See Chapter 9, Section B(3)(c).

implied term. Be that as it may, today the dominant policy driving the development of the implied term is to expand the rights of the vulnerable employee.[35]

The dynamics of the employment relationship make it unavoidable that many gaps and ambiguities will remain in the express terms of the contract; nonetheless, it is submitted that greater predictability and certainty could be infused into this area if Canadian provinces adopted the British model of legislating an obligation on the employer to give the employee written particulars of the major terms and conditions of employment at the date of hiring and thereafter when any changes are made.[36]

1) Liability for Misstatements in the Law of Tort

So far we have considered the position where the representations of either party are enforced in the law of contract as express or implied terms of the employment contract. However, the parties' representations can be legally enforced in the law of tort as fraudulent or negligent misrepresentations. The tort of fraudulent misrepresentation (or deceit) occurs where one side makes a statement of existing fact—either knowing it to be untrue or being reckless as to its truth—and the other party relies on the representation to its detriment.[37] The tort of negligent misrepresentation occurs where two parties have a judicially recognized "special relationship," and one side makes a statement of existing fact to the other without taking reasonable care to verify its accuracy, inducing the other side to suffer detrimental reliance. A special relationship normally exists where one party has superior expertise and knowledge that it can reasonably foresee the other party will rely on.

The employment relationship clearly provides a fruitful field for the operation of these torts—the more so with negligent misrepresentation, since fraud occurs infrequently and is difficult to prove. Thus, employers have been found liable for negligently misrepresenting, during recruitment interviews, the nature of the job being applied for and

---

35   See generally G. England, "The Impact of the *Charter* on Individual Employment Law in Canada: Rewriting an Old Story" (2006) 13 C.L.E.L.J. 1; G. England, "Recent Developments in Individual Employment Law: Tell Me the Old, Old Story" (2002) 9 C.L.E.L.J. 43.

36   *Employment Protection (Consolidation) Act 1978* (U.K.), 1978, c. 44, ss. 1–11. This practice was recommended in Canada, Commission on the Review of Federal Labour Standards, *Fairness at Work: Federal Labour Standards for the 21st Century* by H.W. Arthurs (Ottawa: Commission on the Review of Federal Labour Standards, 2006) at 79–83.

37   The seminal authority is *Derry v. Peek* (1889), 14 App. Cas. 337 (H.L.).

its degree of security of tenure,[38] and, for example, the certainty that an employee's overseas qualifications would be accepted by the licensing body in Canada.[39] Similarly, employers have been found liable for negligently misrepresenting the financial impact of an early retirement package on an employee's pension and other retirement benefits.[40] In some of the latter decisions, the employers in question were found liable for negligently failing to advise the employees about their retirement benefits *pro-actively*. This holding appears to be an exception to the traditional rule that the tort of negligent misstatement does not compel the employer to disclose relevant information to the employee proactively; rather, liability arises only if the employer voluntarily chooses to make a representation of fact, or responds to a request from the employee. Here, the courts appear to be giving paramountcy to the employee's need to know vitally important and technically complex information that the employer is in the best position to provide. Because the laws of tort and contract often develop in tandem, it will be interesting to see if future courts rely on these decisions to develop an implied contractual duty on the employer to look after the broad economic well-being of its employees. Traditionally, the English courts have refused to imply such a duty in the employment contract, reasoning that it is too uncertain and potentially too intrusive into managerial prerogatives,[41] but the above-mentioned developments in the tort of negligent misstatement unquestionably hint at such a possibility in Canada.[42]

On the other hand, the employer will not be found liable if it merely expresses its *opinion* on a particular matter to the employee, as opposed to making a statement of existing fact. For example, an employer that mis-estimated its chances of winning a case in arbitration, thus creating

---

38   *Queen v. Cognos Inc.*, [1993] 1 S.C.R. 87.

39   Examples: *De Groot v. St. Boniface Hospital* (1993), 48 C.C.E.L. 271 (Man. Q.B.); *Woolridge v. H.B. Nickerson & Sons Ltd.* (1980), 40 N.S.R. (2d) 388 (S.C.A.D.).

40   Examples: *Allison v. Noranda Inc.* (2001), 9 C.C.E.L. (3d) 280, especially at 290 (C.A.); *Gauthier v. Canada (A.G.)* (2000), 225 N.B.R. (2d) 211 (C.A.); *Spinks v. Canada* (1996), 19 C.C.E.L. (2d) 1, especially at 16 (F.C.A.); *Ford v. Laidlaw Carriers Inc.* (1993), 50 C.C.E.L. 165 (Ont. Gen. Div.); *Lehune v. Kelowna (City)* (1994), 98 B.C.L.R. (2d) 135 (C.A.).

41   *Crossley v. Faithful and Gould Holdings Ltd.*, [2004] I.R.L.R. 377 (C.A.); *Hagen v. ICI Chemicals and Polymers Ltd.*, [2002] I.R.L.R. 31 (Q.B.).

42   See, for example, *Menard v. Royal Insurance Company of Canada* (2000), 1 C.C.E.L. (3d) 96 at para. 44 (Ont. S.C.J.), where the employer was found liable for breaching an implied contractual duty to explain proactively to an emotionally distraught employee during a termination interview that she could apply for certain post-termination disability benefits within a specified deadline. The court held that the employer has a contractual obligation ". . . to be honest, forthright, candid and to act in good faith."

a vacancy for the employee, was found not liable on this basis.[43] Moreover, the doctrine of contributory negligence applies to these torts, so that the innocent party's damages will be reduced commensurate with the degree of carelessness in failing to verify the representations in question.[44] In addition, there will be no liability if the representor clearly disclaims responsibility for the accuracy or reliability of statements made,[45] or if the innocent party does not rely on them in making the decision that results in the harm. Finally, nothing in theory prevents an employer from suing an employee for negligent misstatements, but this rarely happens since the employee usually lacks the funds to make such an action worthwhile, and the employer can usually summarily dismiss the employee for serious negligence and misconduct.

There may be practical advantages to bringing an action in tort as opposed to contract. For example, the rules of remoteness of damages are broader in tort than in contract. The object in tort is to restore the employee to the position he or she would have been in had the tortious representation never been made (*restitutio in integrum*). In comparison, the object in contract is to compensate the employee for the value of the promise.[46] The limitations periods normally differ between contract and tort, as well.[47]

Finally, section 8 of the *British Columbia Employment Standards Act* is noteworthy in giving legislative effect to the torts of fraudulent and negligent misrepresentation. The main practical advantage to the employee is the ability to pursue a relatively cheap and expeditious remedy under the statute's administrative machinery, rather than bringing a tort action in the courts.

2) Modifying the Terms of the Employment Contract and the Problem of Consideration

The dynamic nature of the employment relationship is such that the terms of the employment contract will often change. Contract law dictates that any amendment to the terms of a contract must be supported

---

43 *Williams v. Saanich School District No. 63* (1986), 11 C.C.E.L. 233 (B.C.S.C.), aff'd (1987), 17 C.C.E.L. 257 (B.C.C.A.).
44 Example: *Lewis v. Coles* (1993), 47 C.C.E.L. 302, especially at 306 (B.C.S.C.).
45 Example: *Lipczynska-Kochany v. Gillham* (2001), 14 C.C.E.L. (3d) 304 at 317 (Ont. S.C.J.).
46 See W.H. Charles, "Torts and Contract—Merging Areas?" (1987) 8 Advocates' Q. 222 at 236–37.
47 See J. Blom, "Concurrent Liability in Tort and Contract—Start of Limitation Period: *Central Trust Co. v. Rafuse*" (1987) 21 U.B.C. L. Rev. 429.

by fresh consideration over and above the performance of existing contractual obligations.[48] Thus, if the employer reduces the length of the working week, reduces the employee's severance entitlements, reduces the employee's compensation, or substantially changes the employee's job duties or place of employment, the employee is required to provide something of value in return in order to render the variation of the term in question legally enforceable. Ordinarily, simply continuing to perform work will not constitute adequate consideration, since the employee will be under a pre-existing contractual duty to do so.[49] Cementing contractual variations, therefore, can be problematic.

One solution is to include a term in the employment contract that expressly permits the employer unilaterally, and at its unfettered discretion, to modify some or all of the terms of the contract in a prescribed manner by giving the employee written notice, for example. Either the employment contract itself could contain such a term, or the contract could expressly incorporate an ancillary document, such as a work's rule book or policy manual, that expressly gives the employer this right. Provided that such a term is sufficiently unambigous to pass the muster of judicial *contra proferentem* interpretations[50] and that the employee has given informed consent to it forming part of the contract, there is no doctrinal reason why the courts should not enforce it.[51] Effectively, such a provision would play the same role in the private employment contract as a "management's rights" provision plays in a collective agreement.

Another solution is to find fresh consideration in the forbearance of the employee to exercise the legal privilege of lawfully resigning or, in the case of the employer, of giving lawful notice of termination.[52] Al-

---

48   Examples; *Stilk v. Myrick* (1809), 2 Camp. 317, 170 E.R. 1168 (C.P.); *Gilbert Steel Ltd. v. University Construction Ltd.* (1976), 67 D.L.R. (3d) 606 (Ont. C.A.), which involved a construction contract. But *quaere* the effect on the traditional rule of *Williams v. Roffey Bros. & Nicholls (Contractors) Ltd.* (1990), [1991] 1 Q.B. 1 (C.A.).

49   Example: *Singh v. Empire Life Insurance Co.* (2002), 19 C.C.E.L. (3d) 29 at 34 (B.C.C.A.), involving reduced termination entitlements.

50   Example: *Corker v. University of British Columbia* (1990), 33 C.C.E.L. 246 at 253 (B.C.S.C.), where a *contra proferentem* interpretation of a job description was applied to disallow the employer's right unilaterally to change the employee's job duties.

51   Examples: *Belton v. Liberty Insurance Company of Canada*, [2003] C.L.L.C. ¶210-006 (Ont. S.C.J.); *Pathak v. Royal Bank of Canada* (1996), 18 C.C.E.L. (2d) 266 at 270 (B.C.C.A); *Long v. Delta Catalytic Industrial Services Inc.*(1998), 35 C.C.E.L. (2d) 70 at 78 (Alta. Q.B.), where Furman J. stated that he would have upheld the clause if it had been properly included in the contract.

52   *Sloan v. Union Oil Co. of Canada*, [1955] 4 D.L.R. 644 at 679 (B.C.S.C.); *Maier v. E & B Exploration Ltd.*, [1986] 4 W.W.R. 275 at 281–82 (Alta. C.A.).

though this solution is technically plausible, in reality, it has a somewhat hollow ring: the possibility of terminating their relationship will often not be in the parties' minds when they are negotiating an amendment to a contract. Indeed, the courts have prevented employers from using this device to make changes that would significantly disadvantage a vulnerable employee unless the employer can show that it definitely would have terminated the contract had the employee not assented to the change, and that the employee agreed to the change in return for an undertaking of ongoing employment.[53] Alternatively, in some circumstances, the parties might be said to have mutually rescinded the employment contract. Doing this involves bringing the first employment contract to an end and replacing it with an entirely new contract that contains the changed terms. A mutual rescission generates its own consideration.[54] The main limitation with rescission, however, is that the courts normally require a substantial majority of the first contract's terms to be replaced, which is not always the case. If the employer gives advance notice of a contractual variation equal to the period of lawful notice of termination, it can be argued that the notice can serve as a notice of termination coupled with an offer to renew the contract on changed terms.[55] Again, however, this reasoning will often have an implausible ring, and it restricts the employer's flexibility to implement a modification if it must be preceded by a possibly lengthy and uncertain notice period. Finally, promissory estoppel could come into play if one party changes a term of the employment contract and the other party continues to work as before without protest, thereby inducing the first party to incur a detriment in the belief that the second party is relinquishing strict contractual rights.

Whichever of the above methods is invoked to enforce a contractual modification, it is clear that both parties to the employment contract must have full knowledge of the scope and nature of the change in question and must assent to it without duress or coercion in order for the modification to be legally binding.[56]

---

53 Examples: *Hobbs v. TDI Canada Ltd.*, [2005] C.L.L.C. ¶210-031, especially at 141,251 (Ont. C.A.); *Techform Products Ltd. v. Wolda* (2001), 12 C.C.E.L. (3d) 184 at 193 (Ont. C.A.).

54 See G.H. Treitel, *The Law of Contract*, 8th ed. (London: Stevens, 1991) at 94–95.

55 Examples: *Chambers v. Axia Netmedia Corporation* (2004), 30 C.C.E.L. (3d) 243 at 263–64 (N.S.T.D.); *Morgan v. Fry*, [1968] 2 Q.B. 710 (C.A.), Davis L.J., construing strike notice; *Hill v. Peter Gorman Ltd.* (1957), 9 D.L.R. (2d) 124 at 136 (Ont. C.A.) [*Hill*], Gibson J.A. in a dissenting judgment.

56 Examples: *McLaren v. Pacific Construction Savings Credit Union*, [2000] C.L.L.C. ¶210-023 (B.C.S.C.); *Hill, ibid.*; *Sagkeeng Education Authority Inc. v. Guimond*, [1996] 1 F.C. 387 at 399–400 (T.D.); *Chilagan v. Island Lake Band No. 161*, [1994] 5 W.W.R. 308 at 316 (Sask. Q.B.).

3) Defective Contracts of Employment

An employment contract is subject to the general principles of contract law regarding misrepresentation;[57] mistake;[58] duress, undue influence, and unconscionability; illegality;[59] and frustration.[60]

For employment lawyers, the most interesting area is duress, undue influence, and unconscionability since the disequilibrium of bargaining power in most employment contracts can provide a fertile ground for these doctrines. The doctrine of duress states that a contract is voidable if it is procured by a threatened illegal act, including a threatened breach of contract.[61] The greatest potential for duress is the situation where an employer threatens to break a term in the employment contract, such as dismissal without due notice, unless the worker agrees to modify other terms and conditions of employment. The English courts, however, have suggested that duress can be established even in the absence of unlawful means if the "will" of one party is "overborne" by another.[62] The ambit of this new development remains untested in the context of employment law.

The doctrine of undue influence rests on the notion that in certain kinds of relationships, one party will be unduly swayed by the other. As yet, the courts have not recognized the employment relationship as falling within this category, despite the power imbalance in most employment contracts.

The doctrine of unconscionability allows a court to rescind a contract if one party has exploited its dominant bargaining position to extract a manifestly improvident agreement from the other. In recent years, the Supreme Court of Canada has often reiterated the importance of protecting the employee against the asymmetry in bargaining power that typifies most employment relationships.[63] Yet, these *obiter*

---

57   See Section B(1), above in this chapter, where the burgeoning importance of the tort of negligent misstatement is reviewed.

58   Example: *Littleleaf v. Peigan Board of Education*, [2001] C.L.A.D. No. 396 (England), aff'd 2002 FCT 1300, involving mutual mistake.

59   This doctrine most frequently arises in the context of restrictive covenants limiting post-employment competition by employees: see Chapter 9, Section G.

60   Chapter 9 examines this in detail.

61   *Pao On v. Lau Yiu Long* (1979), [1980] A.C. 614 (P.C.).

62   Examples: *B. & S. Contracts and Designs Ltd. v. Victor Green Publications Ltd.*, [1984] I.C.R. 419 (C.A.); *Barton v. Armstrong* (1973), [1976] A.C. 104 (P.C.). See generally P.S. Atiyah, "Economic Duress and the 'Overborne Will'" (1982) 98 L.Q. Rev. 197; K.W. Wedderburn, "Comment" (1982) 45 Mod. L. Rev. 556.

63   See generally England, "The Impact of the *Charter* on Individual Employment Law in Canada: Rewriting an Old Story," above note 35 at 17–34.

dicta have not resulted in an aggressive application of the doctrine of unconscionability to one-sided or harsh terms in the employment contract. The courts are reluctant to substitute judicial fiat for market forces in setting the terms and conditions of employment contracts, and perhaps wisely so since judicial over-exuberance in this area would augur badly for economic efficiency. At this juncture, most courts have applied the doctrine of unconscionability relatively cautiously to those situations where the employer has taken an unfair advantage of a clear vulnerability of the worker.[64] For instance, the doctrine was applied to vitiate a separation agreement that the employer pressured the worker to sign when the employer knew that the worker was psychologically traumatized after his termination, was in extreme financial distress, and had not obtained professional legal advice.[65] The doctrine has also been applied to vitiate unduly harsh termination clauses, where the fundamental nature of the employment contract has changed since the clause was first included, and the worker has not been given a fair opportunity to bargain the clause out of the contract.[66]

C. STATUTORY RESTRICTIONS ON THE EMPLOYER'S FREEDOM TO HIRE

The common law principles examined in the previous section leave the employee exposed to the full rigours of market forces when entering into an employment relationship. In order to safeguard the employee against abuse by the employer of its superior market power, extensive legislation restricts the employer's conduct during the recruitment process.

Foremost among these is the human rights legislation common to all jurisdictions. Human rights statutes prohibit employers from refusing to hire potential employees or from discriminating against them in regard to their terms and conditions of employment on designated "human rights" grounds, such as race, sex, religion, and disability. These

---

64 Examples: *Howell v. Reitmans (Canada) Ltd.* (2002), 21 C.C.E.L. (3d) 208 at 214 (Nfld. S.C.); *Dolter v. Media House Productions Inc.*, [2002] S.J. No. 366 (Q.B.); *Matthewson v. Aiton Power Ltd.* (1985), 8 C.C.E.L. 312 at 314 (Ont. C.A.); *Jobber v. Addressograph Multigraph of Canada Ltd.* (1980), 1 C.C.E.L. 87 at 91 (Ont. C.A.). But compare the broader formulation by Lambert J.A., *obiter*, in *Harry v. Kreutziger* (1978), 95 D.L.R. (3d) 231 at 241 (B.C.C.A.).

65 *Howell v. Reitmans (Canada) Ltd.*, *ibid.* at 214; *Blackmore v. Cablenet Ltd.* (1994), 8 C.C.E.L. (2d) 174 at 184 (Alta. Q.B.); *Waterman v. Frisby Tire Co. (1974) Ltd.* (1995), 13 C.C.E.L. (2d) 184 at 199–200 (Ont. Gen. Div.).

66 The cases are examined in detail in Chapter 9, Section B(3)(a).

protected grounds differ considerably between the provinces, requiring that each statute be consulted individually. A key element to the concept of "discrimination" under this legislation is that it encompasses not only the situation where an employer intentionally discriminates out of personal spite or disaffection towards a protected group — "direct" discrimination, in human rights parlance — but also the situation where an employer's recruitment policies and practices have the unintended result of disproportionately disadvantaging members of a protected group — "indirect" discrimination. The legislation also prohibits employers from discriminating on proscribed grounds in job advertisements, job interviews, or otherwise during the recruitment process.

The employer is allowed to discriminate against a person where the discriminatory qualification is necessary for the effective performance of the job — this is called the defence of "*bona fide* occupational qualification." For example, in the case of sperm donors, an employer can make maleness a condition of employment. But even here, the employer must prove that it has made reasonable attempts to accommodate someone up to the point of undue hardship before it can refuse to employ him or her — this is called the "duty of reasonable accommodation." For example, a retail store would have to consider providing a stepladder so that unusually short employees could reach the higher shelves before it could set a minimum height requirement for the job in question. Perhaps most controversially, the human rights legislation generally authorizes a human rights tribunal to order that the employer impose affirmative action hiring and promotion policies, including job quotas, as a remedy for unlawfully discriminating in hiring. This legislation is so important to all facets of the employment relationship that it is dealt with in detail in a chapter of its own.[67]

The collective bargaining legislation in all jurisdictions makes it an "unfair labour practice" for an employer to refuse to employ a person, or otherwise discriminate against a person in regard to the terms and conditions of employment, because he or she is a member or supporter of or has participated in the lawful activities of a trade union.[68] Labour relations boards are empowered to apply "make whole" remedies to compensate workers and unions whose rights have been violated, including ordering the employer to hire a job applicant.

In addition, privacy legislation in most jurisdictions limits the employer's freedom to canvass personal information about a job applicant from his or her previous employers or other acquaintances, but this is

---

67   See Chapter 7.
68   Example: Alberta *Labour Relations Code*, S.A. 2000, c. L-1, s. 149(a).

not as comprehensive as the human rights and collective bargaining legislation.[69] As well, Manitoba is unique in having a *Personal Investigations Act*.[70] This Act makes it unlawful for an employer to canvass information about a prospective employee without that person's written consent, subject to an extensive list of exceptions. Section 4, the cornerstone of the Act, prohibits an employer from collecting in a "personal report" the following information about a prospective employee:

> No personal report shall contain
>
> (a) any reference to race, religion, ethnic origin, or political affiliation of the subject unless this information is voluntarily supplied by the subject; or
>
> (b) information about any bankruptcy of the subject if the personal report is made more than six years after the date of the discharge in bankruptcy, unless the subject has been bankrupt more than once; or
>
> (c) information regarding any writs, judgments, collections or debts that are statute barred; or
>
> (d) information regarding writs issued against the subject more than 12 months prior to the making of the report if the present status of the action is not ascertained; or
>
> (e) information as to any judgment against the subject unless mention is made of the name and, except in the case of information provided by the designated officer under *The Family Maintenance Act*, the address of the judgment creditor as given at the date of entry of the judgment and the amount of the judgment; or
>
> (f) any other adverse factual or investigative information that is more than six years old unless it is voluntarily supplied by the subject or is otherwise permitted by this Act; or
>
> (g) any investigative information regarding the subject unless reasonable efforts have been made to corroborate the information.

It is an offence for any person to breach the Act.

---

69   See Chapter 6.
70   C.C.S.M. c. P34.

FURTHER READINGS

ADAMS, J., & R. BROWNSWORD, "Contract, Consideration and the Critical Path" (1990) 53 Mod. L. Rev. 536

CLARK, J., & M. HALL, "The Cinderella Directive: Employee Rights to Information about Conditions Applicable to Their Contract or Employment Relationship" (1992) 21 Indus. L.J. 106

CORNISH, M., E. MCINTYRE, & A. PASK, "Strategies for Challenging Discriminatory Barriers to Foreign Credential Recognition" (2000) 8 C.L.E.L.J. 17

ENGLAND, G., R. WOOD, & I. CHRISTIE, *Employment Law in Canada*, 4th ed., looseleaf (Markham, ON: LexisNexis Canada, 2005–) cc. 4 & 7

FREEDLAND, M.R., *The Personal Contract of Employment* (Oxford: Oxford University Press, 2003)

HONEYBALL, S., "The Enforcement of Illegal Contracts" (1992) 21 Indus. L.J. 143

LONGFORD, M., "Family Poverty and the Exploitation of Child Labour" (1995) 17 Law & Pol'y 471

MILGROM, P.R., & R. ROBERTS, *Economics, Organization, and Management*, 6th ed. (Englewood Cliffs, NJ: Prentice-Hall, 1992) at 333–41, 349–53, & c. 11

RAFFERTY, N.S., "Liability for Pre-Contractual Misstatement" (1984) 14 Man. L.J. 63

RAFFERTY, N.S., "Torts—Negligent Misstatement—Recovery for Purely Economic Loss" (1991) 70 Can. Bar Rev. 381

THE COMMON LAW OBLIGATIONS OF THE EMPLOYEE UNDER THE CONTRACT OF EMPLOYMENT

An employee owes his or her employer obligations under both the express and the implied terms of the employment contract.[1] Regarding the employee's express obligations, in Chapter 3 we saw that employment contracts generally do not contain a detailed and comprehensive list of the employee's duties, except perhaps for higher echelon executives, sports stars, and entertainers. Usually, the contract of employment will state little about the employee's obligations beyond providing a brief job description and summarizing the basic pay, the basic hours of work, and annual vacations. The most common exception is a restrictive covenant that prevents the employee from competing with his or her employer within a defined area and for a defined time after the employment relationship ends. We examine the law on restrictive covenants in this chapter. The explanation for the relative dearth of express terms in employment contracts is that the parties cannot, when they are negotiating their contract, foresee all possible contingencies that might occur over the lifetime of their relationship and deal with them in advance. Consequently, the courts have had to fill the gap by implying terms into the employment contract, and the scope of the employee's obligations to the employer at common law depends almost exclusively on these implied terms.

---

1   For further detailed elaboration on this topic, see G. England, R. Wood, & I. Christie, *Employment Law in Canada*, 4th ed., looseleaf (Markham, ON: Lexis-Nexis Canada, 2005–) c. 11 (II–III).

According to the general principles of contract law, terms must be implied into a contract in order to give effect to the unstated factual intentions of the parties; otherwise "freedom of contract" would be jeopardized. In reality, courts often imply terms into contracts in order to reflect the *judges'* perceptions of what the parties' respective rights and obligations *ought* to be as a matter of public policy. This has clearly happened in the case of the employee's implied obligations under the employment contract. The courts have, over the years, developed a standardized body of particular obligations that are implied into all employment contracts. The cornerstone of these particular obligations, however, is an overriding residual duty of the employee to conduct himself or herself in the best interests of the employer, usually referred to as the "duty of fidelity."[2] This duty is critically important for employers. Because the employer cannot predict and set specific rules in advance for the myriad circumstances that can arise during the course of a long-term employment relationship, it is essential that the employer have the flexibility to command obedience from its employees as new circumstances arise.[3] Plainly, it would be grossly inefficient if the employer had to renegotiate the express terms of the employment contract every time an unexpected occurrence arose! The implied duty of fidelity, therefore, delineates the scope of "managerial prerogative" at common law.

Most of the cases on the implied obligations of the employee arise in the context of litigation over wrongful dismissal, since the employer's usual reaction to a perceived breach of duty is to fire the worker summarily without notice or wages in lieu. Consequently, the scope of the employee's implied obligations becomes inextricably interwoven with the issue of whether the employer had "just cause" for summary dismissal. We shall see in our examination of just cause how the rigour of the employee's implied duty of fidelity has been tempered to reflect modern notions of proportionality, equality, and fairness.[4] The *Charter* has indirectly influenced the development of the common law greatly

---

2   The historical antecedents of the employee's duty of fidelity can be traced to the pre-Industrial Revolution law of master and servant in England. See, for example, A. Fox, *Beyond Contract: Work, Power and Trust Relations* (London: Faber, 1974) at 154–59, 178–81, 184–88; D. Hay, "England, 1562–1875: The Law and Its Uses" in D. Hay & P. Craven, eds., *Masters, Servants and Magistrates in Britain and the Empire, 1562–1955* (Chapel Hill, NC: University of North Carolina Press, 2004) at 59.

3   The centrality of this point cannot be overemphasized. See, for example, J. Godard, "The Progressive HRM Paradigm: A Theoretical and Empirical Re-Examination" (1991) 46 Rel. Indus. 378 at 383.

4   See Chapter 9.

in this respect. Although the *Charter* does not apply directly to private contracts of employment, the courts have transposed its fundamental values of fairness, equality, and proportionality into the contract of employment under the rubric of malleable contract law principles, such as the implied duty of fidelity, "just cause" for dismissal, and others.[5] However, an employer may sometimes sue an employee for damages to recoup losses it has suffered as a result of the employee's breach of implied obligations, and may seek an injunction to restrain breaches of particular obligations, such as the duty not to compete or divulge confidential information.

A. THE EMPLOYEE'S EXPRESS CONTRACTUAL OBLIGATIONS: RESTRICTIVE COVENANTS

Any express terms in the employment contract regarding the employee's obligations to the employer will be enforced by the courts according to their literal meaning. Only where the express terms are ambiguous can the courts rely on extrinsic evidence, such as the parties' past practices in interpreting contractual language. If the contractual language is unambiguous, however, the court normally applies the terminology in question as it stands, no matter how unfair the judge might feel the outcome to be.[6] The courts will interpret contractual language *contra proferentem* the interests of the employer if the clause in question appears to be unduly onerous for the employee, normally the weaker party to the bargain. Frequently, the employment contract will expressly state that the employee's obligations, along with other terms and conditions of employment, are to be found in a personnel manual or in some other documentation, in which case such documentation will be expressly incorporated into the employment contract. Next, we examine the most frequently litigated express term in the employment contract: the "restrictive covenant."

A restrictive covenant seeks to prevent an employee from exploiting an employer's trade secrets, confidential information, or general business goodwill, or from competing with the employer after their employment relationship has ended. Not surprisingly, such clauses are

---

5   G. England, "The Impact of the *Charter* on Individual Employment Law in Canada: Rewriting an Old Story" (2006) 13 C.L.E.L.J. 1.

6   Subject, of course, to the doctrines of unconscionability and duress, which allow unambiguous terms to be avoided in limited circumstances. See Chapter 3, Section B(3).

generally found in the employment contracts of managers, professionals, and salespersons. The treatment of such clauses necessitates striking a balance between (1) the employer's interest in safeguarding the possibly substantial investment it has made in its confidential information, general know-how, and business goodwill; (2) the employee's interest in securing replacement employment and pursuing his or her career in an occupation in which he or she may have invested heavily; and (3) the general "public interest" in facilitating labour mobility and promoting competition among suppliers for goods and services.

Currently, the courts strike the balance by presuming that any restrictive covenant is void as being in restraint of trade unless the following conditions are all met:[7] (1) the covenant must protect a "proprietary interest" of the employer that the courts recognize as worthy of protection, rather than merely limit the employee's general ability to compete with the employer; (2) the covenant must be "reasonable" in terms of duration and geographical location; (3) there must be minimal impairment of the employee's interests, in the sense that there must be no alternative method available for protecting the employer's specific interests that is less harmful to the employee than a full-scale prohibition against engaging in post-employment competition;[8] and (4) the covenant must not otherwise be contrary to the public interest. Essentially, these four requirements boil down to the principle of proportionality. Normally, since it will be seeking to enforce the covenant, the employer will carry the burden of proving that these requirements are met.[9] Moreover, courts resolve any doubts about these requirements being met in favour of the employee by application of the *contra proferentem* method, given that restrictive covenants are often the product of a disequilibrium of bargaining power in favour of the employer.[10] Only if the power between the parties is evenly balanced will the courts dispense with the *contra proferentem* method.[11]

---

7   The general principles can be found in *Lyons v. Multari*, [2001] C.L.L.C. ¶210-011 at 141,056–59 (Ont. C.A.) [*Lyons*]. The leading English authorities are *Mason v. Provident Clothing and Supply Co.*, [1913] A.C. 724 (H.L.) and *Morris (Herbert) Ltd. v. Saxelby*, [1916] 1 A.C. 688 (H.L.) [*Saxelby*].

8   *Lyons*, ibid.; *Atlantic Business Interiors v. Hipson and MPP Office Interiors Ltd.*, [2005] C.L.L.C. ¶210-034, especially at 141,314 (N.S.C.A.) [*Atlantic Business Interiors*].

9   Example: *Friesen v. McKague* (1992), 44 C.C.E.L. 280 at 284 (Man. C.A.), citing *Rapid-Med Plus Franchise Corp. v. Elliot* (1991), 73 Man. R. (2d) 150 at 152 (C.A.), Twaddle J.A.

10   Examples: *Button v. Jones* (2001), 11 C.C.E.L. (3d) 312 at 317 (Ont. S.C.J.); *Ernst & Young v. Stuart* (1993), 46 C.C.E.L. 161 (B.C.S.C.) [*Ernst & Young*].

11   *Ipsos S.A. v. Reid* (2005), 43 C.C.E.L. (3d) 117 at 134 (B.C.S.C.).

The courts have held that a legitimate proprietary interest of the employer must involve confidential information, trade secrets, or business goodwill; merely eliminating competition from an employee after he or she has left the firm will not suffice.[12] An express term in the contract describing certain material, information, or trade relationships as a "legitimate business interest" of the employer will not automatically bind the court to such a finding; rather, the courts recognize that such clauses are often the product of disparate bargaining power and accordingly determine whether there is a "legitimate business interest" as a matter of fact.[13] Furthermore, a line is drawn between firm-specific confidential information, which can be protected by a restrictive covenant, and the general expertise and skills that the employee has learned on the job, which cannot be restricted.[14]

In order to be reasonable in terms of geographical coverage, a covenant must protect the employer's interests only within that area where competition exists for the employer's product or service. For example, a covenant precluding an accountant from competing within a 50 mile (80 kilometre) radius of the employer's premises was held to be unreasonably broad, since the employer drew its clients from a far smaller catchment area.[15] In order to be reasonable in terms of duration, a covenant must protect the employer only so long as is necessary for the employer to recover from the employee's influence. For instance, a covenant that forbade a photographer from competing with his former employer for one year in a small town in Northern Ontario was ruled temporally reasonable, since it would take approximately one year for the employee's replacement to build up a relationship of trust and confidence with the firm's clientele.[16]

The requirement that a restrictive covenant must cause minimal harm to the employee is exemplified by the leading case of *Lyons*.[17] In that case, a covenant prohibiting the employee from competing as an oral surgeon after his employment had ended was struck down. The employer could have adequately safeguarded its interest in protecting

---

12 A useful checklist is provided in *Winnipeg Livestock Sales Ltd. v. Plewman*, [2001] C.L.L.C. ¶210-003 at 141,015 (Man. C.A.).

13 *Management Recruiters of Toronto Ltd. v. Bagg*, [1971] 1 O.R. 502 (H.C.J.).

14 Example: *Mercury Marine Ltd. v. Dillon* (1986), 30 D.L.R. (4th) 627 (Ont. H.C.J.).

15 *Ernst & Young*, above note 10. See also *Semiconductor Insights Inc. v. Kurjanowicz* (1996), 16 C.C.E.L. (2d) 98, especially at 105 (Ont. Gen. Div.).

16 *Jostens Canada Inc. v. Gendron* (1993), 1 C.C.E.L. (2d) 275 (Ont. Gen. Div.) [*Gendron*].

17 Above note 7. See also *Atlantic Business Interiors*, above note 8, especially at 141,314.

its clients by inserting a less draconian clause in the employment contract. It could simply have prohibited the employee from soliciting former clients in his new firm.

Regarding the requirement that a restrictive covenant must be in the public interest, Canadian courts have held that it will not suffice that the restraint is reasonable between the employer and the employee; rather, the public interest is a separate requirement that must be satisfied in its own right. Thus, a restrictive covenant that prohibited an obstetrician from practising any form of medicine or surgery within 5 miles (8 kilometres) of St. Catharines, Ontario, was avoided: the prohibition would have been against the public interest due to a shortage of obstetricians in that region.[18] In contrast, most (but not all) English courts hold that any restraint that is reasonable between the parties must *ipso facto* be harmonious with the public interest.

If a restrictive covenant is found to be an unreasonable restraint of trade, the courts will not necessarily avoid the *entire* provision in question, but may simply expunge the offending part of the provision and leave the remainder intact. This will only be done, however, if it is possible to sever the offending part without rendering the remainder of the provision absurd or meaningless, for, out of deference to the principle of freedom of contract, the courts will not rewrite the terms of the contract in order to facilitate the excision.[19] This principle is commonly referred to as the "blue-pencil" test.[20] Some employers attempt to exploit this exception by including so-called "Russian doll" clauses in the contract.[21] These clauses specify a list of alternative diminishing areas and times governing the restrictive covenant, and invite the court to go down the list, striking out offending areas and times until the court finds one that it can uphold as reasonable.

The English courts have held that an otherwise valid restrictive covenant ceases to bind the employee if the employer summarily dismisses him or her in breach of contract.[22] This rule is normally justified

---

18   *Sherk v. Horwitz*, [1972] 2 O.R. 451 (H.C.J.), aff'd on other grounds (1972), [1973] 1 O.R. 360 (C.A.), leave to appeal to S.C.C. refused, [1972] 2 S.C.R. xiv.
19   Compare *Jones v. Prostar Painting and Restoration Ltd.*, [2006] B.C.J. No. 1556 at para. 41 (S.C.) where the court substituted a two-year term for a five-year term "on the basis of fairness." Other courts, however, have not followed this exceptional approach.
20   Examples: *Gordon v. Ferguson* (1961), 30 D.L.R. (2d) 420 (N.S.S.C.), aff'd [1962] S.C.R. vii; *Attwood v. Lamont*, [1920] 3 K.B. 571 (C.A.); *R.C. Young Insurance Ltd. v. Bricknell*, [1955] 5 D.L.R. 487 at 488 (Ont. H.C.J.), aff'd [1955] 5 D.L.R. 490 (Ont. C.A.).
21   Example: *Community Credit Union Ltd. v. Ast*, [2007] A.J. No. 156, 2007 ABQB 46.
22   *General Billposting Co. v. Atkinson*, [1909] A.C. 118 (H.L.).

on the grounds that, first, the employer's repudiatory breach brings to an end any outstanding obligations on the employee, including a restrictive covenant, and second, that it would be morally indefensible to allow the employer to benefit under a contract that it has just repudiated. On the other hand, it can be persuasively argued that the employer has a valid moral claim to enforce the restrictive covenant, notwithstanding having wrongfully dismissed the employee. The employee will have been paid extra wages in return for agreeing to include the covenant in the employment contract, so the employer would simply be receiving its reciprocal expectation. Furthermore, there is no technical reason why particular rights and obligations in contracts cannot survive a repudiatory breach if such is the parties' intention. If arbitration clauses, liquidated damages clauses, and exclusion clauses can survive a repudiatory breach,[23] there is no theoretical barrier to a restrictive covenant surviving wrongful dismissal if that is what the parties intend. Although some Canadian courts have expressed doubts concerning the principle that wrongful dismissal automatically eliminates a restrictive covenant,[24] the majority of cases continue to follow it.[25] It can be argued that the ideal solution is to adopt a flexible approach of upholding a restrictive covenant following a wrongful dismissal only if it is just and equitable in the circumstances to do so.[26] This approach would enable the courts to strike a fair balance between the parties' respective interests on the facts of each case. Thus, a restrictive covenant would be more likely to be struck down if the employee is unable to find replacement work after a wrongful dismissal than if replacement work is readily available, or if the employer has acted egregiously in dismissing the employee so that deterrence comes into play. Indeed, the courts have adopted this flexible approach where employers seek to enforce a restrictive covenant against a fiduciary employee following wrongful dismissal.[27] The principle does not apply, however, where the employee commits a repudiatory breach that gives the employer just cause for summary dismissal.[28]

---

23 Examples: *Photo Production Ltd. v. Securicor Transport Ltd.*, [1980] A.C. 827 (H.L.); *Moschi v. Lep Air Services Ltd.*, [1973] A.C. 331, especially at 350 (H.L.), Lord Diplock.

24 See, for example, the remarks in *Jostens Canada Ltd. v. Zbieranek* (1993), 42 C.C.E.L. 264 at 267 (Ont. Gen. Div.); *Murrell v. Burns International Security Services Ltd.* (1994), 5 C.C.E.L. (2d) 123 at 130 (Ont. Gen. Div.).

25 Example: *Gerrard v. Century 21 Armour Real Estate Inc.* (1991), 35 C.C.E.L. 128 at 135–36 (Ont. Gen. Div.).

26 See M.R. Freedland, "Comment" (2003) 32 I.L.J. 48–52.

27 *Harris Scientific Products Ltd. v. Araujo*, 2005 ABQB 603 [*Harris*].

28 *Robinson (William) & Co. v. Heuer*, [1898] 2 Ch. 451 at 458 (C.A.).

The courts could take a similar approach to other express terms in the contract. For example, the principle of proportionality applied to post-employment restrictive covenants would appear to be especially apt in the context of express "no-love" pacts, often used by American employers.[29] Such a clause states that the employee consents to be terminated for just cause, without any severance entitlements, if he or she conducts a romantic affair with another employee. While employees unquestionably have a right to follow the tug of the heart, employers also have a legitimate interest in ensuring that romances are conducted in a manner that avoids harm to the production process. The balance of interests might be struck by presuming an automatic dismissal clause to be void as unduly impinging on the employee's civil liberty unless the employer can prove that dismissal is proportional in all the circumstances. For example, if the employee has disregarded measures that the employer has established to ensure that the morale of other employees is not undermined by the romance, or to ensure that there is no conflict of interest in affairs between a supervisor and a subordinate. If the romantic relationship falls within the definition of "marital status" under the human rights legislation, the employer would have to make these sorts of arguments in order to prove the defence of *bona fide* occupational requirement.[30]

B. THE EMPLOYEE'S IMPLIED CONTRACTUAL OBLIGATIONS

The courts imply terms imposing duties on employees into employment contracts on the same theoretical basis as they imply terms into any other contract.[31] Thus, a term will be implied in order to give effect to the unexpressed factual intentions of both parties as evidenced from all the circumstances, such as their precontractual negotiations, their past practices, and the customary way of doing things in the firm—or even the industry—in question. As well, courts imply standardized terms into contracts in order to reflect the judges' perceptions of what the parties' rights and obligations *ought* to be as a matter of public policy. These principles also operate in the context of implying obligations on employees into employment contracts. The courts may imply

---

29 V. Schultz, "The Sanitized Workplace" (2003) 112 Yale L.J. 2061. See also Chapter 9, Section C(9).

30 See Chapter 7.

31 For further elaboration, see Chapter 3, Section B.

particular firm- or person-specific obligations into the contract of a given employee on the basis of evidence that this is what the parties expect the employee to do. In addition, the courts have developed a broad set of standardized employee obligations that they imply into all employment contracts, reflecting the standards of behaviour that courts expect of employees in a modern industrialized society. In the latter sense, it can fairly be said that the courts have created a "status" for working people.[32] Nevertheless, this point must not be exaggerated, since it is always possible, at least in theory, for employees to modify a standardized implied obligation by insisting on an express clause in the contract to that effect. In this section of the book, attention is focused on the employee's *implied* obligations.

When faced with a perceived breach of implied obligations by an employee, the primary remedy of the employer is summary dismissal, whereupon the question of the precise nature of the employee's obligations becomes interwoven with the issue of whether or not just cause for summary dismissal exists.[33] This point is critically important: whereas the content of the employee's contractual duties may sometimes appear to modern eyes to be unduly strict, the standard may often be tempered by the court ruling that the breach in question does not provide just cause for dismissal because of some other factor, such as procedural unfairness on the employer's part, the presence of mitigating circumstances, or the disproportionate severity of dismissal with regard to the relative triviality of the employee's breach.

In addition to dismissing an employee, the employer is entitled to sue the employee for damages for losses caused by the breach of duty. This occurs infrequently, however, due to the relatively small sums of money generally involved, the difficulty of quantifying the employer's losses accurately enough to found a damages claim, and the practical obstacle of collecting substantial amounts of damages from relatively impecunious employees. Damages actions are most likely to occur when an employee has misused an employer's confidential business information—for example, by misappropriating the employer's client list or inventions—and the employer seeks to recover its losses flowing therefrom, or where the court wants to signal its disapproval at egregious conduct on the employee's part. Furthermore, an employer may seek an injunction to restrain certain breaches on the employee's part—for example, to prohibit the employee from continuing to

---

32   The debate over whether the employment relationship is predominantly one of "status" or "contract" is reviewed in Chapter 1.

33   The common law standards of just cause are examined in Chapter 9.

exploit the employer's confidential business information. Finally, the employer may seek an order of accounting from an employee (or other third party) who misappropriates its confidential business information, directing such a person to disgorge any monies obtained from using the information in question and to remit them to the employer. We examine these remedies in further detail below in the context of specific implied obligations.

1) The Residual Obligation to Advance the Employer's Business Interests

The cornerstone of the employment relationship is the employer's expectation that, in return for receiving wages, the employee undertakes to submit himself or herself to the employer's authority to issue lawful and reasonable orders, and to act in furtherance of the organization's business goals. Employers do not bargain with employees for the supply of specific amounts of labour; they bargain for the right to command the employee and to receive his or her undivided loyalty.[34] In order to reflect this expectation, the courts imply a term into all employment contracts obliging the employee to act in the best interests of the firm, as determined by the employer, in carrying out his or her duties. The employee's duty to obey the lawful and reasonable orders of the employer is a subset of this pervasive obligation to further the employer's interests.

An Alberta trial judge described the duty as follows:

> It has long been accepted that . . . the employee is expected to serve his employer honestly and faithfully during the term of employment. This duty of fidelity permeates the entire relationship between the employer and the employee. It is a flexible concept that is paramount to the basic relationship. There is an implied obligation on the employee to act in the best interests of his employer at all times. The employee shall not follow a course of action that harms or places at risk the interests of the employer.[35]

The duty means, for example, that an employee who wishes to express displeasure at the employer's actions or to pressure the employer into granting a concession cannot perform his or her work with a degree of

---

34   This critically important truth about the nature of the employment contract is brought home by P.R. Milgrom & J. Roberts, *Economics, Organization, and Management* (Englewood Cliffs, NJ: Prentice-Hall, 1992) at 329–30.

35   *CRC-Evans Canada Ltd. v. Pettifer* (1997), 26 C.C.E.L. (2d) 294 at 303 (Alta. Q.B.), Sanderman J. [*CRC-Evans*].

meticulous attention to detail that is designed to disrupt operations.[36] Moreover, the employer is not bound to pay wages for work that falls short of the contractual requirements regarding quality.[37] It is significant that the duty persists even during the employee's personal time. Here, the courts have ruled that the employee must not conduct himself or herself during off-duty hours in a manner that undermines the employer's business reputation with its clients and customers, that undermines the symbolic legitimacy of managerial authority, or that otherwise substantially harms the employer's operations.[38] Nevertheless, there are limitations on what the employer can order the worker to do, as we shall see next.

2) Obedience to Orders and Insolence

The employee is impliedly bound to carry out the employer's orders so long as they are lawful, reasonable, and within the scope of employment. Disobedience to such an order—commonly referred to as "insubordination"—may entitle the employer to dismiss the employee summarily, provided that the requirements of just cause are met.[39] An order would not be "lawful" if carrying it out would involve the employee committing a criminal offence, such as driving an uninsured vehicle, or a civil wrong, such as defaming a third party. Similarly, an order would not be lawful if it would infringe on the employee's personal legal rights under employment standards or health and safety legislation—for example, an order to perform unsafe work. If an employee is ordered to perform tasks that he or she has not expressly or impliedly undertaken to perform under the employment contract, the employee can disobey the order as beyond the "scope of employment."[40] Indeed, such an order may well entitle the employee to resign and sue the employer for damages for constructive dismissal if it amounts to a repudiatory breach on the employer's part.[41] Of course, the dearth

---

36 A work-to-rule campaign by railway workers aimed at winning a collective bargaining dispute was held to breach the implied duty: *Secretary of State for Employment v. Associated Society of Locomotive Engineers & Firemen (No. 2)*, [1972] 2 All E.R. 949 (C.A.) [*A.S.L.E.F.*].

37 *A.S.L.E.F.*, *ibid.* at 966.

38 Example: *Strowbridge v. Re/Max United Inc.* (1992), 42 C.C.E.L. 51 at 55 (Nfld. S.C.T.D.).

39 These requirements are analyzed in Chapter 9.

40 Examples: *Adams v. Comark Inc.* (1992), 42 C.C.E.L. 15, especially at 23 (Man. C.A.); *Dooley v. C.N. Weber Ltd.* (1994), 3 C.C.E.L. (2d) 95 at 100 (Ont. Gen. Div.), aff'd (1995), 80 O.A.C. 234 (C.A.) [*Dooley*].

41 Constructive dismissal is analyzed in Chapter 9.

of comprehensive, express descriptions of an employee's job duties in most employment contracts makes it difficult to define exactly what she is legally bound to do. An order that causes substantial harm to the employee while recouping relatively little benefit to the employer can be disobeyed as being "unreasonable." For instance, an employer was held not to have the right to order a manager to refrain from having an intimate relationship with a consenting subordinate outside working hours because the firm's operations were not harmed in any tangible way by such a relationship, while the intrusion into the manager's private life was extreme.[42]

Technically speaking, insubordination is a separate offence from "insolence." In practice, though, insubordination (refusal to obey orders) is often accompanied by insolence (profanity directed at the employer). Uttering profanities against the employer constitutes a breach of the employee's implied duty of loyalty because such conduct undermines the symbolic authority of the employer in the workplace. Usually, courts will not ground cause for summary dismissal on a single instance of profanity, especially where there is provocation on the employer's part, but even a single act of insolence may establish just cause if it is accompanied by actual or threatened physical assault on the employer.

3) Absenteeism and Lateness

An employee is impliedly bound to report for work when assigned by the employer in a timely manner.[43] Again, litigation normally centres on whether or not the employee's breach gives cause for summary dismissal; the existence of the duty is indisputable. Nevertheless, it must be remembered that the employee's contractual duty at common law may be modified by human rights legislation. Thus, if the reason an employee refuses to attend work relates to his or her protected status under the human rights legislation—for example, the worker's absence may be due to a "disability" or a "religious" requirement—the contractual obligation will be qualified by the employer's statutory duty to reasonably accommodate the employee up to the point of "undue hardship."[44] This means, for example, that an employer must try to rearrange shift schedules to allow a Jewish employee to take off Yom Kippur day. As well, if the employee's absence is due to an event that operates to frustrate the employment contract, there will be no breach of contract

---

42   *Dooley*, above note 40 (Gen. Div.).
43   Examples: *Aspinall v. Mid-West Collieries Ltd.*, [1926] 3 D.L.R. 362 (Alta. C.A.); *Bratti v. F. & W. Wholesale Ltd.* (1989), 28 C.C.E.L. 142 (B.C. Co. Ct.).
44   This is examined in Chapter 9, Section G.

on his part.[45] It is interesting that while most courts have ruled that an employee whose absence from work results from imprisonment can be summarily dismissed for breaching the implied term of attendance,[46] MacPherson J. (as he then was) has intimated that the employer may be required to accommodate such an employee up to the point of undue hardship by assigning other workers to cover that person's duties, at least if the employee has lengthy seniority.[47] This trend illustrates the growing influence of the human rights acts' duty of reasonable accommodation on Canadian employment contract law.

4) Dishonesty

An employee is impliedly bound not to act in a deceitful, fraudulent, or otherwise dishonest manner towards the employer. The gravamen of "dishonesty" is not the economic harm that the employer may suffer as a result of the employee's misconduct, but the impact of dishonesty in shattering the psychological bond of loyalty and trust between the parties. Therefore, the courts have held that the dishonesty may justify summary dismissal even though the employer suffers no economic losses as a result of the employee's actions.[48] Indeed, the implied duty of honesty is so pivotal to the employment relationship that courts usually treat a single instance of dishonesty as justifying summary dismissal.[49] They respond this way especially if the dishonesty involves a manager or a person involved in sensitive industries and occupations, such as banking, investments, or baggage handling.[50] The Supreme Court of Canada has ruled, however, that dishonesty never automatically justifies dismissal as a rule of law; rather, the test of proportionality always applied, and mitigating circumstances may result in dismissal being

---

45 Frustration is examined in Chapter 9.

46 *Hare v. Murphy Bros.*, [1974] I.C.R. 603 (C.A.).

47 *Heynan v. Frito-Lay Canada Ltd.* (1997), 32 C.C.E.L. (2d) 183 at 192–93 (Ont. Gen. Div.).

48 *Lake Ontario Portland Cement Co. v. Groner*, [1961] S.C.R. 553; *Jewitt v. Prism Resources Ltd.* (1980), 110 D.L.R. (3d) 713 (B.C.S.C.), aff'd (1981), 127 D.L.R. (3d) 190 (B.C.C.A.).

49 Examples: *Ferguson v. Allstate Insurance Co. of Canada* (1991), 35 C.C.E.L. 257 at 265 (Ont. Gen. Div.) [*Ferguson*], where the court described honesty as being the "fundamental function and obligation" of any employee; *Carrol v. Emco Corp.*, 2006 BCSC 861, esp. para. 25 [*Emco*], where a manager lied to his employer on one occasion when asked if he was conducting an affair with a subordinate.

50 Example: *Pinto v. BMO Nesbitt Burns Inc.* (2005), 40 C.C.E.L. (3d) 293 at 308 (Ont. S.C.J.), involving an investments adviser.

ruled too harsh.[51] As well, many employees fall into the trap of lying to their employer when asked to explain their involvement in a particular incident, instead of making a clean breast of it. Here, the courts will uphold summary dismissal for the lie even though the employee's involvement in the incident might be innocent.[52] Employees are well-advised, therefore, not to attempt to deceive their employers.

It does not constitute culpable dishonesty for a regular employee to refrain from disclosing past misdeeds with a previous employer during the recruitment process. The employment relationship is not *uberrimae fidei*, so non-disclosure does not amount to misrepresentation.[53] However, if the employee owes a superadded "fiduciary" duty to his or her employer, there is a duty proactively to divulge such material.[54] Of course, if a regular employee lies about his or her prior record when asked by the employer during the recruitment process, this will constitute a serious breach of contract, usually justifying summary dismissal.[55] The logic of the general implied obligation of loyalty towards the employer would appear to militate in favour of requiring employees to proactively report known wrongdoing on the part of co-workers. However, the courts have been reluctant to impose such a duty,[56] probably because the employer is in the best position to develop express policies, clarifying in advance the myriad of practical difficulties that could potentially arise with the scope of such a duty, rather than placing the resolving of any uncertainties on the employee. Occasionally, though, exceptions have been made to this rule.[57] Noteworthy among these is

---

51 *McKinley v. B.C. Tel*, [2001] 2 S.C.R. 161, especially at 187–90. On the relevance of mitigating circumstances and procedural fairness under "just cause," see Chapter 9.

52 Example: *Di Vito v. Macdonald Dettwiler & Associates Ltd.* (1996), 21 C.C.E.L. (2d) 137 (B.C.S.C.).

53 Examples: *Zadorozniak v. Community Futures Development Corp. of Nicoal Valley* (2005), 38 C.C.E.L. (3d) 70 (B.C.S.C.); *Bell v. Lever Bros. Ltd.*, [1932] A.C. 161 (H.L.); *Grove v. Domville* (1877), 17 N.B.R. 48 (C.A.).

54 Example: *Courtright v. Canadian Pacific Ltd.* (1983), 4 C.C.E.L. 152 (Ont. H.C.J.), aff'd (1985), 18 D.L.R. (4th) 639 (Ont. C.A.) [*Courtright*].

55 Example: *Clarke v. Coopers and Lybrand Consulting Group* (2002), 19 C.C.E.L. (3d) 186 (Ont. C.A.) [*Coopers and Lybrand*]. But compare *Islip v. Coldmatic Refrigeration of Canada Ltd.* (2002), 17 C.C.E.L. (3d) 169 at 175–76 (B.C.C.A.) where it was held that the dismissal of an employee who deliberately overstated his previous salary in a recruitment interview was too severe.

56 *Tesco Stores v. Pook*, [2004] I.R.L.R. 618 (Ch. D.); *Tyrrell v. Alltrans Express Ltd.* (1976), 66 D.L.R. (3d) 181 (B.C.S.C.). See generally G. Davenport, "To Speak or Not to Speak: What if There Is No Question?" (1998) 6 C.L.E.L.J. 185.

57 In favour of such a duty are these: *Re I.W.A., Local 1-118 and Sooke Forest Products Ltd.* (1968), 1 D.L.R. (3d) 622 (B.C.C.A.); *Swain v. West Butchers Ltd.*, [1936] 3 All E.R. 261 at 264–65 (C.A.).

the requirement on a manager to proactively divulge to his or her superiors any romantic affair with a subordinate whom he or she supervises: the rationale is that this enables procedures to be established to avoid any appearance of a conflict of interest that might undermine the morale of other employees whom the individual also supervises.[58]

5) Drunkenness, Sexual Harassment, and Moral Impropriety

The employee is impliedly bound to report for work in a sufficiently sober condition to perform the job effectively and without endangering the safety of other persons in the workplace.[59] The rationale for this duty, therefore, is not the moral opprobrium sometimes attached to drinking, but the potential damage to the production process. The same applies to employees who come to work under the influence of drugs. The common law duty has been qualified by the human rights legislation where such employees are concerned. Alcoholism and drug addiction commonly constitute protected disabilities under human rights acts, so that the employer must reasonably accommodate the employee up to the point of undue hardship prior to invoking dismissal for inability to perform the job by reason of drugs or drunkenness.[60] This accommodation will usually involve participating with the employee in an alcohol or drug rehabilitation program.

Sexually harassing other employees in the workplace also violates the implied terms of the employment contract, such as to ground just cause for summary dismissal, especially if the perpetrator is a supervisor.[61] Indeed, if an employer fails to dismiss or discipline employees whom it knows, or ought reasonably to know, have committed sexual harassment as defined in the human rights legislation, the employer will be liable to the victim in its own name under that legislation.[62] Again, employers must be mindful of the requirements of just cause when dismissing employees for alleged sexual harassment. In particular, the courts have imposed relatively strict standards of procedural

---

58   *Emco*, above note 49 at para. 25.
59   Examples: *McEdwards v. Ogilvie Milling Co.* (1886), 4 Man. R. 1 at 5 (C.A.); *Rose v. Marystown Shipyard Ltd.* (1985), 52 Nfld. & P.E.I.R. 144 (Nfld. C.A.).
60   See Chapter 7.
61   Examples: *Gonsalves v. Catholic Church Extension Society of Canada* (1998), C.L.L.C. ¶210-032 (Ont. C.A.); *Simpson v. Consumers Assn. of Canada* (2001), 13 C.C.E.L. (3d) 234 (Ont. C.A.).
62   This aspect of the law of sexual harassment is examined in Chapter 7.

fairness on the manner of dismissal, and the ultimate penalty of dismissal cannot be invoked for relatively minor acts of harassment.[63]

Historically, courts have held that the employee is impliedly bound not to commit any moral impropriety that would likely diminish the employer's reputation in the community. Some judges based the implied duty on moral grounds alone, whereas others based it on the likelihood that the employer would suffer tangible economic harm if the general public ceased doing business with the firm because of the employee's actions. Modern courts would almost certainly take the latter approach. Thus, a business school professor who committed unlawful income tax evasion in his personal business accounts was held liable for summary dismissal because such behaviour would clearly undermine public confidence in the business school, thereby endangering student enrolment and funding.[64] Tax evasion is a crime and there is no doubt that such conduct conflicts with contemporary moral standards. However, standards of moral propriety have changed and will change further with time, rendering many of the old precedents obsolete under modern conditions.[65]

6) Incompetent or Negligent Performance of the Job

An employee impliedly guarantees that he or she has the requisite expertise and capacity to effectively perform contractual duties.[66] Failure to fulfill this expectation will give the employer just cause for summary dismissal. Moreover, if an employee deliberately misrepresents his or her qualifications, skills, or experience during the recruitment process, this would constitute dishonesty, justifying summary dismissal.[67] The implied duty of competence may seem rather harsh for the employee in a situation where the employer radically changes the employee's job duties—for example, by introducing complicated technology to replace the old way of doing the job, which the employee simply cannot master despite his or her best efforts to learn and despite comprehensive train-

---

63   Example: *Brazeau v. International Brotherhood of Electrical Workers*, [2004] C.L.L.C. ¶210-032 (B.C.S.C.), aff'd [2005] C.L.L.C. ¶210-011 (B.C.C.A.).These safeguards are examined in Chapter 7 of this book.

64   *Pliniussen v. University of Western Ontario* (1983), 2 C.C.E.L. 1 (Ont. Co. Ct.).

65   For example, the ruling on a fireman's dismissal for living with a woman out of wedlock in *McPherson v. Toronto (City of)* (1918), 43 D.L.R. 604 (Ont. C.A.) was overruled in *Reilly v. Steelcase Canada Ltd.* (1979), 26 O.R. (2d) 725 (H.C.J.).

66   Example: *Bridgewater v. Leon's Manufacturing Co.* (1984), 6 C.C.E.L. 55 (Sask. Q.B.).

67   Example: *Clarke v. Coopers and Lybrand Consulting Group* (2002), 19 C.C.E.L. (3d) 186 (Ont. C.A.).

ing from the employer. After all, the employee is not "at fault"; indeed, if any fault exists, it probably lies with the employer in the recruitment process for failing to properly assess the employee's capacity to learn and innovate. Be that as it may, the common law does not expect the employer to "subsidize" a non-productive employee in these circumstances; rather, the burden falls on the employee and the state welfare and unemployment schemes. Nevertheless, the courts temper the rigour of the implied obligation under the rubric of just cause. Thus, the employer is bound under an implied term in the employment contract to provide personalized assistance to an employee who is encountering difficulty in learning new technology introduced into the workplace.[68] In addition, summary dismissal for unsatisfactory work performance will only be for cause if the employee's degree of incapacity amounts to "gross incompetence"[69] and the employer has cooperated with the employee in establishing a rehabilitative program designed to appropriately train the employee.[70] Of course, if an employer wishes to dispose of a marginal performer who does not meet the threshold of gross incompetence or avoid the costs of attempting to rehabilitate a grossly inadequate performer, the employer can still dismiss the employee by giving him or her due notice of termination, or wages in lieu.

In addition, the employer can sue to recover damages from an employee who breaches his or her implied duty of competence. For example, an employee who did a shoddy concreting job for his employer was found liable for $45 000, or the employer's cost of refinishing the job.[71] Moreover, punitive damages may also be awarded if the employee's conduct is egregious.[72] A damages action can be brought whether or not the employee's breach is repudiatory in nature. Historically, there have

---

68 Example: *Levesque v. Sherwood Credit Union*, [2000] C.L.L.C. ¶210-038, especially at 141,303–4 (Sask. Q.B.). English courts have ruled that there is no such duty on the employer. See, for example, *Woods v. W.M. Car Services (Peterborough) Ltd.*, [1982] I.C.R. 693 (C.A.), Lord Watkins.

69 *Woodward v. Sound Insight Ltd.* (1986), 13 C.C.E.L. 177 at 181 (N.S.S.C.T.D.).

70 *Chester v. Pepsi-Cola Canada Ltd.*, [2005] C.L.L.C. ¶210-035 at 141,324 (Sask. Q.B.) where the court stated, "Perfection is a laudable goal but not likely attainable by many." The components of rehabilitative programs are examined in greater detail in Chapter 9, Section C, which deals with just cause and progressive discipline.

71 *Petrone v. Marmot Concrete Services Ltd.* (1996), 18 C.C.E.L. (2d) 170 at 185 (Alta. Q.B.). See also *Ferguson*, above note 49, where an insurance agent who falsified the information on an automobile policy was found liable for $125,000, the amount her employer had to pay out to the victim of an accident.

72 Example: *Connor v. Shaparrall Ltd.* (1998), 34 C.C.E.L. (2d) 208 at 266–67 (Ont. Gen. Div.), where $10,000 in punitive damages was awarded against a financial administrator who fraudulently falsified her compensation over a lengthy time.

been relatively few reported cases of employers suing for damages, but several such decisions have been reported. These decisions may herald a trend towards such actions by employers who perceive the pendulum to have swung too far in favour of employees in wrongful dismissal actions. Thus, employers may calculate that counterclaiming for damages will act as a disincentive to an employee who is considering suing for wrongful dismissal because the employee may have to pay such damages, even though the court rules that his or her incapacity and/or misbehaviour, while a breach of implied contractual duties, is insufficiently serious to ground just cause for summary dismissal. In order to succeed in an action for damages, the employer must be able to quantify its losses reasonably exactly, and the employer will have to weigh the chance of collecting a judgment debt from a possibly impecunious employee.

Closely related to the implied obligation of competence is the employee's implied duty to perform work in a non-negligent manner.[73] Generally, a single instance of negligence will not give just cause for summary dismissal unless the resulting harm to the employer or a third party is extremely serious.[74] Again, the employer can sue the employee for damages in respect to any losses sustained as a result of the employee's breach of the implied duty, but this occurs infrequently.

The position is more complicated where the employee negligently injures a third party in the course of his or her employment and the third party recovers damages from the employer by virtue of the doctrine of vicarious liability. Subsequently, the employer may sue the employee for breach of the implied duty not to be negligent in order to recover the damages it has paid out to the third party. Here, the accepted view until recently was that the employee is liable for such damages, even if the employer has taken out insurance coverage for the loss in question.[75] (In the latter scenario, the insurance company would assume the employer's legal right to sue the worker under the doctrine of subrogation, with or without the employer's consent.) The rationale for this ruling was to provide employees with an incentive to be careful in their work. Of course, employers already have adequate incentives available for this purpose: they can invoke dismissal, summarily or otherwise, or suspend negligent workers without pay. More problematic is the fact that the financial cost of an accident will ultimately fall

---

73   *London Drugs Ltd. v. Kuehne & Nagel International Ltd.*, [1992] 3 S.C.R. 299 at 341, La Forest J. [*London Drugs*]; *Dominion Manufacturers Ltd. v. O'Gorman* (1989), 24 C.C.E.L. 218 at 222 (Ont. Dist. Ct.).

74   *Tracey v. Swansea Construction Co.* (1964), 47 D.L.R. (2d) 295 (Ont. H.C.J.), aff'd without written reasons (1965), 50 D.L.R. (2d) 130n (Ont. C.A.).

75   *Lister v. Romford Ice & Cold Storage Ltd.*, [1957] A.C. 555 (H.L.).

on the employee, thereby defeating the main objective of the doctrine of vicarious liability, which is to spread the financial cost of accidents over as broad a segment of the community as possible through the medium of insurance.

This approach has been shaken, if not formally overruled, by the landmark decision of the Supreme Court of Canada in 1993 in *London Drugs*.[76] *The ratio decedendi* of that case is that an employee cannot be personally sued in tort by a third party whose person or property he or she negligently damages during the course of employment if the employer and the third party have a contract that exempts or limits the employer's liability to the third party, even though the employee may not be privy to the contract in question. However, La Forest J. went further in an important *obiter dictum* by suggesting that an employee is not liable to the employer for breach of the employment contract if he or she negligently injures a third person during the course of employment, unless the employee is guilty of gross negligence.[77] It remains to be seen whether or not future courts will take up this gauntlet.

7) The Obligation Not to Wrongfully Exploit or Abuse the Employer's Business Interests

This all-encompassing implied obligation is generally taken to include the following non-exhaustive list of specific sub-duties:

- the duty of an employee not to make a secret profit from his or her employment;
- the employer's presumptive right to ownership of any inventions or copyrights made by the employee;
- the employee's duty not to compete with the employer's business;
- the employee's duty not to misuse the employer's trade secrets or "confidential" information; and
- the superadded fiduciary obligation owed by employees in a fiduciary relationship with their employer.

It must be emphasized that this list is not closed, so that any conduct deemed unduly damaging to the employer's business interests could amount to a breach of the employee's implied obligation.[78]

---

76 Above note 73. See M.G. Baer, "Case Comment on *London Drugs v. Kuehne & Nagel International Ltd.*" (1993) 72 Can. Bar Rev. 385.

77 *London Drugs*, *ibid.* at 341–45.

78 See, for example, *Courtright*, above note 54, where a non-fiduciary employee occupying a sensitive position was bound to a duty of pro-active disclosure even

The issue of remedies can become quite complicated for breaches of the above duties, since they often involve the employee depriving the employer of a rightful economic advantage. For example, the employee might divulge the employer's confidential business information to a competitor who subsequently exploits it for its own financial advantage, or the employee may make a secret profit by illicitly dealing with the employer's customers. While summary dismissal of the employee is clearly in order in such circumstances,[79] the employer might also seek an interlocutory injunction to stop the employee or a third party from continuing to exploit its confidential business information.[80] However, the unauthorized use of the employer's confidential business information is not a criminal offence.[81]

In order to obtain such an interlocutory injunction, the employer must establish the following prerequisites. First, there must be a *prima facie* case of illegality on the employee's part. Generally, the employer will plead breach of the employee's implied contractual duty not to misuse its business information, but an action can also be brought in the tort of conversion if the employee misappropriates material or information in which the employer has a proprietary interest, such as trade secrets, copyrights, customer lists, and other confidential business information. Second, the employer must adduce concrete evidence to show that it will suffer irreparable harm unless an injunction is granted immediately. Third, the so-called balance of convenience must favour issuing an injunction. This means that the degree of harm that the employer would suffer if the injunction were refused must exceed the degree of harm that the employee would suffer if the injunction were granted. Fourth, it must be fair and equitable in all circumstances to grant the injunction pending a full trial.[82] An injunction can be granted against a third party, such as the employee's new employer, to prevent it from exploiting the previous employer's confidential business infor-

---

though such duties have traditionally been restricted to fiduciary relationships *stricto sensu*.

79   Example: *O'Callahan v. Transair Ltd.* (1975), 58 D.L.R. (3d) 80 (Man. C.A.), subject to the requirements of just cause examined in Chapter 9.

80   *Ashburton (Lord) v. Pape*, [1913] 2 Ch. 469 at 475 (C.A.).

81   *R. v. Stewart* (1988), 50 D.L.R. (4d) 1 (S.C.C.).

82   The seminal authority is *American Cyanamid Co. v. Ethicon Ltd.*, [1975] A.C. 396 (H.L.), involving an interlocutory injunction to restrain wrongful exploitation of a patent. See also *Khan v. RDMI* (2001), 5 C.C.E.L. (3d) 303 (Ont. S.C.J.) [*Khan*]; *Zesta Engineering Ltd. v. Cloutier*, [2001] C.L.L.C. ¶210-024 (Ont. S.C.J.), quashed and a new trial ordered because of the discovery of new evidence, [2002] O.J. No. 3738 (C.A.).

mation that the employee has passed on to it.[83] It appears that an injunction will be issued against a third party only if it knows, or ought reasonably to know, that the information in question was wrongfully appropriated from the previous employer.[84]

If the employer suspects that an employee after termination has removed trade secrets or other confidential business information from the workplace, and considers that the imminent exploitation of the material will cause it irreparable harm, the employer can apply for an *Anton Pillar* allowing it to enter the employee's private residence and remove the material in question.[85] These orders are granted by application to the Master on an *ex parte* basis — that is, without the employee being notified and given a right to particpate in the proceedings. They are extraordinary orders and are only given in exceptional circumstances where the employer can prove that there is an extremely strong *prima facie* case of illegality; that the potential exists for serious harm to the employer from misuse of the material; that there is clear evidence showing that the employee has removed the material from the workplace; and that there is a real possibility of the employee destroying, hiding, or otherwise misusing it before an *inter partes* hearing can take place. The employer must come to the court with "clean hands" and undertake to pay to the employee any damages that might result from a wrongful implementation of the order. The order identifies the material that can be taken from the employee's home, and the employer must strictly limit itself to removing only that material. The employer must be accompanied to the employee's residence by his or her lawyer (and usually also by a police offer), who will ensure that the order is properly complied with.

In addition, the employer may sue the employee for damages for any lost profits it has suffered as a result of the employee's breach of the

---

83   Example: *International Tools Ltd. v. Kollar* (1968), 67 D.L.R. (2d) 386 (Ont. C.A.), var'g (1966), 56 D.L.R. (2d) 289 (H.C.J.) [*Kollar*].

84   There is, however, some uncertainty on this point. See H.G. Fox, *The Canadian Law and Practice Relating to Letters Patent for Inventions*, 4th ed. (Toronto: Carswell, 1969) at 619, citing *London Joint Stock Bank v. Simmons*, [1892] A.C. 201 at 215 (H.L.), and *Printers & Finishers Ltd. v. Holloway* (1964), [1965] R.P.C. 239 at 253 (Ch.) [*Printers & Finishers*].

85   The name derives from the seminal English authority *Anton Pillar KG v. Manufacturing Processes Ltd.*, [1976] Ch. 55 (C.A.). Useful Canadian authorities are *Netsmart Inc. v. Poelzer* (2002), 20 C.C.E.L. (3d) 195 (Alta. Q.B.); *Harris*, above note 27, which Veit J. described as being " a poster case for what should not be done in the execution of these orders"; *Ridgewood Electric Ltd. (1990) v. Robbie* (2005), 74 O.R. (3d) 514 (S.C.J.).

implied terms of the employment contract.[86] The question of compensation is complicated, however, if the employee exploits information or material in which the employer has a recognized proprietary interest; then, the employer is allowed to sue for an "accounting" of all profits that the employee has obtained using the information or material in question.[87] An action for accounting is distinguishable from an action for damages. The latter arises from the employee's breach of his or her employment contract and is subject to the general contract law principles governing the measure of damages. An action for accounting, however, lies in equity[88] and requires the wrongful exploiter of the employer's property to disgorge all the profits it has obtained therefrom as a matter of "unjust enrichment." The employer is entitled to pursue whichever option—straight damages or an accounting—is most advantageous to it in the circumstances.[89] Again, the employer can seek an accounting for profits from a third party, such as the employee's new employer, if the third party knows, or ought reasonably to know, that the employee wrongfully appropriated the material in question.[90] The picture is further complicated by the possibility that the employer, clearly having a proprietary interest in its confidential business information, may sue either or both the employee and the third party in the tort of conversion. In this case, the measure of damages will be governed by the principles of the law of tort rather than the law of contract.[91] Finally, the courts may award the employer punitive damages if the employer or a third party has deliberately misappropriated its confidential business material.[92]

Next, we examine in greater detail the various subsets of the employee's implied duty to respect the employer's business interests.

---

86   Examples: *Billows v. Canarc Forest Products Ltd.* (2003), 27 C.C.E.L. (3d) 188, especially at 220–21 (B.C.S.C.) [*Billows*]; *Crawley v. Trans-Power Construction Ltd.* (1996), 23 C.C.E.L. (2d) 34 at 41 (B.C.S.C.); *Monarch Messenger Services Ltd. v. Houlding* (1984), 5 C.C.E.L. 219 (Alta. Q.B.) [*Monarch*]; *Kollar*, above note 83.

87   Examples: *Anderson Preece and Associates Inc. v. Dominion Appraisal Group Inc.* (2001), 309 A.R. 124 (Q.B.); *Lake Mechanical Systems Corp. v. Crandell Mechanical Systems Inc.* (1985), 9 C.C.E.L. 52 (B.C.S.C.); *57134 Manitoba Ltd. v. Palmer* (1985), 8 C.C.E.L. 282 at 297 (B.C.S.C.), aff'd (1989), 37 B.C.L.R. (2d) 50 (C.A.) [*57134 Manitoba Ltd.*].

88   *Seager v. Copydex Ltd.*, [1967] 2 All E.R. 415 at 417 (C.A.) [*Seager*].

89   Examples: *KJA Consultants Ltd. v. Soberman*, [2004] O.J. No. 4560 at para. 52 (C.A.) [*KJA*]; *57134 Manitoba Ltd.*, above note 87 at 298 (S.C.).

90   There is, however, some uncertainty on this point: *Seager*, above note 88; *57134 Manitoba Ltd.*, ibid. at 58 (C.A.).

91   Example: *Cline v. Don Watt & Associates Communications Inc.* (1986), 15 C.C.E.L. 181 at 196–98 (Ont. Dist. Ct.) [*Cline*].

92   Example: *57134 Manitoba Ltd.*, above note 87.

a)   Secret Profits and Other Dishonest Profit-Making

An employee is bound by an extremely rigorous obligation not to take bribes or gifts or make otherwise unauthorized profits from his or her position. The duty will be breached and summary dismissal will normally be warranted even though the employer suffers no economic loss as a result of the employee's actions.[93] Moreover, the employer is entitled to recover from the worker the full amount of the secret profit, even though the employer would have been unwilling or unable to exploit the opportunity in question on its own account.[94]

b)   Inventions and Copyright

The traditional view of English and Canadian courts is that an employee impliedly undertakes to hold in trust for the benefit of the employer any inventions made during his or her employment.[95] According to the traditional view, this presumption could be displaced only by either an express term in the contract or an implied term based on crystal clear evidence that the parties intended otherwise. However, in *Comstock Canada v. Electec Ltd.*,[96] the Federal Trial Court reversed the presumption and held that the employee is deemed to own any inventions unless either the express terms of the contract provide otherwise or there is clear evidence that the parties impliedly intended otherwise. The court cited the following examples of such evidence:

(a) whether the employee was hired for the express purpose of inventing;

(b) whether the employee at the time he was hired had previously made inventions;

(c) whether the employer had incentive plans encouraging product development;

(d) whether the conduct of the employee once the invention had been created suggested ownership was held by the employer;

---

93   Examples:,*Rupert v. Greater Victoria School District No. 1*, [2002] C.L.L.C. ¶210-001 (B.C.S.C.), aff'd [2004] C.L.L.C. ¶210,026 (B.C.C.A.); *Standard Life Assurance Company v. Horsburgh* (2005), 39 C.C.E.L. (3d) 19 (B.C.C.A.); *Connolly v. General Motors of Canada Ltd.* (1993), 50 C.C.E.L. 247 (Ont. Gen. Div.).

94   *Reading v. A.G.*, [1951] A.C. 507 (H.L.); *Boston Deep Sea Fishing & Ice Co. v. Ansell* (1888), 39 Ch. D. 339 (C.A.).

95   Examples:, *W.J. Gage Ltd. v. Sugden* (1967), 62 D.L.R. (2d) 671 at 685–86 (Ont. H.C.J.) [*Sugden*]; *Sterling Engineering Co. v. Patchett*, [1955] A.C. 534, especially at 542–45 (H.L.). See generally R. Brait & B. Pollock, "Confidentiality, Intellectual Property and Competitive Risk in the Employment Relationship" (2004) 83 Can. Bar Rev. 585.

96   (1991), 38 C.P.R. (3d) 29 (F.C.T.D.) [*Comstock*].

(e) whether the invention is the product of the problem the employee was instructed to solve (i.e., whether it was his duty to make
inventions);

(f) whether the employee's invention arose following his consulta-
tion through normal company channels (i.e., was help sought?); .

(g) whether the employee was dealing with highly confidential information or confidential work;

(h) whether it was a term of the servant's employment that he could
not use the ideas which he developed to his own advantage.[97]

In particular, the court stated that it would be unusual for the presumption to shift in favour of the employer owning an invention unless
the employee was engaged specifically because of his or her "inventive
skills . . . [and] creates something in the ordinary course of his [or her]
duties."[98] This places the employee in a more favourable position than
under the traditional rule, which gave the employer the exclusive benefit to an invention made tangentially to the core functions performed
by the employee.[99] However, the court added that if the employee owes
a superadded fiduciary duty to the employer, then the employer will
be presumptively entitled to any inventions, unless the parties clearly
intend otherwise.[100] Also, inventions made by employees of the federal
government in the course of their employment are owned by their employer under section 3 of the *Public Servants Inventions Act.*[101]

The traditional common law rule in relation to copyright is that the
employer is presumptively entitled to the exclusive copyright in any
works produced by the employee in the course of employment, unless
the parties clearly intend otherwise.[102] This rule has also been enacted
under the *Copyright Act.*[103]

The above-mentioned rules illustrate the primacy accorded to the
employer's interests under the common law implied duty of loyalty.
Some countries have tempered the rigour of the implied term by introducing legislation that entitles the employee to a bonus if he or she

---

97 *Ibid.* at 53–54, Muldoon J.

98 *Ibid.* at 54.

99 As in *Sugden,* above note 95, where inventing mathematical paper was ancillary
to the worker's main duties, but the employer happened to ask him to turn his
mind to it.

100 *Comstock,* above note 96 at 60.

101 R.S.C. 1985, c. P-32.

102 See ss. 13(2) & (3) of the *Copyright Act,* R.S.C. 1985, c. C-42, and *BBM Bureau
of Measurement v. Cybernauts Ltd.* (1992), 8 C.P.C. (3d) 293 (Ont. Gen. Div.). See
generally D. Vaver, *Copyright Law* (Toronto: Irwin Law, 2000).

103 R.S.C. 1985, c. C-42, ss. 13(2) & (3).

produces an "outstanding" invention or work, but as yet no Canadian province has adopted such a scheme.[104]

c) Working in Competition with the Employer's Business

The implied duty of loyalty prohibits the employee from taking another job — either during working hours or in his or her spare time — with a firm that completes with his or her employer's business. Traditionally, the implied term has been framed with the utmost strictness to outlaw working for a competitor even though the employer may have suffered no economic harm as a result.[105] The basis of the duty, therefore, is psychological, aimed at guaranteeing the employer the undivided trust and loyalty of its employees. The dangers with formulating the implied duty too strictly, of course, are that employees will be deprived of extra earning opportunities, that labour mobility will be impaired, and that competition for goods and services will be restricted. Recently, some courts have tempered the employee's position by holding that there will be no just cause for summary dismissal if the outside competition results in relatively minor harm to the employer, and the employee has not tried to conceal his or her activities.[106]

It does not breach the duty of fidelity for an employee to plan to leave his or her employer to take up competing employment, by applying for other positions and going for job interviews, for example; so, too, if the employee commences to establish the infrastructure of a *future* competing business of his or her own, for example, by purchasing equipment and supplies, persuading fellow employees to lawfully quit in order to work for him or her, and entering into contracts with suppliers and customers.[107] After all, given that the law permits the employee to engage in post-employment competition with a former employer, it would be illogical to prohibit the employee from preparing to do that which is lawful once done. Therefore, the courts have ruled that breach of the

---

104 See, for example, the English scheme under the *Patents Act, 1977* (U.K.), 1977, c. 37, described in K.R. Wotherspoon, "Employee Inventions Revisited" (1993) 2 Indus. L.J. 119.

105 Examples: *Cinema Internet Networks Inc (c.o.b. Cinemaworks) v. Porter*, [2006] B.C.J. No. 3200 (S.C.) [*Porter*]; *Knowlan v. Trailmobile Parts and Service Canada Ltd.*, [2006] B.C.J. No. 457 (S.C.); *Millard v. Seven Continents Enterprises Inc.* (1992), 92 C.L.L.C. ¶14,052 (Ont. Gen. Div.). The leading English authorities are *Hivac Ltd. v. Park Royal Scientific Instruments Ltd.*, [1946] Ch. 169, especially at 176–77 (C.A.); *Wessex Dairies Ltd. v. Smith*, [1935] 2 K.B. 80 at 84 (C.A.).

106 Examples: *Segin v. Hewitt* (1993), 1 C.C.E.L. (2d) 5 (Ont. Gen. Div.); *Isopo v. Kobe Fabrics Ltd.* (1994), 5 C.C.E.L. (2d) 172 at 174 (Ont. Gen. Div.).

107 *Westcan Bulk Transport v. Stewart* (2005), 38 C.C.E.L. (3d) 194, especially at 211–15 (Alta. Q.B.).

duty will only occur at the moment the employee either firmly resolves to misappropriate the employer's confidential information, or actually begins to canvass the employer's customers and clients.[108] Nor is the employee obliged to proactively divulge to his or her employer that he or she is planning to quit to take up competing employment.[109]

Once the employment relationship has ended, the employee is free to work for another firm or to set up a business in competition with a former employer. Here, the common law accords paramountcy to encouraging competition and labour mobility. Naturally, the former employee must continue to respect the employer's confidential information and trade secrets after the employment relationship has ceased. If the employee owes the employer a superadded fiduciary duty, he or she will also be prohibited from engaging in competition for a reasonable time after the employment relationship has ended.[110] Some (but not all[111]) decisions have blurred the line between fiduciary and non-fiduciary relationships by holding that even a non-fiduciary employee cannot engage in "unfair" competition with a former employer for a reasonable time after employment has ceased.[112] However, it is unclear exactly what makes for unfair competition. Finally, we saw earlier that an express restrictive covenant in the employment contract may limit the employee's freedom to engage in post-employment competition.[113]

d) Protecting the Employer's Confidential Information, Trade Secrets, and Customer Lists, and the Right to Whistleblow

The employee is impliedly bound under the employment contract not to misappropriate the employer's confidential business information, both during employment and after it has ceased. This contractual duty on the employee's part is reinforced by other laws designed to safeguard the employer's proprietary interest in such material. Thus, misusing confidential information may constitute the torts of conversion

---

108 Examples: *Porter*, above note 105; *CRC-Evans*, above note 35 at 333–34 (Alta. Q.B.); *Restauronics Services Ltd. v. Forster* (2004), 32 C.C.E.L. (3d) 50, especially at 63 and 65 (B.C.C.A.).

109 *ATI Technologies Inc. v. Henry* (2000), 5 C.C.E.L. (3d) 101 (Ont. S.C.J.).

110 For further elaboration, see Section B(7)(c), above in this chapter.

111 This proposition was firmly rejected by Southin J.A. in her majority judgment in *RBC Dominion Securities Inc. v. Merrill Lynch Inc.*, 2007 BCCA 22 at paras. 65–66 [*RBC*].

112 Examples: *Monarch*, above note 86; *Sure-Grip Fasteners Ltd. v. Allgrade Bolt & Chain Inc.* (1993), 45 C.C.E.L. 276 at 288 (Ont. Gen. Div.) [*Sure-Grip*]; *Tomenson Saunders Whitehead Ltd. v. Baird* (1980), 7 C.C.E.L. 176 (Ont. H.C.J.) [*Baird*]; *57134 Manitoba Ltd.*, above note 87 at 56.

113 See Section A, above in this chapter.

and detinue, and equitable principles of unjust enrichment require the employee or a third party to disgorge any profits it has made from such information to the employer.[114]

The main difficulty with this area of the law is defining what constitutes the employer's confidential information. The English Court of Appeal encapsulates the essence of the matter as follows:

> First, I think that the information must be information the release of which the owner believes would be injurious to him or of advantage to his rivals or others. Second, I think the owner must believe that the information is confidential or secret, i.e., that it is not already in the public domain. It may be that some or all of his rivals already have the information: but as long as the owner believes it to be confidential I think he is entitled to try and protect it. Third, I think that the owner's belief under the two previous heads must be reasonable. Fourth, I think that the information must be judged in the light of the usage and practices of the particular industry or trade concerned. It may be that information which does not satisfy all these requirements may be entitled to protection as confidential information or trade secrets: but I think that any information which does satisfy them must be of a type which is entitled to protection.[115]

Specific examples of protected confidential information would include computer programs relating to the operation of the business, lists of suppliers with the employer's assessment of their reliability and efficiency, lists of clients and customers, operating instructions for the firm's manufacturing processes, and lists of employees containing personal information about their health and disciplinary records.[116] The information in question must be obviously secret. Thus, if the employer's competitors have already discovered the information through their own research, it cannot be regarded as confidential.[117]

Information that forms part of the employee's accumulated experience and knowledge does not constitute protected confidential information. Indeed, a major incentive for employees to accept employment with particular firms is precisely to augment their skills and expertise, and consequently their market value to future employers. It is clear that

---

114   For the remedial implications of these overlapping illegalities, see above in this chapter.

115   *Marshall (Thomas) (Exports) Ltd. v. Guinle* (1978), [1979] Ch. 227 at 248 (C.A.), cited with approval in Canada in *R. v. Stewart* (1983), 24 B.L.R. 53 at 78 (Ont. C.A.) [*Stewart*]. See also *Khan*, above note 82 at 310.

116   *Stewart, ibid.* at 73–74.

117   *Kollar*, above note 83 (C.A.).

the courts do not want to discourage employees from investing in their future careers in this way.[118] However, it is often difficult to distinguish between general know-how and firm-specific confidential information. An Ontario trial judge, Barr J., expressed the spirit of the inquiry rather colourfully as follows:

> To use a simple analogy, a beginning cook can be given a recipe for apple pie but it will be a long time before, by trial and error, he can produce a pie like grandmother does. Baking a good pie is no secret process but it is one that requires a skilled and experienced baker.[119]

The cases sometimes turn on seemingly hairsplitting distinctions. For example, it has been held to breach the implied duty of loyalty for an employee to copy or deliberately memorize customer lists while still employed by his or her employer and to subsequently use such information after the employment relationship has terminated to canvass business from those customers.[120] However, it does not breach the duty if the employee, after employment ends, obtains the names of the customers from a public telephone directory, a personal notebook not used as a regular part of the employee's work, a list compiled by the employee while in the employment of previous companies, or non-deliberate memorization.[121] Nor does it breach the duty for a financial adviser to remove his or her book of client names and addresses—not least because clients will want to know that their adviser is changing employment. However, it will breach the duty if he or she removes the clients' personal portfolios and accounts information.[122] While an employee, generally speaking, is entitled to canvass the customers of a former employer *after* his or her employment has ended—subject to any express restrictive covenant in the employment contract or a superadded fiduciary duty, and provided that he or she does not canvass on the basis of confidential customer lists—the employee is not allowed to actively solicit the employer's customers for his or her own business during the employment relationship.[123] The key distinction here is whether "enticement" occurred. The courts have held that simply notifying customers of the

---

118 *Saxelby*, above note 7 at 714.
119 *Genesta Manufacturing Ltd. v. Babey* (1984), 6 C.C.E.L. 291 at 309–19 (Ont. H.C.J.).
120 *Billows*, above note 86; *Faccenda Chicken Ltd. v. Fowler* (1986), [1987] Ch. 117 (C.A.); *Anderson, Smyth & Kelly Customs Brokers Ltd. v. World Wide Customs Brokers Ltd.* (1993), 1 C.C.E.L. (2d) 57 at 69 (Alta. Q.B.), rev'd (1996), 20 C.C.E.L. (2d) 1 (Alta. C.A.) [*Anderson, Smyth & Kelly*].
121 *Baird*, above note 112; *Sure-Grip*, above note 112 at 290.
122 *RBC*, above note 111 at paras. 139–42.
123 Example: *McCormick, Delisle and Thompson Inc. v. Ballantyne* (2001), 9 C.C.E.L. (3d) 50 (Ont. C.A.).

fact that he or she will be leaving employment and working elsewhere does not breach the implied duty on the employee's part. After all, it is in the public interest for customers to be able to make informed choices about whom to do business with. Enticement, on the other hand, involves actively inducing or persuading customers to change their allegiance to the employee.[124] Usually, in borderline cases, the courts will lean towards the employee, not least because the employer can readily protect its interests by including an express restrictive covenant in the contract if it thinks the matter is important enough.[125]

An exception is made to the prohibition against divulging the employer's confidential information where disclosure is necessary to expose an "iniquity.[126] Indeed, deliberately failing to disclose such information would violate the employee's duty of fidelity, possibly even justifying summary dismissal.[127] "Whistleblowing" refers to the unauthorized disclosure by the employee of information that he honestly and reasonably believes violates the law or professional standards, or that involves mismanagement, corruption, abuse of authority, or danger to the public, other employees, or individuals or bodies outside the firm. The law must strike a balance between the interests of employers, who want to protect their business against false, malicious, or otherwise irresponsible disclosures that would harm their reputation; employees, who want, in good conscience, to exercise their right to free speech without fear of retaliation by their employers; and members of the general public who want disclosure of information that could possibly harm them.[128]

There are no recently reported cases on this point, probably because the costs of civil litigation are beyond the reach of most employees. Collective agreement arbitrators, however, have developed a comprehensive jurisprudence in the area that has been approved by the Supreme

---

124 *Atlantic Business Interiors*, above note 8. Compare the broad meaning given to "inducement" in the context of the economic torts involving trade union picketing and hot cargo declarations, summarized in K.W. Wedderburn, *The Worker and the Law*, 3d ed. (London: Sweet & Maxwell, 1986) at 588–89.

125 *Printers & Finishers*, above note 84 at 256–57.

126 *Gartside v. Outram* (1856), 3 Jur. N.S. 39 (Ch.); *Initial Services Ltd. v. Putterill*, [1967] 3 All E.R. 145 (C.A.); *Merk v. I.A.B.S.O.I. Local 771*, 2005 SCC 70 especially paras. 15, 18, 20, 23–27, and 37 [*Merk*].

127 *Merk, ibid.* at paras. 23–27 and 37.

128 See generally C. Dubin, "Whistleblowing Study" (Ottawa: Industry Canada Competition Bureau, 1997); L. Sossin, "Speaking Truth to Power? The Search for Bureaucratic Independence in Canada" (2005) 55 U.T.L.J. 1; L.J.E. Callahan, T. Dworkin, & D. Lewis, "Whistleblowing: Australian, U.K. and U.S. Approaches to Disclosure in the Public Interest" (2003–04) 44 Va. J. Int'l Law 879.

Court of Canada for the purposes of individual employment contract law.[129] The leading decision is that of arbitrator Weiler, who said:

> The duty of fidelity does not mean that the Daniel Ellsbergs and Karen Silkwoods of the world must remain silent when they discover wrongdoing at their place of employment. Neither the public nor the employer's long-term best interests are served if these employees, from fear of losing their jobs, are so intimidated that they do not bring information about wrongdoing at their place of employment to the attention of those who can correct such wrongdoing. However, the duty of fidelity does require the employee to exhaust internal "whistleblowing" mechanisms before "going public". These internal mechanisms are designed to ensure that the employer's reputation is not damaged by unwarranted attacks based on inaccurate information. Internal investigation provides a sound method of applying the expertise and experience of many individuals to all problems that may only concern one employee.[130]

(The Supreme Court of Canada's decision provides yet another example of the growing congruence between the common law and arbitral standards of "just cause" for dismissal.)

In several jurisdictions, there are various statutory safeguards for whistleblowers, but these are piecemeal: they do not provide a general and comprehensive right to whistleblow. Thus, the labour standards legislation in Saskatchewan prohibits the employer from dismissing or otherwise penalizing an employee who reports to a "lawful authority" conduct that "is or is likely to result in an offence" under an Act.[131] The courts have held that reporting fraud on the part of a superior to top-level managers falls within this section.[132] Other provinces do not include this provision in their labour standards acts, but do commonly safeguard the employee against reprisals for taking part in proceedings under the labour standards acts against the employer.[133] Other protective employment legislation, including the human rights acts and the occupational

---

129 *Merk*, above note 126 at para. 23. The arbitral jurisprudence is reviewed by M. Myers & V.J. Matthews-Lemieux, "Whistleblowing, Employee Loyalty and the Right to Criticize: The Employee's Perspective" (1991) Labour Arbitration Yearbook 211; R. Heenan & C. De Stefano, "Whistleblowing, Employee Loyalty and the Right to Criticize: A Management Perspective" (1991) Labour Arbitration Yearbook 199.

130 *Ministry of Attorney-General, Corrections Branch*, [1981] B.C.C.A.A.A. No. 9 at para. 44, 3 L.A.C. (3d) 140 (Weiler).

131 *Saskatchewan Labour Standards Act*, R.S.S. 1978, c. L-1, s. 74(a).

132 *Merk*, above note 126.

133 Example: *British Columbia Employment Standards Act*, R.S.B.C., 1996, c. 113, s. 83.

health and safety acts, also commonly include no-reprisal protections,[134] as does environmental protection legislation.[135] Furthermore, legislation has been introduced in the federal jurisdiction and many provinces to safeguard whistleblowers who expose wrongdoings in the public services. For example, the federal *Public Servants Disclosure Protection Act* of 2005 allows civil servants to divulge wrongdoings to the Public Sector Integrity Commissioner and protects them against reprisals.[136] In addition, section 425.1 of the *Criminal Code* makes it an offence for an employer or other person in authority over an employee to penalize or threaten to penalize the employee in regard to employment status, or other terms and conditions of employment, for reporting to the appropriate authorities any violations of federal or provincial laws on the part of the employer. The crime carries a maximum period of five years imprisonment.

e) Fiduciary Duties

Employees in a special fiduciary relationship with their employer owe the firm a far more rigorous duty of loyalty than that imposed on regular employees. In this section, we first examine the circumstances wherein a fiduciary relationship exists and then discuss the nature of the duties owed by a fiduciary employee to the employer. In order to understand the law on these points, it is necessary to appreciate the underlying policy goals of the law on fiduciary relationships. Professor Flannigan describes these policies as follows:

> The traditional rationale for fiduciary responsibility is straightforward. People trust others to act on their behalf or to perform tasks for them. This normally involves the trusted party acquiring access to assets of the trusting party. The mischief that can occur in such circumstances is that the trusted party will divert value away from the trusting party. The trust placed in the trusted party, in other words, will be abused. Public morality is offended by this kind of conduct. The courts, openly asserting this public morality or policy, formulated a liability rule to deter the abuse. A special rule was constructed which required more than compensation; the trusted party had to disgorge any benefit gained by the breach. The effect of such a rule is intensely prophylactic. If the trusted party cannot benefit at all, the conduct is less likely to occur.

---

134 Examples: Alberta *Human Rights, Citizenship and Multiculturalism Act*, R.S.A. 2000, c. H-14, s. 10(1); Ontario *Occupational Health and Safety Act*, R.S.O. 1990, c. O.1, s. 50.

135 Example: *Ontario Environmental Protection Act*, R.S.O. 1990, c. E.19, s. 174(2).

136 *Public Servants Disclosure Protection Act*, S.C. 2005, c. 46.

The desire to deter opportunistic behaviour, and to do so effectively, required a second special feature for the liability rule. In addition to requiring the trusted party to disgorge, the rule had to be strict. The trusted party could not be allowed to attempt to excuse or justify the conduct. Often the trusted party controls the circumstances surrounding the abuse and is able to manipulate them both before and after the event to sanitize their appearance. At other times the trusted party may have intended no wrongdoing, yet may have subconsciously preferred a personal interest. A strict disgorgement rule captures any gain from either intentional or innocent self-interested conduct. This strictness further contributes to what is clearly and intentionally a vigorously prophylactic rule.

These are the policies that operate in the fiduciary context. We want to regulate the abuse of trust. We want to do so vigorously. We are so concerned with maintaining the integrity of these trusting relationships that we will admit our inability to detect abuse in the greater number of instances and dispense with the need to establish that objectionable conduct actually occurred.[137]

Regarding the first issue of when a fiduciary relationship will be found to exist, Professor Flannigan argues that, strictly speaking, a fiduciary obligation arises where A entrusts B with access to resources that can be used only for a limited purpose as defined and authorized by A. The duty is breached when B acts opportunistically and uses those resources to further personal interests rather than the interests of A.[138] It follows that even the most lowly employee could be found to owe, and to have breached, a fiduciary duty. However, the courts have not adopted this approach in the context of the employment relationship, much to Professor Flannigan's chagrin.[139] Rather, the courts generally require that (1) a fiduciary must exercise a relatively broad and independent discretion in handling the critical aspects of an employer's business, and (2) the employer's business interests must be especially vulnerable to the actions of the fiduciary.[140] Although this test leaves room for some uncertainty, typically fiduciary relationships are re-

---

137 R. Flannigan, "Fiduciary Obligation in the Supreme Court" (1990) 54 Sask. L. Rev. 45 at 46–47.

138 R. Flannigan, "The Boundaries of Fiduciary Accountability" (2004) 83 Can. Bar Rev. 35 at 36.

139 R. Flannigan, "The Fiduciary Accountability of Ordinary Employees" (2007) 13 C.L.E.L.J. 283, where the learned author criticizes the courts' approach as creating too much uncertainty and unpredictability into the law.

140 This synthesis of the law can be gleaned from *Frame v. Smith*, [1987] 2 S.C.R. 99 at 136, Wilson J.; *LAC Minerals Ltd. v. International Corona Resources Ltd.*, [1989]

stricted to executives at the top levels of the organizational hierarchy who have the responsibility and authority to make decisions about the fundamentals of the firm.[141] Nevertheless, even middle- to low-level managers may be characterized as fiduciaries if their knowledge and expertise make the employer extremely vulnerable to competition after such an employee ceases employment there.[142] (As outlined below, a fiduciary is precluded from engaging in post-termination competition with a former employer for a reasonable time.) In applying the above-mentioned test, the courts will have regard to what the employee does in practice, not just to the employee's formal job description.

Regarding the second issue of what the precise components of a fiduciary duty are, the law is again somewhat unclear. However, the underlying thrust is that ". . . upon the essential point of integrity to their employer . . . [fiduciaries'] conduct must stand unimpeached."[143] More specifically, a fiduciary is bound by the following duties:

- A fiduciary cannot quit his or her employment in order to exploit a business opportunity discovered during the course of that employment, but must offer the employer the first opportunity of exploiting it.[144] Moreover, the fiduciary must first disclose the opportunity to the employer, even though he or she knows that the employer will not elect to exploit it.
- A fiduciary relationship is *uberrimae fidei*, which means that the employee is bound proactively to divulge to the employer any information that can reasonably be expected to have an impact on the employer's business interests — for example, blemishes in the employee's work record with previous employers, wrongdoings committed by the employee or by co-workers during the employment

---

2 S.C.R. 574, Sopinka and La Forest JJ.; *Canadian Aero Service Ltd. v. O'Malley* (1973), [1974] S.C.R. 592.

141 Examples: *Fraser v. ProScience Inc.* (2005), 42 C.C.E.L. (3d) 245 at 259 (Ont. S.C.J.) [*Fraser*]; *R.W. Hamilton Ltd. v. Aeroquip Corp.* (1988), 65 O.R. (2d) 345 at 351; *Sure-Grip*, above note 112 at 287.

142 *White Oaks Welding Supplies Ltd. v. Tapp* (1983), 42 O.R. (2d) 445 at 449 (H.C.J.), where a relatively low-level sales manager was found to be a "fiduciary" because of his "encyclopedic" knowledge of the firm's customers and their needs. But compare *Gendron*, above note 16 at 291, where Valin J. cautioned that vulnerability does not count as much as the employee's position in the hierarchy.

143 *Wilcox v. GWG Ltd.* (1985), 8 C.C.E.L. 11 at 12 (Alta. C.A.), quoting *State Vacuum Stores of Canada Ltd. v. Phillips*, [1954] 3 D.L.R. 621 (B.C.C.A.). See generally *C.H.S. Air Conditioning Ltd. v. Environmental Air Systems Inc.* (1996), 20 C.C.E.L. (2d) 123 at 133–36, Adams J. (Ont. Gen. Div.).

144 *Berkey Photo (Canada) Ltd. v. Ohlig* (1983), 2 C.C.E.L. 113 at 127–28 (Ont. H.C.J.) [*Berkey Photo*].

relationship, or plans on the employee's part to resign and set up a competing business or work for a competitor.[145]

- A fiduciary cannot compete with a former employer for a reasonable time after the employment has ceased.[146] This restriction encompasses not enticing the employer's customers to shift their loyalty to the fiduciary's new firm and also not enticing fellow employees to resign and come to work with the fiduciary. Presumably, however, a fiduciary can simply convey information to customers and other employees that he or she is quitting to work elsewhere, so that the individuals concerned can make informed market choices. What constitutes a reasonable time for banning such post-termination competition will depend on how long the court feels it ought reasonably to take the former employer to safeguard itself against the vulnerability in question, and to take the fiduciary to develop a replacement career without recourse to the sensitive information upon which the fiduciary relationship rests. In other words, the courts must balance the respective interests of the fiduciary in getting on with a career and of the former employer in protecting its vulnerable spot.

It deserves emphasis that the foregoing list of the specific duties of fiduciary employees is not exhaustive. Rather, a fiduciary obligation is all-pervasive and residual in nature, so that each case must turn on its own circumstances.

Breach of a fiduciary obligation allows the employer to pursue the remedies mentioned earlier: summary dismissal of the employee (subject to the requirements of just cause); a damages action for lost profits or an accounting for profits obtained by the employee or another third party, whichever is most favourable to the employer; and an injunction against the employee or another third party.[147]

8) The Employee's Duty to Give Notice of Termination

An employee is impliedly bound to give the employer reasonable notice of resignation. We examine this topic in detail in Chapter 9 on termination of employment.

---

145 Example: *Fraser*, above note 141 at 259–60, where the employee was making plans to resign and establish a competing business.
146 Examples: *KJA*, above note 89; *Sure-Grip*, above note 112 at 290; *Berkey Photo*, above note 144 at 128; *Cline*, above note 91 at 192.
147 See Section B(7), above in this chapter.

FURTHER READINGS

BRAIT, R., & B. POLLOCK, "Confidentiality, Intellectual Property and Competitive Risk in the Employment Relationship" (2004) 83 Can. Bar Rev. 585

CALLAHAN, L.J.E., T. DWORKIN, & D. LEWIS, "Whistleblowing: Australian, U.K. and U.S. Approaches to Disclosure in the Public Interest" (2003–04) 44 Va. J. Int'l Law 879

DUBIN, C., "Whistleblowing Study" (Ottawa: Industry Canada Competition Bureau, 1997)

ENGLAND, G., "Recent Developments in Individual Employment Law: Tell Me the Old, Old Story" (2002) 9 C.L.E.L.J. 37

ENGLAND, G., "Recent Developments in the Law of the Employment Contract: Continuing Tension between the Rights Paradigm and the Efficiency Paradigm" (1995) 20 Queen's L.J. 557

ENGLAND, G., "The Impact of the *Charter* on Individual Employment Law in Canada: Tell Me the Old, Old Story" (2006) 13 C.L.E.L.J. 1

ENGLAND, G., R. WOOD, & I. CHRISTIE, *Employment Law in Canada*, 4th ed., looseleaf (Markham, ON: LexisNexis Canada, 2005–) c. 11

FLANNIGAN, R., "The Fiduciary Accountability of Ordinary Employees" (2007) 13 C.L.E.L.J. 283

FREEDLAND, M.R., *The Personal Employment Contract* (Oxford: Oxford University Press, 2003)

HAY, D., "England, 1562–1875: The Law and Its Uses" in D. Hay & P. Craven, eds., *Masters, Servants and Magistrates in Britain and the Empire, 1562–1955* (Chapel Hill, NC: University of North Carolina Press, 2004) at 59

NAPIER, B., "Working to Rule: A Breach of the Contract of Employment?" (1972) 1 Indus. L.J. 125

SOSSIN, L., "Speaking Truth to Power? The Search for Bureaucratic Independence in Canada" (2005) 55 U.T.L.J. 1

CHAPTER 5

THE COMMON LAW OBLIGATIONS OF THE EMPLOYER UNDER THE CONTRACT OF EMPLOYMENT

The employer's obligations to its employees derive from the express and implied terms of the contract of employment.[1] As we saw in Chapter 4, which dealt with the common law obligations of the employee,[2] express contractual terms are generally of secondary importance in delineating the employer's duties. Because the parties cannot foresee at the date of hiring all the contingencies that might occur over the course of their future relationship, and therefore cannot bargain comprehensively and precisely about them,[3] the field is left in large measure to the standardized implied terms. Typically, the express duties of the employer will be found in its written and verbal offer and the employee's written and verbal acceptance of that offer; they will also be found in any ancillary documentation that the parties expressly agree will be incorporated into the contract, personnel manuals, works rule books, benefit handbooks, and other personnel memoranda among them. In contrast, in some countries such as Britain, legislation requires the employer to provide the employee with a written statement describing a comprehensive range of contractual matters, including the legal identity of the employer, job title, wages, vacation and holiday pay, sick pay, notice of termination, length of vacations, pension benefits, disciplinary rules

---

1   See generally on this topic G. England, R. Wood, & I. Christie, *Employment Law in Canada*, 4th ed., looseleaf (Markham, ON: LexisNexis Canada, 2005–) c. 10.
2   See Chapter 4.
3   See the illuminating analysis by P.R. Milgrom & J. Roberts, *Economics, Organization and Management* (Englewood Cliffs, NJ: Prentice-Hall, 1992) at 329–30.

and procedures, and dispute resolution machinery.[4] This information must be given to the employee within thirteen weeks of the date of hiring and must be updated regularly thereafter. As yet, no Canadian jurisdiction has enacted equivalent legislation, although in 2006 the Arthurs Report recommended that it be incorporated into the federal Code.[5] The report also suggested an innovative remedy for employer violations of the provision, namely, that the employee's recollection of the terms of the contract shall be presumed to be accurate unless the employer can prove otherwise.

The disparity of bargaining power between many low- and mid-skilled workers and their employer may be reflected in express contractual provisions that impose harsh termination entitlements on the employee or confer broad, unfettered discretionary powers on the employer in key areas, such as changing job duties and granting or withholding bonuses or other perquisites. Most courts will interpret harsh termination clauses *contra proferentem* the interests of the employer.[6] Furthermore, several courts have held that clauses giving the employer a broad discretion to adversely affect the employee's interests are subject to an implied term requiring that such discretion be exercised reasonably and in good faith. For example, in one case where an express term permitted the employer to unilaterally modify a salesperson's territory, it was held that the parties impliedly understood that any modifications would be for "good and valid" business reasons and would be implemented "reasonably."[7] However, the Alberta courts have refused to imply a residual proviso of reasonableness and fairness into express discretionary clauses that permit employers to terminate the employ-

---

4   *Employment Protection (Consolidation) Act 1978* (U.K.), 1978, c. 44, ss. 1–11. There is also a directive of the European Economic Community to similar effect: "An Employer's Obligation to Inform Employees of the Conditions Applicable to the Contract or Employment Relationship," Directive 91/533/E.C.; O.J. No.L 288/32, 18/10/91. For a criticism of this directive, see J. Clark & M. Hall, "The Cinderella Directive? Employee Rights to Information about Conditions Applicable to Their Contract or Employment Relationship" (1992) 21 Indus. L.J. 106.

5   Canada, Commission on the Review of Federal Labour Standards, *Fairness at Work: Federal Labour Standards for the 21st Century*, by H.W. Arthurs (Ottawa: Commission on the Review of Federal Labour Standards, 2006) at 80–84 [Arthurs Report].

6   See Chapter 4.

7   *Snelling v. Tenneco Canada Inc.* (1992), 40 C.C.E.L. 122 at 128 (B.C.S.C.). In a similar vein, see *Truckers Garage Inc. v. Krell* (1994), 3 C.C.E.L. (2d) 157 (Ont. C.A.); *Greenberg v. Meffert* (1985), 18 D.L.R. (4th) 548 (Ont. C.A.); *Cohnstaedt v. University of Regina*, [1989] 1 S.C.R. 1011 at 1019. All of these cases are authority for the principle that the employer's express discretionary powers must, by implication, be exercised in good faith and fairly.

ment relationship without notice or pay in lieu, reasoning that both understand the purpose of such clauses is to provide for a "clean break" in the relationship.[8]

The gap in express terms has been filled by a set of standardized obligations on the employer, which the courts imply into all employment contracts across the board. As we saw in earlier chapters of this book, the theoretical basis for these implied terms is to give effect to the unexpressed factual intentions of both parties, but in practice, that test has become a vehicle for the courts to formulate obligations on the employer that the judges perceive to be appropriate as a matter of general policy in light of changing managerial practices. A major theme in modern Canadian employment law is how most (but not all) courts are applying the standardized implied terms in order to give increasing weight to safeguarding the rights of vulnerable employees. Many societal factors have propelled this trend, but unquestionably the *Canadian Charter of Rights and Freedoms* has had a major indirect impact.[9] Although the *Charter* does not apply directly to the terms of private employment contracts, its underlying values of fairness, equality, and proportionality have been incorporated into the employment contract under the rubric of general contract law principles, such as implied terms and defining what constitutes a repudiatory breach for the purposes of constructive dismissal and summary dismissal. As we shall see below, the leading issue in this area of the law is whether the courts should imply a standardized term in all employment contracts requiring the employer to treat the employee fairly and decently. If this step is taken, such an implied term would play the same role for the employer's implied contractual duties as the implied duty of fidelity plays for the employee's implied contractual duties:[10] it would establish the residual and overarching bedrock obligation from which the employer's particularized implied obligations would derive.

Before analyzing the specific implied obligations of the employer, a cautionary note must be sounded. In practice, since civil litigation is beyond the financial reach of most employees, the common law entitlements of the employee described in this chapter exist only on paper. It is no surprise that the majority of reported cases on the employer's common law duties to the employee have involved relatively high-level

---

8   Examples: *Meyer v. Partec Lavalin Inc.* (2001), 11 C.C.E.L. (3d) 56 at 61 (Alta. C.A.); *Goering v. Mayfair Golf and Country Club Co. Ltd.*, [2001] C.L.L.C. ¶210-038 (Alta. Q.B.).

9   G. England, "The Impact of the *Charter* on Individual Employment Law in Canada: Tell Me the Old, Old Story" (2006) 13 C.L.E.L.J. 1.

10   This issue is examined in Chapter 4.

managers, professionals, and sports and entertainment stars. The reality for most workers is that the employment standards legislation provides them with their rights and the means of enforcing them. As well, the common law cases almost invariably involve constructive dismissal, since only a very brave or foolhardy employee would contemplate suing his or her employer for damages for breaching an implied term in the contract while continuing in the job. We examine this issue next.

A. AN IMPLIED DUTY OF FAIRNESS

The courts traditionally have refused to imply as a standardized term in the employment contract a requirement that the employer treat the employee "fairly" in regard to employment-related matters.[11] An exception used to exist for employees of statutory bodies who occupy a judicially recognized "office" — the administrative law duty of fairness required such employers to exercise their statutory authority in a procedurally fair manner.[12] However, in its 2008 decision in *Dunsmuir v. New Brunswick*,[13] the Supreme Court of Canada substantially narrowed this exception. The Court held that an office holder who is employed under a contract of employment is generally restricted to common law rights and remedies, thereby excluding the administrative law duty of fairness. The Court ruled that the administrative law duty of fairness would only apply to an office holder if either (1) he has no contract of employment, for example, if hired "at pleasure" or (2) if the empowering statute necessarily implies that the duty of fairness should apply.[14] Of course, the parties may incorporate into the employment contract, either expressly or by implication based on their past practices, a complaints or disciplinary procedure from a personnel manual or other works rule book, and this may include the main features of a duty of fairness.[15] Otherwise, at common law the employer is not contractually bound to treat the employee fairly and decently.

11 Examples: *Knight v. Indian Head School Division No. 19*, [1990] 1 S.C.R. 653 at 670–74; *Ridge v. Baldwin* (1963), [1964] A.C. 40 (H.L.).
12 Most of the cases arise in the context of dismissal, examined in Chapter 9, but the duty of fairness applies to all decisions that potentially harm the employee's interests.
13 2008 SCC 9, especially paras. 85–116.
14 *Ibid.* at paras. 115–16.
15 Example: *Bruce v. Region of Waterloo Swim Club* (1990), 31 C.C.E.L. 321 (Ont. H.C.J.).

This traditional rule has been shaken severely during the last decade or so. Critics have argued that modern courts should imply a standardized duty of fairness for several reasons.[16] First, contemporary personnel management techniques emphasize the importance of treating employees fairly in order to enhance their morale, and ultimately, the firm's productivity. The employee's expectation of fair dealing, it is argued, now forms part of the general climate of contracting that employers and employees can safely be deemed to intend to incorporate into their employment contracts, unless a contrary intention is clearly present. Second, employees have long owed their employer an implied contractual duty to act reasonably in advancing the best interests of the firm, so that imposing a reciprocal duty on the employer would bring symmetry into the common law.[17] The implied duty of fairness, therefore, would serve as the cornerstone obligation on employers equivalent to the implied duty of fidelity on employees.[18] Third, implying a standardized duty of fairness into employment contracts would mirror the long-standing practice of implying into commercial contracts a reciprocal duty to act reasonably and in good faith in furthering the objectives of the contract.[19] Fourth, contemporary public opinion, especially as manifested in the duty of reasonable accommodation under human rights legislation and in the values of fairness, equality, and proportionality underpinning the *Charter*,[20] expects employers to treat their employees fairly. Fifth, the courts have imposed on employers most of the components of a duty of fairness under the rubric of other common law doctrines, such as the requirement that summary dismissal be for just cause, the determination of reasonable notice of termination, and the award of punitive damages against employers who act in a high-handed manner. Sixth, recognizing an independent contractual term of fairness would provide a convenient legal technique for the purpose of compensating an employee for psychological harm

---

16 See, for example, G. England, "Recent Developments in the Law of the Employment Contract: Continuing Tension between the Rights Paradigm and the Efficiency Paradigm" (1995) 20 Queen's L.J. 557 at 585–91; G. England, "The Impact of the *Charter* on Individual Employment Law in Canada: Tell Me the Old, Old Story," above note 9 at 21–25; G. England, "Recent Developments in Individual Employment Law: Tell Me the Old, Old Story" (2002) 9 C.L.E.L.J. 37 at 50–56.

17 See Chapter 4, especially Section B(1).

18 This matter, too, is examined in Chapter 4.

19 Example: *Dawson v. Helicopter Exploration Co.*, [1955] S.C.R. 868.

20 See Chapter 7. See also G. England, "The Impact of the *Charter* on Individual Employment Law in Canada: Tell Me the Old, Old Story," above note 9.

in a wrongful dismissal action. As it is, under the *Vorvis* doctrine,[21] such compensation can be awarded only if the employer commits an independent actionable wrong unconnected with the contractual duty to give the employee due notice of termination, the latter forming the sole basis of a common law action for wrongful dismissal. Tort law, too, has come into play when the employer treats the employee unfairly, especially when a brutally handled discharge causes the employee mental distress.[22] Critics have argued that implying an independent contractual duty of fairness on employers would be consistent with the trend exemplified in these doctrines.

On the other hand, there are risks with implying a duty of fairness. Employers fear the uncertainty and unpredictability of such a legal standard. Not only would they potentially be exposed to endless litigation by aggrieved employees, but they would also face the spectre of widespread judicial second-guessing of the fairness of their decisions in all areas of the employment relationship. The latter risk need not materialize, however, if courts interpret the duty of fairness in a predominantly procedural rather than substantive sense, taking care not to substitute their decisions for those of the employer on matters requiring sensitive business judgment and expertise. Thus, an employee could not use the duty of fairness to argue that wages are unreasonably low, that vacations are unreasonably short, or that employer efforts to increase profits by introducing a technological change or implementing labour subcontracting are unreasonable. Furthermore, the expense of civil litigation and the risk of paying the employer's solicitor-client fees would probably deter most employees from launching spurious lawsuits. Opponents of a duty of fairness also argue that it would clash with the traditional common law principle that an employer need not show just cause if it terminates an employee by giving due notice or wages in lieu.[23] This principle, employers argue, is essential to preserving their flexibility to discard unwanted labour. This need not be the case, however, if the duty of fairness is formulated cautiously, with due regard to the employer's interests as well as to the employee's.

These arguments came to a head in the 1997 decision of the Supreme Court of Canada in *Wallace v. United Grain Growers Ltd.*[24] There,

---

21 *Vorvis v. Insurance Corporation of British Columbia*, [1989] 1 S.C.R. 1085 [*Vorvis*]: examined in Chapter 9, Section F(1).

22 Chapter 9 of this book outlines the law in these areas.

23 See the authorities cited in above note 7.

24 [1997] 3 S.C.R. 701 [*Wallace*]. See J. Fudge, "The Limits of Good Faith in the Contract of Employment: From *Addis* to *Vorvis* to *Wallace* and Back Again?" (2007) 32 Queen's L.J. 529; K. VanBuskirk, "Damages for Improvident Employer

the plaintiff was wrongfully dismissed from his job at age 59 after fourteen years of service with the defendant and suffered severe mental distress as a result. The defendant had explicitly promised the employee during the recruitment process that he would be given a secure job and be treated fairly, and the plaintiff would not have quit his previous secure job and accepted employment with the defendant had it not been for these undertakings. This breach of faith was partially responsible for the employee's mental distress. In addition, the employer handled the discharge callously, raising spurious allegations of incompetence on employee Wallace's part to cloak the real reason for the termination and using hardball tactics before the trial in order to pressure him into dropping his suit. One issue before the Court was whether the plaintiff could recover damages for such mental distress. As seen above, *Vorvis* [25] held that such damages can be awarded only if the employer commits an independent actionable wrong separate from the contractual duty to give the employee due notice of termination, the latter forming the sole basis of a common law action for wrongful dismissal. The plaintiff argued that the employer had breached an implied term in the employment contract obliging it to treat him fairly in regard to his dismissal. Alternatively, the plaintiff argued that a co-terminous duty of fairness existed under a tort of "bad faith discharge." The majority of the Court rejected both these propositions.

Justice Iacobbuci, delivering the majority decision, held that there is no standardized implied term in employment contracts requiring employers to treat their employees in good faith or fairly. He reasoned that such a term would be "overly intrusive" into the employer's freedom to manage its business affairs; it would also be inconsistent with the recognized right of the employer to terminate employees without just cause by giving due notice or wages in lieu.[26] Similar concerns led him to deny the existence of a tort of bad faith discharge. Nevertheless, he held that bad faith or unfair treatment of an employee during the dismissal process can be taken into account in determining the length of reasonable notice of termination. Accordingly, he extended the period of reasonable notice to twenty-four months to take account of the callous manner of dismissal. Justice Iacobbuci stated that the rules of the employment contract must take account of the "special" nature of

---

Behaviour" (2004) 83 Can. Bar Rev. 755; L. Steusser, "Wrongful Dismissal—Playing Hardball: *Wallace v. United Grain Growers*" (1998) 25 Man. L.J. 547; J. Swan, "Damages for Wrongful Dismissal: Lessons from *Wallace v. United Grain Growers Ltd.*" (1998) 6 C.L.E.L.J. 313.

25 Above note 21, examined in Chapter 9, Section F(1).
26 *Wallace*, above note 24 at 735–36.

the employment relationship, which makes the employee "vulnerable" to the employer by virtue of the parties' disparity in bargaining power, especially in dismissal situations when the employee's psychological stake in his or her job is jeopardized. Thus, Iacobbuci J. held that employers are under an "obligation of good faith and fair dealing in the manner of dismissal," which, while "incapable of precise definition," requires employers, as a "minimum," to be ". . . candid, reasonable, honest and forthright with their employees and . . . [to] . . . [r]efrain from engaging in conduct that is unfair or is in bad faith by being, for example, untruthful, misleading or unduly insensitive."[27]

There are three potentially serious limitations with the approach of Iacobucci J. First, if the employment contract contains a relatively short express notice period, such a clause would presumably preclude the award of a lengthier "reasonable" notice period. Indeed, express notice clauses may become more popular with employers than is now the case if employers see them as a defence against the *Wallace* doctrine. The courts may consider that the duty of fairness is sufficiently akin to a fundamental human right that cannot be abridged by express terms in the employment contract, by analogy with the *jus cogens* doctrine in international law. As yet, though, the courts have not taken this radical step.[28] Second, if there is no independent implied term in the employment contract requiring the employer to treat its employees fairly and in good faith, then presumably the employee could not resign in response to such mistreatment on the employer's part and sue for damages for constructive dismissal.[29] This result would appear to be at odds with the tenor of Iacobbuci J.'s judgment, which explicitly recognizes the vulnerable position of the employee. It is fortunate that, as yet, *Wallace* has not been applied in this way by other courts in constructive dismissal litigation. Third, Iacobucci J. failed to clarify whether an extension of the notice period can be granted on the basis of the employer's mistreatment of the employee *prior* to the moment of dismissal, and, if so, how far back in time the courts can go in reviewing the employer's improprieties. Subsequently, most courts have been prepared to review the employer's actions for a lengthy time prior to the moment of dismissal in order to

---

27   *Ibid.* at 743.

28   *Barnard v. Testori Americas Corp.* (2001), 11 C.C.E.L. (3d) 42 at 45 (P.E.I.S.C.A.D.). Compare *Smith v. Casino Rama Services Inc.*, [2004] O.T.C. 653 (S.C.J.), where Loukidelis J. overrode an express notice term in granting a *Wallace* extension, but the lack of any reasons for this ruling weakens its authoritative weight.

29   This doctrine is examined in Chapter 9, Section D.

protect the vulnerable employee.[30] It is submitted that in doing so, these courts are tacitly recognizing an independent contractual term of fairness: it is illogical to say that the employer's conduct amounts to bad faith at the moment of dismissal without also saying that it constitutes bad faith at the time it actually occurs.

In her dissenting judgment, McLachlin J. held that the duty of fairness in dismissal situations should exist as an independent implied term in all employment contracts and not, as Iacobbuci J. preferred, be imposed under the rubric of the reasonable notice test.

Despite the *Wallace* ruling, numerous subsequent decisions appear to be explicable only on the basis of the employer having breached an implied term in the contract requiring it to treat the employee fairly and decently. All of these decisions involve employees who have resigned in response to unfair treatment by their employer and successfully sue for constructive dismissal. Thus, the courts have grounded constructive dismissal on failing proactively to advise a psychologically depressed employee of her rights to disability benefits during a termination interview;[31] systematically marginalizing an employee and building a paper trail of his performance deficiencies in the hope that he would quit;[32] conducting performance appraisals in a callous and insensitive manner;[33] setting unreasonably high performance targets that are beyond the employee's capacity;[34] scheduling work without attempting to accommodate the employee's family-care needs;[35] refusing to make reasonable efforts to train the employee to use new technologies;[36] failing to protect the employee against personal intimidation, harassment, and

30   Examples: *Keays v. Honda Canada Inc.*, [2005] O.J. No. 1145 (S.C.J.), var'd in part (2006), 82 O.R. (3d) 161 (C.A.), where the *Wallace* extension was granted on the basis of five years of ongoing mistreatment of a disabled employee; *Miller v. ICO Canada Inc.*, [2005] A.J. No. 335 (Q.B.) [*Miller*], where a *Wallace* extension was granted on the basis of two years of mistreatment of the employee. Only a minority of courts have limited their review to the actual moment of dismissal: see, for example, *Marlowe v. Ashland Canada Inc.*, [2002] C.L.L.C. ¶210-004, especially at 141,049 (B.C.S.C.).
31   *Menard v. Royal Insurance Company of Canada* (2000), 1 C.C.E.L. (3d) 96 (Ont. S.C.J.).
32   Example: *Miller*, above note 30 at 61 (Alta. Q.B.).
33   Example: *Lavinskas v. Jacques Whitford and Associated Ltd.*, [2005] C.L.L.C. ¶210-045, especially at 141,457–58 (Ont. S.C.J.).
34   Example: *Mark v. Westend Development Corp.* (2002), 18 C.C.E.L. (3d) 90 (Ont. S.C.J.).
35   Example: *Hanni v. Western Road Rail Systems (1991) Inc.* (2002), 17 C.C.E.L. (3d) 79 (B.C.S.C.).
36   Example: *Levesque v. Sherwood Credit Union*, [2000] C.L.L.C. ¶210-038 at 141,303–4 (Sask. Q.B.).

bullying;[37] and deliberately deceiving an employee into believing that she was being promoted into a permanent position when the employer knew the posting was temporary.[38] Influential courts in other countries, including the English House of Lords, have also recognized the existence of an independent implied duty of fairness.[39] The final word has not been said on the existence of such a duty in Canada.

If an employer does treat an employee unfairly in breach of an express or implied term in the employment contract, difficulties may arise with remedying the breach. Regarding damages, it may be difficult to ascertain exactly what financial losses an employee will have sustained as a consequence of the employer violating a procedural requirement, such as to afford the employee an opportunity to voice an opinion before taking disciplinary action. Indeed, nominal damages might be appropriate if the employer's decision would have been the same, even if the proper procedure had been followed. Yet, it would surely erode the symbolic legitimacy of procedural rights not to award substantial compensation in such circumstances. Perhaps the courts could award a hefty sum of punitive damages in order to deter employers from disregarding procedural rights in the employment contract. If a procedural violation results in the worker suffering mental distress, a damages award would present fewer difficulties. Ordering the employer to rescind its decision and review the matter in accordance with the proper procedure seems to be to the most effective way of "making whole" a procedural violation; however, the courts do not traditionally order specific performance of employment contracts, especially entailing the reinstatement of a wrongfully dismissed employee.[40] Such an order might seem pointless if the employer is likely to go through the procedural motions with its mind already fixed on repeating the original decision. Again, the courts might award punitive damages in these circumstances in order to underscore the symbolic importance of maintaining procedural justice. It remains to be seen how Canadian courts would respond to these questions.

37 Example: *Stamos v. Annuity Research and Market Services Ltd.*, [2002] C.L.L.C. ¶210-036 at 141,404 (Ont. S.C.J.) [*Stamos*].
38 *Wilson v. New Westminster Chamber of Commerce*, [2004] C.L.L.C. ¶210-001 at 141,006 (B.C. Prov. Ct.).
39 *Malik v. BCCI*, [1998] A.C. 20 (H.L.), examined in D. Brodie, "A Fair Deal at Work" (1999) 19 Oxford J. Legal Stud. 83. The Australian courts have followed suit: see, for example, *Russell v. The Trustees of the Roman Catholic Church for the Archdiocese of Sydney*, [2007] NSWSC 104.
40 However, some English courts have relaxed the no specific performance rule in such circumstances. Example: *Robb v. Hammersmith and Fulham London Borough Council*, [1991] I.C.R. 514 (Q.B.). See generally Chapter 9, Section F(2).

B. THE IMPLIED DUTY TO PAY FOR WORK DONE, GRATUITIES, AND EMPLOYEE EXPENSES

The employer is impliedly bound to pay wages for all work performed by the employee. In practice, common law actions are rarely used by employees to recover unpaid wages, since the employment standards legislation typically requires employers to pay wages for work done and provides special administrative machinery for enforcing that obligation.[41] The common law usually comes into play in determining the threshold question of whether the employee is legally entitled under the employment contract to be paid for the work in question. If the contract contains an express clause disentitling the employee to compensation in defined circumstances—for example, contracts may disallow a salesperson from receiving commissions that have been earned, but not yet paid out prior to the date of quitting or resignation[42]—such clauses are generally construed *contra proferentem* the employer's interests. The parties to an employment contract are presumed to intend that services performed by the employee are to be compensated, not provided gratuitously. If the employer takes the benefit of services that it has not specifically ordered the employee to perform, the employee is entitled to recover the fair market value of such services on a *quantum meruit*;[43] otherwise, the employer would be unjustly enriched at the employee's expense.

The employee's right to receive payment is subject to the condition precedent that the quality of his or her services satisfies the minimum level for acceptable performance.[44] The employee cannot demand payment for substandard work. Nevertheless, the employee may be entitled to recover some reduced compensation on a *quantum meruit* even for inferior work, so long as the employer has derived some value from it and the employee has expended some effort in carrying it out.[45]

---

41   See Chapter 6, Section B(6).

42   *Morrison v. Deschambault Bertoldi & Associates Ltd.* (1993), 46 C.C.E.L. 187 at 191 (Ont. Gen. Div.). Contrast *Graycombe Associates Ltd. v. Northern Stag Industries Ltd.* (1976), 14 O.R. (2d) 201 (H.C.J.).

43   *Deglman v. Brunet Estate*, [1954] S.C.R. 725; *Alyea v. South Waterloo Edgar Insurance Brokers Ltd.* (1994), 50 C.C.E.L. 266 (Ont. Gen. Div.).

44   *Miles v. Wakefield Metropolitan District Council*, [1987] A.C. 539 (H.L.) [*Miles*]. See generally P. Sayles, "Contract and Restitution in the Employment Relationship: No Work, No Pay" (1988) 8 Oxford J. Legal Stud. 301.

45   *Miles*, ibid. at 553 and 561.

The courts have held that the employer's implied obligation to pay wages extends to tips and other gratuities.[46] As well, English and Australian authorities have held that the implied obligation extends to reimbursing the employee for any expenses reasonably incurred in performing the job.[47] However, it is unclear whether the latter obligation would require the employer to reimburse an employee who works out of a personal residence the expenses of maintaining an office or other workplace in the home.

C. THE IMPLIED DUTY TO GIVE NOTICE OF TERMINATION

The common law presumes that the parties to an employment contract intend their agreement to be for an indefinite term that can only be terminated by either party giving due notice of that intent.[48] This contrasts with the position in the United States, where hiring is presumed to be on an "at will" basis so that either side can terminate the relationship without giving notice. In Canada, the default position is that the employer must, in the absence of a clear mutual agreement to the contrary, provide the employee with reasonable notice to terminate the relationship. The jurisprudence on reasonable notice is examined at length elsewhere in this book.[49]

D. THE IMPLIED DUTY TO PROVIDE WORK OPPORTUNITIES AND JOB SATISFACTION

Traditionally, the courts have not implied a term into the employment contract requiring the employer to provide the employee with actual working opportunities.[50] The employee has no guaranteed "fallback" pay during layoffs at common law. Instead, layoff operates as a repudiatory breach of the employment contract that entitles the employee

---

46 *Shabinsky v. Horwitz* (1971), 32 D.L.R. (3d) 318 (Ont. H.C.J.).

47 B.A. Hepple & P. O'Higgins, *Employment Law*, 3d ed. (London: Sweet & Maxwell, 1979) at 153; *Pupazzoni v. Fremantle Fishermen's Co-op Society Ltd.* (1981), 23 A.I.L.R. para. 168 (W. Austl. S.C.).

48 *Wallace*, above note 24.

49 See Chapter 9.

50 Examples: *Turner v. Sawdon & Co.*, [1901] 2 K.B. 653 (C.A.); *Burmeister v. Regina Multicultural Council* (1985), 8 C.C.E.L. 144 at 155 (Sask. C.A.).

to damages for constructive dismissal, unless the employment contract expressly or impliedly entitles the employer to lay off without giving notice of termination or wages in lieu.[51] Exceptionally, however, the courts will imply an obligation on the employer to provide the employee with working opportunities where the nature of the employment in question, or other surrounding circumstances, clearly show that such opportunities are a core part of the consideration for which the employee bargained. Thus, courts have held that professional entertainers and sports personalities implicitly bargain for a high public profile and are therefore entitled to extra damages for being denied the opportunity to work.[52] The courts have also held that employees paid "by the piece," or on a pure commission basis, are entitled to reasonable working opportunities in order to enable them to make a living wage.[53]

The traditional approach was questioned by a 1974 judgment of Lord Denning, holding that all employees implicitly bargain for a "right to work" — namely, the personal satisfaction of doing their jobs well — so that the employer must provide them with adequate opportunities.[54] Although courts at that time did not endorse Lord Denning's radical view, today it appears to be gaining support among Canadian courts. Thus, in several recent decisions, constructive dismissal has been grounded on the employer breaching a contractual duty to provide the employee with job satisfaction. The common element in these decisions is that the psychological satisfaction of doing the job was plainly of central importance to the employee, making it a core component of the parties' bargain rather than a peripheral or ancillary feature of the job.[55] This development should not be surprising since the Supreme Court of Canada has trumpeted the importance of the psychological component of the employment contract on numerous occasions,[56] and modern

---

51 Example: *Turner v. Uniglobe Custom Travel Ltd.*, [2005] C.L.L.C. ¶210-039 (Alta. Q.B.).

52 Examples: *Cranston v. Canadian Broadcasting Corp.* (1994), 2 C.C.E.L. (2d) 301 at 309 (Ont. Gen. Div.); *Clayton (Herbert) & Jack Waller Ltd. v. Oliver*, [1930] A.C. 209 (H.L.).

53 *R. v. Welch* (1853), 3 E. & B. 357, 118 E.R. 800 (M.C.); *Devonald v. Rosser & Sons*, [1906] 2 K.B. 728 (C.A.); *Browning v. Crumlin Valley Collieries Ltd.*, [1926] 1 K.B. 522.

54 *Langston v. A.U.E.W.*, [1974] I.C.R. 180 at 190 (C.A.), Lord Denning.

55 Examples: *Tanton v. Crane Canada Inc.*, [2001] C.L.L.C. ¶210-023 (Alta. Q.B.); *Michaud v. R.B.C. Dominion Securities*, [2001] C.L.L.C. ¶210-032 (B.C.S.C.); *Bowen v. Ritchie Bros. Auctioneers Ltd.* (1999), 47 C.C.E.L. (2d) 232, especially at 236–37 (Ont. C.A.); *Wilkinson v. T. Eaton Co.* (1992), 44 C.C.E.L. (2d) 287 (Alta. Q.B.).

56 The seminal judgment is that of Dickson C.J. in *Reference Re Public Service Employee Relations Act (Alberta)*, [1987] 1 S.C.R. 313 at 368. His remarks regard-

personnel management practice places great importance on providing the employee with job satisfaction. As yet, all the cases have involved constructive dismissal, but there is no doctrinal reason preventing an employee from suing for damages for loss of the psychological satisfaction derived from work.

E. THE IMPLIED DUTY TO PROVIDE SICK PAY

Many employers will carry insurance coverage that entitles the employee to specified payments during defined short- and long-term periods of sickness and disability, and these provisions will be incorporated, expressly or impliedly, into the employment contract. In the absence of insurance, the obligation of the employer to make payments during periods of sickness is unclear. The consensus of opinion among Canadian courts appears to be that the employer is presumed to intend to provide sick pay, at least for absences of a relatively short duration.[57] Of course, if the evidence discloses a contrary intention, the presumption will be rebutted and the employee will not be entitled to sick pay.[58] These Canadian authorities, however, are relatively old. In contrast, modern English authorities have presumed the opposite, namely, that the employer does *not* intend to provide sick pay.[59] In England, the employee must prove a reliable past practice of providing sick pay in order to rebut the presumption. There are no recent Canadian decisions on point. In order to avoid any ambiguities, Canadian employers and employees are well advised to bargain express contractual terms about the matter.

---

ing the psychological and social importance of work to the employee are now treated as authoritative, even though they were made in a dissenting judgment. See *Slaight Communications Inc. v. Davidson* (1989), 59 D.L.R. (4d) 416 (S.C.C.); *Machtinger v. HOJ Industries Ltd.*, [1992] 1 S.C.R. 986; *Wallace*, above note 24 at 742–46; *Re Rizzo and Rizzo Shoes Ltd.*, [1998] 1 S.C.R. 27 at 35–36; *McKinley v. B.C. Tel*, [2001] C.L.L.C. ¶210-027 at 141,206 (S.C.C.).

57 *Heinbigner v. Kinzel*, [1931] 2 W.W.R. 539 (Sask. Dist. Ct.); *Montague v. Grand Truck Pacific Ry.* (1915), 8 W.W.R. 528 (Man. C.A.); *Colman v. Naish* (1914), 28 W.L.R. 487 (B.C. Co. Ct.). But *quaere* the effect of *Low v. Toronto (City of)*, [1947] 2 D.L.R. 718 (Ont. C.A.) [*Low*].

58 It is submitted that *Low*, *ibid.*, is best explained as turning on the fact that the employer did not intend temporary workers to receive sick pay.

59 *Mears v. Safecar Security Ltd.* (1982), [1983] Q.B. 54, especially at 77–79 (C.A.). Prior to this decision, the English courts presumed that sick pay was payable: e.g., *Orman v. Saville Sportswear Ltd.*, [1960] 3 All E.R. 105 at 111 (C.A.).

F. THE IMPLIED DUTY TO PREVENT PERSONAL HARASSMENT AND INTIMIDATION

Modern Canadian courts recognize an implied contractual duty on the employer to prevent employees from being harassed, bullied, or otherwise personally intimidated by other employees, customers, or other visitors to the worksite.[60] The impetus for this development is clearly the employer's obligation under the human rights legislation to safeguard the employee against sexual harassment,[61] and the law in both areas is similar. Thus, the employer must take all reasonable steps to eliminate any personal harassment of which it knows or ought reasonably to know, including disciplining and dismissing the perpetrator[62] and removing visiting offenders from the worksite. The rationale is that since the employer has the power to control all aspects of work operations, the employer is expected to use it to eliminate any harassment. In order to demonstrate that they have taken reasonable steps to eliminating such conduct in the event of possible future litigation, employers are advised to adopt an express anti-harassment policy parallelling their sexual harassment policy.[63]

The definition of what constitutes personal intimidation is uncertain and potentially broad.[64] It encompasses physical threats, verbal abuse, and the spreading of rumours that demean the employee's personal character or professional capabilities. It also appears to encompass deliberately making life unpleasant for the employee by a wide variety of means, such as by scheduling the person for degrading or unpleasant working hours or job duties, by giving negative performance appraisals, by excluding the employee from training and career development opportunities, or by otherwise acting out of spite or ill

---

60   Examples: *Saunders v. Chateau des Charmes Ltd.* (2002), 20 C.C.E.L. (3d) 220, especiall at 248–50 (Ont. S.C.J.); *Stamos*, above note 37, especially at 141,404. See generally D. Doorey, "Employer 'Bullying': Implied Duties of Fair Dealing in Canadian Employment Contracts" (2005) 30 Queen's L.J. 542.

61   The treatment of sexual harassment under human rights legislation is examined in Chapter 7, Section D(1).

62   Summary dismissal is justified for harassment and intimidation of fellow workers. See, for example, *Holwen v. Alberta Plywood Ltd.* (2005), 42 C.C.E.L. (3d) 264 (Alta. Q.B.).

63   The contents of such a policy are examined in Chapter 7.

64   G. Friedman & J. Whitman, "The European Transformation of Harassment Law: Discrimination versus Dignity" (2003) 9 Colum. Jo. of Eur. Law 241 at 249. See also R. Yuen, "Beyond the Schoolyard: Workplace Bullying and Moral Harassment Law in France and Quebec" (2005) 38 Cornell Int'l L.J. 625.

will to make the person's life intolerable in the workplace. The definition in section 81.18 of the Quebec *Labour Standards Act*—Quebec is the only province so far to have enacted a right not to be personally harassed—is also consistent with a broad approach:

> Any vexatious behaviour in the form of repeated and hostile or unwanted conduct, verbal comments, actions or gestures, that affects an employee's dignity or psychological or physical integrity and that results in a harmful work environment for the employee. A single incident of such behaviour that has a lasting effect on an employee may also constitute psychological harassment.[65]

The duty, therefore, penetrates to the very core of managerial prerogatives.

It is debatable whether the duty ought properly to be regarded as an independent and distinct term of the contract, or as a subset of a general contractual duty to treat the employee fairly and decently. (As we shall see below, it may also be viewed as a subset of the ancient implied contractual duty to safeguard the employee's personal health and safety.) The language used by the courts in all of the judgments is certainly more consistent with a residual implied term requiring fair and decent treatment of employees than with a narrowerer prohibition against personal harassment *simpliciter*. Be that as it may, an employee who is harassed in violation of contractual rights can resign and sue for constructive dismissal and can sue for damages for any physical or mental harm resulting from the harassment. (In theory, an employee could sue for such damages without resigning from the job, but in practice, few employees choose to risk retaliation from their employer.) Punitive damages could also be awarded for egregious abuse of the employee. One potential obstacle to such a damages action, though, would be if the employee's injuries are compensable under workers' compensation legislation (the extent to which psychological harm is covered varies between the provinces), in that case, the employee is precluded from bringing a common law action against the employer.[66] In addition, the employee cannot be reinstated at common law. It is submitted that incorporating the right not to be personally harassed in the employment standards legislation, as Quebec has done, would be preferable in terms of cost, speed, and efficacy of remedies.

---

65 *An Act respecting Labour standards*, R.S.Q. c. N-1.1, s. 81.18, definition of "psychological harassment."

66 See Chapter 6.

G. THE IMPLIED DUTY TO PROVIDE A REASONABLY SAFE WORKPLACE

Traditionally, courts have implied a term into the employment contract obliging the employer to provide a reasonably safe system of work.[67] A similar duty exists under the tort of negligence. The interesting question at common law is whether it is more advantageous for an injured worker to sue the employer in contract than in tort, since the measure of damages, the limitation periods,[68] and the conflict of law rules are different, and in tort doctrine of *res ipsa loquitur* facilitates the worker's task of discharging the burden of proof. Interesting as these issues may be, they are irrelevant to most modern workers because workers' compensation legislation eliminates the employee's right to bring a common law damages action for illnesses and injuries occurring during employment, substituting a system of no-fault compensation. The common law, therefore, only applies to employees who are disqualified from receiving compensation under the legislation—a relatively narrow field. Furthermore, the employee's implied right under the employment contract to refuse unsafe work has been overtaken by occupational health and safety legislation in all provinces: the employee is entitled to refuse to perform work that he or she genuinely and reasonably believes will present danger on the worksite. The statutory "right to refuse," unlike its common law counterpart, is buttressed by effective administrative enforcement machinery.

Fresh life has been breathed into this largely dormant implied term by a recent decision holding that the implied term obliges the employer to prevent its employees from being bullied, harassed, or otherwise intimidated in the workplace by fellow employees and/or customers.[69] Theorists may debate whether this obligation ought properly to be categorized as a subset of a general contractual duty to treat the employee fairly, as a separate and distinct implied term, or as a subset of the venerable implied duty to provide a reasonably safe workplace. In practice, however, for common law purposes little seems to turn on the theoretical categorization of the obligation. As seen earlier in this chapter, the

---

67   *Marshment v. Borgstrom*, [1942] S.C.R. 374; *Ainslie Mining & Railway Co. v. Mc-Dougall* (1909), 42 S.C.R. 420.

68   The period within which an action for breach of an ordinary contract must be brought in six years; a tort action must be commenced within two years. See, for example, the Alberta *Limitations Act*, S.A. 1996, c. L-15.1, s. 3(1)(a). See also S.M. Waddams, *The Law of Contracts*, 3d ed. (Toronto: Canada Law Book, 1993) at 140.

69   *Haggarty v. McCullough*, [2002] C.L.L.C. ¶210-022 at 141,265 (Alta. Prov. Ct.).

definition of proscribed personal harassment is potentially broad.[70] An employee who is personally harassed can resign and sue for constructive dismissal, in which case he or she will receive compensation for the period of notice of termination. The person can also sue for damages to compensate the psychological harm caused by the harassment. (The employee can sue for the damages while remaining employed, but practical obstacles would make this a rarity.) However, a potential obstacle to such a damages action would be the bar on common law actions against an employer under a workers' compensation act.[71] If an employee is entitled to receive compensation under the workers' compensation act of a province for the psychological harm caused by the personal harassment—the acts generally limit compensation to psychological harm that represents an "acute reaction to a traumatic event" in the workplace[72]—the employee is prohibited from seeking a common law remedy against the employer. In addition, personal harassment causing psychological harm almost certainly constitutes a workplace hazard under the occupational health and safety acts,[73] given that section 15 of the Charter precludes differentiating between mental and physical injuries.[74] These acts contain an arsenal of remedies to eliminate workplace hazards, including the right to refuse unsafe work, the right to have a departmental officer issue a fast-track order directing the employer to make the work safe, and the right to reinstatement and compensation for reprisals the employer takes against the employee.

H. THE IMPLIED DUTY TO PROVIDE TESTIMONIALS

Traditionally, the courts have not implied an obligation into the employment contract that the employer must provide the employee with a reference for use in seeking alternative employment. By so doing, they largely limit the employer's liability in the tort of negligence to persons

---

70   See Section F, above in this chapter.
71   See Chapter 6, Section D.
72   Example: New Brunswick *Workers Compensation Act*, R.S.N.B. 1973, c. W-13, s. 1 "accident," interpreted relatively narrowly in *W.(D.) v. New Brunswick (Workplace Health, Safety and Compensation Commission)* (2005), 42 C.C.E.L. (3d) 163 (N.B.C.A.). For further elaboration, see Chapter 6, Section D. See also B. Barrett, "Employer's Liability for Stress at the Workplace: Neither Tort nor Breach of Contract?" (2004) 33 Indus. L.J. 343.
73   See Chapter 6, Section D.
74   *Nova Scotia (Workers' Compensation Board) v. Martin*, [2003] 2 S.C.R. 504.

who rely on a reference. Recent Canadian authorities have endorsed this principle,[75] even though requiring employers to provide references would appear to serve the public interest in facilitating labour mobility.[76] On the other hand, the English House of Lords held in 1994 that there is an implied contractual obligation on the employer to provide the employee with a reference where the employee's trade, profession, or occupation is such that a new employer would require a testimonial from a previous employer as a precondition of employment.[77] The court held that the reference must be fair and be given within a reasonable period of the employee quitting or being fired.

Although no Canadian court as yet has followed this approach, the traditional rule has been tempered somewhat by holding that if an employer either refuses to give a reference or provides an unfair one resulting in the employee's job search being impeded, the length of reasonable notice of termination will be extended to reflect the increased period of unemployment.[78] Moreover, if the refusal to give a reference, or providing an unfair one, amounts to "bad faith" on the employer's part within the meaning of the *Wallace*[79] doctrine, the reasonable notice period may also be extended.[80] The reasonable notice doctrine provides the courts with a useful catch-all for safeguarding against unfairness on the employer's part. Furthermore, the employee can sue in the law of tort if a reference is defamatory, or if a reference tortiously interferes with contractual relations between the employee and a future employer.[81]

---

75   Example: *Shinn v. TBC Teletheatre B.C.* (2001), 6 C.C.E.L. (3d) 244 (B.C.C.A.) [*Shinn*].

76   For an excellent analysis of how the interests of the public, the employer, and the employee can be balanced, see P. Winward, "The Need for Change in Idaho's Reference Immunity Statute: A Proposal to Minimize Idaho Employers' Exposure to Negligent Hiring Claims after *Doe v. Garcia*" (1999) 35 Idaho L. Rev. 343.

77   *Spring v. Guardian Assurance Plc.*, [1994] I.C.R. 596 (H.L.), Lords Woolf and Slynn. See generally S. Middlemiss, "The Truth and Nothing But the Truth: The Legal Liability of Employers for Employee References" (2004) 33 Indus. L.J. 59; T. Allen, "Liability for References: *Spring v. Guardian Assurance*" (1994) 57 Mod. L. Rev. 111.

78   Examples: *Ditchburn v. Landis & Gyr Powers Ltd.* (1995), 96 C.L.L.C. ¶210-002 at 141,021 (Ont. Gen. Div.); *Gillman v. Saan Stores Ltd.* (1992), 45 C.C.E.L. 9 at 19 (Alta. Q.B.).

79   Above note 24 and accompanying text. The *Wallace* doctrine is examined in Chapter 9, Section B.

80   Examples: *Shinn*, above note 75 at 249; *Barakett v. Lévesque Beaubien Geoffrion Inc.* (2001), 12 C.C.E.L. (3d) 24 at 39 (N.S.C.A.).

81   Example: *Drouillard v. Cogeco Cable Inc.* (2005), 42 C.C.E.L. (3d) 222 (Ont. S.C.J.).

FURTHER READINGS

ALLEN, T., "Liability for References: *Spring v. Guardian Assurance*" (1994) 57 Mod. L. Rev. 111

BALL, S., "Bad Faith Discharge" (1994) 39 McGill L.J. 568

DOOREY, D., "Employer 'Bullying': Implied Duties of Fair Dealing in Canadian Employment Contracts" (2005) 30 Queen's L.J. 500

ENGLAND, G., "Recent Developments in Individual Employment Law: Tell Me the Old, Old Story" (2002) 9 C.L.E.L.J. 37

ENGLAND, G., "Recent Developments in the Law of the Employment Contract: Continuing Tension between the Rights Paradigm and the Efficiency Paradigm" (1995) 20 Queen's L.J. 557

ENGLAND, G., "The Impact of the *Charter* on Individual Employment Law in Canada: Tell Me the Old, Old Story" (2006) 13 C.L.E.L.J. 1

ENGLAND, G., R. WOOD, & I. CHRISTIE, *Employment Law in Canada,* 4th ed., looseleaf (Markham, ON: LexisNexis Canada, 2005–) c. 10

FREEDLAND, M.R., *The Personal Employment Contract* (Oxford: Oxford University Press, 2003)

FUDGE, J., "The Limits of Good Faith in the Contract of Employment: From *Addis* to *Vorvis* to *Wallace* and Back Again?" (2007) 32 Queen's L.J. 529

MIDDLEMISS, S., "The Truth and Nothing But the Truth: The Legal Liability of Employers for Employee References" (2004) 33 Indus. L.J. 59

SALIPANTE, P.F., "The Practical View of Employee Rights" (1991) 4 Employee Resp. & Rts. J. 87

WEIR, T., "The Case of the Careless Referee" (1993) 52 Cambridge L.J. 376

CHAPTER 6

THE EMPLOYER'S STATUTORY OBLIGATIONS TO ITS EMPLOYEES

A. INTRODUCTION

This part of the book examines the employer's duties to its employees under the floor of rights legislation, which establishes certain irreducible protections for the employee that the parties cannot abridge in their employment contracts, but are free to improve upon. An enormous number of statutes comprise this floor of rights.[1] Here, attention is focused on the following particularly important ones: (1) the employment standards legislation, which deals with minimum wages, hours of work and overtime, regulation of the mode and interval of wage payments and of deductions and charges, daily rest and meal periods, weekly rest periods, advance notice of work schedules, statutory holidays, annual vacations, time off to vote, maternity and child-rearing leave, family leave, compassionate leave, sick leave, bereavement leave, lie-detector tests, protection against personal intimidation and harassment, the regulation of part-time, casual, and home-based work, and the regulation of work supplied through an employment agency; (2) equal pay legislation contained in the employment standards acts, human rights acts, and specialized pay equity acts; (3) industrial standards acts, which allow for the "extension" of terms and conditions of

---

1 For further detailed elaboration on this topic, see G. England, R. Wood, & I. Christie, *Employment Law in Canada*, 4th ed., looseleaf (Markham, ON: LexisNexis Canada, 2005–) c. 8 [*Employment Law in Canada*].

employment from one segment into broader segments of the labour market; (4) occupational health and safety and workers' compensation legislation; and (5) privacy legislation, which limits the employer's right to intrude into the employee's personal privacy. Other protective legislation governing termination of employment[2] and human rights[3] is examined elsewhere in this book.

The statutory floor of rights reflects the general public consensus that has emerged in Canada since the Second World War, namely, that the worker is entitled to be treated decently by the employer. The Arthurs Report defines the right to decency as follows:

> Labour standards should ensure that no matter how limited his or her bargaining power, no worker . . . is offered, accepts or works under conditions that Canadians would not regard as "decent." No worker should therefore receive a wage that is insufficient to live on; be deprived of the payment of wages or benefits to which they are entitled; be subject to coercion, discrimination, indignity or unwarranted danger in the workplace; or be required to work so many hours that he or she is effectively denied a personal or civic life.[4]

The fundamental importance of safeguarding the worker's right to decency explains why the Supreme Court of Canada[5] has ruled that the floor of rights legislation must be construed generously, broadly, and liberally in order to expand rather than abridge the protections available to employees. Legislating the right to decency is necessary for three reasons. First, in most employment relationships, the employer has a superiority in bargaining power *vis-à-vis* the employee, which creates the potential for unfair exploitation. The common law principles governing the employment contract may assume that "free" contracting takes place between parties with relatively equal bargaining power, but this assumption is only legal fiction. Of course, there are exceptions—such as highly skilled technicians, professionals, senior managers, entertainers, and sports stars, who are in short supply in the market—but most employees do not fall into these categories. As well, depending on fluctuating economic cycles in particular industries,

---

2   See Chapter 9.

3   See Chapter 7.

4   Canada, Commission on the Review of Federal Labour Standards, *Fairness at Work: Federal Labour Standards for the 21st Century* by H.W. Arthurs (Ottawa: Commission on the Review of Federal Labour Standards, 2006) at 47 [Arthurs Report].

5   *Re Rizzo and Rizzo Shoes Ltd.*, [1998] 1 S.C.R. 27 at 36, involving the employment standards acts.

such as construction, mining, and trucking, even relatively low- to mid-skilled workers may have substantial bargaining power during high points in the cycle, but see their power erode during downswings. Indeed, when it comes to designing statutory benefits, the right to decent treatment in the workplace is widely (but not universally) regarded as something of paramount importance, not least because relatively generous employment benefits provide the gateway to enjoying the fruits of political liberty. Accordingly, the Arthurs Report described the right to decency as "the pre-eminent principle" that "trumps" other principles, such as maximizing economic efficiency, when a conflict emerges between them.[6] While the latter conclusion is controversial—some would argue that economic efficiency should be paramount in the event of a conflict—protecting the right to decency is undeniably a fundamental goal of modern Canadian employment law.

Second, legislation is necessary because trade unionism has not succeeded in protecting most workers. In 2007, the density of trade union organization in Canada was approximately 29 percent—17 percent in the private sector and 71.7 percent in the public sector—and it appears to be falling under the pressures of the "new economy."[7] Moreover, even where employees are unionized, some groups may lack the bargaining power to win benefits significantly in excess of the statutory minima.

Third, legislation is necessary because the legal protections that the non-unionized employee enjoys under his or her employment contract may exist on paper only; the costs and delays of civil litigation frequently preclude the employee from enforcing them. Indeed, the availability of relatively expeditious and cheap enforcement machinery is pivotal to the success of the floor of rights legislation. Unfortunately, enforcing the legislation has proven to be problematic, as we shall see later.

The social, economic, and political conditions operating in Canada since the Second World War have resulted in an almost continuous expansion in the statutory floor of rights. The impetus for this trend has been a combination of factors:[8] the dominant influence of pro-rights

6   Arthurs Report, above note 4 at 47.
7   See generally G. Murray, "Unions: Membership, Structures and Actions" in M. Gunderson, A. Ponak, & D. Taras, *Union–Management Relations in Canada*, 5th ed. (Don Mills, ON: Pearson Addison-Wesley, 2005) at 79.
8   The most recent example of the process for formulating new employment standards is the Arthurs Report, above note 4, especially chapters 2, 3, and 11. Previous useful examples include British Columbia, Ministry of Skills, Training and Labour, *Rights and Responsibilities in a Changing Workplace: A Review of Employment Standards in British Columbia* by M. Thompson (Victoria: Ministry of Skills, Training and Labour, 1994) at 25–27 [Thompson Commission]; Ontario Task Force on Hours of Work and Overtime, *Working Times: The Report of the*

philosophers in all walks of life, especially of those who regard the enjoyment of employment benefits as the gateway to enjoying the fruits of political liberty;[9] the success of most trade unions in bargaining relatively generous benefits for their members in the favourable economic conditions prevailing until the early 1980s; and the influence of international labour standards, especially the conventions and recommendations of the International Labor Organization (ILO).[10] Regarding the latter, ratification by the federal government of ILO conventions binds the federal government under international law to implement them, but since the regulation of employment relations falls within the jurisdiction of the provinces in Canada,[11] provincial governments are not legally bound to follow suit—there is, however, much moral pressure on them to do so. At this juncture, the federal government has ratified thirty ILO conventions.[12] Moreover, the 1998 ILO *Declaration on Fundamental Principles and Rights at Work* obliges all ILO members, regardless of whether they have ratified conventions ". . . to respect, to promote and to realize, in good faith and in accordance with the . . . [ILO] . . . Constitution, the principles concerning the fundamental rights which are the subject of those Conventions." Currently, the employment standards legislation in all Canadian provinces meets the ILO requirements in virtually all respects, the most notable exceptions being that only three jurisdictions—Nova Scotia, Quebec, and the federal government—have enacted protection against unjust discharge in line with the 1963 *Termination of Employment Convention* No. 119.[13]

The floor of rights legislation also recognizes the indisputable need of Canadian employers to operate in an economically efficient manner, not least because society as a whole depends on the benefits of

---

Ontario Task Force on Hours of Work and Overtime by A. Donner (Toronto: Ontario Ministry of Labour, 1987) at 23–25 [Donner Report].

9   See H. Collins, *Justice in Dismissal: The Law of Termination and Employment* (Oxford: Clarendon Press, 1992), especially at 16–20, citing from J. Raz, *The Morality of Freedom* (Oxford: Clarendon Press, 1986).

10 For useful reviews of ILO standards, see L. Betten, *International Labour Law: Selected Issues* (Deventer, Neth.: Kluwer, 1993), which also reviews the European Economic Community standards; R. Plant, *Labour Standards and Structural Adjustment* (Geneva: International Labour Office, 1994).

11 *Canada (A.G.) v. Ontario (A.G.)*, [1937] A.C. 326 (P.C.); *Toronto Electric Commissioners v. Snider*, [1925] A.C. 396 (P.C.) [*Toronto Electric Commissioners*].

12 A list of these conventions is provided in the Arthurs Report, above note 4 at 283–84.

13 This convention was strengthened in 1982 by the *Termination of Employment Convention* No. 158. The statutory unjust discharge schemes in Canada are examined in Chapter 9, Section E(1).

economic success. Before the 1980s, the proliferation in legislated employment rights was made possible by the lack of foreign competition on Canadian employers and by the ease with which Canadian provincial and federal governments could borrow money in the international bond market. These economic conditions have now disappeared with the advent of the "new economy."[14]

Today, the burning question facing Canadian governments is whether to halt the expansion of the statutory floor—or even to rescind existing protections—due to the cost to employers of paying for and administering the statutory benefits. Thus, employers frequently claim that employment legislation impedes the movement of wages and benefits down to the equilibrium point where the forces of supply and demand would otherwise intersect in the labour market. They claim that the result is to decrease employment opportunities for the unemployed, something both economically inefficient and unjust, since those lucky enough to have the jobs to which the statutory benefits attach are in a sense taking a ride on the backs of the unemployed. This view is challenged, however, by those who claim that legislating generous employment benefits enhances economic efficiency: it improves the morale of employees and avoids the costs to the state social welfare system of providing for the "working poor."[15] As well, they argue that a country's international competitiveness is influenced almost entirely by technological and other productivity-related factors, not by its labour rules.[16] That is why there has been no economic "race to the bottom" between countries repealing their labour laws in order to attract global business investors.[17] Nevertheless, the need to be eco-

---

14 The impact of the "new economy" is summarized in the Arthurs Report, above note 4 at 24–35 and 48–50.

15 See, for example, F. Wilkinson, "Equality, Efficiency and Economic Progress: The Case for Universally Applied Equitable Standards for Wages and Conditions of Work" in W. Sengenberger & D.C. Campbell, eds., *Creating Economic Opportunities: The Role of Labour Standards in Industrial Restructuring* (Geneva: International Institute for Labour Studies, 1994) 61; D.C. Campbell & W. Sengenberger, "Labour Standards, Economic Efficiency and Development: Lessons from Experience with Industrial Restructuring" in Sengenberger & Campbell, eds., *ibid.* at 422; J. Bivens & C. Weller, *Rights Make Might, Ensuring Workers Rights as a Strategy for Economic Growth* (Washington: Economic Policy Institute, 2003); H. Collins, "Regulating the Employment Relationship for Competitiveness" (2001) 30 Ind. Law J. 17.

16 M. Huberman, *Are Canada's Labour Standards Set in the Third World? Historical Trends and Future Prospects*, C.D. Howe Institute Commentary No. 209 (Ottawa: Renouf, 2005) at 21–23.

17 Arthurs Report, above note 4 at 32. On the contrary, globalization has generally had a positive effect on labour conditions: R. Flanagan, *Globalization and Labor*

nomically competitive has caused Canadian employers to adopt various work practices that have a negative impact on employment rights, notably "outsourcing" their operations to non-employee third parties; using "precarious" forms of labour, such as casuals and agency workers who can be brought in and released on short notice; substituting self-employed contractors for employees; using part-time workers; and generally seeking to enlarge their flexibility to schedule hours of work and to modify terms and conditions of employment.[18]

In his 2006 study for the Arthurs Task Force, Prof. Morley Gunderson, a leading labour economist, concluded that there is a sufficiently high risk of damaging the competitiveness of employers in the federal jurisdiction, arising from continued expansions to the statutory floor of rights, to warrant the federal government taking a cautious approach to enacting new rights for employees.[19] Accordingly, the Arthurs Report recommended that "federal policy makers should be cautious about adopting labour standards that impose significant costs on employers without the prospect of providing corresponding productivity gains."[20]

Of course, as the Arthurs Report indicates, there will be many instances where legislating employee rights will also serve to increase economic efficiency. For example, in all Canadian provinces, workplace participation rates among women, Aboriginals, immigrants from different ethnic and cultural backgrounds, disabled persons, single parents, and elderly persons continue to increase significantly.[21] Canadian workers are also more highly educated and more willing to change careers than ever before. Shaping the floor of rights legislation (in conjunction with the human rights legislation) to ensure that employers respect and accommodate the differing needs and interests of these workers would clearly enhance the efficient use of the Canadian labour force, as well as protect the right to decency. Nevertheless, on some occasions, the right to decency and maximizing economic efficiency will collide, and hard choices will have to be made. In this situation, as we saw earlier, the Arthurs Report made the controversial recommenda-

---

Conditions: Working Conditions and Worker Rights in the Global Economy (New York: Oxford University Press, 2006).

18   Arthurs Report, *ibid.* at 24–34.

19   M. Gunderson, *Social and Economic Impact of Labour Standards*, Executive Summary of a Report to the Federal Labour Standards Review Panel (Ottawa: Human Resources and Social Development Canada, 2005), online: www.hrsdc. gc.ca/en/labour/employment_standards/fls/research/research01/page01.shtml.

20   Arthurs Report, above note 4 at 34.

21   *Ibid.* at 18–24 and 51.

tion that the right to decency should always win out.[22] Be that as it may, there can be no doubt that the impact of the "new economy" will require legislators to calculate carefully the economic costs and benefits of any future reforms to the statutory floor of rights.

It is sometimes claimed that the 1992 *North American Free Trade Agreement (NAFTA)* will hasten the dismantling of Canada's statutory floor of rights. There is no *direct* legal obligation on signatory states under *NAFTA* to reduce the level of protection afforded to workers under their employment laws. However, Canadian legislators could be pressured *indirectly* to do so in order to create a level playing field for Canadian employers, on which to compete with U.S. and Mexican firms that are not burdened with equally generous employment protections.[23] As yet, this has not occurred.

On the other hand, *NAFTA* contains an *Agreement on Labor Cooperation*,[24] the so-called Labour Side Agreement, which may make it somewhat more difficult for signatory states to reduce legislated employment protections. First, the Labour Side Agreement obliges signatories to explicitly delineate their domestic labour policies and to publicly communicate about labour law matters and labour-market conditions within their jurisdiction. The Commission for Labour Cooperation, formed to administer the Labour Side Agreement, can publicize this information. Such publicity, it is thought, will encourage signatories—especially Mexico—to enforce, and perhaps even improve, their own employment laws. Since Canada's statutory floor of rights is more extensive than that of Mexico and United States,[25] the Labour Side Agreement is unlikely to

---

22   *Ibid.* at 47.

23   G. Betcherman & M. Gunderson, "Canada–U.S. Free Trade and Labour Relations" (1990) 41 Lab. L.J. 454. For a detailed analysis of the impact of *NAFTA* on U.S. labour law, see J.F. Perez-Lopez, "Labor and the *North American Free Trade Agreement*" (1993) 11 Dick J. Int'l L. 565.

24   *North American Agreement on Labor Cooperation*, 17 December 1992, 107 Stat. 2057, reprinted in 32 I.L.M. 1499 (entered into force 1 January 1994). For a detailed examination of this agreement, see J. Stensland, "Internationalizing the *North American Agreement on Labor Cooperation*" (1995) 4 Minn. J. Global Trade 141; R.J. Adams & P. Singh, "Early Experience with *NAFTA*'s Labour Side Accord" (1997) 18 Comp. Lab. L.J. 161; L. Campa, "*NAFTA*'s Labour Side Agreement and International Labour Solidarity" (July 2001) 33 Antipode: A Radical Journal of Geography 451; G. Gesser, "Why *NAFTA* Violates the Canadian Constitution" (1998) 27 Denver J. Int'l L. & Pol'y 121

25   For an overview of Mexican labour law, see M.E. Zeleck & O. de La Vega, "An Outline of Mexican Labor Law" (1992) 43 Lab. L.J. 467. Federal employment law in the United States, along with the state law of Florida—the latter, of course, is a so-called sunshine state attracting new industries, partly due to a comparative advantage in cheap labour, making the comparison particularly

stimulate further protections in this country. Second, the Labour Side Agreement merely obliges each signatory to enforce its *own* laws, not to adopt externally authored labour standards. At most, the Labour Side Agreement commits the signatories to "promote to the maximum extent possible" eleven designated labour principles, namely,

(1)   freedom of association and the right to organize;
(2)   the right to bargain collectively;
(3)   the right to strike;
(4)   prohibition of forced labour;
(5)   labour protection for children and young persons;
(6)   minimum employment standards;
(7)   elimination of discrimination in employment;
(8)   equal pay for both sexes;
(9)   prevention of occupational injuries and illnesses;
(10) compensation for occupational injuries and illnesses; and
(11) protection of migrant workers.[26]

The main obstacle to legislating improved standards is that emerging countries, such as Mexico, suspect that the real aim of such standards is to eliminate the competitive advantage derived from their comparatively low labour costs.[27] Indeed, the hue and cry among Canadian

---

insightful—is summarized in C.L. Hyland, "Labor and Employment Law: 1994 Survey of Florida Law" (1994) 19 Nova Law Rev. 161. See also R. Block & K. Roberts, "A Comparison of Labour Standards in the United States and Canada" (2000) 55 R.I./I.R. 273, who conclude that Canada has more generous laws than the United States regarding paid leave, unemployment insurance, termination benefits, unjust dismissal, collective bargaining, and workers' compensation, and less generous laws regarding the minimum wage, overtime, and health and safety. Laws regarding human rights and pay equity are roughly equivalent.

26   *North American Agreement on Labour Cooperation*, above note 24, Article 1(b) and Annex 1.

27   The advantages and disadvantages of legislating minimum labour standards in international trade agreements are examined by J. Baumert *et al.*, *International Cooperation on Trade and Labor Issues* Working Paper (Washington, DC: Office of Industries, U.S. International Trade Commission, 2008); B. Hepple, *Labour Laws and Global Trade* (Oxford: Hart, 2005); A. Verma, "Global Labour Standards: Can We Get from Here to There?" (2003) 19 Int'l J. Comp. Lab. L. & Ind. Rel. 515; M. Trebilcock, "Trade Policy and Labour Standards: Objectives, Instruments and Institutions," Law and Economics Research Paper No. 02-01 (University of Toronto, Faculty of Law, 2001), online: http://ssrn.com/abstract_id=307219; G. Van Liemt, "Minimum Labor Standards and International Trade: Would a Social Clause Work?" (1989) 128 Int'l Lab. Rev. 433; M. Hart, "The Social Dimension of Freer Trade and Globalization" (1996) 1 World Economic Affairs 39.

trade unions against *NAFTA* has created the strong suspicion that self-protection, not humanitarian concern with improving the lot of Mexican workers, is the principal driving force of the campaign. Third, the Labour Side Agreement contains a complicated dispute resolution procedure that can be resorted to if the preferred method of political persuasion fails to settle a complaint. Thus, dispute settlement panels can be established with the authority to issue action plans and, ultimately, to impose fines and trade sanctions[28] in the case of persistent refusal by a signatory to enforce its domestic employment laws.

The Labour Side Agreement has had little direct impact on Canadian employment law, since all provinces make efforts in good faith to enforce their employment standards legislation, albeit without much success. Furthermore, the Labour Side Agreement is legally binding only on those provinces that choose to adhere to its provisions, since employment relations are within provincial jurisdiction under Canadian constitutional law.[29] So far, only Alberta, Prince Edward Island, Quebec, and Manitoba have signed the Labour Side Agreement. However, if it has the desired effect of forcing Mexico to enforce its labour laws, Canadian employers could benefit indirectly by the corresponding reduction in the competitive advantage of Mexican employers. Moreover, the Labour Side Agreement at least symbolizes for the future that the internal labour legislation of signatory states is a legitimate matter for regulation under international trade agreements, even if the agreement's substantive provisions seem somewhat insipid.

Finally, the floor of rights legislation must accord with the *Charter of Rights and Freedoms*.[30] The *Charter* directly supervises the contents of the legislation, thereby defusing the risks that politicians would curtail employees' rights to curry favour with powerful employers or anti-labour political groups.[31] The most important right in this context is section 15, which states that every individual is equal before and under the law and has the right to equal protection and benefit of the law, without discrimination on the specifically enumerated grounds of race, national or ethnic origin, colour, religion, sex, age or mental or physical disability, as well as on analogous grounds, such as sexual orientation.

---

28   However, trade sanctions can be imposed only for failure to enforce domestic laws relating to child labour, minimum wages, and occupational health and safety, and such sanctions can never be imposed against Canada.

29   See above note 10.

30   *Canadian Charter of Rights and Freedoms*, Part 1 of the *Constitution Act, 1982*, being Schedule B to the *Canada Act 1982* (U.K.), 1982, c. 11 .[*Charter*].

31   See generally G. England, "The Impact of the *Charter* on Individual Employment Law in Canada: Rewriting an Old Story" (2006) 13 C.L.E.L.J. 1.

Section 6(2)(b), which provides the right "to pursue the gaining of a livelihood in any province," is also important. If a right is violated by a provision in floor of rights legislation, the government carries the burden of justifying the abridgement as a reasonable limit in a free and democratic society under section 1 of the *Charter*. Section 1 basically evaluates an abridgement according to the standards of proportionality, and the government must adduce concrete evidence that there truly are valid policy reasons for its actions. So far, the *Charter* has been used to strike down several offending provisions in floor of rights statutes, including these:

- disqualifying the employee from receiving statutory severance pay if the employment contract has been frustrated by reason of sickness, even if the employee had otherwise accrued the continous service with the employer needed to qualify for the pay;[32]
- excluding employees with chronic back pain from the general statutory benefits and limiting them to a shorter benefit period of four weeks under the Functional Restoration Program contained in the workers compensation' act;[33]
- repealing the "proxy" provisions in the Ontario *Pay Equity Act* that allowed for comparison of female job classes to male job classes in different organizations of the public sector in situations where no internal male job class comparators existed;[34]
- imposing an annual cap of 1 percent of payroll on pay equity liability under the Manitoba *Pay Equity Act*;[35]
- reducing the minimum wage for employees who are undergoing occupational rehabilitation or taking part in a therapeutic work program under the employment standards acts.[36]

Other statutory provisions are particularly susceptible to challenge under the *Charter*. For example, the requirement in most employment standards acts that the employee must have accrued a substantial period of continuous employment in order to qualify for designated benefits, as in Nova Scotia where an employee must have ten years

---

32   *O.N.A. v. Mount Sinai Hospital* (2005), 75 O.R. (3d) 245 (C.A.).

33   *Nova Scotia (Workers Compensation Board) v. Martin*, [2003] 2 S.C.R. 504.

34   *S.E.I.U. Local 204 v. Ontario (A.G.)* (1997), 35 O.R. (3d) 508 (Gen. Div.).

35   *Manitoba Council of Health Care Unions v. Bethesda Hospital* (1992), 88 D.L.R. (4d) 60 (Man. Q.B.) [*Bethesda*].

36   There is an *obiter dictum* to this effect in *Fenton v. British Columbia (Forensic Psychiatric Services Commission)* (1989), 29 C.C.E.L. 168 (B.C.S.C.), rev'd on other grounds (1991), 91 C.L.L.C. ¶14,030 (B.C.C.A.), leave to appeal to the S.C.C. refused (1992), 39 C.C.E.L. 289n [*Fenton*].

of continous service to qualify for protection against unjust dismissal, appear to discriminate indirectly against women and members of visible minorities who predominantly occupy short-term jobs that prevent them from qualifying.[37] Another example is the plethora of provincial regulations that deal with access to trades and professions through licensing and registration requirements, many of which are barriers to foreign-trained workers.[38] However, the courts will defer to reasoned and principled abridgements of rights under the *Charter*. Thus, the Supreme Court of Canada in 1991 upheld a Newfoundland statute that postponed the commencement date of a promised pay equity increase for female health-care workers as a proportionate response to the fiscal exigency then facing the province.[39] The province eventually paid the increase in 2006 ,by which time it could afford to do so.

Next, we analyze the individual components of the Canadian statutory floor of rights in greater detail.

B. THE EMPLOYMENT STANDARDS ACTS

All provinces and the federal jurisdiction have adopted employment standards legislation establishing a floor of rights for the worker that cannot be undercut by the provisions of an employment contract or a collective agreement, but can be improved upon in such instruments.[40] Before examining the substantive benefits conferred by these acts, the crucial threshold issues of the enforceability of the legislation and its scope of coverage must be addressed.

---

37 See, by analogy, *Rinner-Kuhn v. FWW Spezial-Gebaudereinigung GmbH and Co. KG*, [1989] I.R.L.R. 493 (E.C.J.), where a German law exempting part-timers from sick benefits was found to violate the sex discrimination prohibition under European Economic Community law.

38 See generally M.Cornish, E. McIntyre, & A. Pask, "Strategies for Challenging Discriminatory Barriers to Foreign Credential Recognition" (2000) 8 C.L.E.L.J. 17.

39 *Newfoundland (Treasury Board) v. N.A.P.E.*, [2004] 3 S.C.R. 381 [*N.A.P.E.*].

40 The employment standards acts commonly prohibit the negotiation of contractual benefits below the statutory minimum, thereby rendering any such contractual provisions void, e.g., *Canada Labour Code*, R.S.C. 1985, c. L-2, s. 168 [*CLC*]. But the employee can enforce benefits in excess of the statutory floor: e.g., *Re Queen's University and Fraser* (1985), 51 O.R. (2d) 140 (Div. Ct.); *Johnston v. Frontier Realty (1971) Ltd.* (1985), 39 Sask. R. 131 (C.A.).

1) Enforcing the Employment Standards Legislation

The most impressive code of substantive legal rights is only as good as the machinery enforcing it. Securing compliance with employment standards acts has always proven to be extremely difficult, especially for part-timers, casuals, and homeworkers; members of visible minorities; women; and employees of small businesses.[41] Since a major purpose of employment standards acts is to provide workers with a practical means of enforcing their employment rights — civil litigation to enforce the employment contract being beyond the financial means of most workers — this failure is most serious.

Generally, the enforcement process begins with an aggrieved employee filing a personal complaint of breach of the act with the provincial department of labour. Often, the departmental officer who investigates the complaint will unearth a broader pattern of non-compliance on the employer's part, which will result in the filing of further complaints. As well, provincial departments of labour are usually empowered to conduct spot checks of employers, which may unearth violations of the act. The efficacy of spot checks seems to be slight due to the understaffing of employment standards inspectorates.[42] Primacy is accorded to settling complaints voluntarily by conciliation conducted by the departmental inspector, but formal adjudication and even criminal sanctions can be deployed where conciliation is not possible. Conciliation is well suited to settling a complaint involving an employer that does not understand the full extent of its legal obligations, but full-scale legal enforcement, perhaps reinforced by criminal penalties, is undoubtedly necessary when the employer is deliberately avoiding its statutory duties.

Although considerable differences of detail exist under each province's employment standards act, the procedure under the British Columbia *Employment Standards Act* is illustrative. There, an employee must file a complaint with the director of employment standards, usually within six months of the alleged violation of the Act.[43] A depart-

---

41   Numerous studies show that this problem remains persistent. See, for example, the Arthurs Report, above note 4 at 190–95; the Thompson Commission, above note 8 at 113–19; *Report of the Advisory Group on Working Time and the Distribution of Work* (Ottawa: Minister of Supply and Services Canada, 1994) at 58 (Chair: A. Donner) [*Advisory Group Report*], where it was recommended that the legislation be "vigorously enforced" in relation to these groups; R.J. Adams, "Employment Standards in Ontario: An Industrial Relations System Analysis" (1987) 42 R.I./I.R. 46 [Adams].

42   See, for example, Thompson Commission, *ibid.* at 116.

43   British Columbia *Employment Standards Act*, R.S.B.C. 1996, c. 113, s. 74 [*B.C. ESA*].

mental inspector conducts an investigation[44] and attempts to negotiate a consensual settlement between the parties, failing which the inspector reports his or her findings to the director. If the director determines that the complaint is unfounded, it will be dismissed. If, however, the director determines that the complaint is founded, the employer can be ordered to carry out its duties under the Act, compensate the employee for any monetary losses incurred as a result of the violation, and reinstate an employee who has been wrongfully discharged.[45] In addition, the director can order that the employer pay a penalty for violating the worker's rights.[46] The director is also empowered to vary or cancel an earlier determination.[47]

An aggrieved party can appeal the director's decision to the Employment Standards Tribunal, a standing body appointed by the government, which conducts a hearing into the matter and can confirm, vary, or cancel the director's decision or refer it back to the director for reconsideration.[48] The Employment Standards Tribunal, too, is authorized to reconsider its earlier determinations.[49] Its decisions are legally binding and cannot be appealed on their merits in a court of law,[50] but an appeal to the courts can be launched on the usual administrative law grounds of breach of natural justice or other jurisdictional error.

The employment standards legislation generally contains special machinery to enable an employee to recover unpaid wages and benefits against the employer. This special machinery is necessary because recalcitrant employers in the past have often simply refused to comply with judgment orders of courts or employment standards tribunals to pay unpaid wages, and the usual methods for enforcing such orders have proven to be ineffective. The topic of wage recovery systems is examined elsewhere.[51]

The hallmark of the employment standards machinery is that a public official, usually the provincial director of employment standards, collects the monies owing from the employer on behalf of the employee. The process is much faster and cheaper than the traditional civil law methods for enforcing unpaid judgment debts. The main drawback of the schemes, from the employee's viewpoint, is that each

---

44   *Ibid.*, ss. 76, 77, 83, 84, & 85.

45   *Ibid.*, ss. 79 & 80.

46   *Ibid.*, ss. 79(3)(c), 81(1)(c), and 98.

47   *Ibid.*, s. 86.

48   *Ibid.*, Parts 12–13.

49   *Ibid.*, s. 116.

50   *Ibid.*, s. 110.

51   For a detailed analysis, see *Employment Law in Canada*, above note 1, c. 19.

province's statute imposes a cap on the maximum amount that can be claimed against an employer. In Ontario, for instance, the maximum amount under the scheme for any one employee is fixed at $10,000.[52]

The British Columbia *Employment Standards Act*, like its counterparts elsewhere, makes it unlawful for an employer to dismiss or otherwise penalize an employee because he or she has filed a complaint under the Act, or has otherwise participated in the statutory complaints procedure.[53] Nevertheless, in his study of how the Ontario act operates, Prof. Adams found that a major weakness with the statutory complaints machinery is that, because of the fear of retaliation, virtually no complaints are filed by workers who wish to remain in the employ of their employer.[54] The "no-reprisal" provisions are clearly not doing their job.

Several suggestions for improving the statutory enforcement mechanisms have been advanced.

• Plainly, greater emphasis must be placed on deterrence. Typically, consent to prosecute for violating the employment standards acts is given by the minister of labour or another government official and is usually reserved for employers who are repeat offenders or who are deliberately flaunting their statutory obligations, if it is granted at all. The Arthurs Report found that no prosecution for breach of the federal legislation had been brought for twenty years![55] The efficiency of deterrence depends on the likelihood of being detected as well as on the costs of being found liable. One way of increasing the probability of catching offenders is to track employers previously identified as violators and monitor their compliance level on an ongoing basis, at employer expense.[56] Doing this would enable the department of labour to focus its limited resources on high-risk employers. Indeed, high-risk employers could even be required proactively to file performance audits with the department of labour at their expense.

• A points system could be introduced whereby employers earn demerit points if they commit a specified number of violations, much like drivers receiving demerit points for committing traffic offences. Employers with the specified number of demerit points could be subject to ongoing monitoring and made liable for more serious criminal penalties if they re-offend, than an employer with a clean record. An

---

52   Ontario *Employment Standards Act, 2000*, S.O. 2000, c. 41, s. 103(4) [*Ont. ESA*].
53   *B.C. ESA*, above note 43, s. 83.
54   See Adams, above note 41 at 50.
55   Above note 4 at 220.
56   This recommendation was made in the Arthurs Report, *ibid.* at 211–13.

employer could reduce its demerit points by committing no further violations over a specified period. Another way of increasing the chance of catching offenders could be to involve employers in high-risk sectors in monitoring the compliance levels of their competitors. After all, no employer wants to see a competitor obtain an advantage by avoiding its statutory obligations to its workers. Thus, a partnership could be formed between the department of labour and an employers' association in designated areas, for example, restaurants in Saskatoon, and the parties could collaborate in identifying renegade employers, as well as in improving training and education regarding the legislation.

• Imposing automatic fines for all violations would increase the financial cost of being caught. For example, in 2004, Ontario introduced a scheme that permits employment standards officers to issue $300 "tickets" for run-of-the-mill violations that do not involve complex issues of fact or law.[57] It is significant that the issuance of a "ticket" does not preclude a more serious penalty from being applied if the employer is subsequntly found to have committed more serious violations. Also, some provinces have introduced systems of graduated fines, which involve increasingly severe penalties on repeat violators. In Saskatchewan, for example, a maximum fine of $2,000 is specified for a first offence, $5,000 for a second offence, and $10,000 for a third offence committed within six years of the first.[58] Moreover, in order to facilitate securing convictions, the prosecution in Saskatchewan need only overcome the civil law standard proof—the "balance of probabilities"—not the more rigorous criminal law standard of "beyond any reasonable doubt" that applies in other jurisdictions.[59] Even these amounts, however, appear to be too low. Thus, in comparison with Saskatchewan, Ontario imposes a maximum fine of $100,000 for a corporation that commits a first offence, $200,000 for a second offence, and $500,000 for a third or subsequent offence.[60] The Arthurs Report recommended a maximum fine of $50,000 for a first

---

57   The scheme was introduced by amending R.R.O. 1990, Reg. 950 under the Ontario *Provincial Offences Act*.

58   Saskatchewan *Labour Standards Act*, R.S.S. 1978, c. L-1, s. 85(1.1) [*Sask. LSA*]. See also British Columbia *Employment Standards Regulation*, B.C. Reg. 396/95, s. 29 [*B.C. ESR*], in respect to the "specific" violations under Appendix II.

59   *Sask. LSA*, ibid., s. 85(2). In *R. v. Wholesale Travel Group Inc.*, [1991] 3 S.C.R. 154 [*Wholesale Travel Group*], it was held that "strict liability" measures, such as reversing the burden of proof on the accused, can be used to enforce public welfare statutes such as employment standards acts without breaching s. 7 of the *Charter*.

60   *Ont. ESA*, above note 52, ss. 132(b) & (c).

offence, $100,000 for a second offence, and $250,000 for a third or subsequent offence. These amounts could be substantially increased by the additional recommendation that a separate offence should be deemed to be committed for every day that a previous offence continues.[61]

- The deterrent effect of criminal sanctions would be magnified if the officers of a company are made personally liable in their own names, subject to a defence of due diligence, rather than the company being liable in its corporate name — an approach most provinces have taken.[62] Indeed, in most provinces, the additional deterrent of imprisonment of company officers is also available.
- The deterrent effect could be intensifed by requiring proven violators to reimburse the department of labour's administrative costs in processing the complaint, as well as any legal costs incurred by the employee.
- Imposing reputational costs on employers could also intensify the deterrent effect. For example, one proposal is to publish in a government data bank, and circulate in the media, the names of employers who have violated the legislation; such information would be accessible to potential employees, business clients, customers, and other government agencies responsible for awarding contracts.[63]
- Against hard-core violators, various pre-emptive measures could be taken, such as requiring them to post bonds to be available to reimburse employees in the event of future violations; to undergo regular audits at their own expense; to be disqualified from receiving government contracts; or even to lose their right to engage in businesses requiring government permits.[64]
- Measures could be taken to preserve complainants' confidentiality, at least to a point consistent with the employer's right under the principles of natural justice to know the nature of the complaint.[65] As well, complaints could be initiated and processed by third parties on behalf of employees who otherwise might be unwilling to file individual complaints, for example, advocacy groups, legal clinics, trade unions, or even private contractors.

---

61 Arthurs Report, above note 4 at 222. The report also recommended that serious violations, referred to as "unfair labour practices," be processed through a separate, more formal administrative procedure than that in place to handle minor infractions (see 222–27).
62 Example: *Ont. ESA*, above note 52, ss. 136–37.
63 Thompson Commission, above note 8 at 115.
64 Arthurs Report, above note 4 at 225.
65 Example: *B.C. ESA*, above note 43, s. 75.

- Greater efforts could be made to make employers and employees aware of their rights and duties under the employment standards legislation.[66] The Arthurs Report, for example, suggested that posting a summary of the appropriate act and regulations in the workplace, along with a toll-free phone number and website for immediate advice regarding rights, should be mandatory.[67] Similarly, the department of labour could establish partnerships with employer associations in designated sectors and geographical areas that would collaborate in educating employers and employees as to their rights and duties, and in identifying employers that are violating the legislation. As well, such sectoral groups of employers could develop voluntary codes of conduct for promoting employee rights among their members.[68]
- Funding to the departments of labour could be increased to assist them with all of their activities, but especially with regard to improving education about the legislation and increasing their capacity to do spot audits.[69]
- Employment standards adjudicators should be granted a broad panoply of remedies, including cease-and-desist orders, reinstatement, and "make whole" compensation awards, with expedited interim orders being available for employees with urgent financial needs who would be unduly prejudiced by waiting for a final hearing.[70]
- Employers could be encouraged to voluntarily adopt corporate codes of conduct, namely, written sets of standards and principles pertaining to relations with employees (and, for that matter, other parties with whom there are dealings). These could be complemented by adopting a Social Labelling Program, which involves labels being attached to a firm's products or services, verifying the firm's compliance record under the employment standards legislation. Evidence shows that such measures work best when legal compulsion is made available to bolster the voluntary programs.[71]

---

66 Thompson Commission, above note 8 at 116–19, where various ways of promoting education are examined, including the particularly sensible one of including employment standards within high school curricula.
67 Above note 4 at 197. In several jurisdictions, a posting requirement exists: e.g., B.C. ESA, above note 43, s. 6, where the posted statement must be in the form specified by the director of employment standards.
68 Arthurs Report, ibid. at 198–99.
69 Ibid. at 199.
70 In Ontario, for example, expedited interim relief is provided for under the Ont. ESA, above note 52, s. 119(11).
71 P. Macklem & M. Trebilcock, "New Labour Standards Compliance Strategies: Corporate Codes of Conduct and Social Labeling Programs," Research Report

- Prof. Adams recommends that safeguards against discharge without just cause should be legislated—as they currently are in Quebec, Nova Scotia, and the federal jurisdiction—in order to make it more difficult for an employer to cloak its true motive of penalizing a worker for exercising statutory rights.[72]
- Prof. Adams also recommends the compulsory establishment of joint employee–employer parity committees in each workplace to enforce employment standards, similar to European works councils or the joint health and safety committees already in place in most provinces.[73]

Clearly, much remains to be done to improve compliance with employment standards acts.

Although the primary method for enforcing employment standards claims is the statutory machinery itself, it is not the only one—the courts, too, can become involved (see Chapter 8, Section A).

2) The Coverage of the Legislation

One might expect that the strong influence of human rights philosophies on the development of employment standards legislation would have resulted in virtually universal coverage. On the contrary, many groups of employees are excluded from the coverage of the legislation. Depending on the jurisdiction, the main exclusions are as follows: persons attending school; secondary school or advanced education students engaged in a work study, work experience, or training program; sitters; persons engaged in jobs that are financed by defined government job creation funding programs; newspaper vendors who are still in school; prison inmates engaged in cooperative or rehabilitative work programs; criminal offenders performing work or services under a court order; defined agricultural workers; defined professional occupations, such as architecture, accounting, dentistry, law, medicine, chiropody, optometry, pharmacy, engineering, psychology, surveying, and veterinary work; defined salespersons; domestics employed in a private residence; police; employees who provide care on a non-profit basis to children or handicapped, aged, or disabled persons in their residences; construction workers; inmates of medical facilities who are working for their "physical, mental or social rehabilitation"; defined

---

Prepared for Commission on the Review of Federal Labour Standards (Ottawa: Commission on the Review of Federal Labour Standards, 2006).

72   These schemes are examined in Chapters 8 and 9.
73   See Section D(2), below in this chapter.

schoolteachers and instructors in colleges and universities; employees whose wages are fixed by legislation; employees in an undertaking where only members of the employer's immediate family are employed; and voluntary workers in religious, patriotic, philanthropic, or political organizations. The courts have held that these exclusions should be construed narrowly in furtherance of the remedial nature of employment standards statutes.[74]

Furthermore, other industries and occupations are frequently either exempted from the coverage of designated sections under the employment standards statutes or have special variances made for them, as we shall see below when we consider the substantive rights accorded under the legislation. Finding these exclusions, exemptions, and variances is often no easy matter, since they are frequently enacted in the form of regulations made pursuant to an enabling section in the main act. It is advisable to carefully scrutinize the act and any regulations made thereunder in one's province since the specifics differ enormously in each jurisdiction.

The economic justification for some of these exemptions and exclusions is questionable, leaving the impression that political lobbying is sometimes the dominant factor. Possibly, an exclusion, exemption, or variance that disadvantages a protected group under section 15 of the *Charter* could be challenged as a form of "indirect discrimination" — the vast majority of domestics, for instance, are women — in which case the government would have to advance concrete policy justifications for the differential treatment under section 1 of the *Charter.*[75] So far, one such challenge has succeeded.[76]

Next, we examine the major substantive rights conferred under the employment standards legislation.

3) Minimum Wage

Every province[77] has enacted a minimum wage, and employees in the federal jurisdiction[78] are entitled to receive the minimum wage that

---

74 Example: *Saskatoon Horses and the Handicapped Inc. v. Thibeault* (1995), 8 C.C.E.L. (2d) 28 at 33 (Sask. Q.B.).
75 Above note 30. The concept of "indirect" discrimination in examined in Chapter 7.
76 *Fenton*, above note 36, but not on the *Charter* points. This case involved the exclusion of mentally disabled persons working in rehabilitation centres from the minimum wage under the former British Columbia *Employment Standards Act*. The exclusion is now removed.
77 Examples: *B.C. ESA*, above note 43, s. 16, and *B.C. ESR*, above note 58, ss. 15–19.
78 *CLC*, above note 40, ss. 178, 179, and 181.

applies in the province in which they work. The current average minimum wage across Canada (including the territories) is $8.16 per hour, with the maximum amount being $8.75 per hour in Ontario and the lowest being $7.50 per hour in Prince Edward Island. In the mid-2000s, about 4.6 percent of Canadian employees worked for minimum wages: 2 percent in Alberta compared to 8.7 percent in Newfoundland; 3.7 percent for men compared to 6 percent for women; and 44 percent for teenagers compared to under 3 percent for those between 25 and 64. Minimum wage workers are concentrated in the services sector.[79] There is a lively debate on whether a legislated minimum wage is justifiable at all, and if so, how much it should be.

On one side of the coin, proponents of legislated minimum wages argue that employees are morally entitled to receive wages that enable them to have a decent lifestyle, regardless of economic or political considerations.[80] Proponents of the minimum wage usually argue that any adverse economic effects of legislating increased minimum wages are part of the price that must be paid for the advancement of individual human rights.

On the other side of the coin, opponents of legislated minimum wages claim that they have several negative effects:[81]

- Minimum wages have a disemployment effect, with the groups affected worst being women, youth, and visible minorities — ironically, the very groups the minimum wage is supposed to help. The conventional view is that a 10 percent increase in the minimum wage results in a short-term decline in employment of between 1 percent and 3 percent. However, some studies from the United States (but not yet replicated in Canada) have recently challenged this view by contending that increasing minimum wages can result in *more* workers being hired (in the case of employers exercising a high degree of monopsony power).
- Minimum wages are a disincentive for employers to invest in training for their employees, who accordingly tend not to advance out of entry-level minimum wage positions.

---

79   M. Gunderson, "Minimum Wages in Canada: Theory, Evidence and Policy," Report Prepared for the Canadian Federal Labour Standards Review (2005), online: www.hrsdc.gc.ca/en/labour/employment_standards/fls/research/research11/page00.shtml [*Minimum Wages in Canada*].
80   See, for example, the Arthurs Report, above note 4 at 247.
81   The literature, largely from the United States but also from Canada, is reviewed in M. Gunderson, *Minimum Wages in Canada*, above note 79. See also the excellent analysis of the British experience following the introduction of a minimum wage in 1997 by G.S. Bain, "The National Minimum Wage: Further Reflection" (1999) 21 Employee Relations 15.

- Minimum wages are too blunt an instrument for the effective elimination of low pay, although they do tend to reduce wage inequality
and disproportionately benefit low-income families.

It is difficult to escape the conclusion that the current policy on
minimum wages in Canada achieves the worst of both worlds: low pay
persists and the negative economic impact of minimum wages continues
to be felt. Clearly, alternative solutions must be sought to the problems
of low pay, high unemployment, and low investment in training.

The reader is advised to consult the details of each province's legislation to determine which categories of employee are either excluded
altogether from the minimum wage legislation or are entitled to a reduced minimum wage. Typical exclusions from the minimum wage
include defined agricultural workers; domestics who work in private
residences; caregivers in private homes; handicapped persons who work
in sheltered workshops as part of a rehabilitation or care program;[82]
persons employed in defined training or apprenticeship programs;
members of or trainees for entry into defined professions; managers,
supervisors, and employees performing managerial functions; persons
employed in non-profit recreational programs and camps for children;
defined commission salespersons; resident janitors, caretakers, and
building supervisors; noon-hour school supervisors; persons employed
in hunting or fishing; and persons employed in positions funded under
government assistance programs.

In several provinces, the amount of the minimum wage varies depending on the industry, occupation, or work in question and even on
geographical zones within the province, but the trend is away from
such separate rates. Differentials typically involve young persons under
a specified age, normally 18; defined agricultural workers; domestics
who reside in a private residence; persons working from their own
homes; inexperienced employees, apprentices, and trainees; home-
makers; school bus drivers; residential caretakers; people employed in
children's camps; and employees who normally receive gratuities.

Some of these exclusions and variances will disproportionately affect groups protected by section 15 of the *Charter*, such as youth and females, and therefore, are susceptible to a constitutional challenge under
that section. Such a challenge succeeded before the Trial Division of the

---

82   Today, this exclusion is found only in the Saskatchewan *Labour Standards Regulations, 1995*, R.R.S. 1995, c. L-1, O.C. 89/95, s. 13 [*Sask. LSR*]. Previously, it was
also found in British Columbia, Newfoundland, and Quebec, but the probability
of a *Charter* challenge seems to have caused the latter provinces to rescind the
exclusion. See *Fenton*, above note 36.

British Columbia Supreme Court in *Fenton v. British Columbia (Forensic Psychiatric Services Commission)*,[83] where the reduced minimum wage payable to mentally disabled employees working in rehabilitation centres was ruled unconstitutional. The British Columbia government subsequently repealed the provision in question.

In addition to the minimum wage, the federal jurisdiction and some provinces have enacted "fair wages acts"[84] under which any person who contracts with the government to perform defined services (normally[85] limited to construction work) is required to pay the going rate (normally the unionized rate) for the area in which he or she is working. However, the fair wages legislation does not allow the worker to sue his or her employer directly in order to recover remuneration in excess of the regular statutory minimum wage.[86]

4) Payment of Wages

Canadian employment standards acts commonly require that the employee be paid in cash, with a defined negotiable instrument, or by an order to pay credited to the employee's bank account.[87] The rationale is to safeguard the employee against the potentially abusive practice of so-called "tommyshopping," whereby employers would compensate their workers in the form of the goods or services—frequently of inferior quality—provided by the company itself. The employment standards legislation also requires that wages be paid at regular and frequent intervals—in Prince Edward Island, for example, a semi-monthly payment must be made[88]—but employers wishing to be excused from the normal obligation can usually apply to officials within the employment standards department for a variation order.[89] Typically, the legislation

---

83 *Ibid.*.
84 British Columbia *Skills Development and Fair Wage Act*, R.S.B.C. 1996, c. 427; New Brunswick *Public Works Act*, R.S.N.B. 1973, c. P-28, s. 4. In the federal jurisdiction, see *Fair Wages and Hours of Labour Act*, R.S.C. 1985, c. L-4; *Fair Wages and Hours of Labour Regulations*, C.R.C. 1978, c. 1015; *Fair Wages Policy Order*, C.R.C. 1978, c. 1621.
85 Only the New Brunswick statute extends to defined areas beyond construction.
86 *R. v. Baert Construction Ltd.* (1974), 51 D.L.R. (3d) 265 (Man. C.A.).
87 Example: Prince Edward Island *Employment Standards Act*, R.S.P.E.I. 1988, c. E-6.2, s. 30(2) [*P.E.I. ESA*].
88 *Ibid.*, s. 30(2)(a).
89 Example: *B.C. ESA*, above note 43, ss. 72(b) & (c), but note the safeguard, *inter alia*, that a majority of the employees affected must consent: New Brunswick *Employment Standards Act*, S.N.B. 1982, c. E-7.2, s. 35 [*N.B. ESA*]; Nova Scotia *Labour Standards Code*, R.S.N.S. 1989, c. 246, s. 79(3) [*N.S. LSC*].

contains special rules for the situations when an employee is absent from work on a regular payday or when an employee's employment has been terminated. Again, the legislation excludes certain occupations from the wage payment sections—for instance, designated mining and construction workers in Manitoba.[90]

The basic rule in all provinces is that the employer cannot make deductions from wages earned by the employee.[91] Thus, if the employer wishes to recover sums owed to it by an employee or to indemnify itself against losses caused by an employee's inferior workmanship or wrongful resignation, it is incumbent on the employer to sue the employee for damages in court; the employer cannot deduct the amounts in question from the employee's wages. The rationale is to make the employer bear the costs of initiating civil litigation to enforce its claim, since the employer will normally be best able to afford it.[92] Nevertheless, and depending on the jurisdiction, certain deductions may be permitted by the employment standards act. In Saskatchewan, for example, the legislation permits the employer to make "lawful" deductions,[93] and deductions for goods or services produced by the employer that the employee has voluntarily agreed to purchase. In Ontario, a deduction can be made if it is permitted by a judicial order or a statute, or if the employee authorizes it in writing.[94] However, the latter exception does not apply to a deduction in respect to "faulty workmanship" or to cash shortages or loss of property where persons other than the employee have access to the cash or property. In contrast, section 49(1) of the Quebec *Act Respecting Labour Standards* broadly permits any deduction so long as the worker has agreed to it in writing, but the employee is allowed to revoke consent at any time. In British Columbia, the employee can also give written authorization for any deduction, but subject to the safeguard that the director of employment standards must be satisfied

---

90   Manitoba *Construction Industry Wages Act*, C.C.S.M. c. C190, s. 3.

91   Depending on the province, this prohibition may be implicit in the statutory requirement to pay wages at the specified intervals (e.g., *CLC*, above note 40, s. 247) or may be expressly legislated (e.g., Alberta *Employment Standards Code*, R.S.A. 2000, c. E-9, s. 12(1)) [*Alta. ESC*].

92   *Meyers v. Walter Cycle Co. Ltd.*, [1990] 5 W.W.R. 455 (Sask. C.A.); *Antelope Inspection Services Ltd. v. Alberta (Director of Employment Standards)* (1996), 24 C.C.E.L. (2d) 316, especially at 319 (Patterson A.C.J. Prov. Ct., Umpire).

93   *Sask. LSA*, above note 58, ss. 58 & 59. "Lawful" has been construed narrowly to mean deductions that are expressly authorized or mandated by another statutory provision, not those permitted by the parties' own private arrangements: *Hillcrest Contractors Ltd. v. McIntyre* (1987), 88 C.L.L.C. ¶14,012 (Sask. Q.B.).

94   *Ont. ESA*, above note 52, s. 13.

that the deduction is for the employee's "benefit."[95] Other provinces allow deductions to be made for insurance and pension plan premiums
payments to a former spouse and/or children under statutory maintenance orders, trade union dues, and charities.

The employment standards acts typically contain detailed regulation on what constitutes "wages" for statutory purposes. For example,
in most provinces tips and gratuities are excluded from the definition
of wages, thereby rendering lawful the widespread practice of mandatory "tip sharing" under which employers require waiters to share tips
with other workers in the restaurant, such as cooks and dishwashers.
It could be argued that if an employer's practice is to discount faulty
workmanship or shortages from the till when calculating the wages
the employee has earned, such a deduction from wages is not illegal:
the amounts in question will not have been earned in the first place.
Although this argument appears to conflict with the underlying policy
of the statutory no-deduction ban, at least one Ontario court has approved it.[96]

Normally, an employer can factor into the calculation of wages an
amount for room and board provided to the employee. In order to avoid
abuse of this practice, some provinces legislate a maximum value for
such meals and lodgings.[97]

In order to keep the employee abreast of how much remuneration
he or she is entitled to, the employment standards legislation commonly obliges the employer to issue a periodic wage statement containing
comprehensive information on the hours worked, the rate of pay, and
any deductions.[98] Normally, such a statement is given to the worker
with each wage payment. As well, the employer must keep comprehensive records of its employees' wage entitlements for inspection by the
department of labour.[99] Plainly, this obligation is pivotal to the effective
enforcement of the legislation.

The employment standards legislation makes breach of the above-
mentioned obligations regarding payment of wages an offence that can
result in the employer being liable for a fine or even imprisonment.

---

95 *B.C. ESA*, above note 43, s. 22(2).
96 *Toronto Transit Commission v. A.T.U., Local 113* (1992), 92 C.L.L.C. ¶14,047, espe-
    cially para. 12,294 (Ont. Gen. Div.). See, by analogy, *Sagar v. H. Ridehalgh & Son
    Ltd.*, [1931] 1 Ch. 310 (C.A.).
97 For example, in Alberta, the maximum value of a meal is $2.76 per day and
    lodging is $3.65 per day—rather modest amounts: *Employment Standards Regu-
    lation*, Alta. Reg. 14/97, s. 12.
98 Example: *CLC*, above note 40, s. 254.
99 Examples: *Alta. ESC*, above note 91; *Sask. LSA*, above note 58, s. 70.

However, the employee's most important practical remedy to deal with an employer's failure to pay wages or wrongful deduction from wages is to proceed under the special wage collection machinery contained in the employment standards legislation.

5) Work Scheduling

The employment standards legislation in all provinces and the federal jurisdiction contains detailed regulation of the maximum number of hours of work that an employee can work during specified periods; the number of hours of work that can be paid at straight time before an overtime premium is payable; the scope of the employer's right unilaterally to assign overtime work and of the employee's right to refuse to work overtime; the minimum rest periods that an employee must be given daily and weekly; and the employer's obligation to give the worker advance notice of his or her work schedule. The legislation seeks to provide employees with a satisfactory balance of work and life, while simultaneously affording employers sufficient flexibility to meet their production needs.[100]

The main problems that many employees are experiencing with work scheduling pertain to the assignment of excessive amounts of work; the assignment of irregular working hours outside the traditional eight-hour Monday through Friday box; the unpredictability of their future work assignments; the intrusion of work on their personal time, resulting from new communications technology, such as cell phones and Blackberries that enable their employer to contact them at will; and their inability to accommodate personal needs to be absent from work for emergency, family, or other reasons within their employer's work schedule. Paradoxically, while large numbers of employees are working excessively long overtime hours, many part-time and casual workers desperately want more opportunities to work. A knee-jerk reaction to this problem is to legislate severe restrictions on how many hours employees can work, so that the employer would have to fill the gap by hiring unemployed workers or by engaging part-timers and casuals on a regular full-time basis. However, the 1994 Advisory Group Report to the federal government advised against this solution: it would take draconian cuts in permissible working hours before any appreciable reduction in unemployment would result, and such cuts would be un-

---

100 Arthurs Report, above note 4, at 108–15. See also J. Fudge, "Control over Working Time and Work Life Balance: A Detailed Analysis of the *Canada Labour Code* Part III" (Ottawa: Human Resources and Skills Development Canada, 2006).

duly costly to both employers and employees, whose overtime earnings would diminish.[101] Given that employers generally assign substantial overtime work in lieu of hiring more labour with the related, perhaps excessive costs posed by employment protection and social welfare legislation, it would appear to be more sensible to stimulate employment opportunities by reducing these costs, rather than by arbitrarily limiting the permissible hours of work.

For employers, it is frequently cheaper to assign employees substantial overtime work than to hire employees to meet upswings in the production cycle and unexpected emergencies. Employers, therefore, vigorously promote their need for legislation that will maximize their "timing flexibility."

The general public, too, has an interest in ensuring that the physical and pyschological health of citizens is not imperilled by excessive work. The concern is not only to avoid overburdening the health-care system, but also to recognize that a healthy workforce is more productive than an unhealthy one. It is interesting that British Columbia is the only province that expressly prohibits an employer from working hours that are "detrimental to the employee's health or safety."[102]

Four models for balancing these interests are currently used, either singly or in various combinations, in the legislation across Canada.[103]

First, the "ministerial" model involves the statute setting rules of general application, but allowing for exceptions and variations to be made to these rules, either permanently or temporarily, by means of one or a combination of the following methods: (1) authorizing the executive branch of government, by express terms in the main statute, to make regulations permitting exclusions or variances for designated occupations, industries, sectors, or individual employers; (2) authorizing the issuance of *ad hoc* ministerial permits that exempt employers, in specified circumstances, from compliance with the general rules, subject to specified safeguards to ensure that the affected employees are not being unjustly prejudiced, and subject to ministerial review to ensure that the permit is not being abused by the employer; and (3) excusing the employer, by express terms in the statute, from compliance with the general rules in broadly defined "emergency or other exceptional circumstances," subject to an administrative review of the validity of an alleged "emergency or other exceptional circumstances."

---

101 Donner Report, above note 8, especially at 108. This point was also emphasized by the *Advisory Group Report*, above note 41, especially at 4, 8, 52, and 76–77.
102 *B.C. ESA*, above note 43, s. 39.
103 For a detailed elaboration of these models, see the Arthurs Report, above note 4 at 116–35.

Typically, the employer will initiate one of these exceptions, although the minister of labour can also act on his or her own initiative.

The main disadvantages of this model are as follows. It is too slow to respond to the rapid pace of change in the workplace. It is too remote from the unique circumstances of individual enterprises, especially at shop floor level, where the employer and the employees are often the best judges of how to resolve their own problems. It imposes excessive administrative costs on governments. The lack of transparency and vagueness in the process creates the potential for political gerrymandering by influential employers, and finally, employees generally perceive that the process does not adequately safeguard their interests and is biased against them.

Second, the "sectoral" model is based on the assumption that because certain sectors or industries, such as trucking or construction, encounter common operational problems pertaining to work scheduling, all the participants in a sector or industry—employers, employees, unions, and possibly even independent contractors—could combine as a single group to formulate exclusions and variances from the general rules in the statute, subject to final approval of the minister of labour. The main advantages are that economies of scale derive from combining the participants' knowledge and expertise; the participants have superior knowledge of their particular operational circumstances; the employers are assured a level playing field; the process is transparent; the process can react quickly to changing circumstances in the industry or sector in question; and the employers will likely have a strong sense of commitment to rules that they helped to make.

Third, the "workplace" model involves each employer agreeing with its own employees on the appropriate variances and exemptions from the general rules that are best suited for their own workplace, subject to final approval of the minister of labour The main advantages are that local-level parties have superior knowledge about their own unique needs; the parties can react quickly to sudden changes in their own enterprise; the process is transparent; the employer will likely comply with rules that it has voluntarily made with its employees; and the level of job satisfaction among employees will likely increase due to their having an effective voice in formulating the rules. The main disadvantage here is that non-unionized employees will be coerced by the superior power of their employer into accepting modifications to the general standards with which they do not genuinely and freely agree. This risk is minimized, however, by giving the minister of labour ultimate authority to approve any modifications that an employer alleges its employees have accepted.

Fourth, the "consensual flexibility" model involves the individual employee and the employer agreeing to modify the general standards contained in the statute. Despite its attractions in terms of potentially maximizing the flexibility of both sides, this model holds the risk that the vulnerable employee will be coerced into making undesired modifications. Accordingly, in order to safeguard the employee, provision for final ministerial approval is required.

Next, we examine in greater detail how the various elements of these models are used in the legislation across Canada in the context of hours of work and overtime pay, weekly and daily rest periods, and advance notice of work schedules.

a) Hours of Work and Overtime Pay

All provinces and the federal jurisdiction legislate the number of hours that an employee can work during a specified period at straight time before an overtime premium is payable; they also impose ceilings on the total number of hours that can be worked during a specified period. There are two popular approaches to curtailing working hours and the use of overtime.[104]

First, some statutes do not directly legislate a ceiling on the number of hours that can be worked, but instead require the employer to pay an overtime premium of 1.5 times the regular rate of pay for any hours it chooses to assign beyond the "standard working hours" defined in the act.[105] Payment of the overtime premium, therefore, operates as a disincentive on market principles to assigning extra amounts of work. The number of standard working hours that activates the overtime premium is defined as 8 hours per day or 40 hours per week in five provinces and the federal jurisdiction,[106] while two provinces have opted for

---

104 The strengths and weaknesses of the two approaches are analyzed in the Donner Report, above note 8 at 56.
105 Examples: *CLC*, above note 40, s. 174, and *CLSR*, below note 111, ss. 6(6)(c) and 7. The Newfoundland *Labour Standards Act*, R.S.N. 1990, c. L-2, s. 25 [*Nfld. LSA*], and *Labour Standards Regulations, 1996*, C.N.L.R. 781/96, s. 9(4) [*Nfld. LSR*] are exceptional in providing for a specific dollar amount of $12 per hour as the minimum overtime rate. In British Columbia, the premium increases to two times the regular rate for work in excess of 12 hours per day: *B.C. ESA*, above note 43, s.40(1)(b).
106 Examples: *CLC*, above note 40, s. 169(1); *B.C. ESA*, above note 43, ss. 35, 40, and 41; *Nfld. LSR, ibid.*, s. 5(1); Manitoba *Employment Standards Code*, C.C.S.M. c. E110, s. 10 [*Man. ESC*]; Quebec *Act Respecting Labour Standards*, R.S.Q., c. N-1.1, s. 52 [*Quebec LSA*]; Sask. *LSA*, above note 58, ss. 6(1), (2), and 9(1).

48 hours per week,[107] and two for 44 hours per week.[108] An employee is generally deemed to be "working" for overtime if the employer knows, or ought reasonably to know, that he or she is working, but does not send the person home;[109] the same is true if the employee is at home, but is required to commence work at the employer's call.[110] In addition, if the employer does call an employee in to work during what was personal time, most provinces and the federal act require the employer to pay for a minimum number of hours, generally three, even if no work is available for them at that time.[111]

Second, in addition to requiring employers to pay the above-mentioned overtime premium for hours assigned in excess of the defined standard working hours, some statutes legislate a "cap" on the number of hours that an employee is permitted to work during a defined period.. Thus, in the federal jurisdiction, the ceiling is 48 hours per week;[112] in Alberta,[113] 12 hours per day; in Newfoundland,[114] 16 hours per day; and in Ontario,[115] 8 hours per day or 48 hours per week. British Columbia is unique in providing that the employer cannot require or "directly or indirectly allow" an employee to work "excessive hours" or hours "detrimental to the employee's health or safety."[116]

Some provinces, however, combine the two approaches by legislating an overtime premium "trigger" along with a cap on hours.[117] Less commonly, four provinces bolster the above-mentioned approaches by expressly entitling the employee to refuse to perform overtime work in excess of a specified amount. In Saskatchewan, for example, the cap is normally 44 hours per week, but is subject to an "emergency circumstances" override. Oddly, the Saskatchewan act enables the employer to exceed this amount if the employee "consents," thereby raising the spectre of coerced agreements. The Arthurs Report favoured enact-

---

107 Nova Scotia *Minimum Wage Order*, N.S. Reg. 5/99, s. 9; *P.E.I. ESA*, above note 87, s. 15(1).
108 *Alta. ESC*, above note 91, s. 21; *Ont. ESA*, above note 52, s. 22.
109 Example: *Sask. LSA*, above note 58, s. 8.
110 *Watson v. Wozniak* (2004), 36 C.C.E.L. (3d) 202, especially at 205–6 (Sask. Q.B.).
111 Examples: *Canada Labour Standards Regulations*, C.R.C., c. 986, s. 11.1 [*CLSR*]; *Man. ESC*, above note 106, s. 51(1)(b).
112 *CLC*, above note 40, s. 171, but note that subsection (2) of s. 171 allows hours to be "averaged" for this purpose.
113 *Alta. ESC*, above note 91, s. 16(1).
114 *Nfld. LSA*, above note 105, s. 23, but the "ceiling" can be exceeded in cases of "imminent hazard to life or property."
115 *Ont. ESA*, above note 52, s. 17(1).
116 *B.C. ESA*, above note 43, s. 39.
117 Example: *Ont. ESA*, above note 52, ss. 17–18.

ing a personal right to refuse overtime in excess of 12 hours a day or 48 hours a week, or if the employee has a significant family commitment, an educational commitment, or another work commitment (in the case of part-time workers).[118] In most provinces, the legislation expressly allows the employee to agree with the employer that overtime be "banked" and subsequently taken as time off with pay (at the rate of one and a half hours for every hour worked as overtime) within a specified period, instead of being paid out at the overtime premium. Even in jurisdictions where the legislation does not technically allow this, employers and employees sometimes agree to the arrangement, and the department of labour generally turns a blind eye to it, so long as the employer is not abusing the practice.[119]

The employment standards legislation typically contains highly detailed provisions delineating the exemptions and variances to the above-mentioned general standards, utilizing various combinations of the four models described above.[120] Thus, the employment standards acts—or, more commonly, regulations made under the acts—generally either totally exclude or specify variances for a broad spectrum of industries, occupations, and sectors. In Saskatchewan,[121] for example, these include city newspapers, commercial hog operation workers, oil truck drivers, defined construction workers, defined professionals, travelling salespersons, residential service facility workers, highway workers, employees who work in specified areas of northern Saskatchewan, firefighters, teachers, and supervisors who perform exclusively managerial duties.[122] Interestingly, in Ontario and British Columbia, defined high-technology workers are excluded. The goal is to foster the development of high-technology companies, whose start costs are notoriously high and whose employees normally work for lengthy and irregular periods of time during the start-up phase.[123]

The acts also generally allow the employer to apply to the minister of labour (or, depending on the jurisdiction, the director of labour standards) for a permit authorizing the employer to "average" the hours

---

118 Above note 4 at 145–46.
119 *Ibid.* at 147–48.
120 See Section B(5), above in this chapter.
121 *Sask. LSA*, above note 58, ss. 4(2) and (4); *Sask. LSR*, above note 82, ss. 4–9.
122 The employee's duties must be exclusively managerial in nature, subject only to *de minimis* exceptions: *TriRoc Electric Ltd. v. Butler and Minister of Labour*, [2003] C.L.L.C. ¶210-046 (O.L.R.B.).
123 British Columbia *Employment Standards Regulation*, B.C. Reg. 396/95, s. 37.8; Ontario Regulation *Exemption, Special Rules and Establishment of Minimum Wage*, O. Reg. 285/01, s. 8(1) [*Ontario Exemption Reg.*].

worked by its employees over several weeks or months: the purpose is to accommodate production cycles that do not fit the traditional mould of eight hours per day, Monday to Friday. In Saskatchewan, for example, the director of labour standards has broad discretion under section 9 of the *Labour Standards Act* to issue such a permit, subject to any terms and conditions, including duration, that he or she sees fit; there are no guidelines in the Act or the Regulations delineating the factors that govern the exercise of this discretion. The Arthurs Report was highly critical of the equivalent "averaging" provisions in the federal act on account of their lack of transparency, their failure to give affected employees an adequate voice in the process, their inaccessibility to review, and the slowness with which they are issued.[124] In contrast, in Ontario, an employer seeking an "averaging" permit from the director of Employment Standards must obtain the written consent of the employees affected, and an "averaging" permit cannot last for more than two years.[125]

As well, most statutes allow the employer to exceed the normal maximum hours, without obtaining prior administrative approval, if there is an "emergency" or other "exceptional" circumstance as defined in the statute.[126] In Alberta, for example, section 16(1)(a) of the *Employment Standards Code* allows the employer unilaterally to exceed the maximum of twelve hours of work per day if "an accident occurs, urgent work is necessary to a plant or machinery or other unforeseeable or unpreventable circumstances occur." It is incumbent on the employee to challenge the validity of alleged "emergency" conditions.

The sectoral model is used in several jurisdictions. For example, in the Quebec clothing industry, the minister of labour is empowered to establish by decree special rules regarding *inter alia* the standard work week, following consultations with employers and trade unions in the industry.[127] In the federal jurisdiction, too, special rules exist for motor transport, shipping, railway running trades, and commission salespersons in banking and broadcasting. Most controversially, perhaps, maximum hours of work for road transport drivers are not dealt with under the *Commercial Vehicle Drivers Hours of Service Regulations*, enacted by Transport Canada and enforced by the provinces. It is argued that Transport Canada gives undue weight to the employers' interests

---

124 Above note 4 at 142.

125 *Ont. ESA*, above note 52, s. 22.

126 *CLC*, above note 40, s. 18; *Alta. ESC*, above note 91, s. 16(1)(a); *Man. ESC*, above note 106, s. 19; *Nfld. LSA*, above note 105, s. 23; *N.S. LSC*, above note 89, s. 63; *Ont. ESA*, *ibid.*, s. 19.

127 *Quebec LSA*, above note 106, s. 92.1.

in formulating these regulations and that this sector should be brought under the umbrella of the specialized employment standards that are part of the *Canada Labour Code*.[128]

The workplace model is best exemplified[129] by section 37 of the *British Columbia Employment Standards Act* that permits an employer to adopt a "flexible work schedule" so long as at least 65 percent of the affected employees agree to it voluntarily. The schedule is posted in the workplace for at least ten days before it is submitted to the director of Employment Standards for approval; it must be submitted to the director within seven days of being approved by the employees; and the schedule must remain in force for at least twenty-six weeks. The maximum duration of a schedule is two years, after which it must be approved again by 65 percent of the affected employees. The director can rescind a schedule at any time if he or she is satisfied that the employees' approval was procured by undue influence, intimidation, or coercion of any employee by the employer, or if the employer violated the other above-mentioned statutory prerequisites. A review can be initiated by any single employee filing a complaint about a schedule with the director.

The Arthurs Report recommended a variant of the workplace model where the employer forms a workplace consultative committee of affected employees to review proposals for adopting flexible work schedules, as formulated by the employer.[130] There would be legislated safeguards against the employer attempting to coerce or unduly influence committee members, and the members would be paid for their committee work. The committee would be empowered to bring forward suggestions on the employer's proposals. Only if an employer proposal won majority support in a secret ballot of the committee, would it be allowed to proceed to the director of employment standards for approval. The director would monitor implementation of the schedule on an ongoing basis to ensure that the employer is acting properly. The maximum duration of a flexible work schedule would be three years.

As yet, no province has enacted this recommendation, but the approach is important symbolically. It recognizes that non-union employees should be afforded group representational rights *vis-à-vis* their employer without having to join a union to bargain collectively on their behalf.

---

128 Arthurs Report, above note 4 at 140–42.
129 See also the variant of this model in the *CLC*, above note 40, s. 170(2)(b), which provides that 70 percent of the employees affected by the employer's proposed flexible work schedule must approve it.
130 Above note 4 at 131–35.

The consensual flexibility model under which an employee can make a personal agreement with the employer to depart from the general standards without ministerial supervision is rarely found in Canada because of the risk of employer undue influence over a vulnerable employee. One exception is section 12(1) of the *Saskatchewan Labour Standards Act*[131] which allows the employer to make a personal agreement with the employee, subject to his or her "consent" to work for more than the normal maximum of 44 hours per week. Even then, "consent" presumably would be vitiated by coercion or undue influence on the employer's part, but this would have to be determined *ex post facto*, and only if the employee elects to file a complaint. In contrast, Ontario imposes stringent safeguards on personal agreements between an employee and an employer to work in excess of the standard 8 hours per day/48 hours per week: the employer must give the employee an information sheet, prepared by the director of employment standards, that outlines the employee's statutory rights; the employee must agree to the proposal in writing; the employer must apply to the director of employment standards for approval prior to implementing the agreement; and the employer must post all applications to the director in conspicuous places in the workplace so that all affected employees know what is going on. The director has broad discretion about whether to grant approval, with specific reference being made to the employer's record of prior contraventions of the Act and the need to protect the employee's health and safety; the director can also impose any conditions he or she sees fit on the agreement in order to safeguard the employee. A maximum duration of one year is imposed on agreements allowing the employee to work in excess of 60 hours per week; in the case of agreements to work fewer than 60 hours per week, the duration is three years.[132]

b) Daily and Weekly Rest Periods
In order to secure a satisfactory balance between work and life for the employee, the employment standards legislation in all provinces (but not the federal jurisdiction[133]) limits the number of hours that any employee is permitted to work during a day. These provisions complement the statutory limit examined above on the number of hours that can be worked in a day.[134] Generally, the employee is allowed 8 con-

---

131 Above note 58.
132 *Ont. ESA*, above note 52, s. 17.1.
133 The Arthurs Report recommended introducing similar rights in the federal act: above note 4 at 160–61.
134 See Section B(5)(a) in this chapter.

secutive hours of rest in any period of 24 hours, [135] but in Ontario, 11 hours is mandated.[136] The employee is also generally allowed one half-hour break in every 5 hours of continuous work[137]—usually without pay[138]—but there are exceptions to accommodate the employer's need for flexibility that are based on various combinations of the four models described above.[139] Accordingly, in several provinces the employer can apply to a designated government official, usually the director of employment standards, for a permit varying the rest break requirements, reflecting the "ministerial" model.[140] In some provinces, including Saskatchewan,[141] the director can grant such a permit only if the majority of the employees affected by it approve the exemption, reflecting the "workplace" model. Most provinces also define "emergency" and other "exceptional circumstances" allowing the employer to depart from the general rules. In Alberta,[142] for example, the employer is excused if an "accident" occurs, "urgent" work is "necessary," "unforeseeable or unpreventable" circumstances occur, or if a rest break would not be "reasonable." Saskatchewan also provides broad exceptions where (1) it is not "reasonable" for the employee to take a meal break, (2) medical reasons justify the employee taking the break at a different time,[143] or (3) where there may be other circumstances specified by regulation in the future.[144] The broadest exception, however, is in Newfoundland,[145] where an employee and an employer can agree in writing in the contract of employment to dispense with the employee's entitlement to a one hour break after five consecutive hours of work; this exception reflects the "consensual flexibility" model. As well, in all provinces, defined occupations, industries, and sectors are excluded from the general rule, as in Newfoundland where crew members on ferry boats are

---

135 Example: *Sask. LSA*, above note 58, s. 13.2(1).

136 *Ont. ESA*, above note 52, s. 18(1).

137 Example: *B.C. ESA*, above note 43, s. 32(1).

138 Except in Saskatchewan under the *Minimum Wage Board Order, 1997*, R.R.S. 1997, c. L-1, O.C. 417/97, s. 3.

139 See Section B(5)(a), above in this chapter.

140 Examples: *Man. ESC*, above note 106, s. 50(2)(b).

141 *Sask. LSA*, above note 58, s. 13.3(1)(b).

142 *Alta. ESC*, above note 91, s. 18.

143 In other provinces, the employer's duty under human rights legislation to reasonably accommodate an employee's "disability" to the point of sustaining an "undue hardship" is roughly similar in effect (assuming that the employee's medical condition constitutes a defined disability under the legislation). See Chapter 7, Section A..

144 *Sask. LSA*, above note 58, ss. 13.3(1)(a), (d), (e), and (2).

145 *Nfld. LSA*, above note 105, s. 24.

excluded.[146] This type of exclusion reflects a combination of the "ministerial" and "sectoral" models.

Furthermore, in all provinces and the federal jurisdiction, the worker is entitled under the employment standards acts to a minimum period of continuous rest, normally 24 hours over seven days.[147] The Arthurs Report recommended that the minimum rest period be increased to 32 consecutive hours over a seven-day period.[148] Usually, Sunday is the recommended day of rest wherever "practicable."[149] This recommendation is not religiously inspired; instead, it reflects the reality that in Canada, Sunday is the day when most family members are free from their work and school obligations and can relax together. Indeed, the legislation in Ontario, New Brunswick, and Manitoba is unique in entitling employees engaged in defined retail business establishments to refuse to work on Sunday; in the latter two provinces, however, this is subject to the proviso that the employee gives the employer at least fourteen days advance notice.[150] In Ontario, the right to refuse is qualified by the requirement that the refusal be reasonable in the circumstances. These provisions resulted from the expansion of Sunday shopping during the last two decades after the Supreme Court of Canada's ruling that the federal *Lord's Day Act* was unconstitutional.[151]

Again, the weekly rest provisions are modified to accommodate the employer's need for flexibility, reflecting various combinations of the four models described above.[152] Accordingly, designated industries, sectors, and occupations may be excluded from the weekly rest requirements by regulations, such as supervisors and managers; domestics; forest-fire-fighters; agricultural workers; workers in the retail trade; workers who are employed for relatively few hours per day; over-

---

146 *Nfld. LSR*, above note 105, s. 7(a).
147 Examples: *CLC*, above note 40, s. 73; *Ont. ESA*, above note 52, s. 18(4).
148 Above note 4 at 161.
149 *CLC*, above note 40, s. 73.
150 *Man. ESC*, above note 106, s. 81; *N.B. ESA*, above note 89, s. 17.1; *Ont. ESA*, above note 52, s. 73(2). In New Brunswick, s. 7.11 of the *Days of Rest Act*, S.N.B. 1985, c. D-4.2, reinforces this right by avoiding any term in an employer's lease that obliges it to stay open on a weekly day of rest.
151 R.S.C. 1970, c. L-13, ruled unconstitutional in *R. v. Big M Drug Mart*, [1985] 1 S.C.R. 295. Subsequently, several provinces, including Ontario, enacted Sunday closing laws with a secular rather than a religious orientation, which were generally ruled to be constitutional: e.g., *R. v. Edwards Books & Art Ltd.*, [1986] 2 S.C.R. 713 at 779, especially Dickson C.J. For more detailed analysis of the constitutional dimension, see M. Brundrett, "Demythologizing Sunday Shopping: Sunday Retail Restrictions and the *Charter*" (1992) 50 U.T. Fac. L. Rev. 1.
152 See Section B(5)(a), above in this chapter.

night security, janitors, and superintendents; and employees engaged in "emergency" work, such as repairing breakdowns in machinery, reflecting a combination of the "ministerial" and "sectoral" models.[153]

Furthermore, in some jurisdictions, the employer can apply to a designated government official for a permit excusing it from the weekly rest provisions in defined "exceptional" circumstances, reflecting the "ministerial" model. For example, in Manitoba the director of employment standards can issue such a permit if the employer stands to suffer an "undue hardship" by virtue of the remote location of the work site, the seasonal nature of operations, or other factors.[154] In British Columbia, the issuance of such a permit by the director is subject to the safeguard that the majority of workers affected know and approve of it, reflecting a combination of the "ministerial" and "workplace" models.[155] In addition, in some provinces, employers have the added flexibility of being able to postpone the weekly rest day, which then accumulates and becomes due later,[156] or to "average" the number of days worked over a specified period to take account of non-traditional shift systems.[157]

The Arthurs Report recommended that further rest periods be introduced in order to safeguard better the employee's right to decency, namely "short breaks" for the purposes of breastfeeding and nursing infants, and personal medical needs, such as injecting medication or visiting a physician.[158] According to Chair H.W. Arthurs, the balance between the employee's personal interests and the employer's operational needs should be struck by legislating that no such leave can be "unreasonably" denied. As yet, this recommendation has not been enacted in any Canadian jurisdiction.

Finally, the employment standards legislation may intersect with the human rights legislation in determining an employee's entitlement to take breaks from work. For example, if the employee requests time off work for medical, family, religious or other purposes covered by the human rights legislation, the employer must attempt to reasonably accommodate the employee's request up to the point of undue hardship.[159]

---

153 The broadest list of exemptions is in the *B.C. ESR*, above note 58, ss. 34 and 41.
154 *Man. ESC*, above note 106, s. 46. See the similar safeguards in the *B.C. ESA*, above note 43, ss. 73(1)(b) & (2).
155 *B.C. ESA, ibid.*, s. 73(1)(a).
156 Example: *N.B. ESA*, above note 89, s. 17(1), but approval of the director of Labour Standards is required.
157 Example: *CLSR*, above note 111, s. 9.
158 Above note 4 at 161–62.
159 See Chapter 7.

c) Advance Notice of Work Schedules

In order to enjoy an appropriate work and life balance, an employee needs to be able to predict future work obligations in order to make plans for personal life. Clearly, the employee needs as much advance notice as possible of any changes to an existing work schedule.

It seems surprising that only two provinces require the employer to notify the employee in advance of changes to his or her work schedule.[160] Saskatchewan affords the employee the greatest protection, requiring the employer to provide the employee with one week's advance written notice of his or her work schedule or of any changes to it, and to post the notice in conspicuous spots in the workplace.[161] The employer's need for flexibility is accommodated in several ways, reflecting the four models described above.[162] For example, the employer can apply to the director of labour standards for a permit exempting it from the requirement, thereby reflecting the "ministerial" model. That model is also reflected in statutory language permitting the employer to override the requirement where "any sudden or unusual occurrence or condition arises that could not, by the exercise of reasonable judgement have been forseen by the employer." As well, oral notice can replace the written form when the latter is "impractical" for any reason, including the "small" size of the employer's operations. In Alberta, the employer's obligation is limited to giving the employee at least twenty-four hours notice of a shift change.[163]

6) Statutory Holidays

The employment standards acts in all jurisdictions designate a number of days upon which employers are obliged to grant their employees a holiday or, where the employees do work, to pay them at a designated premium rate.[164] Depending on the jurisdiction, the following holidays are recognized under the employment standards legislation: New Year's

---

160 The Arthurs Report recommended the enactment of this safeguard in the federal *Code*: above note 4 at 151–52.

161 *Sask. LSA*, above note 58, s. 13.1(1).

162 See Section B(5)(a), above in this chapter.

163 *Alta. ESC*, above note 91, s. 17(2).

164 *CLC*, above note 40, ss. 166 and 191–202; *Alta. ESC, ibid.*, ss. 25–33; *B.C. ESA*, above note 43, ss. 1(1) and 44–49; *Man. ESC*, above note 106, ss. 1(1)(d) and 21–30; *N.B. ESA*, above note 89, ss. 1, 18–23; *Nfld. LSA*, above note 105, ss. 15–20; *N.S. LSC*, above note 89, ss. 37–43; *Ont. ESA*, above note 52, ss. 1(1) and 29–32; *P.E.I. ESA*, above note 87, ss. 6–10; *Quebec LSA*, above note 106, ss. 60–65; *National Holiday Act*, R.S.Q., c. F-1.1, ss. 2 and 4; *Sask. LSA*, above note 58, ss. 2, 38–41; and *Sask. LSR*, above note 82, ss. 18–22. In all Canadian juris-

Day; Good Friday; Victoria Day; Canada Day; Labour Day; Thanksgiving Day; Remembrance Day; Christmas Day; Boxing Day, in Ontario only; the first Monday in August; Memorial Day; Family Day; Louis Riel Day in Manitoba; and, in Quebec, a national holiday on 24 June.

The statutory holiday provisions are aimed only partially at giving the employee time off from the stress of work; rather, a major objective is to generate employment opportunities for the unemployed and underemployed. It is thought that reducing the number of hours that an employee can be ordered to work, or imposing a wage premium for ordering an employee to work on a holiday will give employers an incentive to recall employees on layoff or to hire new employees to fill the gap.[165] (Currently, the going premium is 1.5 times the regular rate of pay for the holiday in question, save in Newfoundland where the rate is double time and in British Columbia, where double time must be paid after eleven hours of work on the holiday.[166]) However, some argue that rather than tinkering with the statutory holiday provisions to reduce unemployment, this laudable goal would be achieved more successfully by tackling the root cause: the excessive costs of hiring employees under employment protection and social welfare legislation generally.

The following issues are generally dealt with under the holiday provisions:

- Normally, employers are not prohibited from assigning work to an employee on a statutory holiday provided that they pay the above-mentioned wage premium or give the employee banked time off in lieu.[167] In most provinces, the employee can choose between time off and extra pay, except in several provinces where employers with defined continuous work operations can unilaterally decide to give time off.[168]
- In several provinces, the legislation gives the parties the flexibility to substitute alternate days for the statutory holidays if the majority of affected employees agree.[169] In order to safeguard against employer

---

dictions, the minimum of two weeks' vacation established under article 2.2 of the *European Social Charter*, 1965, 529 U.N.T.S. 89, Eur. T.S. No. 35, is met.
165 Donner Report, above note 8 at 114.
166 *B.C. ESA*, above note 43, s. 46(1); *Nfld. LSA*, above note 105, s. 17(a).
167 In the federal jurisdiction, Nova Scotia, and Saskatchewan, the legislation does not provide for a *general* right to take time off in lieu, but only in relation to employees engaged in defined continuous operations.
168 Examples: *CLC*, above note 40, ss. 191 and 198(b); *Man. ESC*, above note 106, s. 25(2); *N.B. ESA*, above note 89, ss. 18(5) & (6); *N.S. LSC*, above note 89, ss. 41(2) & (3); *Sask. LSR*, above note 82, ss. 18–20.
169 Example: *Man. ESC*, ibid., s. 28(1)(b) where the majority of affected employees must agree in writing.

coercion, these provinces generally require that a designated government official be satisfied that any such agreement has been approved by a majority of employees affected by it.[170] A drawback to having a majority vote of employees determine a substitutition is that the unique cultural or religious needs of an employee from a minority group might not be adequately safeguarded. Although human rights legislation requires employers to make reasonable accommodation for the individual in these circumstances, it would simplify enforcement if the employment standards legislation also included this protection.

- The legislation commonly deals with what might be called various "housekeeping" matters, such as substituting for statutory holidays that fall on a non-working day[171] or during the employee's annual vacation; calculating the "regular wages"[172] of employees who are paid other than on an hourly, weekly, or monthly basis;[173] and disqualifying an employee who was absent without reasonable cause on a statutory holiday on which he or she was supposed to work.[174]

- The legislation typically describes the prerequisites that an employee must satisfy in order to qualify for a statutory holiday. These usually include a requirement that the employee have a minimum period of continuous employment with the same employer;[175] have worked a minimum number of hours for the employer during a specified period preceding the holiday—normally fifteen working days during the preceding thirty calendar days;[176] and have worked on the last day before and the first day after the statutory holiday, unless he or she has a reasonable excuse for not doing so.[177]

- In the interest of employer efficiency, defined industries, sectors, and occupations may be excluded from the statutory holiday provisions by regulations; these vary between the provinces. Thus, Ontario excludes the following: fishing and hunting guides; full-time firefighters; defined lansdcape, horticultural, and agricultural workers; students employed in camps, recreational facilities, or charitable

---

170   Example: *CLC*, above note 40, s. 195(b), where the minister of labour verifies such approval.

171   Generally, the employer and the employee must arrange a mutually agreeable substitute day, which must precede the employee's next annual vacation or occur within some other specified period.

172   Examples: *CLC*, above note 40, s. 196, and *CLSR*, above note 111, ss. 18, 20; *N.B. ESA*, above note 89, ss. 21(1) and 19(1.1); *N.S. LSC*, above note 89, ss. 40(2) & (3).

173   Example: *CLSR*, *ibid.*, s. 17(a).

174   Example: *N.B. ESA*, above note 89, s. 18(1)(d).

175   Example: *Nfld. LSA*, above note 105, s. 19(1)(a), thirty days seniority.

176   Example: *B.C. ESA*, above note 43, s. 45(a).

177   Example: *Man. ESC*, above note 106, s. 22.

programs or instructing children; janitors, superintendents, or care-takers of residential buildings who reside in the building; taxi drivers; seasonal employees of hotels, tourist resorts, taverns, or restaurants who receive room and board; and construction workers who receive more than 7.3 percent of their hourly rate or wages for vacation or holiday pay.[178] Again, these exclusions reflect the "ministerial" model described above.[179] Many of them seem to be the product of political expediency rather than thorough cost-benefit analysis. Any exclusion that disproportionately prejudices a protected group under section 15 of the *Charter* is susceptible to constitutional challenge.[180]

7) Annual Vacations

The employment standards legislation in all jurisdictions entitles qualified employees to an annual vacation. Although the purpose of this provision might seem to be to provide the employee with a reasonable break from the physical and psychological stress of working, the facts that the legislation generally allows the employee to forego vacation and continue working for pay in lieu[181] and to take alternate employment during a vacation belie this. These allowances are justified out of respect for the employee's personal freedom of choice, but the justification only holds good if the legislation effectively safeguards the employee against coercion or undue influence by the employer. Therefore, in provinces that expressly permit the parties to make such agreements, the agreements are subject to approval by the director of labour standards.

Today, approximately 25 percent of Canadians do not use their full vacation entitlement, while about 10 percent do not use any of it.[182] The length of the vacation is generally two weeks, but in several provinces, the length increases with the employee's period of continuous employ-

---

178 *Ontario Exemption Reg.*, above note 123, s. 9.
179 See Section B(5)(a), above in this chapter.
180 See, by analogy, *Fenton*, above note 36; *Charter*, above note 30.
181 In some jurisdictions, express terms in the statute permit this practice: eg., *CLSR*, above note 111, s. 14; *N.S. LSC*, above note 89, s. 33; *Ont. ESA*, above note 52, s. 41; *Sask. LSA*, above note 58, s. 37, but only if there is a "shortage of labour." Elsewhere, it is implicit in the statutory provision allowing the parties to agree on arrangements that are more or equally as beneficial to the worker as the statutory *minima*: e.g., *Alta. ESC*, above note 91, s. 3(1)(b); *N.B. ESA*, above note 89, s. 27; *Nfld. LSA*, above note 105, s. 4; *P.E.I. ESA*, above note 87, s. 11(4). Only in Quebec is the employer expressly prohibited from giving pay in lieu of the vacation, under the *Quebec LSA*, above note 106, s. 73.
182 Arthurs Report, above note 4 at 164.

ment with the employer. For example, in Saskatchewan, employees are entitled to three weeks of vacation after each year of service with any one employer, increasing to four weeks after ten years of service.[183] In Alberta, two weeks of vacation vests after each of the first four years of service, increasing to three weeks after five years of continuous employment.[184]

In order to qualify for an annual vacation, the employee must generally have accrued at least twelve consecutive months of continuous employment with an employer.[185] In order to be continuous, a period of employment need not involve the ongoing performance of actual work; it suffices that the contractual nexus remains intact for the duration of an absence from work, such as a disciplinary suspension, a sickness, or a layoff. This requirement can be especially harmful for casual workers whose employment contracts terminate after each period of hiring with an employer. In order to temper this effect, some acts state that interruptions in service up to a specified duration will not interfere with the accrual of continuous employment for the purpose of designated statutory benefits, such as annual vacations.[186]

The costs to employers of administering annual vacation entitlements can be reduced if the employer, instead of calculating each employee's *personal* length of service for vacation purposes, can choose a *common* anniversary date that suits the firm's particular circumstances.[187] Several provinces currently give employers the flexibility to designate such a common anniversary date.[188] Under this model, an employee who has not worked for the full designated year, so as to become entitled to the full two weeks of vacation, will receive a vacation payment (or time off) pro-rated according to time worked during that year. The following issues are generally dealt with under the vacation provisions:

- Typically, the employer has the right to decide when an employee takes vacation, so long as this occurs within a designated period — usually

---

183 *Sask. LSA*, above note 58, s. 30(1).
184 *Alta. ESC*, above note 91, s. 34.
185 Example: *N.S. LSC*, above note 89, s. 32(1).
186 For instance, the *Alta. ESC*, above note 91, s. 36 provides for a maximum hiatus of three months for the purpose of determining whether an employee has been continuously employed for five years or more.
187 This recommendation came from the Thompson Commission, above note 8 at 111.
188 *CLC*, above note 40, s. 183, and *CLSR*, above note 111, ss. 12, 13; *Alta. ESC*, above note 91, s. 35; *B.C. ESA*, above note 43, s. 60; *Man. ESC*, above note 106, s. 42; *Quebec LSA*, above note 106, ss. 66 & 67, which designates a "reference year" as 1 May to 30 April; *Sask. LSR*, above note 82, s. 16.

ten months—of the vacation having been earned.[189] The Thompson Commission disagreed with this model and recommended that the employee and the employer aim to mutually settle the matter, with the director of employment standards being empowered to resolve any disagreements.[190] No province as yet has endorsed this recommendation, presumably because of the resulting costs to employers and the public purse. However, in two jurisdictions, the legislation expressly prevents vacations from being scheduled to coincide with an employee's period of paid sick leave.[191] Elsewhere, the employee would be safeguarded in this situation by the employer's duty of reasonable accommodation under the human rights legislation if he or she is absent due to a protected "disability."

- In several provinces, the employee can fraction his or her vacation into two or more segments rather than take it in one block. This opportunity allows the employee to take leaves for short-term personal needs, cultural reasons, emergencies, or a series of long weekends.[192] The consent of the employer is usually required for this arrangement, save in Saskatchewan, Quebec, and British Columbia, where the employee can decide unilaterally. The legislation generally states how much advance notice of when they can take their vacations the employer must give its employees. In Alberta, for instance, at least two weeks must be given, unless the parties agree otherwise.[193]

- The legislation commonly regulates in detail how much vacation pay must be paid and how it is to be calculated. In most jurisdictions, the employee is entitled to 4 percent of his or her regular earnings over the qualifying period,[194] but in several provinces and the federal jurisdiction, this amount increases with the employee's period of continuous employment with the employer.[195]

- Normally, the employer must give the employee the appropriate vacation pay within a specified period before the vacation period commences.[196]

---

189 Examples: *Nfld. LSA*, above note 105, s. 8(1); *Ont. ESA*, above note 52, s. 35.
190 Above note 8 at 111.
191 *B.C. ESA*, above note 43, s. 59(1)(a); *P.E.I. ESA*, above note 87, s. 11(4).
192 Example: *Sask. LSA* above note 58, s. 31(c). However, the federal jurisdiction, Manitoba, New Brunswick, and Prince Edward Island are silent on this matter.
193 *Alta. ESC*, above note 91, s. 38.
194 Example: *Ont. ESA*, above note 52, s. 35.2.
195 Examples: Alberta, British Columbia, Newfoundland, Quebec, Saskatchewan, and the federal jurisdiction.
196 Example: *B.C. ESA*, above note 43, s. 58(2)(a), where the pay must be given at least one week before the vacation falls due.

- The legislation customarily deals with the effect of termination of employment on annual vacation entitlements. Clearly, if an employee is terminated before his or her vacation vests, the individual is entitled to any vacation pay credits due, either immediately or within a specified period.[197] It is less clear, however, whether an employer can treat time spent on vacation as part of the required period of notice of termination. Although this practice is expressly prohibited in Manitoba and Saskatchewan, it is expressly allowed in Newfoundland if the parties agree to it in writing. Elsewhere, it could be argued that permitting the employee to have time off work facilitates searching for another job and is therefore consistent with the remedial goal of the legislation; however, this principle remains unclear.
- The effect of a statutory holiday during an employee's vacation is usually dealt with in this legislation. The basic rule is that the employer must add an extra day to the employee's vacation or give an extra day's pay.[198]
- In most provinces, there are detailed (but differing) exemptions from the annual vacation provisions for designated industries, sectors, and occupations, all designed to safeguard the employer's interest in efficiency. In Ontario, for example, the exclusion covers defined practising professionals, namely, architects, lawyers, engineers, accountants, vets, and surveyors; defined registered health-care practitioners, namely, chiropodists, chiropractors, dentists, massage therapists, medical doctors, optometrists, pharmacists, physiotherapists, and psychologists; teachers; students in training for the above-mentioned designated professions; commercial fishers; real estate brokers; defined commission salespersons; and defined agricultural workers. As well, Ontario has enacted special rules for fruit, vegetable, and tobacco harvesters.[199] These provisions are commonly contained in regulations made under the main act and reflect the "ministerial" model described earlier.[200]

8) Leaves of Absence

In order to afford employes a decent work and life balance, the employment standards legislation generally establishes the following leaves of absence: pregnancy; parental; adoption; compassionate care; family needs; bereavement; voting in elections; and sickness. As well, we

---

197 Example: *Ont. ESA*, above note 52, s. 38.
198 Example: *Sask. LSA*, above note 58, s. 34.
199 Example: *Ontario Exemption Reg.*, above note 123, ss. 2 and 26.
200 See Section B(5)(a), above in this chapter.

examine leaves of absence for other purposes that could be introduced in the foreseeable future.

a) Pregnancy Leave

The increasingly important role of women in the Canadian labour market makes it necessary to protect them when they bear children. Accordingly, in all provinces and the federal jurisdiction, legislation entitles women to a leave of absence for childbirth and safeguards them from being penalized by their employer with respect to their job tenure and other terms, conditions, and benefits of employment by reason of their pregnancy. Four kinds of protective legislation can come into play in this area: employment standards, employment insurance, health and safety, and general human rights statutes. The following issues are normally of critical importance.

i)   How Much Pregnancy Leave Is the Worker Allowed?

In six provinces and the federal jurisdiction, the basic entitlement is 17 weeks of unpaid leave;[201] in three provinces, the amount is 18 weeks;[202] in Alberta, the amount is 15 weeks.[203] However, in most provinces this period may be extended up to a specified maximum if the employee's medical condition renders her unfit to resume work,[204] or, in some provinces, if the infant's medical condition requires care by the mother.[205] The employee can commonly increase the basic maternity leave period by adding to it the statutory "parental" leave period,[206] which is commonly of equal duration, up to a maximum of 52 weeks.[207] Typically, any parental leave must begin immediately upon the expiry of the maternity leave, unless the employer and the employee agree otherwise.

ii) Is Maternity Leave with Pay?

All Canadian jurisdictions have adopted the recommendation of the International Labour Organization[208] that the state, not the employer,

---

201 *CLC*, above note 40, s. 206; *Man. ESC*, above note 106, s. 54(5); *Nfld. LSA*, above note 105, s. 40(2); *N.B. ESA*, above note 89, s. 43(1); *N.S. LSC*, above note 89, s. 59(1); *P.E.I. ESA*, above note 87, s. 20(1); *Ont. ESA*, above note 52, s. 46(2).

202 *B.C. ESA*, above note 43, s. 50(1); *Quebec LSA*, above note 106, s. 81.4; *Sask. LSA*, above note 58, s. 23(3).

203 *Alta. ESC*, above note 91, s. 46(1).

204 Examples: six weeks under the *B.C. ESA*, above note 43, ss. 50(2) & (3), and under the *Sask. LSA*, above note 58, s. 24.

205 Example: *Quebec LSA*, above note 106, s. 81.7(2).

206 Considered Section B(8)(b), below in this chapter.

207 Example: *N.S. LSC*, above note 89, s. 59B(4).

208 *ILO Maternity Protection Convention Revised*, No. 103 (1952).

should be responsible for ensuring the financial security of employees during maternity leave. Accordingly, the employment standards legislation acts do not oblige employers to grant maternity pay, but the *Employment Insurance Act*[209] entitles a biological mother who has worked the requisite 600 hours during the previous 52 weeks to receive employment insurance benefits at the rate of 55 percent of her insurable earnings, up to a maximum of $435 per week, for a maximum period of 15 weeks. (The $435 ceiling increases if the employee is within the definition of a low income family, currently $25,921 per year.) An employee can begin to receive benefits up to eight weeks before the expected date of birth.

Benefits cease to be payable seventeen weeks after either the actual birthdate or the expected birthdate, whichever is later. However, if the child is hospitalized due to a medical condition, benefits remain payable for the period of hospitalization, up to fifty-two weeks after the week of confinement. Furthermore, the mother can obtain additional income under the "parental benefits" provisions of the *Employment Insurance Act*, which allow the parents of a child to share, as they see fit, the statutory parental benefit of ten weeks' pay (calculated at the same rate as maternity benefits). The employee is also entitled to an additional five weeks of parental benefits if the child is six months of age or older upon arrival at home or if the child suffers from a physical, emotional, or psychological condition. Quebec is unique in providing qualified employees (and independent contractors) with additional money from a special government-administered fund, financed from contributions by all employers, employees, and independent contractors in the province.[210]

The employment standards statutes are generally structured so as to mesh with the *Employment Insurance Act*, thereby permitting employees to take full advantage of the Act's benefits. Furthermore, many employers "top up" these statutory benefits so that the mother suffers no financial loss as a result of having a child.

iii) When Does Maternity Leave Begin and End?
The employment standards acts commonly specify that a leave must commence within a stated time before the anticipated date of delivery[211] and must include a period of at least six weeks immediately after the

---

209   S.C. 1996, c. 23, ss. 12(3)(a) and 22. Because the federal government constantly amends the details of the system, the reader is advised to consult the regularly updated Service Canada website, online: www.hrsdc.gc.ca/en/ei/types/special. shtml#Maternity3.

210   The Quebec scheme is contained in *An Act Respecting Parental Insurance*, R.S.Q., c. A-29.011.

211   Example: 17 weeks under the *P.E.I. ESA*, above note 87, s. 20(1).

birth, unless the mother can obtain a medical certificate showing that she is fit to resume work before the six-week deadline. Otherwise, the employee is free to choose when her leave will begin and end, always assuming that she is capable of performing her job to the satisfaction of her employer. If the employer determines that the employee's pregnancy (or pregnancy-related sickness) incapacitates her from performing the duties of her position, and there is no alternative method of reasonably accommodating the employee short of causing the firm undue hardship, the employer can lay off the pregnant employee without offending the employment standards[212] or the human rights legislation.[213]

iv) Which Employees Are Qualified for Maternity Leave?

All jurisdictions except New Brunswick, Quebec, and British Columbia require a minimum period of continuous employment with the employer in order to qualify for maternity leave.[214] Casual workers who are hired for intermittent periods by several different employers may be prejudiced by this requirement. The Saskatchewan statute gives such workers some protection by entitling an employee to a maternity leave provided that she has been employed for at least twenty weeks by her current employer during the fifty-two weeks before the commencement date of her leave, even though the weeks may be broken up.[215] In order to qualify for maternity leave, the employee must normally give her employer written notice of her planned leave, supported by medical certification, within a specified period before her leave is to begin, although this requirement may be waived or varied in defined circumstances depending on the jurisdiction.[216]

v) Is the Employee Who Takes Maternity Leave Safeguarded against Penalization in Respect to Her Job Security and Other Terms and Conditions of Employment?

The employment standards and human rights legislation, in combination, afford extensive protections for the employee. First, the employee

---

212 Example: *CLC*, above note 40, ss. 208(2) and (4). The burden of proving such incapacity is generally placed on the employer under the employment standards acts.

213 The treatment of pregnancy under human rights statutes is examined in Chapter 7.

214 Examples: *CLC*, above note 40, s. 206 — 6 consecutive months; *Alta. ESC*, above note 91, s. 45 — 12 consecutive months; *Man. ESC*, above note 106, s. 53 — 7 consecutive months; *Nlfd. LSA*, above note 105, s. 40(1) — 20 consecutive weeks; *Ont. ESA*, above note 52, s. 46(1) — 13 weeks prior to the estimated date of delivery.

215 *Sask. LSA*, above note 58, s. 23(1)(a).

216 Example: *N.B. ESA*, above note 89, ss. 43(1) & (2).

is commonly entitled, at the end of her maternity leave, to be reinstated in her former position or to be re-engaged in a "comparable position with no less favourable wages and benefits."[217] Most employment standards acts reinforce this by specific provisions that prohibit employers from dismissing or laying off an employee due to her pregnancy or her application for maternity leave.[218] Sometimes, these provisions reverse onto the employer the legal burden of proving that its motive for penalizing the worker was unrelated to her pregnancy, the rationale being that the employer is best able to explain why it acted as it did.[219]

One might expect that if the employer has mixed motives for its actions—partially related to pregnancy and partially to some other factor—the actions would be unlawful, with the presence of a contributory factor being taken into account in fashioning an appropriate penalty. (For example, if a pregnant employee punches her boss and is fired because of the assault and the pregnancy, the dismissal would be unlawful as being partially related to pregnancy, but compensation would be reduced significantly due to her contributory misconduct and she might be denied reinstatement.) Nevertheless, some provinces' employment standards acts state that dismissal, suspension, or layoff is unlawful where the employer's reasons "solely" relate to pregnancy, which has been interpreted as exempting liability in mixed-motive situations.[220] Of course, in these provinces a mixed-motive dismissal, suspension, or layoff could still be successfully challenged under the human rights legislation, which clearly encompasses such conduct,[221] but human rights proceedings are extremely slow compared with proceedings under employment standards acts.

The above-mentioned provisions in employment standards and human rights statutes do not prevent an employer from refusing to reinstate an employee for legitimate business reasons—for example, if her job has been eliminated for *bona fide* economic reasons or if the

---

217 *B.C. ESA*, above note 43, s. 54(3); *Ont. ESA*, above note 52, s. 53.

218 Example: *Sask. LSA*, above note 58, s. 27.

219 Examples: *Nfld. LSA*, above note 105, s. 43.9(2); *Sask. LSA*, above note 58, s. 27(2).

220 *R. v. Pacific Western Airlines Ltd.* (1975), 75 C.L.L.C. ¶14,287, upheld (trial *de novo*) (*sub nom. C.A.L.F.A.A. v. Pacific Western Airlines Ltd.*) (1979), 105 D.L.R. (3d) 477 (B.C.S.C.), aff'd (1981), 81 C.L.L.C. ¶14,121 (B.C.C.A.), interpreting the word "solely" in s. 59.4 of the *CLC*, the predecessor to the current s. 209.3: see above note 40. Provinces currently using the "solely" formulation or its equivalent are *N.B. ESA*, above note 89, ss. 42, 44.04(1)(b); *Nfld. LSA*, above note 105, s. 43.9(1)(a), but, oddly, subsection (1)(b) omits this word; *P.E.I. ESA*, above note 87, s. 18.

221 Example: *Scott v. Foster Wheeler Ltd.* (1987), 16 C.C.E.L. 251 (Ont. Div. Ct.); see generally Chapter 7.

firm has suspended production during a market downswing. In such circumstances, the employment standards legislation in several provinces entitles the employee to first recall in her old position when work resumes or, if her position has disappeared, to re-engagement in a reasonably comparable alternative position if and when work resumes, subject only to any seniority system in place in the organization.[222] By the same token, the fact that an employee is on maternity leave does not prevent her from being dismissed if she commits an act of misconduct or gross incompetence.

The employment standards legislation prevents the employer from penalizing an employee in regard to other terms and conditions of employment by reason of her pregnancy. Thus, where a pregnant employee is reinstated in her position at the end of her leave, she is entitled to any increases in pay or benefits that were applied to the position during her absence, provided, of course, that such increases were attached to the position rather than given as a reward for the personal efforts of the temporary incumbent.[223] Conversely, if the wages and benefits in the position were reduced during the leave, she would presumably receive the lower amount.[224] If the employee has to be re-engaged in a different position than that which she previously occupied—for example, if her old position has been eliminated for economic reasons—the terms and conditions of employment must be no less favourable to her than before and the new position must be "comparable" to the old one in regard to status, effort, responsibility, skill, physical and psychological working conditions, and geographical location. The employer also cannot treat a maternity leave as rupturing the accrual of continuous service for the purpose of seniority-related benefits, and the employee's seniority continues to accrue during the leave.[225] Indeed, in most provinces the employment standards acts require the employer to continue paying its share of the contributions to benefit plans, provided that the employee still pays her share.[226] This requirement is the nearest the employment standards acts come to forcing employers to give "paid" maternity leave. As well, the human rights legislation (and, in the federal jurisdiction, the employment

---

222 Example: Alberta, where the right to recall lasts for one year only. In British Columbia, Nova Scotia, Prince Edward Island, Quebec, and Ontario no time limitation on the right to recall applies.

223 Example: *Ont. ESA*, above note 52, s. 53(3).

224 This is expressed in *Quebec LSA*, above note 106, s. 81.17. .

225 Examples: *N.S. LSC*, above note 90, s. 59G(1)(b); *Sask. LSA*, above note 58, s. 26.

226 However, the *N.S. LSC*, above note 89, s. 59F(2) is unique in making the employee responsible for paying the employer's costs if she wishes to maintain benefits during her leave.

standards legislation[227]) compels employers to notify employees taking maternity leave of any training or promotion opportunities.

The foregoing are quite obvious ways in which a pregnant employee could be penalized because of taking a pregnancy leave. However, less obvious forms of penalization may also occur, especially in regard to the treatment of pregnancy under sickness and disability insurance plans. Traditionally, many such plans have not only excluded pregnancy from the list of compensable conditions, but have also disqualified pregnant employees from receiving benefits for non–pregnancy-related illnesses that coincide with a maternity leave. In its landmark decision in *Brooks v. Canada Safeway Ltd.*,[228] the Supreme Court of Canada held that the ban on "sex" discrimination in the human rights legislation, which the Court ruled to implicitly encompass pregnancy, prohibits employers from treating non-pregnant employees more favourably than pregnant employees under sickness and disability plans. The rationale underlying the *Brooks* decision is that women should not suffer any employment disadvantage by virtue of choosing to have children.[229] Thus, a plan that disentitles employees from receiving sickness benefits if they become pregnant is unlawful.[230] Furthermore, a plan that exempts pregnancy from insurance coverage is unlawful.[231] Employers must take the initiative in ensuring that pregnancy is included under their sickness and disability plans.

vi) What Is the Role of Occupational Health and Safety Legislation in Protecting the Pregnant Employee?[232]

If an employee honestly and reasonably believes that performing a work assignment may endanger her health and safety or that of her baby, she can refuse to perform the assignment under the provisions of

---

227 *CLC*, above note 40, s. 209, if the employee requests are in writing.
228 [1989] 1 S.C.R. 1219 [*Brooks*]. See also *Alberta Hospital Assn. v. Parcels* (1992), 1 Alta. L.R. (3d) 332 (Q.B.); *Stagg v. Intercontinental Packers Ltd.* (1992), 18 C.H.R.R. D/392 (Sask. Bd. Inq.); *Crook v. Ontario Cancer Treatment and Research Foundation (No. 3)* (1996), 96 C.L.L.C. ¶230-044, especially para. 145,461 (Ont. Bd. Inq.).
229 For the argument that market solutions afford more just and efficient safeguards of pregnant employees than human rights legislation, see R. Knopff & T. Flanagan, *Human Rights and Social Technology: The New War on Discrimination* (Ottawa: Carleton University Press, 1989) 149; and R.A. Epstein, *Forbidden Grounds: The Case against Employment Discrimination Laws* (Cambridge, MA: Harvard University Press, 1992) 329–50.
230 *Brooks*, above note 228 at 1236.
231 *Ibid.* at 1237–38.
232 This legislation is examined in Chapter 8.

the health and safety legislation in all jurisdictions. On the other side of the coin, the employer can unilaterally reassign or lay off a pregnant employee because the employer reasonably and honestly believes that the health and safety of the employee herself, her baby, or other workers is endangered.[233]

b) Parental Leave

In all jurisdictions the employment standards acts provide for parental leave.[234] The parental leave provisions are identical to the maternity leave provisions in respect of the requisite qualifying service and the protections against dismissal or other penalization. The only differences are in the length of parental leave—which, depending on the province, may be longer or shorter than maternity leave—and in various housekeeping matters, such as when parental leave begins. In most jurisdictions, any employee, male or female, who is responsible for caring for the child can elect to take parental leave,[235] except in Nova Scotia and New Brunswick where it appears that only natural parents or parents who are legally adopting the child qualify.[236] Either parent may use the statutory parental leave, and parents can agree to share it between themselves if they so choose. The mother may use parental leave to top up her statutory maternity leave up to a maximum of fifty-two weeks.[237] Parental leave is unpaid under the employment standards legislation, but the employee can claim benefits under the *Employment Insurance Act*, as is also the case with maternity leave.[238]

c) Adoption Leave

All Canadian jurisdictions entitle the employee who adopts a child to a leave of absence. Typically, adopting a child would be encompassed by the parental leave provisions described above; however, Newfoundland and Saskatchewan have separate adoption leave sections, albeit substantially similar to the parental leave provisions.[239] As with pregnancy and parental leaves, there are provisions in respect of the requisite qualifying service and the protections against dismissal or other penalization. They dovetail with the *Employment Insurance Act*.

---

233 See also the *Quebec LSA*, above note 106, s. 122, which allows the employer unilaterally to transfer a pregnant employee if the employer judges that the safety of the employee or her baby are threatened.

234 Examples: *CLC*, above note 40, s. 206(1); *Man. ESC*, above note 106, s. 58(1).

235 *CLC, ibid.*, s. 206(1)(b).

236 *N.B. ESA*, above note 89, s. 44.02(2); *N.S. LSC*, above note 89, s. 59B(i).

237 Example: *N.S. LSC, ibid.*, s. 59B(4).

238 See Section B(8)(a), above in this chapter.

239 *Nfld. LSA*, above note 105, s. 43; *Sask. LSA*, above note 58, s. 29.2.

d) Compassionate Care Leave

The federal jurisdiction and four provinces entitle the employee to an unpaid leave of absence of up to eight weeks to care for or support a family member who has a serious medical condition as defined in the statute, generally an illness having a "significant risk of death."[240] The Arthurs Report recommended that requiring the illness to have a "significant risk of death" within a proscribed time is unduly callous and should be replaced by making reference to a "serious" illness or accident.[241] Except for the federal jurisdiction and British Columbia, where no qualifying period of prior employment applies, the individual must have been employed with an employer for a minimum time to qualify for this leave—three months of continuous employment in Nova Scotia, compared with thirty days, continuous or not, in Newfoundland and Manitoba. The employee must provide the employer with advanced notice of the leave, supported by a physician's certificate corroborating the family member's illness. Although the leave is unpaid, the employee is entitled to receive prescribed benefits under the *Employment Insurance Act*.[242] The federal statute is unique in requiring that compassionate leave be shared between two or more employees who work for the same employer.[243] As with pregnancy and parental leaves, employees who take compassionate leave are protected against dismissal or other penalization.

e) Family Leave

Seven provinces allow the employee to take unpaid family leave to deal with emergencies involving medical, dental, educational, and other personal-care needs, including those of defined immediate family members.[244] The growing number of working women with children badly

---

240 *CLC*, above note 40, s. 206.3, where the illness must have a significant risk of death within 26 weeks; *B.C. ESA*, above note 43, s. 52.1, where the illness must have a significant risk of death within 26 weeks; *Man. ESC*, above note 106, s. 59.2, where the illness need only be serious; *Nfld. LSA*, above note 105, ss. 43.13–43.16, where the illness must have a significant risk of death; *N.S. LSC*, above note 89, s. 60E, where the illness must have a significant risk of death.

241 Above note 4 at 158–59.

242 The details of these rules change constantly, the latest updates being collated on the Service Canada website, online: www.hrsdc.gc.ca/en/ei/types/compassionate _care.shtml.

243 The Arthurs Report recommended the removal of this requirement: see above note 4 at 158–59.

244 *B.C. ESA*, above note 43, s. 52; *Man. ESC*, above note 106, s. 59.3; *N.B. ESA*, above note 89, s. 44.022; *Nfld. LSA*, above note 105, s. 43.11; *N.S. LSC*, above note 89, s. 60E; *Ont. ESA*, above note 52, s. 51(1); *Quebec LSA*, above note 106, s. 81.2.

need the flexibility that such a leave would give them.[245] Typically, the maximum period of leave is relatively short, ranging from ten days per year in Quebec to three days per year in Manitoba and New Brunswick. The employee is obliged to give the employer reasonable advance notice of an intention to take such a leave. Because these leaves are short term, the employee is disallowed from receiving benefits under the *Employment Insurance Act*, unlike in the case of the lengthier leaves described above. In addition, in all jurisdictions the prohibition against "family status" discrimination under the human rights legislation requires the employer to reasonably accommodate an employee who requests leave of absence to deal with the personal needs of immediate family members.[246] Again, the employer cannot dismiss or otherwise penalize an employee for taking such a leave.

f) Sick Leave

An employee who is absent due to sickness may claim an unpaid "family" leave in those provinces conferring this right.[247]As well, the employment standards acts in the federal jurisdiction, Newfoundland, and Saskatchewan[248] make it unlawful for an employer to dismiss, suspend, lay off, or otherwise discipline an employee "because" he or she has been absent from work due to an illness or injury for less than the maximum period specified in the statute.[249] In Newfoundland the maximum period of protected sick leave is five days;[250] in the federal jurisdiction, 12 weeks;[251] and in Saskatchewan, twelve days in the case of a "non serious illness or injury," increasing to 12 weeks in the case of a "serious" one or to 26 weeks where the employee is receiving compensation under the province's *Workers' Compensation Act*.[252] In all three jurisdictions, the employee must have the requisite continuous service with his or her employer—six months in Newfoundland, three months

---

245 Thompson Commission, above note 8 at 92; *Advisory Group Report*, above note 41 at 60–61.
246 See Chapter 7.
247 See Section B(8)(e), above in this chapter.
248 *CLC*, above note 40, s. 239; *Nfld. LSA*, above note 105, s. 43.10(2); *Sask. LSA*, above note 58, s. 44.2. Note that in the federal jurisdiction, special provisions come into play where the employee is absent from work due to a "work related illness or injury." See the *CLC*, *ibid.*, s. 239.1, and *CLSR*, above note 111, s. 34.
249 However, the *CLC*, *ibid.*, s. 239(1.1) provides that if the employee cannot do the old job when he or she resumes work by reason of an illness, the employer can assign the employee to a different job at different rates of pay and benefits.
250 *Nfld. LSA*, above note 105, s. 43.10(2).
251 *CLC*, above note 40, s. 239(1)(b).
252 *Sask. LSA*, above note 58, s. 44.2(1)(b) & (2).

in the federal jurisdiction, and thirteen weeks in Saskatchewan—in order to qualify for this protection.

Even though other provinces have not included express sick leave entitlements in their employment standards acts, an employee who is dismissed or otherwise penalized for absence from work due to sickness may have legal recourse under other legislation—for example, the human rights legislation if the sickness is a protected "disability" as defined therein[253]—and may be able to sue for wrongful dismissal at common law.[254]

g)   Bereavement Leave

In the federal jurisdiction and all provinces (except for Alberta), the employee is entitled to a defined leave of absence—three days is the norm, but there are variations— upon the death of defined relatives.[255] The recent proliferation in multi-generational families and common law relationships has resulted in a broadening of the definitions of which relatives will qualify the employee for a leave, the traditional view being that only members of the employee's natural family or family by marriage or adoption would count. [256] In Saskatchewan, for example, a "spouse" is defined as a person with whom the employee has cohabitated for at least two years or for a lesser period if the employee has cohabitated with the person "in a relationship of some permanence" and they are the parents of a child.[257] Even more broadly, in British Columbia the list includes "any person who lives with an employee as a member of the employee's family."[258]

Bereavement leave is generally unpaid, except in the federal jurisdiction, Quebec, and Newfoundland, where payment is required in

---

253   See Chapter 7.

254   See Chapter 9, Section C(6).

255   *CLC*, above note 40, s. 210 and *CLSR*, above note 111, s. 33; *B.C. ESA*, above note 43, s. 33 and 1(i) "immediate family"; *Man. ESC*, above note 106, s. 59.4; *N.B. ESA*, above note 89, s. 44.03; *Nfld. LSA*, above note 105, s. 43.10(1); *N.S. LSC*, above note 89, s. 60(A)(i); *P.E.I. ESA*, above note 87, s. 23; *Quebec LSA*, above note 106, ss. 80–80.2; *Sask. LSA*, above note 58, s. 29.3. In Ontario, there is no specific bereavement leave provision, but the employee could use an "emergency" leave under the *Ont. ESA*, above note 52, s. 50.

256   Thompson Commission, above note 8 at 91.

257   *Sask. LSA*, above note 58, s. 29.3(1)(b)(ii). In a similar vein, see the definition of "consort" in the *Quebec LSA*, above note 106, which includes unmarried persons who have been living together as husband and wife for at least one year.

258   *B.C. ESA*, above note 43, s. 1(i) "immediate family." In a similar vein, see the *CLSR*, above note 111, s. 33(f), which includes "any relative of the employee who resides permanently in the employee's household or with whom the employee permanently resides."

relatively narrowly defined circumstances. Generally, there is no minimum seniority requirement for bereavement leave, except in Saskatchewan and the federal jurisdiction, where three continuous months of employment must have been served, and in Newfoundland, where the period is one month of continuous employment. The maximum length of leave varies, ranging from one day in Nova Scotia to five days in Saskatchewan and New Brunswick. Generally, the leave must commence immediately after the death of the relative and be taken in one block, something that could be problematic for employees whose cultural values entail more protracted or fragmented funeral celebrations.[259] Although the human rights legislation would require the employer to reasonably accommodate such employees under the prohibitions against religion, creed, and ethnicity,[260] enforcement would be simpler if a similar duty were included in the employment standards acts.

h) Time off to Vote

In order to facilitate the operation of our democratic electoral processes, legislation is in place at the federal and provincial levels to ensure that employers give employees reasonable time off work to vote in federal,[261] provincial,[262] and municipal elections.[263] Normally, the employer is allowed to decide precisely when the requisite time off must be taken. Breach of the legislation is a criminal offence that may result in the employer being fined or even imprisoned.

i) Possible New Leaves

In order to secure a decent balance between work and life for the employee, as well as advance the general public interest, the enactment of further leaves of absence for other purposes, such as those outlined below, requires serious consideration.

---

259 Arthurs Report, above note 4 at 154–55.
260 See Chapter 7.
261 *Canada Elections Act*, R.S.C. 1985, c. E-2, which entitles eligible voters in federal elections to have four consecutive hours off work with no loss of pay while the polls are open.
262 All provinces have election acts governing provincial elections: e.g., British Columbia *Election Act*, R.S.B.C. 1996, c. 106, s. 74(1), which allows four hours off with pay to vote. However, there are variations among the provinces that must be consulted.
263 Most provinces have special statutes regulating municipal elections: e.g., Alberta *Local Authorities Election Act*, R.S.A. 2000, c. L-21; Ontario *Municipal Elections Act, 1996*, S.O. 1996, c. 32.

- Canada's military commitments cannot be effectively implemented without a significant reserve force. Legislation is necessary in order to protect reservists whose duties require them to be absent from their civilian jobs. So far, Manitoba and Prince Edward Island provide that a reservist who is called up for military duty is entitled to an unpaid leave of absence "for the period necessary to accommodate the period of military service."[264] Thus, in Manitoba the employee must give the employer as much advance notice as is "reasonable and practicable" in the circumstances. The employee must also give the employer at least two weeks of notice of his or her return to the workplace; the employer can defer re-entry for up to two weeks. In order to qualify for this protection, the employee must have seven consecutive months of prior service with the employer. This model could be usefully adopted in other Canadian jurisdictions.
- In the "new economy," where highly skilled jobs, lifelong learning, and frequent career changes are essential, it would benefit the employee, employers, and society in general to provide the employee with periodic leaves of absence for advancing his or her education and professional training. Indeed, an ILO convention endorses this form of leave, as did the 1994 federal Advisory Committee.[265] Currently, the closest any Canadian jurisdiction comes to providing educational leave can be found in some health and safety acts, where health and safety representatives are entitled to time off work for training and education.
- It would enhance labour mobility if employees were entitled to take unpaid leaves of absence to attend job interviews.
- Legislating public emergency leaves of absence for employees who may be quarantined as a result of flu pandemics or SARS would be helpful; such leaves would also benefit employees unable to come to work due to a natural disaster, such as a flood or earthquake.[266]
- Court leaves of absence are legitimately required for employees who participate in legal proceedings, whether as voluntary litigants, subpoenaed witnesses, or jurors, in order to ensure that the legal process operates fairly and efficiently.[267]
- Leaves for residual, multiple purposes were recommended as far back as 1987. The Donner Report recommended that an employee with ten years of prior service with an employer be entitled to one

---

264 *Man. ESC*, above note 106, s. 59.5; *P.E.I. ESA*, above note 87, s. 23.1.
265 *Advisory Group Report*, above note 41 at 61; *International Labour Organisation Convention of Paid Educational Leave, 1974* (No. 140).
266 Arthurs Report, above note 4 at 159.
267 *Ibid.*

week's unpaid leave annually for each subsequent year of service, increasing to four weeks of leave in the four years immediately preceding retirement.[268] The employee could use this leave for whatever purpose he or she sees fit. Legislating the leave would also enhance job creation.

9) "Precarious" Work

The term "precarious" work usually refers to working arrangements that give the employer the flexibility to call in the employee on demand; to release the employee without notice or other severance benefits; to compensate the employee on a payment-by-results basis; to require the employee to provide necessary tools, equipment, and materials; and even to require the employee to work from home. Typically, these arrangements do not fit the traditional pattern of forty hours of work, fifty-two weeks per year with the same employer who guarantees its employees a reasonable measure of economic and job security.

The term encompasses a wide variety of working relationships, notably self-employed contractors, casuals, part-timers, homeworkers, employees in government-subsidized job creation programs, and temporary employees of labour supply agencies. Typically, these workers are relatively low paid and they frequently receive less pay for work equivalent to that performed by regular employees; they have no job security or severance entitlements; they do not receive the same economic fringe benefits, seniority rights, and career advancement opportunities as regular employees; and because of their large supply in the labour market, they have minimal bargaining power to negotiate decent terms and conditions of employment. These working arrangements predominate among women, immigrants, members of visible minorities, and the relatively young, giving the problem a distinct human rights hue.

The incidence of this type of work has expanded substantially in Canada (and elsewhere) with the advent of the "new economy."[269] Several factors have contributed to this spread: the increasing popularity of

268 Donner Report, above note 8 at132.
269 Arthurs Report, above note 4 at 24–31, 61–66, 230–50; R. Chaykowski, *Canadian Workers Most in Need of Labour Standards Protection: A Review of the Nature and Extent of Vulnerability in the Canadian Labour Market and Federal Jurisdiction*, Research Study Prepared for the Federal Labour Standards Review Commission (Ottawa: Human Resources and Skills Development Canada, 2006); K. Rittich, *Vulnerability at Work: Legal and Policy Issues in the New Economy*, Report for the Law Commission of Canada (Ottawa: Law Commission of Canada, 2004).

just-in-time production systems pioneered in Japan; technological advances that allow firms to complete short-term customized orders for their buyers and that allow firms to outsource their labour needs; the growth of service industries, where irregular hours and short-term fluctuations occur to meet the needs of customers; the pressure from overseas competitors on Canadian employers to reduce their labour costs by substituting cheaper "precarious" workers for regular employees; and the growing supply of females, students, immigrants, Aboriginals, early retirees, and other groups in the labour market who are willing to accept these forms of work out of necessity or to suit their lifestyles. As a result of these forces, many modern organizations have an inner core of permanent full-time employees who perform the key functions of the enterprise, surrounded by concentric circles of part-timers, casuals, self-employed contractors, agency-supplied "temporaries," and others who are only called upon when needed. Put simply, these archetypal vulnerable workers provide the *raison d'etre* for labour law's existence.[270] The problem for employment standards legislation, therefore, is to ensure that these groups of atypical workers are not exploited, while at the same time ensuring that the competitiveness of Canadian employers, from which society as a whole benefits, is not jeopardized.

This section focuses on the following forms of precarious work: (1) part-time work, wherein the employee regularly works significantly less than the standard weekly or monthly hours of work for the firm;[271] (2) casual work, wherein the employee is called upon to work intermittently, in order to meet an employer's short-term need for extra workers;[272] (3) homeworkers, who carry on their employment duties primarily in their private residence;[273] and (4) temporaries supplied by an employment agency. Clearly, these categories can overlap, so that an employee may fall within two or more of them simultaneously.

---

270 The seminal analysis of this role of labour law is enunciated by O. Kahn-Freund, *Labour and the Law* (London: Stevens, 1972) c. 1.

271 This definition follows that of the International Labor Organization, namely, "regular, voluntary employment carried out during working hours distinctly shorter than normal," cited by H. Krahn, "Non-Standard Work Arrangements" (1991) 3 Perspectives on Labour and Income 35 at 41, online: www.statcan.ca/english/studies/75-001/archive/e-pdf/e-9145.pdf. However, Statistics Canada defines "part-time" workers as those persons who usually work fewer than 30 hours per week: Statistics Canada, *Guide to The Labour Force Survey* (Ottawa: Statistics Canada, 1994).

272 This definition is contained in Commission of Inquiry into Part-Time Work, *Part-Time Work in Canada: Report of the Commission of Inquiry into Part-Time Work* by J. Wallace (Ottawa: Labour Canada, 1983) at 37 [Wallace Report].

273 This definition of "homework" is contained in the *Ont. ESA*, above note 52, s. 1.

a) Part-Timers[274]

Not all part-timers fit the mould of vulnerable "precarious" employment described above. Many of them prefer part-time work due to its
flexibility, and their employers treat them decently.[275] However, this
reality is not universal. Many part-timers are relatively low paid;[276]
they receive less remuneration than full-time workers for performing
equivalent work; they are not entitled to the same fringe benefits as
full-timers; and they have less security of tenure, fewer career advancement opportunities, and reduced seniority protection.

In some provinces, the employment legislation treats part-timers
less advantageously than full-timers.[277] Given the fact that most part-
time work is done by females, such legislation is potentially susceptible to challenge under section 15 of the *Charter* as a form of "indirect"
discrimination.[278] Most provinces have now removed from their employment standards statutes many of the provisions that particularly
disadvantage part-timers[279] and have required employers to allow part-
timers with defined minimum seniority to participate in private occupational pension plans.[280]

Nevertheless, the response of most provinces to the other problems
of part-time work has been slow. Only Saskatchewan has taken the
major step of requiring employers to provide defined part-timers with
the same medical, dental, disability, and life insurance coverage, on a

---

274 Useful analyses from the enormous literature on this topic include the Wallace
Report, above note 272; I. Zeytinoglu & G. Cooke, "Non-Standard Work and
Benefits: Has Anything Changed since the Wallace Report?" (2005) 60 R.I./I.R.
29 ["Anything Changed?"].

275 Arthurs Report, above note 4 at 237.

276 "The plight of part-timers was originally exposed in 1983 by the Wallace
Report, above note 272. The problem still persists: see "Anything Changed?,"
above note 274 at 29.

277 As in Saskatchewan, where the Minimum Wage Board is empowered to fix
a reduced minimum wage for part-timers under *Sask. LSA*, above note 58, s.
15(4)(b). As yet no such regulation has been issued.

278 By analogy, see *Fenton*, above note 36. See also *Rinner-Kuhn v. FWW Spezial
Gebaudereinigung GmbH & Co. KG*, [1989] I.R.L.R. 493 (E.C.J.), where a German law exempting part-timers from sick benefits was found to violate the sex
discrimination ban under EEC labour law.

279 The disadvantageous treatment of part-timers under employment standards
acts in the past is examined in G. England, *Part-time, Casual and Other Atypical
Workers: A Legal View*, Research and Current Issues Series No. 48 (Kingston,
ON: Queen's University Industrial Relations Centre, 1987) at 8–10. Almost all
of those disadvantages have now been removed from the legislation.

280 Example: New Brunswick *Pension Benefits Act*, S.N.B. 1987, c. P-5.1, s. 29(5).

pro-rated basis, as is made available to their full-time employees.[281] In Quebec,[282] employers are prohibited from paying an employee a lower rate of wages than that granted to other employees for the "sole reason" that he or she "usually works less hours each week." The Quebec statute also prohibits employers from discriminating against part-timers regarding vacation benefits.[283] Several public inquiries into part-time work have unanimously recommended that employers be legally obliged to pay part-timers the same wages for performing substantially similar work as full-timers and to make available to part-timers, on a pro-rated basis where applicable, the same fringe benefits and other employment opportunities that full-timers are entitled to.[284] The reluctance of provincial governments to adopt these measures is probably explained by the fear that the added costs to employers would weaken their competitiveness and cause them to hire fewer part-timers.

b) Casuals

Most casuals squarely fit the mould of vulnerability described above. The fact that they work for short-term periods with one or more employers creates additional disadvantages under employment standards acts.[285] For example, they may be unable to accrue seniority with an employer for the purpose of important statutory benefits, such as notice of termination, leaves of absence, and annual vacations: entitlement to such benefits and their amounts usually depend on an employee having an uninterrupted relationship with an employer. Some provinces have sought to ameliorate this problem by deeming successive periods of employment with the same employer to be "continuous," so long as the hiatus between periods does not exceed specified durations.[286]

---

281 *Sask. LSA*, above note 58, s. 45.1.

282 *Quebec LSA*, above note 106, s. 41.1. But this obligation is qualified by the *Regulation Respecting the Lifting of the Suspension and the Application of Section 41.1 of the Act Respecting Labour Standards for Certain Employees*, O.C. 570-93, 21 April 1993, G.O.Q. 1993.II.2607.

283 *Quebec LSA, ibid.*, s. 74.1.

284 Wallace Report, above note 272; Thompson Commission, above note 8 at 101; *Advisory Group Report*, above note 41 at 59; Economic Council of Canada, *Good Jobs, Bad Jobs: Employment in the Service Economy* (Ottawa: Economic Council of Canada, 1990). In contrast, the Arthurs Report recommended that part-timers receive the same pay as full-timers who perform equivalent jobs, but failed to recommend that they be entitled to receive the same fringe benefits on a pro-rated basis: above note 4 at 238.

285 Arthurs Report, *ibid.* at 238–39.

286 For example, under the *Alta. ESC*, above note 91, s. 54, the maximum hiatus is three months, but this applies only to the individual notice of termination provisions. The employment standards acts in Ontario, Nova Scotia, Saskatchewan,

Casual workers may suffer in provinces where entitlement to a paid statutory holiday depends on the employee having worked a designated minimum number of hours preceding the holiday. The British Columbia statute has responded to this problem by entitling employees who have worked fewer than fifteen of the thirty days prior to a statutory holiday to receive holiday pay on a pro-rated basis; an employee's total wages, excluding overtime pay, are divided by fifteen for the thirty-day period.[287] Moreover, in some jurisdictions, the employment standards legislation may exclude casual workers, exempt them from specified benefits under it, or provide them with benefits inferior to those of regular employees. Again, given that the casual work is dominated by women, immigrants, and members of visible minorities, legislation that disadvantages casual workers is potentially susceptible to challenge of indirect discrimination under section 15 of the *Charter*.[288] In order to address the problem of casual workers not having fringe benefits, such as medical, dental and life insurance, and pensions, the Arthurs Report recommended establishing a "benefits bank" through which employment-related benefits could be purchased by workers or by their various employers.[289] The model would resemble the current Registered Retirement Savings Plan under which the employee and any of his or her employers can make periodic contributions to a mutual fund on the employee's behalf.

c)   Homeworkers[290]

Today, the main area of growth in homeworking is data processing on a home-based computer (commonly referred to as "telecommuting"), although the phenomenon also persists in more familiar areas, such as textiles and light manufacturing. The main disadvantage with homeworking is the difficulty in enforcing the employee's rights under the employment standards and other protective legislation. Indeed, the individual homeworker may deliberately disregard legislated standards on hours of work, rest breaks, and health and safety, in order to earn as much as possible in the minimum time.

---

and the federal jurisdiction also contain "bridging" provisions, but with different maximum durations and applying to different benefits provided under the acts.

287 *B.C. ESR*, above note 58, s. 24.

288 Above note 30.

289 Above note 4 at 239–41.

290 See generally G. Schneider de Villegas, "Home Work: A Case for Social Protection" (1990) 129 Int'l Lab. Rev. 423; C. Lipsig-Mummé, "The Renaissance of Homeworking in Developed Economies" (1983) 38 R. I. 545; *Advisory Group Report*, above note 41 at 33–35.

The 1994 *Advisory Group Report* recommended that all provinces establish a registry for the purpose of reporting information on the numbers and identities of homeworkers and the details of their wages, working hours, and other terms and conditions of employment. Doing so would facilitate enforcement of employment standards legislation.[291] Manitoba and Ontario are the only provinces to have established government-maintained registries of homeworkers, but these were dismantled in 1998 and 2000, respectively, presumably to minimize public expenditures. Today, no Canadian jurisdiction operates such a registry.

Homeworkers are covered by the employment standards acts in all Canadian jurisidictions, assuming they have "employee" status under the general test. Generally homeworkers are entitled to the same rights under the legislation as other employees. Indeed, some provinces have enacted special safeguards for homeworkers, such as in Ontario where the employer must provide the employee with written particulars of the compensation system, especially regarding how pay is calculated under a system of piece work.[292] Similarly, in Manitoba the employer not only must maintain comprehensive records of the names, addresses, hours of work, and compensation earned by homeworkers whom it employs, but also the director of employment standards has the discretion to impose any conditions and limitations on an employer regarding the wages paid to homeworkers that he or she considers are necessary to ensure compliance with the legislation.[293] As well, Ontario entitles homeworkers to 110 percent of the standard minimum wage to cover the additional costs of working out of their residences.[294]

d) Agency Workers

In 2000, of the 2.8 million temporary workers in Canada (representing almost 19 percent of the Canadian workforce), between 20 and 25 percent of those temporary workers were assigned to user firms through temporary work agencies.[295] These employees are predominantly women, immigrants, young persons, members of ethnic minorities, and older workers.[296] Many of these workers may be self-employed con-

---

291 *Ibid.* at 58.

292 *Ontario Exemption Reg.*, above note 123, s. 12.

293 *Man. ESC*, above note 106, s. 80.

294 *Ontario Exemption Reg.*, above note 123, s. 5(4).

295 T. Newton, "Report on the 2000 Survey of Employment Services" (2000) at 7, online: www.statcan.ca/english/sdds/document/4718_D3_T9_V1_E.pdf.

296 P. Andersson, "Other Forms of Employment: Temporary Employment Agecies and Self Employment" (Institute for the Study of Labour, 2004) at 3, online: www.ssrn.com/abstract=556142.

tractors and therefore excluded from the employment standards legislation.[297]

The problem with agency-supplied labour is when it is used as a disguised form of "permanent" employment to evade the worker's statutory and common law protections; otherwise, it is legitimate for employers to use it to find specialized workers, to provide training for their own employees, to meet periods of peak demand, or to cover temporary leaves of absence. Agency workers face an array of disadvantages compared to permanent employees: they receive less pay for doing comparable work; they receive few fringe benefits or career development opportunities from the agency or the user firm; and they are sometimes prevented from applying for permanent positions by the user firms.[298]

Nevertheless, as yet the employment standards legislation in Canada does almost nothing to safeguard these workers. Saskatchewan and Quebec are exceptional in making the user company vicariously liable for unpaid wages that the agency owes its employees.[299] This provision is aimed at the fly-by-night labour contractor that is either unwilling or unable to fulfill its statutory and common law obligations to its employees. The effect is to give the user company an incentive to verify that the agency is reliable, and the user may even require the agency to post a security bond as a condition to obtaining the contract.

In British Columbia, too, the user is made jointly and severally liable for unpaid wages, but only in the case of "farm labour contractors" as defined in the Act.[300] The British Columbia act also establishes a licensing system for farm labour contractors that seeks to ensure their reliability. If an employer uses the services of an unlicensed contractor, the employer is deemed to "employ" the contractor's workers for the purpose of providing them with all rights and benefits under the *Employment Standards Act*.[301]

The Arthurs Report recommended that the user company and the agency be made jointly and severally liable for unpaid wages owed to the agency's employees.[302] In additon, it recommended that the disguised "permanent" employment problem be addressed by deeming temporary employees who have been employed for one year by a user company, whether on a continuous basis or not, to have passed the

---

297 See Chapter 2.
298 See the Arthurs Report, above note 4 at 233–37.
299 *Quebec LSA*, above note 106, s. 95; *Sask. LSA*, above note 58, s. 53.
300 *B.C. ESA*, above note 43, s. 30.
301 *Ibid.*, s. 13(2).
302 Above note 4 at 236.

probation period and to be considered for permanent employment on the same basis as the regular employees. The employer would also have to give temporary employees written notice of the duration of their employment and the conditions under which they may become eligible for permanent employment. As well, the report recommended that temporary workers who have worked for the same employer for periods that cumulatively total at least one year should be entitled to the same pay as regular employees receive for equivalent jobs, and should be deemed to have completed the period of continuous employment required for all statutory benefits, so long as the interval between successive periods of service does not exceed sixty days.[303] As yet, these recommendations have not been enacted in any Canadian jurisdiction.

The safeguards that exist for temporary agency workers are found almost exclusively in legislation requiring that employment agencies be registered and monitored by a designated government department.[304] This legislation, however, is more concerned with assuring the financial and organizational viability of the agency than with directly regulating its substantive employment practices; however, it does commonly prohibit agencies from charging the employee a fee. As well, in some provinces designated sectors are subject to special regulation, as in British Columbia where extensive monitoring (including a requirement of compulsory licensing) by the director of employment standards is imposed on "farm labour contractors" and "silviculture contractors" because of the past history of exploitation and abuse of employees in these sectors.[305]

10) Wage Discrimination: Equal Pay Legislation

In Canada, there is a difference between the amount of remuneration received by male and female employees. In 2005, the level of female earnings was approximately 64 percent of the level of male earnings.[306] The difference between the two levels is commonly referred to as the "wage gap." Despite strenuous legislative attempts to narrow this wage

303   *Ibid.* at 237.
304   Examples: Alberta *Employment Agency Business Licensing Regulations*, Alta. Reg. 189/1999; *B.C. ESR*, above note 58, ss. 2–4; Manitoba *Employment Services Act*, C.C.S.M. c. E100, and *Employment Agencies Licensing Regulation*, Man. Reg. 98/87 R; Saskatchewan *Employment Agencies Act*, R.S.S. 1978, c. E-9.
305   *B.C. ESA*, above note 43, ss. 12.1 and 13, and *B.C. ESR*, above note 58, s. 5.
306   Canadian Labour Congress, *Equality for All: Women in the Workforce; Still a Long Way from Equality* (Ottawa: Canadian Labour Congress, 2008) at 8, citing data from the 2005 Statistics Canada Survey.

gap over the past twenty-five years, the gap persists. For example, in 2005 average annual earnings of full-time women workers equalled 64 percent compared with 61.7 percent in 2000 and 64 percent in the early 1980s.[307] The problem is exacerbated by the fact that the wage gap is highest among females who are Aboriginal, from visible minorities, or disabled. Although the wage gap exists across all occupations and levels of education, it is highest among private sector firms with 100 or fewer employees.

Economists disagree about the precise size of the wage gap as well as its causes. Recent studies suggest that the proportion of the wage gap that is attributable to the discriminatory undervaluation of female work within the same organization appears to be somewhere between 5 and 10 percent.[308] The remainder is attributable to productivity differences between males and females caused by factors such as their different qualifications, education, and work experience, and by the tendency of women to crowd into relatively low-paid occupations.[309] There is legislation in all Canadian provinces and the federal jurisdiction that seeks to eradicate discrimination caused by the discriminatory undervaluation of female work.[310] It deserves emphasis that despite the lofty nomenclature often attached to this legislation—in many jurisdictions, for example, it is called "pay equity" legislation—it deals with only a relatively small cause of wage inequality—namely, sex discriminatory job evaluation—and consequently, will not eliminate the wage gap. The attraction of the nomenclature, of course, is its political appeal; who, after all, can oppose *equity*? Indeed, there is a plethora of international

---

307 *Ibid*; *Pay Equity: A New Approach to a Fundamental Right*, Pay Equity Task Force Report by B. Bilson (Ottawa: Pay Equity Task Force, 2004) at 12 [Pay Equity Task Force Report].

308 M. Gunderson, "Discrimination, Equal Pay and Equal Opportunities in the Labour Market" in W.C. Riddell, ed., *Work and Pay: The Canadian Labour-Market* (Toronto: University of Toronto Press, 1985) at 229–31; N. Weiner & M. Gunderson, *Pay Equity: Issues, Options and Experiences* (Toronto: Butterworths, 1990) at 6 [Weiner & Gunderson].

309 See, for example, the *Target Group Project*, above note 306 at 14–15. Some argue that this occupational crowding is primarily the outcome of cultural conditioning of and discrimination against women, while others attribute it to their personal career choices. The former view is argued, for example, by P. England, *Comparable Worth: Theories and Evidence* (New York: de Gruyter, 1992) at 120–21 and 283–85 [*Comparable Worth*], whereas the latter view is taken by S. Rhoads, *Incomparable Worth: Pay Equity Meets the Market* (Cambridge: Cambridge University Press, 1993) at 8, 14–15, 218, and 233 [*Incomparable Worth*].

310 For further detailed elaboration on this topic, see *Employment Law in Canada*, above note 1, c. 8 (IV)(O).

covenants and conventions, some of which have been ratified by the government of Canada, that make it strongly arguable that women have a fundamental human right to receive the same compensation as men for work of equal value.[311]

Today, three basic models of "equal pay" legislation are in use across Canada: (1) the "equal work" model, which requires the employer to pay identical wages for the performance of identical or substantially similar job duties; (2) the "equal value" model, which requires the employer to pay identical wages for the performance of job duties that are judged to be of the same or substantially similar worth to the organization, even though the job duties may be dissimilar in nature; and (3) the "pay equity" model, which requires employers to take the initiative in achieving pay equity as defined by the legislation within specified time limits. We examine these models in greater detail next.

a) The "Equal Work" Model

This form of equal pay legislation typically prohibits the employer from paying female employees at a rate of pay less than that received by male employees "for substantially the same work performed in the same establishment, the performance of which requires substantially equal skill, effort and responsibility and which is performed under similar working conditions."[312] The legislation then provides a list of factors that justify a wage differential, for example: "(a) a seniority system; (b) a merit system; (c) a system that measures wages by quantity or quality of production; or (d) another differential based on a factor other than sex."[313]

In order to safeguard employers against having to pay potentially crippling compensation awards for past wage discrimination, the legislation usually imposes a maximum retroactive period of one year during

---

311 These instruments are reviewed in the Pay Equity Task Force Report, above note 307 at 49–62.

312 *N.S. LSC*, above note 89, s. 57(1). Alberta is unique in including the equal pay obligation in its human rights act: Alberta *Human Rights, Citizenship and Multiculturalism Act*, R.S.A. 1980, c. H-11.7, s. 6. Useful judicial interpretations of the equivalent provisions in Saskatchewan include *Pasqua Hospital v. Harmatiuk* (1987), 87 C.L.L.C. ¶17,021 (Sask. C.A.), aff'g (1983), 83 C.L.L.C. ¶17,023 (Sask. Q.B.).

313 *N.S. LSC*, *ibid.*, s. 57(2). Useful judicial interpretations of these exceptions include *Alta. (A.G.) v. Gares* (1976), 76 C.L.L.C. ¶14, 016 (Alta. S.C.T.D.); *Derouin Opticians Ltd. v. Fraser* (1982), 83 C.L.L.C. ¶14,028 (Ont. Div. Ct.); *Brantford General Hospital v. Ontario (Director of Employment Standards)* (1986), 86 C.L.L.C. ¶14,022 (Ont. Div. Ct.).

which compensation is recoverable,[314] along with a one-year limitation period for commencing an action for breach of the equal pay obligation. However, such limitations violate the right to equality under section 15 of the *Charter* and will be ruled unconstitutional unless the government can justify them under section 1.[315] Doing this may not always be easy, as the Manitoba government discovered in 1992 when the courts ruled that imposing an annual cap of 1 percent of payroll on pay equity liability contravened the *Charter*.[316]

This model applies to the private sector in all provinces except Quebec and the federal jurisdiction, where the "equal value" model is universal, as well as to public sector employers in Alberta, British Columbia, Newfoundland, and Saskatchewan. In Ontario, the "equal value" model applies to both private and public sector employers under the *Pay Equity Act*,[317] but the "equal work" model also exists in section 42 of the *Employment Standards Act*. The main drawbacks of the "equal work" model are, first, that it depends on a male occupying the same or a substantially similar position as a female, thereby leaving untouched those positions that are exclusively staffed by women, and second, that it depends on a female plaintiff having the knowledge and fortitude to file a complaint against her employer for wage discrimination. Accordingly, studies show that this model has had virtually no effect in reducing the wage gap.[318]

b) The "Equal Value" Model

This model involves determining the value to the organization of a given job that is currently held by a female and ensuring that other jobs of equal value to the organization and held by males receive identical pay. The usual criteria for determining how much value a job contributes to an organization are the degree of skill, effort, and responsibility in-

---

314 Example: British Columbia *Human Rights Code*, R.S.B.C. 1996, c. 210, s. 7(5)(b).

315 Above note 30.

316 *Bethesda*, above note 35. Compare *N.A.P.E.*, above note 39, where the Court upheld under section 1 legislation introduced in 1991 by the government of Newfoundland to defer for three years the commencement date of a promised pay equity increase for female health-care workers. The Court found the legislation to be a proportionate response to the extraordinarily severe fiscal crisis facing the province at that time. On 23 March 2006, the government announced that it could now honour its commitment by making a $24 million *ex gratia* payment to the affected employees.

317 R.S.O. 1990, c. P-7 [*Ont. PEA*], examined below.

318 M. Gunderson, "Spline Function Estimates of the Impact of Equal Pay Legislation: The Ontario Experience" (1985) 40 R.I./I.R. 775, especially at 781 ["Spline Function Estimates"].

volved in performing the work and the physical and psychological conditions under which it is carried out. The main attraction of this model is that jobs involving quite different work functions can be compared for pay purposes. For example, if a gardener is determined to be of equal value to the firm as a receptionist, both jobs should receive equal pay even though their functions are dissimilar. However, this method cannot be used if there are no male-occupied jobs in the firm whose value can be compared with the female-occupied jobs. Since women tend to dominate certain occupations—daycare workers, for instance, are almost exclusively female—this is a real drawback to the "equal value" model. One possibility in the latter situation is to compare the female jobs in one firm with male jobs in a *different* firm,[319] but the danger with this approach is that market forces external to each firm may influence wage rates and distort the evaluation process.

The strengths and weaknesses of the "equal value" model have been hotly debated. The main disadvantages are alleged to be the following:[320]

- The job evaluation process will likely result in females being awarded wage increases above the market rate, resulting in unjustifiable increases in labour costs for the employer.
- The legal and administrative costs to employers of complying with equal value laws are likely to be substantial, resulting in further inefficiencies for the employers.
- Employment opportunities will decrease as a result of the previously mentioned inefficiencies, which will ultimately harm the very group whom the legislation is designed to protect.
- The job evaluation process is so subjective that it can easily be tainted by the political preferences of those involved in it, including the tribunals that administer the legislation.
- There is a risk of reduced morale among male and female employees who may feel cheated by the process.
- The regulatory edifice required to monitor the "equal value" model imposes an unwarranted cost on the public purse at a time of restraint in public sector spending.

---

319 As we shall see below, the Ontario government has taken this approach with public sector organizations under the "proxy" amendment to the *Ont. PEA*, above note 317

320 See, for example, S. Shamie, *Narrowing the Gender Wage Gap: Is Equal Value Legislation the Answer?* (Kingston, ON: Industrial Relations Centre, Queen's University, 1986) at 33–36; *Incomparable Worth*, above note 309.

- Firms are less likely to invest in provinces with equal value laws for all of the foregoing reasons.
- Such laws are unnecessary since market forces are gradually narrowing the wage gap anyway.

On the other hand, proponents of equal value laws argue that the above-mentioned dangers are generally overstated and that the moral importance of eradicating gender-discriminatory job evaluation — equal pay for work of equal value is regarded by its proponents as a "fundamental human right"[321] — justifies incurring some inefficiencies on a temporary basis until the problem is gone.[322] However, they acknowledge that equal value legislation will affect only a small part of the wage gap, namely, that portion attributable to the undervaluation of female jobs; the remainder, they argue, can be eliminated only by broader measures, such as adopting affirmative action programs for females and altering general societal myths about the role of women in the workforce. For the present it seems fair to conclude that the social science jury remains undecided on the whole question of whether the "equal value" model is justifiable.

Be that as it may, the Canadian federal government has adopted this model, having ratified the *Equal Remuneration Convention* (No. 100) of the International Labor Organization on 16 November 1972.[323] Although the provinces are not legally bound to follow suit,[324] six provinces have done so, but of these, only Quebec and Ontario have extended the obligation to private sector employers.[325] Elsewhere, only the public service and designated public and parapublic organizations are covered by the legislation. Presumably, this restriction aims to minimize the possible negative economic effects of such legislation mentioned above, the assumption being that the public purse is better able to withstand the cost of possible inefficiencies than private firms are. Nevertheless, even

---

321 Pay Equity Task Force Report, above note 307 at 49–62.
322 The best analyses in favour of this model are by England, *Comparable Worth*, above note 309, and Pay Equity Task Force Report, above note 307, especially cc.4 & 5
323 165 U.N.T.S. 303 (1951). The various international instruments supporting the "equal value" model are examined in Pay Equity Task Force Report, *ibid.* at 49–62.
324 *Toronto Electric Commissioners*, above note 11.
325 *Canadian Human Rights Act*, R.S.C. 1985, c. H-6, s. 11(1) [*Can. HRA*]; Manitoba *Pay Equity Act*, C.C.S.M. c. P13 [*Man. PEA*]; New Brunswick *Pay Equity Act*, S.N.B. 1989, c. P-5.01 [*N.B. PEA*]; Nova Scotia *Pay Equity Act*, R.S.N.S. 1989, c. 337 [*N.S. PEA*]; *Ont. PEA*, above note 317; Prince Edward Island *Pay Equity Act*, R.S.P.E.I. 1988, c. P-2 [*P.E.I. PEA*]; Quebec *Charter of Human Rights and Freedoms*, R.S.Q., c. C-12, s. 19 [*Quebec Charter*], and *Pay Equity Act*, R.S.Q., c. E-12.001 [*Que. PEA*].

in provinces without explicit equal value legislation, it would seem that the general prohibition against sex discrimination under the human rights acts could be used in those provinces to compel employers to pay women equal pay for work of equal value. If statistics show that an employer's compensation system results in women being paid less than men for work of equal value, this would constitute indirect sex discrimination, and the human rights tribunal could order, as the appropriate "make whole" remedy, that the employer implement a gender-unbiased job evaluation system that pays women the same as men for performing work of equal value and that sets time limits within which the employer must achieve pay equality.[326]

Several issues are commonly dealt with under legislation establishing the "equal value" model, a key issue being to determine who the "employer" is for the purpose of making equal pay comparisons. Determining the identity of the employer can be critical to the successful implementation of the "equal value" model because the broader the definition of the employer is, the more occupations can be compared for equal pay purposes. Suppose, for example, that female nurses employed in a hospital operated under the authority of a municipality claim that they are underpaid compared with male police officers employed by the same municipality. If the hospital is taken to be the employer of the nurses, it may be impossible to find male occupations to compare them with. However, if the municipality is taken to be the employer, the nurses could be compared with the police officers.[327] Furthermore, an employer may deliberately try to limit the scope for making comparisons by breaking up its operations into several corporate entities.

Equal pay statutes rarely define in detail the term "employer," leaving it to the tribunal that administers the act to flesh out the precise meaning on a case-by-case basis. The approach of tribunals is consistent with that generally taken under all employment protection statutes. Thus, there must be a sufficient degree of control exercised by one entity over another in regard to the key activities of the organization in order for the first entity to be the employer. The Ontario Pay Equity Tribunal recently summarized the key factors as follows:

---

326 The Saskatchewan courts have accepted this argument in *Canada Safeway Ltd. v. Saskatchewan (Human Rights Commission) (No. 2)* (1999), 99 C.L.L.C. ¶230-011 at 145,094 (Sask. Q.B.).

327 These are the facts of *Haldimand-Norfolk (Regional Municipality) Commissioners of Police v. O.N.A.* (1989), 30 C.C.E.L. 139 (Ont. Div. Ct.), aff'd (1990), 41 O.A.C. 148 (C.A.) [*O.N.A.*]. See also on this issue Pay Equity Commission of Ontario *Definition of Employer*, Revised Guideline No. 2 (Toronto: Pay Equity Commission, 1994).

(1) Who bears the overall financial responsibility, including budget preparation, ultimate responsibility for paying wages and benefits, financial administration, and ownership or shareholder investment structure?

(2) Who is responsible for determining employee compensation and administering job evaluation?

(3) What is the nature of the business, service or enterprise, including whether or not there is a "core" activity or business; whether or not the work under pay equity review is integral or severable from the organization; who decides what labour is to be undertaken and what are the employees' perceptions as to who is their employer?[328]

First, as with all protective legislation, a purposive approach is taken to defining the terms: a definition of employer that seeks to facilitate the achievement of pay equity will be chosen. Thus, in the example of the nurses and police officers given above, it makes sense to hold the municipality to be the employer because this enables a comparison to be made between a traditionally male-dominated occupation—police officer—and a traditionally female-dominated occupation—nurse.[329] Tribunals will "pierce the corporate veil" to ensure that employers do not attempt to restructure their legal identity in order to avoid their statutory obligations. For example, the Nova Scotia courts have ruled that a tribunal order issued against a municipality to increase the pay of its female school crosswalk employees continued to bind a company that hired the employees in question after the municipality had contracted-out the work in question to it.[330] In Quebec, section 42 of the *Pay Equity Act* is unique in expressly stating that a predecessor employer's pay equity obligations are automatically transferred to a successor employer in the event of the "alienation of the enterprise or the modification of its juridical structure."[331]

Second, if an organization consists of two or more separate establishments, it must be determined which are relevant for job evaluation purposes. Equal pay acts normally state that job comparisons must be

---

328 Cited in *O.N.A.*, *ibid.* See also *Kingston-Frontenac Children's Aid Society (No. 2)* (1992), 3 P.E.R. 117 at 118 (P.E.H.T.), where the Ministry of Community and Social Services was held to be the employer. This approach has also been applied in the private sector: e.g., *Thomson Newspapers* (1993), 4 P.E.R. 21 (P.E.H.T.). See generally on the definition of employer Chapter 2.

329 *O.N.A.*, *ibid.*

330 *Dartmouth (City of) v. Nova Scotia (Pay Equity Commission)* (1995), 134 N.S.R. (2d) 308 (S.C.A.D.).

331 *Que. PEA*, above note 325.

made within defined sectors—or "establishments"—of a firm, to ensure that the job evaluation process is not tainted by different wage administration conditions. Normally, the legislation specifies that, in the public sector, the provincial civil service and designated public and parapublic organizations constitute separate establishments for job evaluation purposes. The picture can be more complicated in regard to private sector employers. In Ontario, for instance, the *Pay Equity Act* states that an establishment consists of all employees hired by the employer in a "geographical division," defined as a "county, territorial district or regional municipality."[332] All workplaces of the employer within the geographical division are encompassed within the establishment for pay equity purposes.

Further complications arise where one or more trade unions have bargaining rights in an organization. Professor Paul Weiler has argued in favour of making the pay equity unit coterminous with each bargaining unit in order to avoid the practical difficulties that would be encountered by employers and trade unions having to negotiate pay equity comparisons across the lines of several different bargaining unit.[333] However, in 2006 the Supreme Court of Canada rejected this view by ruling that employees who are subject to a common wage and personnel policy fall within one "establishment" for pay equity purposes, regardless of whether they are in different bargaining units with different collective agreements. This decision arose in the federal jurisdiction where the legislation does not directly clarify the issue.[334] In contrast, in Ontario, the trade union's "bargaining unit" operates as the establishment for pay equity purposes, and the Act provides that a separate pay equity plan must be prepared for each bargaining unit in a unionized employer's establishment, as well as for any non-union employees.[335]

Third, the legislation commonly describes how an employer must determine which male jobs to compare with which female jobs. In order to spare the costs of comparing every job held by a female with every job held by a male, employers are allowed to compare female-dominated classes of jobs with male-dominated classes of jobs. A "job class"

---

332 Section 1(1). See generally "establishment" in Pay Equity Commission of Ontario, *Definition of Establishment*, Revised Guideline No. 4 (Toronto: Pay Equity Commission, 1994).

333 Paul C. Weiler, "Presentation by Professor Paul Weiler to the Federal Task Force on Pay Equity," Ottawa (28 June 2002), especially at 10, online: www.payequityreview.gc.ca/4481-e.html.

334 *Canada (Human Rights Commission) v. Canadian Airlines International Ltd.*, 2006 SCC 1, especially at paras. 36–42.

335 *Ont. PEA*, above note 317, ss. 14(1), 15(1), & 15(2).

is usually defined as a group of positions whose duties, responsibilities, and qualifications are sufficiently similar to be covered by the same wage schedule.[336] The risk with defining a job class too broadly is that the unique qualities of an individual position can become submerged, resulting in that position being undervalued. Therefore, the legislation permits an employee to file a complaint with the applicable tribunal that his or her particular position is undervalued, despite the presence of a class-based evaluation scheme.

The legislation usually contains detailed rules for determining when a job class is dominated by either gender for pay evaluation purposes. Thus, in non-unionized organizations in Ontario, a job class is deemed to be "male dominated" if 70 percent or more of its incumbents are men and "female dominated" if 60 percent or more of its incumbents are women.[337] In contrast, in Nova Scotia, Quebec, and Prince Edward Island, the relevant percentages are 60 percent for both male and female job classes.[338] Also, the legislation usually states that a job class must include a minimum number of incumbents in order to qualify as a female- or male-dominated job class—for example, ten persons in Nova Scotia.[339]

A particular job class that is currently not female dominated may nonetheless be undervalued because in the past it was female dominated. For example, a hospital may employ roughly equal numbers of male and female nurses, but previously have employed a vast majority of women as nurses. In order to safeguard against this risk, several statutes provide that "historical incumbency" must be taken into account in determining whether or not a job class is gender dominated.[340] However, the phrase is undefined in the legislation. As well, in some provinces, "gender stereotypes of fields of work"[341] must be taken into account in determining whether or not a job class is gender dominated. This phrase, too, is undefined.[342] The federal Pay Equity Task Force Re-

---

336 *Ibid.*, s. 1. See also Pay Equity Commission of Ontario, *Determining Job Class*, Revised Guideline No. 5 (Toronto: Pay Equity Commission, 1994).

337 *Ont. PEA, ibid.*, s. 1(1). In unionized plants, the matter can be negotiated between the union and the employer.

338 *N.S. PEA*, above note 325, ss. 3(1)(f) and 3(1)(m); *P.E.I. PEA*, above note 325, ss. 1(g) & (h); *Que. PEA*, above note 325, s. 55.

339 *N.S. PEA, ibid.*

340 *N.B. PEA*, above note 325, s. 1; *Ont. PEA*, above note 317, s. 1(5); *P.E.I. PEA*, above note 325, s. 2(4); *Que. PEA*, above note 325, s. 55(2)

341 *Ont. PEA, ibid.*, s. 1(5); *Que. PEA, ibid.*, s. 55(3); *P.E.I. PEA, ibid.*, s. 2(4).

342 But see the suggestions in Pay Equity Commission of Ontario, *Determining Gender Predominance*, Revised Guideline No. 7 (Toronto: Pay Equity Commission, 1994) [*Determining Gender Predominance*]. The guidelines are not legally

port recommended that ". . . a job class may be deemed female or male dominated when it is commonly associated with women or men due to occupational stereotype."[343]

In Ontario, the administrative costs of conducting pay evaluations are further minimized by allowing employers to compare "groups of jobs."[344] Thus, an employer can select the single job class containing the greatest number of employees from within a defined group of job classes as the representative comparator for all of the remaining job classes in the group. The rate of pay accorded to the representative female job class, following its evaluation and comparison with a matching male job class, applies to all other job classes within the group. Nevertheless, this group of jobs approach can be used only if at least 60 percent of incumbents in the group as a whole are female.[345] Also, in order to qualify as a group of jobs, the constituent job classes must "bear a relationship" to each other because of the nature of the work they perform and be "organized in successive levels."[346] Of course, with such a broadly based approach to job evaluations, the risk increases that the unique characteristics of individual positions will be overlooked, leaving some pockets of wage discrimination untouched.

Fourth, the legislation commonly describes how work is to be accorded "value" for the purpose of wage comparisons. Deciding how much value a job provides to a firm is inescapably a subjective matter, depending on the perceptions of the evaluator. Given the essential subjectivity of the process, the risk of female jobs being undervalued as a result of sex stereotyping is considerable. The legislation commonly obliges employers to ensure that the job evaluation process is "gender unbiased," and tribunals will scrutinize the employer's conduct in minute detail to ensure that this requirement is met.[347] In Ontario, Prince

---

binding, but the Pay Equity Tribunal takes them into account in applying the express provisions of the Act.

343 Pay Equity Task Force Report, above note 307 at 267.
344 *Ont. PEA*, above note 317, s. 6(6). See also *Determining Gender Predominance*, above note 342.
345 *Ont. PEA, ibid*, s. 6(6).
346 *Ibid.*, s. 6(10).
347 Canada *Equal Wage Guidelines*, 1986, SOR/86-1082, ss. 9 and 17 [EWG]; *Man. PEA*, above note 325, ss. 9(1)(a)(i) and 14(1)(a)(i); *N.B. PEA*, above note 325, s. 11(1)(a)(i); *N.S. PEA*, above note 325, s. 12; *Ont. PEA*, above note 317, s. 12; *P.E.I. PEA*, above note 325, ss. 1(j), 2, 8, 14(1)(a)(1); *Que. PEA*, above note 325, s. 51. See, for example, the close scrutiny of the process in *Dare Foods Ltd.* (1992), 3 P.E.R. 142, especially at 163–66 (Ont. P.E.H.T.); *Women's College Hospital (No. 4)* (1992), 3 P.E.R. 61 (Ont. P.E.H.T.); and *Haldimand-Norfolk (No. 6)* (1991), 2 P.E.R. 105 (Ont. P.E.H.T.) [*Haldimand-Norfolk*].

Edward Island, Quebec, and the federal jurisdiction, the employer is free to select whichever job evaluation system best suits its particular circumstances,[348] but a uniform system seems to be mandated in other jurisdictions.[349] There is a vast body of specialized writing on how to safeguard against the risk of bias when conducting job evaluations.[350] The following practical tips should prove useful.

The job evaluation process begins with the implementation of a "job analysis," something that entails finding out precisely which work duties employees perform. Apparently, stereotypical attitudes towards women's work cause employers to overlook certain characteristics of "female" jobs, such as communicating, coordinating, handling emotional crises, listening, record keeping, meeting deadlines under stress, maintaining confidentiality, lifting, and handling public relations.[351] Employers must take particular care that such characteristics are given their due regard.

The next stage of the job evaluation process involves determining what will constitute the applicable "compensable factors." The equal pay acts usually define these broadly as "skill," "effort," "responsibility," and "working conditions," but it is permissible for employers to break them down into more detailed components, such as "customer relations" or "maintaining confidential records." Typically, the employer will then assign points for each compensable factor representing the degree of benefit that each factor is deemed to give to the organization. The risk of gender bias is reduced if a formalized system of points is used rather than implicit judgments being made about the worth of each compensable factor.[352] The risk of bias is further reduced if job evaluators receive training in the process; joint evaluation committees consisting of equal numbers of employer and employee representatives of both sexes make the decisions; such committees make decisions by unanimity rather than by majority votes; and care is taken to avoid giving undue weight to the decisions of previous evaluators, whose judgment may have been tainted by gender bias.

---

348 Explicitly or implicitly, in the *Ont. PEA, ibid.*, s. 13(2)(a); *P.E.I. PEA, ibid.*, s. 14(1)(a)(i); *EWG, ibid.*, s. 9; *Quebec Charter,* above note 325, s. 19.

349 *Man. PEA*, above note 325, ss. 9(1)(a)(i) and 14(1)(a)(i); *N.S. PEA*, above note 325, s. 12; *N.B. PEA*, above note 325, s. 11(1)(a)(i).

350 Examples: Pay Equity Task Force Report, above note 307, c. 10; Weiner & Gunderson, above note 308, cc. 3 & 4; *Comparable Worth*, above note 309, c. 4; and Pay Equity Commission of Ontario, *Gender-Neutral Job Comparison*, Revised Guideline No. 9 (Toronto: Ontario Pay Equity Commission, 1994).

351 See, for example, the useful checklist provided by Ontario Pay Equity Tribunal in *Haldimand-Norfolk*, above note 347.

352 This is advised by Weiner & Gunderson, above note 308 at 63–64.

In several provinces, the equal pay acts expressly define several factors that justify wage differentials between men and women.[353] Although there are variations among the provinces, these factors may include a merit pay system based on formal performance appraisals, which have been brought to the attention of employees; a formal seniority system, wherein compensation increases with length of service; a temporary training or development assignment for career advancement purposes; a skills shortage causing a temporary increase in the cost of skilled labour; and a defined red-circling system. Ontario[354] is unique in allowing pay differences attributable to "bargaining strength," but only after the initial pay equity plan has been implemented in the organization, so that gender-based wage inequalities presumably have been eliminated. Nevertheless, the legislation commonly imposes an overriding proviso that none of these factors can be gender biased in content or application. All the exceptions are interpreted narrowly in furtherance of the remedial goal of the legislation.[355]

Fifth, the legislation commonly deals with how equality should be implemented in the pay structure, once male and female jobs have been evaluated. This involves making the initial determination of exactly which benefits constitute "pay" for the purpose of achieving "equal pay." Typically, the legislation defines pay broadly to include all monetary benefits derived from employment. For example, the *Canadian Human Rights Act*[356] defines "wages" as including "any form of remuneration," including commissions, bonuses, vacation pay, dismissal payments, payments "in kind," and "reasonable value" for board and lodge; employer contributions to pension and health and disability plans; and "any other advantage received directly or indirectly" from the employer.

When it comes to determining exactly how equality is to be implemented, there are two basic methods: the job-to-job method, and the proportional value method. The Nova Scotia *Pay Equity Act*[357] makes the former method compulsory; the Manitoba, New Brunswick, and Prince

---

353 *Can. HRA*, above note 325, s. 11(4) and *EWG*, above note 347, ss. 16, 18, 19; *N.S. PEA*, above note 325, s. 12(4); *Ont. PEA*, above note 317, s. 8(1); *P.E.I. PEA*, above note 325, s. 8(1); *N.B. PEA*, above note 325, s. 4; *Quebec Charter*, above note 325, s. 19. For a detailed analysis of how the exceptions are applied, see *Pay Equity Commission of Ontario, Permissible Differences in Compensation*, Revised Guideline No. 12 (Toronto: Ontario Pay Equity Commission, 1994).

354 *Ont. PEA, ibid.*, s. 8(2). This is the case whether the organization is unionized or not.

355 Example: *Law Society (No.2)* (1998–99), 9 P.E.R. 35 at 41 (Ont. P.E.H.T.), involving the Ontario merit pay exception.

356 Above note 325, s. 11(7).

357 Above note 325, s. 6(1).

Edward Island pay equity acts make the latter method compulsory.[358] The Ontario, Quebec, and federal statutes allow the employer to select whichever method it deems most satisfactory in the circumstances. All jurisdictions disallow employers from reducing an employee's wages in order to achieve equality.[359]

The job-to-job method involves matching each female-dominated job class in the firm with a male-dominated job class that has been determined to be of equal value in the job evaluation process (known as the "male comparator"). The next step is to award all positions within the relevant job classes the same pay.

Despite its apparent simplicity, difficulties can arise with this method. For example, if a female job class matches with two or more male comparators with different pay rates, the question arises which pay rate to accord to the female job class. The pay equity acts of Ontario and Nova Scotia have opted, somewhat controversially, for the lower paying male job class, whereas the Quebec *Pay Equity Act* makes the average wage of the male job classes the applicable rate. Moreover, in female-dominated industries, there may well be no suitable male comparators in an organization. The response under the Nova Scotia *Pay Equity Act* is to match the pay rate of the female job class to that of any male-dominated job class in the organization that has a higher rate of pay than the female job class, even though the male job class in question may have received a lower value in the evaluation process than the female job class.[360] In the event that two or more male job classes are better paid than the female job class, the Nova Scotia act awards the female job class the highest pay rate among them. In the event that no male comparators can be found using this approach, the Nova Scotia act denies any pay equity adjustment. In contrast, the Ontario and Quebec pay equity acts require an employer confronted with the problem of lack of male comparators to resort to the proportional value method, rather than deny any pay equity adjustment. As well, the position in Ontario is complicated somewhat by the fact that several different pay equity plans can exist in the same firm—for example, if there are several unionized bargaining units alongside a non-union group. The Ontario *Pay Equity Act* states that if a female job class cannot be matched with a male comparator within the boundaries of its own pay

358 *Man. PEA*, above note 325, s. 6(2); *N.B. PEA*, above note 325, s. 8; *P.E.I. PEA*, above note 325, s. 7(2).
359 Example: *Ont. PEA*, above note 317, s. 9(1).
360 *N.S. PEA*, above note 325, s. 17(1)(c).

equity plan, it can be matched with an equally valued male job class within other pay equity plans in the firm.[361]

The proportional value method essentially involves calculating a "wage line" representing the pay rates of all male-dominated job classes according to points allotted by the job evaluation process and plotting it against the wage line of the applicable female job classes. Any female job classes at lower pay rates than the average difference between the male and female wage lines are adjusted up to the level of that average.[362] Depending on what seems most suitable for the circumstances of a case, one of five forms of the proportional value method may be used:[363]

- The job-to-line method involves using statistical regression to calculate a wage line for male dominated jobs and for female dominated jobs, and increasing the females' compensation up to the level of the male line.
- The job-to-segment method involves selecting groups (or "segments") of male jobs having a value points score roughly similar to the score for the female job and using statistical regression to calculate a male wage line for the jobs in the segment. The females' wages are then increased to this male wage line.
- The level-to-line method involves grouping female jobs according to their level of compensation, calculating the average value points score for these jobs, and ensuring that this level of compensation is no less than that corresponding with the average value points score on the male wage line.
- The level-to-segment method involves calculating the male line on the basis of a "segment" of male jobs and comparing it with equivalent value points score on the female wage line so as to ensure wage equality.
- The line-to-line method involves using statistical regressions to calculate wage lines for male and female jobs, and raising the wages on the female line to correspond with those on the male line.

The main attraction of using one of these proportional value methods is that every female job can be accorded a pay equity adjustment,

---

361 *Ont. PEA*, above note 317, ss. 6(4), (5).
362 For detailed elaboration on this method, see Weiner & Gunderson, above note 308 at 77–81; *Proportional Value Comparison Method: Using the Step by Step to Pay Equity* (Toronto: Ontario Pay Equity Commission, 1993).
363 For a detailed elaboration of these methods, see J. Kervin, "Wage Adjustment Methodologies," submission to the Federal Pay Equity Task Force, January 2003, online: www.payequityreview.gc.ca/2316-e.html.

even though it may not match with a specific male comparator. On the other hand, because the approach deals with averages, it could result in a particular female job of equal or comparable value to a male job being paid below the wage line, while the male job in question is paid above the wage line. As well, the complexity of the methodology has spawned protracted litigation, often involving battles between each side's statisticians.[364]

The Ontario and Quebec pay equity acts are unique in requiring employers, in limited circumstances, to make pay equity comparisons with the employees of *other* employers where insufficient male comparators exist in their own organizations. The so-called proxy provisions of the Ontario *Pay Equity Act*, introduced in 1993,[365] stated that if an employer in the provincial public service could not find male comparators for its female job classes within its own organization by using either or both of the job-to-job and proportional value methods, the employer could seek a job match for its female job classes with male comparators in other public service organizations. Organizations would be designated as "proxies" for this purpose. In order to qualify as a proxy, an organization had to be within the Ontario public service, to include enough jobs to enable comparisons to be made, and to either perform similar work functions within the same geographical area as the employer or pattern its compensation practices on those of the employer. The latter requirement sought to ensure that the proxy process would not distort an employer's compensation system by tainting it with external labour-market factors that are unsuitable to that employer's situation. The province's Pay Equity Commission had to approve applications for proxy status to ensure that these preconditions were met. In 1996, the newly elected Progressive Conservatives repealed these provisions, but the courts subsequently ruled the repeal to be unconstitutional,[366] whereupon the government reinstated them into the Act in 1997.

The Quebec *Pay Equity Act* also contains proxy provisions, but these differ dramatically from the Ontario model in that they apply to

---

364 Example: *Canada (A.G.) v. Public Service Alliance of Canada*, [2000] C.L.L.C. ¶230-002 (F.C.T.D.), examined by P. Hughes, "*P.S.A.C. v. Canada (Treasury Board)*: The Long and Winding Road to Equity" (2000) 8 C.L.E.L.J. 55.
365 Part III.2 of the *Ont. PEA*, above note 317, as am. by S.O. 1993, c. 4, s. 13.
366 *Savings and Restructuring Act*, S.O. 1996, c. 1, Sch. J, s. 4 (effective 7 January 1997), ruled unconstitutional as violating the ban against sex discrimination in the *Charter*, s. 15, in *S.E.I.U., Local 204 Ontario (A.G.)* (1997), 97 C.L.L.C. ¶230-035 (Ont. Gen. Div.).

private sector employers as well as public sector organizations.[367] The federal Pay Equity Task Force Report strongly endorsed this model.[368] Allowing proxy comparisons to be made between different private sector firms, however, runs the risk of making unduly distorting market forces the preferred determinant of wages. In order to minimize this risk, proxy comparisons should be allowed in the private sector only when the respective firms share demonstrably homogeneous market circumstances.

Sixth, the role of employees in the pay equity process is commonly dealt with in equal value statutes. One might expect that the same concern with advancing human rights that inspired the "equal value" model would also result in employers being obliged to give employees a collective voice in formulating and administering the process for achieving pay equity, even though the employees are not unionized.[369] Yet, the trailblazing Ontario *Pay Equity Act* does not compel employers to involve their non-unionized employees, either individually or collectively, in any facets of the pay equity process.[370] Nevertheless, since the Act requires that all facets of the pay equity process must be gender unbiased, and since the risk of gender bias can be significantly reduced if employers establish joint committees of employee and employer representatives, there is some indirect legal pressure on employers in Ontario to give their employees participation rights.[371] Elsewhere, non-unionized employees are given broad participation rights, as in Quebec where at least two-thirds of the membership of pay equity committees must be employees who are selected by their fellow workers.[372] Similarly, in provinces where the pay equity legislation is limited to the public sector, the employer is required to negotiate in good faith

---

367   *Que. PEA*, above note 325, s. 114(2).

368   Pay Equity Task Force Report, above note 307 at 334–46.

369   Employee participation in the process was described as essential in the Pay Equity Task Force Report, *ibid.* at 221 and c. 8. See also R. Adams, "Efficiency Is Not Enough" Research and Working Paper Series No. 360 (Hamilton, ON: McMaster University, Faculty of Business, 1991) at 2–3, 15; and R. Adams, "The Unorganized: A Rising Force" Research and Working Paper Series No. 201 (Hamilton, ON: McMaster University, Faculty of Business, April 1983), especially at 9–19. Prof. Adams advocates group representational rights for non-unionized employees.

370   Unionized employees, of course, are given a voice through their union's status as exclusive bargaining agent.

371   Indeed, most employers have established joint committees with their non-unionized employees: see Avebury Research & Consulting, *What Works . . . Experiences with Implementation of the Pay Equity Legislation, Final Report* (Toronto: Ontario Pay Equity Commission, 1991) at 7.

372   *Que. PEA*, above note 325, ss. 16, 17, 19, and 28, and note that the employee representatives continue to receive their pay.

and make every reasonable effort to reach an agreement on a pay equity plan with its non-unionized "employee representatives."[373] The statutes do not describe how these representatives are to be selected. Of course, in Ontario, any individual employee—or for that matter, any group of employees—can complain to the Pay Equity Commission that a pay equity plan prepared unilaterally by the employer does not satisfy the statutory requirements, in which case mediation and ultimately adjudication of the matter can follow.[374]

Seventh, the legislation must address what government services are available to help employers implement pay equity. Since implementing the "equal value" model pay equity legislation is complex and expensive (especially for relatively small employers), all jurisdictions provide the services of specialized government officials free of charge. In provinces with specialized pay equity acts, there are pay equity commissions whose officers will give the necessary help. In all cases, these bodies will provide their assistance regardless of whether or not a formal complaint has been filed against an employer. Special mention must be made of the extremely helpful pay equity guidelines published by the Ontario Pay Equity Commission, which give comprehensible practical advice on all aspects of the process.[375] The guidelines are not legally enforceable, but are taken into account by the Ontario Pay Equity Tribunal in interpreting the express provisions in the Act. Employers in all jurisdictions can benefit from the general advice provided in the guidelines on implementing the "equal value" model.

Last, the legislation must specify whether any particular employers or employees are excluded from equal pay provisions. Although there are differences between the provinces, the main exclusions are as follows:

• The equal value model binds private sector employers only in Quebec, Ontario, and the federal jurisdiction; elsewhere, only the public service and designated public and parapublic organizations are bound to adopt the "equal value" model.

---

373 *Man. PEA*, above note 325, s. 1, "employee representative," and ss. 13(2)(a)–(d), (3); *N.B. PEA*, above note 325, s. 1(1), "employee representative," "bargaining agent," and s. 10(1)(a); *P.E.I. PEA*, above note 325, s. 1(f) "employee representative," s. 1(a) "bargaining agent," and s. 13; *N.S. PEA*, above note 325, s. 3(1)(g), "employee representative," and s. 18(1).

374 *Ont. PEA*, above note 317, ss. 15(7), 16(3), 16(4), and 17.

375 Pay Equity Implementation Series, Revised 1994, Guidelines Nos. 1–16 (Toronto: Ontario Pay Equity Commission, 1994). See also the Pay Equity Commission's useful *Annual Reports*, and the Pay Equity Reports, which contain the full decisions of the Pay Equity Hearing Tribunal.

- The acts often exclude small businesses—for example, in Ontario and Quebec, firms must hire at least ten employees in order to be covered by the pay equity acts. The rationale is presumably that such employers can ill afford the costs of complying with the equal value obligation, but the result of the exclusion could be to deny pay equity to significant numbers of workers, since small business is the largest growth area for future employment. The Federal Pay Equity Task Force Report recommended repealing the small business exclusion and suggested that small employers could combine on sectoral pay equity committees in female-dominated occupations to pool their resources and expertise.[376]
- Casual or transient employment relationships, such as with summer students, may also be excluded.[377]

Next, we examine the third model that equal pay legislation can take, namely, the proactive "pay equity" model.

c)   The "Pay Equity" Model

The hallmark of this model is that employers are bound to proactively achieve defined pay equity goals within specified time limits and to regularly report their progress to a government-appointed Pay Equity Commission.[378] The rationale for requiring employers to take the initiative in achieving pay equity is that the complaints-based approach to enforcing equal pay legislation has proven to be relatively unsuccessful in achieving the desired goals.[379]

The proactive statutes commonly endorse the "equal value" model of achieving pay equity described above. Each act contains detailed time limits—which vary among the provinces—within which the various steps in the pay equity process must be completed. In Nova Scotia, for instance, the entire process must be completed within four years of its commencement.[380] Private sector employers and small businesses are usually given longer to accomplish pay equity than public sector and larger employers.[381] Indeed, in Ontario, private sector firms employing between zero and one hundred workers are not compelled to formulate

---

376 Pay Equity Task Force Report, above note 307 at 181–84.
377 Example: *Ont. PEA*, above note 317, s. 8(3), (4).
378 Provinces with this model are Manitoba, New Brunswick, Ontario, Nova Scotia, Quebec, and Prince Edward Island.
379 The case for the proactive model is forcefully advocated in Pay Equity Task Force Report, above note 307 at 84–113.
380 *N.S. PEA*, above note 325, ss. 14(1), 15.
381 Example: *Ont. PEA*, above note 317, ss. 10, 13(2), and 13(4).

a pay equity plan, but may do so if they wish.[382] The rationale seems to be that such organizations are less able to absorb the costs of complying with the Act than the others.

The proactive model does not preclude employees from filing complaints that their employer has breached its statutory obligations. Rather, the legislation commonly contains machinery for resolving such complaints. Typically, the initial thrust is towards settling complaints voluntarily through mediation conducted by an officer of the Pay Equity Commission, but adjudication by either a standing Pay Equity Tribunal or a neutral ad hoc tribunal is available in the last resort. The criminal law normally plays a minimal role.[383] Thus, breach of the acts is generally not made a criminal offence, although violation of certain key obligations may sometimes be made an offence. In Ontario,[384] for example, breaches of the prohibitions against penalizing employees for exercising their rights under the Act, against obstructing an officer of the Pay Equity Commission in the performance of his or her duties, and against disobeying an order of the Pay Equity Hearing Tribunal are criminal offences.

It remains to be seen whether or not the proactive "equal value" model of legislation will be applied to private sector employers outside the federal jurisdiction, Ontario, and Quebec. In view of the pressure now being felt on Canadian private sector businesses to become more competitive and the seemingly convincing economic arguments against such legislation, it is unlikely that this model will be applied more widely in the near future.

C. INDUSTRIAL STANDARDS LEGISLATION

Separate industrial standards acts were enacted in several provinces during the 1930s, before today's relatively expansive employment standards codes and collective bargaining statutes were in force. The common thrust of these acts was for the executive branch of government to promulgate by regulation defined minimum wages, hours, and working conditions for a designated trade, industry, or geographical zone. Typically, the legislation did not specify in detail how such wages, hours, and conditions were to be set, but established "advisory com-

---

382 *Ibid.*, ss. 18–20.
383 The role of the criminal law appears to be most pronounced in Quebec: see *Que. PEA*, above note 325, ss. 115–18.
384 *Ont. PEA*, above note 317, s. 26.

mittees" consisting of knowledgeable employers and trade union officials charged with providing guidance to the minister of labour, who made the final decision. In practice, if a union was established in the trade, industry, or zone in question, the wages and benefits it bargained for became the standard extended to all employers in the applicable trade or industrial zone. Today, only Nova Scotia operates an "industrial standards" scheme, with wages being extended for a limited range of employment, namely, the major construction industry trades.[385]

Somewhat similar to the industrial standards acts is the "extension" scheme under the Quebec *Collective Agreement Decrees Act*.[386] In Quebec, the lieutenant-governor in council may order that a collective agreement respecting any trade, industry, commerce, or occupation shall be extended to bind all members of a stated class of employees and employers in the province or in a region of the province. In 1993, 15,300 employers and 125,000 workers in Quebec were covered by twenty-nine such decrees in the following industries: construction; garages; services, such as security, building services, bread distribution, and solid waste and road haulage; clothing and other apparel; hairdressing; woodworking; and the manufacture of furniture, petroleum equipment, corrugated paper boxes, and non-structural metals. These industries are dominated by relatively small employers who traditionally pay low wages. In contrast, the industrial standards acts in the common law provinces are considerably narrower in scope. Generally, only the construction industry and selected trades are subject to an industrial standards order, but in Ontario, a somewhat broader range of industries, including defined sectors of the garment industry and beauty culture, is covered.

Employers generally fear the extension system because it reduces their flexibility to reduce pay and benefits in order to compete with firms from outside the province with lower standards. Trade unions may fear them, too, since non-unionized workers will have no incentive to organize if they receive the prevailing union rate by virtue of legislated extension. On the other hand, if the changing economic conditions result in a decline in trade union representation among low- and mid-skilled workers and a concomitant reduction in their pay and benefits, legislators may revisit the extension model contained in these industrial standards acts as a possible means of protecting these workers' interests.

---

385 The scheme is contained in *N.S. LSC*, above note 89, s. 11.
386 R.S.Q., c. D-2, s. 2. See J.-G. Bergeron & D. Veilleux, "The Quebec Collective Agreement Decrees Act: A Unique Mode of Collective Bargaining" (1996) 22 Queen's L.J. 135.

D. OCCUPATIONAL HEALTH AND SAFETY LEGISLATION

All provinces have enacted comprehensive legislation designed to prevent accidents and illnesses in the workplace and to compensate employees who are injured or become sick during the course of their employment. At common law, the employer has always been impliedly bound under the employment contract to make the workplace reasonably safe, and the tort of negligence is to the same effect. Legislative intervention has been necessary, however, because of major gaps in the protection afforded by the common law, namely, the following:

- An employee is presumed to consent to being injured by risks that he or she knows or ought reasonably to know of.
- Contributory negligence by an employee constitutes a complete defence to an action in negligence against the employer.
- The notorious "common employment" doctrine deems that an employee agrees to being injured by the negligence of his or her workmates.
- The cost of civil litigation and the problems of proving "fault" on the employer's part result in too many injured employees going uncompensated and weakens the potency of a damages award as an incentive for the employer to improve health and safety.
- Compulsory reinstatement and comprehensive "make-whole" compensation awards to safeguard the employee who is wrongfully dismissed for refusing to perform hazardous work are unavailable at common law.[387]

In this section, we examine the legislative response to preventing accidents and illnesses, and then the legislation dealing with the compensation of injured workers.

1) Preventing Accidents and Injuries at Work under the Occupational Health and Safety Legislation[388]

Preventive legislation falls into two categories. First, there is "external" legislation, which fixes minimum health and safety standards of general

---

387 For detailed analysis on the defects in the common law, see E. Tucker, "The Law of Employers' Liability in Ontario 1861–1990: The Search for a Theory" (1984) 22 Osgoode Hall L.J. 213, especially at 217–21.

388 *CLC*, above note 40, Part II; Alberta *Occupational Health and Safety Act*, R.S.A. 2000, c. O-2 [*Alta. OHSA*]; British Columbia *Workers Compensation Act*, R.S.B.C.

application to all employers or to specific employers within designated industries and occupations, and creates special machinery for enforcing them. Second, there is "internal" legislation, which requires employers to establish mechanisms within their own organizations—such as joint employer–employee committees to combat hazards within their own workplace—and which afford employees the rights to "know of" and to "refuse" unsafe work. Both categories of legislation interrelate in furthering the goal of improving workplace health and safety—internal health and safety committees, for instance, will ensure that external standards are honoured—but the distinction is useful for the purpose of exposition.

a)   "External" Health and Safety Standards

The external legislation includes extensive and detailed minimum health and safety standards applicable to all employers, to particular industries, and to particular trades and occupations.[389] Frequently, these standards are enacted as regulations by the executive arm of government pursuant to a general enabling power in an occupational health and safety or other act. Typically, in drawing up the requisite standards, the executive will consult with expert agencies in the area. Standards may address specified sanitary, first aid, and fire regulations; procedures for operating and maintaining defined machinery and equipment; periodic medical checkups for employees; protective clothing requirements; minimum standards of light, ventilation, temperature, and air cleanliness; installation and maintenance of guard

---

1996, c. 492 [B.C. WCA]; Manitoba Workplace Safety and Health Act, C.C.S.M. c. W210; New Brunswick Occupational Health and Safety Act, S.N.B. 1983, c. O-0.2; Nova Scotia Occupational Health and Safety Act, R.S.N.S. 1989, c. 320; Newfoundland Occupational Health and Safety Act, R.S.N.L. 1990, c. O-3 [Nfld. OHSA]; Prince Edward Island Occupational Health and Safety Act, R.S.P.E.I. 1988, c. O.1; Ontario Occupational Heath and Safety Act, R.S.O. 1990, c. O.1 [Ont. OHSA]; Quebec Act Respecting Occupational Health and Safety, R.S.Q., c. S-2.1; Saskatchewan Occupational Health and Safety Act, 1993, S.S. 1993, c. O-1.1 [Sask. OHSA]. See generally E. Kelloway, L. Francis, & J. Montgomery, Management of Occupational Health and Safety, 3d ed. (Toronto: Nelson Thomson, 2006); Canadian Employment Safety and Health Guide, 4 volumes, looseleaf (Don Mills, ON: CCH Canadian, 1980–); M. Grossman, The Law of Occupational Health and Safety in Ontario, 2d ed. (Toronto: Butterworths, 1993); N.A. Keith, Canadian Health & Safety Law: A Comprehensive Guide to the Statutes, Policies and Case Law, looseleaf (Aurora, ON: Canada Law Book, 1997–); E. Tucker, "Diverging Trends in Worker Health and Safety Protection and Participation in Canada 1985–2000" (2003) 58 Indus. Rel. L.J. 395.

389 The regulations in each province are reproduced in full in Canadian Employment Safety and Health Guide, ibid..

rails, steps, and walkways; minimum exposure levels for designated chemicals and substances; and defined training and supervision programs for certain kinds of work.

The extent to which the health and safety legislation should restrict the right to smoke in the workplace has generated a heated public debate. Some provinces have sought to curtail smoking in the workplace by specific regulations in the health and safety legislation, as in Saskatchewan where *Occupational Health and Safety Regulations* compel employers to ensure that workers do not smoke in an "enclosed place" and that workers are not exposed to second-hand smoke.[390] The employer can, however, designate smoking areas (including vehicles) so long as no smoke escapes to contaminate other parts of the workplace. Otherwise, the employer's general statutory duty to eliminate workplace hazards under the health and safety legislation historically has not been interpreted as requiring the employer to ban or restrict smoking, despite the increasing number of scientific studies showing the health risks of second-hand smoke.[391] Nevertheless, in order to safeguard employees against the harmful effects of second-hand tobacco smoke, and to minimize the economic costs on employers resulting from smoking in the workplace, all provinces have introduced special statutes that prohibit employees and other persons present at the worksite from smoking.[392]

As long ago as 1989, Ontario enacted the *Smoking in the Workplace Act*, which disallowed smoking in "enclosed spaces" and gave employers the discretion to permit smoking in a designated area not larger than 25 percent of the entire workplace area.[393] The Act also obliged employers to reasonably accommodate requests from employees to work in a smoke free area. However, this Act has been replaced by the 2005 *Smoke-Free Ontario Act*, which is much tougher.[394] The new Act is

---

390 Saskatchewan, *Occupational Health and Safety Regulations, 1996*, R.R.S., c. O-1.1, Reg. 1.

391 See National Cancer Institute, "Secondhand Smoke: Questions and Answers," online: www.cancer.gov/cancertopics/factsheet/Tobacco/ETS.

392 Examples: Alberta *Smoke-Free Places Act*, S.A. 2005, c. S-9.5; Manitoba *Non-Smokers Health Protection Act*, C.C.S.M. c. S125; Newfoundland *Smoke-Free Environment Act*, S.N.L. 2005, c. S-16.2; New Brunswick *Smoke-Free Places Act*, S.N.B. 2004, c. S-9.5; Nova Scotia *Smoke Free Places Act*, S.N.S. 2002, c. 12; Prince Edward Island *Smoke-Free Places Act*, R.S.P.E.I. 1988, c. S-4.2; Quebec *Tobacco Act*, R.S.Q. c. T-0.01; Saskatchewan *Tobacco Control Act*, S.S. 2001, c. T-14.1. In British Columbia, the equivalent protections are contained in the *Occupational Health and Safety Regulation*, B.C. Reg. 296/97, ss. 4.81 & 4.82.

393 R.S.O. 1990, c. S.13, now repealed.

394 S.O. 2005, c. 18.

similar to the smoke-free legislation now in force in all other jurisdictions, subject to some relatively minor differences in detail between the provinces. Thus, the Act prohibits outright smoking in all "enclosed workplaces," including all buildings and roofed vehicles used by employees in the course of their employment, on the part of employees as well as all visitors to the worksite. Unlike its predecessor, the new Act disallows employers from establishing designated smoking areas. An exception is made for patients in residential and psychiatric care facilities who can smoke in a properly ventilated designated room, but not when employees are present. Another exception is made for Aboriginals in hospital or in a residential or psychiatric facility who can smoke for "traditional aboriginal cultural or spiritual purposes." The employer is prohibited from penalizing an employee for exercising his or her rights under the Act. Violation of the Act makes an individual liable to a maximum fine of $4,000 for a first offence, $10,000 for a second offence, $20,000 for a third offence, and $100,000 for a subsequent offence, whereas a company is liable to a maximum fine of $10,000 for a first offence, $20,000 for a second offence, $50,000 for a third offence, and $150,000 for a subsequent offence.

Special considerations come into play if an employer wishes to discipline, dismiss, or refuse to hire a person who smokes because nicotine addiction is a protected "disability" under the human rights legislation.[395] In order to escape liability, the employer must prove that its actions constitute a *bona fide* occupational requirement under the Act, which entails reasonably accommodating smokers up to the point of undue hardship. As yet, no employer has sought to defend a policy of not hiring smokers on the basis of the economic costs resulting from possible increased absenteeism and increased medical insurance premiums. Even if these costs can be verified, the employer must still reasonably accommodate smokers, for example, by offering to hire them if they undertake to stop smoking, possibly with the employer's assistance in providing nicotine counselling or nicotine patches.

Although such detailed external regulation is unquestionably necessary to further the goal of improving health and safety, its limitations must be acknowledged. Foremost is the fact that many health and safety hazards can be most effectively identified and combatted within the firm at the workplace level; internal procedures, therefore, are essential to perform this role. Also, legislating external standards is often a slow and cumbersome process, with political considerations some-

395 Example: *Cominco Ltd. v. U.S.W.A. Local 9705*, [2000] B.C.C.A.A.A. No. 62 (Arb. Bd.), involving a collective agreement arbitration. See also Chapter 7.

times appearing to count as much as objective scientific evidence.[396] Finally, even if state-of-the-art external standards are legislated, they may not be implemented by employers—enforcing the external legislation has proven to be extremely difficult.

The external legislation also imposes "performance" duties on employers and workers, obliging them to take reasonable steps to secure a safe workplace. The Nova Scotia *Occupational Health and Safety Act*, for instance, provides that the employer must "take every precaution that is reasonable to . . . ensure the health and safety of persons at or near the workplace." The Nova Scotia Act buttresses this general duty by imposing on the employer detailed duties to provide the prescribed training and information in health and safety; to supervise the workforce to ensure that health and safety requirements are being complied with; to ensure that equipment and machinery are being properly maintained and that protective clothing and other devices are being properly used; to notify the workforce of any workplace hazards; and to cooperate with any health and safety committee in the plant, and with health and safety representatives from government and its own workforce. Similarly, the Nova Scotia Act obliges every "worker"—independent contractors as well as "employees" *stricto sensu*—to "take every reasonable precaution in the circumstances to protect his [or her] own health and safety and that of other persons at or near the workplace." The Act also obliges workers to cooperate with the employer, co-workers, and health and safety representatives within the firm or from government in enhancing health and safety; to properly use any health or safety clothing or devices; and to report hazards to the employer. Furthermore, the Nova Scotia Act requires suppliers of material, tools, and equipment to ensure that their products are safe to use and that the hazard notification requirements for their products are satisfied.

In several provinces, such as Alberta, the statutes explicitly require a principal contractor operating at the worksite to ensure that any subcontractors it brings onto the site abide by its health and safety obligations to its own employees. The federal jurisdiction and such provinces as Saskatchewan have even introduced specific statutory duties to combat violence in the workplace, a problem that seems to be increasingly serious throughout North America.[397] As well, Saskatchewan specific-

---

396 See, for example, E. Tucker, "The Persistence of Market Regulation of Occupational Health and Safety: The Stillbirth of Voluntarism" in G. England, ed., *Essays in Labour Relations Law* (Don Mills, ON: CCH Canadian, 1983) 219.

397 *CLC*, above note 40, s. 125(z.16); Saskatchewan *Occupational Health and Safety Regulations, 1996*, R.R.S., c. O-11, Reg. 1. See generally E. Roher, *Violence in the Workplace*, 2d ed. (Toronto: Carswell, 2004).

ally requires employers to ensure that their workers are not exposed to sexual harassment.[398] Elsewhere, sexual harassment appears to fall within the definition of a "hazard" or "danger," at least if it it involves actual or threatened physical assault or serious psychological harm.[399] The advantage of encompassing sexual harassment within the health and safety acts is that the victim has access to fast and effective remedies, including the right to refuse unsafe work; procedures under the human rights legislation are notoriously slow.

These statutory performance duties typically do not create a system of absolute liability; rather, they parallel the common law[400] duties in requiring that reasonable measures be taken. The determination of reasonableness involves balancing the state of knowledge of the hazard in question, the magnitude of the harm likely to be suffered, the probability of the accident or injury occurring, and the costs and inconvenience to the employer and other persons at the worksite of eliminating the risk.[401] Any statutory provision that potentially results in the imprisonment of an offender and that does not recognize, either explicitly or implicitly, a defence of "due diligence" would almost certainly be ruled unconstitutional, offending section 7 of the *Charter*.[402]

b) The "Internal" System for Improving Health and Safety

The centrepiece of all Canadian occupational health and safety statutes is the establishment of the "internal" system, which gives employers and employees at worksite-level the pivotal role in identifying and combatting hazards unique to their particular labour processes.[403] There

---

398 *Sask. OHSA*, above note 388, c. 3(c).

399 Examples: *Au v. Lyndhurst Hospital*, (1996), 31 C.L.R.B.R. (2d) 298 (O.L.R.B.); *Pieters v. Toronto Board of Education* (1997), 36 C.L.R.B.R. (2d) 120 (O.L.R.B.).

400 *Latimer v. AEC Ltd.*, [1953] A.C. 643 (C.A.) illustrates this interest balancing process. Today, the common law has been supplanted by workers' compensation legislation as the preferred means for compensating most (but not all) workplace accidents and injuries.

401 *Ibid.*

402 See *R. v. Cancoil Thermal Corp.* (1986), 52 C.R. (3d) 188 (Ont. C.A.); *R. v. Ellis-Don Ltd.*, [1992] 1 S.C.R. 840, rev'g (1990), 1 O.R. (3d) 193 (C.A.), a health and safety case; *Wholesale Travel Group*, above note 59, var'g (1989), 70 O.R. (2d) 545 (C.A.), a competition case.

403 See generally K.E. Swinton, "Enforcement of Occupational Health and Safety: The Role of the Internal Responsibility System" in K.P. Swan & K.E. Swinton, eds., *Studies in Labour Law* (Toronto: Butterworths, 1983) 143. Despite its undoubted advantages, the internal responsibility system has not been as successful in reducing the level of accidents and illnesses at work as its advocates had originally hoped . See, for example, D. Smith, *Consulted to Death* (Winnipeg: Arbeiter Ring Publishing, 2000).

are three elements to an effective internal responsibility system: the right of employees to participate in health and safety decisions, the right of employees to refuse unsafe work, and the right of employees to know of workplace hazards.

The cornerstone of the "right to participate" is the plant-level health and safety committee. In most provinces,[404] the establishment of a joint committee consisting of equal numbers of employer and employee representatives is mandatory, provided that the firm hires a specified minimum number of employees, usually twenty. In smaller firms, the employer is required to deal with employee health and safety representatives. The mandate of such committees is spelled out in detail in each province's legislation, but typical functions include investigating and resolving health and safety complaints, conducting periodic health and safety audits in the plant, cooperating with government health and safety officers in the discharge of the latters' statutory duties, keeping abreast of health and safety developments in the industry by consulting with other companies and specialists in the area, and maintaining education and training programs in health and safety for the workforce. The employer is required to cooperate with the committee in the discharge of its functions. The legislation commonly requires that employees be paid for time spent on committee activities that occur during regular working hours, but often does not address the issue of payment for committee work outside of regular working hours.

Studies have shown that health and safety improves substantially in workplaces with a joint health and safety committee;[405] nevertheless, several criticisms can be made of the present system. One is that committee decisions are not legally binding on the employer, but are merely recommendations. It is true that an employer that disregards a committee recommendation in bad faith or arbitrarily will likely be held in breach of the statutory duty to cooperate with the committee, but it is less clear whether an employer would be ruled in breach of this duty if it refused to implement a recommendation because it would unreasonably impede operations or result in unreasonable costs. In Ontario, however, the legislation was amended in 1990 to permit committees to issue legally enforceable stop-work orders, where both the employer and the employee representatives on the committee agree with the issuance of the order.[406] Moreover, if a government-appointed

---

404 The establishment of a committee is at the discretion of the executive branch of government in Alberta, Newfoundland, and Prince Edward Island.

405 G.K. Bryce & P. Manga, "The Effectiveness of Health and Safety Committees" (1985) 40 R. I. 257. Compare with *Consulted to Death*, above note 403.

406 *Ont. OHSA*, above note 388, s. 49.

adjudicator has declared that the foregoing process is still insufficient to safeguard health and safety in the plant, the adjudicator can authorize the employee representatives of the committee to unilaterally issue a legally binding stop-work order. So far, no other province has followed this innovative approach.

Other criticisms of the committee system are that inadequate training in health and safety is provided for committee members, on the management as well as the employee side; that committee members often have inadequate systems for communicating with government health and safety agencies and outside specialists in the field; and that too many employers fail to comply with their statutory obligations to establish and cooperate with the committees.[407] Ontario attempted to address these problems by creating a Workplace Health and Safety Agency in 1990 to provide education and training to employers and employees throughout the province. The agency was authorized to "certify" employees and managers who had successfully completed the designated programs. Certified individuals would return to sit on the health and safety committee in their own plant. The agency operated under the aegis of the provincial government, but it was jointly controlled by labour and management representatives. Abolished in 1997, its functions were taken over by the Workplace Safety and Insurance Board.[408]

The second pillar of the internal responsibility system — the "right to refuse unsafe work" — has always existed at common law in the sense that an employee who is summarily fired for exercising this right will be ruled to have been wrongfully discharged without just cause.[409] However, this right is illusory in practice, since reinstatement is normally unavailable and the common law measure of damages does not make the employee's financial and emotional losses fully whole. The occupational health and safety legislation, in contrast, attempts to give teeth to the right to refuse.[410]

The general model is for the statute to state explicitly that any worker is entitled to refuse to perform work that he or she honestly and reasonably believes may endanger health and safety, his or her own or that of another person.[411] The "honesty" limb establishes a subjective criterion: the employee must genuinely intend to refuse for a health and

407 See, for example, Ontario Advisory Council on Occupational Health & Safety, *Ninth Annual Report* (Toronto: Ministry of Supply and Services, 1987), especially 49–57.
408 *Workplace Safety and Insurance Act, 1997*, S.O. 1997, c. 16, Sch. A, s. 4(1)5.
409 Example: *Ottoman Bank v. Chakarian*, [1930] A.C. 277 (P.C.).
410 See R. Brown, "The Right to Refuse Unsafe Work" (1983) 17 U.B.C. L. Rev. 1.
411 Example: *CLC*, above note 40, s. 128.

safety reason rather than for some unrelated purpose, such as to pressure the employer into giving a wage increase. The "reasonableness" limb establishes an objective criterion: the average employee in similar circumstances must conclude that an unacceptable level of risk exists. Accordingly, an employee whose assessment of the degree of risk subsequently turns out to be incorrect will be protected, provided that the assessment was reasonable in the circumstances at the time of the refusal.[412] In determining what is reasonable, account is taken of any peculiar sensitivities unique to the worker in question, such as a weak heart or a bad back. In the nomenclature of tort law, this is referred to as the "egg shell skull" doctrine.[413] In some provinces, the test seems somewhat more restrictive in that the risk must be "unusually dangerous"[414] or "imminent"[415] in order to warrant a refusal.

The exact procedure for exercising the statutory right to refuse differs in detail among the provinces. Typically, the first step is for the employer and a representative of the health or safety committee (or a health and safety representative in small firms) to investigate the refusal and attempt to resolve the problem. If an internal settlement cannot be reached to the satisfaction of the employer, the employee, and the health and safety committee (or a health and safety representative in small firms), a complaint can be filed with the appropriate government department and an inspector will be called to the plant. The inspector will conduct an inquiry into the refusal and determine whether or not it was justified, and if it was, direct the employer as to what measures must be implemented to make the job safe. Either party is given a right to appeal an inspector's ruling to a neutral third party, such as the labour relations board or a government-appointed adjudicator. The employer is expressly prohibited from dismissing or otherwise penalizing an employee for exercising the right to refuse — or, for that matter, any other right conferred by the act — and a neutral third party can order reinstatement and full compensation. Nevertheless, non-unionized employees appear to be extremely reluctant to exercise their statutory right of refusal, the vast majority of refusals occurring in the unionized sector. This suggests that the legislation must be given more teeth.

The third pillar of the internal responsibility system — the "right to know" of safety hazards —is largely contained in the *Workplace Hazardous Materials Information System (WHMIS)*, which was adopted in

---

412 Examples: *Cole v. Carey Limousine Canada* (2000), 4 C.C.E.L. (3d) 94 (O.L.R.B.); *Sidbec Dosco Inc.*, [1988] O.L.R.B. Rep. 1334.
413 Example: *Owens v. Liverpool Corp.* (1938), [1939] 1 K.B. 394 at 400–1 (C.A.).
414 *Sask. OHSA*, above note 388, s. 23.
415 *Alta. OHSA*, above note 388, s. 35(1)(a); *Nfld. OHSA*, above note 388, s. 29.

all jurisdictions in the late 1980s.[416] The basic model for the *WHMIS* is contained in the federal *Hazardous Products Act*,[417] which has been incorporated by reference into each province's occupational health and safety statutes so as to provide a uniform national system. Space constraints limit this book to providing only a general outline of this complicated system.

There are four components to the *WHMIS*. First, suppliers of designated hazardous products—called "controlled products" under the legislation—are obliged to provide "labels" and "material safety data sheets" with their products identifying the chemical composition of any material the supplier reasonably believes to be hazardous along with a description of the appropriate procedure for handling the products safely. Second, the employer is required to make an assessment in the manner prescribed by the regulations of whether any material produced in the plant is hazardous and to notify the workforce thereof. Third, employers must provide employees and supervisors with a copy of the regulations. Fourth, any manufacturer who fears that complying with the *WHMIS* disclosure requirements would involve disclosing confidential information can appeal to the federal Hazardous Materials Information Review Committee, which is empowered to excuse the employer from disclosing such information. However, even confidential information must be disclosed in medical emergencies.

2) The Problem of Enforcing Occupational Health and Safety Legislation

The occupational health and safety legislation, as is the case with other floor of rights statutes, has proven extremely difficult to enforce. Although there are differences in detail among the provinces, generally the primary aim of the statutory enforcement machinery is to settle violations by mediation. Thus, a government health and safety officer who discovers a health and safety violation during a spot check of a firm, or who conducts an investigation in response to a complaint from an employee or from the health and safety committee at the firm, will

---

416 The details are examined in P.L.S. Simon, *Hazardous Products: Canada's WHMIS Laws*, 2d ed. (Don Mills, ON: CCH Canadian, 1989); Canadian Centre for Occupational Health and Safety, "WHMIS: General," online: www.ccohs.ca/osh-answers/legisl/intro_whmis.html.

417 R.S.C. 1985, c. H-3, and *Controlled Products Regulations*, SOR/88-66. The Act is complemented by the *Hazardous Materials Information Review Act*, R.S.C. 1985 (3d Supp.), c. 24 and *Hazardous Materials Information Review Regulations*, SOR/88-456.

inform the employer about its statutory obligations and strive to persuade the employer to remedy the situation. Mediation is clearly useful in the case of an employer that simply does not understand its legal obligations and inadvertently violates the act, but it is useless if the employer has made a calculated decision that it is more profitable to breach the act than to honour it. For the latter—the hard-core violator—an effective deterrent is necessary.

When it comes to deterrence, Canadian occupational health and safety legislation features two distinct approaches: the "criminal prosecution" approach and the "administrative penalty" approach.[418] The main advantage of bringing a regular criminal law prosecution against hard-core violators is the added deterrent effect of the social taint of criminality. On the other hand, there are disadvantages with this method: the criminal law burden of proof of beyond any reasonable doubt may make it difficult to secure convictions; regular judges may be unfamiliar with the intricacies of health and safety legislation; and criminal trials are costly, invite esoteric procedural defences, and are prone to lengthy delay. All of the latter weaknesses were vividly highlighted in the prosecution of senior managers at the Westray Mine in Nova Scotia, after an underground explosion killed twenty-six miners in May 1992.[419] As a result of the Westray disaster, in 2004, section 217.1 was included in the *Criminal Code* to make it easier to prosecute companies for criminal negligence. It provides:

> Every one who undertakes, or has the authority, to direct how another person does work or performs a task is under a legal duty to take reasonable steps to prevent bodily harm to that person, or any other person, arising from that work or task.[420]

Nevertheless, it was not until March 2008 that the first conviction was recorded under this section: a paving stone company was fined $110,000 for criminal negligence in the death of an employee in 2005.[421]

---

418 See R.M. Brown, "Administrative and Criminal Penalties in the Enforcement of Occupational Health and Safety Legislation" (1992) 30 Osgoode Hall L.J. 691 ["Administrative and Criminal Penalties"].

419 E. Tucker, "The Westray Mine Disaster and Its Aftermath: The Politics of Causation" (1995) 10 Can. J.L. & Soc. 91 ["The Westray Mine Disaster"]; C.R. McCormick, *The Westray Chronicles: A Case Study in Corporate Crime* (Halifax: Fernwood, 1999); Westray Mine Public Inquiry, *The Westray Story: A Predictable Path to Disaster* by Justice K.P. Richard (Halifax: Westray Mine Public Inquiry, 1997).

420 *Criminal Code*, R.S.C. 1985, c. C-46.

421 Graeme Hamilton, "Safety Ruling Likely to Set Legal Precedent: Company Fined" *National Post* (18 March 2008) A6.

Most Canadian provinces have adopted the "criminal prosecution" approach.

In contrast, the "administrative penalty" approach authorizes the government health and safety department that investigates the complaint to impose a financial penalty on violators, subject to an appeal to a superior body within the department. British Columbia currently adopts this model, with the provincial Workers' Compensation Board being charged with both investigating complaints and levying penalties. An internal appeal is provided to the appeal division of the board. According to Brown, this approach has three main advantages over the "criminal prosecution" approach: the incidence of successful convictions is increased owing to the application of the balance of probabilities standard of proof; proceedings are faster and cheaper; and penalties can be levied before a serious accident occurs (unlike under the "criminal prosecution" approach, where the tendency is to delay prosecuting until a patently winnable case exists—usually after someone has been seriously hurt).[422] Brown's preference is for the administrative model to be used for commonplace violations, with criminal prosecution being used sparingly for the most serious violations.

A common criticism of the present system is that provincial departments of labour are too reluctant to initiate prosecutions. Usually, prosecution is commenced only where the consequences of an accident are severe or the employer is a repeat violator. In any criminal prosecution that could potentially result in imprisonment, the employer can escape liability by showing that it exercised "due diligence" in attempting to avoid the incident.[423] Furthermore, it is argued, the fines are too low to provide an effective deterrent. In this regard, fines are higher in British Columbia under the administrative model than in most other provinces that adopt the "criminal prosecution" approach.[424] During the 1990s, however, most provinces increased the fines in response to this criticism. In Ontario, for example, the Act was amended to increase the maximum fine on corporations to $50,000 from $25,000. The maximum penalty for an individual is one year's imprisonment and a fine of $25,000.

It remains to be seen whether the deterrent impact of fines alone will encourage greater compliance with the legislation; furthermore, several provinces empower courts to impose broader remedies designed to improve health and safety in addition to imposing fines. In Alberta,

---

422 See "Administrative and Criminal Penalties," above note 418.
423 See the authorities cited in note 402, above.
424 See "Administrative and Criminal Penalties," above note 418.

for example, the statute allows the court to impose a training or educational program in the workplace at the employer's expense or take any other "specific action to improve health and safety at work sites."[425] Some commentators have argued that prosecuting senior managers of firms in their personal capacity for general crimes, such as manslaughter or even homicide, might be necessary.[426] However, the difficulties of securing convictions against such individuals may limit the usefulness of this option, as the Westray Mines saga confirms.[427]

3) Compensating Employees Injured at Work

All Canadian provinces have workers' compensation acts that compensate employees who are injured or contract a disease in the course of their employment.[428] Employees in the federal jurisdiction are subject to the workers' compensation act of the province in which they work. The legislation is administered by a state-appointed Workers' Compensation Board. Its essential feature is that it compensates employees without requiring them to prove fault on the part of the employer or other tortfeasor, in return for eliminating the right to pursue a common law action for damages.[429] It was thought that trading off the common

425 Examples: *Alta. OHSA*, above note 388, s. 41.1(1); *Nfld. OHSA*, above note 388, s. 69(1). Examples of the various innovative sentencing measures that courts have imposed are examined by T. Tull, "From the Courtroom, Alternative Sentencing in OHS Prosecutions" *Occupational Health and Safety Magazine* (September 2004) at 15. See also A. Stelmakowich, "A Spoonful of Sugar" *Occupational Health and Safety Canada* (April/May 2003) at 4.

426 H. Glasbeek & S. Rowland, "Are Injuring and Killing at Work Crimes?" (1979) 17 Osgoode Hall L.J. 506.

427 "The Westray Mine Disaster," above note 419.

428 Alberta *Workers' Compensation Act*, R.S.A. 2000, c. W-15; *B.C. WCA*, above note 388; Manitoba *Workers Compensation Act*, C.C.S.M. c. W200; New Brunswick *Workplace Health, Safety and Compensation Commission Act*, S.N.B. 1974, c. W-14; Newfoundland *Workers' Compensation Act*, R.S.N.L. 1990, c. W-11; Nova Scotia *Workers' Compensation Act*, S.N.S. 1994–95, c. 10; Ontario *Workers' Compensation Reform Act, 1997*, S.O. 1997, c. 16; Quebec *Act Respecting Industrial Accidents and Occupational Diseases*, R.S.Q., c. A-3.001; Prince Edward Island *Workers' Compensation Act*, S.P.E.I. 1994, c. 67; Saskatchewan *Workers' Compensation Act, 1979*, S.S. 1979, c. W-17.1.

429 The best analysis is the series of three volumes produced by P. C. Weiler for the Ontario provincial government: *Reshaping Workers' Compensation for Ontario* (Toronto: Ministry of Labour, 1980); *Protecting the Worker from Disability: Challenges for the Eighties* (Toronto: Ministry of Labour, 1983); and *Permanent Partial Disability: Alternative Models for Compensation* (Toronto: Ministry of Labour, 1986). See also M Gunderson & D.Hyatt, eds., *Workers Compensation: Foundations of Reform* (Toronto: University of Toronto Press, 2000).

law right to sue in return for a guarantee of compensation was in the best interests of workers because the obstacles to succeeding in a common law action result in many workers receiving no compensation for their accident or illness.[430] The courts have confirmed the contemporary justification of this trade-off by holding that workers' compensation acts do not violate the *Charter* by eliminating an employee's common law right to sue, at least so long as the level of statutory benefits is maintained at or about the current relatively generous levels.[431] However, critics have argued that giving the employee a choice of either suing at common law or recovering under the statute would provide a potent incentive for employers to improve health and safety, since the employee stands a chance of receiving a substantial damages award in a common law suit.

Although the details of the workers' compensation legislation cannot be examined in this introductory book, its main characteristics are as follows.

First, the scheme is funded almost entirely by contributions from employers to a state-operated "accident fund"; employees do not make any contributions, but in some provinces the accident fund is topped up from general government revenues. The employee is compensated out of the accident fund, not out of the employer's assets.

Second, the amount that the employer must pay into the fund is determined by a blend of collective and individual factors. Thus, a collectively determined contribution is assessed on the basis of the rate of accidents and diseases in the particular industrial group to which the employer belongs. The weakness of the collective method, of course, is that individual firms with poor health and safety records can take a free ride on the backs of firms that are seriously attempting to improve health and safety in their plants. Consequently, this method is normally complemented by making an individual experience rating for each firm and reducing the level of a firm's contributions commensurate with its record. One risk with the individual method, however, is that it may encourage unscrupulous employers to pressure sick or injured employees not to file a claim for compensation in order to keep the firm's contribution rate down.[432] Such pressure is clearly illegal but,

---

430 The history of the legislation is examined by T.G. Ison, "A Historical Perspective on Contemporary Challenges in Workers' Compensation" (1996) 34 Osgoode Hall L.J. 807.

431 *Piercey Estate v. General Bakeries Ltd.* (1986), 61 Nfld. & P.E.I.R. 147 (Nfld. S.C.T.D.), aff'd (1987), 67 Nfld. & P.E.I.R. 16 (Nfld. S.C.A.D.), aff'd [1989] 1 S.C.R. 922.

432 See T.G. Ison, "The Significance of Experience Rating" (1986) 24 Osgoode Hall L.J. 723.

regrettably, enforcing employee rights under protective employment statutes in practice is no easy matter.

Third, the workers' compensation legislation specifies in great detail the categories of compensation that an injured or sick employee can claim from the fund. The main categories are the following:

- *Income replacement benefits* are granted for permanent and temporary absences from work, ranging from 75 percent of the employee's net earnings loss in Nova Scotia to 90 percent in Alberta, Manitoba, Ontario, Quebec, and Saskatchewan. The rationale for not paying 100 percent of lost earnings is presumably to discourage malingering.
- *Permanent impairment benefits* are given for the "pain and suffering" an employee experiences as a result of injuries, with larger awards being given for more serious injuries. Since regulations specify a dollar amount for defined injuries, they have been nicknamed "meat charts." Usually, the amount of such benefits is less than the worker would receive in a common law tort action for pain and suffering. But the *quid pro quo* is that the employee does not run the risk of losing a tort action.
- *Survivor benefits* are paid to the surviving dependants of an employee who dies as a result of an injury or illness sustained at work.
- *Medical aid costs* arising from an injury or illness are payable out of the workers' compensation fund.
- *Rehabilitation benefits and services* are awarded to employees who cannot resume their former work due to a permanent injury and who require training, education, and other assistance in finding replacement work within their physical capacity.

Fourth, in five provinces the workers' compensation legislation entitles the employee to return to work with the employer after recovering from an illness or injury.[433] If the employee can no longer do his or her old work, the employer is bound under these provisions to offer other work that is within the employee's physical capacity. Only where the employee is unable to perform *any* work because of a medical condition is the employer entitled to refuse an offer of re-employment. Moreover, the employer is required to reasonably accommodate the employee up to the point of undue hardship—for example, by reassigning work duties among other employees or making alterations to the layout of the plant and equipment—so as to make available work that the employee

---

433 Ontario, Quebec, New Brunswick, Prince Edward Island, and Nova Scotia.

can perform.[434] Usually, there is a time limit on the exercise of the right to resume work, normally two years after the injury or illness.

Fifth, the procedure for filing a workers' compensation claim generally begins with the employee's claim being adjudicated by an official of the workers' compensation department. If the adjudicator denies the claim, it is usually remitted to the workers' compensation board for a hearing. If the workers' compensation board also rejects the claim, a right of appeal is made available either to an appellate division of the board or to an unconnected outside tribunal, depending on the jurisdiction. The advantage of having an "in-house" appellate body is to ensure consistency of policy, but the downside is the appearance of bias. The courts can intervene in the decision of the appellate body only if it breaches natural justice or involves an error of jurisdiction; no appeal can be made to the courts on questions of fact.

Sixth, the workers' compensation legislation does not provide a fully comprehensive system of no-fault liability; there are excluded categories of accidents and illnesses and excluded categories of employees. Only those categories of accidents and illness occurring "during the course of employment" are compensable. Many claims fail because difficult questions of causation arise, especially where the symptoms of an industrial disease take a long time to become manifest or where the worker leads an unhealthy personal lifestyle. Moreover, some provinces explicitly exclude from coverage defined injuries or illnesses, even if they occur during employment. For example, psychological stress is generally excluded from coverage, unless the stress is "an acute reaction to a traumatic event." [435] The New Brunswick Court of Appeal has ruled that this language allows stress to be compensated in the following, relatively narrow circumstances:

> First, the traumatic event must have arisen out of and in the course of employment. Second, a traumatic event is defined as an event that is sudden and unexpected: one that is outside the range of usual human experience. Third, an employment decision affecting the terms and conditions of employment does not qualify as a traumatic event. Fourth, cases of chronic or gradual onset stress, being cumulative in

---

434 This duty is also required under human rights legislation if the employee's illness or injury constitutes a "disability" as defined under that legislation. See Chapter 7.

435 New Brunswick *Workers' Compensation Act*, R.S.N.B. 1973, c. W-13, s. 1, "accident." All provinces, save for Alberta and Saskatchewan, have similar legislation regarding stress.

nature, do not qualify as a traumatic event. Fifth, what is or is not a traumatic event must be measured objectively.[436]

The adoption of a purely objective standard for determining what constitutes a "traumatic" event means that an employee whose personal sensitivity level is above average will not be covered.[437] As well, the courts have ruled that verbal abuse does not cross the "traumatic" threshold under the objective test unless it also involves a real and imminent threat of physical violence.[438] This reluctance to cover mental stress is justified in order to safeguard the financial health of the fund against a possible tidal wave of spurious claims.

Any exclusions of or differential treatment between specified injuries or illnesses can be challenged under section 15 of the *Charter*, in which case the provincial government would have to justify them under section 1. Thus, in 2003 the Supreme Court of Canada struck down provisions in the Nova Scotia Act excluding employees with chronic back pain from the general statutory benefits and limiting them to a shorter benefit period under the Functional Restoration Program.[439] The Court ruled that the government's policy reasons for this differential treatment, namely, budgetary constraints, administrative convenience, the difficulty of identifying malingerers, and the medical benefits of participating in the Functional Restoration Program, were insufficient to justify the discrimination.

Furthermore, in limited circumstances, compensation can be denied if the accident or illness resulted "solely" from the worker's "serious and wilful misconduct,"[440] a vestige of the common law contributory negligence doctrine. Typically excluded categories of employees, depending on the jurisdiction, include homeworkers, domestics, casuals, educators, and taxidermists. However, the legislation usually empowers the workers' compensation board, either at the motion of the employees in question or at its own initiative, to extend the act's coverage to an excluded group on conditions to be determined by the board.

---

436 *W.(D.) v. New Brunswick (Workplace Health, Safety and Compensation Commission)* (2005), 42 C.C.E.L. (3d) 163 at para. 181–82 (N.B.C.A.).
437 *Ibid.* at 185–86.
438 *Children's Aid Society of Cape Breton-Victoria v. Nova Scotia (Workers' Compensation Appeals Tribunal)*, [2005] N.S.J. No. 75 (C.A.).
439 *Nova Scotia (Workers' Compensation Board) v. Martin*, [2003] 2 S.C.R. 504.
440 Example: Saskatchewan *Workers Compensation Act, 1979*, S.S. 1979, C. W-17.1, s. 31.

E. PRIVACY LEGISLATION

Historically, Canadian legislation has not gone far in protecting the employee's personal privacy; nor has the common law.[441] However, the advent of new computer technology that gives employers broad access to extensive personal information about their employees and that allows the employer to monitor closely employee activities both during and outside working hours, has spurred legislative intervention. Safeguards are now established under (1) employment standards acts, (2) special privacy acts, and (3) the Canadian *Criminal Code*.

1) Employment Standards Acts

Except for the Ontario and New Brunswick acts that prohibit employers from either asking or requiring an employee or a job applicant to take a "lie detector test" as defined in the acts, employment standards acts do not contain comprehensive safeguards against undue interference by employers with the privacy of their employees.[442] Not only is the employee expressly entitled to refuse to submit to such a test, but the employer cannot "require, enable or influence, directly or indirectly,"[443] an employee to take a test. It is perhaps surprising that the latter wording has been held to permit an employer to suggest to an employee that he or she consider submitting voluntarily to a test and even to arrange an appointment for the employee.[444] Even in provinces without the express statutory prohibition, courts in civil litigation normally give little or no weight to the results of lie detector tests. Polygraph evidence is notoriously unreliable in scientific terms,[445] so the courts want to avoid

---

441 On the general law of privacy, see B. McIssac, R. Shields, & K. Klein, *The Law of Privacy in Canada*, looseleaf (Toronto: Carswell, 2000). On the law of privacy specifically in the employment relationship, see I. Turnbull, *Privacy in the Workplace: The Employment Perspective* (Toronto: CCH Canadian, 2004); J. De Beer, "Employee Privacy: The Need for Comprehensive Protection" (2003) 66 Sask. L. Rev. 383; K. Eltis, "The Emerging American Approach to E-mail Privacy in the Workplace: Its Influence on Developing Caselaw in Canada and Israel: Should Others Follow Suit?" (2004) 24 Comp. Lab. L. & Pol'y J. 487; M. Geist, "Computer and E-mail Surveillance in Canada: The Shift from Reasonable Expectation of Privacy to Reasonable Surveillance" (2003) 82 Can. Bar Rev. 151.

442 *N.B. ESA*, above note 89, s. 44.1; *Ont. ESA*, above note 52, ss. 68–70.

443 *Ont. ESA, ibid.*, s. 47(2).

444 *Haldimand-Norfolk (Regional Municipality) (Grandview Lodge) v. Health, Office & Professional Employees, Local 206* (1985), 22 L.A.C. (3d) 123 at 126 (Samuels).

445 In criminal proceedings, polygraph results are inadmissible: e.g., *R. v. Béland*, [1987] S.C.J. No. 60, 43 D.L.R. (4d) 641.

bogging down proceedings with conflicting scientific debates. As well, the test is often not taken voluntarily, and usually there is other, more reliable evidence available upon which to base a judgment.

2) Specialized Privacy Acts

There are two kinds of specialized legislation aimed at safeguarding the employee's privacy: (a) the *Personal Information Protection and Electronic Documents Act* and (b) privacy acts.

a) The *Personal Information Protection and Electronic Documents Act*

In 2000, the federal government enacted the *Personal Information Protection and Electronic Documents Act* which establishes how employers in the private sector can collect, use, and disclose personal information about their employees.[446] Initially, the Act applied only to employers within the federal jurisdiction, but as of 1 January 2004, coverage was extended to employers within provincial jurisdictions as well, unless a province shows that it has enacted its own "substantially similar" safeguards. As yet, only Quebec, Alberta, British Columbia, Manitoba, and Ontario have enacted equivalent legislation.[447] The federal statute illustrates the common approach.

The Act establishes a code of principles for the collection, use, and disclosure of "personal information," broadly defined as any "information about an identifiable individual" except name, title, business address, or telephone number. The ten principles are outlined below.

- Principle 1: "Accountability" requires the employer to designate an officer responsible for implementing the Act.
- Principle 2: "Identifying Purpose" requires the employer to specify the business purposes for which personal information is being collected and restricts the use of the information to these purposes.

---

446 S.C. 2000, c. 5 [*PIPEDA*]. For a detailed analysis analysis of the Act, see Office of the Privacy Commissioner of Canada, *PIPEDA: Leading by Example: Key Developments in the First Seven Years of the Personal Information Protection and Electronic Documents Act* (Ottawa: Office of the Privacy Commissioner of Canada, 2008); S. Perrin *et al.*, *The Personal Information Protection and Electronic Documents Act* (Toronto: Irwin Law, 2001).

447 Alberta *Personal Information Protection Act*, S.A. 2003, c. P-6.5; British Columbia *Personal Information Protection Act*, S.B.C. 2003, c. 63; Manitoba *Personal Health Information Act*, C.C.S.M. c. P33.5; Ontario *Personal Health Information Protection Act*, S.O. 2004, c. 3; Quebec *Act Respecting the Protection of Personal Information in the Private Sector*, R.S.Q., c. P-39.1.

- Principle 3: "Consent" obliges the employer to make "reasonable efforts" to inform the employee of the purposes for which the information is being used and to obtain the employee's consent to using the information for those purposes unless it would be "inappropriate."
- Principle 4: "Limiting Collection" restricts an employer to collecting information needed for "reasonable"[448] business purposes and requires that such information be collected "by fair and lawful means."
- Principle 5: "Limiting Use, Disclosure, and Retention" prohibits the use, disclosure, or retention of personal information for purposes other than those for which it was collected, except with the consent of the individual or "as required by law."
- Principle 6: "Accuracy" obliges the employer to maintain accurate, complete, and updated information.
- Principle 7: "Safeguards" requires that the employer protect personal information by security measures that are "appropriate to the sensitivity of the information."
- Principle 8: "Openness" obliges the employer to notify its employees of its policies respecting the handling of personal information.
- Principle 9: "Individual Access" entitles an employee to be informed of the existence, use, and disclosure of personal information and to contest its accuracy.
- Principle 10: "Challenging Compliance" permits an employee to complain to the employer's officer in charge of personal information administration that his or her rights have been violated.

The Act provides relatively broad and vague exceptions where personal information can be collected, used, or disclosed without the consent of the individual.[449] Thus, information can be collected (but not used or disclosed) without an employee's agreement where doing so is "clearly in the interests" of the employee and consent cannot be obtained in a "timely" fashion. Information can also be secretly collected (but not used or disclosed) where it is "reasonable" to expect that obtaining consent would "compromise the availability or accuracy" of the information, or if it is "reasonable" for the purpose of investigating a breach of "an agreement" or the laws of the land. Employee consent is also not required if the information is being disclosed to a lawyer who is representing the employee, or where another party needs the

---

448 The "reasonableness" limitation on the range of purposes for which personal information may be collected, used, or disclosed is imposed under s. 5(3) of the Act: see *PIPEDA*, above note 446.
449 The exceptions are contained in s. 7: see *PIPEDA*, *ibid.*

information because of an "emergency the life, health or safety of an individual" (provided the party in question notifies the employee in writing of the disclosure "without delay.")

The Act is enforced by filing a complaint to the Privacy Commissioner who conducts an investigation, attempts to mediate a voluntary settlement of the complaint, and if necessary, issues a written, but not legally binding recommendation to settle the complaint. However, if the complainant remains unsatisfied, he or she can proceed in the Federal Court for an order compelling the employer to comply with the Act and to provide compensation for any losses suffered, including injury to dignity. In order to protect the integrity of the statutory process, the Act makes it unlawful for an employer to penalize any employee or other person for having exercised his or her rights. Compliance with the Act is also achieved by authorizing the Privacy Commissioner to initiate an audit of an employer's personal information practices if the commissioner has "reasonable grounds" to believe that a firm is violating the law. The commissioner is entitled to conduct an investigation and make a report of findings within a year. If necessary the commissioner can also file a complaint against the employer in the Federal Court, and the Court may issue any affected employees a remedy as outlined above.

As yet, the exact scope of the Act remains unknown, but given the vague statutory language, its impact on personnel practices is potentially enormous. At this juncture, the Act has been applied to give employees the right to examine material in their personnel files, such as performance appraisals, training records, disciplinary reports, letters of complaint written by third parties, letters from a doctor concerning the employee's medical condition, and reports of investigations involving the employee.[450] Furthermore, the Act restricts the employer's use of workplace video surveillance to situations where the employer can demonstrate that video surveillance is a necessary, effective, and proportional method of meeting a specific need, such as to avoid theft of company property, to reduce vandalism, to avoid assaults on employees, or to discourage malingering; and that there are no less intrusive methods available to achieve the need in question.[451] Similarly, employers cannot secretly monitor an employee's use of a computer during working time unless the employer can prove that unauthorized

450 Examples: *Rousseau v. Canada (Privacy Commissioner)*, [2008] F.C.J. No. 151 (C.A.); PIPEDA Case Summary #44, 8 April 2002; PIPEDA Case Summary #50, 10 May 2002; PIPEDA Case Summary #88, 31 October 2002.
451 Examples: PIPEDA Case Summary #114, 23 January 2003; PIPEDA Case Summary #279, 26 July 2004.

computer use is interfering with productivity, and that less intrusive solutions have been tried before resort is had to secret surveillance, for example, warning employees to cease unauthorized computer use.[452]

b) Privacy Acts

In four provinces, special privacy acts establish a tort for willfully and without justification violating the privacy of another person, for which damages are available.[453] These acts, which are of general application, are rarely used in the employment relationship, probably because the costs of civil litigation are too high for a vulnerable employee relative to the amount of compensation that he or she stands to recover if successful. Furthermore, most provinces have privacy acts that regulate the collection of personal information about an individual by government bodies and that allow the individual to have access to that information.[454] Again, these acts apply generally, including in the workplace, but they are used infrequently by employees.

3) Canadian *Criminal Code*

Section 184(1) of the *Criminal Code* makes it an offence for anyone, including an employer, to willfully intercept a private communication "by means of any electro-magnetic, acoustic, mechanical or other device." This would appear to cover email or telephone monitoring by an employer. However, since section 184(2)(a) states that the offence is not committed if the originator of the communication or the recipient expressly or impliedly consent, employers can easily avoid liability if there are company policies giving them the right to monitor the employee's computer and telephone communications. After all, few employees would have the power to oppose the introduction of such policies.

---

452 *Order No. F07-18; University of British Columbia (Re)*, [2007] B.C.I.P.C.D. No. 30 (Information and Privacy Commission), interpreting section 26 of the British Columbia *Freedom of Information and Protection of Privacy Act*, R.S.B.C. 1996, c. 165.

453 British Columbia *Freedom of Information and Protection of Privacy Act, ibid.*; Manitoba *Privacy Act*, C.C.S.M. c. P125; Newfoundland *Privacy Act*, R.S.N.L. 1990, c. P-22; Saskatchewan *Privacy Act*, R.S.S. 1978, c. P-24.

454 Examples: Alberta *Freedom of Information and Protection of Privacy Act*, R.S.A. 2000, c. F-25; Nova Scotia *Freedom of Information and Protection of Privacy Act*, S.N.S. 1993, c. 5.

FURTHER READINGS

ABBOTT, M.G., *Pay Equity: Ends and Means*. Policy Forum Series No. 20 (Kingston, ON: John Deutsch Institute for the Study of Economic Policy, Queen's University, 1991)

ADAMS, R.J., "Employment Standards in Ontario: An Industrial Relations System Analysis" (1987) 42 R.I./I.R. 46

ADAMS, R., "The Unorganized: A Rising Force" Research and Working Paper Series No. 201 (Hamilton, ON: McMaster University, Faculty of Business 1983) at 977

ADDISON, J.T., & W.S. SIEBERT, "The Social Charter of the European Community: Evolution and Controversies" (1991) 44 Indus. Lab. Rel. Rev. 597

BASU, K. *et al.*, eds., *International Labour Standards: Histories, Theories and Policy Options* (Oxford: Blackwell, 2003)

BAUMERT *et al.*, *International Cooperation on Trade and Labor Issues*, Working Paper (Washington, DC: Office of Industries, U.S. International Trade Commission, 2008)

BETTEN, L., *International Labour Law: Selected Issues* (Deventer, Neth.: Kluwer, 1993)

BROWN, C., C. GILROY, & A. KOHEN, "The Effect of the Minimum Wage on Employment and Unemployment" (1982) 20 J. Econ. Lit. 487

BROWN, R.M., "Administrative and Criminal Penalties in the Enforcement of Occupational Health and Safety Legislation" (1992) 30 Osgoode Hall L.J. 691

CANADA, COMMISSION ON THE REVIEW OF FEDERAL LABOUR STANDARDS, *Fairness at Work: Federal Labour Standards for the 21st Century* by H.W. Arthurs (Ottawa: Commission on the Review of Federal Labour Standards, 2006)

Canadian Employment Health and Safety Guide, 4 vols., looseleaf (Don Mills, ON: CCH Canadian, 1980–)

CANADIAN LABOUR CONGRESS, *Equality Once and for All: Women in the Workforce: Still a Long Way from Equality* (Ottawa: Canadian Labour Congress, 2008), online: www.onceandforall.ca

COLLINS, H., "Regulating the Employment Relationship for Competitiveness" (2001) 30 Indus. L.J. 17

COLLINS, H., "Vertical Disintegration to Employment Protection Laws" (1990) 10 Oxford J. Legal Stud. 331

DEAKIN, S., & F. WILLIAMSON, "Rights versus Efficiency? The Economic Case for Transnational Labour Standards" (1994) Indus. L.J. 289

ENGLAND, G., *Part Time, Casual and Other Atypical Work: A Legal View* (Kingston, ON: Industrial Relations Centre, Queen's University, 1987)

ENGLAND, G., R. WOOD, & I. CHRISTIE, *Employment Law in Canada*, 4th ed., looseleaf (Markham, ON: LexisNexis Canada, 2005–) cc. 8 & 9

ENGLAND, P., *Comparable Worth: Theories and Evidence* (New York: de Gruyter, 1992)

EWING, K., "Homeworking: A Framework for Reform" (1982) 11 Indus. L.J. 94

GUNDERSON, M., "The Evolution and Mechanics of Pay Equity in Ontario" (May 2002) 46 Can. Pub. Pol'y Supplement: Occupational Gender Segregation: Public Policies and Economic Forces S117–31

GUNDERSON, M., "The Social and Economic Impact of Labour Standards," Executive Summary of a Report to the Federal Labour Standards Review Panel (Ottawa: Human Resources and Social Development Canada, 2005), online: www.hrsdc.gc.ca/en/labour/employment_standards/fls/research/research01/page01.shtml

GUNDERSON, M., & D. HYATT, eds., *Workers Compensation: Foundations of Reform* (Toronto: University of Toronto Press, 2000)

HEPPLE, B., *Labour Laws and Global Trade* (Oxford: Hart, 2005)

ISON, T.G., *Workers Compensation in Canada,* 2d ed. (Toronto: Butterworths, 1989)

KEITH, N.A., *Canadian Health & Safety Law: A Comprehensive Guide to the Statutes, Policies and Case Law*, looseleaf (Aurora, ON: Canada Law Book, 1997–)

KELLOWAY, E., L. FRANCIS, & J. MONTGOMERY, *Management of Occupational Health and Safety*, 3d ed. (Toronto: Nelson Thomson, 2006)

KELLY, J.G., *Pay Equity Management*, 2d ed. (Don Mills, ON: CCH Canadian, 1996)

MALLES, P., *Canadian Labour Standards in Law: Agreement and Practice* (Ottawa: Economic Council of Canada, 1976)

MAYER, F., "Temps Partial et Precarite" (1996) 51 R.I./I.R. 524

McCLURE, JR., J., "Minimum Wages and the Wessels Effect in a Monopoly Model" (1994) 15 J. Lab. Res. 271

ONTARIO PAY EQUITY COMMISSION, *Ontario Pay Equity Commission's Series of Guidelines under the Pay Equity Act* (Toronto: Ontario Pay Equity Commission, 1994)

Part-Time Work in Canada: Report of the Commission of Inquiry into Part-Time Work (Ottawa: Labour Canada, 1983) (Chair: J. Wallace)

OFFICE OF THE PRIVACY COMMISSIONER OF CANADA, *PIPEDA: Leading by Example: Key Developments in the First Seven Years of the Personal Information Protection and Electronic Documents Act* (Ottawa: Office of the Privacy Commissioner of Canada, 2008)

POSNER, R.A., "Some Economics of Labour Law" (1984) 51 U. Chi. L. Rev. 988

Report of the Advisory Group on Working Time and the Distribution of Work (Ottawa: Ministry of Supply and Services Canada, 1994) (Chair: A Donner)

RHOADS, S., *Incomparable Worth: Pay Equity Meets the Market* (Cambridge: Cambridge University Press, 1993)

Rights and Responsibilities in a Changing Workplace: A Review of Employment Standards in British Columbia (Victoria: Ministry of Skills, Training and Labour, 1994) (Chair: M. Thompson)

SCHNEIDER DE VILLEGAS, G., "Home Work: A Case for Social Protection" (1990) 129 Int'l Lab. Rev. 423

SIMON, P.L.S., *Hazardous Products: Canada's WHMIS Laws*, 2d ed. (Don Mills, Ont.: CCH Canadian Ltd., 1989)

SMITH, D., *Consulted to Death* (Winnipeg: Arbeiter Ring Publishing, 2000)

STENSLAND, J., "Internationalizing the North American Agreement on Labor Cooperation" (1995) 4 Minn. J. Global Trade 141

TUCKER, E., "Diverging Trends in Worker Health and Safety Protection and Participation in Canada 1985–2000" (2003) 58 R.I./I.R. 395

TUCKER, E., "The Westray Mine Disaster and Its Aftermath: The Politics of Causation" (1995) 10 C.J.L.S. 91

TURNBULL, I., *Privacy in the Workplace: the Employment Perspective* (Toronto: CCH Canadian, 2004)

WEILER, P.C., *Protecting the Worker from Disability: Challenges for the Eighties* (Toronto: Ministry of Government Services, 1983)

WEILER, P.C., *Reshaping Workers' Compensation for Ontario* (Toronto: Ministry of Labour, 1980)

WEINER, N., & M. GUNDERSON, *Pay Equity: Issues, Options and Experiences* (Toronto: Butterworths, 1990)

Working Times: The Report of the Ontario Task Force on Hours of Work and Overtime (Toronto: Ontario Ministry of Labour, 1987) (Chair: A. Donner)

CHAPTER 7

HUMAN RIGHTS LEGISLATION IN THE WORKPLACE

All Canadian provinces and the federal jurisdiction have enacted human rights statutes designed to eliminate discrimination on proscribed grounds from all walks of life, including employment.[1] The development of this legislation has been inspired by the growing concern in Canada and at the international level since the Second World War with protecting human rights; by the increasingly important role of women, immigrants, and visible minorities in the Canadian labour force; and by the enactment of the *Canadian Charter of Rights and Freedoms*, which, although it does not apply directly to the terms of private employment contracts, has nonetheless fuelled the expectation of all workers for greater "rights" in their employment relationships.[2]

---

1   *Canadian Human Rights Act*, R.S.C. 1985, c. H-6 [*Can. HRA*]; Alberta *Human Rights, Citizenship and Multiculturalism Act*, R.S.A. 2000, c. H-14 [*Alta. HRCMA*]; British Columbia *Human Rights Code*, R.S.B.C. 1996, c. 210 [*B.C. HRC*]; Manitoba *Human Rights Code*, C.C.S.M. c. H175, s. 9(2) [*Man. HRC*]; New Brunswick *Human Rights Act*, R.S.N.B. 1973, c. H-11 [*N.B. HRA*]; Newfoundland and Labrador *Human Rights Code*, R.S.N.L. 1990, c. H-14 [*N.L. HRC*]; Nova Scotia *Human Rights Act*, R.S.N.S. 1989, c. 214 [*N.S. HRA*]; Ontario *Human Rights Code*, R.S.O. 1990, c. H.19 [*Ont. HRC*]; Prince Edward Island *Human Rights Act*, R.S.P.E.I. 1988, c. H-12 [*P.E.I. HRA*]; Quebec *Charter of Human Rights and Freedoms*, R.S.Q. c. C-12 [*Quebec Charter*]; Saskatchewan *Human Rights Code*, S.S. 1979, c. S-24.1 [*Sask. HRC*]. For further elaboration on the employment dimension of this legislation, see G. England, R. Wood, & I. Christie, *Employment Law in Canada*, 4th ed., looseleaf (Markham, ON: LexisNexis Canada, 2005–) c. 5 at 1.

2   G. England, "The Impact of the *Charter* on Individual Employment Law in Canada: Rewriting an Old Story" (2006) 13 C.L.E.L.J. 1 ["Impact of the *Charter*"].

It is important to understand from the outset that the concept of "discrimination" espoused by modern human rights legislation goes beyond the situation where an employer deliberately penalizes a worker out of distaste for a protected characteristic—for example, where an employer refuses to hire Jews out of anti-Semitism. This situation is referred to in human rights parlance as "direct" or "intentional" discrimination. Rather, the human rights acts seek to eliminate the disadvantages that women and visible minorities are perceived as suffering, even though their current employer or potential employer may not harbour any personal animosity towards them. Accordingly, the employment practices and policies of an employer can be regarded as "discriminatory" in the latter sense if they simply have a deleterious impact on a protected group, even though the practices and policies in question, on their face, treat non-protected and protected groups identically. This situation is referred to in human rights parlance as "indirect" discrimination. Much of the public controversy generated by the fact that human rights acts accord "preferential treatment" to protected groups—for example, by means of affirmative action hiring and promotion remedies—springs from a widespread misunderstanding of or disagreement with the notion that discrimination encompasses non-intentionally produced societal disadvantages.

It is also important to appreciate from the outset the potentially enormous influence of human rights legislation on other areas of Canadian employment law. A central feature of modern human rights acts is the duty of "reasonable accommodation," which obliges employers to attempt to rearrange work schedules, job assignments, and other facets of the production process up to the point of causing the firm "undue hardship," in order to avoid disadvantaging protected employees—for example, by laying off employees whose disabilities incapacitate them from performing some of their duties. This duty goes to the very heart of the employer's managerial prerogatives, allowing human rights tribunals to dictate how much economic harm the employer must sustain in order to safeguard an employee's personal rights. Conceivably, this precedent—that an employer's interests must give way to the employee's claim to be treated fairly—has influenced courts to develop a broad duty of fairness on employers, possibly under the rubric of established doctrines, such as "constructive dismissal," "reasonable notice," and "just cause," or even as an independent implied term in the employment contract.[3]

Furthermore, the human rights legislation brings to the fore the issue of where to strike the balance between, on the one hand, advan-

---

3   Ibid. at 26.

cing employee rights, and on the other hand, avoiding the imposition of extra costs on employers that would imperil their competitiveness to the disadvantage of their existing and potential employees and society as a whole. Although legislating safeguards for human rights almost certainly will achieve some efficiency gains for employers, there will clearly be a point at which legal intervention will create inefficiencies. Unfortunately, there is a dearth of empirical evidence on the economic costs and benefits of modern Canadian human rights laws. Social stability could be jeopardized if workers' expectations for ever-increasing rights cannot be met by employers.

An assessment of Canadian human rights legislation must also take into account the notorious slowness of current enforcement procedures. This slowness is an important limitation on the success of the legislation, for any body of substantive rights is only as good as its enforcement machinery. Not only is the employee harmed by delays, but the employer, too, may suffer from the uncertainty and public stigma associated with a human rights complaint. The *raison d'être* of all protective employment legislation is to provide employees with an accessible, cheap, and expeditious method of enforcing their employment rights compared with common law litigation, which is unaffordable for most workers.

This chapter begins by outlining the protected grounds under Canadian human rights acts and then examines what conduct on the employer's part constitutes proscribed discrimination. We then analyze the defences to discrimination, especially the crucially important defence of "*bona fide* occupational requirement" and the employer's duty of reasonable accommodation. These general principles are then examined in the context of sexual harassment. Finally, the enforcement machinery and available remedies under human rights acts, including those of affirmative action, are examined. The reader should refer to one of the specialized human rights texts for further elaboration of these matters.[4]

A. PROHIBITED GROUNDS OF DISCRIMINATION

Depending on the jurisdiction, the following grounds of discrimination are explicitly protected in human rights statutes: race; mental[5]

---

4   The leading text is W.S. Tarnopolsky, *Discrimination and the Law: Including Equality Rights under the Charter*, rev. ed., by W.F. Pentney, looseleaf (Don Mills, ON: DeBoo, 1988).

5   Example: *Lane v. ADGA Group Consultants Inc.*, 2007 HRTO 34, where bipolar disorder was ruled to be a protected "disability" or "handicap."

and physical disability,[6] including alcohol and drug dependency,[7] and (arguably) other addictions, such as nicotine, food, gambling, and sex; religion; creed; age;[8] national or ethnic origin; place of origin; ancestry; colour; sex; pregnancy and childbirth;[9] marital status;[10] criminal convictions; political beliefs; family status; source of income; sexual orientation; and social origin. Quebec is unique in specifically protecting the individual's language,[11] civil status, and right to "dignity, honour and reputation";[12] "respect for his [or her] private life"; confidentiality; and the freedoms of opinion, expression, peaceful assembly, conscience, religion, and association. Currently, twenty-three different protected grounds exist across Canada. Since the above-mentioned grounds may overlap, particular discriminatory conduct may simultaneously fall within several different protected grounds.

These express grounds have been added to by judicial implication. For example, in provinces where sexual orientation is not an expressly protected ground—namely, Alberta and the federal jurisdiction—the courts have ruled that sexual orientation must be "read into" the human rights legislation in order to comply with section 15 of the *Charter*,[13] the rationale being that homosexuals and lesbians are disadvantaged

---

6   On "disability" discrimination, see generally Michael S. Lynk, "Disability and Work: The Transformation of the Legal Status of Employees with Disabilities in Canada" (December 2007), online: http://papers.ssrn.com/sol3/papers. cfm?abstract_id=1068403.

7   It has been held that alcohol/drug dependency constitutes a "disability": e.g., *Entrop v. Imperial Oil Ltd.* (2000), 50 O.R. (3d) 18 (C.A.) [*Entrop*]. In some jurisdictions, alcohol/drug dependency is expressly protected. See generally J. Craig, "*Entrop v. Imperial Oil Ltd.*: Employment Drug and Alcohol Testing Is Put to the Test" (2002) 9 C.L.E.L.J. 141.

8   The "age" protection commonly is available only to those who are either 18 or 19. In several provinces protection formerly ceased at age 65, but this exception has been removed.

9   This is expressly protected in all jurisdictions save British Columbia, New Brunswick, and Newfoundland, where it is implied under the rubric of "sex" discrimination following *Brooks v. Canada Safeway Ltd.*, [1989] 1 S.C.R. 1219, especially at 1241–50.

10 In all provinces except Saskatchewan, this ground prohibits discrimination on the ground of being married to a particular person, as opposed simply to being married: e.g., *B. v. Ontario (Human Rights Commission)*, [2002] 3 S.C.R. 403.

11 Elsewhere, if an employer uses language as a pretext to discriminate against an employee on an expressly protected ground, such as race or place of origin, this will be unlawful: e.g., *Fletcher Challenge Canada Ltd. v. British Columbia (Council of Human Rights)* (1993), 18 C.H.R.R. D/422 at D/428 (B.C.S.C.).

12 Section 4 of the *Quebec Charter*, above note 1, ss. 3–5.

13 *Canadian Charter of Rights and Freedoms*, Part I of the *Constitution Act, 1982*, being Schedule B to the *Canada Act 1982* (U.K.), 1982, c. 11 [*Charter*].

groups "analogous" to the groups specifically protected under section 15.[14] Other protected grounds that could be "read in" to the legislation in the future include gender identity,[15] criminal conviction, and social condition,[16] but not political opinion.[17]

The human rights acts of three provinces—Alberta, Nova Scotia, and Prince Edward Island—expressly state that a protected ground can apply to "any other person," not just to the employee who is directly harmed by an employer. In that case, it would seem that a healthy employee could ask to have his or her work schedule modified in order to care for a "disabled" child. Arguably, in other provinces the legislation could be interpreted in a similar fashion, because the courts have held that human rights acts must be given a broad and liberal meaning in favour of protecting the individual's interests.

The courts have ruled that "disability" discrimination can exist where an employer subjectively believes that an employee is unable to perform the job based on "perception, myth and stereotypes," even though the person is not in fact disabled, in order to further the statutory purpose of eliminating negative attitudes towards disabled persons within society.[18] Therefore, it would appear to constitute unlawful "disability" discrimination for an employer to refuse to hire a person on the basis of a genetic test showing that the individual will probably contract a serious disease later in life whose symptoms are not yet manifest. This notion of "perceived disability" also explains why imposing compulsory drug and alcohol testing on non-addicted drinkers and drug users constitutes "disability" discrimination; the general public, it is believed, will perceive that non-addicted employees are being penalized because they are addicts, thereby casting a negative taint on addicts as a group.[19] Only rarely have courts questioned this analysis as, for example, where the Alberta Court of Appeal ruled that a mandatory drug and alcohol testing policy imposed at the giant Syncrude oil

---

14   *Vriend v. Alberta*, [1998] 1 S.C.R. 493, quashing (1996), 181 A.R. 16 (C.A.).

15   Although gender identity has been included under disability, sex, and sexual orientation, arguably it deserves independent recognition out of respect for the uniqueness of transgendered people.

16   These recommendations are made in Canada, Canadian Human Rights Review Panel, *Promoting Equality: A New Vision—Report of the Canadian Human Rights Review Panel* by G.V. La Forest (Ottawa: Department of Justice, 2000) at 105 and 113 [La Forest Panel].

17   This ground was rejected in *Jazairi v. Ontario (Human Rights Commission) (No. 1)* (1999), 36 C.H.R.R. D/1 at D/6 (Ont. C.A.).

18   *Quebec (Commission des droits de la personne et des droits de la jeunesse) v. Montreal (City)*, [2000] C.L.L.C. ¶230-020 at 145,233 (S.C.C.).

19   *Entrop*, above note 7.

plant did not constitute proscribed "disability" discrimination because the reasonable person would regard ensuring health and safety at the worksite as the exclusive purpose of the policy.[20]

The definition of "age" discrimination has now been modified in all provinces to remove the exemption that permitted employers to discriminate against persons who reach age 65. The result of this is to disallow policies requiring workers to retire at age 65 or above. Therefore, employers must now prove the defence of *bona fide* occupational requirement if they wish to terminate an employee on account of age. Abolishing compulsory retirement raises other discrimination issues, for example, whether employers can reduce the level of benefits (or increase the level of contributions) under pension, medical/dental, and other insurance policies for workers who plan to continue working beyond the former compulsory retirement date.

Among the above-mentioned grounds, the experience in Ontario between 2006 and 2007 was that the most frequently specified complaints related to disability (30 percent of all discrimination complaints), race (19 percent), sexual harassment (9 percent), ethnic origin (7 percent), sex or pregnancy (6 percent), age (5 percent), family status (3 percent), creed (2 percent), sexual orientation (2 percent), marital status (1 percent), and public assistance (1 percent).[21] The picture is probably similar in other provinces and has not changed significantly over the years.

B. THE PROSCRIBED CONDUCT: WHAT CONSTITUTES "DISCRIMINATION"?

Modern human rights acts draw a pivotal distinction between direct discrimination (sometimes called "intentional" or "disparate treatment" discrimination) and indirect discrimination (sometimes called "systemic" or "disparate impact" discrimination). Roughly speaking, the former is concerned with eradicating conduct on the part of an employer that intends on its face to penalize a person on a protected ground—for example, an employment rule that denies employment to

---

20   *Alberta (Human Rights and Citizenship Commission) v. Kellogg Root and Brown (Canada) Company*, 2007 ABCA 426. The unofficial subtext of this decision is to spare employers in such safety-sensitive industries the costs of reasonably accommodating individuals who fail the drug or alcohol test.

21   Ontario Human Rights Commission, *Annual Report, 2006–2007* (Toronto: Human Rights Commission, 2007) Table 1, online: www.ohrc.on.ca/en/resources/annualreports/ar0607?page=eng-Tables_.html#Heading433.

spouses of existing employees or an unspoken policy of not hiring Jews due to the anti-Semitic views of the employer. The latter, on the other hand, is concerned with eliminating ostensibly neutral policies and practices that have a disproportionately harmful effect on members of a protected group — for example, a minimum height rule for entry into the police service, which would exclude more women and Asians than it would white males. There is also a third category of discrimination, one that combines elements of both the direct and the indirect forms to create a "poisoned work environment" for the employee.

Regarding direct discrimination, most human rights acts contain a provision prohibiting an employer, or any person acting on behalf of an employer, from refusing to employ or to continue to employ a person, or otherwise discriminate against him or her in regard to terms and conditions of employment, because that person is a member of a protected group.[22] It might be thought that competitive market forces would have eliminated this kind of discrimination, since discriminatory employers would miss out on hiring or promoting the most productive workers by arbitrarily excluding members of protected groups from consideration. Regrettably, however, the necessity of legal intervention remains.[23] The concept of "intent" has been applied purposively by courts and tribunals in order to further the policy goal of eradicating discrimination from the workplace. Accordingly, an illegitimate intent will be found not only where an employer penalizes a worker out of personal hatred for his or her minority characteristics, but also where an employer acts on the basis of a non-malicious stereotypical assumption about that person's capabilities and characteristics — for example, by laying off a pregnant cashier who could perform her job satisfactorily out of the misconception that customers would not find it right for a pregnant woman to be lifting product boxes.[24] Moreover, if an employer acts on the basis of a combination of several factors, some of which are legitimate and others not, liability will be grounded; the employer's motive

---

22 Examples: *Can. HRA*, above note 1, s. 7; *Sask. HRC*, above note 1, s. 16(1).

23 For a detailed analysis of the economics of anti-discrimination laws, see R.L. Paetzold & R. Gely, "Through the Looking Glass: Can Title VII Help Women and Minorities Shatter the Glass Ceiling?" (1995) 31 Hous. L. Rev. 1517, especially at 1518–28; J.J. Donahue III, "Is Title VII Efficient?" (1986) 134 U. Pa. L. Rev. 1411; D. Charny & M. Gulati, "Efficiency Wages, Tournaments, and Discrimination: A Theory of Employment Discrimination Law for 'High Level' Jobs," Discussion Paper Series No. 182 (Cambridge, MA: Harvard Law School, 1996); and W.Z. Hirsch, *Law and Economics: An Introductory Analysis*, 2d ed. (Boston: Academic Press, 1988) c. 11.

24 *Holloway v. MacDonald* (1983), 83 C.L.L.C. ¶17,019 (B.C. Bd. Inq.).

must be totally devoid of discriminatory intent.[25] If liability depended on the employer's *predominant* motive being illicit, many complaints would fail because of the difficulty of proving such a motive. The presence of legitimate contributory factors can be taken into account in fashioning the appropriate remedy under the human rights tribunals' flexible "make whole" remedial authority. Thus, if a job applicant is denied the position partially because of race but partially because his or her qualifications and experience were inadequate to have won the competition anyway, the applicant would not receive compensation for lost wages, but be limited to damages for personal humiliation.[26]

The location of the burden of proof is of critical practical importance whenever liability turns on motive. In most Canadian jurisdictions, the ultimate legal burden of proving discrimination rests with the claimant. This contrasts with the position in unjust dismissal at common law, in statutory adjudication, and in collective agreement arbitration, where the employer carries the legal onus of proving just cause for dismissal.[27] It seems odd that the human rights legislation would not follow the latter practice, given its remedial thrust. In some provinces, including Saskatchewan,[28] there is a statutory reversal of the onus of proof on to the employer. Elsewhere, courts and tribunals have considerably ameliorated the position of complainants under human rights statutes by obliging the complainant to establish only a *prima facie* case of discrimination, whereupon the evidentiary onus shifts to the employer to adduce a credible and convincing reason for its actions that bears no discriminatory taint. It is relatively easy to establish such a *prima facie* case. Thus, if an applicant was denied a job or a promotion, he or she need only prove that he or she is a member of a protected group and has the requisite qualifications, and that the employer either hired or promoted someone who was no better qualified or continued the employee search. If an employee was dismissed, disciplined, or laid off, he or she need only prove membership in a protected group and the fact of dismissal, discipline, or layoff. If the employee was denied

25   Example: *Ontario (Human Rights Commission) v. Gains Pet Foods Corp.* (1993), 50 C.C.E.L. 315, especially at 318 (Ont. Gen. Div.) [*Gains Pet Foods*]; *Gauvreau v. National Bank of Canada* (1992), 17 C.H.R.R. D/25 at D/59 (Can. H.R.T.).

26   Example: *Hammad v. Baiton Enterprises Ltd.* (1991), 16 C.H.R.R. D/36, especially at D/39 (Sask. Bd. Inq.). See also *Gains Pet Foods*, *ibid.*, where the court limited the claimant's period of compensation for lost wages to six months because she likely would have been lawfully dismissed during that time anyway due to her record of excessive non-cancer–related absences.

27   See Chapter 9.

28   *Sask. HRC*, above note 1, s. 39(1).

an employment-related benefit, he or she need only prove membership in a protected group and denial of the benefit in question. The onus then shifts to the employer explain its actions. If the employer fails to explain why it treated the complainant as it did, or if the explanation lacks credibility, the tribunal will infer that a discriminatory motive exists.[29] As one tribunal puts it, circumstantial evidence must often be resorted to "in order to identify . . . the subtle scent of discrimination."[30] From the employer's perspective, the best defence to such a *prima facie* case of intentional discrimination is if it can honestly say that it would have made the same decision regarding the complainant whether or not protected status was a factor. However, even that may not provide a defence against indirect discrimination, under which, as we shall see, an illicit motive on the employer's part is not a necessary condition for liability.

All jurisdictions also prohibit indirect discrimination, where an employer's practices and policies, while neutral on their face and motivated by legitimate business concerns, nonetheless result in disproportionately harmful consequences for members of a protected group. This form of discrimination is often referred to as "adverse effect" or "disparate impact" discrimination. The legislation uses various formulations to entrench it,[31] but the end result is that it is universally prohibited in Canada. The landmark authority is the decision of the Supreme Court of Canada in *Ontario (Human Rights Commission) v. Simpsons Sears Ltd.*,[32] where a full-time salesperson who refused to work on Saturdays pursuant to the dictates of her religion—she became a Seventh-day Adventist long after she was hired—was advised by her employer that she would have to work part-time or quit. She worked part-time for awhile, but eventually resigned and claimed compensa-

---

29   Examples: *Aboucher v. Ontario (Human Rights Commission)* (1998), 31 C.H.R.R. D/411, especially D/4425–26 (Ont. Bd. Inq.); *Canada (A.G.) v. Grover (No. 1)* (1992), 18 C.H.R.R. D/1 at D/ 46 (Can. H.R.T.) [*Grover*]; *Ontario (Liquor Control Board) v. Ontario (Human Rights Commission)* (1988), 19 C.C.E.L. 172 at 192 (Ont. Div. Ct.) [*L.C.B.O.*]; *Base-Fort Patrol Ltd. v. Alberta (Human Rights Commission)* (1982), 83 C.L.L.C. ¶17,010 (Alta. Q.B.).

30   *Grover, ibid.* at D/48.

31   Thus, some acts contain an explicit, positive right to "equality" and declare it unlawful for an employer to violate that right: *Man. HRC*, above note 1, s. 9(1); *Ont. HRC*, above note 1, s. 5(1); *Quebec Charter*, above note 1, ss. 10 and 16; *N.S. HRA*, above note 1, s. 3; *P.E.I HRA*, above note 1, s. 6(1). Also, some acts explicitly refer to this form of discrimination as "unintentional," "systemic," "adverse impact," "disparate impact," or "constructive" discrimination: *Man. HRC, ibid.*, s. 9(3); *Can. HRA*, above note 1, s. 10(a); and *Ont. HRC, ibid.*, s. 11(1).

32   [1985] 2 S.C.R. 536 [*Simpsons Sears*].

tion for the difference between her full-time and part-time earnings. The Court upheld her complaint, even though the employer bore no personal malice towards the employee because of her religion, but was motivated by legitimate business concerns. The Court stated that the general statutory prohibition against discrimination is breached "where an employer for genuine business reasons adopts a rule or standard which is on its face neutral, and which will apply equally to all employees, but which has a discriminatory effect upon a prohibited ground on one employee or group of employees in that it imposes, because of some special characteristic of the employee or group, obligations, penalties or restrictive conditions not imposed on other members of the work force."[33] The Court reasoned that the adoption of this principle was necessary, first, in order to make it more difficult for employers to disguise an illicit intent behind the veneer of legitimate business concerns, and second, because the goal of the legislation is to secure the elimination of discrimination from the workplace, not to punish employers with guilty minds. As McIntyre J. explained:

> The Code aims at the removal of discrimination .... Its main approach, however, is not to punish the discriminator, but rather to provide relief for the victims of discrimination. It is the result or the effect of the action complained of which is significant. If it does, in fact, cause discrimination; if its effect is to impose on one person or group of persons obligations, penalties, or restrictive conditions not imposed on other members of the community, it is discriminatory.[34]

The Court held that in order to avoid liability for indirect discrimination, the employer would have to prove that it had made reasonable efforts to accommodate the employee's religious practices — for example, by arranging for her to switch her Saturday shifts — up to the point of causing the company undue hardship.[35] On the facts of the case, the employer was found to have made no such efforts. The employer's "duty of reasonable accommodation" is examined in detail later in this chapter.[36]

As the examples that follow suggest, the potential ambit of indirect discrimination is extremely broad, penetrating to the heart of traditional managerial prerogatives, because all practices and policies of a company that disproportionately disadvantage potential or actual employees with

---

33   *Ibid.* at 551, McIntyre J.
34   *Ibid.* at 547.
35   *Ibid.* at 555.
36   See Section C(1)(a), below in this chapter.

protected status are susceptible to challenge.[37] In traditionally male-dominated firms, seniority systems that govern the order of layoffs and recall, or that govern access to promotion may indirectly discriminate against females and visible minorities. Work schedules that require employees to work at times when their children are out of school or daycare may indirectly discriminate against women under the "sex" head, or against women and men under the "family status" head. Work schedules that require members of religious groups to work on their holy days indirectly discriminate on the basis of religion. Benefits that depend on accrued periods of continous and/or active employment, such as vacations, leaves of absence, insurance benefits, severance payments, and probationary periods, may indirectly discriminate against the disabled who are often absent from work. Hiring policies favouring recent graduates in order to "renew" an organization may indirectly discrimate on the basis of age. Compulsory dress codes may indirectly discriminate against on the basis of religion, for example, if a Sikh is required to wear a hard hat. Minimal physical height, fitness, and strength tests may indirectly discriminate against women, the disabled, the aged, or certain ethnic groups. Pre-employment tests, such as general integrity and intelligence tests, language tests, and professional credential tests, that disadvantage immigrants and visible minorities may constitute indirect discrimination. Job evaluation systems that result in women receiving less pay than men for performing the same work or work of equal value constitute indirect "sex" discrimination.[38] Automatic termination policies providing that employees will be deemed to be dismissed for just cause for specified periods of absence from work or for violating a "last chance" agreement for drug or alcohol abuse indirectly discrimate against the disabled, and disabled employees may be indirectly discriminated against if the physical layout of the plant or the available machinery and equipment, prevents them from performing the job.

---

37   Useful reviews of the caselaw can be found in L. Dulude, *Seniority Systems and Employment Equity for Women* (Kingston: Queen's University Industrial Relations Centre, 1995); M. Kaye Joachim, "Seniority Rights and the Duty to Accommodate" (1998) 24 Queen's L.J. 131; M. Lynk, "Accommodating Disabilities in the Canadian Workplace" (1999) 7 C.L.E.L.J. 183; L. Chabursky, "The *Employment Equity Act*: An Examination of Its Development and Direction" (1992) 24 Ottawa L. Rev. 305 at 310–29. Pay equity legislation is examined in Chapter 6.
38   Significantly, this means that the "equal value" model of pay equity legislation applies in all provinces, including those that do not expressly legislate it in special pay equity legislation or in their human rights act. See, for example, *Canada Safeway Ltd. v. Saskatchewan (Human Rights Commission) (No. 2)* (1999), 34 C.H.R.R. D/409 at D/413 (Sask. Q.B.).

Of course, the costs to employers of defending such actions may be substantial. In order to avoid these costs, employers may elect to implement practices that give preferential treatment to protected persons, such as hiring and promotion quotas. Furthermore, the concept of indirect discrimination inevitably leads tribunals to fashion affirmative action remedies that are designed to eradicate the discriminatory consequences of the employer's practices and policies. It is precisely these remedies that have generated the greatest degree of public controversy about indirect discrimination.

One especially important way of establishing indirect discrimination is to adduce statistics showing that a firm's employment practices, such as hiring or promotion, result in an under-representation of protected groups. (Of course, such statistical evidence can also provide important circumstantial evidence that an employer is intentionally discriminating.) There has been relatively little case law in Canada concerning the use of statistics in discrimination cases,[39] but useful insights can be gleaned from the extensive American jurisprudence on the topic.[40] Most of the American cases concern discrimination in hiring and promotion. Here, the first step is usually to compare the number of protected group members employed in target positions by the company with an appropriate comparator group. The latter group could be taken as the number of protected group members in the general population of the community in question. However, this would be misleading where specialized jobs are concerned, since one would not expect everyone in the general population of a region to have the requisite qualifications for the target positions. Where specialized work is concerned, the comparator group can be taken as those persons who have the requisite qualifications in the city or region from which the firm normally recruits.[41] Of course, this approach can be criticized as

---

39   The leading Canadian example is *Canadian National Railway v. Canada (Human Rights Commission)*, [1987] 1 S.C.R. 1114 [*Canadian National Railway*], where statistical evidence of female under-representation in blue-collar positions on the railway was held to ground indirect discrimination. The company was ordered to institute a female hiring quota in order to rectify this imbalance. This aspect of the case is considered in Section E(1)(d) of this chapter.

40   See, for instance, A.R. Vining, D.C. McPhillips, & A.E. Boardman, "Use of Statistical Evidence in Employment Discrimination Litigation" (1986) 64 Can. Bar Rev. 660 [Vining *et al.*]; P.N. Cox, *Employment and Discrimination* (Salem, NH: Butterworths, 1991) 18–20 [Cox]; J.L. Gastwirth, "Employment Discrimination: A Statistician's Look at Analysis of Disparate Impact Claims" (1992) 11 Law Ineq. J. 151 [Gastwirth].

41   Example: *Persad v. Sudbury Regional Police Force (No. 2)* (1993), 19 C.H.R.R. D/336, especially at D/340–41 (Ont. Bd. Inq.).

entrenching past discrimination if the reason most protected group members remain unqualified is because they have been discriminated against previously. Alternatively, the comparator group can be taken as those persons with protected status who apply for the target positions with the employer in question over a designated time.[42] This comparison should portray any given employer's hiring and promotion practices more accurately than the previous method, but care must be taken to ensure that in the past the employer has not deliberately discouraged protected persons from applying for jobs.

The second step in cases of statistical discrimination is to ensure that any disparities in the representation rates of protected persons and others are statistically "significant" for the purpose of drawing meaningful conclusions about a firm's practices. Statisticians take a variance of 0.05 as establishing significance, so that an employer's hiring or promotion practices must result in a disproportionate imbalance against protected applicants at least 5 percent of the time in order to be significant proof of discrimination.[43] The *United States Equal Employment Opportunity Guidelines* recommends as a useful rule of thumb the "four-fifths" rule, under which discrimination is presumed to exist if the hiring or promotion rate of the protected group is less than four-fifths of the comparator group's.[44] However, critics have emphasized that this rule of thumb cannot be applied automatically as proof of discrimination.[45] The bottom line is that statistics can never be treated as being determinative *ipso facto* of illegal discrimination: rather, they merely provide one piece of evidence that must be weighed into the balance with all the other relevant facts in order to determine whether any particular employer, in the circumstances of each case, practises illegal discrimination. So far, Canadian tribunals have avoided the danger of allowing the intricacies of statistical methodology to become the end instead of a *means* to the end of proving discrimination, along with all other circumstantial evidence.

---

42   This method was utilized, for example, in *Dhaliwal v. B.C. Timber Ltd. (No. 1)* (1983), 4 C.H.R.R. D/1520 (B.C. Bd. Inq.). A leading American example is *Hazelwood School District v. United States*, 433 U.S. 299 (1977).

43   See Gastwirth, above note 40 at 154.

44   The Uniform Guidelines on Employee Selection Procedures (1978), 29 C.F.R. § 1607, 4D (1982) state: "A selection rate for any race, sex, or ethnic group which is less than four-fifths (4/5, or 80 percent) of the rate for the group with the highest rate will generally be regarded by the federal enforcement agencies as evidence of adverse impact, while a greater that four-fifths rate will generally not be regarded by Federal enforcement agencies as evidence of adverse impact."

45   Vining *et al.*, above note 40 at 689–90; Cox, above note 40 at para. 19.05.

The distinction between direct and indirect discrimination used to be of critical practical importance with regard to the employer's duty of reasonable accommodation. Prior to the Supreme Court of Canada's landmark decision in *Meoirin* in 1999,[46] the courts held that the employer was under a duty to reasonably accommodate the claimant up to the point of causing the firm undue hardship only in situations of indirect discrimination, but not if the discrimination was characterized as direct. The unfortunate consequences of this view were removed by the *Meoirin*[47] case, which authoritatively ruled that the duty of reasonable accommodation applies to both direct and indirect discrimination.

In "poisoned work environment" discrimination, an employee is made to feel ill at ease as a result of a combination of work policies and practices, harassment, intimidation, and insults that the perpetrators know or ought reasonably to know would make the employee feel uncomfortable and unwelcome on account of his or her protected characteristics.[48] The offending conduct also does not have to be committed by the victim's colleagues or managers in order to make the employer liable; rather, if customers or clients of the employer engage in the conduct, the employer will be liable unless it takes reasonable steps to stop it. For example, it could remove the clients or customers from the premises or cease to deal with them.[49] The rationale is that the employer has the power to control what goes on and therefore can readily take measures to stop the offending activity. Opinions have differed on whether the test for liability is the subjective reaction of the particular victim to the conduct in question—this would protect the hypersensitive employee—or the objective reaction of the reasonable person.[50] Of

---

46   *British Columbia (Public Service Employment Relations Commission) v. British Columbia Government and Service Employees Union*, [1999] 3 S.C.R. 3 [*Meoirin*]. See K. Schucher, "Weaving Together the Threads: A New Framework for Achieving Equality in Workplace Standards" (2000) 8 C.L.E.L.J. 325 [Schucher].

47   *Ibid.*

48   Example: *Naraine v. Ford Motor Company of Canada (No. 4)* (1996), 27 C.H.R.R. D/230 at D/238–39 (Ont. Bd. Inq.) [*Naraine*], involving racial harassment; *Espinoza v. Coldmatic Refrigeration of Canada Ltd.* (1995), 95 C.L.L.C. ¶230-026 at 145,296–97 (Ont. Bd. Inq.) [*Espinoza*], where harassment against Central South Americans was held to be grounded on their "ethnicity" under s. 10 of the *Ont. HRC*, above note 1; *Canada (A.G.) v. Uzoaba* (1994), 94 C.L.L.C. ¶17,201, especially at 16,228 (Can. H.R.T.), aff'd (1995), 26 C.H.R.R. D/428 (F.C.T.D.) [*Uzoaba*] involving racist taunts by inmates against a black prison guard.

49   *Uzoaba, ibid.*, especially at 16,228 (Can. H.R.T.), where the employer failed to protect a black prison guard against racist abuse by inmates.

50   *Dhanjal v. Air Canada* (1996), 28 C.H.R.R. D/367 at D/414 (Can. H.R.T.).; *Ghosh v. Domglas Inc. (No. 2)* (1992), 17 C.H.R.R. D/216 at D/221 (Ont. Bd. Inq.) [*Ghosh*].

course, under the subjective approach, if a reasonable person would not feel offended by the conduct in question, it could be inferred that the employee's alleged reaction was not honestly held.

C. THE DEFENCES TO DISCRIMINATION

There are four main defences to discrimination provided under the human rights statutes in most jurisdictions. Foremost among these is the defence of *bona fide* occupational requirement (BFOR). This defence has become closely linked with the employer's duty of reasonable accommodation, which we also examine in this part of the book. Second, some provinces excuse discrimination on the part of an employer that meets the statutory definition of a non-profit fraternal or social organization. Third, some provinces exempt employees engaged in defined industries or occupations, such as domestics employed in a private residence. Fourth, in most jurisdictions, discrimination on the grounds of sex, age, and/or disability in the operation of pension or insurance plans is permitted in defined circumstances. These defences are construed narrowly on furtherance of the remedial goal of the human rights acts.[51]

1) The Defence of *Bona Fide* Occupational Requirement

The human rights legislation in all jurisdictions provides a defence to what would otherwise be unlawful discrimination if there exists a *"bona fide* occupational qualification,"[52] a *"bona fide* occupational requirement,"[53] a "reasonable occupational qualification and requirement,"[54] a "genuine occupational qualification,"[55] or *"bona fide* and reasonable requirements or qualifications."[56]

The test for a BFOR was authoritatively stated by McLachlin J. (as she then was) of the Supreme Court of Canada. It is as follows:[57]

---

51   Example: *Crook v. Ontario Cancer Treatment and Research Foundation of Ontario* (1998), 98 C.L.L.C. ¶230-011 at 145,071 (Ont. Gen. Div.), involving the pension benefit plans exemption.

52   Example: *Ont. HRC,* above note 1, ss. 11(1)(a), 24(1)(b).

53   Examples: *Can. HRA,* above note 1, s. 15(a); *Alta. HRCMA,* above note 1, s. 7(3), which is buttressed by s. 10 "reasonable and justifiable in all the circumstances."

54   *Sask. HRC,* above note 1, s. 16(7); see also the comprehensive definition contained in the *Human Rights Code Regulations,* Sask. Reg. 216/79, s. l(b), (d).

55   *P.E.I. HRC,* above note 1, s. 4(a).

56   *Man. HRC,* above note 1, s. 14(1).

57   *Meoirin,* above note 46 at para. 54. See Schucher, above note 46.

... I propose the following three-step test for determining whether a prima facie discriminatory standards is a BFOR. An employer
may justify the impugned standard by establishing on the balance of
probabilities:

(1) that the employer adopted the standard for a purpose rationally
    connected to the performance of the job;

(2) that the employer adopted the particular standard in the honest
    and good faith belief that it was necessary to the fulfillment of
    that legitimate work-related purpose; and

(3) that the standard is reasonably necessary to the accomplishment
    of that legitimate work-related purpose. To show that the stan-
    dard is reasonably necessary, it must be demonstrated that it is
    impossible to accommodate individual employees sharing the
    characteristics of the claimant without imposing undue hard-
    ship upon the employer."

It has been held that the BFOR defence must be applied "narrowly"[58] in order to maximize the reach of the anti-discrimination ban in
the legislation.

Regarding the subjective limb of this test, the employer has the
legal burden of proving that its motive for making the contested decision is a genuine desire to advance the legitimate goals of the organization. Regarding the test's objective limb, the employer must prove
that the contested decision will result, as a matter of objective fact, in
furthering the legitimate goals of the enterprise. The standard of proof
under the objective limb is rigorous: authoritative and updated empirical evidence is normally required, not unsubstantiated assertions of
the employer's personal opinion.[59] This means that employers must try
to base their BFOR on state-of-the-art economic, sociological, statistical, or medical knowledge whenever possible. Only if no such body
of evidence exists, or if the employer's costs of collating it would be
unduly onerous, should an employer resort to reasoned speculation in
order to establish a BFOR.

When an employer does choose to rely on a statistically based
"group" generalization as a proxy for individual performance—for

58   Example: *Ontario (Human Rights Commission) v. London Monenco Consultants
     Ltd.* (1992), 18 C.H.R.R. D/118 at D/121 (Ont. C.A.).

59   Example: *Ontario (Human Rights Commission) v. Etobicoke (Borough of)*, [1982] 1
     S.C.R. 202, where a mandatory retirement policy for firefighters was held not to
     be a BFOR because the employer failed to adduce concrete statistical evidence to
     substantiate its opinion that firefighting is a "young man's game," even though a
     considerable body of research existed on the effects of aging on job performance.

example, minimum health requirements for applicants to particular positions—the issue arises whether the employer must test the performance capacity of each member of the group. It has been held that if an accurate personal testing mechanism is available at an affordable cost to the employer, then the employer cannot rely on generalized standards in order to establish a BFOR, but must conduct an individual assessment of each employee.[60]

The *Meoirin* test is especially important for removing two obstacles to advancing equality that limited the pre-1999 law. First, *Meoirin* authoritatively holds that the employer is bound to reasonably accommodate an employee as a condition precedent to establishing the BFOR defence in both the direct and indirect forms of discrimination. Thus, if a job advertisement states: "Truck driver wanted; disabled people need not apply due to heavy lifting component of the job," this is direct discrimination. The employer would have to investigate the cost of purchasing a mechanical device to enable disabled persons to do the lifting component of the job or of reallocating the lifting duties to other employees who are strong enough to do them; it would then be obliged to determine that the cost in question imposes an undue hardship before it could refuse to hire a disabled person. Prior to *Meoirin*, the employer would only have to reasonably accommodate a disabled applicant in these ways if the discrimination was indirect. Consider, for example, "Truck driver wanted: must be able to lift 100 lb deadweights, ten repetitions in three consecutive sets."

Second, *Meoirin* leaves no doubt that the determination of a BFOR must take into account the *personal* circumstances and characteristics of the individual complainant, rather than the characteristics of the *class* to which the complainant belongs.[61] Suppose, for example, that an applicant for a railway company has a rule against hiring insulin-dependent diabetics for the position of track person and that employing such persons would pose a risk to public safety, so as to ground a BFOR. Suppose, however, that a particular job applicant has his diabetic condition under control, so that he would pose no greater threat to public safety than any healthy job applicant. If the existence of a BFOR can be

---

60   Example: *Delamare v. Inter-Mountain School Division* (1984), 7 C.H.R.R. D/3147 (Man. Bd. Adj.), where the compulsory retirement of a school bus driver who reached age 65 was held not to be a BFOR because an affordable individual testing mechanism was available. In contrast, in *Saskatchewan (Human Rights Commission) v. Saskatoon (City)*, [1989] 2 S.C.R. 1297, a mandatory retirement policy for firefighters at age 60 was upheld because no reliable tests existed to assess how the claimant, personally, would perform in an emergency.

61   *Meoirin*, above note 46 at 23–24.

tested according to the personal circumstances of the particular claimant, the defence would be unavailable since hiring that person for the position would not create a special safety risk. But if the existence of a BFOR must be tested solely at the level of the class of persons covered by the rule—namely, insulin-dependent diabetics in general, who may not have their condition under control—refusing to hire the particular job applicant would constitute a BFOR.

a) The Duty of Reasonable Accommodation

We saw earlier in this section that the duty of reasonable accommodation applies either implicitly as part of the general statutory BFOR defence, or explicitly by virtue of the provisions of the legislation in Manitoba and Ontario, in both direct and indirect forms of discrimination.[62] Essentially, the duty of reasonable accommodation reflects the notion of proportionality, namely, that an employer must make reasonable attempts to accommodate the employee's protected characteristics before causing the person any disadvantage, up to the point of causing the firm undue hardship. The burden of proving that it has discharged its duty of reasonable accommodation is on the employer.[63] In order to discharge this burden, the employer must furnish concrete evidence of any financial or production losses, workforce morale problems, or health and safety risks it asserts will result from accommodating the employee; mere subjective assertions of such harms will not suffice. The following synthesis of the general principles governing the duty may be useful.[64]

First, in determining what constitutes undue hardship on the employer, Canadian tribunals have declined to adopt the American practice of holding that a "minimal degree"[65] of harm will constitute undue hardship. Rather, as Sopinka J. explains:

> More than mere negligible effort is required to satisfy the duty to accommodate. The use of the term "undue" infers that some hardship is acceptable; it is only "undue" hardship that satisfies this test. . . . [therefore] more than minor inconvenience must be shown before the complainant's right to accommodation can be defeated.[66]

---

62 *Man. HRC*, above note 1, ss. 9(d), 12; *Ont. HRC*, above note 1, s. 11(2), (3).
63 Example: *O.P.S.E.U. v. Ontario (Ministry of Community and Social Services)* (1996), 96 C.L.L.C. ¶230-016 at 145,181 (Ont. Div. Ct.).
64 Practical advice on the application of the BFOR defence and the duty of reasonable accommodation can be obtained from the guidelines that most provincial and federal human rights commissions publish.
65 Example: *Trans World Airlines Inc. v. Hardison*, 432 U.S. 63 at 84–85 (1977).
66 *Central Okanagan School District No. 23 v. Renaud*, [1992] 2 S.C.R. 970 at 985–86.

In Canada, therefore, an undue hardship connotes the imposition of an excessive or disproportionately severe degree of harm for the employer.

Second, an employer's costs can take many forms. For example, accommodating an employee's work schedule or work assignments may increase the employer's labour costs by compelling it to assign extra overtime to other employees, to hire substitute employees, or even to increase general wage levels to reflect the extra work. The amount of such costs will obviously depend on the size of the workforce and the nature of the job. Large firms employing many workers, for instance, will probably find it easier to rearrange schedules and assignments than smaller firms, and it will normally be cheaper to find substitutes for relatively low-skilled jobs than for high-skilled, specialized ones. Account must also be taken of any extra administrative or supervisory burden that the accommodation places on the employer. In the latter regard, one would expect such costs to increase commensurately with the number of requests from employees for accommodation. In addition, account must be taken of any negative impact on the morale, or even the legal rights, of other employees who may be required to participate in the accommodation. The employer may have to incur extra expenses by modifying machinery, equipment, or the physical layout of the plant in order to accommodate, say, a disabled or pregnant employee.

Third, any economic benefits that the employer stands to recoup from accommodating an employee must be discounted from the costs of implementing the accommodation. For example, the accommodation may be deductible as an income tax expense; government subsidies may be available; general employee morale, and therefore labour productivity, may increase if employees are reasonably accommodated; and the employer may find it easier to recruit and retain employees if it has a reputation for treating its workforce decently.

Fourth, any potential disruption or legal liability to other employees or to a trade union must be taken into account. Regarding the role of trade unions in the duty of reasonable accommodation, it must be emphasized that the mere fact a union opposes a particular form of accommodation is not automatically a defence for the employer. The union itself is also bound by the statutory duty of reasonable accommodation and may face liability, jointly and severally, with the employer for failing to reasonably accommodate an employee.[67] Similarly, fellow employees of the claimant are bound by the general no-discrimination

---

67   Example: *Gohm v. Domtar Inc. (No. 4)* (1990), 12 C.H.R.R. D/161 (Ont. Bd. Inq.). For a comprehensive analysis of trade union liability in human rights cases, see generally M. Mac Neil, M. Lynk, & P. Engelmann, *Trade Union Law in Canada* (Aurora, ON: Canada Law Book, 1994) c. 11.

ban in the legislation, so must therefore make reasonable efforts to accommodate their colleague.[68]

Fifth, any health and safety risk to the claimant, to other employees, or to the public involved in a proposed accommodation is taken into account under the undue hardship test.

Sixth, if the employer is facing tough economic times, the degree of harm that an employer can be expected to sustain in order to cross the threshold of undue hardship would clearly be less than in good times.[69]

Seventh, the employer must handle a request for reasonable accommodation in a procedurally correct way. Thus, the employer must investigate a proposal in good faith, comprehensively, and promptly; invite the claimant to participate fully in the process; and ensure consistent treatment of like requests. Tribunals have held that the employer must take the initiative in proposing ways of accommodating the employee; it is not enough for an employer to respond to proposals formulated by the employee.[70] The rationale is that the employer's superior expertise about the production process will normally enable it to devise accommodation techniques that the employee could not have thought of. This does not absolve the employee from participating in the process—a claimant must disclose promptly to the employer the full details of his or her personal circumstances so that an appropriate form of accommodation can be arranged[71] and must generally cooperate in the process in a constructive manner.[72]

In *Meoirin*, McLachlin J. provided further guidance on the nature of the duty, as follows:

> Some of the important questions that may be asked include:

---

68 Tribunals have generally held that it would be an undue hardship to "bump" another permanent employee out of a job: e.g., *Beznochuk v. Spruceland Terminals Ltd* (1999), 37 C.H.R.R. D/259 at D/264 (B.C.H.R.T.). *Quaere*: What if a permanent, long-service employee seeks to "bump" a casual employee with no long-standing relationship with the company?

69 See, for example, the cautionary remarks to this effect by Cory J. in *Commission scolaire régionale de Chambly v. Bergevin*, [1994] 2 S.C.R. 525.

70 Example: *Zaryski v. Loftsgard* (1995), 95 C.L.L.C. ¶230-038 at 145,112 (Sask. Bd. Inq.).

71 Example: *Metsala v. Falconbridge Ltd., Kidd Creek Division*, [2001] C.L.L.C. ¶230-29 at 145,322 (Ont. Bd. Inq.), where the worker was required to provide the employer with detailed medical information so that an appropriate accommodation could be devised.

72 Example: *Handfield v. North Thompson School District No. 26* (1995), 95 C.L.L.C. ¶230-015, especially at 145,168 (B.C.C.H.R.), where an alcoholic employee refused to cooperate in a rehabilitation program.

(a) Has the employer investigated alternative approaches that do not have a discriminatory effect, such as individual testing against a more individually sensitive standard?

(b) If alternative standards were investigated and found to be capable of fulfilling the employer's purpose, why were they not implemented?

(c) Is it necessary to have all employees meet the single standard for the employer to establish its legitimate purpose or could standards reflective of group or individual differences and capabilities be established?

(d) Is there a way to do the job that is less discriminatory while still accomplishing the employer's legitimate purpose?

(e) Is the standards properly designed to ensure that the desired qualification is met without placing an undue burden on those to whom the standard applies?

(f) Have other parties who are obliged to assist in the search for possible accommodation fulfilled their roles . . . ?[73]

It should be evident from the foregoing that the law on what constitutes reasonable accommodation is uncertain and unpredictable, with each case ultimately turning on its own unique facts. Employers complain that such a high degree of legal uncertainty (especially combined with the notorious delays in processing complaints through the human rights machinery) operates as a significant cost item for them, jeopardizing their competitive position. Unfortunately, there are as yet no published case studies of the economic costs and benefits of the duty of reasonable accommodation. Furthermore, employers fear that because the duty of reasonable accommodation invites tribunals to make decisions in substantive areas of traditional management prerogatives, tribunals risk becoming "absentee managers" whose decisions will undermine business efficiency. Plainly, such a risk exists, since the duty is extremely open-ended, but so far the reported cases suggest that tribunals have generally proceeded quite cautiously in applying the duty and have not acted arbitrarily in second-guessing employers' judgments about how their firms should best be organized.[74]

---

73 Above note 46 at para. 65.

74 A measure of this relatively conservative approach is that human rights tribunals have interpreted the duty of reasonable accommodation in much the same way as collective agreement arbitrators, assumed to be relatively conservative because of their long-standing respect for the "reserved rights" of management under collective agreements. See, for example, A. Griffin, "The Duty to Accommodate: An Arbitrator's Perspective" (1996–1997) Lab. Arb. Y.B. 291.

Next, we outline the other three main defences to discrimination under the human rights legislation.

2) Employment by Social and Fraternal Organizations

In several provinces, the human rights legislation expressly states that an employer that is an "exclusively religious, fraternal or sororal organisation that is not operated for private profit"[75] is exempt from the no-discrimination requirement. Other provinces have enacted a similar provision, with the significant difference that the employer must be able to justify the exclusion of any groups as a BFOR.[76] In order to fall within this exemption, all provinces require that the employer in question must be devoted *solely* to social or fraternal purposes.[77]

3) Exempted Industries and Occupations

As is the case with most protective employment legislation, the human rights statutes typically exempt from coverage defined industries or occupations, the details of which vary among the provinces. Examples include domestic workers engaged in the employer's private residence;[78] religion instructors in religious schools;[79] and persons who are employed primarily to look after the medical and/or personal needs of their employers, sick children, or a spouse or other relative who is infirm or ill.[80] Any such exemption must pass the muster of a constitutional challenge under section 15 of the *Charter*,[81] especially if a protected group comprises the majority of the exempted occupation or industry—for example, domestics, most of whom are probably women.[82] No such challenge has yet been launched.

---

75   N.L. *HRC*, above note 1, s. 9(6)(a). The language is similar in Quebec, Newfoundland and Labrador, and Prince Edward Island.

76   As in Nova Scotia, Saskatchewan, and Ontario.

77   Example: *Canadian Corps of Commissionaires (Toronto & Region) v. Barnard* (1986), 13 C.C.E.L. 1 (Ont. Div. Ct.).

78   *Man. HRC*, above note 1, s. 14(9); *N.L. HRC*, above note 1, s. 9(5)(b); *N.S. HRA*, above note 1, s. 9(4)(a); *Sask. HRC*, above note 1, s. 16(8).

79   *Sask. HRC, ibid.*, s. 16(5).

80   *Ont. HRC*, above note 1, s. 24(1)(c).

81   Above note 13.

82   See an analogy, *Fenton v. British Columbia (Forensic Psychiatric Services Commission)* (1989), 29 C.C.E.L. 168 (B.C.S.C.), rev'd (1991), 37 C.C.E.L. 225 (B.C.C.A.).

4) Employee Insurance and Pension Benefit Plans

The human rights acts typically provide an exception to the general no-discrimination prohibition in regard to the operation of a *bona fide* pension or medical/disability insurance scheme.[83] Protected grounds, such as sex, age, and disability, are commonly used in the insurance industry as cost-efficient proxies for an individual's risk level. Clearly, if the employer or its insurance company had to conduct a personal medical examination of each employee covered by a pension or insurance plan, the administrative costs would be enormous, which would have to be reflected by either increasing the price of the coverage in question or reducing the value of the benefits payable to employees. Nevertheless, human rights tribunals will scrutinize any discriminatory provisions in pension or insurance plans to ensure that they are based on "sound actuarial practice" and that there are no "practical" alternatives to such provisions.[84] In some jurisdictions, there are complex regulations governing the circumstances under which discrimination is permitted in the operation of pension and insurance plans.[85]

In addition, other legislation may have to be considered in examining the legality of discriminatory provisions in pension and insurance plans. Thus, pension and insurance benefits generally constitute "wages" for the purposes of the "equal pay" legislation, so that any differential payouts or contribution rates for males and females *prima facie* violate the equal pay obligation.[86] The equal pay legislation may contain an express exception for the operation of *bona fide* pension and insurance plans, or if not, an exception may be implied under the residual "any other factor justifying a distinction" provision usually found in equal pay acts. Specialized pension benefits legislation may also come into play: in Manitoba, for example, the *Pension Benefits Act* disallows

---

83   *Alta. HRCMA*, above note 1, s. 7(2); *B.C. HRC*, above note 1, s. 8(3); *N.B. HRA*, above note 1, s. 6(1)(b); *N.L. HRC*, above note 1, s. 9(5)(c); *P.E.I. HRA*, above note 1, s. 11; *Quebec Charter*, above note 1, s. 20; *Sask. HRC*, above note 1, s. 16(4).

84   *Zurich Insurance Co. v. Ontario (Human Rights Commission)*, [1992] 2 S.C.R. 321, Sopinka J. See, for example, *O' Neill v. C.P.U.* (1996), 96 C.L.L.C. ¶230-049 at 145,533 (B.C.C.H.R.), involving discriminatory survivor benefits under a pension plan; *Ontario (Human Rights Commission) v. North American Life Assurance Co.* (1995), 123 D.L.R. (4th) 709 (Ont. Div. Ct.), aff'g (1992), 93 C.L.L.C. ¶17,002 (Ont. Bd. Inq.), involving the exclusion of an AIDS sufferer from medical disability insurance.

85   Examples: *Can. HRA*, above note 1, s. 22 and *Canadian Human Rights Benefit Regulations*, SOR/80-68; *Ont. HRC*, above note 1, ss. 25(2) & (3), which incorporate the *Benefit Plans Regulation*, R.R.O. 1990, Reg. 321.

86   Equal pay legislation is examined in Chapter 6.

differentiation by sex in determining the amount of pension contributions to plan members, the variety of options available to members, the amount of benefits payable, and the eligibility for coverage.[87]

D. SELECTED PRACTICAL APPLICATIONS OF ANTI-DISCRIMINATION LEGISLATION

It should be apparent from the material examined so far in this chapter that the statutory no-discrimination ban, along with the BFOR defence (and its concomitant duty of reasonable accommodation) are of potentially enormous reach in the employment relationship. Indeed, virtually no aspect of an employer's decision-making power is unaffected by these doctrines. Thus, there already exists a substantial body of case law on the employer's freedom to choose how to advertise vacancies and conduct job interviews; how to administer pre-employment credential, intelligence, aptitude, integrity, and medical tests; how to set minimum qualifications for the job; how to avoid discrimination in performance appraisal and job evaluation processes; how to structure the compensation and benefit package to avoid discrimination in insurance and other employment-related benefits; how to structure retirement policies; how to organize work schedules and job assignment; how to implement layoffs and recalls; how to promote employees; how to dismiss or otherwise discipline employees; how to structure the physical layout of the plant, machinery, and equipment; and how to sensitize its employees, and even its customers and clients, to avoiding discrimination in the workplace. A useful review of the law in most of these areas can be found in the guidelines published by each province's human rights commission.[88] In this section, attention is focused, for

---

87   Manitoba *Pension Benefits Act*, C.C.S.M. c. P32, s. 21(18). See generally D. Brown, "Sex Discrimination in Pension Plans" (1977) 4 Dal. L.J. 189.

88   For example, the Ontario Human Rights Commission, based in Toronto, publishes the following useful guidelines: (1) "Policy Statement on Height and Weight Requirements"; (2) "Exceptions to the Equality Rights Provisions of the Ontario Human Rights Code as They Relate to the Workplace"; (3) "Policy on HIV/AIDS-Related Discrimination"; (4) "Policy on Discrimination and Harassment Because of Gender Identity"; (5) "Policy on Drug and Alcohol Testing"; (6) "Policy on Requiring a Driver's Licence as a Condition of Employment"; (7) "Policy on Employment-Related Medical Information"; (8) "Developing Procedures to Resolve Human Rights Complaints within Your Organization"; (9) "Policy and Guidelines on Discrimination Because of Family Status"; (10) "Policy and Guidelines on Racism and Racial Discrimination"; (11) "Policy on Discrimination and Language"; (12) "Policy on Discrimination against Older

the purpose of illustration, on an area of the employment relationship where human rights legislation has had an especially important practical effect, namely, in combatting sexual harassment.

1) Combatting Sexual Harassment in the Workplace

There appears to be a signficant problem with workplace sexual harassment[89] in Canada. For example, a 1990 study found that there was a probability of between 30 and 60 percent that female employees would be sexually harassed at work.[90] Human rights statutes combat sexual harassment in two ways. First, some acts have express sections specifically defining and outlawing sexual harassment. These provisions should be checked carefully because, depending on the jurisdiction, they may not include certain forms of conduct that would normally be understood as constituting sexual harassment.[91] In Newfoundland, for example, the definition of sexual harassment appears to require that an advance for sexual favours be made, thereby arguably excluding from the definition a "poisoned work environment" resulting from generally told sexual profanities and insults, which are encompassed by the definition elsewhere.[92] Second, the general statutory prohibition against "sex" discrimination common to all jurisdictions was held to include

---

People Because of Age"; (13) "Policy and Guidelines on Disability and the Duty to Accommodate"; (14) "Policy on Discrimination and Harassment Because of Sexual Orientation"; and (15) "Guidelines on Special Programs." These documents are online: www.ohrc.on.ca/en/resources/Policies.

89 The leading Canadian reference work is A.P. Aggarwal & M. Gupta, *Sexual Harassment: A Guide for Understanding and Prevention*, 2d ed.. (Markham: Lexis-Nexis/Butterworths, 2006). The human rights legislation also outlaws harassment on other protected grounds. See *Espinoza*, above note 48 at 145,296–97, where harassment against Central South Americans was held to be grounded on their "ethnicity" under s. 10 of the *Ont. HRC*, above note 1; *Uzoaba*, above note 48, involving racial discrimination against a black correctional officer. See the discussion of "poisoned work environment" discrimination in Section B, above in this chapter.

90 D. Savoie & V. Larouche, "Le harcelement sexuel au travail: resultats de deux etudes quebecoises" (1990) 45 R.I./I.R. 38. This corroborates the 1983 study by the Canadian Human Rights Commission, *Unwanted Sexual Attention and Sexual Harassment: Results of a Survey of Canadians* (Ottawa: Canadian Human Rights Commission, 1983) at 5–6. The picture is equally as grim in other countries: see, for example, B.H. Earle & G.A. Madek, "An International Perspective on Sexual Harassment Law" (1993) 12 Law & Ineq. J. 43.

91 *Can. HRA*, above note 1, ss. 14(1), (2); *Man. HRC*, above note 1, s. 19(2)(b), (c); *N.L. HRC*, above note 1, s. 13; *N.B. HRC*, above note 1, s. 7.1; *N.S. HRA*, above note 1, ss. 5(2), 3(o); *Ont. HRC*, above note 1, ss. 7(2), s. 10, "harassment."

92 *N.L. HRC, ibid.*, s. 13.

sexual harassment in the leading Supreme Court of Canada decision in *Janzen v. Platy Enterprises Ltd.*[93] According to the Court, the discrimination element is found in the fact that those employees who are sexually harassed are subject to a different and more onerous psychological burden in the workplace than those who are not. Presumably, any gaps in specific legislative definitions of sexual harassment — such as the above-mentioned exclusion of "poisoned work environment" sexual harassment in Newfoundland — would be captured by the general prohibition against sex discrimination, given that human rights legislation is normally given a broad and liberal interpretation.

The *Canadian Human Rights Act* contains a uniquely worded provision giving employees the right to work in an environment that is "free of sexual harassment."[94] In order to give effect to this right, the Act requires employers to take proactive measures to eradicate sexual harassment by issuing a policy statement with the following features to their employees:

(a) a definition of sexual harassment that is substantially the same as the definition in [the Code];

(b) a statement to the effect that every employee is entitled to employment free of sexual harassment;

(c) a statement to the effect that the employer will make every reasonable effort to ensure that no employee is subjected to sexual harassment;

(d) a statement to the effect that the employer will take such disciplinary measures as he deems appropriate against any person under his direction who subjects any employee to sexual harassment;

(e) a statement explaining how complaints of sexual harassment may be brought to the attention of the employer;

(f) a statement to the effect that the employer will not disclose the name of a complainant or the circumstances related to the complaint to any person except where disclosure is necessary for the purposes of investigating the complaint or taking disciplinary measures in relation thereto; and,

(g) a statement informing employees of the discriminatory practices provisions of the *Canadian Human Rights Act* that pertain to

93   [1989] 1 S.C.R. 1252, especially at 1276, rev'g (1986), 33 D.L.R. (4th) 32 (Man. C.A.) [*Janzen*].
94   Above note 1, ss. 247.1–247.4.

rights of persons to seek redress under that Act in respect of sexual harassment.[95]

The rationale for imposing these measures is that the employer is in the best position, by virtue of its authority over its employees' conduct, to ensure that sexual harassment does not occur, or if it does, that it is treated seriously.[96] As we shall see below, this rationale also explains why the Supreme Court of Canada held the employer to be *automatically* liable for sexual harassment committed by its employees in its landmark 1987 decision in *Robichaud*; such liability, it is thought, will provide an incentive to the employer to use its disciplinary and other powers to eradicate sexual harassment from its organization.[97] In other provinces where the legislation does not compel employers to have a sexual harassment policy, it is nevertheless advisable to have one since it shows that the employer treats sexual harassment seriously and may reduce the extent of the employer's liability for any sexual harassment that does occur. Indeed, it is possible that a human rights tribunal could order an employer not having such a policy to introduce one as part of a "make whole" remedy to combat sexual harassment in the firm.

The occupational health and safety legislation also comes into play since sexual harassment involving actual or threatened physical assault, or significant psychological injury to the victim, appears to constitute a workplace "hazard" or "danger" in breach of the legislation.[98] Not only is the employer bound to eliminate a proscribed "hazard" or "danger" as soon as possible — a government inspector can issue a fast-

---

95 *Ibid.*, s. 247.4(2). For additional practical recommendations on how employers should handle sexual harassment complaints, see Ontario Human Rights Commission, *Guidelines for Internal Human Rights Complaint Resolution Procedures* (Toronto: Ontario Human Rights Commission, 1991); C. Cohen & M. Cohen, "Defending Your Life: When Women Complain about Sexual Harassment" (1994) 7 Employee Resp. & Rts. J. 235; M. Waxman, "Constructive Responses to Sexual Harassment in the Workplace" (1994) 7 Employee Resp. & Rts. J. 243.

96 *Canada Labour Code*, R.S.C. 1985, c. L-2, s. 147.4(3).

97 *Robichaud v. Canada (Treasury Board.)*, [1987] 2 S.C.R. 84 [*Robichaud*]. As we shall see, this ruling has subsequently been modified by making available to employers the defence of "due diligence."

98 See *Au v. Lyndhurst Hospital*, [1995] O.L.R.B. Rep. November 1371, supporting reasons at [1995] O.L.R.B. Rep. May/June 456, application for judicial review refused, [1996] O.L.R.B. Rep. 902 (Ont. Div. Ct.). In Saskatchewan, the *Occupational Health and Safety Act*, S.S. 1993, c. O-1.1, s. 3(c) expressly provides that the employer must "insofar as is reasonably practicable" ensure that the employees are not exposed to sexual harassment in the workplace. The health and safety legislation is examined in Chapter 6, Section D.

track order directing this to be done almost immediately—but also, the employee is entitled to say no to performing any work that he or she honestly and reasonably believes to constitute a "hazard" or "danger." A major advantage of the occupational health and safety acts is that complaints are processed much more quickly than under the notoriously slow machinery in the human rights acts.

Regarding the definition of proscribed sexual harassment, the main difficulty has proven to be drawing the line between, on the one hand, socially acceptable flirtation and jocularity, and on the other hand, unjustifiable intimidation and oppression. Plainly, if an overly censorious definition is adopted, the law could be brought into disrepute, with possibly serious repercussions for the legitimacy of human rights legislation in general.[99] The standard, however, is whether a "reasonable woman" would perceive the conduct in question as making the work atmosphere uncomfortable, not whether a "reasonable man" or a "reasonable person" would do so.[100] There are two wings to the current definition.[101] The first outlaws conduct that involves one employee granting or withholding an employment benefit to another employee in return for sexual favours. This is often called *"quid pro quo"* sexual harassment. A leading case on this form of sexual harassment is *Kotyk v. Canada (Employment & Immigration Commission)*,[102] where the supervisor of one of the complainants insinuated that he would not approve her probationary review unless she had an affair with him. It is usually fairly easy for tribunals to detect this form of harassment.

The second wing of sexual harassment proscribes sexually related conduct that makes the workplace oppressive or intimidating for the victim. This "poisoned work environment" sexual harassment can sometimes be difficult to define exactly when the line is crossed between socially acceptable jocularity and impermissible harassment. The following examples cited in the Ontario Human Rights Commission's guidelines convey the essence of this form of discrimination:

---

99 Example: *Marinaki v. Canada (Human Resources Department)*, [2000] C.L.L.C. ¶230-032 at 141,365–6 (Can. H.R.T.), where a male who told a female co-worker to "fuck off" in a heated argument was held not to have committed sexual harassment.

100 *Stadnyk v. Canada (Employment and Immigration Commission)*, [2001] C.L.L.C. ¶230-002 at 145,012 (F.C.A.).

101 See the comprehensive analysis of these two forms of sexual harassment in *Janzen*, above note 93.

102 (1983), 83 C.L.L.C. ¶17,012 (Can. H.R.T.), aff'd (*sub nom. Chuba v. Kotyk*) (1983), 84 C.L.L.C. ¶17,005 (Can. H.R.R.T.). In a similar vein, see *Strauss v. Canada Property Investment Corp. (No. 2)* (1995), 24 C.H.R.R. D/43, especially at D/49 (Ont. Bd. Inq.).

- gender-related comments about an individual's physical attributes, mannerisms, or characteristics;
- unwelcome physical contact;
- suggestive or offensive remarks or innuendos about members of a specific gender;
- propositions about physical intimacy;
- gender-related verbal abuse, threats, or taunting;
- leering or inappropriate staring;
- bragging about sexual prowess;
- demands for dates or sexual favours;
- offensive jokes or comments of a sexual nature about an employee;
- display of sexually offensive pictures, graffiti or other materials;
- questions or discussions about sexual activities;
- paternalism based on gender which a person feels undermines his/ her self-respect or position of responsibility;
- rough and vulgar humour or language related to gender;
- sexual assault.[103]

These guidelines do not have the force of law in and of themselves, but they reflect the spirit with which human rights tribunals in Ontario and elsewhere apply the express terms of the legislation.

In order to constitute proscribed sexual harassment, the conduct in question must be unwelcome. This condition means either that the victim must have informed the harasser that the conduct is unwelcome or that the harasser, as a reasonable person, ought to have reasonably foreseen that the conduct would be unwelcome to a reasonable person in the victim's position. If the employer would clearly pay no heed to a complaint of harassment by an employee — for example, if the perpetrator is the employer or a close personal friend of the employer[104] — the victim need not go through the motions of formally complaining. If the harassment has been going on for some time with the consent of the victim, the perpetrator must cease the conduct in question immediately upon being notified that it is no longer welcome. If the harassment is committed by an employee's supervisor, tribunals require clear and cogent evidence to support an assertion that the employee consented to the activity in view of the inherent power imbalance between a

---

103 *Policy Statement on Sexual Harassment and Inappropriate Gender-Related Comment and Conduct* (Toronto: Ontario Human Rights Commission, 1993) at 7, online: www.ohrc.on.ca/en/resources/Policies/PolicySexHarrCommentsENG?page=PolicySexHarrCommentsENG-3_.html#Heading85.

104 *Zarankin v. Johnstone* (1984), 84 C.L.L.C. ¶17,015 at 16,125 (B.C. Bd. Inq.).

supervisor and a subordinate.[105] The harassment must occur during the course of employment, for the employer cannot be expected to control what its workers do in their private time. However, the course of employment is not restricted to actual working hours, but can include off-duty time when the employee is going about the employer's business in circumstances in which it would be reasonable to expect the employer to be able to control the behaviour of its workers. For instance, if the harassment occurs at a party in a hotel after the employees have attended a company workshop, it may fall within the course of employment, but not if the party has ended and the employees have retired to their rooms.[106]

Furthermore, an employer may be held responsible for sexual harassment committed against one of its employees by its clients and customers. Although this might appear at first to be unfair to the employer, since it cannot discipline non-employees, the employer can take steps to protect the employee against such harassment—for example, requesting the perpetrators to stop, by refusing to deal with them further unless they stop, or reassigning the victim to work duties that do not involve coming into contact with the perpetrator.[107]

The legal burden of proving sexual harassment lies with the employee (or, more accurately, with the human rights commission, which commonly carries complaints on behalf of the aggrieved employee).[108] However, the claimant's position is ameliorated by the tribunal's practice of imposing on the employer a *de facto* evidentiary onus of explanation once the claimant has established a *prima facie* case of sexual harassment. In order to raise such a *prima facie* case, the claimant need only prove that he or she was employed by the company, that the alleged harassment took place during the course of employment, that he or she did not willingly consent, and that the conduct falls within the statutory definition of sexual harassment.[109] If the employer cannot present a plausible explanation for its behaviour, the tribunal will draw the inference that the employer did, in fact, engage in sexual harassment. If the conduct is motivated partially by legitimate business

---

105 *Simpson v. Consumers Assn. of Canada*, [2001] O.J. No. 5058 at para. 64 (C.A.) [*Simpson*].

106 See *Cluff v. Canada (Department of Agriculture)* (1992), 20 C.H.R.R. D/61 (Can. H.R.T.), aff'd (1993), [1994] 2 F.C. 176 (T.D.) [*Cluff*]; *Simpson, ibid.*.

107 *Greensides v. Human Rights Commission (Saskatchewan)* (1992), 20 C.H.R.R. D/469 (Sask. Bd. Inq.), aff'd (1993), 21 C.H.R.R. D/474 (Sask. Q.B.).

108 The enforcement procedures under human rights acts are examined below in Section E of this chapter.

109 *Singson v. Pasion* (1996), 26 C.H.R.R. D/435 at D/440 (B.C.C.H.R.) [*Singson*].

reasons, but also by an intention to harass the employee, it is unlawful; the employer's motive must be totally devoid of an intent to harass.[110] The standard of proof regarding sexual harassment is the usual civil law "balance of probabilities" standard.[111]

The policy of the legislation is to eliminate sexual harassment from the workplace, not solely to punish employers who willingly intend or condone harassment. In order to achieve this goal, the Supreme Court of Canada held in 1995 that employers are automatically liable for acts of harassment committed by their workers or by their clients and customers, even though top management may be innocent of what is going on.[112] The rationale is that this will provide employers with a strong incentive to proactively ensure that harassment does not occur. The Court ruled that although employers cannot escape this absolute liability, the amount of compensation that the employer will be ordered to pay may be reduced if it has adopted efficacious measures to prevent harassment from occurring, to deal with complaints of harassment and to punish the perpetrators.[113] The measures contained in the *Ontario Human Rights Commission* policy statement on combatting sexual harassment quoted above[114] will, if implemented by an employer, be taken into account by tribunals to reduce the employer's level of blame, and therefore the amount of compensation payable to the victim. It is doubtful, however, that this form of automatic and absolute liability could survive a constitutional challenge under sections 7 and 11(d) of the *Charter* if the employer could show that the harassment occurred despite it having acted with "due diligence" to ensure that the workplace was harassment free[115]—for example, by implementing all of the measures in the Canada Human Rights Commission policy statement described above. Indeed, it is no surprise that the federal and Manitoba human rights acts have subsequently been amended in order to include an explicit defence of due diligence to sexual harass-

---

110 Example: *Wales-Callahan v. CN Office Cleaning Ltd.* (1993), 26 C.H.R.R. D/64 at D/69 (Ont. Bd. Inq.).

111 *Mahmoodi v. Dutton (No. 4)* (1999), 36 C.H.R.R. D/8 at D/22–23 (B.C.H.R.T.), where the tribunal declined to apply the more rigorous standard of "clear and convincing evidence" despite the stigma attached to being found liable for sexual harassment.

112 *Robichaud*, above note 97, especially at 85.

113 *Ibid.*

114 Above note 103 and accompanying text.

115 See, by analogy, *R. v. Ellis-Don Ltd.* (1990), 34 C.C.E.L. 130 (Ont. C.A.) and *R. v. Cancoil Thermal Corp.*, [1986] O.J. No. 290 (C.A.), both holding that the "due diligence" was constitutionally required under the health and safety legislation.

ment. In other jurisdictions, tribunals would almost certainly have to imply a due diligence defence into the statute in order to comply with the *Charter*.

The procedure for enforcing complaints of sexual harassment under human rights acts is identical to that for enforcing any other complaint of breach of the act. These procedures are examined in the next section of this chapter. However, it deserves emphasis at this juncture that human rights tribunals may award special remedies to make whole the victim's losses where an employer is found liable for sexual harassment in addition to the usual remedies of reinstatement and financial compensation for lost wages and benefits. Frequently, the victim of sexual harassment will suffer emotional trauma as a result of his or her experiences. If the medical evidence shows that the claimant's traumatic condition makes it more difficult to find replacement work at the same pay after the employment ends — normally, victims of sexual harassment will resign before commencing legal proceedings against their employers — the tribunals will increase the level of compensation to take account of this impediment.[116] Counselling or other medical services that the victim pays for in order to restore mental health are compensable against the employer.[117] Furthermore, compensation will be awarded for the personal humiliation that the victim suffers in having his or her legal rights violated. Although the basis of such awards in theory is supposed to be compensatory,[118] some awards appear to have a punitive orientation. The following factors have been held to be relevant in determining the amount awarded:

(a) The nature of the harassment, that is, was it simply verbal or was it physical as well. (b) The degree of aggressiveness and physical contact in the harassment. (c) The ongoing nature, that is, the time period of the harassment. (d) The frequency of the harassment. (e) The age of the victim. (f) The vulnerability of the victim.[119] (g) The psychological impact of the harassment upon the victim.[120]

---

116 Example: *Burton v. Chalifour Bros. Construction Ltd.* (1994), 21 C.H.R.R. D/501 (B.C.C.H.R.) [*Burton*].

117 Example: *Clarke v. Command Record Services Ltd.* (1996), 27 C.H.R.R. D/73 at D/86 (B.C.C.H.R.) [*Clarke*].

118 Examples: *Clarke, ibid.* at D/85; *Burton*, above note 116 at D/507.

119 See, for instance, *Singson*, above note 109, where the sum awarded was $3,500 where the victim was a relatively young immigrant from the Philippines working as a live-in domestic whom the perpetrator threatened to have deported if she complained.

120 *Donaldson v. 463963 Ontario Ltd.* (1994), 26 C.H.R.R. D/335 at D/342 (Ont. Bd. Inq.) [*Donaldson*], citing from *Shaw v. Levac Supply Ltd.* (1990), 14 C.H.R.R.

Generally, the amount awarded for relatively non-serious instances of sexual harassment is between $1,000 and $2,000, but awards of approximately $5,000 are commonplace for more serious occurrences.[121] Some tribunals, however, have grasped the nettle and awarded compensation explicitly on a punitive basis, reasoning that their make whole remedial mandate implicitly allows such awards in order to deter employers who maliciously, flagrantly, or recklessly disregard their statutory obligations.[122] Thus, one tribunal has awarded $10,000 in punitive damages for persistent and serious physical harassment combined with threats of violence if the employee notified the police.[123] Although the make whole philosophy would not normally be understood as encompassing the goal of deterrence, it can be strongly argued that the urgency of eradicating sexual harassment from the workplace justifies making an exception in these circumstances. Any doubts about the jurisdiction of human rights tribunals to award punitive damages for sexual harassment are resolved in those provinces whose legislation specifically allows such awards in defined circumstances—typically where the perpetrator has acted maliciously or recklessly—and up to a specified maximum.[124] Furthermore, the make whole mandate has been applied to order employers to implement sensitivity training programs in sexual harassment for their employees and managers, and to report regularly to the provincial human rights commission on the firm's progress in combatting sexual harassment.[125] Finally, the make whole remedy appears to be sufficiently broad to allow the tribunal to order an employer to transfer, discipline, and even dismiss a perpetrator of sexual harassment who shows an unwillingess or inability to respond to rehabilitation.[126] (At common law, committing sexual ha-

---

D/36 at D/61–62 (Ont. Bd. Inq.) [*Shaw*]. See also *Miller v. Sam's Pizza House* (1995), 23 C.H.R.R. D/433 (N.S. Bd. Inq.) [*Sam's Pizza House*].

121 Examples: *Shaw, ibid.*, where $5,000 was awarded for egregious verbal harassment that persisted for fourteen years; *Donaldson, ibid.*, the relatively high amount of where $5,000 was awarded for aggressive and persistent verbal and physical harassment that resulted in the victim's needing psychological counselling.

122 Examples: *Sam's Pizza House*, above note 120 at D/456–57; *Torres v. Royalty Kitchenware Ltd.* (1982), 3 C.H.R.R. D/858 at D/870 (Ont. Bd. Inq.).

123 *Sam's Pizza House, ibid.*

124 Examples: *Can. HRA*, above note 1, s. 53(3), ceiling of $5,000; *Man. HRC*, above note 1, s. 43(2)(d); *Sask. HRC*, above note 1, s. 31(8), ceiling of $5,000.

125 *Scott v. Lou's Moving and Storage Ltd.* (1992), 18 C.H.R.R. D/143 at D/145 (Man. Bd. Adj.), where the employer was also ordered to post the tribunal's decision and a sexual harassment policy on the firm's notice board.

126 By analogy with *Re Tenaquip Ltd. and Teamsters Local 419* (2002), 112 L.A.C. (4th) 60 (Newman) [*Re Tenaquip*], where an arbitrator applied the make whole

rassment constitutes serious misconduct that generally provides just cause for summary dismissal, unless there are compelling mitigating factors present.[127]) It is significant that financial remedies for sexual harassment can be made against the officers, directors, agents, and employees of a company in their personal capacity as well as against the company in its own name, thereby providing an additional incentive to eradicate sexual harassment from the workplace.[128]

E. ENFORCING THE HUMAN RIGHTS LEGISLATION

Human rights statutes are supposed to provide employees with a cheap and expeditious means of safeguarding their legal rights, a means that meets the generally recognized standards of due process, to fill the void created by civil litigation being beyond the financial reach of most workers; however, human rights legislation has failed miserably to fulfill its promise. A plethora of studies have shown that human rights commissions, nationwide, have performed poorly over many years in enforcing the legislation, especially in the following areas:[129]

- Delays are excessive in all phases of the enforcment process, but especially in investigating complaints, in obtaining discovery of documents from employers, and in completing the mediation process that must precede adjudication. Most statutes do not include time limits for completing the various stages of the enforcement process, or, if they do, the time limits are excessively long. In 2000, the La Forest Panel reported that the federal Human Rights Commission takes, on

---

remedial mandate under the collective agreement to discipline a supervisor who assaulted and harassed a subordinate. See also *McKinnon v. Ontario (Ministry of Correctional Services) (No. 3)* (1998), 32 C.H.R.R. D/1 at D/70 (Ont. Bd. Inq.), where the employer was ordered to transfer employees who racially harassed the claimant to a different facility away from the claimant's workplace.

127 *Leach v. Canadian Blood Services* (2001), 7 C.C.E.L. (3d) 205 (Alta. Q.B.), where just cause for dismissal was found. Compare *Brazeau v. International Electrical Workers*, [2004] C.L.L.C. ¶210-032 at 141,302 (B.C.S.C.), where mitigating factors resulted in finding no just cause for dismissal.

128 *Katsiris v. Isaac*, [2001] C.L.L.C. ¶230-014, especially at 145,133 (Sask. Q.B.); *Curling v. Tomimoro (No. 2)* (1999), 36 C.H.R.R. D/468 (Ont. Bd. Inq.).

129 La Forest Panel, above note 16, Part 2. In a similar vein, see J. Payne & C. Rootham, "Are Human Rights Commissions Still Relevant?" (2005) 12 C.L.E.L.J. 199; R.B. Howe & M. Andrade, "The Reputations of Human Rights Commissions in Canada" (1994) 9 C.J.L.S. 1 at 3 and 10.

average, two years to investigate a complaint and forty-five months to decide to reject or remit a case to adjudication once the mediation process is finished.[130]

- An unhealthy public perception exists that the human rights commissions deliberately reject many complaints that are meritorious merely to save the commissions' scarce resources.

- The human rights commissions often fail to prioritize cases so that more urgent ones are often left to languish in line with less urgent ones.

- Employers and employees distrust the neutrality of the human rights commissions because of the commissions' multiple roles as "judge" in accepting or rejecting complaints at the intake stage and in determining whether to remit a complaint to adjudication, as "advocate" in taking carriage of the claimant's case in adjudication, and as "neutral" in investigating and mediating a case and in preparing guidelines and other educational material on how the statute should be interpreted and applied. The appearance of a conflict of interest undermines the efficacy of commissions in the performance of all their functions.

- Employers and employees often see injustice in the fact that a quintessentially "administrative" body such as the human rights commission should perform the quintessentially "judicial" task of deciding whether or not to remit a complaint to adjudication: the adjudicative tribunal is supposed to have the specialized expertise in deciding legal questions involving the interpretation and application of the legislation — not the commission.

Exactly how these deficiencies have occurred (and how they might be remedied) requires an understanding of the "traditional" Canadian model of enforcement under the human rights acts. Although there are considerable differences in the details of each province's statutory enforcement machinery, certain common general principles can be identified.

- The human rights acts are normally enforced exclusively through specialized human rights commissions and tribunals, with the courts declining to hear civil complaints of breach of the acts in order to bolster the integrity of the administrative machinery.[131] Neverthe-

---

130 *Ibid.*

131 Examples: *Moore v. British Columbia* (1988), 88 C.L.L.C. ¶17,021 at 16,184 (B.C.C.A.), breach of the statute *simpliciter; Tenning v. Manitoba* (1983), 3 C.C.E.L. 72 (Man. C.A.), breach of the statute as incorporated as a term of the employment contract; *Seneca College of Applied Arts and Technology v. Bha-*

less, over the years the courts have gradually enlarged the scope for bringing human rights issues as part of other civil complaints, such as wrongful dismissal, to enable employees to avoid the excessive delays in the statutory enforcement machinery.

- A complaint of breach of the act can normally be filed not only by the victim personally, but also independently by the human rights commission, often with or without the consent of the employees affected. Typically, the commission itself will initiate a complaint if there is evidence of systemic discrimination in the workplace. The commission's mandate is to eliminate discrimination from society, not just to compensate particular victims who have chosen to complain. When a complaint is first received, an intake officer makes a preliminary determination whether or not it is sufficiently meritorious to proceed, usually on the basis of information supplied by the claimant and communications with the employer and other key witnesses. Usually, there is no appeal against an intake officer's decision to reject a complaint. The legislation commonly imposes time limits for filing complaints, usually one year or six months, depending on the jurisdiction, but these are generally waived by the commissions, pursuant to their statutory discretion to allow late claims, in furtherance of the remedial goal of the legislation. As a result, the problem of delay is exacerbated by overburdened caseloads.[132]

- The human rights commission usually takes carriage of the employee's complaint on his or her behalf, up to and including adjudication where necessary.[133] However, the employee is kept fully informed and has a right to participate at all stages of the procedure. At the outset, the investigation officer conducts a comprehensive examination of all the evidence pertaining to the complaint, and has extensive powers under the legislation to order discovery of documentation, to enter workplaces, and to interview witnesses.[134] The investigator is bound by the administrative law duty of procedural fairness in dealings with the parties, so investigations must be con-

---

dauria, [1981] 2 S.C.R. 181, a residual tort of discrimination. See generally A.L. Mactavish & A.J.F. Lenz, "Civil Actions for Conduct Addressed by Human Rights Legislation: Some Recent Substantive and Procedural Developments" (1996) 4 C.L.E.L.J. 375. For further elaboration of the enforceability of human rights issues in the courts, see Chapter 8.

132 La Forest Panel, above note 16 at 61–62. The Panel recommended limiting extensions to situations where the claimant could not file on time due to "serious reason" such as disability, or where the claimant could not reasonably have known that his or her rights had been violated until after the expiry of the time limit.

133 Example: *Sask. HRC,* above note 1, s. 30(1)(a).

134 Example: *ibid.,* s. 28.1.

ducted in a "neutral" and "thorough" manner, and each party given an opportunity to examine and respond to all material evidence.[135] However, employers are often unduly slow, or even outright unwilling to produce documents or be interviewed when requested by the investigator. A key function of the investigator is to seek a voluntary settlement of the complaint by mediation. Mediation is very successful in resolving complaints in all jurisdictions.[136] In some provinces, including Ontario, a private mediator from outside the human rights commission can be appointed if the parties both agree, and this approach seems to be more successful in producing voluntary settlements than in-house mediation.[137] The human rights commission can unilaterally decide to proceed with a complaint, even though the employee is willing to settle it, if the complaint involves issues of general public importance or affects the interests of other workers. While mediation is ideal in securing compliance in the case of employers that do not understand their statutory obligations—a likely scenario, given the uncertainty of the law in the area—it is clearly insufficient in the case of employers that deliberately disregard their legal obligations out of malice or because they consider breaching the legislation to be more profitable than honouring it. For such employers, penal sanctions are required.

- If the investigation officer cannot secure a mutually acceptable settlement in mediation, the officer reports to the human rights commission, which has the discretion to dismiss the complaint as non-meritorious or to remit it for adjudication. Alternatively, the human rights commission can generally elect to defer the complaint to an alternative remedial procedure, such as collective agreement arbitration (in the case of unionized employees)[138] or adjudication under

---

135 *Boliden Westmin (Canada) v. Bonneau* (1999), 35 C.H.R.R. D/173 (B.C.S.C.).

136 For example, in Nova Scotia between 2006 and 2007, 75 percent of attempted mediations by the Human Rights Commission produced a settlement, and 75 percent of claimants and respondents stated that they were satisfied with the mediation process: Nova Scotia Human Rights Commission, *Annual Accountability Report for the Fiscal Year 2006–2007* (Halifax: Nova Scotia Human Rights Commission, 2007) at 6 and 11, online: www.gov.ns.ca/humanrights/publications/nshrc_accountabilityreport2006_07.pdf.

137 The La Forest Panel strongly endorsed making private mediation available, preferably as early as possible in the complaints process: above note 16.

138 For several years in Ontario, the Human Rights Commission automatically deferred complaints to arbitration, but in 2001 the Court of Appeal ruled that automatic deferral was unlawful; rather, the commission had to examine the circumstances of each case in order to evaluate whether or not arbitration is the most suitable forum for resolving the complaint in question: *Thomas v.*

another statute. The latter avenues, of course, may well be much faster than adjudication under the human rights legislation. Also, deferral to another forum reduces the human rights commission's caseload, thereby alleviating delays under the statutory procedure, and reduces the commissions' operating costs. On the other hand, it is questionable whether these administrative benefits outweigh the complainant's right to have his or her complaint dealt with by the specialized human rights agency. Some human rights acts give the complainant a right to appeal to the human rights commission itself[139] or to some other superior authority in the human rights apparatus[140] for "reconsideration" of the decision to dismiss a complaint. Newfoundland is unique in entitling a complainant to appeal to the courts for a full review of the merits of the commission's dismissal of a complaint.[141] Furthermore, the usual administrative law safeguards against abuse of discretion and procedural unfairness apply to a human rights commission in deciding whether or not to dismiss a complaint.[142] Accordingly, the courts have held that, prior to finalizing its decision, the commission must provide each party with a copy of the investigator's report, along with any other material taken into account in reaching its decision, and must give each party a reasonable opportunity to respond in writing to all the relevant documentation.[143] Interestingly, the courts have ruled that the investigator must have prepared any report to the commission in a "neutral" and "thorough" manner in order for it to constitute the basis for the commission's decision.[144]

Ontario (Human Rights Commission) (2001), 12 C.C.E.L. (3d) 14 (Ont. C.A.). In contrast, in Saskatchewan, the Human Rights Commission automatically defers to arbitration: *Cadillac Fairview Corp. v. Saskatchewan (Human Rights Board of Inquiry)* (1999), 34 C.H.R.R. D/133 (Sask. C.A.). See the critique by B. Etherington, "Promises, Promises: Notes on Diversity and Access to Justice" (2000) 26 Queen's L.J. 43. 62.

139 Example: Prince Edward Island *Human Rights Act*, R.S.P.E.I. 1988, c. H-12, s. 25, where the Commission's chairperson conducts the review.

140 Examples: *Alta. HRCMA*, above note 1, s. 22; *B.C. HRC*, above note 1, s. 24.

141 *N.L. HRC*, above note 1, s. 21(4).

142 Examples: *Slattery v. Canada (Human Rights Commission)* (1994), 22 C.H.R.R. D/205 (F.C.T.D.); *Ontario (Human Rights Commission) v. Ontario (Human Rights Board of Inquiry)* (1993), 20 C.H.R.R. D/498, especially at D/500 (Ont. Gen. Div.).

143 *Syndicat des employés de production du Québec & de l'Acadie v. Canada (Human Rights Commission)* (1986), 16 C.C.E.L. 275 at 284 (F.C.A.), aff'd [1989] 2 S.C.R. 879 at 895–96, Sopinka J. [*Syndicat des employés*]; *Zutter v. British Columbia (Council of Human Rights)* (1993), 21 C.H.R.R. D/164 at D/169–70 (B.C.S.C.).

144 *Syndicat des employés, ibid.* at 283 (F.C.A.). See, for example, the biased investigation in *Shreve v. Windsor (City of) (No. 2)* (1993), 18 C.H.R.R. D/363 (Ont. Bd. Inq.).

- Adjudication of complaints is commonly provided for by a neutral tribunal, which, depending on the jurisdiction, may be either a standing tribunal or an *ad hoc* one. Although tribunal proceedings are more informal than civil litigation before the courts, the tribunal must comply with the principles of natural justice and procedural fairness[145] since its decisions are commonly legally binding.[146] The federal legislation provides a right to appeal a tribunal decision to a superior review tribunal;[147] otherwise, tribunal decisions generally cannot be appealed on their merits, only by judicial review for breach of natural justice or other jurisdictional error.[148] Depending on the jurisdiction, the courts have generally applied the standard of either "reasonablness" or "patent unreasonabless" when reviewing issues within the purview of a tribunal's specialized expertise.[149]
- Delay in processing a human rights complaint through the various stages outlined above can result in the complaint being dismissed by the tribunal if it results in either party not receiving a "fair hearing."[150] Thus, if key witnesses have died or if their recollections have irreversibly dulled with the passage of time and no other reliable evidence on which the tribunal can evaluate the complaint is available, it will be dismissed. The tribunals will not readily dismiss cases on this ground, however, since the individual's fundamental human rights are at stake. In particular, a case will not be dismissed because of the personal stigma and injury to reputation that a respondent may suffer as a result of being cited as an alleged human rights violator.[151] Of course, if one side

145 In Saskatchewan, for instance, a human rights tribunal is empowered to conduct its proceedings under The *Public Inquiries Act*, R.S.S. 1978, c. P-38, ss. 3 & 4, while in British Columbia, the tribunals have the powers conferred under that province's *Inquiry Act*, R.S.B.C. 1996, c. 224.

146 Example: *B.C. HRC*, above note 1, s. 28(8).

147 *Can. HRA*, above note 1, ss. 55–56.

148 Example: *Pushpanathan v. Canada (Minister of Citizenship and Immigration)*, [1998] 1 S.C.R. 982 at 1004–5.

149 *Entrop*, above note 7, where "reasonableness" was applied; *University of British Columbia v. Berg*, [1993] 2 S.C.R. 353, where "patent unreasonableness" was applied. However, as a result of the 2008 decision of the Supreme Court of Canada in *Dunsmuir v. New Brunswick*, 2008 SCC 9, eliminating the "patently unreasonable" test, the courts must now apply either the test of "correctness" or "reasonableness."

150 *Nisbett v. Manitoba (Human Rights Commission)* (1993), 93 C.L.L.C. ¶17,022 at 16,123 (Man. C.A.). The caselaw is examined fully in *Simms v. Seetech Metal Products* (1993), 20 C.H.R.R. D/477, especially at D/479–81 (Ont. Bd. Inq.).

151 *Blencoe v. British Columbia (Human Rights Commision)*, [2000] C.L.L.C. ¶230-040 (S.C.C.), involving an allegation of sexual harassment of a female personal assistant by a male cabinet minister in the N.D.P. provincial government. The tribunal subsequently found the respondent guilty of the alleged harassment: *Willis v. Blencoe*, [2001] C.L.L.C. ¶230-032 (B.C.H.R.T.).

deliberately engineers a delay in the hope that the complaint will be dismissed by the tribunal or withdrawn by the complainant, the tribunal will proceed and not let that party benefit from its wrongdoings.[152]

Several useful recommendations have been made for improving the performance of the statutory enforcement machinery.[153]

- Increase government funding for the human rights commissions and tribunals.
- Have complaints made directly to the appropriate adjudicative tribunal instead of going to a human rights commission first. Doing this would end the human rights commissions' monopoly on deciding which cases go to adjudiction, thereby freeing up the commissions' resources to do what they best: research, education, and advocacy on human rights issues. The tribunal would then be able to do what it does best—namely, deciding the legal merits of complaints and attempting to mediate settlements.[154] This model was adopted in Ontario in 2006.[155] There, the legislation creates a new Human Rights Tribunal to perform the adjudicative functions and restricts the role of the Human Rights Commission to initiating complaints of systemic discrimination or of widespread public interest, and to intervening before the tribunal in particular cases as an independent third party of interest. To assist claimants in preparing and presenting their cases to the tribunal, and in enforcing the tribunal's orders, Ontario also established a publicly funded and publicly accountable Legal Support Centre.[156] In 2003, British Columbia introduced a somewhat similar model that also places complaints exclusively within the domain of an adjudicative tribunal, but unlike Ontario, British Columbia abolished the human rights commission outright.[157]

---

152 Example: *Patel v. Minto Developments Inc. (No. 2)* (1996), 26 C.H.R.R. D/444 at D/448 (Ont. Bd. Inq.), arising under the Ontario *Statutory Powers Procedure Act*, R.S.O. 1990, c. S.22, s. 23(1).

153 The most extensive list of recommendations is that suggested by the La Forest Panel, above note 16, summarized at 156–68.

154 LaForest Panel, *ibid.* at 52–53.

155 In Ontario, the new system was introduced under the *Human Rights Code Amendment Act*, S.O. 2006, c. 30. See generally *Moving Forward: Ontario Human Rights Commission Annual Report 2006–2007* (Toronto: Queen's Printer, 2008), online: www.ohrc.on.ca/en/resources/annualreports/ar0607?page=eng-MOVING.html#Heading81; The changes are examined in Ontario Human Rights Commission, News Release, "Human Rights Changes Take Effect" (30 June 2008), online: www.ohrc.on.ca/en/resources/news/newsystem.

156 This is based on the recommendation of the La Forest Panel, above note 16 at 76–77.

157 *B.C. HRC*, above note 1, s. 21.

- In order to reduce delays, the legislation should incorporate short and strictly enforced time limits for completing all phases of the complaints procedure, including time limits on filing complaints; provide for alternative dispute resolution methods, such as the private mediation at the earliest stage in the process; allow for two or more individual complaints to be joined as a single complaint where appropriate; establish expedited adjudication procedures for relatively straightforward cases that do not need a full-scale, formal tribunal hearing; allow for fast-track interim remedial orders to be issued pending a full hearing before the tribunal in cases where speed is of the essence; and empower the tribunal to award costs against a party who has either deliberately delayed the complaints process or otherwise acted inappropriately.[158]
- In order to overcome the weaknesses of a statutory process that does not respond to discrimination until a complaint is made, the legislation should require employers, where feasible, to establish joint worker–management anti-discrimination committees to identify and resolve discriminatory practices at workplace level. These would resemble joint health and safety committees under the occupational health and safety legislation. To buttress an effective "internal responsibility system" for eliminating discrimination, individual employees could also be given the statutory right to refuse unsafe work in a disciminatory environment, equivalent to the right to refuse unsafe work under the health and safety acts.[159] As we saw earlier, some discriminatory conduct will violate the health and safety legislation as the law currently stands.[160]
- More dramatically, the legislation could take a proactive stance and require employers to take the initiative in achieving designated standards and measures of equality in the workplace within specified times. This type of legislation would resemble the pay equity acts in some jurisdictions where employers are required to eradicate gender-based wage discrimination within specified times:[161] As well, this model is featured under the federal *Employment Equity Act*, considered below.

A key to successful adjudication is the availability of remedies that effectively compensate the victim for the harm suffered as a result of having his or her human rights violated. We examine these remedies next.

---

158 La Forest Panel, above note 16 at 158–61.
159 *Ibid.* at 27–29.
160 See Section D(1), above in this chapter.
161 See Chapter 6, Section B.

1) Remedying Breach of Human Rights Legislation: The "Make Whole" Approach

In all jurisdictions, human rights tribunals have broad remedial authority which is supposed to be applied in order to further two objectives:
(1) to make whole the claimant's economic losses and psychological
harm suffered due to the employer's violation of his or her statutory
rights—that is, to restore the claimant to the position he or she would
have been in had the unlawful discrimination not occurred;[162] and (2)
to eliminate discrimination from the workplace for the benefit of all
future workers there. The "make whole" method does not mean that
causation *simpliciter* is the basis for awarding compensation (that the
claimant should be compensated for all losses and injury that would
not have been suffered "but for" the discrimination) because hairsplitting distinctions would have to be drawn between which factual links
in the chain of causation are or are not sufficiently "direct" to justify
making the employer liable. (As chaos theorists are wont to remind
us, who can predict the consequences of a butterfly in the Amazonian
rainforest spreading its wings?) Rather, in order to avoid the risk of
overburdening the employer with financial liability, the make whole
approach, as applied by most human rights tribunals, makes the employer liable only for "reasonably foreseeable" losses. The reasonable
foresight formula has a venerable pedigree in tort law, where it is used
as a vehicle for making policy decisions about who ought to bear the
financial risk in question, having regard to all of the moral and economic circumstances of each case.[163] It follows that human rights tribunals using the reasonable foresight test should squarely address the
relevant policy considerations in fashioning remedies. These include
determining the most efficient manner of combatting the various forms
of discrimination, how much financial liability employers can bear before a disemployment effect or other negative economic consequences
occur, whether employers should take out insurance coverage against
discrimination liability so as to distribute the loss broadly throughout
society,[164] and the cheapest and fastest ways of reintegrating a victim

---

162 See, for instance, the strikingly explicit endorsement of this philosophy in *B.C.
    HRC*, above note 1, s. 32(2).
163 See J.G. Fleming, *The Law of Torts*, 7th ed. (Sydney: Law Book Company, 1987)
    at 186–94.
164 Loss distribution is generally recognized as justifying making the employer
    liable for the torts of its employees committed in the course of their employ-
    ment under the vicarious liability doctrine, and employers commonly insure
    against this risk. In the United States, employers often insure against the risk

of discrimination into the workforce. Unfortunately, tribunals often do not address these questions openly in their judgments, and little guidance is provided by the academic literature. Furthermore, since the human rights legislation also aims to eradicate discrimination from the workplace for the future, consideration must be given to deterring employers who are unwilling to comply with their legal responsibilities through punitive damages awards and criminal or administrative penalties.

a) Loss of Future Earnings, Benefits, and Opportunities

The make whole approach frequently involves compensating the claimant for loss of future earnings and other employment-related benefits. Clearly, this will be the case where the claimant is either dismissed or refused employment for a discriminatory reason, but it will also apply where the employee voluntarily resigns in order to escape a poisoned work environment. Suppose, for example, that a claimant has been unlawfully refused employment or a promotion. In order to make the claimant whole, the tribunal would ensure compensation for all the wages, benefits, and other opportunities that would have been received had he or she been awarded the position.[165] However, this action should be taken only if the tribunal determines that the claimant likely would have been awarded the position in the absence of discrimination. Therefore, the tribunal would have to assess the merits of the claimant's application and compare it with others received by the employer in order to determine whether or not the individual would likely have won the competition.[166] The process also requires the tribunal to engage in reasoned speculation regarding the claimant's likely career progress had he or she been given the position. Thus, the tribunal must assess the probability that the claimant would have received not only general wage increases and economic benefits given to the whole workforce, but also personal benefits, such as individual performance bonuses,

---

of discrimination law suits: F. Mootz III, "Insurance Coverage of Employment Discrimination Claims" (1997) 52 U. Miami L. Rev. 1.

165 Examples: *Green v. Canada (Public Service Commission)* (1998), 34 C.H.R.R. D/166 (Can. H.R.T.) [*Green*]; *Nkwazi v. Correctional Service of Canada*, [2001] C.L.L.C. ¶230-022 (Can. H.R.T.) [*Nkwazi*]; *Singh v. Canada (Statistics Canada)* (1998), 34 C.H.R.R. D/203 (Can. H.R.T.) [*Singh*]; *Randhawa v. Yukon (Territory)* (1994), 96 C.L.L.C. ¶230-035 (Can. H.R.T.) [*Randhawa*].

166 On the requisite degree of probability, see the different formulations of each judge in *Canada (A.G.) v. Morgan* (1994), 21 C.H.R.R. D/87 (F.C.A.). Subsequently, in *Wardair Canada Inc. v. Cremona (No. 3)* (1993), 20 C.H.R.R. D/398 at D/408 (Can. H.R.T.) [*Wardair*], the tribunal held that the consensus of judicial pronouncements favoured the "serious possibility" test.

the right to apply for promotion to higher positions, and other training and career advancement opportunities. On the other hand, compensation will be cut off if the claimant would have resigned, retired, or been laid off from the position in question; otherwise, he or she would be unjustly enriched. Making these projections can be a complex process and the amount of compensation may be substantial since there is often a lengthy delay between the date of the discrimination and the date of the tribunal hearing.[167]

Similarly, suppose that a claimant seeks compensation for lost earnings and benefits that would have been obtained had he or she not been unlawfully fired or forced to resign from a position. In order to make the claimant whole, the tribunal would have to predict how much wages and other benefits he or she would have received by remaining with the employer. Again, this will sometimes require making difficult estimates about what the normal career ladder is for persons in the claimant's position,[168] and whether or not the claimant would have resigned anyway[169] or been lawfully fired for incompetence or misconduct.[170] It will also require making difficult predictions about the future economic health of the firm: if the future looks bright, the claimant's wages would likely have increased, but if the future looks grim, the claimant would likely have received no increase or a decrease, or even have been laid off.[171] An amount must be discounted from this sum to reflect the chance of the claimant finding replacement employment, something that will entail examining general labour-market conditions and considering the claimant's personal employability, which encom-

---

167 Examples: *Green*, above note 165; *Nkwazi*, above note 165; *Singh*, above note 165.
168 *McKinnon v. Ontario (Human Rights Commission) (No. 3)* (1998), 32 C.H.R.R. D/1 at D/68 (Ont. Bd. Inq.), aff'd (*sub nom. Ontario v. McKinnon*) [2004] O.J. No. 5051 (C.A.). The long and tortuous history of this case is reviewed in V. Verma & M. Wente, "Systemic Remedies to Address Institutional Racism: Lessons Learned from *McKinnon v. Ontario (Ministry of Correctional Services)*," online: www.cavalluzzo.com/publications/Reference%20documents/Systemic_remedies_paper.a16.pdf.
169 Example: *Andrews v. (Canada) Treasury Board* (1994), 95 C.L.L.C. ¶230-005 at 145,089–90 (Can. H.R.T.).
170 Examples: *Gains Pet Foods*, above note 25, especially at 320; *British Columbia v. Tozer (No. 2)* (2000), 36 C.H.R.R. D/393 at D/401 (B.C.H.R.T.); *Courchaine v. aahh ... Balloon Delights Inc.* (1994), 24 C.H.R.R. D/76 at D/82 (B.C.C.H.R.) [*Courchaine*].
171 *Whitehead v. Servodyne Canada Ltd.* (1986), 15 C.C.E.L. 5 (Ont. Bd. Inq.); *Morano v. Nuttal* (1988), 88 C.L.L.C. ¶17,008 (Ont. Bd. Inq.); *Switzer v. Jim Pattison Industries Ltd.* (1996) 26 C.H.R.R. D/449 at D/459–60 (B.C.H.R.T.) [*Switzer*].

passes skills and experience, health,[172] and age.[173] The earnings level in any replacement job must be taken into account; if the new level is less than in the old job, the claimant's compensation will increase—and vice versa. Significantly, the make whole approach differs completely from the common law measure of damages for wrongful dismissal, which compensates the employee solely for wages and benefits that would vest during the period of notice of termination.[174] Consequently, common law doctrines, such as the unofficial ceiling of two years' reasonable notice,[175] the irrecoverability of non-contractually binding, but "expected" benefits, and the extra notice premium attached to high-status positions, are irrelevant under the make whole theory.[176] Rather, the make whole approach of human rights tribunals has more in common with the similar approach of adjudicators under the statutory "unjust discharge" schemes in the federal jurisdiction, Quebec, and Nova Scotia.[177] It seems surprising that human rights tribunals and statutory unjust discharge adjudicators have not as yet referred to each other's jurisprudence in applying their respective remedial authorities.

The usual common law duty of mitigation applies under the human rights legislation. This duty requires the claimant to make reasonable efforts to minimize the harm caused by the unlawful act, for example, by making reasonable efforts to find replacement work if he or she has been unlawfully dismissed. It is quite compatible with the make whole philosophy not to compensate claimants for avoidable losses.

b) Reinstatement, Re-engagement, and Hiring Orders

Reinstatement, re-engagement, and hiring orders have traditionally been unavailable at common law.[178] Nevertheless, they are clearly pivotal to the make whole approach under the human rights legislation. Thus, if an employer unlawfully refuses to hire or promote an employee, the obvious way of making the employee personally whole is to direct the employer to hire the individual for the position in ques-

---

172 Example: *Canada (A.G.) v. Thwaites* (1994), 3 C.C.E.L. (2d) 290 at 317 (F.C.T.D.) [*Thwaites*], where an AIDS sufferer's damages were reduced because he would not remain employable for long.
173 Examples: *McKee v. Hayes-Dana Inc. (No. 1)* (1992), 17 C.H.R.R. D/79 at D/84 (Ont. Bd. Inq.); *Switzer*, above note 171 at D/459–60.
174 See Chapter 9, Section F(1).
175 Some, but not all provinces apply this unofficial ceiling. See Chapter 9, Section B.
176 *Smith v. Ontario (Human Rights Commission)* (2005), 195 O.A.C. 323 (Div. Ct.).
177 See Chapter 9, Section E(1)(c).
178 See Chapter 9, Section F(2).

tion or, if no vacancy exists, in the next one that comes open.[179] Also, forcing the employer to hire the individual would emphasize the importance of creating a discrimination-free atmosphere in the general workplace; such an order would be an especially strong disincentive against discriminatory hiring and promotion. It is surprising, therefore, that a federal court trial judge has described this as an "extraordinary" remedy.[180] Similarly, reinstatement with full back pay would appear to be the obvious make whole remedy for a claimant who has been dismissed for a discriminatory reason; it would also seem to help in the creation of a discrimination-free atmosphere in the general workplace. Nevertheless, claimants will often not seek reinstatement because they fear reprisals by their employer, especially in the non-organized sector, where claimants will not have a professional trade union representative safeguarding their interests. Alternatively, claimants who do request the remedy will frequently trade it off in negotiations in return for a more generous cash settlement of their complaint. As we shall see later, this factor has proven to be a major obstacle to the success of reinstatement orders by adjudicators under statutory unjust discharge schemes. It also explains why many adjudicators are reluctant to grant the remedy.[181] Unfortunately, there is no easy solution to the problem.

Human rights tribunals, however, have taken a very robust approach to ordering reinstatement in dismissal cases, regarding it as the primary remedy for making whole the claimant's personal losses and for eliminating discrimination from the general workplace. Accordingly, where an employer seeks to persuade a human rights tribunal that reinstatement would be inappropriate due to the souring of personal relationships in the workplace, the tribunals are reluctant to agree, arguing that the employer has the authority and the responsibility to put its house in order.[182] Furthermore, in order to facilitate the claimant's reintegration into the workplace following reinstatement, the tribunal can order the employer to transfer other employees who persist in their ill will towards the claimant to work in other locations separate from the claimant, and even to dismiss or otherwise discipline them if their discriminatory conduct

---

179 This was done in *Nkwazi*, above note 165 at 145,223; *Wardair*, above note 166 at D/408; *Uzoaba*, above note 48 at D/423 (Can. H.R.T.); *Randhawa*, above note 165 at paras. 145 and 374–75.
180 *Uzoaba, ibid.* (F.C.T.D.).
181 See Chapter 9, Section E(1)(c).
182 Examples: *Pitawanakwat v. Canada (Attorney General)* (1994), 21 C.H.R.R. D/355 at D/361–62 (F.C.T.D.) [*Pitawanakwat*]; *Naraine*, above note 48.

persists.[183] Exceptional circumstances may justify not reinstating the claimant, however. For instance, if claimant misdeeds significantly contributed to the dismissal and he or she shows no rehabilitative potential, there would likely not be reinstatement; also, if someone's position has been declared redundant or if a replacement worker has occupied the claimant's position in good faith and for a significant time such that it would be an undue hardship to "bump" that person out of the job, there would not be reinstatement. If the claimant's job has disappeared, the tribunal can order that he or she be re-engaged in a position for which he or she is qualified, if and when a vacancy arises.[184]

c)   Ancillary Relief

Victims of discrimination stand to suffer a variety of losses. Psychological harm, for example, can be compensated provided that the claimant can adduce medical evidence to prove that the symptoms in question were caused by the discrimination and not by other factors, such as personal lifestyle.[185] In some provinces, the human rights act limits the amount of compensation that can be awarded for mental distress or places other restrictions on the conditions under which such awards can be made. Section 41(b) of the *Ontario Human Rights Code*, for instance, not only limits compensation for mental anguish to situations where the employer has acted willfully or recklessly against the claimant, but also fixes a ceiling of $10,000 on the award. However, the $10,000 limit applies to each separate act of unlawful discrimination, so that an employer who engages in a pattern of discriminatory conduct may end up paying substantially more than $10,000.[186] In contrast, the limit in the federal jurisdiction was raised from $10,000 to $20,000 in 1998.[187] These limits are susceptible to challenge under section 15 of the *Charter* as offending the claimant's right to equality.[188]

---

183   In *McKinnon v. Ontario (Human Rights Commission) (No. 3)*, above note 126 at D/69–70; *McKinnon v. Ontario (Ministry Of Correctional Services) (No. 4)*, above note 126; *Re Tenaquip*, above note 126, where an arbitrator applied the "make whole" remedial mandate under the collective agreement to discipline a supervisor who sexually assaulted and harassed a subordinate.

184   *Armstrong v. Crest Realty Ltd.* (1998), 31 C.H.R.R. D/156 at D/164 (B.C.H.R.T.); *Bernard v. Waycobah Board of Education* (1999), 36 C.H.R.R. D/51 (Ont. Bd. Inq.).

185   Examples: *Entrop v. Imperial Oil Ltd.* (1995), 96 C.L.L.C. ¶230-001 (Ont. Bd. Inq.) [*Entrop* – Bd. Inq.]; *Jenner v. Pointe West Development Corp.* (1993), 21 C.H.R.R. D/336 at D/ 341 (Ont. Bd. Inq.).

186   *Ghosh*, above note 50.

187   *Can. HRA*, above note 1,, s. 53(2)(e), as am. by S.C. 1998, c. 9, s. 27.

188   The La Forest Panel, above note 16 at 71, recommended removing any such arbitrary limits on compensation for mental suffering.

Compensation for mental distress must be distinguished from compensation for the personal humiliation and loss of self-respect that victims of discrimination are presumed to suffer. The latter need not be specifically proven by a claimant, but the former must. As of 2008, the going rate for mental distress is between $1,000 and $2,000 for run-of-the-mill discrimination, but the amount may increase substantially to reflect the vulnerability of the victim, the persistence and offensiveness of the employer's conduct, and the presence of malice and deliberateness on the employer's part.[189] It has been held that compensation for mental distress cannot be reduced to reflect a claimant's contributory fault in the events leading up to dismissal or discipline,[190] even though the latter practice is commonplace with other types of compensation.[191] Again, some human rights acts set ceilings on this category of compensation.[192]

Some courts have held that the make whole philosophy is inconsistent with awarding punitive damages aimed at punishing the employer and deterring the employer and others from discriminating in the future; as a result, such awards are impermissible in the absence of express statutory empowerment.[193] Based on an understanding that punitive damages can provide a potent disincentive to hard-core discriminators, the legislation in most jurisdictions now expressly permits tribunals to award punitive damages in cases where the employer's misconduct is "willful" or "reckless," but typically imposes a limit of $10,000 or $20,000, depending on the jurisdiction.[194] Tribunals are especially disposed towards awarding punitive damages if the employer's misconduct seriously harms the employee, as in the earlier example of persistent sexual harassment involving violent physical assault.[195] It has been suggested that punitive damages should be used, wholly or partly, to help finance the work of the human rights commissions

---

189 Example: *Lane v. ADGA Group Consultants Inc.*, 2007 HRTO 34 at paras. 154–57, where $10,000 was awarded to an employee who was discriminated against because of bipolar disorder. One of the largest awards is $20,000 against an employer who subjected a black employee to a persistent, intense, and long-term regime of racial harassment that included physical assaults: *Naraine v. Ford Motor Company of Canada (No. 5)* (1996), 28 C.H.R.R. D/267 at D/273 (Ont. Bd. Inq.).

190 *Pitawanakwat*, above note 182 at D/371.

191 Example: *Gains Pet Foods*, above note 25.

192 Example: *Sask. HRC*, above note 1, section 31.4(b): the limit is $10,000.

193 *York Condominium Corp. No. 216 v. Dudnik*, [1991] O.J. No. 638 (Div. Ct.).

194 Thus, $10,000 is the limit under the *Sask. HRC*, above note 1, s. 31.4(a); $20,000 is the maximum under the *Can. HRA*, above note 1, s. 53(3).

195 *Sam's Pizza House*, above note 120 and text accompanying note: $10,000 punitive damages were awarded.

and tribunals—government underfunding is a perennial problem for these agencies, we saw earlier—rather than being given outright to the claimant for personal use.[196]

Many tribunals have held—rightly, it is submitted—that the make whole philosophy encompasses awarding the successful claimant his or her solicitor-client costs.[197] However, this view has not been universally accepted.[198] Some human rights acts expressly allow such costs to be awarded in defined circumstances, such as when the employer has deliberately delayed proceedings or lied to the investigator or the tribunal,[199] but others impose no express limitations.[200]

Ancillary remedies of a non-pecuniary nature take a variety of forms. These include requiring the employer to write a letter of apology to the claimant,[201] to remove discriminatory material from the claimant's personnel file, to post the tribunal's decision in conspicious places throughout the workplace,[202] and to combat discrimination with educational programs and sensitivity training for its managers and employees.[203] The latter can be regarded as a form of affirmative action remedy, since the objective is to modify general attitudes in the workplace. Next, we examine affirmative action remedies in greater detail.

d) Affirmative Action Remedies

Few topics have generated a livelier public debate in recent years than whether employers should be legally obliged to implement affirmative

---

196 M. Mankes, "Combatting Individual Employment Discrimination in the U.S.A. and Britain: A Novel Remedial Approach" (1994) 16 Comp. Lab. L.J. 67 at 113.

197 Example: *Thwaites*, above note 172 at 319.

198 Examples: *L.C.B.O.*, above note 28 at 191; *Courchaine*, above note 170 at D/83.

199 Example: *B.C. HRC*, above note 1, s. 37(4), applied in *Hendrickson v. Long and McQuade Ltd. (No. 2)* (1999), 34 C.H.R.R. D/36 at D/39 (B.C.H.R.T.), additional reasons [1999] B.C.H.R.T.D. No. 4. This approach is consistent with the recommendation of the La Forest Panel, above note 16 at 71.

200 Example: *P.E.I. HRA*, above note 1, s. 28.4(6).

201 Example: *Nkwazi*, above note 165. *Quaere*: Under what conditions would such an order violate the employer's right to freedom of speech under s. 2(b) of the *Charter*? By analogy, see *National Bank of Canada v. R.C.I.U.*, [1984] 1 S.C.R. 269 at 295–96; *Slaight Communications Inc. v. Davidson*, [1989] 1 S.C.R. 1038.

202 Example: *Aboucher v. Ontario (Human Rights Commission) (No. 4)* (1999), 35 C.H.R.R. D/175 at D/182 (Ont. Bd. Inq.).

203 Examples: *McKinnon v. Ontario (Human Rights Commission) (No. 3)*, above note 126; *McKinnon v. Ontario (Human Rights Commission) (No. 4)*, above note 168; *Bolton v. Cancoil Thermal Corp.* (1994), 26 C.H.R.R. D/490 at D/493–94 (Ont. Bd. Inq.). *Quaere*: Are such measures effective in combatting "unconscious" discrimination? See A. Wax, "Discrimination as Accident" (1999) 74 Indiana L.J. 1129 at 1184–86.

action measures for groups protected under the human rights legislation. The term "affirmative action," however, is frequently misunderstood. In its mildest form, affirmative action means that employers should introduce measures that make protected groups feel comfortable when applying for jobs or having their performance appraised for the purposes of probation, merit pay, and so on. Such measures would typically include having members of the protected group participate in the hiring or performance appraisal process and ensuring that supervisors are sensitized to the interests of protected groups. These measures are non-controversial. But affirmative action can also include requiring employers to restructure the labour process to accommodate the interests of protected groups—for example, by introducing flexible work schedules for mothers with families to raise or for particular religious groups, or modifying the physical layout of the plant or equipment for disabled employees. This form of affirmative action is legally mandated under the employer's duty of reasonable accommodation described above.[204] Although employers often express their concern that the costs of implementing such measures may impair their efficiency, the duty of reasonable accommodation has not generated widespread public concern. The same cannot be said, however, for affirmative action measures that involve giving preferential treatment to protected groups in the areas of hiring, promotion, and job security.

Here, affirmative action measures may entail the following: (1) giving preference to the protected group member whose personal merit, reflected in his or her qualifications, experience, and other skills and abilities, is *roughly equal* to that of the non-protected person; (2) giving preference to the protected group member who meets the minimum standard of performance set for the job, even though non-protected persons may have greater merit; or even (3) reducing the standard of acceptable performance set for the job in order to ensure that a protected group member can qualify when otherwise he or she would not, notwithstanding non-protected persons with greater merit being available. The public controversy over these affirmative action measures has largely focused on whether it is justifiable to *force* employers to implement them by legislation. Generally, it is considered acceptable for employers to voluntarily choose to adopt these measures if they evaluate them as being beneficial to the firm. Space constraints regrettably preclude an in-depth analysis of the debate here.[205]

---

204 Section C(1)(a), above in this chapter.
205 There is a huge body of literature on this topic. Useful materials in favour of affirmative action include H. Holzer & D. Newmark, "Assessing Affirmative Action" (2000) 38 J. of Economic Literature 483; D.A. Grossman, "Voluntary

It is probably fair to conclude that the Canadian public opposes legislated affirmative action measures that would require employers proactivly establish "quotas" giving preference to protected group members who are less meritorious than non-protected persons. For example, in 1995 the Progressive Conservatives in Ontario won a resounding electoral victory on a platform that highlighted the repeal of the predecessor NDP government's *Employment Equity Act*, which established a relatively mild form of quota system.[206] The Ontario Court of Appeal ruled that repealing the Act did not violate section 15 of the *Charter* because section 15 does not oblige a provincial government to enact special affirmative action measures when the make whole remedial provisions in the general human rights legislation allow tribunals to issue comprehensive affirmative action orders to combat systemic discrimination.[207]

The human rights legislation in all provinces permits employers to voluntarily adopt all of the above-mentioned affirmative action programs. Thus, the legislation commonly provides a defence to complaints of discrimination by non-protected persons that an employer has afforded preferential treatment to a member of a protected group on a prescribed ground, such as race or sex, either under the residual BFOR defence[208] or by express provisions in the Act.[209] Moreover, in

---

Affirmative Action Plans in Italy and the United States: Differing Notions of Gender Equality" (1992) 14 Comp. Lab. L.J. 185; *Report of the Commission on Equality in Employment* (Ottawa: Supply and Services Canada, 1984) at 40 (Chair: R.S. Abella), and R. Wasserstrom, "A Defense of Programs of Preferential Treatment" (1978) 58 Nat'l Forum 15. Useful arguments for the case against affirmative action include R.A. Posner, *The Economics of Justice* (Cambridge: Harvard University Press, 1981) at 364–74; T. Sowell, *Preferential Policies: An International Perspective* (New York: Morrow, 1990); and E.W. Block & M.A. Walker, eds., *Discrimination, Affirmative Action, and Equal Opportunity* (Vancouver: Fraser Institute, 1982).

206 *Employment Equity Act, 1993*, S.O. 1993, c. 35 (as rep. by S.O. 1995, c. 4). For a review of the Act's operation, see Office of the Employment Equity Commission, *Employment Equity in Action: An Overview of Ontario's Employment Equity Regulations* (Toronto: Ministry of Citizenship, 1994); Employment Equity Commission, *Getting Ready: Preparing for Ontario's Employment Equity Act* (Toronto: Employment Equity Commission, 1994). The Act was repealed by S.O. 1995, c. 4, s. 1.

207 *Ferrel v. Attorney General of Ontario* (1998), 99 C.L.L.C. ¶230-005, especially at 145,047–48 (Ont. C.A.).

208 Affirmative action hiring quotas for Aboriginal people have been held to be a BFOR in *Athabasca Tribal Council v. Amoco Canada Petroleum Co.*, [1981] 1 S.C.R. 699.

209 Example: *Ont. HRC*, above note 1, s. 14(2).

some provinces the human rights legislation expressly empowers officials of the human rights commissions to assist employers in formulating affirmative action programs.[210] Nevertheless, the affirmative action
defence almost certainly does not give employers a *carte blanche* to
implement preferential policies; rather, preferential measures for protected groups must not disproportionately harm the interests of either
non-protected persons or of the employer itself.[211] For example, it is
strongly arguable that in a layoff, the employer should not be permitted
to advance a newly hired protected employee to the head of the seniority list, bumping a white employee with decades of seniority, in order
to maintain a predetermined ethnic/gender balance in the composition
of the workforce—usurping of the white employee's seniority would be
disproportionately severe for that person compared with the benefit to
the workplace of maintaining the balance.[212] It is also arguable that the
BFOR defence would fail if an affirmative action policy eliminates personal merit from being considered in hiring and promotion decisions;
so too, if the policy is not scheduled to be rescinded once the designated standard of equality has been met. An affirmative action policy
that causes undue harm to the employer's productive efficiency—for
example, by requiring the employer to create vacancies that are not economically justifiable or to hire/promote individuals who are unqualified for the position—would clearly establish the BFOR defence.[213]

Furthermore, the human rights legislation in all provinces allows
tribunals to order, as remedies for unlawful discrimination, all of the
affirmative action measures described above, including preferential
hiring and promotion quotas. The Supreme Court of Canada, in the
famous case of *Canadian National Railway*,[214] ruled that ordering an
employer to implement a hiring quota can help eliminate discrimination in three ways: (1) it overcomes the difficulty of proving an illicit,

---

210 As in the federal jurisdiction under the special proactive *Employment Equity Act*,
    S.C. 1995, c. 44, ss. 8(1)–(3), considered below.
211 See, for example, *Roberts v. Ontario* (1994), 117 D.L.R. (4th) 297, especially
    at 303 and 306 (Ont. C.A.), Houlden J.A.; *Tomen v. O.T.F. (No. 4)* (1994), 20
    C.H.R.R. D/257 (Ont. Bd. Inq.).
212 The argument is made forcefully by K. Swinton, "Accommodating Women in
    the Workplace: Reproductive Hazards and Seniority Systems" (1992) 1 Can.
    Lab. L.J. 125 at 139. *Quaere*: Can the same be said of preferential policies in pro-
    motions, where the long-seniority, white employee's interest is an expectancy of
    future higher earnings?
213 Indeed, the proactive affirmative action program enacted under the federal
    Employment Equity Act, above note 210, ss. 8(1)–(3) specifies most of these
    exceptions.
214 Above note 39.

discriminatory intent on the employer's part; (2) it undermines stereo-typical attitudes among workers and supervisors if protected group members are seen to succeed on the job; and (3) it creates a "critical mass" of protected group members in the workforce, which will encourage other protected persons to apply for jobs and pursue their careers with the employer in question. In that case, the employer's workforce comprised only 0.7 percent of women in blue-collar positions in the St. Lawrence region and 13 percent in Canada as a whole compared with a female representation rate in blue-collar jobs of 40.7 percent across Canada and 39 percent in Quebec. The Supreme Court upheld an order of the federal Human Rights Tribunal that the employer hire at least one woman for every four non-traditional vacancies until women occupied 13 percent of the non-traditional positions. This one-to-four quota had to be achieved on a quarterly basis. As well, the company was directed to establish an information and publicity campaign to recruit women in non-traditional occupations and to report-in periodically on its progress to the tribunal. Although this decision clearly mandates human rights tribunals to order affirmative action hiring and promotion quotas as a remedy for unlawful discrimination, relatively few subsequent decisions have done so.[215]

In the federal jurisdiction, the *Employment Equity Act* requires employers, among other things, to proactively achieve designated representation rates of protected group members in their workforces within specified time limits. This model seeks to rectify the main weakness of the complaints based system contained in the general human rights act, namely, that one or more individual victims of discrimination will rarely have the intestinal fortitude and knowledge of their legal rights to file a complaint against their current employer.[216] At this juncture, only Quebec[217] has adopted this proactive model of affirmative action legislation, but this is limited to organizations in the public sector hav-

---

215 A notable exception is the comprehensive quota ordered in *National Capital Alliance on Race Relations v. Canada (Health and Welfare)* (1997), 97 C.L.L.C. ¶230-015 (Can. H.R.T.)

216 The best analysis of the advantages of the proactive model of human rights legislation is Canada, Pay Equity Task Force, *Pay Equity: A New Approach to a Fundamental Right*, Pay Equity Task Force Final Report 2004 (Ottawa: Department of Justice, 2004), cc. 4 & 5. Although this study concerns wage discrimination, the arguments apply equally to general human rights legislation.

217 An Act respecting equal access to employment in public bodies and amending the Charter of human rights and freedoms, R.S.Q. c. A-2.01 As well, Quebec's *Act to Secure the Handicapped in the Exercise of their Rights*, R.S.Q. c. E-20.1, s. 63 obliges firms that hire fifty or more workers to establish an affirmative action hiring program in favour of the disabled.

ing one hundred or more employees. Elsewhere, eight provinces provide for some kind of employment equity policy under the "special program" provisions of their general human rights legislation, but typically these depend on the employer voluntarily agreeing to participate in the process.[218]

The federal Act is therefore unique in applying to both public sector organizations and to private sector employers of a minimum size.[219] The protected groups under the Act are women, Aboriginal persons, the disabled, and members of visible minorities, or "persons . . . who are non-Caucasian in race or non-white in colour." Section 5 of the Act states that employers must take the following measures to achieve "equity" in their organizations:

(a) identifying and eliminating employment barriers against persons in designated groups that result from the employer's employment systems, policies and practices that are not authorized by law; and

(b) instituting such positive policies and practices and making such reasonable accommodations as will ensure that persons in designated groups achieve a degree of representation in each occupational group in the employer's organization that reflects their representation in

(i) the Canadian workforce, or

(ii) those segments of the Canadian workforce that are identifiable by qualification, eligibility or geography and from which the employer may reasonably be expected to draw employees.

However, the Act seeks to strike a balance of proportionality. It provides that employers will not be compelled to adopt any measures that would cause their firms undue hardship, cause them to hire or promote "unqualified" persons or to create new positions, or result in the abridgement of accrued seniority rights in layoffs and recalls.[220]

---

218 British Columbia, Manitoba, Ontario, Saskatchewan, Quebec, Nova Scotia, New Brunswick, and Prince Edward Island. For example, the Saskatchewan "special program" scheme under the *Sask. HRC*, above note 1, s. 47, is examined in Saskatchewan Human Rights Commission, *Affirmative Action: A Case Book of Legislation and Affirmative Action Programs in Saskatchewan* by Ken Norman (Saskatoon: Saskatchewan Human Rights Commission, 1983).

219 Section 3 of the *Employment Equity Act*, above note 210, makes it applicable to private sector employers who employ 100 or more workers.

220 *Employment Equity Act, ibid.*, ss. 6, 8(1)–(3).

The Act imposes substantial administrative costs on employers. The employer must collect, analyze,[221] and continuously update[222] data on the composition of its workforce as prescribed by regulations in order to determine whether or not protected group members are under-represented in the various occupations within the firm. As well, the employer must proactively review all of its employment policies and practices in order to identify any "employment barriers" in the firm that disadvantage protected group members.[223] If a protected group is found to be under-represented, the employer is obliged to prepare an "employment equity plan" in the manner prescribed by the Act and regulations.[224] Roughly speaking, such a plan must specify what measures the employer intends to implement in the short and long term in order to increase the representation of protected groups, including short-term numerical goals for hiring and promoting protected persons. The employer is required to "consult" and "collaborate" with representatives of its employees, whether or not they are unionized, in preparing its employment equity plan.[225] Significantly, this is one of the relatively few instances where protective employment legislation gives non-unionized employees a collective right to representation. The Act also imposes ongoing obligations on employers to monitor the operation of their employment equity plan; to revise the plan where necessary; to maintain and update comprehensive records on all facets of the employment equity process in the prescribed manner;[226] and to file an annual report with the minister, along with a copy to its employee representatives, containing comprehensive information about the workforce composition and the firm's progress towards achieving employment equity.[227] The minister must table in Parliament every year a consolidated analysis of all such annual reports, the rationale being that negative publicity will provide employers with an incentive to take the pursuit of employment equity seriously.

More important, however, the minister passes on each employer's annual report to the Canadian Human Rights Commission for inspec-

---

221 *Ibid.*, s. 9; and *Employment Equity Regulations*, SOR/96-470, ss. 1(1), 3.

222 *Employment Equity Regulations, ibid.*, s. 5.

223 *Employment Equity Act*, above note 210, s. 9(1)(b).

224 *Ibid.*, s. 10, and *Employment Equity Regulations*, above note 221, ss. 8–9.

225 *Employment Equity Act, ibid.*, s. 15. However, s. 15(4) states, rather oddly, that this duty to consult is not a form of "co-management": this seems to be mere political window dressing.

226 The details are prescribed in the *Employment Equity Act, ibid.*, s. 17, and *Employment Equity Regulations*, above note 221, ss. 5, 11, and 12.

227 *Employment Equity Act*, above note 210, ss. 16–18.

tion. Doing this potentially allows the commission to commence a complaint of systemic discrimination under the *Canadian Human Rights Act* against any employer that is remiss in pursuing employment equity. (Of course, the Canadian Human Rights Commission can also become involved if an employee files a complaint of discrimination against his or her employer or if a spot check by the commission unearths discrimination in the organization.) The possibility of such a complaint was the most potent incentive for complying with the Act prior to 1995, but in that year the Act was amended to include administrative (as opposed to criminal) fines against employers for violating its provisions.[228] Presumably, the reasons criminal prosecution is not included are to avoid souring the employment equity process and to avoid the problem of securing criminal convictions under the tough criminal law burden of proof "beyond any reasonable doubt." Nevertheless, the administrative fines are hefty, with a maximum of $10,000 being levied for single violations and a maximum of $50,000 for continuing or repeat violations.[229] The minister has the discretion to select the appropriate penalty, having regard to the "nature, circumstances, extent and gravity" of the violation; whether the employer acted willfully; and any prior history of violations.[230] An employer is given the right to appeal a penalty to a single-member tribunal selected by the president of the Human Rights Tribunal established under the *Canadian Human Rights Act*, whose decision is declared to be final and binding.[231] It must be emphasized, however, that these penalties will be applied only in the last resort after attempts to mediate a settlement have failed.[232]

The procedure for handling complaints that an employer has not prepared an appropriate employment equity plan in the manner prescribed under the Act begins with investigation and mediation by an officer of the Canadian Human Rights Commission. If no acceptable resolution of the matter can be made at this stage, the Human Rights Commission issues a direction as to what the plan must contain. The employer may appeal the commission's direction to the Employment Equity Review Tribunal for adjudication.[233] The tribunal may quash the commission's directive, uphold it in its entirety, vary it, or substitute "any other order it considers appropriate and reasonable in the cir-

---

228 *Ibid.*, s. 35(3).
229 *Ibid.*, s. 36(2).
230 *Ibid.*, s. 36(3).
231 *Ibid.*, s. 39.
232 The paramountcy of voluntarism is emphasized in the *Employment Equity Act, ibid.*, s. 22(2).
233 *Ibid.*, ss. 27–29.

cumstances to remedy the non-compliance."[234] However, the tribunal is expressly disallowed from making an order that would, *inter alia*, cause the employer undue hardship, force the employer to hire or promote an unqualified person, force the employer to create new positions, force a public sector employer to ignore merit in hiring or promotion, or impose a quota on an employer.[235] In the latter regard, the Act defines a quota as "a requirement to hire or promote a fixed and arbitrary number of persons during a given period."[236] Accordingly, it seems to be permissible to order a "non-arbitrary" quota, but not an "arbitrary" one. It remains to be seen how the term "arbitrary" will be defined in this context. The inclusion of such an uncertain standard is perhaps explained as a form of political expediency to shelter federal legislators against flak from advocates and opponents of affirmative action quotas. An order of the tribunal is final and binding and can be enforced as an order of the Federal Court.[237]

A serious flaw in the *Employment Equity Act* is that it relies on employees to identify themselves voluntarily in their employer's workforce survey as a member of a protected group. There is no legal mechanism for the employer or the Human Rights Commission to ensure that employees have identified themselves correctly. Presumably, an employer cannot interrogate employees about their protected status, since this would arguably breach the human rights statutes, subject to the possibility of the BFOR defence applying. Moreover, an employer's data relating to the group identification of workers must be kept confidential.[238] The seriousness of this flaw is shown by a study which reported that self-identification under the predecessor employment equity act resulted in an under-reporting of protected status of approximately 50 percent.[239]

It is difficult to assess how successful the Act has been. On the twentieth anniversary of its introduction, a federal government spokesman, the Rt. Hon. Minister Blackburn, stated that there had been "undeniable progress"[240] in improving representation of the four protected

234 *Ibid.*, s. 30(1).
235 *Ibid.*, s. 33(1).
236 *Ibid.*, s. 33(2).
237 *Ibid.*, ss. 30 & 31.
238 *Ibid.*, s. 9(3). However, s. 4 of the *Employment Equity Regulations*, above note 221, requires the employer to use some method for identifying which questionnaire belongs to which worker.
239 Canada, *A Matter of Fairness: Report of the Special Committee on the Review of the Employment Equity Act* (Ottawa: Queen's Printer, 1992) (Chair: A Redway).
240 Labour, News Release, "Minister Blackburn releases 2005 Annual Employment Equity Report," (15 June 2006) online: http://news.gc.ca/web/view/en/index.

groups. Thus, between 1985 and 2005, female representation increased from 40.9 percent to 43.4 percent; visible minorities from 5.0 percent to 13.3 percent; Aboriginals from 0.7 percent to 1.7 percent; and the disabled from 1.6 percent to 2.5 percent. It is unknown how much of this improvement was due to the Act and how much was due to other economic and social factors.

In the federal jurisdiction, mention must also be made of the Federal Contractors Program,[241] which requires all suppliers of services and goods who employ 100 or more workers and are seeking federal government contracts worth $200,000 to implement a defined affirmative action program in order to qualify for the contract. This scheme is administered by the Canada Employment and Immigration Commission. Manitoba, too, has a roughly similar program for provincial contracts.[242]

2) Enforcing the Human Rights Legislation: Punishing Perpetrators and Safeguarding Complainants

A cornerstone of all employment protection acts is the "no-reprisal" provisions, which prohibit employers from penalizing an employee in regard to terms and conditions of employment because he or she has filed a complaint, or otherwise participated in proceedings under the act in question. Human rights acts commonly contain this safeguard.[243]

Plainly, without such provisions the legislation would be extremely difficult to enforce. Regrettably, the no-reprisal provisions in the employment standards acts have been largely ineffective in protecting employee complainants,[244] but no direct empirical evidence shows whether this is also the case under human rights acts. In the relatively few re-

---

jsp?articleid=220479&. See also *Employment Equity Act Review: A Report to the Standing Committee on Human Resources Development and the Status of Persons with Disabilities* (Ottawa: Human Resources and Social Development Canada, December 2001), online: www.hrsdc.gc.ca/en/lp/lo/lswe/we/review/report/main.shtml.

241 Treasury Board Directive No. 802984, "Federal Contractors Program for Employment Equity — Departmental Responsibilities Concerning Contracting for Goods and Services of $200,000 or More" (25 August 1986) (Circular Letter No. 1986–44). See also Canada Employment Equity Branch, *Employment Equity: The Federal Contractors Program* (Ottawa: Employment and Immigration Canada, 1994).

242 *Man. HRC*, above note 1, s. 56.

243 Example: *Can. HRA*, above note 1, s. 59.

244 R.J. Adams, "Employment Standards in Ontario: An Industrial Relations System Analysis" (1987) 42 R.I./I.R. 46 at 50, examined further in Chapter 6.

ported cases involving the human rights acts' no-reprisal sections, the tribunals have been strict in protecting complainants. Thus, it has been held that the test for liability is whether a "reasonable person" in the complainant's position would "reasonably perceive" the employer's conduct to be retaliatory in nature.[245] One tribunal explained the test as follows:

> In assessing the reasonableness of the complainant's fears and perceptions, boards of inquiry must be sensitive to the particular difficulties that confront complainants, many of whom experience great fear and anxiety surrounding the lodging and pursuit of a human rights complaint. This is exacerbated where the complainant continues in an ongoing relationship with the respondent, especially where that relationship is complicated by a difference in power such as is undeniably manifest in the employer-employee setting. In such a context, otherwise innocuous events, conversations and correspondence may take on an overtly intimidating aura, with an impact out of all proportion to any original intent or understanding on the part of the respondent. The damage may, however, be enormous.[246]

If an employer breaches the no-reprisal section, the employee is compensated for any losses he or she thereby sustains under the make whole approach—including a hefty sum for infringement of his or her statutory rights.[247] In addition, the legislation commonly makes the breach an offence for which the employer can be prosecuted,[248] subject, generally, to the consent of the minister or the attorney general, depending on the jurisdiction.

In order to punish and deter employers from deliberately flaunting their statutory obligations, most human rights acts make breach of the act a criminal offence punishable by maximum specified fines.[249] Normally, consent to prosecution is required from a government official, such as the minister or the attorney general, and will be granted only as a last resort against hard-core violators for whom mediation and education have failed. However, a different approach is taken in Alberta and British Columbia in that breach of the act in and of itself is not made a criminal offence, but breach of an order of a human rights tribunal is. In the federal jurisdiction, it is a criminal offence to breach designated key sections of the act, including the no-reprisal provision and the obli-

245 *Entrop*, above note 7 at 145,008.
246 *Ibid.*
247 *Ibid.*, where $10,000 was awarded under this head.
248 Example: *Can. HRA*, above note 1, s. 60(4).
249 Example: *N.B. HRA*, above note 1, s. 23.

gation not to obstruct a human rights officer in the execution of his or her duties.[250] The emphasis on downplaying the role of prosecution is to avoid the possible souring effect of such sanctions on the parties' future relationships.

FURTHER READINGS

AGGARWAL, A.P., *Sex Discrimination, Employment Law and Practice* (Toronto: Butterworths, 1994)

AGGARWAL, A.P., *Sexual Harassment in the Workplace*, 2d ed. (Toronto: Butterworths, 1992)

BLOCK, W.E., & M.A. WALKER, eds., *Discrimination, Affirmative Action, and Equal Opportunity: An Economic and Social Perspective* (Vancouver: Fraser Institute, 1982)

CANADA, COMMITTEE ON THE REVIEW OF THE EMPLOYMENT EQUITY ACT, *A Matter of Fairness: Report of the Special Committee on the Review of the Employment Equity Act* by A. Redway (Ottawa: Queen's Printer, 1992)

CANADIAN HUMAN RIGHTS REVIEW PANEL, *Promoting Equality: A New Vision — Report of the Canadian Human Rights Review Panel* by G.V. La Forest (Ottawa: Department of Justice, 2000)

CHOTALIA, S.P., *Human Rights Law in Canada*, looseleaf (Agincourt, ON: Carswell, 1995)

COX, P.N., *Employment and Discrimination* (Salem, NH: Butterworths, 1991)

CRAIG, J.D., "*Entrop v. Imperial Oil Ltd.*: Employment Drug and Alcohol Testing Is Put to the Test" (2002) 9 C.L.E.L.J. 141

EARLE, B.H., & G.A. MADEK, "An International Perspective on Sexual Harassment Law" (1993) 12 Law & Ineq. J. 43

ENGLAND, G., R. WOOD, & I. CHRISTIE, *Employment Law in Canada*, 4d ed., looseleaf (Markham, ON.:LexisNexis Canada, 2005–) c. 5, 1

EPSTEIN, R.A., *Forbidden Grounds: The Case against Employment Discrimination Laws* (Cambridge, MA: Harvard University Press, 1992)

---

250 *Can. HRA*, above note 1, s. 60(1).

ETHERINGTON, B., "Promises, Promises: Notes on Diversity and Access to Justice" (2000) 26 Queen's L.J. 43

GUNDERSON, M., "Implications of the Duty to Accommodate for Industrial Relations Practices" (1992) 2 Can. Lab. L.J. 294

KNOPFF, R., *Human Rights and Social Technology: The New War on Discrimination* (Ottawa: Carleton University Press, 1989)

LYNK, MICHAEL S., "Disability and Work: The Transformation of the Legal Status of Employees with Disabilities in Canada" (December 2007), online: http://papers.ssrn.com/sol3/papers.cfm?abstract_id=1068403

ONTARIO HUMAN RIGHTS COMMISSION, *Ontario Human Rights Commission's Policy Statements on Various Aspects of Ontario Human Rights Law* (Toronto: Ontario Human Rights Commission, 1996–2008)

PAYNE, J., & C. ROOTHAM, "Are Human Rights Commissions Still Relevant?" (2005) 12 C.L.E.L.J. 65

SCHUCHER, K., "Weaving Together the Threads: A New Framework for Achieving Equality in Workplace Standards" (2000) 8 C.L.E.L.J. 325

TARNOPOLSKY, W.S., *Discrimination and the Law: Including Equality Rights under the Charter*, rev. ed. by W.F. Pentney, looseleaf (Don Mills, ON: De Boo, 1988)

CHAPTER 8

MULTIPLE FORUMS AND THE ENFORCEMENT OF EMPLOYMENT RIGHTS

Protective employment statutes, such as the human rights and labour standards acts examined in the preceding two chapters, normally contain special administrative procedures for enforcing the rights established thereunder. These administrative procedures may potentially intersect with civil litigation in the courts in at least two situations: (1) when an employee attempts to bring a civil action to enforce claims conferred by the statute in question; and (2) when an employee has commenced proceedings in one forum and subsequently launches a complaint in a different forum. There is also the question of an unsuccessful party seeking judicial review to quash the decision of a statutory tribunal, but that is beyond the scope of this book, properly falling within the purview of general administrative law.[1]

A. THE ROLE OF THE COURTS IN ENFORCING EMPLOYMENT STANDARDS AND HUMAN RIGHTS CLAIMS

Regarding claims under employment standards acts, courts permit employees to launch civil actions to enforce their statutory rights in-

---

1   The leading authority is *Dunsmuir v. New Brunswick*, 2008 SCC 9. See generally D. Mullan, *Administrative Law* (Toronto: Irwin Law, 2001); R. Charney & T. Brady, *Judicial Review in Labour Law*, looseleaf (Aurora, ON: Canada Law Book, 1997–).

stead of proceeding under the special statutory machinery. There are several possible bases for a civil action: straightforward breach of the act; breach of a term in the contract of employment, the term in question being the statutory entitlements that may have been expressly or impliedly incorporated into the contract; the tort of breach of statutory duty; or breach of a constructive trust under which the employer arguably holds the statutory entitlements as a trustee in favour of the employee.[2] Provisions in the employment standards acts of most provinces expressly preserving the civil remedies of employees covered by the acts seem to allow court actions to enforce statutory benefits.[3] Nevertheless, the acts may specify restrictions on the choice of forum, as in Ontario where the *Employment Standards Act* states that an employee who has filed a complaint under the statutory procedure is precluded from subsequently launching a civil action for wrongful dismissal, subject to a two-week window of opportunity in which the statutory complaint may be withdrawn and a civil action commenced.[4] If the employee initially files a complaint under the statute, then a subsequent civil action is barred.

Regarding civil actions to enforce claims under human rights legislation courts, the Supreme Court of Canada ruled in the leading case *Seneca College of Applied Arts and Technology v. Bhadauria*[5] that the courts cannot enforce claims under human rights acts, either in a direct action to enforce the statute in question or in a common law action — such as the tort of breach of statutory duty — based solely on the statute. The rationale is to ensure that human rights complaints, which usually involve sensitive matters of human rights policy, are handled by specialized tribunals rather than by judges. Unfortunately, the enforcement of human rights complaints is excruciatingly slow so many complainants would prefer running the gauntlet of civil proceedings to becoming entangled in the web of the human rights apparatus. This factor possibly explains why some courts have subsequently relaxed the *Bhadauria* principle to permit a common law action in tort on a contract involving behaviour on the employer's part that potentially

---

2   Examples: *Kolodziejski v. Auto-Electric Service Ltd.*, [1999] 10 W.W.R. 543 (Sask. C.A.); *Beaulne v. Kaverit Steel and Crane U.L.C.* (2002), 19 C.C.E.L. (3d) 252 at 272–76 (Alta. Q.B.).

3   Example: Alberta *Employment Standards Code*, R.S.A. 2000, c. E-9, s. 3(1).

4   *Employment Standards Act, 2000*, S.O. 2000, c. 41, ss. 97(1) & (2). However, the courts have discretion to extend the time limit but "only in very limited circumstances": Sachs J. in *Galea v. Wal-Mart Canada Inc.* (2003), 24 C.C.E.L. (3d) 294 at 302 (Ont. S.C.J.).

5   [1981] 2 S.C.R. 181, especially at 189 [*Bhadauria*].

runs afoul of the human rights act, so long as the cause of action is defensible in its own right and does not depend exclusively on breach of the act.[6] For example, a female employee who quit in response to verbal and physical harassment from her employer was allowed to sue for constructive dismissal, even though the employer's conduct also constituted sexual harassment under the human rights act: the harassment clearly amounted to a repudiatory breach of the employment contract according to established common law principles.[7] In a similar vein, if the employer's mistreatment of the employee constitutes an actionable tort according to established common law principles, the employee can launch a civil action in tort despite the possibility that a complaint could also be filed under the human rights act.[8] In 2006, the *Ontario Human Rights Code* was amended to empower courts in a wrongful dismissal suit involving breach of the Code to award its full panoply of "make whole" remedies, including compulsory reinstatement.

B. STATUTORY TRIBUNALS

If an employee has the option of launching a civil action in the courts or of filing a complaint under one (or possibly more[9]) statutory enforcement procedures, the choice will be dictated by practical exigencies, such as the comparative speed, cheapness, and remedial efficacy of the competing forums. However, an employee who has commenced an action to enforce benefits under one statute's enforcement machinery may be required to recommence the action under another statute's enforcement machinery. Generally, administrative tribunals have the discretion to defer a claim to a different statutory procedure if the tribunal

---

6   See generally A.L. Mactavish & A.J.F. Lenz, "Civil Actions for Conduct Addressed by Human Rights Legislation: Some Recent Substantive and Procedural Developments" (1996) 4 C.L.E.L.J. 375; T. Witelson, "Retort: Revisiting *Bhadauria* and the Supreme Court of Canada's Rejection of a Tort of Discrimination" (1999) 10 N.J.C.L. 149. See also B.L. Adell, "Jurisdictional Overlap between Arbitration and Other Forums: An Update" (2000) 8 C.L.E.L.J. 179.

7   *L'Attiboudeaire v. Royal Bank of Canada* (1996), 17 C.C.E.L. (2d) 86, especially at 88 (Ont. C.A.). See also *Alpaerts v. Obront* (1993), 46 C.C.E.L. 218 (Ont. Gen. Div.).

8   Example: *Galea v. General Motors of Canada Ltd.* (1993), 94 C.L.L.C. ¶17,015, especially at 16,163 (Ont. Gen. Div.).

9   For example, a pregnant employee who is fired for refusing to perform work that she reasonably believes is endangering her baby may complain under the occupational health and safety legislation as well as under the human rights and employment standards legislation.

considers that the alternative forum has superior expertise to handle the matter or can grant more effective remedies.[10] Thus, tribunals usually defer cases involving human rights violations to the human rights legislation procedures, but only where the human rights issues are relatively complex.[11]

The doctine of "issue estoppel" may come into play. By virtue of this doctrine, an employee who has obtained a ruling on his or her complaint from a statutory tribunal might be precluded from subsequently commencing a civil action in the courts to enforce the claim. In the converse situation, where a civil action is initiated and the employee subsequently wishes to take the statutory route, the employee might similarly be precluded from action.

The purposes of issue estoppel are to avoid the administrative inconvenience of multiple proceedings and to safeguard against a complainant being doubly compensated for the same wrongdoing. The requirements for the doctrine are as follows: (1) the "same question" must have been decided in one forum, (2) the decision in question must have been "final and binding," (3) the parties to both proceedings must be identical, and (4) it must be just and equitable in all the circumstances to apply issue estoppel.[12]

Regarding the "same question" requirement, a good example is *Rasanen v. Rosemount Instruments Ltd.*, where the Ontario Court of Appeal ruled that the decision by an employment standards referee—that a worker was not "terminated" for the purpose of receiving statutory termination pay because he unreasonably refused his employer's offer of alternative employment—precluded the worker from subsequently bringing a civil action for constructive dismissal.[13] The court was satisfied that the same question was involved for the purpose of issue

---

10   Examples: *Pieters v. Toronto Board of Education* (1997), 36 C.L.R.B.R. (2d) 120 (O.L.R.B.), and *Musty v. Meridean Magnesium Products. Ltd.*, [1996] O.L.R.B. Rep. November/December 964, where the Labour Relations Board deferred complaints of racial and sexual harassment filed with it under the *Occupational Health and Safety Act* to the superior expertise of the *Human Rights Act*.

11   This practice is consistent with the recommendation in the La Forest Report: Canada, Canadian Human Rights Review Panel, *Promoting Equality: A New Vision—Report of the Canadian Human Rights Review Panel* by G.V. La Forest (Ottawa: Department of Justice, 2000) at 88.

12   *Danyluk v. Ainsworth Technologies Inc.*, [2001] C.L.L.C. ¶210-033 at 141,250–51 (S.C.C.) [*Danyluk*]. See generally C. Flood, "Efficiency v. Fairness: Multiple Litigation and Adjudication in Labour and Employment Law" (2001) 8 C.L.E.L.J. 383.

13   (1994), 1 C.C.E.L (2d) 161 at 178 (Ont. C.A.) [*Rasanen*]. See generally G. Demeyere, "Issue Estoppel in Employment Law Disputes: *Rasanen v. Rosemount Instruments* and Its Aftermath" (1998) 6 C.L.E.L.J. 299.

estoppel because the core issue at stake in both actions was whether or not the employer's offer of alternative employment was sufficiently unreasonable to warrant the employee turning it down and quitting his job. Other courts have followed this decision where the common law doctrine and a statutory provision turn on essentially similar matters.[14] The courts generally rule that the decisions of a board of referees under the *Employment Insurance Act* regarding whether the employee is disqualified from receiving unemployment insurance benefits on account of his or her wrongdoings is not the same question as whether the employee has been dismissed for just cause under a common law wrongful dismissal suit.[15]

Regarding the requirement for a final and binding judicial decision, the courts' approach is again exemplifed by the the Ontario Court of Appeal's decision in *Rasanen*.[16] There, the court considered the procedure under the *Employment Standards Act* as final and binding for the purpose of issue estoppel, even though the usual safeguards available to an employee in civil litigation—such as the right to pretrial discovery and the opportunity to have the case pursued with the utmost vigour by his or her lawyer—are normally relaxed in proceedings under employment standards acts. The court was clearly concerned with preserving the legitimacy of employment standards proceedings, which are purposefully designed to maximize informality, speed, and cheapness. It would appear to be implicit in this ruling that issue estoppel will not apply if the employee's rights are greater under the legislation than under the common law: for example, if the tribunal can award "make whole" compensation awards or order reinstatement. Indeed, this circumstance would also cause the courts to refuse to apply issue

---

14 Examples: *Stewart v. Tarpline Products Inc.* (2002), 16 C.C.E.L. (3d) 271 at 280 (B.C.S.C.), involving the method of calculating a sales commission under a statutory claim for unpaid wages and under a civil action for breach of the employment contract; *Wong v. Shell Canada* (1996), 15 C.C.E.L. (2d) 182 at 187 (Alta. C.A.), involving whether an employee's performance deficiencies ground just cause for summary dismissal at common law and under the statutory notice of termination providions. Compare *Piercey v. Brennan Pontiac Buick GMC Ltd.* (1999), 48 C.C.E.L (2d) 287 (Ont. S.C.J.), where the determination of reasonable notice in a common law wrongful dismissal action was held not to be the same question as the employee's entitlement to statutory notice of termination since the factors that determine the common law notice period are completely different from those that determine eligibility to the statutory notice period.

15 Example: *Minnot v. O'Shanter Development Co.* (1999), 168 D.L.R. (4d) 270 at 280–81 (Ont. C.A.) [*Minott*]. See generally J.E. Goodman, "Approach with Caution: Issue Estoppel and Employment Insurance Adjudications" (2001) 8 C.L.E.L.J. 461.

16 Above note 13.

estoppel under the requirement of general justice and equity considered below. However, if the tribunal does not conduct a hearing in which the employee is allowed to participate actively, there will not be a final and binding judicial decision.[17] This circumstance would also lead the courts to reject issue estoppel under the general justice and equity requirement described below.

Regarding the requirement of similarity of parties, the courts consider this to be satisfied when proceedings are brought under the employment standards acts, even though in many jurisdictions, including Ontario, the employment standards department carries an employee's complaint before the tribunal.[18] The courts reason that a complainant will not be prejudiced in statutory proceedings so long as he or she is allowed to adduce testimony and argument in person to the tribunal, to participate fully in all preadjudication steps, and to appear at the hearing with a lawyer. If these safeguards are not present, the courts will reject issue estoppel under the general justice and equity requirement described next.

The Supreme Court of Canada has identified seven relevant factors in determining whether it is just and equitable to apply issue estoppel.[19] These are outlined here.

1) *The circumstances giving rise to the proceedings.* If the employee was compelled to commence proceedings under the statute because he or she was financially vulnerable and needed to recover the statutory benefits with the utmost dispatch, this situation militates against applying issue estoppel to bar a subsequent claim, and vice versa.[20] The likelihood of issue estoppel being applied will be further reduced if there is a gross disparity between the amount of money being claimed under the statute and the amount being claimed in the subsequent common law action.[21]

2) *Procedural flaws in the earlier statutory proceedings.* If the statutory process involved breach of the duty of procedural fairness, such as failing to allow the employee to respond to material taken

---

17   Example: *Ferrare v. Kingston Interval Home* (2002), 19 C.C.E.L. (3d) 59 at 61 (Ont. S.C.J.).

18   Example: *Rasanen*, above note 13 at 176–77.

19   *Danyluk*, above note 12.

20   Examples: *Danyluk, ibid.* at 141,257; *Perez v. G.E. Capital Technology Management Services Canada Ltd.* (1999), 47 C.C.E.L. (2d) 145 at 157 (Ont. S.C.J.) [*Perez*].

21   As in *Danyluk, ibid.*, where the employee received $2,300 as a result of her claim under the *Employment Standards Act* compared with her subsequent claim for approximately $300,000 under her common law action for breach of the contract of employment.

into account in reaching a decision, this situation militates against applying issue estoppel.[22] The same would be true where other shortcomings in the statutory procedures, such as the absence of pre-hearing discovery mechanisms, laxity in applying the rules of evidence when admitting testimony, or the lack of legal representation for the employee, exist.[23]

3) *The administrative tribunal's level of legal expertise.* If the statutory authority making the initial determination lacks specialized expertise in the legal matter that is the subject of the subsequent action, this militates against applying issue estoppel.[24]

4) *The overall adequacy and suitability of the statutory procedures for determining the contested issue.* The courts are unlikely to apply issue estoppel if the statutory procedures unduly disadvantage the employee, for example, by failing to provide for efficacious remedies[25] or by involving unresolved legal ambiguities.[26]

5) *The availability of an appeal.* If the statutory procedure contains a right to appeal and the employee elects not to use it, this militates against issue estoppel.

6) *The overall policy of the legislation.* Issue estoppel will not be applied if the effect is to frustrate the objectives of the legislation. Thus, employment standards legislation is designed to produce fast, cheap, and relatively informal determinations, usually for fairly small monetary claims. If an employer believes that it could bar a subsequent common law claim for a substantially greater amount of money than that involved in the statutory claim, the employer probably would contest the statutory claim with the full legal resources at its disposal. The effect would be to bog down the statutory procedure with the very sort of legalisms it was intended to avoid. Therefore, the courts are reluctant to apply issue estoppel if doing so would have this effect.[27]

---

22   Examples: *Danyluk, ibid.* at 141,253–54 and 141,257; *Fuggle v. Airgas Canada Inc.* (2002), 22 C.C.E.L. (3d) 224 at 235 (B.C.S.C.).

23   Examples: *Perez,* above note 20 at 157–58; *Minnot,* above note 15 at 291.

24   As in *Danyluk,* above note 12 at 141,257, where the legal issue in the subsequent common law action for breach of the employment contract was whether a sales commission was implied into the contract, a complex matter of general employment law beyond the expertise of the employment standards officer who was charged with determining whether the commission comprised "wages" under the Act.

25   Example: *Baird v. Lawson* (1996), 22 C.C.E.L. (2d) 101 (Sask. Q.B.).

26   Example: *Apotex Ltd. v. Merck and Co.* (2002), 214 D.L.R. (4th) 429 (F.C.A.).

27   Examples: *Danyluk,* above note 12 at 141,256–57; *Minnot,* above note 15 at 290.

7) *The terminology of the statute.* The legislation may expressly restrict the right to bring a subsequent common law action—which is the case in Ontario, as we saw above[28]—and the courts must respect such provisions.

It might well be concluded from this review of the difficulties arising from multiple forums that the sensible solution would be to have a single "labour court" charged with handling all employment-related complaints, whether they arise under common law or by virtue of legislation—or even, for that matter, under a collective agreement in the unionized sector.[29] Some steps in this direction have been taken in New Brunswick, where the Labour and Employment Board has jurisdiction over employment standards, collective bargaining, and pension benefit legislation, but not over the highly specialized areas of human rights and health and safety.[30] This may well be the wave of the future. In 2000, Ontario considered going even further by establishing a single board to handle collective bargaining, employment standards, health and safety, workers compensation, pay equity, human rights, and employment relations in the education sector, but the proposal was dropped in the face of opposition from vested interests.

FURTHER READINGS

ABRAMSKY, R.H., "The Ontario Law Reform Commission Report on Delay and Multiple Proceedings: A Critique" (1996) 4 C.L.E.L.J. 353

CHARNEY, R., & T. BRADY, *Judicial Review in Labour Law*, looseleaf (Aurora, ON: Canada Law Book, 1997–)

DEMEYERE, G., "Issue Estoppel in Employment Law Disputes: *Rasanen v. Rosemount Instruments* and Its Aftermath" (1998) 6 C.L.E.L.J. 299

ENGLAND, G., R. WOOD, & I. CHRISTIE, *Employment Law in Canada*, 4th ed., looseleaf (Markham, ON: LexisNexis Canada, 2005–) c. 20

28 See text accompanying notes 13–15 above.
29 See generally B.L. Adell, "Adjudication of Workplace Disputes in Ontario: A Report to the Ontario Law Reform Commission," March 1991 [unpublished].
30 *Labour and Employment Board Act*, S.N.B. 1994, c. L-0.01.

FLOOD, C., "Efficiency v. Fairness: Multiple Litigation and Adjudication in Labour and Employment Law" (2001) 8 C.L.E.L.J. 383

GOODMAN, J.E., "Approach with Caution: Issue Estoppel and Employment Insurance Adjudications" (2001) 8 C.L.E.L.J. 461

GOODMAN, J.E., & J. MURRAY, "Ties That Bind at Common Law: Issue Estoppel, Employment Standards and Unemployment Insurance Adjudication" (1997) 24 C.C.E.L. (2d) 291

MACTAVISH, A.L., & A.J.F. LENZ, "Civil Actions for Conduct Addressed by Human Rights Legislation: Some Recent Substantive and Procedural Developments" (1996) 4 C.L.E.L.J. 375

ONTARIO LAW REFORM COMMISSION, *Report on Avoiding Delay and Multiple Proceedings in the Adjudication of Workplace Disputes* (Toronto: Ontario Law Reform Commission, 1995)

TERMINATION OF EMPLOYMENT

This chapter examines the main ways in which the employment relationship can be terminated. First, the relationship may be terminated by agreement of the parties, for example, where employment is specified to last for a fixed term or for the performance of a defined task, and the term expires or the task is completed. It also includes the situation where the employee reaches the retirement age designated by the employer. Second, the employer may terminate the relationship by giving the employee the requisite notice, or wages in lieu thereof, as specified by the contract of employment or the applicable employment standards legislation. Third, the employee may be summarily dismissed without notice or wages in lieu thereof for misconduct or incompetence. Fourth, the relationship may be terminated by the employee resigning. This way includes situations where the employee quits by giving due notice as required by the employment contract or applicable employment standards legislation and where the employee quits in response to a "repudiatory breach" of the employment contract on the employer's part (normally referred to as "constructive dismissal"). Fifth, termination of the employment relationship may involve breach of special legislation. Relevant here are the role of the "unjust discharge" legislation in the federal jurisdiction, Quebec, and Nova Scotia, and the unique position of public "office holders" who are dismissed in breach of a statutory procedure or the administrative law duty of fairness. Other specialized statutes, such as health and safety, human rights, and collective bargaining legislation, can also come into play when an employee is terminated, but these are examined in detail either elsewhere in this book or in other specialized texts. The statutory unjust discharge legislation is especially significant in regard to the availability of broad "make whole" remedies. Sixth, in the case of wrongful dismissal, the employee may avail himself or herself of the remedies available at common law. These are examined and compared with the statutory "make whole" remedies. And seventh, the employment relationship may be terminated by operation of the doctrine of frustration of contract.

Today, the critical question in the law of termination of employment is where to strike the point of balance between, on the one hand, safeguarding the employee's interest in being treated fairly in termination situations and receiving adequate severance payments, and, on the other hand, safeguarding the employer's interest in enhancing profitability by minimizing the costs of terminating employees. We shall see, for example, that several courts have sought to reduce the length of common law notice periods in order to enable employers to better weather the storm of increasing foreign competition. Unfortunately, more empirical investigation of the economic effects of most of the termination laws examined in this chapter is needed in order to guide legislators and judges in fixing the point of balance.[1] Some commentators argue that providing overly generous termination protections to employees will deter employers from laying off redundant workers in economic downturns; deter employers from replacing overpriced employees with cheaper workers; induce employers in economic upswings to use easily disposable "non-employee" contract labour or introduce labour-saving technology as a substitute for hiring employees who will be expensive to dismiss in the future; and impede labour mobility by discouraging employees in declining sectors from resigning—thereby prejudicing their termination benefits—so as to enter growth sectors. However, other commentators argue that generous termination protections may improve the productivity of employees by increasing their loyalty and commitment to the firm; facilitate the labour readjustment process by making layoffs more palatable to employees; induce employers to make

---

1 See R. Di Tella & R. MacCulloch, "The Consequences of Labour Market Flexibility: Panel Evidence Based on Survey Data," Harvard Business School [unpublished], available from authors at rditella@hbs.edu or robertmacculloch@compuserve.com; J. Friesen, "The Response of Wages to Protective Labour Legislation: Evidence from Canada" (1996) 49 Indus. & Lab. Rel. Rev. 243; S.R.G. Jones & P. Kuhn, "Mandatory Notice and Unemployment" (1995), 13 J. Lab. Econ. 599; N. Leckie, *An International Review of Labour Adjustment Policies and Practices* (Kingston, ON: Industrial Relations Centre, Queen's University, 1993), especially at 7–8 and 39–45; E. Lazear, "Job Security Provisions and Employment" (1990) 105 Q. J. Econ. 699.

fundamental changes to their organizations with a long-term payoff, instead of resorting to the quick fix of implementing layoffs; and reduce the costs of unemployment to society as a whole.

A. TERMINATION BY AGREEMENT OF THE PARTIES

The contract of employment can be brought to an end by express consent of both parties at any time in accordance with general contract law principles. The difficult question in the employment context is ensuring that the employee genuinely consents to a termination settlement rather than having it imposed on him or her by the employer's superior power. The courts will strike down an ostensibly consensual termination settlement if it is "unconscionable" — if the employer has unfairly exploited the employee's inferior bargaining position in order to negotiate terms that are substantially less favourable to the employee than the prevailing industry standard. For example, unconscionability will likely be found if the employee is forced to accept the offered terms because of a serious financial problem, agrees under protest or at a time of emotional distress, or has not consulted a lawyer.[2] Furthermore, if the employer has threatened the employee with discharge unless he or she agrees to resign, or if the employee resigns because the employer has unilaterally changed an important term or condition of employment, the employee can sue for damages for constructive dismissal.[3]

Some employment contracts expressly state that they will terminate automatically after the expiry of a fixed term, or upon completion of a defined project. There is no wrongful dismissal on the employer's part or wrongful resignation upon the employee's part when the contract terminates in this way.[4] Furthermore, non-renewal of the employment contract after the expiry of the term or completion of the task is lawful. Since the effect of finding a contract to be for a fixed term or task is to deprive the employee of entitlement to "reasonable" notice of termination, the courts require unequivocal and explicit language to establish

---

2   Examples: *Howell v. Reitmans (Canada) Ltd.* (2002), 21 C.C.E.L. (3d) 208 at 214 (Nfld. S.C.T.D.); *Lambert v. Digital Rez Software Corp.*, [2002] B.C.J. No. 915 (S.C.); *Stephenson v. Hilti (Canada) Ltd.* (1989), 29 C.C.E.L. 80 at 89 (N.S.S.C.T.D.). Compare *Dolter v. Media House Production Inc.* (2002), 227 Sask. R. 153 (C.A.), where no unconscionability was found.

3   See Section D, below in this chapter.

4   Examples: *Flynn v. Shorcan Brokers Ltd.*, [2006] O.J. No. 470 (C.A.); *Lambert v. Canadian Assn. of Optometrists* (1994), 6 C.C.E.L. (2d) 129 at 131 (Ont. Gen. Div.).

such a contract and will interpret any ambiguities strictly against the employer's interests.[5]

Nevertheless, if the employer terminates the relationship before the term expires or the project is completed, this constitutes wrongful dismissal, entitling the employee to recover damages. The measure of damages is the wages and benefits the employee would have earned over the balance of term, subject to the duty of mitigation.[6] Thus, the employee cannot sit in the sun following a premature termination, but must make reasonable efforts to find replacement work—otherwise his or her damages will be reduced. Similarly, any earnings from a replacement job received during the balance of the term will be deducted from the employee's damages. The exception to this rule is where the employment contract expressly states that the employee is entitled to receive an unequivocally identifiable severance payment in the event of early termination, as a money debt rather than as compensation for breach, in which case the duty to mitigate is inapplicable and the full sum is recoverable.[7] It is simply a question of construction of the contractual language whether or not the parties intend the severance payment to be money debt rather than damages for breach.

It is possible for the parties to make an employment contract under which the employee will work for a specified period and then be laid off, without severing the contractual nexus, until he or she is subsequently recalled for work. An example would be a snow remover who is hired each winter and laid off over the summer over a lengthy time. Under such an arrangement, the employment contract would be suspended during the layoff and the employer would have to give reasonable notice of termination if it intends not to recall the worker for the winter season.[8] Similarly, the employee would have to give reasonable notice of resignation if he or she plans not to report for work over the winter. However, the courts require strong evidence showing that the parties intend to create an ongoing employment relationship where seasonal or other short-term work is involved.[9]

---

5   Example: *Ceccol v. Ontario Gymnastic Federation* (2001), 11 C.C.E.L. (3d) 167 at 177 (Ont. C.A.).

6   *Vondette v. Vancouver Port Corp.* (1987), 21 B.C.L.R. (2d) 209 (S.C.).

7   *Graham v. Marleau Lemire Securities Inc.* (2000), 49 C.C.E.L. (2d) 289 at 305–6 (Ont. S.C.J.); *Paquin v. Gainers Inc.* (1991), 37 C.C.E.L. 113, especially at 115 (Alta. C.A.).

8   Example: *Gray v. Manvers (Township)* (1992), 93 C.L.L.C. ¶14,023, especially at 12,139 (Ont. Gen. Div.).

9   Example: *Lawton v. Peter Bowden Drilling Ltd.* (1990), 33 C.C.E.L. 99, especially at 101 (Alta. Q.B.), where the court refused to find an indefinite term contract.

Legislation has relatively little to say about fixed-term contracts. The employment standards acts commonly exempt employers from having to give the minimum notice of termination where work ceases as a result of expiry of a fixed term or completion of a specified task.[10] The statutes of frauds require that employment contracts for a term in excess of one year be evidenced in writing, failing which the contract will be unenforceable. Nevertheless, since the default position in the event that if the contract is unenforceable is the common law reasonable notice period, the employee is not unduly prejudiced. Finally, in Ontario, section 2 of the *Employers and Employees Act* prohibits the making of employment contracts for a fixed, non-determinable term of nine years.

Perhaps the most common arrangement for terminating employment contracts by mutual assent is when the employee attains the age of retirement mutually agreed upon by the parties. Negotiated early retirement arrangements, in particular, have become popular as a more human way for companies to engage in downsizing. At common law, the fact that an employee reaches age 65 or any other age recognized for retirement, does not *ipso facto* provide the employer with cause for dismissing the employee without due notice or wages in lieu thereof.[11] In order to excuse the employer from giving such notice, either the contract of employment must contain a term express or implied whereby both parties agree that employment will automatically end at a specified retirement age, or the employee must expressly agree to waive rights to due notice in a separate termination agreement. If the employee continues to work beyond a contractually agreed-upon retirement date, the employment relationship is deemed to be for an indefinite term and the employer cannot rely retroactively on the retirement provision to terminate the employee, but must give reasonable notice or wages in lieu thereof.[12] If, however, job performance becomes impaired by reason of advancing age, the employer can summarily dismiss the employee for incompetence, subject to the usual requirements of "just cause," considered in Section C(1), (2), and (6) of this chapter.

The legislative regulation of retirement has changed dramatically in recent years, with the human rights statutes in all provinces being amended to prohibit mandatory retirement policies at age 65 or at any other age.[13] Under the human rights legislation, termination by reason

---

10   Example: Ontario *Termination and Severance of Employment Regulation*, O. Reg. 288/01, s. 2(1)1 [*Ont. Termination and Severance Reg.*].

11   *Heslop v. Cooper's Crane Rental Ltd.* (1994), 6 C.C.E.L. (2d) 252 (Ont. Gen. Div.).

12   *Stock v. Best Form Brassiere Canada Inc.* (1986), 15 C.C.E.L. 298 (Que. Sup. Ct.).

13   The policy reasons justifying this approach are examined in J.R. Kesselman, *Mandatory Retirement and Older Workers: Encouraging Longer Working Lives*

of the employee reaching a specified age constitutes discrimination of the basis of "age." In order to avoid liability, the employer would have to establish the defence of *bona fide occupational requirement* (BFOR), which entails having to reasonably accommodate the employee up to the point of undue hardship.[14] The burden of proving that the worker's age is a BFOR is on the employer.[15] The employer normally must make an individual assessment of each worker's mental and physical capacity as it affects the capability to perform job duties. The only exceptions where an employer is permitted to use group characteristics as a proxy for individual performance are where individual testing is not "feasible," "reliable," "practical," or "possible,"[16] or where there exists a demonstrable threat to the safety of the public or other employees. In the latter circumstances, the employer must be able to prove that there is a "factual basis for believing that all or substantially all persons within the class . . . would be unable to perform [the job] safely and efficiently."[17] The standard of proof of a BFOR is rigorous; employers must present concrete medical evidence that age impairs job performance to an unacceptable degree rather than subjective speculation based on their own uncorroborated experience.[18] As well, the employer must reasonably accommodate the employee up to the point of undue hardship, for example, by examining the costs and benefits of reassigning some or all of the worker's job duties, or rescheduling working hours, to reflect diminished capabilities.

Furthermore, a BFOR may be grounded on economic considerations unrelated to the employee's inability to perform the job by reason

---

Commentary No. 200 (Ottawa: C.D. Howe Institute, June 2004); C.T. Gillin, D. MacGregor, & T.R. Klassen, eds., *Time's Up! Mandatory Retirement in Canada* (Toronto: James Lorimer, 2005); M. Krashinsky, "The Case for Eliminating Mandatory Retirement: Why Economics and Human Rights Need Not Conflict" (1988) 14 Can. Pub. Pol'y 40. Compare M. Gunderson, "Banning Mandatory Retirement: Throwing out the Baby with the Bathwater" (2004), online: www.cdhowe.org/pdf/backgrounder_79.pdf.

14   See Chapter 7.

15   The test for BFOR is defined in *British Columbia (Public Service Employee Relations Commission)* v. *British Columbia Government and Service Employees' Union* (1999), 99 C.L.L.C. ¶230-028 at 145,224 (S.C.C.). For further elaboration, see Chapter 6, Section C(1).

16   *Saskatchewan Human Rights Commission* v. *Saskatoon (City of)*, [1989] 2 S.C.R. 1297. See also *Large* v. *Stratford (City of)*, [1995] 3 S.C.R. 733.

17   *Carson* v. *Air Canada* (1983), 5 C.H.R.R. D/1857 (Can. H.R.T.). This part of *Carson* was upheld by the Federal Court of Appeal: [1985] 1 F.C. 209.

18   *Ontario (Human Rights Commission)* v. *Etobicoke (Borough of)*, [1982] 1 S.C.R. 202 at 212; *Rodger* v. *Canadian National Railway* (1985), 6 C.H.R.R. D/2899 at D/2907 (Can. H.R.T.).

of age. For example, if an employer's compensation structure under-pays newly hired employees in their early years relative to the profits the employer makes from them, but overpays employees in their later years, compulsory termination at the agreed-upon age would appear to be economically justifiable in order to avoid an unjust enrichment on the part of the employee who elects to work beyond retirement age. However, the duty of reasonable accommodation would almost certain-ly require that an exception be made in the case of employees who are hired late in life, for example, individuals who take time out from their careers to raise a family, for they will not have derived the full benefit of the compensation structure by the time they reach retirement age. An employer might also seek to justify compulsory termination in or-der to make room for young employees with new skills and ideas, to reduce personnel administration costs by having a predetermined date for employee terminations, to provide elderly workers with a dignified means of exit compared with a possible dismissal for incompetence, to bolster internal "peer review" systems of performance appraisal, and to stimulate opportunities for youth employment. Whether or not these arguments will succeed depends on the unique facts of each case.[19]

B. TERMINATION BY DUE NOTICE OR WAGES IN LIEU THEREOF

A contract of employment that does not come to an end automatically upon the expiry of a fixed term or the completion of a defined task can be terminated lawfully by the employer only if it gives the employee due notice of termination of employment in accordance with the ex-press or implied terms in the contract dealing with the notice period. Of course, such notice may be dispensed with if the employee's miscon-duct or incompetence gives the employer "cause" to invoke summary dismissal, as we shall see later in this book. Moreover, the employer may terminate the contract at any time by giving the worker wages in

---

19 These arguments have been accepted under s. 1 of the *Charter* in the context of s. 15 challenges to provisions in human rights acts that used to allow employ-ers to impose mandatory retirement at age 65: e.g., *McKinney v. University of Guelph*, [1990] 3 S.C.R. 229 [*McKinney*]; and *Dickason v. University of Alberta*, [1992] 2 S.C.R. 1103 [*Dickason*]; *Stoffman v. Vancouver General Hospital*, [1990] 3 S.C.R. 483; *Harrison v. University of British Columbia*, [1990] 3 S.C.R. 451. They have also been accepted in challenges to mandatory retirement policies under the human rights legislation: e.g., *University of Alberta v. Alberta (Human Rights Commission)* (1992), 17 C.H.R.R. D/87 (Alta. Q.B.).

lieu of the contractual notice period, but this almost certainly operates as liquidated damages for what is, technically speaking, a breach of the employment contract by the employer in failing to provide *actual* notice of termination.[20]

This section of the book examines how much notice must be given—an important question, since the amount of compensation an employee receives for wrongful dismissal at common law is determined by the contractual benefits that he or she would have been entitled to during the notice period. In addition, the employment standards legislation in all jurisdictions entitles the employee to a specified minimum notice period, which the parties can exceed, but not undercut in their employment contracts. We examine this statutory floor of rights next.

1) Individual Notice Requirements under the Employment Standards Legislation

The employment standards statutes in all provinces provide for minimum notice periods for all employees covered by the legislation. Typically, the length of notice increases with the employee's period of continuous employment with the employer. This emphasis on seniority appears to reflect a combination of several policies: (1) employees with high seniority are likely to be relatively old and will likely encounter greater difficulty than younger employees in finding replacement work, which justifies providing them with a more generous cushion against unemployment; (2) seniority-based notice entitlements may be regarded as a form of "deferred wages," under which the employee is deemed to postpone part of his or her compensation until terminated; (3) seniority-based notice arguably represents compensation for loss of the employee's "property interest" in his or her job, which accrues with continuous service; and (4) seniority-based notice replicates for the non-unionized worker the same kind of protections that are generally available for unionized workers under collective agreements.

Section 56 of the Alberta *Employment Standards Code*[21] is illustrative, providing for a minimum notice of one week for employees with

---

20 Although there is no complete Canadian judicial analysis, the overwhelming majority of cases support this analysis: e.g., *Taylor v. Dyer Brown*, [2005] C.L.L.C. ¶210-001 at 141,002–3 (Ont. C.A.); *Zaraweh v. Herman, Bunbury and Oke* (2001), 13 C.C.E.L. (3d) 264 at 268 (B.C.C.A.); *Noble v. Principal Consultants Ltd. (Trustee of)* (2000), 1 C.C.E.L. (3d) 77 at 84 (Alta. C.A.). However, the alternative view finds support in *Carson v. Dairy and Poultry Pool* (1966), 56 W.W.R. (N.S.) 629 at 633 (Sask. Dist. Ct.).
21 R.S.A. 2000, c. E-9 [*Alta. ESC*].

seniority between three months and two years; two weeks for those with seniority between two years and four years; four weeks for those with seniority between four years and six years; five weeks for those with seniority between six years and eight years; six weeks for those with seniority between eight years and ten years; and eight weeks for those with seniority of ten years or more. Making the accrual of benefits depend upon working for lengthy periods of continuous employment with one employer prejudices employees who are hired on a short term or intermittent basis with one or more employers. Short-term work has proliferated in the "new economy," especially among women, members of visible minorities, and immigrants. Therefore, these legislative provisions are potentially susceptible to challenge as a form of indirect discrimination under section 15 of the *Charter*,[22] in which case the governments would have to justify the relevant qualifying periods under section 1. As yet, no such challenges have been launched.

There are considerable variations in detail between the notice provisions of each province's statute regarding individual notice of termination, requiring careful examination of each act. Nevertheless, certain common features are identifiable. First, the employer is usually allowed to give the employee wages in lieu of actual notice of termination.[23] This provision enables the employer to avoid the risk of "shirking" on the part of employees who have been told that their employment is to end. Second, the employer is usually prohibited from reducing an employee's wages or otherwise unilaterally changing his or her terms and conditions of employment once notice of termination has been served.[24] Third, the legislation in several jurisdictions provides that if the employee continues to work beyond the date specified in a notice of termination, the notice in question becomes spent and the employer must serve another full notice period if it wants to terminate the employee at a later date.[25] In Ontario, however,[26] the employer need only serve another notice if the period of further employment does not exceed thirteen weeks. Fourth, if the employer files for bankruptcy, it is not absolved from providing

---

22 *Canadian Charter of Rights and Freedoms*, Part I of the *Constitution Act, 1982*, being Schedule B to the *Canada Act 1982* (U.K.), 1982, c. 11 [*Charter*].

23 Example: Ontario *Employment Standards Act, 2000*, S.O. 2000, c. 41, s. 61 [*Ont. ESA*]. For further elaboration of this and other aspects of this topic, see G. England, R. Wood, & I. Christie, *Employment Law in Canada*, 4th ed., looseleaf (Toronto: LexisNexis Canada, 2005–) c. 14(1)(A) [*Employment Law in Canada*].

24 Example: Saskatchewan *Labour Standards Act*, R.S.S. 1978, c. L-1, s. 44(2.1) [*Sask. LSA*].

25 Example: Newfoundland *Labour Standards Act*, R.S.N.L. 1990, c. L-2, s. 56(1) [*Nfld. LSA*].

26 *Ontario Termination and Severance Reg.*, above note 10, s. 6.

statutory termination benefits.[27] Fifth, the legislation specifies circumstances in which the employer is excused from notice obligation. The most widespread exemptions are as follows:

- An employee's acts of misconduct or incompetence give the employer just cause for summary dismissal.[28] The concept of just cause in this context generally carries its common law connotation, unless the particular statutory language provides otherwise.[29]
- Employers in cyclical or seasonal[30] industries with fluctuating labour needs, such as construction,[31] are often exempted in order to minimize their labour costs.
- Employees who are temporarily laid off from work are generally disentitled from receiving notice of termination. The employment standards statutes typically define in great detail which layoffs are deemed to be "temporary" for this purpose. In British Columbia, for instance, a temporary layoff is one where either the layoff does not persist beyond the recall date specified in the employee's employment contract or collective agreement, or does not last thirteen weeks or more.[32] A "week of layoff" is, in turn, defined as one in which the employee earns less than 50 percent of his or her regular average pay over the preceding eight weeks.[33] Of course, if the employment contract is not terminated, but rather suspended for the duration of the layoff according to the general common law principles of contract law, notice of termination need not be given, making the legislative layoff exemption superfluous. The courts have held that the employer has no inherent right to impose a layoff under the law of the employment contract; such conduct operates as a repudiatory breach on the employer's part, entitling the employee to quit and sue for damages for constructive dismissal.[34] The employer can only lay off without breaching the contract if there is an express term in

---

27 *Rizzo and Rizzo Shoes Ltd. (Re)* (1998), 33 C.C.E.L. (2d) 173 (S.C.C.) [*Rizzo Shoes*].
28 Example: *Canada Labour Code*, R.S.C. 1985, c. L-2, s. 230(1) [*CLC*].
29 Example: *Houghton Boston Printers & Lithographers Ltd. v. Abreau* (1988), 69 Sask. R. 275 (Q.B.). In Manitoba, however, use of the word "wilful" in the statute establishes a narrower standard than at common law: *Convergys Consumer Management Inc. v. Luba* (2005), 39 C.C.E.L. (3d) 171 (Man. C.A.).
30 Example: British Columbia *Employment Standards Act*, R.S.B.C. 1996, c. 113, s. 65(4)(b) [*B.C. ESA*].
31 *Ontario Termination and Severance Reg.*, above note 10, s. 2(1)9.
32 *B.C. ESA*, above note 30, s. 1.
33 *Ibid.*, s. 62.
34 Example: *Chen v. Sigpro Wireless Inc.*, [2004] O.J. No. 2280 (S.C.J.). See Section D(3), below in this chapter.

the contract or an implied term based on the parties' past practice permitting it to do so; otherwise, notice of termination or wages in lieu thereof must be given at common law. The courts have also held that the provisions in the employment standards act that exempt an employer from giving statutory termination benefits in defined temporary layoffs do not absolve the employer from giving the employee the requisite notice of termination provided for under the express or implied terms of an employment contract.[35] Indeed, the legislation in some provinces expresses this to be the case,[36] something that accords with the "floor of rights" rationale underpinning the legislation. One Alberta trial court decision holds the opposite,[37] but it is submitted that this decision is incorrect.

- The legislation usually dispenses with the notice requirement if the layoff is caused by unforeseen or unpreventable events such as would normally frustrate the contract at common law—for example, if a fire that destroys the plant.[38] Some provinces limit this exception to cases where the employer has shown "due diligence" in avoiding the events in question.[39] Where the frustrating event is sickness of an employee that constitutes a protected "disability" under section 15 of the *Charter*, the employment standards legislation would have to require the employer to comply with the duty of reasonable accommodation before denying an employee termination entitlements, in order to be constitutional. The employment standards acts of some provinces expressly impose this duty in order to forestall any challenges under the *Charter*.[40]

- Some provinces exempt employees who are engaged under a system of work where they can elect to work or not for a temporary period when requested by their employer.[41]

---

35   Examples: *Emler v. Display Fixtures Ltd.*, [1953] 2 D.L.R. 450 (Man. C.A.); *Style v. Carlingview Airport Inn* (1996), 18 C.C.E.L. (2d) 163 at 167 (Ont. Div. Ct.).

36   Example: Prince Edward Island *Employment Standards Act*, S.P.E.I. 1992, c. 18, s. 29(5) [*P.E.I. ESA*].

37   *Vrana v. Procor Ltd* (2003), 24 C.C.E.L. (3d) 51 at 57–58 (Alta. Q.B.), quashed but not on this point (2004), 25 Alta. L.R. (4d) 201 (C.A.) [*Vrana*]. In the latest case on point, Moore J. stated in an *obiter dictum* that *Vrana* was incorrect and should not be followed: *Turner v. Uniglobe Custom Travel Ltd.*, [2005] C.L.L.C. ¶210-039 at 141,386–87 (Alta. Q.B.).

38   *Polyco Window Manufacturers Ltd. v. Saskatchewan (Director of Labour Standards)* (1994), 3 C.C.E.L. (2d) 101, especially at 103 (Sask. Q.B.) [*Polyco*].

39   Example: Nova Scotia *Labour Standards Code*, R.S.N.S. 1989, c. 246, s. 72(3)(d) [*N.S. LSC*].

40   Example: *Sask. LSA*, above note 24, ss. 44.2 & 44.3.

41   Example: *Ont. Termination and Severance Reg.*, above note 10, s. 2(1)10.

- Employees who are hired for a fixed term or to complete a defined task are generally exempt,[42] except in some provinces where the task or term will exceed twelve months' duration,[43] or in others where work extends for a defined period beyond the completion of the task or term.[44]
- Employees who are laid off as a result of a strike or lockout at their place of employment are often exempt.[45]
- An employee who refuses an offer of "reasonable" alternative employment from the employer is generally precluded from receiving statutory notice of termination.[46]

Because the length of statutory notice of termination to which an employee is entitled depends on the period of continuous employment with the employer, it is important to know which interruptions in service will rupture the accrual of continuous employment. The legislation does not require that actual work be performed in order for seniority to accrue; it suffices that the contractual nexus remains intact. Thus, if the parties to an employment contract provide, expressly or impliedly, that a particular absence from work, such as a sabbatical leave or a layoff, operates to suspend rather than terminate the contract, continuous employment will continue to accrue during the absence in question; otherwise, it will not and the worker will have to rebuild seniority from scratch. In particular, changes in the corporate identity of an employer such as occur in a sale, merger, or amalgamation operate to terminate the employment contract at common law.[47] This poses a considerable risk to the security of employees, given the high incidence of corporate sales, mergers, and amalgamations in recent years.

The courts have responded by presuming that if the employees remain in the employ of the new company, the employees' previous seniority will carry over uninterrupted, unless the new employer clearly

---

42   Example: *ibid.*, s. 2(1)1.
43   Example: New Brunswick *Employment Standards Act*, S.N.B. 1982, c. E-7.2, s. 31(3)(a) [*N.B. ESA*]; *N.S. LSC*, above note 39, s. 72(3)(b)
44   Example: *Ont. Termination and Severance Reg.*, above note 10, ss. 2(1) and 2(2)(b) & (c). In this situation, the entire period of employment from the commencement of the task or term usually counts towards the employee's seniority: *B.C. ESA*, above note 30, s. 65(2); *N.B. ESA*, above note 43, s. 31(3)(b); *N.S. LSC*, above note 39, s. 77(2)
45   Example: *Canada Labour Standards Regulations*, C.R.C., c. 986, s. 30(1)(a) [*CLSR*].
46   Example: *Ont. Termination and Severance Reg.*, above note 10, s. 2(1)5.
47   Example: *Canada (A.G.) v. Standard Trust Co.* (1995), 8 C.C.E.L. (2d) 58 at 64–65 (Ont. Gen. Div., Commercial List).

states otherwise.[48] As well, several jurisdictions have responded by enacting "successor rights" legislation preserving continuity of employment for designated statutory purposes[49] where a business or part thereof is sold, transferred, or otherwise disposed of to a "successor employer."[50] Several provinces have also enacted "common employer" provisions, which allow the corporate veil to be pierced in defined circumstances so that an employee who is hired and fired by a succession of one or more common employers can maintain continuity of employment for statutory purposes with respect to all of the common employers.[51] Furthermore, a few provinces provide that interruptions in employment of up to a designated maximum period will not disturb the accrual of continuous employment. Alberta is the most generous, fixing the maximum permissible hiatus between periods of employment as three months,[52] compared with thirteen weeks in Nova Scotia.[53] In Manitoba, an employee who is re-engaged by the same employer within two months of last hiring is deemed to have been continuously employed, and an employee who is re-engaged by the same employer in two or more consecutive years is treated as having a single period of continuous employment.[54] These provisions are critical for safeguarding the rights of casual and other short-term workers.

In Ontario and the federal jurisdiction, the legislation entitles employees who are terminated to an additional "severance" payment on top of the above-mentioned individual notice of termination. The federal statute provides that every employee with twelve months' continuous service with an employer is entitled upon termination to a payment equal to the greater of either two days' wages for regular hours worked in each completed year of employment or five days' wages for the regular hours actually worked.[55] The rationale for this provision seems to be to provide the displaced employee with a more generous

---

48   *Lingelbach v. James Tire Centres Ltd.* (1994), 7 C.C.E.L. (2d) 297 (Sask. C.A.) [*Lingelbach*]. See generally Chapter 2.
49   But not for non-statutory purposes, such as the determination of reasonable notice in wrongful dismissal actions, e.g., *Lingelbach, ibid.*
50   Example: *Alta. ESC*, above note 21, s. . See also Chapter 2.
51   Example: *Ont. ESA*, above note 23, s. 12(1). See also Chapter 2.
52   *Alta. ESC*, above note 21, s. 54.
53   *N.S. LSC*, above note 39, s. 77(3).
54   Manitoba *Employment Standards Regulation*, Man. Reg. 6/2oo7, ss. 4 & 5.
55   *CLC*, above note 28, s. 235(1); and *CLSR*, above note 45, ss. 31–32. See also Canada, Commission on the Review of Federal Labour Standards, *Fairness at Work: Federal Labour Standards for the 21st Century* by H.W. Arthurs (Ottawa: Commission on the Review of Federal Labour Standards, 2006) at 174–75 [Arthurs Report].

financial cushion than is available under the basic notice of termination provision.[56] The Ontario scheme differs in that it distinguishes between terminations due to the "permanent discontinuance" of all or part of the employer's operations and terminations for other reasons. If the employee is dismissed as a result of the permanent discontinuance of all or part of the employer's operations and has at least five years' continuous service with that employer, and fifty other employees are also terminated within six months, then the employee is entitled to a severance payment of one weeks' regular pay for each complete year of employment up to a maximum of twenty-six weeks.[57] Where termination results from reasons other than discontinuance of all or part of the business and does not involve a "group" termination as defined above, the affected employee is entitled to severance pay only if the employer has a payroll of $2.5 million or more.[58] Both the Ontario and federal statutes contain detailed exceptions where severance pay is not required, which roughly correspond to those applicable to the individual notice of termination provisions considered above. If an employee is absent from work at the time of the layoff due to an illness or injury that he or she is receiving benefits for under the workers compensation legislation, the employee remains entitled to severance benefits.[59]

The Ontario Court of Appeal has held that severance payments received under section 58 of the *Employment Standards Act* are deductible from any damages for wrongful dismissal that the employee receives in a civil action. This supports the view that the statutory severance payment is not a "vested" entitlement that the employee earns with ongoing service, but a "windfall" through legislative largesse.[60]

Furthermore, Ontario courts have ruled that severance pay under section 58 cannot be recovered as part of a civil action for wrongful dismissal; rather, the employee must proceed under the *Employment Standards Act*'s administrative machinery in order to recover his or her statutory entitlement.[61]

---

56 *Mattocks v. Smith and Stone (1982) Inc.* (1990), 34 C.C.E.L. 273 at 278–79 (Ont. Gen. Div.).

57 *Ont. ESA*, above note 23, ss. 63–67, and *Ont. Termination and Severance Reg.*, above note 10, s. 9.

58 *Ibid.*, s. 58(2)(b).

59 *Maple Leaf Foods Inc. v. Alejandro*, [1999] O.J. No. 1790 (C.A.).

60 *Stevens v. The Globe and Mail* (1996), 19 C.C.E.L. (2d) 153 at 163 (Ont. C.A.) [*Stevens*].

61 *Hine v. Susan Shoe Industries Ltd.* (1989), 71 O.R. (2d) 438 (H.C.J.).

2) The Group Termination Provisions in Employment Standards Legislation

The last decade or so has been marked by an increase in mass lay-offs resulting from industrial restructuring, in which numerous workers are displaced at roughly the same time. The federal and provincial governments have responded by adopting a broad range of measures designed to facilitate the readjustment of displaced labour.[62] Part of that response is the group termination provisions contained in the employment standards legislation in all jurisdictions save Prince Edward Island. Depending on the jurisdiction, these provisions may include one or all of the following features: requiring the employer to give advance notice to the affected employees, entitling the affected employees to additional termination pay, requiring the employer to give advance notice to government authorities, and requiring the employer to establish joint management–labour planning committees charged with ameliorating the impact of the layoffs.

Typically, the legislation requires employers to give advance notice of termination to affected employees, the length of notice increasing according to the number of employees being terminated. Empirical studies have shown that increasing the length of advance notice of layoffs signficantly reduces the period of post-displacement unemployment.[63] In Saskatchewan, for example, an employer who plans to terminate between ten and fifty employees must give four weeks' notice, but notice increases to eight weeks if between fifty and one hundred employees are to be released and to twelve weeks if one hundred or more employees are affected.[64] The legislation in four provinces (British Columbia,

---

62   For further elaboration of this and other aspects of this topic, see P. Kumar, *Labour Market Adjustment Issues in Canada: An Industrial Relations Perspective* (Kingston, ON: Industrial Relations Centre, Queen's University, 1991). The leading European models for handling redundancy are reviewed by M. Gunderson, "Alternative Mechanisms for Dealing with Permanent Lay-offs, Dismissals and Plant Closures" in W.C. Riddell, ed., *Adapting to Change: Labour Market Adjustment in Canada* (Toronto: University of Toronto Press, 1986) at 146. See also G. England, "Report to the Federal Government Task Force on Part III of the *Canada Labour Code* Regarding the Termination of Employment Provisions in the *Canada Labour Code*" (Ottawa: Human Resources and Skills Development, October 2005) at 64–73.

63   C. Ruhn, "Advance Notice Job Search and Post-Displacement Earnings" (1994) 12 Journal of Labor Economics 1; A. Zippay, "The Effects of Advance Notice on Displaced Manufacturing Workers: A Case Study" (1993) Lab. St. Jo. 43; S. Jones & P. Kuhn, "Mandatory Notice and Unemployment" (1995) 13 Journal of Labor Economics 599.

64   Section 44.1 of the *Sask. LSA*, above note 24, and *Labour Standards Regulations, 1995*, R.R.S., c. L-1, O.C. 89/95 [*Sask. LSR*].

Nova Scotia, Manitoba, and Ontario) expressly allows the employer to terminate the employee without notice by paying a sum equal to the wages that would have been earned during the extended notice period required under the mass termination provisions, but in New Brunswick this practice is expressly precluded.[65] Empirical studies have shown that "on the job" searches for alternative employment are more efficient than post-discharge searches.[66] The risk for employers, however, is that employees who know they are to be terminated may quit or shirk on the job; empirical evidence, however, suggests that this risk may be overly exaggerated.[67] Moreover, no province requires that advance notice be served as soon as the employer "contemplates" that layoffs are "likely"; rather, notice need not be given until after the employer has finalized its decision. Arguably, it would facilitate the adjustment process if employees and government officials could be involved at the earliest opportunity before the employer's decision is confirmed. Indeed, the International Labor Organization's 1982 *Termination of Employment Recommendation* endorses this approach.

The legislation also requires the employer to cooperate with government officials, the affected employees, and their union (if applicable) in ameliorating the effects of the layoffs. The precise extent of the employer's duty to cooperate varies among the provinces, necessitating detailed examination of each statute. Of particular interest is the provision for the establishment of joint employer–employee planning committees in the federal jurisdiction, British Columbia, Manitoba, and Quebec.[68] In the federal jurisdiction, the employer is automatically bound to create such a committee in accordance with the methodology set out in the *Canada Labour Code* once notice of layoff is issued; in the remaining jurisdictions, the minister of labour has the discretion to order the establishment of the committee. The mandate of the committee, roughly speaking, is to formulate a jointly agreed-upon plan to avoid or minimize the scope of the layoffs and to assist those affected to find re-

---

65   *N.B. ESA*, above note 43, ss. 30 and 34.
66   C. Ruhn, "Advance Notice Job Search and Post-Displacement Earnings," above note 63 at 24.
67   J.T. Adison & P. Portugal, "Advance Notice: From Voluntary Exchange to Mandated Benefits" (1992) 31 R.I./I.R. 159 at 176.
68   *CLC*, above note 28, s. 214(1); *B.C. ESA*, above note 30, s. 71; Manitoba *Employment Standards Code*, CCSM c. E110, s. 71(1) [*Man. ESC*]; Quebec *Act Respecting Manpower Vocational Training and Qualification*, R.S.Q., c. F-5, s. 45(b). Before 2000, the Ontario legislation contained this feature, but it was removed in that year, presumably in order to reduce the employer's costs in implementing mass terminations.

placement work. Each statute defines in great detail how the committee members are to be selected and how business is to be conducted. There is a statutory obligation on the employer and the employee members to cooperate in the preparation of a labour adjustment plan. Employee representatives are commonly entitled to be paid their regular wages while serving on the committee. The legislation in the four provinces assumes that the duty to cooperate will result in the committee's generating a mutually agreeble adjustment plan, and no machinery is provided for resolving impasses. More realistically, perhaps, the federal statute provides for the imposition of an adjustment plan by a neutral arbitrator if the committee members reach an impasse.[69] The arbitrator has broad discretion to formulate the contents of an adjustment plan, but cannot reverse the employer's decision to proceed with layoffs. So far, only three arbitration decisions have been made, and the process is similar to interest arbitration under collective agreements in the unionized sector. Thus, the arbitrator initially attempts to mediate a voluntary agreement between the parties on as many issues as possible. Failing such agreement, the arbitrator makes an award that takes into account comparability with similarly placed employers and employees, the nature and scope of the economic exigency facing the employer, and in the public sector, the notoriously elusive concept of the "public interest." So far, the awards have included severance pay based on length of service; early retirement incentive packages; extended post-discharge medical benefits; relocation and retraining assistance; and recall rights based on seniority for employees who are capable of doing the job.[70] These joint labour adjustment committees are highly significant in recognizing that non-unionized workers have group representational rights that should be secured by employment standards legislation without necessitating full-scale unionization on the employees' part.[71] Traditionally, employment standards legislation has focused almost exclusively on economic benefits, such as minimum wages, overtime, hours of work, and paid leaves, rather than on the individual's right to participate in

---

69   *CLC*, above note 28, ss. 223–24.

70   *Re A Group Termination of Employment by Cape Breton Development Corporation (Devco)* (2 June 2000) (Outhouse); *Re A Group Termination of Employment by Cape Breton Development Corporation (Devco)* (12 October 2001) (Ashley); *Re La Société Energie Atomique du Canada and Les Employés de la Société Energie Atomique du Canada Ltée* (20 October 1983) (Dufresne).

71   See R.J. Adams, "The Unorganized: A Rising Force" Research and Working Paper Series No. 21 (Hamilton, ON: McMaster University, Faculty of Business, April 1983) at 13.

workplace decisions. In this sense, the joint committee provisions can be seen as an embryonic form of European wage councils.[72]

The group termination provisions commonly specify exemptions in favour of the employer, which more or less parallel the exceptions to the individual notice of termination requirement considered earlier in this chapter. Since the details vary among the provinces, each statute should be consulted. Perhaps the most interesting exception is that in Manitoba, Saskatchewan, and the federal jurisdiction, the minister of labour is empowered to waive the employer's statutory obligations if the minister believes that the employer's business or other employees would be seriously harmed by full compliance.[73] Clearly, it would be unwarranted to impose costs on the employer or other employees that would exceed the benefits affected employees stand to obtain from having the provisions applied to them.

Finally, no Canadian province has enacted a right to recall for displaced workers. Under paragraph 24(1) of the ILO's *Termination of Employment Recommendation*, it is stated that redundant employees should have priority of rehiring with their former employer, if the employer again hires workers with comparable qualifications and if they have made known their desire to be rehired within a specified time. Presumably, this requirement is thought to be unduly costly for employers to administer.

3) The Common Law Requirements Regarding Notice to Terminate

There is an enormously detailed caselaw on the determination of the common law notice period. The cases are best understood as revealing a tension between two fundamental perspectives on the employment relationship.

One perspective sees the employment relationship as an economic exchange to which the general principles of contract law should apply, so as to maximize the role of competitive market forces in determining the terms and conditions of employment, including the notice period. According to this perspective, the factual intention of the parties should be the main determinant of the notice period. Express contractual pro-

---

72   Advocates of adopting European work councils include D. Beatty, *Putting the Charter to Work* (Kingston, ON: McGill-Queen's University Press, 1987), c. 13 & 14; P.C. Weiler, *Governing the Workplace: The Future of Labor and Employment Law* (Cambridge: Harvard University Press, 1990) at 282–98.

73   *CLC*, above note 28, ss. 228(a)–(c); *Man. ESC*, above note 68, s. 69; *Sask. LSR*, above note 64, s. 22(3)(b).

visions governing the length of notice must be accorded paramountcy, even though the court might not regard the outcome as being fair to the employee. Such provisions should be interpreted at their face value, not *contra proferentem* the interests of the employer. In the absence of express provisions, the court should imply a notice period based on the unstated factual intentions of both parties. Evidence of such a common intention can be gleaned from the parties' past practices regarding termination; from personnel documentation regarding termination; and from customs and usages in the trade or industry that are "certain, reasonable and notorious."[74] Only if the parties do not factually intend a particular notice period should the court imply a reasonable notice period according to what the court considers to be fair in the circumstances.

On the other hand, the alternative perspective accords paramountcy to the policy-making role of the court in determining what a fair notice period is, having regard to a wide variety of factors beyond the factual intentions of the parties. This perspective regards the factual intention test as unsatisfactory since it generally enables the employer to exploit its superior bargaining power in order to impose an unfair notice period on the employee. Instead, it considers such factors as the employee's need for a financial cushion against unemployment, the employee's seniority and age, the status of the employee's job, whether the employer handled the termination fairly, whether the employee was induced to leave a secure position in order to take the job from which he or she is being dismissed, and whether the employer is experiencing financial exigency. Furthermore, by extending the reasonable notice period to assist an employee who is looking for replacement work, the courts are indirectly making the common law resemble the "make whole" method of determining compensation, which human rights tribunals use.[75] Judges favouring this approach attempt to circumvent any harsh express termination clauses in the contract and proceed directly to the step of fashioning a reasonable[76] notice period; they do not search for evidence of an unstated factual intention of the parties regarding the notice period. The result of this process makes determining the reasonable notice period extremely uncertain and unpredictable.

The tension between these perspectives has been highlighted by the complaint of Canadian employers that the reasonable notice test has

---

74   On these requirements, see *Sagar v. H. Ridehalgh & Son Ltd.* (1930), [1931] 1 Ch. 310 (C.A.); *Gardner v. Fogg Motors Ltd.* (1 April 1980), Vancouver C793894 (B.C.S.C.).

75   See Chapter 7.

76   The leading authority on the "reasonableness" test is *Bardal v. The Globe and Mail Ltd.* (1960), 24 D.L.R. (2d) 140 (Ont. H.C.J.) [*Bardal*].

produced excessively long notice periods over the last twenty years, to the point that their competitive position is now seriously harmed by unduly high termination costs. Some courts have agreed with this concern and have sought to reduce common law notice periods. However, other courts have continued with the trend of the last twenty years to gradually increase notice periods by means of the reasonableness test. The tension persists, but the current mainstream approach is still to award relatively generous notice periods under the reasonableness test.

Before considering the cases on the length of notice to terminate, it must be emphasized that in order to qualify as a valid notice of termination, any communication by the employer must clearly and unequivocally make it known to the worker that his or her employment will definitely cease on an ascertainable date. Although no particular form of words is required, the courts require that the employee be left in no doubt that his or her job will end at a certain time, so that the individual can make the necessary preparations to find replacement work.[77] Furthermore, once notice of termination has been communicated, it cannot be unilaterally withdrawn.[78] Next, we examine how courts determine the length of notice of termination.

a)   Express Notice of Termination Clauses

It is an axiom of contract law that express contractual terms always prevail over implied terms. Strictly speaking, this principle applies to notice clauses in employment contracts, too, but most modern courts have recognized that the employer's superiority of bargaining power creates the danger that unduly harsh notice provisions may be included in an employment contract, something that would be unfair to the employee to enforce. Accordingly, most (but by no means all) courts attempt to circumvent harsh termination clauses by various legal techniques and imply a reasonable notice period as the default position. First, the most common technique is to interpret ambiguous language in such a clause *contra proferentem* the interests of the employer.[79] Almost any words can be interpreted as creating an ambiguity if that is

---

77   *Gibb v. Novacorp International Consulting Inc.* (1990), 48 B.C.L.R. (2d) 28 (C.A.).

78   *Elderfield v. Aetna Life Insurance Co.* (1995), 11 C.C.E.L. (2d) 61 at 65 (B.C.S.C.).

79   Example: *MacAlpine v. Medbroadcast Corporation* (2003), 27 C.C.E.L.(3d) 271 at 276–77 (B.C. Prov. Ct.) [*MacAlpine*], where a clause entitling the employee to "such notice as is required by the termination of employment provisions of the British Columbia *Employment Standards Act* as amended from time to time," was construed as establishing a platform upon which the common law reasonable notice period would build, rather than as establishing a cap on the notice period.

the result a court desires. Not all judges, however, are prepared to interpret termination clauses in this way, especially if they perceive that the parties have relatively equal bargaining power or that the notice period is not blatantly unfair, or if they regard notice periods in general as having become too generous for the employee.[80]

Second, an express termination clause that the employer attempts to introduce into a pre-existing employment contract can be circumvented if the court is not satisfied that the employee has freely agreed to be bound by the clause with full knowledge of its legal significance. Employers frequently include such a clause in policy manuals or other personnel documentation and attempt to incorporate it into the employment contract after the date of original hiring. The courts have refused to find informed consent on the employee's part to such a clause unless the employer has specifically drawn the notice clause to the employee's attention, has explained its legal significance, and has clearly told the employee that the document is to be legally binding as part of the employment contract.[81] Moreover, the employee must positively signify assent to the clause in order for it to be included in the contract; simply continuing to work while remaining silent on the matter will not constitute "deemed" assent.[82] Nor will it suffice that the clause may have been accepted by other workers as part of the custom and practice in the plant; the employee must *personally* assent to being bound by it.[83] One judge has even stated that an employee will not be regarded as having agreed to a harsh termination clause that is "a printed form which would make . . . [the employee] feel that it was a standard paragraph which could not be altered."[84] This would appear to depart radically from general contract law principles.

Third, several courts have refused to enforce a harsh termination clause that is introduced into a pre-existing employment contract on the ground that there is no fresh consideration from the employer to

---

80   Example: *Lloyd v. Oracle Corporation of Canada Inc.*, [2005] C.L.L.C. ¶210-006 at 141,044–45 (Ont. S.C.J.), where the court interpreted a notice provision almost identical to that in *MacAlpine, ibid.*, as precluding the implication of a reasonable notice period. See also *Allen v. Bosley Real Estate Ltd.* (2003), 27 C.C.E.L. (3d) 183 at 185 (Ont. S.C.J.), where a clause providing for one month's notice for each year of service was upheld.

81   Examples: *Burden v. Eastgate Ford Sales and Service (82) Co.* (1992), 93 C.L.L.C. ¶14,002 at 12,012 (Ont. Gen. Div.); *Ellison v. Burnaby Hospital Society* (1992), 92 C.L.L.C. ¶14,042 at 12,268–69 (B.C.S.C.); *Jones v. Consumers Packaging Inc.* (1996), 14 C.C.E.L. (2d) 273 at 181 (Ont. Gen. Div.).

82   Example: *Lyonde v. Canadian Acceptance Corp.* (1983), 3 C.C.E.L. 220 (Ont. H.C.J.).

83   *Brode v. Fitzwright Co.* (1992), 41 C.C.E.L. 289 at 296–97 (B.C.S.C.).

84   *Wegg v. National Trust Co.* (1993), 47 C.C.E.L. 104 at 111 (Ont. Gen. Div.).

support the employee's promise to honour the new notice provision.[85] Of course, general contract law doctrine requires that in order to amend the terms of an existing contract, fresh consideration is required from the promisee over and above the performance of pre-existing contractual obligations. The courts have refused to hold that the employer's forbearance to terminate an employment contract is good enough consideration to support the introduction of a harsh termination clause into the employment contract, in the absence of concrete evidence that the employer really would have lawfully dismissed the employee had he or she not accepted the clause.[86] In the absence of such evidence, it would be fictitious to say that the employer had bargained for the harsh termination clause in exchange for not terminating the contract.

Fourth, the courts may avoid a termination clause as being unconscionable if "an employee's level of responsibility and corresponding status has escalated so significantly during his period of employment that it can be concluded that the substratum of an employment contract entered into at the time of his original hiring has disappeared or it can be implied that that contract could not have been intended to apply to the position in the company ultimately occupied by him."[87] However, a termination clause will not be avoided under these circumstances if the employer clearly brings to the employee's attention at the date of any promotion the fact that the termination clause is to remain in the contract, thereby giving the employee the opportunity to bargain it out of the contract. Of course, the reality is that few employees would avail themselves of such an opportunity in the excitement of a promotion, especially if doing so might tempt the employer to change its mind. Most courts have been reluctant to aggressively use the doctrine of unconscionability to strike down unfair termination clauses. The Ontario Court of Appeal, for example, has rejected the notion (accepted by one British Columbia trial court[88]) that the employment relationship is inherently one-sided such as to raise a presumption of uncon-

---

85 Examples: *Hobbs v. TDI Canada Ltd.*, [2005] C.L.L.C. ¶210-031 at 141,252 (Ont. C.A.) [*Hobbs*]; *Watson v. Moore Corp.* (1996), 20 C.C.E.L. (2d) 21 (B.C.C.A.) See also Chapter 3 for information on modifying the terms of employment contracts.

86 *Ibid.*

87 *Nardocchio v. Canadian Imperial Bank of Commerce* (1979), 41 N.S.R. (2d) 26 (S.C. T.D.); *Wallace v. T.D. Bank* (1983), 83 C.L.L.C. ¶14,031 at 12,141 (Ont. C.A.), rev'g (1981), 39 O.R. (2d) 350 (H.C.J.) [*T.D. Bank*]. See generally B. Etherington, "The Enforcement of Harsh Termination Provisions in Personal Employment Contracts: The Rebirth of Freedom of Contract in Ontario" (1990) 35 McGill L.J. 459.

88 *Dolden v. Clarke Simpkins Ltd.* (1983), 3 C.C.E.L. 153, especially at 163 (B.C.S.C.).

scionability.[89] Instead, the court held that the employee must identify specific "oppressive or unconscionable acts"[90] on the employer's part at the date of hiring in order to render a contractual provision void for unconscionability. In particular, the court has refused to base unconscionability on the fact that the employee had accepted the job out of financial necessity in response to a "take it or leave it" ultimatum by the employer.[91]

Fifth, some courts have held that if an employer terminates an employee upon short or no notice, pursuant to a contractual provision giving the employer a broad discretion to terminate the relationship, there is an implied term in the contract requiring the employer to exercise its discretion in good faith and fairly.[92] This ruling gives the court potentially broad power to control abuse of harsh termination provisions, but as yet few cases have arisen on point. The recognition of an implied duty of fairness on employers in this context is also signficant as part of a movement towards recognizing a general common law duty of fairness on employers under the employment contract.[93] In Alberta, however, the courts refuse to imply the requirement of fairness into these clauses, reasoning that the parties intend them to be clean-break provisions.[94]

Finally, an express termination clause that provides for less notice than required under the employment standards act will be avoided. In its place, the court must imply a reasonable notice period according to the usual factors without drawing any inference from the expunged notice clause that the parties intended a shorter than usual notice period.[95]

The practice of most modern courts to circumvent express notice clauses reflects the dominant tendency in Canadian employment law since the 1950s of extending employee rights. As yet, this practice has not changed despite the increasing pressure on Canadian employers in the "new economy" to improve productive efficiency by (among other

---

89   *T.D. Bank*, above note 87; *Matthewson v. Aiton Power Ltd.* (1985), 8 C.C.E.L. 312 (Ont. C.A.) [*Matthewson*].

90   *Matthewson, ibid.* at 314; *T.D. Bank, ibid.*

91   *Matthewson, ibid.*, especially at 314–15.

92   *Truckers Garage Inc. v. Krell* (1994), 3 C.C.E.L. (2d) 157 (Ont. C.A.) [*Truckers Garage*].

93   Despite pressures to recognize such an implied term, the Supreme Court of Canada refused to recognize it in *Wallace v. United Grain Growers Ltd.*, [1997] 3 S.C.R. 701 [*Wallace*], considered in Section B(3)(c)(vi), below in this chapter.

94   *Meyer v. Partec Lavalin Inc.* (2001), 11 C.C.E.L. (3d) 56 at 61–62 (Alta. C.A.) [*Meyer*]; *Goering v. Mayfair Golf and Country Club Ltd.*, [2001] C.L.L.C. ¶210-038, at 141,282–83 (Alta. Q.B.) [*Goering*].

95   *Machtinger v. HOJ Industries Ltd.*, [1992] 1 S.C.R. 986 [*Machtinger*].

things) minimizing the cost of terminating employees. Indeed, if these competitive pressures intensify, Canadian employers may be induced to have greater resort than before to harsh termination clauses. In addition, an efficiency-oriented government might consider legislating the requirement that employment contracts contain an express notice period to be renegotiated at regular intervals, for example, every two years and upon each promotion.[96] This would reduce the uncertainty of the current law, reduce the amount of litigation, and most likely reduce the reasonable notice periods by making them responsive to market forces instead of judicial fiat. While this scheme would have the advantage of making it easier for employers to terminate employees for *bona fide* economic reasons, it creates the risk of employers abusing short notice clauses in order to fire employees for alleged misconduct or incompetence. In order to protect the employee against this risk, unjust dismissal legislation whereby adjudicators can review the substantive fairness of the employer's allegations and order compulsory reinstatement and other "make whole" remedies would also have to be introduced. Effectively, this scheme would strike a balance between increasing the employer's flexibility to terminate employees for economic reasons and increasing the employee's protection where termination is based on personal misconduct or incompetence. Next, we examine how courts proceed to determine the notice period in the absence of such a clause.

b) Implied Terms Reflecting the Parties' Factual Expectations about the Notice Period

Strict contract law theory dictates that, before proceeding to imply a reasonable notice period according to their perception of what is fair, courts should attempt to ground implied terms concerning the notice period on evidence of the parties' factual intentions, such as their past practices and personnel documentation. However, few courts have done so. Instead, most judges have proceeded directly to fashioning a reasonable notice period without searching for hard evidence of the parties' factual intentions. Possibly this is because the judges wish to preserve their flexibility to fashion a reasonable notice period that will adequately protect the employee's interests, without being hamstrung by the parties' factual intentions for a shorter notice period.

However, several courts have sought to reaffirm the strict contractualist approach by insisting that the length of the notice period must

---

96   See G. England, "Recent Developments in Individual Employment Law: Tell Me the Old, Old Story" (2002) 9 C.L.E.L.J. 37 at 62–65.

be determined according to the parties' factual intentions at the date they originally made their contract or at the date the contract was last amended (for example, if the employee was promoted).[97] The policy underlying this view appears to be to shorten notice periods, which the judges in question clearly regard as having become excessively long.[98] It is submitted that if the real concern with notice periods is their long length, then this should be addressed squarely by the judges rather than attempting to cloak the issue as a debate about contract law doctrine. Indeed, despite what some judges profess, the factual intention approach is not untainted by policy considerations. On the contrary, the quest for a real factual intent is normally illusory, since the parties generally would not have turned their minds to the length of the notice period when they created or last amended their agreement; if asked, they would probably have said that they would go with the prevailing reasonable notice period recognized at common law. The factual intent test, therefore, becomes to a large extent a "fictive formality" to effectuate judicial policy making.

Nevertheless, the strict factual intention approach to implying the notice period has not been adopted by the vast majority of courts.[99] Most judges simply ignore the controversy and determine the reasonable notice period in the usual way. Others have sought to blend factual intent into the reasonableness test by stating that the parties' factual expectations based on their understandings, past practices, and personnel documentation are relevant as one factor in the broader test of reasonableness.[100] It remains unclear under the blended approach

---

97 Southin J.A. of the British Columbia Court of Appeal has been a strong supporter of this approach: see, e.g., *Woodlock v. Novacorp International Consulting Inc.* (1990), 32 C.C.E.L. 245 at 270 (B.C.C.A.); *Foster v. Kockums Cancer Division Hawker Siddeley Canada Inc.* (1993), 83 B.C.L.R. (2d) 207 (C.A.); *Pelech v. Hyundai Auto Canada Inc.* (1991), 40 C.C.E.L. 87 (B.C.C.A.). See also *Bartlam v. Saskatchewan Crop Insurance Corp.* (1993), 49 C.C.E.L. 141 (Sask. Q.B.) [*Bartlam*]; *Yosyk v. Westfair Foods Ltd.* (1988), 49 D.L.R.(4th) 260 at 263 (Man. C.A.), Twaddle J.A., citing *Lazarowicz v. Orenda Engines Ltd.*, [1961] O.R. 141, especially at 144 (H.C.J.). But Twaddle J.A. later changed his mind in *Wiebe v. Canadian Transport Refrigeration (Manitoba) Ltd.*, [1994] 6 W.W.R. 305 at 309 (Man. C.A.) [*Wiebe*].

98 See, for example, the strong economic analysis against excessive notice periods provided by Klebuc J. in *Bartlam, ibid.*, in support of the factual intent approach.

99 Even the British Columbia Court of Appeal has disavowed it in *Porter v. Highmont Operating Corp.* (1991), 36 C.C.E.L. 1 at 4 [*Highmont*].

100 Kroft J.A. in *Wiebe*, above note 97 at 319; Iaccobucci J. in *Machtinger*, above note 95 at 997–98, *obiter*; *Slater v. Sandwell Inc.* (1994), 5 C.C.E.L. (2d) 308 (Ont. Gen. Div.).

which will prevail—the parties' factual intentions or other general policy factors—where an unavoidable conflict exists between what the parties expect their notice period to be and what the reasonableness test would normally dictate.

c) "Reasonable" Notice of Termination at Common Law

The seminal enunciation of the "reasonableness" test is that of McRuer C.J. in *Bardal v. The Globe & Mail Ltd.*,[101] a 1960 decision of the Ontario High Court:

> There can be no catalogue laid down as to what is reasonable notice in particular classes of cases. The reasonableness of the notice must be decided with reference to each particular case, having regard to the character of the employment, the length of service of the servant, the age of the servant and the availability of similar employment, having regard to the experience, training and qualifications of the servant.[102]

Today, most judges continue to apply this test. Contrary to popular belief, the courts do not base the reasonable notice period on one month for each year of prior service with the employer; doing so would impair their flexibility to take account of the different circumstances of each case.[103] Indeed, the test has become the vehicle for effectuating a broad range of policy considerations,[104] including but not limited to those mentioned by McRuer C.J. These are as follows: to cushion the worker against the blow of unemployment, to recognize the employee's seniority, to protect the employee who has been induced to leave a secure job to work for the employer, to discourage employers from handling terminations in an unprofessional manner, to reward employees in high-status occupations, and to relieve the costs of termination for employers who are facing a financial exigency. Many courts also appear to

---

101 Above note 76.

102 *Ibid.* at 145. Empirical evidence on the relative importance of the various factors is provided by S.L. McShane & D.C. McPhillips, "Predicting Reasonable Notice in Canadian Wrongful Dismissal Cases" (1987) 41 Indus. & Lab. Rel. Rev. 108 [McShane & McPhillips].

103 *Minott v. O'Shanter Development Co.* (1999), 168 D.L.R. (4th) 270 at 294–95 (Ont. C.A.); *Royster v. 3584747 Canada Inc.* (2001), 12 C.C.E.L. (3d) 259 at 266 (B.C.S.C.) [*Royster*]; *Milsom v. Corporate Computers Inc.*, [2003] C.L.L.C. ¶210-052 at 141,417 (Alta. Q.B.).

104 In *Erskine v. Viking Helicopter Ltd.* (1991), 35 C.C.E.L. 322 at 326 (Ont. Gen. Div.) [*Erskine*], Matheson J. encapsulated the nature of the inquiry as follows: "Each judge must determine, and from his own experience of life, what appears to be logical, judicious, fair, equitable, sensible and not excessive."

utilize the reasonable notice test as an indirect way of infusing a "make whole" element into the award of damages for wrongful dismissal. The "make whole" theory, commonly applied by tribunals under the human rights legislation and by courts under the *Charter*, seeks to place employees in the position where they would have been but for the wrongful dismissal, that is, to restore the *status quo ante*.[105] At common law, however, damages can be awarded only for entitlements that would vest during the notice period.[106] Thus, most courts will award a lengthy notice period where the employee is unable to find replacement work in order to make the person whole to the fullest extent permissible under the common law rules. Often, these policies are not outwardly enunciated in the courts' judgments and even when specifically addressed, they are not comprehensively examined. Not surprisingly, the law on point is extremely uncertain, making it difficult for potential litigants to predict their precise rights and obligations. Consequently, most lawsuits are settled by negotiation prior to trial, with the financial resources of the respective litigants—rather than jurisprudential niceties—frequently determining the outcome. Of course, employees generally have less financial staying power than their employer, putting them at a disadvantage in the bargaining process.

The general trend since the 1950s has been for courts to lengthen the period of reasonable notice, the paramount objective being to help employees withstand the financial blow of unemployment.[107] For example, while *Bardal* itself was a breakthrough case in awarding twelve months' notice, today awards of twenty-four months are not uncommon in the case of older, high-status workers with little realistic chance of finding replacement work.[108] Indeed, even lengthier notice periods

---

105 See Chapter 7.

106 *Vorvis v. Insurance Corporation of British Columbia*, [1989] 1 S.C.R. 1085 at 1096–97 [*Vorvis*], examined below at note 577 and accompanying text.

107 In *Bramble v. Medis Health and Pharmaceutical Services Inc.*, (1999), 99 C.L.L.C. ¶210-045 at 141,357 (N.B.C.A.) [*Bramble*], Drapeau J.A. described the the cushion policy as being the "primary factor." See also *Mastrogiuseppe v. Bank of Nova Scotia*, [2006] C.L.L.C. ¶210-006 at 141,042 and 141,054 (Ont. S.C.J.) [*Mastrogiuseppe*].

108 *Lowndes v. Summit Ford Sales Ltd.*, [2006] C.L.L.C. ¶210-005 at 141,038–39 (Ont. C.A.), where the court substituted twenty-four months for the trial judge's award of thirty-six months; *Gismondi v. City of Toronto*, [2003] C.L.L.C. ¶210-043 at 141,348 (Ont. C.A.), where twenty-four months was substituted for the trial judge's award of twenty-seven months; *Webster v. British Columbia (Hydro and Power Authority)* (1992), 42 C.C.E.L. 105 at 109 (B.C.C.A) , Legg J.A. where the unofficial ceiling was set at twenty-four months. However, in *Chorny v. Freightliner of Canada Ltd.* (1995), 9 C.C.E.L. (2d) 11 at 21 (B.C.S.C.) [*Chorny*], Wetmore J. suggested that even this limit may be exceeded: "One must wonder

have been awarded in such circumstances as where the employee's chances of finding replacement work are slim or where the employee was induced to leave a previous secure job on the understanding that the new position would be highly secure.[109] Furthermore, this practice is not limited to high echelon employees; rather, the courts have now begun to award increasingly lengthy notice periods for relatively low-skilled workers, as well.[110] (Even an already long notice period may be significantly extended if the court awards a *Wallace* extension to reflect the fact that the employer handled the dismissal in a bad faith or an unprofessional manner.[111]) Currently, the courts still accord primacy to the policy of cushioning the employee, despite Canadian employers wanting to reduce the costs of discarding redundant labour in the face of intense overseas competition. We saw earlier that the economic costs and benefits of providing employees with generous severance payments remain unclear.[112] As of yet, there have been no empirical studies of the costs and benefits of the practice of determining reasonable notice periods under common law. Some judges have, however, expressed concern that common law notice periods have become excessive and have used various legal techniques, such as the factual intention approach described above,[113] to shorten them. Today, a tension exists between two judicial camps—the majority camp that favours awarding gener-

---

why the magic number is twenty-four. Judas found the magic number for his breach of the covenant at thirty."

109 Examples: *Baranowski v. Binks Manufacturing Co.*, [2000] C.L.L.C. ¶210-016 at 141,141 (Ont. S.C.J.) [*Baranowski*], where thirty months' basic reasonable notice was awarded to a senior executive, 54, with twenty-nine years of seniority, who had been explicitly guaranteed a "job for life" ten years previously—the employee was awarded a further six months for bad faith dismissal under the *Wallace* doctrine, examined below in Section B(3)(c)(vi); *Walsh v. UPM-Kymmene Miramichi Inc.* (2003), 25 C.C.E.L. (3d) 13 at 20 (N.B.C.A.) [*Walsh*], where twenty-eight months was awarded to two lower level mill supervisors, both 52 with thirty-one years of seniority, who had little chance of finding replacement work; *Donovan v. New Brunswick Publishing Co.* (1996), 469 A.P.R. 40 (N.B.C.A.) [*Donovan*], where twenty-eight months was awarded to an executive sports editor, 57, with thirty-six years of seniority; *Cowper v. Atomic Energy of Canada Ltd.* (1999), 43 C.C.E.L. (2d) 276 (Ont. S.C.J.), aff'd [2000] O.J. No. 1730 (C.A.) [*Cowper*], where twenty-seven months was awarded to a senior manager, 60, with thirty-five years of seniority.
110 See Section B(3)(c)(ii), below in this chapter.
111 Example: *George v. Imagineering Ltd.* (2001), 14 C.C.E.L. (3d) 102 at 111 (Ont. S.C.J.) [*George*], where 25.5 months basic reasonable notice was awarded, as well as five months for bad faith dismissal; *Baranowski*, above note 109, where 30 months' basic reasonable notice was awarded, as well as a further six months for bad faith dismissal. The *Wallace* doctrine is examined in Section B(3)(c)(vi), below.
112 Above note 1 and accompanying text.
113 See the authorities cited in note 97, above, and accompanying text.

ous notice periods to protect the employee and the minority camp that favours reducing notice periods to minimize the employer's termination costs. The future development of the caselaw in this area will be heavily influenced by the preferences of individual judges belonging to one camp or the other.

i)   The Availability of Replacement of Work: The Cushion Rationale
In determining the period of reasonable notice, the courts have always[114] placed paramount weight on whether or not the employee can reasonably be expected to find replacement work, recognizing that employees need a financial cushion to support them while they conduct a job search.[115] Accordingly, courts will examine the state of the general labour market for persons with the plaintiff's skills, expertise, and experience, along with any personal characteristics of the plaintiff that may impede or facilitate obtaining another job, such as age and the degree to which skills and experience are firm specific rather than of general marketability—the other factors cited above in the *Bardal*[116] case are largely proxies for the worker's employability. Furthermore, many courts have increased the notice period because the employer's handling of the dismissal impaired the plaintiff's chances of finding another job—for example, where the employer did not notify the employee of his or her impending termination without good reason until the last moment,[117] dismissed the employee in a manner that diminished his or her professional reputation,[118] refused to provide the employee with a fair reference,[119] or dismissed the employee in a callous or otherwise unprofessional manner.[120]

---

114 Even nineteenth-century judges acknowledged the importance of this factor, e.g., *Morrison v. Abernethy School Board* (1876), 3 R. 945 at 950, Lord Deas (Ct. Sess., Scot).
115 See above note 107, where, Drapeau J.A. in *Bramble* described this as the "primary factor." Excellent examples include *Mastrogiuseppe*, above note 107; *Leduc v. Canadian Erectors Ltd.* (1996), 96 C.L.L.C. ¶210-024 at 14,1202 (Ont. Gen. Div.); *Baranowski*, above note 109; *Walsh*, above note 109; *Donovan*, above note 109, *Cowper*, above note 109.
116 Above note 76 and accompanying text.
117 *Cagigal v. Mill Dining Lounge Ltd.* (1991), 36 C.C.E.L. 21 at 29 (Ont. Gen. Div.), aff'd (1994), 3 C.C.E.L. (2d) 93 (Ont. C.A.).
118 *Mastrogiuseppe*, above note 107,
119 *Gillman v. Saan Stores Ltd.* (1992), 45 C.C.E.L. 9 at 19 (Alta. Q.B.) [*Gillman*]. However, some judges have declined to increase the notice period on this ground, e.g., *Wadden v. Guaranty Trust Co. of Canada* (1987), 49 Alta. L.R. (2d) 348 at 354, Virtue J. (Q.B.).
120 Example: *Wallace*, above note 93, where the Court emphasized that the notice period can be extended under this heading even though the effect of the

Nevertheless, the cushion rationale is not absolute, and the courts will reduce the notice period if an employee who has received advance notice of termination does not aggressively seek alternative employment[121] or if an employee does not aggressively seek replacement work following his or her termination.[122] Furthermore, several courts have balked at increasing the length of notice periods in order to cushion employees in tough economic times when the employer, too, is being harmed by the same economic conditions. Instead, these courts have sought to share the burden of economic downswings by reducing the notice periods from what they would be if the cushion rationale were applied purely from the employee's perspective. This practice was initiated during the recession of the early 1980s by the decision of the Ontario High Court in *Bohemier v. Storwal International Inc.*[123] The High Court stated that if it awarded the usual notice period based on the cushion policy for a person in the plaintiff's position—he had thirty-five years of seniority and was 59—the effect would be to "unduly impair or render illusory" the company's ability to discard workers in tough economic times. Consequently, the High Court awarded eight months' reasonable notice. The Ontario Court of Appeal[124] increased this to eleven months on the ground that the High Court had undervalued the plaintiff's age, length of service, and proximity to pensionable retirement age. Nonetheless, the Court of Appeal approved of the High Court's remarks that account must be taken of economic hardship on the employer when determining the notice period.

The subsequent history of the *Bohemier* doctrine is significant in showing how changing economic conditions influence the development of the common law of the employment contract. Thus, during the economic boom of the late 1980s, the *Bohemier* doctrine fell into disuse, with most courts either refusing to apply it or merely paying it lip service

---

employer's conduct is not to extend the period of unemployment. See also *Plitt v. P.P.G. Canada Inc.* (1992), 92 C.L.L.C. ¶14,041 at 12,263 (Ont. Gen. Div.), where the employer's actions did exacerbate the plaintiff's difficulties in finding replacement work.

121 Example: *Highmont*, above note 99 at 5.

122 Example: *Shinn v. TBC Teletheatre B.C.* (2001), 6 C.C.E.L. (3d) 244 at 252 (B.C.C.A.), where a marketer of televised betting on horse races who could not find another job in that industry was expected to search for employment as a marketer in other industries.

123 (1982), 142 D.L.R. (3d) 8 (Ont. H.C.J.), var'd while affirming this reason (1983), 44 O.R. (2d) 361 (C.A.), leave to appeal to S.C.C. refused, [1984] 1 S.C.R. xiii [*Bohemier*].

124 *Ibid.*

by professing to seek a "middle ground"[125] between the interests of both parties, without diluting the traditional cushion rationale. But the doctrine was revived during the 1990s, as the sting of foreign competition and other economic forces drove Canadian employers to downsize their labour forces. In a 1991 decision of the Ontario High Court, Matheson J. explained his rationale for applying the doctrine as follows:

> To one who studied economics in the thirties . . . the idea of the courts shielding society from unemployment appears as unreasonable as Canute holding back the tide . . . . If there be any merit in the principle of a market economy it is surely that it enables the factors of production, including the important component of labour, to respond naturally, efficiently, and rapidly to changes in the demand and supply curves. Whatever obstructs natural market forces prolongs disruption and economic hardship. Nor is it reasonable, equitable, fair, or just that when hard times descend like the plague and hundreds or thousands of worthy employees are thrown out of work, the few who rush to the courts are accorded a preferred treatment.[126]

Today, while some courts apply the *Bohemier* doctrine in the strict form outlined by Matheson J.,[127] most either continue to apply the traditional practice of increasing the notice period so as to cushion the employee during tough economic times[128] or seek to balance the hardship felt by both sides.[129] Even when the *Bohemier* doctrine is applied, the courts will safeguard against trumped-up claims of economic adversity

---

125 Example: *Hunter v. Northwood Pulp & Timber Ltd.* (1985), 7 C.C.E.L. 260 (B.C.C.A.).

126 *Erskine*, above note 104.

127 Examples: *Bartlam*, above note 97 at 158; *Atkins v. Windsor Star* (1994), 2 C.C.E.L. (2d) 229 at 236 (Ont. Gen. Div.); *Cronk v. Canadian General Insurance Company* (1995), 95 C.L.L.C. ¶210-038 (Ont. C.A.) [*Cronk*], where Weiler J.A., in an *obiter dictum*, endorsed the principle, at least in "mass termination" situations (at 141,303).

128 Examples: *Lim v. Delrina (Canada) Corp.* (1995), 8 C.C.E.L. (2d) 219 at 226 (Ont. Gen. Div.) [*Lim*]; *Dey v. Valley Forest Products Ltd.* (1995), 11 C.C.E.L. (2d) 1 at 9–10 (N.B.C.A.); *MacDonald v. Royal Canadian Legion* (1995), 12 C.C.E.L. (2d) 211 at 221 (N.S.S.C.).

129 Examples: *Miller v. Fetterly and Associates Inc.* (1999), 44 C.C.E.L. (2d) 11 at 45 (N.S.S.C.T.D.), where the notice period was reduced to reflect the fact that the employer was a small firm that could not afford to pay a substantial damages award. See also *Garvin v. Rockwell International of Canada Ltd.* (1993), 50 C.C.E.L. 295 at 307–8 (Ont. Gen. Div.) [*Garvin*]; *Stewart v. British Columbia Sugar Refinery Co.* (1994), 2 C.C.E.L. (2d) 125 at 131 (Man. Q.B.) [*B.C. Sugar Refinery*]; *Shmyr v. Lakeland Regional Health Authority* (1996), 23 C.C.E.L. (2d) 255 at 262–63 (Alta. Q.B.), but note that the court awarded the worker twenty-four months' notice anyway.

on the employer's part. Accordingly, before reducing the notice period for the benefit of the employer, the courts have examined the veracity of any alleged financial exigency, with the burden of proof falling on the employer;[130] have required the employer to exhaust other reasonable cost-saving methods; have required corporate conglomerates to provide financial assistance to plants that are in trouble from profitable plants;[131] have required the employer to ride out what the courts consider to be short-term economic difficulties;[132] and have disagreed with the employer's assessment that the seriousness of its economic difficulties warrants reducing notice periods.[133] Possibly, the *Bohemier* doctrine may become more popular as a device for minimizing employer's termination costs as the pressure on Canadian employers to increase their competitiveness increases, but as yet, the traditional cushion rationale still reigns supreme.

ii)   *Status of the Job*

Traditionally, courts have increased the length of the notice period for employees in high-status occupations,[134] irrespective of other factors, such as the availability of alternative employment. For example, a company president and chief executive officer was awarded eighteen months' notice on this ground, even though he had been employed by the firm for only two years and was relatively young at age 47.[135] The main yardsticks of occupational status are qualifications, education, responsibility, training, experience, and in particular, salary.[136] The courts are not restricted to a formal job description, but will examine what the employee actually does.[137] The traditional practice is arguably justified on any of three grounds. The length of the notice period can

---

130 *Pauloski v. Nascor Inc.* (2002), 16 C.C.E.L. (3d) 202 at 222 (Alta. Q.B.) [*Pauloski*]; *Russell v. Winnifred Stewart Assn. for the Mentally Handicapped* (1993), 49 C.C.E.L. 177 at 180 (Alta. Q.B.); *B.C. Sugar Refinery, ibid.* at 132; *McCrea v. Conference Board of Canada* (1993), 45 C.C.E.L. 29 at 37 (Ont. Gen. Div.).

131 *Pechenkov v. Borg-Warner (Canada) Ltd.* (1983), 2 C.C.E.L. 237 at 239 (Ont. Co. Ct.).

132 Example: *Carson v. Luncheonette Ltd.* (1987), 65 Nfld. & P.E.I.R. 318 (Nfld. S.C.T.D.).

133 *Plummer v. W. Carsen Co.* (1985), 10 C.C.E.L. 19 (Ont. Dist. Ct.).

134 Example: *Ansari v. British Columbia (Hydro and Power Authority)* (1986), 2 B.C.L.R. (2d) 33 at 38 (S.C.), aff'd (1986), 55 B.C.L.R. (2d) xxxiii (C.A.).

135 *Larsen v. Saskatchewan Transportation Co.* (1992), 47 C.C.E.L. 238 (Sask. Q.B.), var'd (1993), 49 C.C.E.L. 165 (Sask. C.A.). See also *Marshall v. Watson Wyatt and Co.* (2002), 16 C.C.E.L. (3d) 162 at 169 (Ont. C.A.) [*Marshall*], where a senior manager was awarded nine months even though he had been employed for only one year.

136 *Lim*, above note 128 at 222 (Ont. Gen. Div.); *Cronk*, above note 127 at 141,294 and 141,305.

137 *Pioro v. Calian Technology Services Ltd.* (2000), 3 C.C.E.L. (3d) 47 (Ont. S.C.J.).

be seen as part of the package of incentives that firms pay in order to persuade potential recruits to accept and remain in high-status positions that typically demand considerable education and training expenses and involve a relatively high degree of career risk. It also relates to compensating high-status workers for the additional costs they incur in finding replacement work because their skills may be firm specific, their job search and relocation costs may be relatively high, and there may be fewer vacancies in high-level positions than in lower level ones. Finally, it helps compensate high-status employees for the stigma of being dismissed and for the downgrading in their lifestyles that results from being unemployed.

These rationales are controversial, both morally and empirically. Indeed, in its 1999 decision in *Bramble v. Medis Health and Inc.*, the New Brunswick Court of Appeal explicitly rejected them and held that there is no rule of law in New Brunswick that automatically entitles high-echelon employees to a lengthier notice period than low-echelon employees; rather, the cushion policy is paramount in determining the reasonable notice period of all employees, irrespective of their job status.[138] The court followed a 1994 decision of an Ontario trial judge, MacPherson J. (as he then was), who had ruled that low-status employees are entitled to the same notice as high-status employees if the economic and psychological harm of being unemployed is equally as severe for them.[139] According to MacPherson J., occupational status *simpliciter* does not operate to lengthen notice periods; rather, the employee's degree of need alone counts. However, the Ontario Court of Appeal quashed this decision and reaffirmed the traditional principle that occupational status *simpliciter* increases the length of reasonable notice.[140] As can be seen, the law in Ontario today differs from that in New Brunswick.

It may have been unnecessary to launch a frontal assault on the traditional principle in order to alleviate the lot of low-status workers: the reasonableness test has proven to be sufficiently malleable to permit courts to narrow the gap and award relatively long notice periods to low-status workers who are clearly in need of a generous financial cushion.[141] Be that as it may, the traditional practice of increasing the

138 *Bramble*, above note 107 at 141,356–59.

139 *Cronk v. Canadian General Insurance Co.* (1995), 19 O.R. (3d) 515 (Gen. Div.).

140 Above note 127. For a full analysis of this and other aspects of the case, see G. England, "Determining Reasonable Notice of Termination at Common Law: The Implications of *Cronk v. Canadian General Insurance Co.*" (1996) 4 C.L.E.L.J. 115.

141 Examples: *Tanton v. Crane Canada Inc.*, [2001] C.L.L.C. ¶210-023 at 141,154 (Alta. Q.B.) [*Tanton*], where a physically and mentally challenged warehouse labourer,

notice period of high-status employees on the basis of their occupational status *simpliciter* continues to represent the law in all provinces save New Brunswick.

iii) Length of Service

A 1987 study of Canadian wrongful dismissal cases found that the plaintiff's length of service is the most important predictor of reasonable notice, with the plaintiff receiving about three months' notice for every ten years of seniority with his or her employer.[142] The recent proliferation of short-term employment may result in courts giving greater credit to relatively short periods of seniority than they did before in determining the notice period, but they have not done so yet. Most courts treat seniority as a proxy of employability — more senior workers are older and therefore encounter greater difficulty in securing replacement work than younger workers; however, some courts appear to accord intrinsic worth to seniority, outside of the cushion rationale.[143]

In determining how much seniority an employee has accrued for the purpose of reasonable notice, most courts have avoided making a strict contractualist analysis that would mean any severance of the contractual nexus — however brief in duration or technical in nature — rupturing seniority accrual. Instead, these courts have sought to safeguard the employee's cushion by holding that resignations of short duration do not interrupt seniority;[144] that periods of part-time

---

in his mid-fifties and with twenty-five years' service, was awarded twenty-two months' basic reasonable notice, as well as a two-month *Wallace* extension; *Chester v. Pepsi-Cola Canada Ltd.*, [2005] C.L.L.C. ¶210-035 at 141,325 (Sask. Q.B.) [*Chester*], where a 45-year-old delivery driver with a Grade 12 education and twenty years of service, was awarded fourteen months; *Portugal v. Car Park Management Services Ltd.* (2004), 37 C.C.E.L. (3d) 68 at 76 (Ont. S.C.J.), where a car park attendant, 59, with eleven years of service, received twelve months; *Radwan v. Arteif Furniture Manufacturing*, [2002] 11 W.W.R. 559 at 575 (Alta. Q.B.), where a punch press operator, 63, with twenty-five years of service, received twenty months; *Blaikies Dodge Chrysler Ltd. v. Crowe*, [2000] N.S.J. No. 368 (C.A.) [*Blaikies*], where an auto body repairer with sixteen years of service received twelve months.

142 McShane & McPhillips, above note 102 at 115.

143 Examples: *Cronk*, above note 127 at 141,304–5; *Zorn-Smith v. Bank of Montreal* (2004), 31 C.C.E.L. (3d) 267 at 303–4 (Ont. S.C.J.) [*Zorn-Smith*]; *Burry v. Unitel Communications Inc.* (1996), 21 C.C.E.L. (2d) 36 at 42 (B.C.S.C.). But compare *Chorny*, above note 108 at 18. Seniority has a venerable pedigree in the unionized sector.

144 Example: *Immaculate Confection Ltd. v. Claudepierre* (1991), 38 C.C.E.L. 119 (B.C.S.C.), but it is uncertain how long a hiatus is permissible. For example, a one-year absence was held not to rupture continuity in *Krewenchuk v. Lewis Construction Ltd.* (1985), 8 C.C.E.L. 206 (B.C.S.C.).

employment with the same employer count towards seniority accrual, albeit on a pro-rated basis relative to full-time service;[145] that in a situation where one employer is taken over in whole or in part by another company, the parties are presumed to intend that the worker's service with the predecessor employer will count *vis-à-vis* the new employer unless the new employer clearly specifies otherwise;[146] and that absences for child-rearing purposes, even if they are of several years, will not preclude service before the absence from accruing towards seniority.[147] One judge has even suggested, *obiter*, that a plaintiff's previous service with *other* employers can count towards the accrual of seniority for the purpose of reasonable notice, provided that the work previously performed by the employee is so closely "intertwined" with the current employer's business that the employer can be said to obtain a "direct" benefit from the employee's previous work experience.[148]

iv) The Employee's Age

Courts treat age as an important factor in increasing the notice period under the cushion rationale;[149] today, older workers are finding it more difficult to obtain alternative employment than younger workers are, despite the prohibition against age discrimination in the human rights acts.[150]

v) Quality of the Employee's Work Record

An employee will often commit acts of misconduct or incompetence that are not sufficiently serious to warrant summary dismissal under the common law standards of just cause, but are still blameworthy and deserving of some punishment. During the 1980s some courts developed the "near cause" doctrine to deal with this situation. Under this doctrine, the courts would rule that dismissal is wrongful as being without just cause but would reduce the length of the notice period, and therefore the amount of recoverable compensation, in order to reflect

---

145 *Maddocks v. Colonial Management Ltd.* (1991), 35 C.C.E.L. 278 at 280 (N.B.Q.B.T.D.).
146 Examples: *Lingelbach*, above note 48 at 308; *Williams and Pacific Mandate Ltd. v. H.H. Heinz Co. of Canada Ltd.*, [2001] C.L.L.C. ¶210-040 (B.C.S.C.).
147 *Cronk*, above note 127.
148 *Dahdouh v. Hugin Sweda Inc.* (1993), 45 C.C.E.L. 56 at 60 (B.C.S.C.).
149 Example: *Farmer v. Foxridge Homes Ltd.* (1992), 45 C.C.E.L. 144 at 149 (Alta. Q.B.), where Rawlins J. increased the notice period from the norm of nine months in these circumstances to twelve months solely because the plaintiff was 56.
150 See K.J. Gibson, W.J. Zerbe, & R.E. Franken, "Employers' Perceptions of the Re-Employment Barriers Faced by Older Job Hunters" (1993) 48 R.I./I.R. 321.

the employee's contributory blameworthiness.[151] Although this practice appears to make sense—collective agreement arbitrators, for example, typically substitute unpaid suspensions for discharge—it is difficult to square with the contract law principle that an employee's misbehaviour either does or does not constitute a repudiatory breach such as to warrant the employer terminating the contract; there does not appear to be a halfway house at common law. As well, unlike collective agreement arbitrators, who generally reinstate partially blameworthy employees while reducing their compensation, reinstatement is rarely available at common law: the near cause doctrine potentially could deprive a wrongfully dismissed employee of a large part of a cushion against unemployment. Accordingly, most (but not all[152]) courts during the late 1980s and 1990s refused to apply the near cause doctrine,[153] and in 1998, the Supreme Court of Canada unequivocally ruled that it does not form part of the common law.[154] One danger with the latter approach is that courts will now have to take an all-or-nothing approach to employee misbehaviour.[155] Thus, courts might be tempted to find just cause in borderline situations where the employee's conduct comes closer to crossing the line of cause than to not crossing it, rather than allow the employee to recover full compensation. Conversely, the courts might be tempted to find "no cause" where the employee's conduct comes closer to not crossing the line of just cause than it does to crossing it, rather than see the employee go uncompensated. It is unfortunate that the common law cannot accommodate an approach to contributory fault that combines flexibility regarding the substitution

---

151 Example: *Smith v. Dawson Memorial Hospital* (1978), 29 N.S.R. (2d) 277 (S.C.T.D.).

152 Example: *Fleming v. Safety Kleen Canada Inc.* (1996), 20 C.C.E.L. (2d) 140 at 150 (Ont. Gen. Div.) [*Fleming*].

153 The doctrine was forcefully rejected, for instance, in *Helbig v. Oxford Warehousing Ltd.* (1985), 20 D.L.R. (4th) 112, especially at 122 (Ont. C.A.), leave to appeal to S.C.C. refused, [1985] 2 S.C.R. vii; *Steinicke v. Manning Press Ltd.* (1984), 4 C.C.E.L. 294 at 304 (B.C.C.A.), Seaton J.A. [*Steinicke*]; *Skaarup v. Andover & Perth United Farmers' Cooperative Ltd.* (1987), 18 C.C.E.L. 63 (N.B.C.A.); *Rose v. Marystown Shipyard Ltd.* (1985), 6 C.C.E.L. 220 (Nfld. C.A.).

154 *Dowling v. Halifax (City of)*, [1998] 1 S.C.R. 22, rev'g (1996), 136 D.L.R. (4th) 352 (N.S.C.A.) [*Dowling*]; and see G. England, "*Dowling v. Halifax (City of)*: The Shortest Hard Case Ever?" (1998) 6 C.L.E.L.J. 455.

155 See, by analogy, *Port Arthur Shipbuilding Co. v. Arthurs* (1968), [1969] S.C.R. 85, where collective agreement arbitrators were directed by the Court to take such an all-or-nothing approach to just cause clauses in collective agreements. As a result of this decision, the collective bargaining acts in most provinces were amended to permit arbitrators to substitute a lesser penalty than dismissal to reflect contributory fault on the part of the employee.

of a lesser penalty with adequate safeguards of the employee's interest in job security. Be that as it may, anecdotal evidence suggests that
many courts do take account informally of an employee's contributory
fault under the general *Bardal* test, and that practising lawyers generally take account of this factor in negotiating out-of-court settlements,
despite the ruling in *Dowling*. It is unfortunate, albeit perhaps under-
standable, that law and practice appear to diverge in this regard. In
the converse situation, where the employee has an exceptionally good
work record, the courts have generally refused to extend the period of
reasonable notice on this account, reasoning that the the employee was
only doing what he or she was contractually obliged to do.[156]

vi) The Wallace *Doctrine and Other Residual Factors*

The breadth of the reasonableness test has enabled the courts to take
account of a wide variety of residual factors in determining the notice
period according to their perceptions of fairness. Thus, some judges
have increased the notice period if the employee has sustained detrimental reliance as a result of the employer's conduct—for example,
where the employer has induced the employee to resign from a secure
job or to immigrate to Canada[157] on the strength of promises of career
advancement or security of tenure with the employer.[158] However, the
inducement element diminishes in importance the longer the employee
works in the new job.[159] (Precontractual representations made by an
employer regarding the security of the job may be actionable in the
tort of negligent misrepresentation, as terms of the main contract, or
as a collateral contract.[160]) On the other hand, the notice period will
be reduced if the employee knows or ought reasonably to know that

---

156 *Steinicke*, above note 153 at 297 (B.C.C.A.). But compare *Pearl v. Pacific Enercon Inc.* (1985), 7 C.C.E.L. 252, especially at 256 (B.C.C.A.), where it was suggested that an excellent record may be relevant as a secondary factor in lengthening the notice period.

157 Example: *I.S.S. Information System Services Ltd. v. Smyth* (1985), 7 C.C.E.L. 35 (B.C. Co. Ct.).

158 This principle was confirmed by the Supreme Court of Canada in *Wallace*, above note 93 at 737–39. Later examples include *Egan v. Alcatel Canada Inc.* (2004), 33 C.C.E.L (3d) 275 at 282–83 (Ont. S.C.J.), aff'd [2006] C.L.L.C. ¶210-004 (Ont. C.A.); *Antidormi v. Blue Pumpkin Software Inc.* (2004), 35 C.C.E.L. (3d) 247 at 266 (Ont. S.C.J.) [*Antidormi*].

159 Example: *Robinson v. Fraser Wharves Ltd*, [2000] B.C.J. No. 212 (S.C.) [*Robinson*], where the inducement factor was given no weight after the plaintiff had worked in the job for nine years.

160 See Chapter 3.

his or her new job is insecure,[161] something that may be obvious from
from the cyclical nature of the industry, for example.[162] Compassion
has also led some courts to extend the notice period so that the employee can qualify for a vested pension, but only a short extension of a
few days will be granted.[163] Concern with equality has led some courts
to take account of severance payments given to other workers by the
company in determining the plaintiff's notice period.[164] Moreover, we
saw earlier that if the employer's conduct makes it more difficult for the
employee to find replacement work—for example, if an unprofessionally handled termination causes the employee psychological harm or
diminishes the employee's reputation with potential employers, or if
the employer fails to give the employee timely advance notice of layoff
or a fair reference[165]—the notice period may be lengthened.

Furthermore, the Supreme Court of Canada held in its 1997 decision in *Wallace*[166] that the period of reasonable notice can be extended
if the employer handles the dismissal in a callous or insensitive manner or in bad faith. This extension can be made even if the employee's
unemployment is not lengthened by such conduct and even if the employee does not suffer any psychological harm due to the employer's actions.[167] The *Wallace* doctrine, therefore, carries a discernibly punitive
whiff, the intention being to discourage employers from engaging in
socially unacceptable conduct, as well as to compensate the employee
for any harm sustained. According to Fisher, the average length of a

161 *Wansborough v. N.W.P. Northwood Products Ltd.* (1983), 3 C.C.E.L. 177, especially
at 179–80 (Ont. H.C.J.).
162 Examples: construction, as in *Scapillati v. Potvin Construction Ltd.*, [1999] O.J.
No. 2187 (C.A.); and automobile selling, as in *Skene v. Dearborn Motors Ltd.*,
[1990] B.C.J. No. 135 (C.A.).
163 Example: *Holmes v. PCL Construction Management Inc.* (1994), 8 C.C.E.L. (2d)
192 at 197 (Alta. C.A.); *Duncan v. Cockshutt Farm Equipment Ltd.* (1956), 19
W.W.R. (N.S.) 554 (Man. Q.B.).
164 *Garvin*, above note 129; *Gaudry v. Woodward's Ltd.* (1993), 79 B.C.L.R. (2d) 236
at 238 (C.A.).
165 See the authorities cited in above notes 117–20 above and text accompanying
them.
166 Above note 93 at 741–46. See J. Fudge, "The Limits of Good Faith in the Contract of Employment: From *Addis* to *Vorvis* to *Wallace* and Back Again?" (2007)
32 Queen's L.J. 529; K. VanBuskirk, "Damages for Improvident Employer Behaviour" (2004) 83 Can. Bar Rev. 755; L. Steusser, "Wrongful Dismissal—Playing
Hardball: *Wallace v. United Grain Growers*" (1998) 25 Man. L.J. 547; J. Swan,
"Damages for Wrongful Dismissal: Lessons from *Wallace v. United Grain Growers Ltd.*" (1998) 6 C.L.E.L.J. 313.
167 *Silvester v. Lloyds Register North America* (2004), 30 C.C.E.L. (3d) 200 at 212
(N.S.C.A.) [*Silvester*]; *Marshall*, above note 135.

Wallace extension is 33 percent of the basic reasonable notice period.[168] That means that the *Wallace* factor frequently results in an employee receiving a notice period significantly greater than the current unofficial ceiling of twenty-four months.[169]

The process of awarding a *Wallace* extension differs between the provinces. In British Columbia and Nova Scotia, the courts determine a global notice period without specifying how much is comprised of a *Wallace* extension.[170] Elsewhere, the courts determine the basic period of reasonable notice and then add on the *Wallace* extension. The advantage of the former approach is to make it more difficult to appeal on the basis of the judge having misapplied the *Wallace* doctrine, but the major disadvantage is that the punitive impact of the *Wallace* doctrine may be reduced if employers cannot see exactly how much their aberrant behaviour is costing them.

We examined earlier some of the difficulties with the *Wallace* doctrine.[171] Here, attention is focused on the difficulty of predicting the circumstances under which an extension will be awarded. The initial reaction of employers to *Wallace* was trepidation since it was uncertain how the courts would define the scope of proscribed conduct, and employers feared that the doctrine would hamstring them from launching robust defences to wrongful dismissal suits. However, today the scope of the doctrine has become relatively clear, and the courts have explicitly cautioned counsel against bogging down proceedings with spurious claims, thereby signalling that the doctrine will be applied conservatively.[172] Although some uncertainty must necessarily remain, the following examples of misconduct on the employer's part convey the essence of the matter:

- attempting to justify dismissal on grounds that the employer knows, or ought reasonably to know are unfounded, especially where the

---

168 Barry Fisher, "The *Wallace* Factor: An Analysis of the Effect of the Bad Faith Dismissal Doctrine on Reasonable Notice Periods in Wrongful Dismissal Actions" (Paper presented to Canada Law Book's Canadian Empoyment Law Super Congress, 21–22 October 1998).

169 Example: *George*, above note 111 at 111, where 25.5 months' basic reasonable notice was awarded, as well as five months for bad faith dismissal; *Baranowski*, above note 109, where thirty months' basic reasonable notice was awarded, as well as a further six months for bad faith dismissal.

170 *Clendenning v. Lowndes Lambert (B.C.) Ltd.* (2000), 4 C.C.E.L. (3d) 238 at 259 (B.C.C.A.); *Barakett v. Lévesque Beaubien Geoffrion Inc.* (2001), 12 C.C.E.L. (3d) 24 at 40 (N.S.C.A.) [*Barakett*].

171 See Chapter 5.

172 Example: *Yanez v. Canac Kitchens*, [2005] C.L.L.C. ¶210-025 at 141,213–14 (Ont. S.C.J.).

322 INDIVIDUAL EMPLOYMENT LAW

allegations damage the employee's personal integrity or professional capabilities, and especially where the unfounded grounds are maintained up to the date of the trial in order to pressure the employee into dropping the case;[173]
- handling dismissal in a procedurally unfair manner, for example, by failing to give the employee an opportunity to explain alleged wrongdoings, by disregarding an internal disciplinary procedure, by failing to investigate allegations of wrongdoing made against the employee, by failing to comply with progressive disciplinary measures in appropriate circumstances, and by pretending to consider the employee's story when the dismissal decision has already been finalized;[174]
- attempting to force the employee into resigning by deliberately making life unpleasant;[175]
- attempting to force the employee into failure by deliberately sabotaging his or her work, or by setting unattainable targets so as to justify dismissing the employee; [176]
- responding in a callous and brutal way to an employee who is encountering performance difficulties due to personal or work-related problems;[177]
- terminating an employee in a callous and brutal manner, for example, by expelling the employee from an office in the presence of workmates, or by notifying the employee of the termination when the employee is having medical problems and there is no compelling business reason for handling the termination in that manner;[178]
- utilizing hardball tactics, such as withholding vested entitlements, cajoling the employee into signing a settlement offer on the spur of

---

173 Examples: *Di Carlo v. L.I.U.N.A. Local 1089* (2002), 33 C.C.E.L. (3d) 143 at 156 (Ont. S.C.J.); *Mastrogiuseppe*, above note 107.
174 Examples: *Silvester*, above note 167 at 212; *Robinson*, above note 159; *Baughn v. Offierski*, [2001] O.J. No. 280 (S.C.J.) [*Baughn*].
175 Example: *Keays v. Honda Canada Inc.* (2006), 52 C.C.E.L. (3d) 165 (Ont. C.A.) [*Keays* C.A.].
176 Example: *Mark v. Westend Development Corp.* (2002), 18 C.C.E.L. (3d) 90 at 95 (Ont. S.C.J.).
177 Example: *Lavinskas v. Jacques Whitford and Associates Ltd.*, [2005] C.L.L.C. ¶210-045 at 141,577–78 (Ont. S.C.J.) [*Lavinskas*]; *Rinaldo v. Royal Ontario Museum* (2004), 37 C.C.E.L. (3d) 1 at 29–31 (Ont. S.C.J.).
178 Examples: *Tanton*, above note 141; *Geluch v. Rosedale Golf Association*, [2004] C.L.L.C. ¶210-036 at 141,348 (Ont. S.C.J.) [*Geluch*]; *Kaiser v. Duval* (2002), 17 C.C.E.L. (3d) 194 (N.S.C.A.).

the moment and without legal advice, or purposefully prolonging the litigation so as to "bleed the employee white";[179]

- refusing to give the employee a reference or providing an unfair one out of revenge or spite;[180] and
- badmouthing the employee's personal integrity or professional competence to potential employers out of revenge or spite.[181]

A few factors seem to undermine the deterrence impact of the doctrine. Any extension of the notice period under the *Wallace* doctrine is subject to the employee's duty to mitigate losses in the usual way.[182] Also, the doctrine can produce arbitrary results in that two employees who suffer the same kind of psychological harm as a consequence of employer wrongdoing will receive different amounts of compensation if their respective reasonable notice periods differ: factors such as job status, likelihood of re-employment, and seniority affect these. It can therefore be argued that the law should base compensation on the nature of the employee's psychological harm, not on the factors that determine the reasonable notice period. The Supreme Court of Canada has ruled that the employee's duty to mitigate personal losses does not apply to the *Wallace* component of the reasonable notice period because the ability to replace lost income through mitigation does not alter the psychological harm suffered from the bad faith dismissal.[183]

It should be noted that courts will not refuse to interfere with an employer's severance offer to an employee just because the offer is within the range of what the common law would normally provide, even though it is slightly short of the mark. Rather, the courts will always make their own determination of what constitutes "reasonable" notice. Some courts experimented with this practice in the 1980s,[184] but the effect was to reduce the employee's common law entitlements: employers would deliberately make low-end offers knowing that employees could not afford to proceed with litigation.[185]

---

179 Examples: *English v. Alcatel Networks Corp.* (2002), 18 C.C.E.L. (3d) 289 at 292 (Ont. S.C.J.); *McGeady v. Saskatchewan Wheat Pool* (1998), 40 C.C.E.L. (2d) 218 at 228 (Sask. Q.B.); *Antidormi*, above note 158 at 268.

180 Example: *Barakett*, above note 170 at 39.

181 Example: *Silvester*, above note 167 at 212; *Geluch*, above note 178 at 141,349.

182 The duty to mitigate is examined in Section F(1)(d), below in this chapter.

183 *Evans v. Teamsters Local Union No. 31*, 2008 SCC 20 at para. 32 [*Evans*].

184 Examples: *Roden v. The Toronto Humane Society*, [2005] C.L.L.C. ¶210-043 at 141,430–31 (Ont. C.A.) [*Roden*]; *Rupchan v. Simpson Timber Co. (Saskatchewan)* (1988), 71 Sask. R. 143 at 145 (Q.B.).

185 *Garvin*, above note 129 at 302; *Spooner v. Ridley Terminals Inc.* (1991), 39 C.C.E.L. 65 at 75 (B.C.S.C.).

C. SUMMARY DISMISSAL FOR MISCONDUCT OR INCOMPETENCE

The general principles of contract law provide the legal framework governing summary dismissal without notice or wages in lieu thereof. Thus, the courts reason that if an employee's misconduct or incompetence constitutes a repudiatory breach of the employment contract on his or her part, the employer is released from its obligation to provide notice of termination and can terminate the contract forthwith.[186] In addition to summarily dismissing the worker, the employer can sue for damages for breach of contract; however, this rarely occurs in practice because of the relatively small amounts of money that are at stake and the difficulty of enforcing a judgment debt against a relatively impecunious employee.[187] Of course, the employer can waive the breach and treat the employment contract as still existing, in which case the employer cannot subsequently rely on the employee's conduct as grounds for summary dismissal.

The critical question, therefore, is what constitutes a repudiatory breach of contract on the employee's part such as to warrant summary dismissal. This determination is policy driven, the concept being sufficiently malleable to have enabled the courts to reflect the changing norms of personnel practice regarding industrial discipline.[188] It follows that cases decided in an earlier time when the prevailing standards of industrial discipline were much harsher towards employees than they are today have limited precedential weight. As one English judge commented:

> Many of the decisions which are customarily cited in these cases date from the last century and may be wholly out of accord with current social conditions. What would today be regarded as almost an attitude of Czar-serf, which is to be found in some of the older cases . . . would, I venture to think, be decided differently today. We have by now come to realise that a contract of service imposes upon the parties a duty of mutual respect.[189]

---

186 These principles have been endorsed in innumerable employment law cases on summary dismissal, including *Laws v. London Chronicle (Indicator Newspapers) Ltd.*, [1959] 2 All E.R. 285 (C.A.); *Durand v. Quaker Oats Co. of Canada* (1990), 45 B.C.L.R. (2d) 354 at 361–62 (C.A.).

187 However, more such cases have been reported. See Chapter 4, Section B(6).

188 Only rarely have the courts explicitly acknowledged that the contract law nomenclature has been used to disguise their underlying policy choices and have advocated addressing the policy issues openly and frankly: e.g., *Henry v. Foxco Ltd.* (2004), 31 C.C.E.L. (3d) 72 (N.B.C.A.) [*Foxco*].

189 *Wilson v. Racher*, [1974] I.C.R. 428 at 430 (C.A.).

Modern courts have developed a common law doctrine of just cause that emphasizes safeguarding the personal dignity and autonomy of the employee.[190] This doctrine is reflected in the following main features: First, courts require that the decision to dismiss a worker must be taken in good faith, non-arbitrarily, and without discrimination. Essentially, this means that the worker's conduct must have harmed the production process or the symbolic authority of management to command an order to warrant dismissal; the employer cannot fire an employee for extraneous reasons unrelated to legitimate business interests. It also means that the plaintiff must be accorded the same treatment as other workers unless there are legitimate grounds for differentiation. Second, the courts apply a requirement of proportionality, which means that the ultimate sanction of dismissal can be invoked only for conduct on the employee's part that causes a substantial harm to the employer's interests.[191] Also, proportionality involves taking into account any mitigating factors that reduce the degree of blame on the employee's part or any exacerbating factors that increase the degree of such blame. Third, the courts impose relatively stringent standards of "procedural fairness" on the employer as a precondition to dismissal. Fourth, the courts have afforded the non-unionized employee roughly equal protections under the common law doctrine of just cause as are available to unionized workers under the just cause provision found in most collective agreements.[192] It is true that, unlike in the unionized sector where reinstatement is the common remedy for wrongful dismissal, non-unionized employees cannot obtain reinstatement at common law. Nevertheless, the components of just cause under the two regimes are now remarkably similar, with few exceptions.[193] The outcome of this approach is that the modern law of summary dismissal "is weighed in favour of employees."[194]

On the other hand, account must be taken of the potential costs to employers of providing employees with relatively generous safeguards against unjust dismissal. Presumably, there comes a point at which the costs of complying with the requirements of just cause—especially

---

190 *McKinley v. B.C. Tel*, [2001] 2 S.C.R. 161 at para. 53 [*McKinley*].
191 *Ibid.* at para. 57.
192 The arbitral standards of just cause are examined in D.J.M. Brown & D.M. Beatty, *Canadian Labour Arbitration*, 3d ed., looseleaf (Aurora, ON: Canada Law Book, 1997) c. 7 [Brown & Beatty].
193 For further elaboration, see *Employment Law in Canada*, above note 23, c. 15; R. Echlin & M. Certosimo, *Just Cause: The Law of Summary Dismissal in Canada*, looseleaf (Aurora, ON: Canada Law Book, 1998).
194 *Foxco*, above note 188 at 103, Robertson J.A.

326 INDIVIDUAL EMPLOYMENT LAW

overly legalistic procedural safeguards—would induce employers to refrain from hiring new employees and to use cheaper substitutes, such as independent contractors or labour-saving technology. The legal protections of just cause, therefore, would benefit the employed to the detriment of the unemployed. Unfortunately, there are no current Canadian empirical studies on this point.[195]

1) Proportionality: What Degree of Misconduct or Incompetence Is Required for "Just Cause"?

The legal burden of proving that the employee has committed sufficiently serious acts of misbehaviour or incompetence to warrant summary dismissal is on the employer. It would seem that the employer could best adduce evidence of why dismissal was invoked, but the same objective could be readily achieved by imposing an evidentiary onus of disclosure on the employer, without having to go to the extent of reversing the legal burden of proof. An important result of the reversed legal onus is that the employee wins in the event that the scales of evidence or argument are evenly balanced.

Because of the grave consequences of summary discharge for the employee, modern courts require that the employee's misconduct or incompetence cause the employer "substantial"[196] harm in order to justify the penalty. Thus, where misconduct is at issue, the courts hold that a single instance will not usually ground summary dismissal; rather, repetitive instances of misconduct are required.[197] Nevertheless, in

---

195 According to B.A. Hepple, "The Fall and Rise of Unfair Dismissal" in W. Mc-Carthy, ed., *Legal Intervention in Industrial Relations: Gains and Losses* (Oxford: Blackwell Business, 1993) 79 at 94, the enactment of relatively comprehensive just cause protections in Britain in 1971 resulted in "considerable" efficiency gains for employers without causing a disemployment effect. The U.S. literature on point is extensive: e.g., David Million, "Default Rules, Wealth Distribution, and Corporate Law Reform: Employment at Will versus Job Security" (1998) 146 U. Pa. L. Rev. 975; Andrew P. Morriss, "Bad Data, Bad Economics, and Bad Policy: Time to Fire Wrongful Discharge Law" (1996) 74 Tex. L. Rev. 1901; J. Hoult Verkerke, "An Empirical Perspective on Indefinite Term Employment Contracts: Resolving the Just Cause Debate" (1995) Wis. L. Rev. 837; Alan B. Krueger, "The Evolution of Unjust-Dismissal Legislation in the United States" (1991) 44 Indus. & Lab. Rel. Rev. 644 at 645; Richard A. Epstein, "In Defense of the Contract at Will" (1984) 51 U. Chi. L. Rev. 947.

196 *Colliar v. Robinson Diesel Injection Ltd.* (1988), 89 C.L.L.C. ¶14,037 at 12,315, Winner J. (Sask. Q.B.).

197 *Foxco*, above note 188 at 91, 103, and 105; *Nossal v. Better Business Bureau of Metropolitan Toronto Inc.* (1985), 12 C.C.E.L. 85, especially at 90 (Ont. C.A.) [*Nossal*].

exceptional circumstances, even a single instance will suffice where the employer sustains severe economic harm as a result of the misconduct[198] or where the misconduct is intrinsically serious. Examples of the latter include behaviour that destroys the elements of trust and confidence that form the core of any employment relationship, such as theft of the employer's or a customer's property,[199] dishonesty towards the employer,[200] or making a secret profit out of the employment relationship.[201] Furthermore, the seriousness of the misconduct will be exacerbated if the plaintiff holds a relatively high position of trust,[202] if he or she is expected to be a role model to other workers,[203] or if the nature of the industry in question entails an especially rigorous standard of public confidence.[204] Dishonesty is regarded as such a serious fault that, historically, some judges have even held that summary dismissal is automatically justifiable for such behaviour, despite any mitigating circumstances.[205] This view was always in the minority, however, and in 2001 the Supreme Court of Canada overruled those precedents and held that the test of contextual proportionality applies

---

198 Example: *Ferguson v. Allstate Insurance Co. of Canada* (1991), 35 C.C.E.L. 257, especially at 265 (Ont. Gen. Div.), where an insurance agent falsified a client's driving record in order to complete the sale of the policy, resulting in the company having to pay out $125,000 on the void policy. The court also held the employee liable in damages for breach of the employment contract to the employer for that amount.

199 Example: *Godden v. CAE Electronics Ltd. and CAF Newnes Ltd.*, [2002] C.L.L.C. ¶210-035 at 141,395 (B.C.S.C.) [*Godden*]; *Hyland v. Royal Alexandra Hospital* (2000), 5 C.C.E.L. (3d) 63 at 69–71 (Alta. Q.B.); *Letendre v. Deines Micro-Film Services Ltd.* (2001), 9 C.C.E.L. (3d) 296 at 306 (Alta. Q.B.).

200 Example: *Robson v. Thorne, Ernst and Whinney* (2000), 48 C.C.E.L. (2d) 1 (Ont. C.A.), where an accounts manager knowingly participated in income tax fraud with a senior partner for several years; *Marshall v. Pacific Coast Savings Credit Union* (1995), 10 C.C.E.L. (2d) 38 (B.C.S.C.), where the plaintiff lied to the employer in an investigation about misuse of a credit card.

201 Example: *Rupert v. Greater Victoria School District No. 61*, [2002] C.L.L.C. ¶210-001 at 141,008 (B.C.S.C.), aff'd [2004] C.L.L.C. ¶210-026 (B.C.C.A.) [*Rupert*].

202 Example: a senior manager with broad discretionary authority over the expenditure of public funds in *Dowling v. Ontario (Workplace Safety and Insurance Board)*, [2005] C.L.L.C. ¶210-002 (Ont. C.A.).

203 Example: *Lane v. Canadian Depository for Securities Ltd.* (1993), 49 C.C.E.L. 225 at 233 (Ont. Gen. Div.) [*Lane*], where the plaintiff, a vice-president for internal audit, was dismissed for fraudulently misusing a credit card.

204 Example: banking, where "caution is the norm and . . . trust and confidence by the employer in the employee is essential" in *Rowe v. Royal Bank of Canada* (1992), 38 C.C.E.L. 1 at 11–12 (B.C.S.C.), Mackoff J.

205 Example: *McPhillips v. British Columbia Ferry Corporation* (1994), 5 C.C.E.L. (2d) 49 (B.C.C.A.).

to all forms of misconduct and incompetence—summary dismissal is never automatically justifiable.[206] Because of the added moral opprobrium attached to allegations of dishonesty compared with other acts of misconduct, most courts require the employer to meet a more exacting standard of proof than the usual civil law "balance of probabilities," but not so exacting as the criminal law standard of "beyond any reasonable doubt."[207] Collective agreement arbitrators, too, have applied a halfway standard of proof in such circumstances.[208]

There are other examples of single instances of misconduct that justify summary dismissal. These include deliberately disobeying an order of the employer in such a way as to openly flaunt the employer's authority in the workplace,[209] especially if the disobedience is accompanied by insolence towards the employer;[210] engaging in competition with the employer's business, whether during the employee's private time or not;[211] making an aggravated assault against fellow workers or members of management;[212] verbally abusing managers;[213] and sexually harassing fellow employees.[214] It deserves emphasis, however, that none of the above offences automatically justifies summary dismissal; rather, the test of contextual proportionality can result in dismissal being ruled unjust if mitigating factors are present.[215]

206 McKinley, above note 190 at para. 57.
207 Example: Goodkey v. Dynamic Concrete Pumping Inc. (2004), 33 C.C.E.L. (3d) 186 at 190 (B.C.S.C.).
208 This is frequently described as "clear and convincing" proof. See generally H.A. Hope, "Evidence, Proof and Penalty Assessment: An Arbitrator's Viewpoint" (1991) 2 Lab. Arb. Y.B. 111.
209 Examples: Roden, above note 184; Clark v. Horizon Holidays Ltd. (1993), 45 C.C.E.L. 244 (Ont. Gen. Div.).
210 Example: Amos v. Alberta (1995), 9 C.C.E.L. (2d) 69 (Alta. Q.B.).
211 Examples: Rupert, above note 201; Knowlan v. Trailmobile Parts and Services Canada Ltd., [2006] B.C.J. No. 457 (S.C.) [Knowlan].
212 Example: Bell v. General Motors of Canada Ltd. (1989), 27 C.C.E.L. 110 (Ont. H.C.J.), where a supervisor assaulted a female employee, whom he supervised, outside of working hours, but the court held there to be "cause" because the incident would likely undermine good working relations between the supervisor and his supervisees. See also Izzard v. Cosmopolitan Industries Ltd. (2002), 17 C.C.E.L. (3d) 268 (Sask. Q.B.).
213 Examples: Codner v. Joint Construction Ltd. (1989), 27 C.C.E.L. 144 (Nfld. S.C.T.D.); Wankling v. Saskatchewan Urban Municipalities Assn. (1989), 27 C.C.E.L. 31 at 39 (Sask. Q.B.).
214 Examples: Alleyne v. Gateway Co-operative Homes Inc. (2001), 14 C.C.E.L. (3d) 31 (Ont. S.C.J.); Leach v. Canadian Blood Services, [2001] A.J. No. 119 (Q.B.).
215 Example: Brazeau v. International Electrical Workers, [2004] C.L.L.C. ¶210-032 at 141,304 (B.C.S.C.), aff'd [2005] C.L.L.C. ¶210-011 (B.C.C.A.) [Brazeau], where

A single instance of disobedience to work rules may justify summary dismissal. However, the courts have followed the lead of collective agreement arbitrators in requiring that certain prerequisites be satisfied before dismissal will be warranted. These are: (1) the rule in question must have been made known to the employee,[216] (2) the rule must have been consistently applied in the past,[217] (3) a clear order must have been communicated to the employee,[218] (4) the order must be within the scope of the worker's duties under the employment contract,[219] (5) the employee must have been clearly informed that dismissal is the penalty for disobedience,[220] (6) the rule must be lawful and reasonable in content,[221] and (7) the employee must not have a reasonable excuse for disobedience.[222]

The employer's power of summary dismissal is not limited to misconduct committed by the employee during working hours; rather, just cause for dismissal will exist if the employee's off-duty misbehaviour substantially injures the employer's legitimate business interests—including undermining public confidence in the employer's business or service[223] and challenging the employer's symbolic right to command.[224]

---

procedural unfairness in handling allegations of sexual harassment resulted in a finding of wrongful dismissal.

216 Examples: *Quinlan v. Bridgeport Self-Serve Carpet Clinic Ltd.* (1993), 2 C.C.E.L. (2d) 60 at 65 (B.C.S.C.); *Aston v. Gander Aviation Ltd.* (1981), 32 Nfld. & P.E.I.R. 148 (Nfld. S.C.T.D.).

217 Example: *Hill v. Dow Chemicals Canada Inc.* (1993), 48 C.C.E.L. 254, especially at 258 (Alta. Q.B.) [*Hill*].

218 Examples: *Panton v. Everywoman's Health Centre Society*, [2000] B.C.J. No. 2290 (C.A.); *F1 Software Inc. v. Broadview Software Inc.*, [2004] C.L.L.C. ¶210-023 at 141,217 (Ont. S.C.J.).

219 Examples: *Collins v. St. John's Publishing Co.* (1980), 27 Nfld. & P.E.I.R. 45 (Nfld. S.C.T.D.); *Dooley v. C.N. Weber Ltd.* (1994), 3 C.C.E.L. (2d) 95 at 100 (Ont. Gen. Div.).

220 Example: *Lennox v. Arbor-Memorial Services Inc.* (2000), 3 C.C.E.L. (3d) 119 at 125 (Ont. S.C.J.).

221 *Smith v. Worldwide Church of God* (1980), 39 N.S.R. (2d) 430 (S.C.T.D.).

222 Example: *Cox v. Canadian Corps of Commissonaires* (2003), 28 C.C.E.L. (3d) 264 at 273 (Sask. Q.B.) [*Cox*]. It is interesting that it is not a reasonable excuse to disobey orders on the instructions of a supervisor: e.g., *Miller v. Alberta*, [1980] A.J. No. 768 (Q.B.).

223 Examples: *Kelly v. Linamar Corporation and Emtol Manufacturing Ltd.*, [2006] C.L.L.C. ¶210-003 at 141,025 (Ont. S.C.J.) [*Kelly*], where a supplies manager who dealt extensively with customers was arrested and charged with possessing child pornography; *Smith v. Kamloops and District Elizabeth Fry Society* (1996), 20 C.C.E.L. (2d) 303 at 314 (B.C.C.A.), where a counsellor had an intimate relationship with a client in violation of the professional Code of Ethics.

224 Examples: *Brenton v. Potash Co. of America* (1985), 63 N.B.R. (2d) 62 (Q.B.T.D.), where the discharge of the work crew supervisor for sexually assaulting a

But courts require clear evidence of substantial harm to the employer's interests in order to ground cause, since the employee's personal liberty in his or her private life is at stake.[225]

Summary dismissal may also be for just cause if the worker's level of job performance is too low for reasons beyond his or her control—for example, if the employee cannot handle new technology introduced into the labour process. This non-culpable dismissal must be distinguished from culpable dismissal for deliberate and wilful misconduct, considered above. The employee is taken as impliedly guaranteeing under the employment contract that he or she will meet the requisite performance standards, so that even if the employee did not intend to do so, if he or she falls short, the contract is breached. The test of contextual proportionality enunciated in *McKinley* also applies to dismissal for incompetence.[226] In order to give cause for summary dismissal, the employee's quality of performance must demonstrably fall below the average level for the firm; an employer cannot summarily dismiss an employee for not being an above-average performer.[227] Courts sometimes express this notion by stating that only gross incompetence will warrant summary dismissal.[228] There must be objective evidence substantiating an allegation of "gross" incompetence; the employer's subjective perceptions will not suffice.[229] This presents difficulties in jobs where there is no measurable output of production, such as personal counselling. Here, the courts attach considerable weight to the employer's assessment of an employee's "intangibles," but objective evidence of specific instances of impaired performance is nonetheless required to ground summary dismissal.[230] Also, a higher standard of performance is generally expected from employees in higher echelon positions because such positions are associated with greater responsibility than

---

minor was upheld because his ability to control his crew members would be diminished due to their loss of respect in him; *Kelly, ibid.*, where a manager was arrested and charged with possessing child pornography.

225 See, for example, *Strowbridge v. Re/Max United Inc.* (1992), 42 C.C.E.L. 51 at 55 (Nfld. S.C.T.D.) where the court expressly endorsed the approach of collective agreement arbitrators to this effect.

226 *McKinley*, above note 190 at para. 57, applied in the context of dismissal for incompetence in *Mastrogiuseppe*, above note 107 at 141,042.

227 Examples: *Chester*, above note 141; *Stewart v. Intercity Packers Ltd.* (1988), 24 C.C.E.L. 135 (B.C.S.C.).

228 Examples: *Duffett v. Squibb Canada Inc.* (1991), 39 C.C.E.L. 37 at 41 (Nfld. S.C.T.D.) [*Duffett*]; *Niwranski v. H.N. Helicopter Parts International Corp.* (1992), 45 C.C.E.L. 303 at 312 (B.C.S.C.) [*Niwranski*].

229 Examples: *Duffett, ibid.* at 42; *Niwranski, ibid.* at 312.

230 Example: *Blackburn v. Coyle Motors Ltd.* (1983), 3 C.C.E.L. 1 (Ont. H.C.J.).

those in the lower echelon.[231] Furthermore, the courts will ensure that the employer sets reasonable, *bona fide* performance standards in order to forestall surreptitious attempts to get rid of unwanted workers.[232] However, they would presumably not stray too far across the line of dictating to an employer what appropriate job standards are, since determining those is best left to the employer's specialized business expertise, not to a judge's subjective opinion.

2) Rehabilitation of the Employee: The Corrective Theory of Discipline in Misconduct and Incompetence Situations

The corrective theory of industrial discipline is aimed at giving a problem worker a fair opportunity to improve job performance before the ultimate sanction of discharge can be invoked. This not only benefits the employee, but is also thought to benefit the employer by avoiding the costs of recruiting and training a replacement for the terminated worker. This theory has long been applied by collective agreement arbitrators.[233] In order to achieve the goal of rehabilitation, the courts have held that the following corrective measures must normally be taken prior to invoking dismissal in cases related to incompetence:[234]

- The employer has clearly made known to the employee the requisite standards of job performance.
- The employer has clearly warned the employee at the time of any delinquent behaviour on the employee's part *exactly* how he or she has failed to meet the requisite standard.[235] A warning need not be in writing, but if the verbal form is used, the statement "must be given

---

231 Example: the serious negligence of the sea captain in *Savage v. British India Steam Navigation Co.* (1930), 46 T.L.R. 294 (K.B.).

232 Examples: *Hodge v. United Co-Operatives of Ontario* (1993), 49 C.C.E.L. 220 (Ont. Gen. Div.), where the employer increased the plaintiff's workload beyond what was possible for her to achieve in an attempt to drive her from her job. See also *Duffett*, above note 228 at 43, where the court held that the sales target set for the plaintiff was "unreasonable."

233 Brown & Beatty, above note 192 at paras. 7.122.12–7.122.15.

234 There are innumerable judicial enunciations of these measures: e.g., *Brown v. Sears Ltd.* (1988), 88 N.S.R. (2d) 426 at 430 (S.C.T.D.); *Whitford v. Agrium Inc.*, [2007] 1 W.W.R. 621 (Alta. Q.B.); *Mastrogiuseppe*, above note 107 .

235 Accordingly, general exhortations to improve performance will not suffice: e.g., *Wilton v. Alport* (1991), 38 C.C.E.L. 218 at 226 (Sask. Q.B.) [*Wilton*]. See also *Niwranski*, above note 228 at 312.

in clear terms and the employee must understand and appreciate the significance of the warning."[236]
- The warning in question has clearly indicated that the employee's job is on the line unless his or her performance improves.[237]
- The employee has been clearly informed of what is required of him or her in order to constitute satisfactory performance and has been given a reasonable opportunity[238] and reasonable assistance[239] from the employer to meet that standard.

The foregoing measures may be dispensed with in certain circumstances. For example, if the degree of incompetence on the employee's part is extremely serious, the employer is allowed to safeguard its business interests against such harm by dismissing the employee for a first offence.[240] This exception reflects the notion of proportionality, which lies at the heart of just cause. Also, corrective measures can be dispensed with if it is clear from the employee's attitude that he or she would not take the opportunity to self-correct[241] — for example, where the employee refuses to acknowledge any shortcoming on his or her part.

Although the requirements of progressive discipline are routinely applied by the courts, the doctrinal basis for doing so is rarely enunciated. Traditionally, the courts have held that employers have no duty to comply with the requirements of procedural fairness in dismissing employees for wilful misconduct, and this appears to apply equally to dismissals for incompetence. Nevertheless, the courts have consistently ignored this doctrinal obstacle when applying progressive discipline. One possible analysis is that the threshold of a repudiatory breach is not crossed unless the employer has first applied progressive discipline. This analysis seems to have been facilitated by the Supreme Court of Canada's adoption of the contextual proportionality test in *McKinley*.[242] Thus, compliance with progressive discipline can be seen as a relevant

---

236 *Duffett*, above note 228 at 42. In a similar vein, see *Parsons v. N1 Cablesytems Inc.* (1994), 5 C.C.E.L. (2d) 282 at 303 (Nfld. S.C.T.D.) [*Parsons*].
237 It must be unambiguous that the employee's job is in jeopardy: e.g., *Regan v. Chaleur Entrepreneurship Centre Inc.* (1995), 7 C.C.E.L. (2d) 46 at 50 (N.B.Q.B.T.D.); *Wilton*, above note 235 at 225; *Niwranski*, above note 228 at 312.
238 *Robson v. General Motors of Canada Ltd.* (1982), 37 O.R. (2d) 229 at 235 (Co. Ct.) [*Robson*]. The employer must give specific deadlines within which improvements must be made: e.g., *Wilton*, ibid.
239 *George v. Muller Sales & Services Ltd.* (1984), 3 C.C.E.L. 106 (Sask. Q.B.); *Bragg v. London Life Insurance Co.* (1983), 2 C.C.E.L. 57 (N.S.S.C.T.D.) [*Bragg*].
240 Example: *Edwards v. Irwin* (1993), 47 C.C.E.L. 138 at 44 (Ont. Gen. Div.).
241 Example: *Fonceca v. McDonnell Douglas Canada Ltd.* (1983), 1 C.C.E.L. 51 at 57–58 (Ont. H.C.J.) [*Fonceca*].
242 *McKinley*, above note 190 at para. 57.

contextual factor in determining whether dismissal is a proportional response to incompetence so as to constitute a repudiatory breach on the employee's part.[243] Another possible analysis is that an employer who knows of an employee's deficiencies, but fails to take progressive measures to correct them may have waived or condoned the employee's failings.[244] The most interesting analysis, however, is to treat the requirements of progressive discipline as a subset of a general implied contractual duty of fairness. An Alberta trial judge, Greckol J., has taken this approach.[245] The significance of this analysis is that it lends support to the existence of an independent implied term in the employment contract, one that requires the employer to treat the employee fairly and decently. As we saw earlier, the existence of such a duty has been hotly debated in recent years.[246]

3) Mitigating Factors

Because the notion of proportionality underlies just cause, the courts will take account of *any* surrounding circumstances that reduce the severity of an employee's misconduct or incompetence, especially if the employee also shows the propensity to self-rehabilitate. Mitigating factors have been held to include provocation or other mistreatment of the employee by the employer,[247] physical or mental trauma in the employee's personal life,[248] a lengthy record of satisfactory service,[249] a lack of premeditated intent to harm the employer,[250] a mistaken belief on the employee's part that he or she was acting in the employer's best interests,[251] and the employer's failure to handle the dismissal in a procedurally fair

---

243 Example: *Foxco*, above note 188 at 103, where Robertson J.A. stated that rehabilitating the employee is an important factor that must not become submerged beneath the nomenclature of repudiatory breach.

244 Examples: *Jasnoch v. Provincial Plating Ltd.* (2000), 49 C.C.E.L. (2d) 81 at 89 (Sask. Q.B.); *Wilton*, above note 235 at 226.

245 *Henson v. Champion Feed Services* (2005), 40 C.C.E.L. (3d) 5 at 22 (Alta. Q.B.) [*Henson*].

246 See Chapter 5.

247 Example: *Chahal v. Khalsa Community School* (2000), 2 C.C.E.L. (3d) 120 (Ont. S.C.J.) [*Chahal*].

248 *Cox*, above note 222 at 274.

249 Example: *Brazeau*, above note 215. Such a record shows that the employee is unlikely to misbehave again.

250 Example: *McKinley*, above note 190.

251 Example: *Doyle v. London Life Insurance Co.* (1985), 23 D.L.R. (4th) 443 at 453–54 (B.C.C.A.), leave to appeal to S.C.C. refused (*sub nom. London Life Insurance Co. v. Doyle*) (1986), 64 N.R. 318n [*Doyle*].

manner.[252] Presumably, only mitigating circumstances that exist at the date of dismissal can be taken into account. Thus, if an employee is dismissed for an act of violence that constitutes a repudiatory breach at the time it happens, but subsequently takes anger management counselling and is rehabilitated, the latter cannot be relied on retroactively to render dismissal unjust.[253] Since the employment relationship is contractual, the sole issue is not whether the rehabilitation is in the broader public interest, but whether the employee breached an implied duty of fidelity. This view harmonizes with the principle that an employer cannot rely on wrongdoing committed by the employee after the date of summary dismissal to ground just cause. There is little difference between the approaches to mitigation taken by courts and collective agreement arbitrators, with one major exception. Unlike collective agreement arbitrators, courts cannot reinstate an employee who is partially to blame for his or her dismissal, subject to a lesser penalty, such as an unpaid suspension. At common law, reinstatement is normally unavailable and the determination of whether an employee's conduct is repudiatory in nature such as to warrant summary dismissal is "all or nothing"; the courts will not find that dismissal is wrongful and then reduce the employee's damages to reflect contributory blameworthiness.[254]

4) Procedural Fairness in Handling Dismissals

The courts have imposed several procedural safeguards on the employer's power of summary dismissal. First, we saw above that the corrective theory of discipline, widely applied to dismissals for incompetence, includes several components of a duty of procedural fairness, such as the obligations to warn the employee of his or her deficiencies and to help the employee self-correct.[255] It is significant that these measures are normally applied under the rubric of determining whether the employee's conduct is repudiatory in nature, but they can be regarded as

---

252 Examples: *Brazeau*, above note 215; *Bouma v. Flex-N-Gate Canada Company*, [2005] C.L.L.C. ¶210-033 at 141,299 (Ont. S.C.J.) [*Bouma*].

253 This appears to be the position in collective agreement arbitration as a result of *Cie Minière Québec Cartier v. Quebec (Grievances Arbitrator)*, [1995] S.C.J. No. 65, 125 D.L.R. (4d) 577 at 581–82, but many arbitrators have balked at this conclusion and have sought innovative ways of circumventing the decision.

254 Some courts experimented with this practice in the 1980s under the so-called near cause doctrine, but today this doctrine has been unequivocally rejected by the Supreme Court of Canada in *Dowling*, above note 154, considered in Section B(3)(c)(v), above in this chapter.

255 See Section B(3)(c)(v), above in this chapter.

components of an independent implied term in the employment contract obliging employers to treat their workers fairly.

Second, the courts apply the doctrine of condonation, or waiver. The employer is deemed to have relinquished the right to dismiss an employee for an act of misconduct or incompetence that the employer becomes aware of, if it fails to notify the employee within a reasonable time.[256] The rationale for the doctrine is to prevent the employee from being lulled into the misbelief that his or her behaviour is acceptable, only to face summary dismissal later. The burden of proving condonation is on the worker.[257] Obviously, the employer must know of the employee's misdeeds in order to condone them.[258] Common examples of condonation include promoting an unmeritorious employee or giving an undeserved merit bonus or good performance appraisal,[259] falsifying the reason for dismissal as economic exigency to spare the worker's feelings or help the worker get replacement work,[260] and permitting an employee to serve out a notice of termination instead of dismissing him or her on the spot.[261] Although collective agreement arbitrators also apply the doctrine of condonation, there is one critical difference between the approaches of arbitrators and the common law position. Unlike in arbitration, at common law, a further act of misconduct or incompetence by the employee revives previously condoned misdeeds for the purpose of establishing just cause.[262] Accordingly, at

---

256 *McIntyre v. Hockin* (1889), 16 O.A.R. 498, especially at 501–02 (C.A.) [*Hockin*]. See A. Marcotte, "Can Employers Forgive and Forget? Employer Condonation and Wrongful Dismissal in Canada" (1998) 8 Windsor Rev. Legal and Soc. Issues 3.

257 *Connolly v. General Motors of Canada Ltd.* (1993), 50 C.C.E.L. 247 at 258 (Ont. Gen. Div.), Ferguson J.

258 *Tracey v. Swansea Construction Co.* (1964), 47 D.L.R. (2d) 295 (Ont. H.C.J.), aff'd (1965), 50 D.L.R. (2d) 130n (C.A.) [*Tracey*].

259 Examples: *Henson*, above note 245; *Sjerven v. Port Alberni Friendship Centre* (2000), 3 C.C.E.L. (3d) 71 at 101 (B.C.S.C.) [*Sjerven*]; *Chambers v. Omni Insurance Brokers* (2002), 17 C.C.E.L. (3d) 179 at 188 (Ont. C.A.); *Mayhew v. Canron Inc.* (1982), 50 N.S.R. (2d) 278 (S.C.T.D.).

260 Example: *Card v. Emjac Screw Products Ltd.* (1994), 4 C.C.E.L. (2d) 155 at 158 (Ont. Gen. Div.).

261 Example: *Dash v. Hudson's Bay Co.* (1992), 42 C.C.E.L. 278, especially at 283–84 (Alta. Q.B.). But compare *Giancola v. Jo-Del Investments Ltd.*, [2004] C.L.L.C. ¶210-017 (Ont. C.A.), where the court was satisfied that the employer intended to make the severance payment as an act of generosity rather than as an act of condonation.

262 A dictum to this effect in *Hockin*, above note 256 at 501, was affirmed by the Ontario Court of Appeal in *Nossal*, above note 197 at 90, Zuber J.A. See also *Cook v. Halifax (City) School Board* (1902), 35 N.S.R. 405 (C.A.) [*Cook*].

common law the employer is merely precluded from relying on the condoned misbehaviour as the *sole* ground for dismissal. As is the case with corrective discipline, the doctrine of condonation is applied under the rubric of the definition of a repudiatory breach, not as part of an independent implied term in the employment contract requiring the employer to treat its employees fairly.

Third, some (but not all[263]) modern courts require employers to dismiss employees in a procedurally fair manner. That is despite the traditional view at common law that an employer is under no inherent contractual obligation to comply with the standards of natural justice or with any less rigorous duty of procedural fairness when dismissing an employee.[264] According to the traditional view, an employer is bound to a duty of procedural fairness only in the following situations: (1) where the employment contract expressly or impliedly incorporates a disciplinary procedure with such requirements,[265] (2) where a statute imposes a disciplinary procedure,[266] (3) where a public employee does not have a contract of employment that provides a common law action for wrongful dismissal,[267] (4) where a duty of fairness "flows by necessary implication from a statutory power governing the employment relationship,"[268] and (4) where a particular province's employment standards legislation requires the employer to provide employees who are being dismissed for cause with written reasons.[269] However, if the law were to impose a duty of procedural fairness, the employee would have a fair and reasonable opportunity to explain his or her side of the case before the employer invokes dismissal, the employer would conduct a fair and thorough investigation of allegations of wrongdoing against the employee prior to

---

263 The traditional rule was applied, for example, in *Higginson v. Rocky Credit Union Ltd.* (1995), 162 A.R. 369 at 376 (C.A.) [*Higginson*]; *Leach v. Canadian Blood Services* (2001), 7 C.C.E.L. (3d) 205 at 236 (Alta. Q.B.); *Geluch*, above note 178; *Lambert v. Canadian Association of Optometrists* (1994), 6 C.C.E.L. (2d) 129 at 131 (Ont. Gen. Div.), aff'd [1996] O.J. No. 1229 (C.A.); *Hannis v. Teevan* (1998), 98 C.L.L.C. ¶210-026 at 141,146 (Ont. C.A.).

264 The seminal authorities are *Lake Ontario Portland Cement Co. v. Groner*, [1961] S.C.R. 553 [*Groner*]; *Ridge v. Baldwin*, [1964] A.C. 40 at 65 (H.L.) [*Ridge*]; *Malloch v. Aberdeen Corp.*, [1971] 2 All E.R. 1278 at 1294 (H.L.); *Tracey*, above note 258 at 309 (H.C.J.).

265 Example: *White v. Sir Thomas Roddick Hospital* (1991), 91 C.L.L.C. ¶14,044 (Nfld. S.C.T.D.) [*Roddick*].

266 *Ibid.*

267 Example: *Dunsmuir v. New Brunswick*, 2008 SCC 9 at para. 115 [*Dunsmuir*]. See also Section E(2), below in this chapter.

268 *Dunsmuir, ibid.* at para. 116.

269 N.B. *ESA*, above note 43, s. 30(2); *CLC*, above note 28, s. 241; Quebec *Act Respecting Labour Standards*, R.S.Q., c. N-11, s. 125 [*Que. LSA*].

invoking dismissal, and as a result, the employer could unearth information convincing it not to proceed with the dismissal. Fulfilling this duty would avoid the costs to both parties of beginning litigation only to discover the information in question during discovery proceedings or at the trial itself. It therefore seems cost efficient to impose a duty of procedural fairness on the employer before dismissal—unless the circumstances clearly indicate that the employee's input could not conceivably alter the outcome. Indeed, the fact that handling dismissal in a procedurally unfair manner can result in the court awarding a *Wallace* extension strengthens the case for recognizing an implied contractual duty of fairness in dismissal situations.[270] Some courts have accepted these arguments and have required employers to fairly and thoroughly investigate allegations of wrongdoing against employees[271] and to provide fair and reasonable opportunities for employees to explain their side of a case before invoking dismissal.[272]

Remedying breach of the duty of procedural fairness is tricky. Ideally, the employee should be reinstated with a direction to the employer to proceed in a procedurally fair manner, but for that approach to be applied, the traditional reluctance of the common law to order specific performance of employment contracts would have to be relaxed.[273] Moreover, if the effect of such an order is that the employer goes through the motions of acting fairly, but reimposes the dismissal, the exercise would seem to be pointless. In the unionized sector, of course, the presence of a trade union in the workplace ensures that the employer takes reinstatement and other orders seriously. Alternatively, the courts could award substantial punitive damages against employers who dismiss employees in breach of the duty of procedural fairness. As well, an extension of

---

270 Examples: *Mastrogiuseppe*, above note 107; *Baughn*, above note 174; *Robinson*, above note 159.

271 Examples: *Brazeau*, above note 215; *Murrell v. Burns International Security Services Ltd.*, [1994] O.J. No. 1019 (Gen. Div.); *McIntyre v. Rogers Cable T.V. Ltd.* (1996), 18 C.C.E.L. (2d) 116 (B.C.S.C.).

272 Examples: *Baughn*, above note 174; *Seeley v. Bob Brown Pontiac Buick GMC. Ltd.* (2002), 21 C.C.E.L. (3d) 311 (B.C. Prov. Ct.); *Bouma*, above note 252; *Henson*, above note 245 at 22; *Tse v. Trow Consulting Engineers Ltd.* (1995), 14 C.C.E.L. (2d) 132 at 145 (Ont. Gen. Div.); *Quirola v. Xerox Canada Ltd.* (1996), 16 C.C.E.L. (2d) 235 (Ont. Gen. Div.); *Norman v. Coon Bros. Sand and Gravel (1998) Ltd.* (1999), 42 C.C.E.L. (2d) 195 at 200 (Ont. Gen. Div.); *Jardine v. Gloucester (City)*, [1999] O.J. No. 424 (Gen. Div.), by way of *obiter dictum*; *Doyle*, above note 251 at 450, 452; *Shiloff v. Canada* (1994), 6 C.C.E.L. (2d) 177 at 191 (F.C.T.D.); *Robarts v. Canadian National Railway* (1980), 2 C.C.E.L. 168, especially at 172 and 174 (Ont. H.C.J.); *Robson*, above note 238.

273 This policy is examined in Section F(2), below in this chapter.

the reasonable notice period could be awarded under the *Wallace* doctrine.[274] Plainly, there would be real obstacles to overcome in remedying breach of a duty of procedural fairness in dismissals.

5) The "Culminating Incident" Rule

The courts have long held that an employer can take into account previous instances of misconduct or incompetence on an employee's work record in combination with a new offence in order to justify summary dismissal, even though the new offence, in isolation, would not be sufficiently serious to justify that penalty.[275] Collective agreement arbitrators take the same approach, which they call the "culminating incident" doctrine.[276] At common law, the courts will generally allow an employee to offer an explanation of any previous offences that an employer seeks to rely on. This is an important safeguard for the nonunionized employee because, unlike in the unionized sector, the employee will not have grievance and arbitration machinery available to challenge the fairness of a disciplinary warning or suspension at the time it is imposed.

Nevertheless, in some respects, the common law is less advantageous than arbitration to the employee. For example, in arbitration an employer is precluded from reviving previous instances of misbehaviour unless the employee was clearly warned at the time that his or her actions are unacceptable, and if repeated, could result in dismissal. In contrast, at common law the employer can revive previously condoned offences pursuant to a new culminating incident.[277] In addition, the courts permit employers to introduce new grounds *ex post facto* in order to justify a dismissal, even though they knew of those grounds at the time of dismissal.[278]

6) Dismissal for Sickness

Sickness is not grounds for summary discharge at common law—nor, for that matter, in collective agreement arbitration—since the employee

---

274 As in *Mastrogiuseppe*, above note 107 at 141,055–56; *Baughn*, above note 174; *Robinson*, above note 159.

275 Examples: *Parsons*, above note 236 at 301, citing the classic arbitral formulation of the doctrine in *Re Air Canada and I.A.M., Lodge 148* (1973), 5 L.A.C. (2d) 7 (Andrews); *Nossal*, above note 197.

276 Brown & Beatty, above note 192 at para. 7.166.

277 Example: *Nossal*, above note 197 and accompanying text.

278 Example: *Groner*, above note 264.

is not at fault.[279] But if the illness or disability in question is so serious that the worker will probably be unable to perform the core functions of his or her position for the foreseeable future, the employment contract will be discharged lawfully by operation of the doctrine of frustration of contract.[280] However, these common law principles have been largely overtaken by the provisions in modern human rights statutes making it unlawful to dismiss an employee suffering from a defined illness or disability unless the employer can prove that it has reasonably accommodated the employee's medical condition up to the point of "undue hardship."[281] The latter may involve reassigning the employee to job duties within his or her capacity, or renovating the workplace to enable the employee to carry out his or her work procedures. Also, dismissal for sickness may, depending on the jurisdiction, violate special provisions of the employment standards[282] and workers' compensation legislation.

7) Employees Having Probationary Status

The standard of just cause governing the dismissal of probationary workers is summarized as follows by Noble J. of the Saskatchewan Court of Queen's Bench:

> [T]he only onus that rests on an employer to justify the dismissal is that he show the court that he acted fairly and with reasonable diligence in determining whether or not the proposed employee is suitable in the job for which he was being tested. So long as the probationary employee is given a reasonable opportunity to demonstrate his ability to meet the standards the employer sets out when he is hired, including not only a testing of his skills but also his ability to work in harmony with others, his potential usefulness to the employer in the future, and such other factors as the employer deems essential to the viable performance of the position, then he has no

---

279 Examples: *Parks v. Atlantic Provinces Special Education Authority Resource Centre for the Visually Impaired* (1992), 39 C.C.E.L. 155, especially at 181–82 (N.S.S.C.A.D.) [*Parks*]; *Dartmouth Ferry Commission v. Marks Estate* (1904), 34 S.C.R. 366 [*Marks Estate*]; *Yeager v. R.J. Hastings Agencies Ltd.* (1984), 5 C.C.E.L. 266 at 284 (B.C.S.C.) [*Yeager*].
280 Example: *McRae v. Dodge City Auto (1984) Ltd.* (1994), 94 C.L.L.C. ¶14,036 (Sask. Q.B.) [*Dodge City*].
281 The details of this legislation are examined in Chapter 7, Section C(1)(a).
282 Example: *Sask. LSA*, above note 24, s. 44.2, prohibits the imposition of dismissal, discipline, suspension, layoff, or demotion for specified maximum periods of absence from work due to illness or injury to either the employee or a member of his or her "immediate family" who is "dependent" on the employee.

complaint. As for the employer, he cannot be held liable if his assessment of the probationary employee is based on such criteria and a fair and reasonable determination of the question.[283]

This standard of cause is less onerous for the employer than that applying to employees who have passed their probationary review, reflecting the employer's interest in having greater than usual leeway to get rid of unmeritorious performers. Nevertheless, important safeguards exist for the employee: the performance criteria set by the employer must be reasonably necessary for the effective performance of the job, the employer must inform the employee at the beginning of the probationary period what the performance criteria are, the employee must have a fair opportunity to satisfy the performance criteria, the employer must warn the employee that his or her performance is inadequate, and the employer must assist the employee to meet the requisite standards.[284] Again, these requirements *de facto* amount to a duty of procedural fairness on the employer.[285] The common law position is the same as in arbitration.[286]

8) Introducing New Grounds to Justify a Prior Summary Dismissal

Collective agreement arbitrators have long held that an employer cannot attempt to justify its decision to dismiss a worker by adducing new grounds after the fact, save in "exceptional circumstances."[287] This proposition would appear to be consistent with generally understood notions of procedural fairness. Nevertheless, there is Supreme Court of Canada authority[288] to the effect that, for common law purposes, an employer may justify summary dismissal by reliance upon employee

---

283 *Ritchie v. Intercontinental Packers Ltd.* (1982), 14 Sask. R. 206 at 212 (Q.B.). See also *Higginson*, above note 263 at 4.

284 Examples: *Alexander v. Padinox Inc.*, [2000] C.L.L.C. ¶210-018 (P.E.I.C.A.); *Longshaw v. Monarch Beauty Supply Co.* (1995), 15 C.C.E.L. (2d) 232 at 241 (B.C.S.C.); *Mison v. Bank of Nova Scotia* (1994), 6 C.C.E.L. (2d) 146 at 155 (Ont. Gen. Div.); *Benson v. Co-op Atlantic* (1987), 15 C.C.E.L. 239 (Nfld. C.A.).

285 See Section C(4), above in this chapter.

286 Brown & Beatty, above note 192 at para. 7.5000.

287 *Ibid.* at para. 7.15. The exceptions are where the new grounds are implicitly encompassed within the stated grounds so that they can be regarded as part and parcel of the stated grounds, and where the employer did not know, and could not reasonably have been expected to know, of the new grounds at the time of dismissal.

288 *Groner*, above note 264 at 591, applied in *Knowlan*, above note 211; *Godden*, above note 199.

misconduct unknown to the employer at the time of dismissal. It has even been intimated[289] that the employer can introduce new grounds where it has deliberately lied to the worker about the reasons for dismissal at the time of discharge, at least unless the worker then relies, to his or her detriment, on the stated grounds without knowing what the real reasons for dismissal are.[290] Nevertheless, if the employer knows of the new grounds, but fails to rely on them at the time of dismissal, this will be evidence that the employer did not regard those grounds as serious[291] and may have condoned them.[292] Furthermore, despite an intimation in the headnote of the *Groner* case to the contrary, courts generally require that the new grounds must exist at the date of dismissal.[293]

9) The Relevance of Express Contractual Provisions Defining "Just Cause"

According to the general principles of contract law, any express terms in the contract defining the circumstances in which summary dismissal is warranted must be accorded paramountcy over judicially crafted standards of just cause.[294] However, in order to protect employees against the risk of unfair exploitation arising from the employer's superior bargaining power, the courts use various techniques to minimize the effect of unduly harsh express termination provisions. These techniques include interpreting any ambiguities in such clauses *contra proferentem* the interests of the employer,[295] and implying into clauses that give the employer a broad discretion to dismiss a duty to exercise such discretion fairly and in good faith.[296] The doctrine of unconscionability is

---

289 *Carr v. Fama Holdings Ltd.* (1989), 28 C.C.E.L. 30 at 41 (B.C.C.A.), Wallace J.A..

290 As in *Backman v. Hyundai Auto Canada Inc.* (1990), 33 C.C.E.L. 300 at 311–12 (N.S.S.C.T.D.) [*Backman*].

291 Example: *Spong v. Westpres Publications Ltd.* (1982), 2 C.C.E.L. 228 (B.C.S.C.).

292 See Section C(4), above in this chapter.

293 Examples: *Sjerven*, above note 259; *Aasgard v. Harlequin Enterprises Ltd.* (1993), 48 C.C.E.L. 192 at 198 (Ont. Gen. Div.).

294 Examples: *McRae v. Marshall* (1891), 19 S.C.R. 10 at 13; *McNeil v. Swyers* (1949), 23 M.P.R. 407 (N.S.C.A.).

295 *Doyle*, above note 251.

296 *Truckers Garage*, above note 92 at 164, Osborne J.A.; *Greenberg v. Meffert* (1985), 18 D.L.R. (4th) 548 at 555–56, Robins J.A. (Ont. C.A.), leave to appeal to S.C.C. refused (1985), 30 D.L.R. (4th) 768n [*Greenberg*]. However, the Alberta courts have refused to imply a proviso of fairness into such clauses, reasoning that this would frustrate the parties' mutual intention to create a "clean break" provision: e.g., *Meyer*, above note 94 at 61; *Goering*, above note 94.

potentially available to supervise such clauses, but as yet it has rarely been used in this context.[297] Also, courts have the residual power to avoid any express term that is against public policy, and this power might be used to overrule express terms that unreasonably abridge the employee's personal civil liberties, for example, a term whereby the employee agrees that dismissal will be automatically lawful if he or she has a romantic relationship with a co-worker.[298] Courts frequently use this power to avoid restrictive covenants that unreasonably limit employee freedom to engage in post-employment competition with the employer,[299] and there is no doctrinal obstacle to taking a similar approach to other types of express terms. The use by employers of harsh express termination clauses will probably increase if the courts fashion standards of just cause that employers perceive to be unduly costly to them.

10) Economic Dismissals and "Just Cause"

It is an axiom of the common law of summary dismissal that the employee must commit a repudiatory breach of the employment contract in order to relieve the employer from its obligation to give due notice of termination. Consequently, the fact that the firm may be sustaining severe economic difficulties or restructuring its internal operations in order to enhance efficiency does not justify the summary dismissal of employees who are in no way to blame for these circumstances.[300] Rather, the employer can only dismiss an employee without notice for economic reasons if the contract of employment expressly gives it that right, or if there is a reliable custom and practice in the firm from which such a right can be implied into the employment contract.[301] It makes sense to exempt economic dismissals from judicial review under the common law standard of "just cause" because employers, not courts, have the expertise and responsibility for making business deci-

---

297 Compare the application of this doctrine in the analogous context of harsh notice of termination provisions examined in Section B(3), above in this chapter.

298 U.S. firms frequently use these clauses to avoid possible sexual harassment law suits and other disruptions to operations that are associated with workplace romances. See L. Fortado, "Workplace 'Love Contracts' on the Rise" (3 March 2005) *The National Law Journal*; V. Schultz, "The Sanitized Workplace" (2003) 112 Yale L.J. 2061.

299 See Chapter 4.

300 Examples: *Re Optinia Inc.* (2002), 21 C.C.E.L. (3d) 44 at 56–57 (Ont. S.C.J.); *Blaikies*, above note 141.

301 As in *Greene v. Chrysler Canada Ltd.* (1982), 7 C.C.E.L. 166 at 168 (B.C.S.C.), aff'd (1993), 7 C.C.E.L. 166 at 175 (B.C.C.A.).

sions. As well, in a capitalist system, it does not affront the employee's personal autonomy and dignity to be displaced for *bona fide* economic reasons—the flip side to receiving the benefits of capitalism.[302] Recognizing displacement as a legitimate price of capitalist activity, unjust statutory discharge schemes commonly exclude from arbitral review *bona fide* economic dismissals.[303]

D. TERMINATION BY ACT OF THE EMPLOYEE: QUITTING AND CONSTRUCTIVE DISMISSAL

An employee can lawfully bring the employment relationship to an end by giving the employer due notice of resignation as required under the express or implied terms of the employment contract and under the employment standards legislation. This section examines, first, the distinction between a valid resignation on the employee's part and a "disguised" dismissal—for example, where the employer presents the employee with a resign-or-be-fired ultimatum. Second, this section analyzes the length of notice of resignation required at common law and under legislation, and the remedies available to the employer if the employee resigns without giving the requisite notice. And finally, it examines the so-called constructive dismissal doctrine, whereunder an employee is deemed to have been wrongfully "dismissed" if he or she resigns in response to employer conduct that constitutes a repudiatory breach of the terms of the employment contract.

1) The Distinction between a Quit and a Dismissal

Resignation occurs where the employee voluntarily intends to bring the employment relationship to an end and so behaves in such a way that a reasonable person would believe that he or she has resigned.[304] The subjective component of this definition prevents the employer from forcing an employee to resign. Thus, if the employer informs the employee that

---

302 See H. Collins, *Justice in Dismissal* (Oxford: Clarendon Press, 1992) c. 5.

303 Example: *CLC*, above note 28, s. 242(3.1)(a), examined in Section E(1)(a), below in this chapter.

304 *Fitzsimmons v. North Thompson School District No. 26* (1996), 23 C.C.E.L. (2d) 130 (B.C.S.C.); *O'Neil v. Towers Perrin Inc.*, [2002] C.L.L.C. ¶210-011 (Ont. S.C.J.); *Kiernan v. Ingram Micro Ltd.* (2004), 33 C.C.E.L. (3d) 157, especially at 164 (Ont. C.A.). This test is similar to that adopted by collective agreement arbitrators. See Brown & Beatty, above note 192 at para. 7.217.

he or she must choose between being fired or resigning, such a resignation *prima facie* would appear to be invalid because it was procured by duress. This does not mean that an employee faced with the alternative of quitting or being fired can never validly resign—an employee who makes a fully informed and rational assessment that resigning will be less harmful to his or her reputation than being dismissed for misconduct or incompetence can validly resign.[305] Here, the crucial element of a valid resignation is that the employee fully comprehends the legal significance of his or her actions and has made a reasoned cost–benefit analysis of resigning or being dismissed. In a similar vein, if an employee is absent from work and is told by the employer that he or she will be deemed to have quit unless he or she resumes work by a specified date, failure to resume work normally will not constitute a resignation. Rather, there will be a dismissal and the question will be whether or not the absenteeism provides just cause.[306]

The purpose of the objective component of the definition is to prevent the employer from snapping up an ostensible resignation notice given by the employee in the heat of the moment. For example, if an employee storms out of the workplace after a heated confrontation with a supervisor, saying, "I quit" or words to that effect, there will be no valid resignation unless the employee confirms his or her statement by remaining away from work or returning equipment after having had a reasonable time during which to calm down.[307] If the employee's conduct would lead a reasonable person in the employer's position to believe that the employee had quit, the fact that the employee subjectively did not intend to do so will not preclude there being a valid resignation; otherwise, the employer stands to suffer detrimental reliance. At the least, in such circumstances the employee would be estopped from asserting that he or she did not subjectively intend to quit. The courts have ruled that a reasonable employer would not regard the employee as manifesting a clear intention to resign if he or she simply asks to commence severance negotiations and presents the employer with a list of severance demands.[308]

---

305 Example: *Lane*, above note 203 at 232.
306 Example: *Polo v. Calgary (City of)* (1993), 44 C.C.E.L. 257 (Alta. Q.B.).
307 *Widmeyer v. Municipal Enterprises Ltd.* (1991), 36 C.C.E.L. 237 (N.S.S.C.T.D.).
308 *Winkler v. Lower Mainland Publishing Ltd.*, [2003] C.L.L.C. ¶210-007 at 141,061 (B.C.S.C.).

2) The Length of Notice to Quit

The length of notice that an employee must give in order to resign lawfully is determined by the contract of employment and the employment standards legislation.

Regarding the employment standards legislation, in six provinces there is a statutory minimum period of notice of resignation that an employee must give to the employer.[309] The length of notice varies among the provinces. For example, in Alberta and Nova Scotia, the employee is bound to give one week's notice if he or she has been employed for more than three months, but less than two years, and two weeks' notice if he or she has been employed for more than two years.[310] The parties can exceed these statutory minima by the express or implied terms of their employment contract, except in Nova Scotia, where section 6 of the *Labour Standards Code* seems to preclude the parties from contracting for a lengthier notice period. In Manitoba, an employee who has been hired for less than one year must give one week's notice, but the period increases to two weeks' notice after one year or more.[311] Oddly, the legislation does not specify what remedy the employer is entitled to if the employee breaches the notice obligation. Typically, the legislation excuses giving notice of resignation if the employer seriously mistreats the employee in relation to his or her terms and conditions of employment.

Regarding the common law position, the length of notice of resignation is determined, to begin with, by any express terms in the employment contract. In the absence of such terms, the courts can imply a term based on the unexpressed factual intentions of the parties as reflected in the organization's past practice and personnel documentation. Failing this, the courts will imply a reasonable period of notice of resignation. In determining what is reasonable, the courts do not simply mirror the period of reasonable notice of termination that the employer would have to give the worker; rather, the reasonable notice period can differ for the employee and the employer. The purpose of determining reasonable notice of dismissal given by the employer is to provide the employee with a financial cushion to help weather unemployment. However, the purpose of determining reasonable notice of resignation is to afford the employer sufficient time to hire and train a replacement for the employee's position, and otherwise to reorganize

---

309 Namely, Alberta, Prince Edward Island, Ontario (in "mass termination" situations), Manitoba, Newfoundland, and Nova Scotia.

310 *Alta. ESC*, above note 21, s. 58(1); *N.S. LSC*, above note 39, s. 73(1).

311 *Man. ESC*, above note 68, s. 62.1(1).

work schedules so as to cover the employee's absence.[312] It follows that reasonable notice of resignation is usually much shorter than reasonable notice of dismissal, since there will usually be an adequate supply of replacement labour for the employer to tap. Of course, if there is a shortage of labour in the employee's position, the notice period will increase.

If the employee fails to give the requisite notice of resignation, this failure constitutes a breach of the employment contract for which damages are recoverable. Specific performance will not be ordered to force the employee to work out the period of notice of resignation.[313] Rather, the measure of damages at common law is to put the employer in the position it would have been in had the employee honoured the promise to give due notice. Normally, this would amount to the value of the employee's personal lost production minus any savings the employer makes, such as not having to pay the employee's wages during the period he or she should have been serving out the notice of resignation. It may be impossible for the employer to quantify such losses exactly enough to succeed in an action for damages. Moreover, the amount of such damages would often be too small to make litigation worthwhile. These reasons probably explain the relative paucity of caselaw involving successful damages actions against employees for wrongful resignation. Exceptionally, the losses sustained by a wrongful resignation may be sufficiently large and quantifiable to warrant an employer suing for damages—for example, in the case of entertainers, sports stars, senior executives, and professional or technical specialists.[314]

3) Constructive Dismissal, or Quitting for Cause

According to the general principles of contract law, if one party commits a repudiatory breach of the contract, the innocent party is entitled, if he or she so chooses, to terminate the contract and sue for damages. These principles also apply to repudiatory breaches of the employment

---

312 Examples: *Engineered Sound Systems Ltd. v. Klampfer* (1994), 3 C.C.E.L. (2d) 105 at 110–12 (Ont. Gen. Div.); *Tree Savers International Ltd. v. Savoy* (1992), 39 C.C.E.L. 253, especially at 250–60 (Alta. C.A.).

313 Compulsory reinstatement is ordered only in exceptional circumstances. See Section F(2), below in this chapter. But compare the reinstatement order issued by the English Court of Appeal in *Evening Standard v. Henderson*, [1987] I.R.L.R. 64 (C.A.).

314 Example: *Systems Engineering & Automation Ltd. v. Power* (1989), 90 C.L.L.C. ¶14,018 (Nfld. S.C.T.D.), var'd in relation to the order of costs (1991), 92 Nfld. & P.E.I.R. 235 (Nfld. S.C.T.D.).

contract on the part of the employer.[315] When an employee quits in response to repudiation of the contract by the employer, the employee is
deemed to have been constructively dismissed and can sue for damages
for wrongful dismissal.[316] The critical questions are these: What are the
employer's exact contractual obligations to the employee? Is the employee's breach sufficiently serious to be characterized as repudiatory
in nature? And, has the employee elected to terminate the contract in
a timely fashion, or has he or she condoned or affirmed the employer's
breach? We examine these questions in this section of the book.

The constructive dismissal doctrine requires courts to strike a delicate balance between the fundamental interests of the employer and the
employee. From the employer's perspective, management requires the
flexibility to modify job assignments, work schedules, the geographical location of work, the compensation structure, and other terms and
conditions of employment in order to respond to the rapidly changing
economic and technological conditions affecting most Canadian businesses.[317] In particular, intensifying foreign competition is pressuring
Canadian employers to reduce their labour costs by seeking greater
flexibility to change the terms and conditions of employment contracts. Yet, the constructive dismissal doctrine imposes a straitjacket
on employers when it comes to modifying the work process: unless a
change to the terms of the employment contract is preceded by notice
to the employee at least equivalent in length to that required lawfully to
terminate the contract—an impractical constraint given the increasing
length and uncertainty of common law notice periods—the employer
is potentially liable to pay the employee damages for wrongful dismissal. On the other hand, the employee can reasonably expect that the essential nature of his or her job will remain intact, subject to tangential
changes in detail that every worker reasonably expects an employer to
have the authority to make in any dynamic work environment. Therefore, constructive dismissal is a classic arena for the clash between each
party's fundamental interests—the employee's interest in security and
the employer's interest in efficiency—that underlies all labour law. The
constructive dismissal doctrine is to the employment contract what the

315 This "contractualist" analysis of constructive dismissal was endorsed by the
Supreme Court of Canada in *Farber v. Royal Trust Co.*, [1997] 1 S.C.R. 846
[*Farber*].
316 For further elaboration, see R.E. Echlin & J.M. Fantini, *Quitting for Good
Reason: The Law of Constructive Dismissal in Canada* (Aurora, ON: Canada Law
Book, 2001); *Employment Law in Canada*, above note 23, c. 13 (V).
317 A. Dastmalchian & P. Blyton, "Workplace Flexibility and the Changing Nature
of Work: An Introduction" (2001) 18 Can. J. of Administrative Sciences 1.

"reserved management rights" doctrine is to the collective agreement in the unionized sector. Of course, few areas of collective labour law have been as controversial as defining the ambit of permissible management rights under the collective agreement.[318]

The intensification of the pressure on Canadian employers to increase labour productivity has caused some courts to relax the straitjacket of the constructive dismissal doctrine and enhance the employer's flexibility to modify the terms and conditions of employment. It remains to be seen whether this tendency will continue. More radical is the proposal that the employment standards legislation be amended to permit the employer unilaterally to modify terms and conditions of employment by giving the worker "fair" advance notice. In this context, "fair" would not refer to the common law reasonable notice period, but would seek a balance between the urgency of the employer's business reasons for making the change and the provision of adequate time to the employee for preparing for it. The proposal includes requiring the parties to negotiate an express notice of termination period in their employment contract. These reforms, however, should be enacted only as part of a package that also includes a right not to be unjustly dismissed in misconduct and incompetence situations, reinforced by the right to reinstatement and other "make whole" remedies.[319] The proposal, therefore, seeks to make it easier for employers to respond to economic exigencies, but only in return for robust safeguards for the employee in performance-related dismissals.

Next, we examine the various components of the constructive dismissal doctrine along with the employee's duty to mitigate, which is particularly important in this context as it potentially relieves the employer from part of the burden of the constructive dismissal doctrine.

a) Determining the Employer's Contractual Obligations

In an earlier chapter we saw that employment contracts rarely contain a comprehensive set of express terms; rather, the flesh and blood of most employment contracts is provided by specific implied terms based on the parties' unstated factual intentions and by standard rights and dut-

---

318 See Brown & Beatty, above note 192 at paras. 4.42–4.53; A.V.M. Beattie, "Reasonableness in the Administration and Interpretation of Collective Agreements" (1993) Lab. Arb. Y.B. 249; B. Williams & M. Giardini, "Constructive Dismissal at Arbitration" (1992) 3 Lab. Arb. Y.B. 113.

319 G. England, "The Impact of the Charter on Individual Employnent Law in Canada: Rewriting an Old Story" (2006) 13 C.L.E.L.J. 1 at 38–39; G. England, "Recent Developments in Individual Employment Law: Tell Me the Old, Old Story" (2002) 9 C.L.E.L.J. 43 at 68–69.

ies implied into all employment contracts as a matter of course.[320] Not surprisingly, therefore, it is often difficult to say exactly what the employer's contractual obligations are. The following obligations of the employer are most commonly litigated: compensation, reassignment of job duties, reassignment of geographical location, and residual assertions of personal harassment and other unfair treatment.

i)   Amending the Compensation Structure

Traditionally, courts have held employers to be strictly bound to pay the employee any wages or other benefits due under the employment contract; they have also disallowed unilateral modifications to the compensation structure that would result, directly or indirectly, in any diminution of the employee's wages or benefits.[321] Only if the employee's financial losses were "relatively minor"[322] would the courts disallow constructive dismissal on the ground that the employer's breach would be non-repudiatory. Theoretically, the employee could sue his or her employer for a non-repudiatory breach, but in practice few employees would be foolhardy enough to do so.

However, this strict approach has been challenged by the 1993 decision of the Alberta Court of Appeal in *Otto v. Hamilton & Olsen Surveys Ltd.*,[323] which seems to give employers considerably broader scope to reduce compensation than previously. There, an employer that was suffering heavily in an economic downturn withheld its contributions to the registered retirement savings plans of two employees and shortened their paid vacations from six weeks to four. This amounted to a reduction in total compensation of 6.49 percent for one plaintiff and 8 percent for the other. Nevertheless, the court declined to find constructive dismissal when both individuals quit. The court stated that "reductions in the benefit package due to external economic pressures, but where salaries are maintained, have consistently escaped character-

---

320 See Chapter 3.

321 Examples: *Viens v. Suburban Distributors Ltd.*, [2000] O.J. No. 2623 (S.C.J.), involving a pay reduction; *Lahmann v. Mt. Hamilton Baptist Day Care Centre* (1996), 23 C.C.E.L. (2d) 56 (Ont. Gen. Div.), involving a reassignment of the employee from full- to part-time work; *Perrett v. Harrison Galleries* (2001), 18 C.C.E.L. (3d) 140 (B.C.S.C.), involving reducing the number of paid work days per week; *Lemay v. Canada Post Corporation* (2003), 26 C.C.E.L. (3d) 241 at 260 (Ont. S.C.J.), involving the amending of the performance appraisal system governing a group-based merit pay scheme.

322 *Poole v. Tomenson Saunders Whitehead Ltd.* (1987), 18 C.C.E.L. 238 at 248 (B.C.C.A.) [*Poole*]. See also *Pathak v. Jannock Steel Fabricating Co.* (1996), 21 C.C.E.L. (2d) 12 at 20–21 (Alta. Q.B.) [*Pathak*].

323 (1993), 12 Alta. L.R. (3d) 431 (C.A.) [*Otto*].

ization as fundamental breaches."[324] The court was clearly concerned with increasing the employer's flexibility to modify the compensation structure: it stated that it is reasonable to expect employees to take rollbacks in tough times in order to help an employer who shares the benefit of good times by giving them "generous" pay increases.[325] One wonders whether the court would allow an employee to sue an employer for refusing to grant a pay increase during an economic expansion!

The *Otto* decision may herald a widespread relaxation of the constructive dismissal doctrine in relation to changes to compensation. Thus, the spirit of *Otto* clearly underlies the subsequent decision of an Ontario court[326] that there was no constructive dismissal, despite the fact that the plaintiff's annual salary was reduced from $95,000 to $85,000, and the subsequent decision of an Alberta court that there was no constructive dismissal where a bonus was withdrawn.[327] However, there is no suggestion in the most recent Supreme Court of Canada decision on the point that any such relaxation would be in order.[328] It remains to be seen how the law in this area will develop.

ii) *Modifying Work Assignments*

The employer is impliedly bound under the employment contract to maintain the employer's job duties more or less in the same form as they were when the contract was made. The courts have long recognized that employers can unilaterally impose tangential or incidental changes in an employee's work assignments — after all, no employee reasonably expects, given the constantly changing work environment, that a job would be "frozen" for the duration of the employment relationship — but the employer cannot reassign work duties to such an extent as to transform the essential nature of the employee's position.[329]

---

324 *Ibid.* at 433.

325 *Ibid.*

326 *Black v. Second Cup Ltd.* (1995), 8 C.C.E.L. 72, especially at 79 (Ont. Gen. Div.).

327 *Pathak*, above note 322 at 20–21. See also *Rasanen v. Lisle-Metrix Ltd.* (2002), 17 C.C.E.L. (3d) 134 at 145 (Ont. S.C.J.), aff'd (2004), 33 C.C.E.L. (3d) 47 (Ont. C.A.) [*Rasanen*], where a 10 percent reduction in total compensation resulting from amending the bonus system was held not to be ground for constructive dismissal. (An alternative reason for the decision was that the breach had been condoned by the employee.)

328 Example: *Farber,* above note 315, but there the reduction was sufficiently substantial not to test the boundaries of the established principles.

329 See *Zifkin v. Axa Insurance (Canada)* (1996), 20 C.C.E.L. (2d) 272 at 278 (Alta. Q.B.) [*Zifkin*], where Nash J. stated that in order to ground constructive dismissal, "(t)he changes must be fundamental, severe, serious, unilateral and substantial so as to result in the employee performing a different job. . . . An

At what point changing a worker's job assignments goes beyond the purview of an existing position is a question of degree.

The courts have held that if an employee is demoted so that his or her status is significantly diminished, constructive dismissal will be grounded even if the employee does not suffer any loss of income.[330] The question is determined according to whether a reasonable person, objectively speaking, would regard the plaintiff's status as having been reduced; it is not determined according to the plaintiff's subjective perception.[331] In this area of the employment contract, judges acknowledge the importance to the employee of psychological—as opposed to purely monetary—benefits derived from working. This perspective should come as no surprise given the numerous Supreme Court of Canada pronouncements on the importance of safeguarding the psychological benefits that employees can legitimately expect under their employment contract,[332] and the importance attached to improving job satisfaction by modern personnel management specialists.[333] Indeed, in several decisions, constructive dismissal has been grounded on the employer's breach of a contractual duty to provide the employee with job satisfaction, even though there was *no* diminution of pay, status, or responsibility such as would constitute a demotion. The common element in these decisions is that the psychological satisfaction of doing the job was plainly of such importance to the employee as to make it a core component, rather than a peripheral feature of the parties' bargain.[334] In one of these cases, for example, an employee with forty-three

---

employer has some leeway to alter the employee's duties to meet the exigencies of the business."

330 *Lesiuk v. British Columbia Forest Products Ltd.* (1984), 56 B.C.L.R. 216 at 220 (S.C.), aff'd on other grounds (1986), 15 C.C.E.L. 91 (B.C.C.A.).

331 *Farber*, above note 315; *Palumbo v. Research Capital Corporation* (2004), 35 C.C.E.L. (3d) 1 (Ont. C.A.); *Cayen v. Woodwards Stores Ltd.* (1993), 45 C.C.E.L. 264 at 271 (B.C.C.A.) [*Cayen*].

332 The seminal judgment is that of Dickson C.J. in *Reference Re Public Service Employee Relations Act (Alberta)*, [1987] 1 S.C.R. 313 at 368. Dickson C.J.'s remarks regarding the psychological and social importance of work to the employee are now treated as authoritative, even though they were made in a dissenting judgment. See *Slaight Communications Inc. v. Davidson* (1989), 59 D.L.R. (4d) 416 (S.C.C.), aff'g [1985] 1 F.C. 253 (C.A) [*Slaight*]; *Machtinger*, above note 95; *Wallace*, above note 93 at 742–46; *Rizzo Shoes*, above note 27 at 35–36; *McKinley*, above note 190.

333 J. Godard, *Industrial Relations, the Economy and Society*, 2d ed. (North York, ON: Captus Press, 2003) c.6.

334 Examples: *Tanton*, above note 141; *Michaud v. R.B.C. Dominion Securities*, [2001] C.L.L.C. ¶210-032 (B.C.S.C.); *Bowen v. Ritchie Bros. Auctioneers Ltd.* (1999), 47 C.C.E.L. (2d) 232, especially at 236–37 (Ont. C.A.); *Wilkinson v. T. Eaton Co.*

years of seniority as a secretary was held to have been constructively dismissed when she resigned after being transferred to the position of salesperson in an economic downswing.[335] The Alberta Court of Appeal held that even though the employer may be acting in response to genuine business concerns, it has no implied right under an employment contract to transfer an employee from one position to another where doing so would involve substantially changing job duties and thereby eliminating the pleasure the employee derives from the job. The psychological satisfaction rationale also means that an employer cannot unilaterally promote an employee to a higher status or higher paid position if the employee prefers to remain in his or her current position due to the psychological satisfaction it provides.[336] Furthermore, if the parties to an employment contract clearly regard the continuation of certain job duties as essential to their bargain, the employer cannot change those duties, even though such a change might appear to be trivial to an outsider. It is an axiom of contract law that the parties' express or implied intentions as to what constitute the fundamental terms of their agreement must be honoured.[337]

However, it must not be thought that modern courts have ignored the employer's interest in maintaining a reasonable measure of flexibility when changing work assignments. On the contrary, many judges have emphasized the importance of safeguarding the employer in this regard.[338] As the Ontario High Court has stated: "[a]n employee's duties are not totally frozen when a job description is prepared. An employer must be allowed some reasonable leeway in which to alter . . . [its] employees'

(1992), 44 C.C.E.L. 287, especially at 288 (Alta. C.A.) [*Wilkinson*]; *Robinson v. Tingley's Ltd.* (1988), 20 C.C.E.L. 263 at 267 (N.B.Q.B.T.D.); *Corker v. University of British Columbia* (1990), 33 C.C.E.L. 246 at 252 (B.C.S.C.) [*Corker*]; and *Ashton v. Perle Systems Ltd.* (1994), 2 C.C.E.L. (2d) 243 (Ont. Gen. Div.).

335 *Wilkinson, ibid.* at 288.

336 Example: *Knezevic v. Rodger W. Armstrong and Associates Ltd.* (1997), 32 C.C.E.L. (2d) 172 at 182 (Ont. Gen. Div.), where the plaintiff had "a strong tendency to cling to the familiar."

337 *Laakso v. Valspar Inc.* (1990), 35 C.C.E.L. 276 (Ont. Div. Ct.), aff'g (1990), 32 C.C.E.L. 72 (Ont. Dist. Ct.), where introducing shift work for the plaintiff was held to ground constructive dismissal because both sides understood that the plaintiff had accepted the job because it did not involve shift work.

338 Examples: *Pathak*, above note 322 at 19, where Kenny J. stated, "An employer requires some latitude in restructuring the affairs of its operation and such a term . . . [i.e., that prevents an employer from introducing changes that would reduce the employee's level of responsibility] . . . would shift the balance too far in favour of the employee"; *Middleton v. Regal Greetings and Gifts Ltd.* (1996), 23 C.C.E.L. (2d) 61 at 68 (B.C.S.C.) [*Middleton*]; *Zifkin*, above note 329 at 278.

duties."[339] Accordingly, an employer is impliedly permitted to transfer a worker laterally within his or her classification and with no loss of pay, even though there may be some changes to duties, provided that the fundamental nature of the job remains intact;[340] to modify an employee's job duties where the practice in the firm or industry (and *a fortiori* the parties' previous relationship[341]) clearly shows that employers can regularly make the changes in question of their own accord;[342] to alter the job duties of employees in relatively low-level positions that do not have detailed job descriptions to accommodate the "fluctuations and changes within the business";[343] and to demote an employee who is not performing adequately to probationary status for the purpose of rehabilitation.[344] It is submitted that permitting the employer to unilaterally change job duties in the foregoing circumstances would be harmonious with the reasonable expectations of most workers and employers.

In determining the scope of the employer's implicit right to modify work assignments, the courts are more likely to permit a reassignment if the employer is acting in good faith for the sole purpose of enhancing efficiency than if the reassignment is a veiled attempt to drive the employee from the job or otherwise penalize him or her for some extraneous reason.[345]

Indeed, if the employer is experiencing severe economic difficulties, the courts may afford it greater than usual leeway to change employees' job assignments in order to weather a crisis.[346] Furthermore,

---

339 *Cadenhead v. Unicorn Abrasives of Canada Ltd.* (1984), 5 C.C.E.L. 241 at 251 (Ont. H.C.J.). In a similar vein, see *Canadian Bechtel Ltd. v. Mollenkopf* (1978), 1 C.C.E.L. 95 at 98 (Ont. C.A.).

340 See, for example, *Cayen*, above note 331 at 272.

341 Example: *Ally v. Institute of Chartered Accountants of Ontario* (1992), 42 C.C.E.L. 118 at 124 (Ont. Gen. Div.), by way of *obiter dicta*.

342 Example: *Hulme v. Cadillac Fairview Corp.* (1993), 1 C.C.E.L. (2d) 94 at 101 (Ont. Gen. Div.).

343 *Winsor v. Canada Trust Co.* (1993), 49 C.C.E.L. 235 at 245 (Nfld. C.A.), where advances in computer technology gradually made the plaintiff's traditional secretarial functions redundant; the employer eventually reassigned her to clerical and teller duties.

344 Example: *Chambers v. Axia Netmedia Corporation* (2004), 30 C.C.E.L. (3d) 243 (N.S.S.C.T.D.). However, the employer cannot unilaterally insist that the employee's previous period of reasonable notice of termination will be decreased.

345 See, for example, *Colasurdo v. CTG, Inc.* (1988), 18 C.C.E.L. 264 (Ont. H.C.J.), especially at 279–80, where the change was aimed at driving the employee away from the job; *Corker*, above note 334 at 252, where the reassignment was designed to "sidetrack" the plaintiff because of her abrasive personality.

346 As in *Pullen v. John C. Preston Ltd.* (1985), 7 C.C.E.L. 91 at 96 (Ont. H.C.J.), where the employer was held entitled to order a senior executive to perform

the courts are less likely to find a constructive dismissal if the employer handles a work reassignment in a fair manner that is consistent with the prevailing norms of personnel management practice[347] than if the reassignment is processed in a callous or otherwise unprofessional way.[348] It must be emphasized, however, that the presence of a legitimate business purpose and fair handling of the reassignment do not provide a defence to the employer where a modification of job duties is clearly beyond the purview of the worker's existing job or plainly involves a demotion;[349] rather, good faith and reasonableness tip the scales in borderline cases.

In order to escape the straitjacket of the constructive dismissal doctrine, some employers insist on inserting an express clause into the employment contract giving them the discretion to modify work assignments, rather like a management rights clause in a collective agreement.[350] The courts must, of course, give effect to such a provision for there can be no constructive dismissal if the express terms of the contract allow the employer to make the change. However, some courts have interpreted provisions conferring such broad discretion as implicitly requiring the employer to act in good faith for legitimate business reasons.[351] Some have gone further by implying into such clauses a requirement that the employer must act reasonably in making the reassignment, which is a broader standard of review than bad faith.[352] The danger with the reasonableness standard, of course, is that courts will be tempted to second-guess the employer's substantive business decisions in areas of the employer's specialized expertise; after all, the employer is responsible for running the plant, not the courts. Courts are well advised, therefore, to proceed cautiously when applying the reasonableness test. Nevertheless, we saw earlier that the Supreme Court of Canada has refused to imply into the employment contract a

---

substantially increased selling duties in order to see the firm through a severe economic crisis. See also *Fisher v. Eastern Bakeries Ltd.* (1986), 14 C.C.E.L. 123 (N.S.S.C.T.D.), aff'd (1987), 77 N.S.R. (2d) 90 (S.C.A.D.).

347 As in *George v. Morden & Helwig Ltd.* (1988), 20 C.C.E.L. 29 (Ont. H.C.J.).

348 As in *Corker*, above note 334 at 253.

349 Example: *Cox v. Royal Trust Corp. of Canada* (1989), 26 C.C.E.L. 203 at 207 (Ont. C.A.), leave to appeal to S.C.C. refused (1989), 33 C.C.E.L. 224n, where the court found a constructive dismissal on the basis of a demotion even though the employer demoted the employee as an alternative to firing him for performance deficiencies.

350 For further elaboration, see Chapter 3.

351 Example: *Park v. Parsons Brown & Co.* (1989), 39 B.C.L.R. (2d) 107 (C.A.).

352 *Snelling v. Tenneco Canada Inc.* (1992), 40 C.C.E.L. 122 at 126 (B.C.S.C.); *Greenberg*, above note 296.

standardized duty of fairness on employers,[353] even though the above-mentioned decisions appear to lend support for the duty's existence. As well, a reliable custom and practice allowing the employer unilaterally to modify job assignments can be implied into the contract so as to preclude a constructive dismissal.[354]

iii) Relocating the Employee's Place of Work

Traditionally, the courts have held that there is an implied term in all employment contracts that the employee will remain employed within reasonable commuting distance of his or her residence.[355] Therefore, in order to relocate the employee beyond this area, either an express clause must be included in the contract permitting such a relocation, or a term must be implied into the contract to the same effect based on the parties' past dealings, past practice, and/or personnel documentation clearly showing that this is what they intend.[356] The traditional view is that a term allowing the employer to implement a transfer would be implied only if there were hard evidence that this is what the parties factually contemplated. However, some courts have relaxed this view by holding that the parties are *presumed* to intend that the employer has the right to transfer in order to enhance its flexibility in reorganizing the work process.[357] In other words, there must be hard evidence showing that the parties did *not* factually intend the employer to have the right to transfer before a term will be implied into the contract curtailing that right. This new approach clearly reflects the growing cry among Canadian employers to maximize their flexibility. Of course, if

353 *Wallace*, above note 93, considered in Chapter 5, Section A, and in Section B(3)(c)(vi), above in this chapter.
354 Example: *Ferdinandusz v. Global Driver Services Inc.* (1998), 5 C.C.E.L. (3d) 248 at 257–58 (Ont. Gen. Div.), aff'd (2000), 5 C.C.E.L. (3d) 264 (Ont. C.A.).
355 The leading authority is *O'Brien v. Associated Fire Alarms Ltd.*, [1968] 1 W.L.R. 1916 (C.A.), arising under the British *Redundancy Payments Act*. In Canada, see *Weselan v. Totten Sims Hubicki Associates (1977) Ltd.* (2001), 16 C.C.E.L. (3d) 184 (Ont. C.A.); *MacDonald v. Tippet-Richardson Ltd.* (1996), 181 N.B.R. (2d) 61 (Q.B.).
356 Example: *Durrant v. Westeel-Rosco Ltd.* (1978), 7 B.C.L.R. 14 (S.C.), where the employee had been transferred several times in the past and the company policy manual plainly contemplated such transfers. See also *Holgate v. Bank of Nova Scotia* (1989), 27 C.C.E.L. 201 (Sask. Q.B.), where transfers were customary in the banking industry.
357 *Morris v. International Harvester Canada Ltd.* (1984), 7 C.C.E.L. 300 at 305 (Ont. H.C.J.), where the court ruled that employees must "normally" accept a transfer that is required for legitimate business purposes; *Smith v. Viking Helicopter Ltd.* (1989), 24 C.C.E.L. 113 at 118 (Ont. C.A.), where Finlayson J.A. held that employees must expect "reasonable dislocations."

the employer and employer clearly understood when they made their contract that the employee would only accept the job on the condition that the geographical location stays the same, a term will be implied on the basis of the parties' factual intention precluding any relocation.[358]

When implying a right to transfer, courts generally require the employer to act reasonably and in good faith vis-à-vis the worker. As the Saskatchewan Court of Queen's Bench stated in a case involving the lawful transfer of an executive:

> It is difficult to conceive of a company the [large] size of the defendant not having the right to transfer, on an executive level, subject always to bona fides, reasonableness, and a promotion of its own business interests, on the one hand, and absence of undue burden or hardship to the employee, on the other, provided the transfer does not involve a demotion or some other factor demeaning to the employee.[359]

What constitutes undue hardship will be governed by the worker's personal circumstances. It would, for example, probably be unreasonable to expect a worker to relocate if his or her children require special schooling or medical attention that is only available in the worker's current area.

iv) Personal Harassment and Otherwise Treating the Employee Unfairly
As we saw earlier, the Supreme Court of Canada in its 1997 decision in *Wallace* refused to imply a standardized term into all employment contracts that would oblige the employer to treat its employees fairly and reasonably in all aspects of the employment relationship.[360] The Court feared that if such a term were implied into the employment contract, the effect would be to open up to judicial review a potentially enormous range of employer decision-making under the rubric of the constructive dismissal doctrine: an employee could resign and sue for damages if he or she perceived any decision of the employer to be unfair or unreasonable.[361] Plainly, this would not augur well for economic efficiency. This

---

358 Example: *Marshall v. Newman, Oliver and McCarten Insurance Brokers*, [2004] C.L.L.C. ¶210-021 (Ont. C.A.).

359 *Page v. Jim Pattison Industries Ltd.*, [1982] 5 W.W.R. 97 at 107 (Sask. Q.B.), rev'd on another point (*sub nom. Jim Pattison Industries v. Page*) (1984), 4 C.C.E.L. 283 (Sask. C.A.).

360 The existence of such a duty was rejected in *Wallace*, above note 93, considered in Section B(3)(c)(vi), above in this chapter.

361 This risk explains why the Supreme Court of Canada has refused to imply a standardized term into the employment contract requiring employers to handle dismissals fairly in *Wallace*, ibid.

risk need not materialize, however, if the duty of fairness is defined relatively narrowly to encompass only (1) bad faith and procedural, rather than substantive, unfairness; and (2) personal bullying and harassment. Indeed, influential courts in other countries, including the English House of Lords, have recognized the existence of an independent implied duty of fairness and applied it relatively conservatively.[362]

Despite the *Wallace* holding, numerous constructive dismissal decisions seem to be based on breach by the employer of an implied term in the contract requiring it to treat the employee fairly. Thus, the courts have grounded constructive dismissal on failing proactively to advise a psychologically depressed employee of her rights to disability benefits during a termination interview;[363] systematically marginalizing an employee and building a paper trail of his performance deficiencies in the hope that he would quit;[364] conducting performance appraisals in a callous and insensitive manner;[365] setting unreasonably high performance targets that are beyond the employee's capacity;[366] scheduling work without attempting to accommodate the employee's family-care needs;[367] refusing to make reasonable efforts to train the employee to use new technologies;[368] failing to protect the employee against personal intimidation, harassment, and bullying;[369] and deliberately deceiving an employee into believing that she was being promoted into a permanent position when the employer knew the posting was temporary.[370] Prior to *Wallace,* there were numerous decisions in a similar vein.[371] So

---

362 *Malik v. BCCI,* [1998] A.C. 20 (H.L.), examined in D. Brodie, "A Fair Deal at Work" (1999) 19 Ox. J. Legal Stud. 83. The Australian courts have followed suit: e.g., *Russell v. The Trustees of the Roman Catholic Church for the Archdiocese of Sydney,* [2007] NSWSC 104.

363 *Menard v. Royal Insurance Company of Canada* (2000), 1 C.C.E.L. (3d) 96 (Ont. S.C.J.).

364 Example: *Miller v. ICO Canada Inc.* (2005), 40 C.C.E.L. (3d) 49 at 61 (Alta. Q.B.).

365 Example: *Lavinskas,* above note 177, especially at 141,457–58.

366 Example: *Mark v. Westend Development Corp.* (2002), 18 C.C.E.L. (3d) 90 (Ont. S.C.J.).

367 Example: *Hanni v. Western Road Rail Systems (1991) Inc.* (2002), 17 C.C.E.L. (3d) 79 (B.C.S.C.).

368 Example: *Levesque v. Sherwood Credit Union,* [2000] C.L.L.C. ¶210-038 at 141,303–4 (Sask. Q.B.).

369 Example: *Stamos v. Annuity Research and Market Services Ltd.,* [2002] C.L.L.C. ¶210-036 at 141,404 (Ont. S.C.J.) [*Stamos*].

370 *Wilson v. New Westminster Chamber of Commerce,* [2004] C.L.L.C. ¶210-001 at 141,006 (B.C. Prov. Ct.).

371 Example: *Lindsay v. Toronto Transit Commission* (1996), 97 C.L.L.C. ¶210-005 at 141,029 (Ont. Gen. Div.). See also *E.H. Freund Ltd. v. Cogasa Mining Corp.* (1983), 4 C.C.E.L. 60 (B.C.C.A.); *O'Neil v. Hodgins* (1988), 87 N.B.R. (2d) 384 (Q.B.T.D.).

far no court has ruled that this line of judicial reasoning is precluded by *Wallace*. It is highly unlikely, however, that the Supreme Court of Canada intended to preclude an employee exposed to callous mistreatment by the employer from quitting and suing for damages in view of the Court's ringing endorsement of the importance of safeguarding the vulnerable employee.[372]

Some Canadian judges have apparently grounded constructive dismissal on breach of an implied duty of procedural fairness on the employer's part. For example, if the employer failed to conduct a fair investigation of allegations of theft against an employee, or made substantial changes to job duties, there could be a finding of constructive dismissal.

b) Is the Employer's Breach Sufficiently Serious to Be Characterized as Repudiatory?

A breach of contract on the employer's part will only ground constructive dismissal if it is sufficiently serious to be characterized as repudiatory.[373] Otherwise, the employee's remedy will be restricted to damages flowing from the breach in question, not from wrongful dismissal. In practice, of course, few employees who wish to keep their job would sue their employer for damages for a non-repudiatory breach. Courts have used various nomenclatures in an attempt to characterize the essence of a repudiatory breach, including whether or not the breach is "fundamental"[374] or "goes to the root of the contract."[375] The onus of proof rests with the employee.

The vagueness of the definition affords the courts ample scope for policy-making in their determinations. Indeed, in a leading decision on constructive dismissal in 1918, MacCardie J. said that the "doctrine of repudiation must of course be applied in a just and reasonable manner."[376] Not surprisingly, therefore, the definition of "repudiatory" will be influenced by the changing standards of what the courts perceive to be "fair" management practice. One might expect the current preoccu-

---

372 *Wallace*, above note 93 at 141,214–15. The Supreme Court of Canada has subsequently reiterated these sentiments in *Rizzo Shoes*, above note 27 at 35–36; and *McKinley*, above note 190 at 141,206.

373 In *Farber*, above note 315, the Supreme Court of Canada used the equivalent word "resiliatory," that case arising under the *Civil Code of Quebec*.

374 Examples: *Schwann v. Husky Oil Operations Ltd.* (1989), 27 C.C.E.L. 103 at 106 (Sask. C.A.); *Otto*, above note 323.

375 Examples: *Orth v. MacDonald Dettwiler & Associates Ltd.* (1986), 16 C.C.E.L. 41 at 55–56 (B.C.C.A.); *Elliott v. Southam Inc.* (1988), 88 C.L.L.C. ¶14,045 at 12,244 (Alta. Q.B.).

376 *Re Rubel Bronze & Metal Co. and Vos*, [1918] 1 K.B. 315 at 322.

pation with enhancing managerial efficiency to result in courts narrowing the definition of "repudiatory" in order to expand the employer's leeway to change terms and conditions of employment. Certainly, this has happened where the employer modifies the compensation structure; the employee's financial loss has been characterized as being insufficiently substantial to constitute a repudiatory breach.[377] In a similar vein, some courts[378] have held that alterations in an employee's job duties—even those involving a "significant erosion"[379] of the employee's former managerial duties and, therefore, his or her status—are non-repudiatory breaches.

c) Continuing to Work under Altered Terms: Condonation and the Employee's Duty to Mitigate

Instead of quitting immediately in the face of an employer's repudiatory breach, the employee may continue to work under the changed terms and conditions of employment for a period of time before quitting, and by doing so, lose the right to sue for constructive dismissal. An employee may continue to work under changed terms for various reasons: he or she may genuinely accept them as part of the employment contract, may act out of financial necessity while searching for replacement employment, may test the suitability of the new arrangements on a trial basis, or may want to minimize personal losses pursuant to the common law duty to mitigate.

The courts will not deem an employee to have condoned the employer's repudiatory breach unless he or she genuinely consents to relinquishing the right to sue. The test for condonation is the objective intention of the employee: would a reasonable person in the position of the employee believe that the employee intends, voluntarily and without coercion, to give up his or her legal right to sue and agree to the changed terms as forming part of the employment contract? The courts recognize that an employee should be allowed a reasonable trial period in which to assess the suitability of working under the new terms before condonation will be found.[380] Furthermore, when an employee is faced with a Hobson's choice of either continuing to work or being unemployed because there are no replacement jobs available, the courts

---

377 Examples: *Barrett v. Sutherland Motors Ltd.* (1989), 28 C.C.E.L. 239 (N.B.Q.B.T.D.); *Poole*, above note 322; *Otto*, above note 323.

378 Examples: *Middleton*, above note 338 at 68; *Zifkin*, above note 329, especially at 278.

379 *Middleton, ibid.* at 68.

380 Example: *Greaves v. Ontario Municipal Employees Retirement Board* (1995), 15 C.C.E.L. (2d) 94 at 108 (Ont. Gen. Div.) [*Greaves*].

take the realistic view that he or she should be allowed a reasonable
time to conduct a job search without prejudicing the right to sue for
constructive dismissal, with reasonableness being determined by the
availability of alternative work.[381] As Jurianz J.A. of the Ontario Court
of Appeal explains:

> The vulnerability of employees who believe they may have been
> constructively dismissed and the difficult of making the life-alter-
> ing decisions they face must be recognized. In this context, it is
> understandable that such employees may wish to try to adjust to the
> new terms and conditions without affirming the employer's right to
> make these changes before taking the radical step of advancing a
> constructive dismissal claim. Allowing employees reasonable time to
> address the new terms before they are forced to take an irrevocable
> legal position not only addresses the vulnerability but also promotes
> stability and harmonious relations in the workplace.[382]

Accordingly, most courts have been generous to the employee in
finding that he or she has not consented despite sometimes lengthy
periods of work under the new arrangements.[383] Indeed, one court has
even held that an employee who continues to work under the modified
terms while suffering from work-induced stress and depression cannot
be deemed to have assented to the changes without explicitly notifying the employer to that effect.[384] Nevertheless, there clearly comes a
point at which continuing to work under the changed terms would
lead the employer, as a reasonable person, to believe that an employee
has condoned a change; in that situation, it would be unfair to allow
an employee to claim that, subjectively speaking, he or she did not
really intend to accept the changes.[385] Here, the courts will either deem

---

381 *Tilbe v. Richmond Realty Ltd.* (1995), 11 C.C.E.L. (2d) 11 at 20 (B.C.S.C.).

382 *Belton v. Liberty Insurance Company of Canada* (2004), 34 C.C.E.L. (3d) 203 at
     213 (Ont. C.A.).

383 Examples: *Campbell v. Merrill Lynch Canada Inc.* (1992), 47 C.C.E.L. 248
     (B.C.S.C.), where a senior marketing analyst who continued to work in a clerical
     position for four months had not accepted the demotion; *Garcia v. Newmar Win-
     dows Manufacturing* (1996), 25 C.C.E.L. (2d) 114 at 120 (Ont. Div. Ct.), where six
     months of work under the changed terms was held not to be acceptance, given
     the low market demand for the plaintiff's kind of work. But compare *Duplessis v.
     Irving Pulp & Paper Ltd.* (1983), 1 C.C.E.L. 196 at 203 (N.B.C.A.), where Stratton
     J.A. stated that the decision to terminate must be made "promptly" following
     the employer's breach.

384 *Dick v. Canadian Pacific Ltd.* (2000), 4 C.C.E.L. (3d) 6 at 19 (N.B.C.A.).

385 Examples: *Belanger v. Hospital Dietary Service Ltd.*, [1983] O.J. No. 2051 (Dist.
     Ct.), where a hospital director who was demoted to assistant director and con-

condonation to have occurred, or rule that the employee is estopped[386] from denying that he or she has agreed to the new arrangements. Of course, if the employee continues working while explicitly protesting to the employer that he or she does not consent to being bound by the changed terms, there can be no condonation.[387] It has been held that commencing litigation against the employer will constitute an effective protest so as to bar condonation.[388] In addition, condonation presupposes that the employee knows the full scope of any changes to working conditions;[389] plainly, a person cannot consent to relinquish legal rights until and unless he or she knows precisely the full extent to which such rights have been violated.

Continued working under the changed terms may be further complicated by the employee's common law duty to mitigate losses. In an effort to temper somewhat the rigours of constructive dismissal for employers, the courts have held that the employee must continue to work under the changed terms while he or she seeks replacement employment pursuant to the common law duty to mitigate losses flowing from the employer's repudiation of the contract, but only if a reasonable person in the employee's position would regard continuing to work as tolerable in both the economic and psychological senses.[390] Thus, the employee is excused from continuing to work, where doing so would cause undue hardship—for example, if his or her wages are reduced, if the working conditions have substantially changed so as to make them unsatisfying, if the changes have seriously diminished the employee's prestige in the eyes of peers, or if the atmosphere in the workplace is acrimonious or humiliating. Consequently, it will often be difficult to determine whether an employee is continuing to work under changed

---

tinued to work in that position for seven months was held to have accepted the change; *Rasanen*, above note 327 at 145 (Ont. S.C.J.), where an employee who continued to work for two years after a 10 percent reduction in his performance bonus was held to have condoned the breach; *Rosscup v. Westfair Foods Ltd.*, 1999 ABQB 629 at paras. 34–36 [*Rosscup*], where an employee who worked for several years following a unilateral reduction of his severance entitlements was ruled not to have consented to the modification.

386 Example: *Erson v. Gaults Ltd.*, [1930] 2 D.L.R. 999 (Man. C.A.).

387 Example: *Hill v. Peter Gorman Ltd.* (1957), 9 D.L.R. (2d) 124 (Ont. C.A.), where work continued for sixteen months without condonation being found because the plaintiff consistently repeated his protest at the employer's actions.

388 *Lehman v. Davis* (1993), 94 C.L.L.C. ¶14,014, especially at 12,072 (Ont. Gen. Div.) [*Lehman*].

389 *Dauphinee v. Major Foods Ltd.* (1984), 62 N.S.R. (2d) 381 (S.C.A.D.), aff'g (1983), 56 N.S.R. (2d) 517 (S.C.T.D.); *Rosscup*, above note 385.

390 *Evans*, above note 183 at paras. 30–34.

terms because he or she genuinely consents to them or is obliged to work by the duty to mitigate. In order to safeguard the employee's claim to constructive dismissal, the courts impose a "very heavy burden"[391] on the employer to prove that an employee who continues working pursuant to the duty to mitigate intends to relinquish his or her legal rights. Indeed, it has been held that continuing to work beyond the period of notice of termination is a minimal requirement of proof of such an intent.[392]

Finally, several questions of technical contract law doctrine can come into play where an employee consents to continuing the employment relationship on the basis of the changed terms introduced by the employer.[393] These questions relate to the precise manner in which the consensual variation is to be given contractual effect. First, in order to be valid, any consensual modification of the contract must be supported by fresh consideration from the promisee, since it is an axiom of contract law that the performance of a pre-existing contractual obligation cannot provide consideration to support a contractual variation. In order to uphold consensual modifications to employment contracts, the courts have found consideration, depending on the circumstances, in the employer's forbearance to exercise its legal privilege of lawfully terminating the contract and the employee's forbearance to exercise the legal privilege of lawfully resigning.[394] However, this will be possible only if the employee really would have quit or the employer really would have terminated the contract, had the other party not accepted the modification.[395] Second, the parties may be said to have consensually rescinded their old employment contract—an agreement to rescind generates its own consideration—and replaced it with a new one that includes the changed terms. One difficulty with this analysis is that a rescission would not normally be found unless the parties intend to replace a substantial majority of their contractual terms, not to make one or two changes. Difficulties may also arise in determining which provisions of the old contract carry over into the new one. The rescission analysis, therefore, is less likely to hold

---

391 *Cayen*, above note 331 at 275; *Noel v. Little Shuswap Indian Band* (1996), 22 C.C.E.L. (2d) 204 at 207 (B.C.C.A.), where Prowse J.A. stated that this onus would be discharged only "very infrequently."

392 *Cayen*, ibid. at 275.

393 For further elaboration, see Chapter 3.

394 Examples: *Techform Products Ltd. v. Wolda* (2001), 12 C.C.E.L. (3d) 184, especially at 193 (Ont. C.A.); *Hobbs*, above note 85, especially at 141,251–52 (Ont. C.A.). See generally the analysis in A.L. Corbin, *Corbin on Contracts* (St. Paul, MN: West, 1952) at 135.

395 *Ibid.*

than the consensual variation analysis, despite the need to fictionalize consideration under the latter approach.

The future of the constructive dismissal doctrine will be heavily influenced by changing economic conditions. The ongoing intensification of foreign competition on Canadian employers will likely escalate their drive for greater flexibility in changing terms and conditions of employment, resulting in increased pressure on the courts and legislators to relax the constructive dismissal doctrine. Clearly, the law in this area is at a crossroads.

E. LEGISLATIVE RESTRICTIONS ON THE PERMISSIBLE GROUNDS OF AND PROCEDURES GOVERNING DISMISSAL

Dismissal is wrongful if it breaches legislation that either prohibits the employer from dismissing an employee for specified reasons or establishes certain procedures that must be followed before dismissal can be invoked. The human rights legislation in all jurisdictions, for example, prohibits dismissal—or any other form of discrimination regarding the employment relationship—on designated protected grounds, such as race, sex, disability, and religion. This legislation is dealt with in detail in Chapter 7 and will not be re-examined here. The collective bargaining legislation in all jurisdictions makes it unlawful for an employer to dismiss or otherwise penalize an employee because he or she is a trade union supporter or has participated in a trade union's lawful activities.[396] Detailed analysis of this legislation is beyond the scope of this book.[397] The employment standards legislation in all jurisdictions makes it unlawful for an employer to dismiss an employee because he or she takes a leave of absence provided for under the acts such as parental leave,[398] because the employee has filed a complaint against the employer or has participated in any other proceedings under the employment standards legislation,[399] or because garnishment proceedings have been launched against him or her.[400]

---

396 Example: Alberta *Labour Relations Code*, S.A. 1988, c. L-12, ss. 19 and 146–47.
397 See G.W. Adams, *Canadian Labour Law*, 2d ed., looseleaf (Aurora, ON: Canada Law Book, 1993) c. 10 [Adams].
398 See Chapter 6, Section B.
399 Example: *B.C. ESA*, above note 30, s. 83.
400 Example: *CLC*, above note 28, s. 238. The other jurisdictions with this protection are Alberta, Manitoba, Saskatchewan, Nova Scotia, Ontario, and Quebec.

This section of the book focuses attention on the statutory protection against unjust discharge in the federal jurisdiction, Nova Scotia, and Quebec. In addition, the position of employees in the public sector, where legislation frequently limits the grounds on which or procedures by which dismissal can be invoked, is also analyzed, along with the residual administrative law duty of procedural fairness governing the dismissal of public office holders.

1) The Statutory Unjust Discharge Schemes in the Federal Jurisdiction, Nova Scotia, and Quebec

The employment standards legislation in these three jurisdictions is unique in providing the non-unionized employee with access to neutral adjudication at the state's expense in order to challenge the justness of his or her dismissal.[401] There are two critical features of this statutory right not to be unjustly dismissed: (1) the adjudicator may order compulsory reinstatement of the employee, a remedy normally unavailable in a common law suit for wrongful dismissal; and (2) the adjudicator may award compensation (and other non-monetary remedies) in order to make whole the employee's real-world losses flowing from the dismissal, unlike in a common law wrongful dismissal suit, where damages are limited to such contractually binding entitlements as would have vested in the employee during the notice period. This legislation was introduced in response to the International Labor Organization's *Termination of Employment Recommendation* No. 119. The reasons so few provinces have enacted unjust dismissal protections are, first, to spare the public purse the costs of administering the scheme, and second, to maintain the employer's flexibility in dismissing employees.[402] Given the current pressures on Canadian employers

---

401 *CLC*, above note 28, s. 240; *N.S. LSC*, above note 39, s. 71; *Que. LSA*, above note 269, s. 124. See generally G. England, "Section 240 of the *Canada Labour Code*: Some Current Pitfalls" (1999) 27 Man. L.J. 17; G. England, "Unjust Dismissal and Other Termination-Related Provisions," Report to the Federal Labour Standards Review (Ottawa: Human Resources and Social Development Canada, 2006); *Employment Law in Canada*, above note 23, c. 17 (VI); Arthurs Report, above note 55 at 172–88.

402 The economic costs and benefits of unjust dismissal laws have been hotly debated. Proponents argue they increase efficiency by strengthening managerial control over discipline, inducing employers to be more careful when recruiting, training, and disciplining employees, and increasing the stature of personnel managers: e.g., B. Hepple, "The Rise and Fall of Unfair Dismissal" in W.E.J. McCarthy, ed., *Legal Intervention in Industrial Relations: Gains and Losses* (Oxford: Blackwell, 1992) 79 at 94; S. Abraham, "Can a Wrongful Discharge Statute

to minimize labour costs in order to compete with foreign firms and on Canadian provincial governments to reduce their debts and deficits, it is unlikely that unjust dismissal schemes will be introduced elsewhere in the near future.

Here, attention is focused on the federal scheme because it shares the main characteristics of the other schemes, and the jurisprudence on the federal statute is more extensive than in Nova Scotia or Quebec. However, significant differences in the Quebec and Nova Scotia models will be indicated where applicable.

a)   The Rules of Eligibility

In order to file a complaint of unjust discharge under section 240 of the *Canada Labour Code*, the following prerequisites must be met: (1) the claimant must qualify as an "employee,"[403] (2) he or she must not be a "manager,"[404] (3) he or she must have accrued at least twelve consecutive months of continuous employment with the employer,[405] (4) a timely application must have been filed,[406] (5) the claimant must have been dismissed,[407] (6) the claimant must not have been released as a result of a "layoff,"[408] (7) the claimant must not be covered by a collective agreement[409] or have access to some other statutory procedure for redress,[410] (8) the claimant must have exhausted preadjudication conciliation,[411] and (9) the claimant must have received ministerial approval

---

Really Benefit Employers?" (1998) 37 R.I./I.R. 499. Opponents argue that they unduly increase employers' termination costs: e.g., D. Million, "Default Rules, Wealth Distribution, and Corporate Law Reform: Employment at Will versus Job Security," above note 195; A.P. Morriss, "Bad Data, Bad Economics, and Bad Policy: Time to Fire Wrongful Discharge Law," above note 195; J.H. Verkerke, "An Empirical Perspective on Indefinite Term Employment Contracts: Resolving the Just Cause Debate," above note 195; A.B. Krueger, "The Evolution of Unjust-Dismissal Legislation in the United States," above note 195 at 645; R.A. Epstein, "In Defense of the Contract at Will," above note 195; B. Ewing, C. North, & B. Taylor, "The Employment Effects of a 'Good Cause' Discharge Standard in Montana" (2005) 59 Indus. & Lab. Rel. Rev. 17.

403 Although s. 240 reads "person," this has been interpreted as "employee": e.g., *Pilling v. Southern Alberta Broadcasting Ltd.* (22 June 1987), Alta. Ref. No. 776 (Rooke) [*Pilling*].

404 *CLC*, above note 28, s. 167(3).

405 *Ibid.*, s. 240(1)(a).

406 *Ibid.*, ss. 240(2) & (3).

407 *Ibid.*, s. 240(1).

408 *Ibid.*, s. 242(3.1)(a).

409 *Ibid.*, s. 240(1)(b).

410 *Ibid.*, s. 242(3.1)(b).

411 *Ibid.*, s. 241(2).

for adjudication.[412] All of these requirements must be met in order for an adjudicator to have jurisdiction to hear the complaint of unjust dismissal. In order to protect the employee's access to adjudication, the courts have held that the prerequisites must be construed narrowly,[413] as is usually the case with remedial legislation, such as employment standards statutes. In order to further the protective thrust of the legislation, adjudicators have ruled that if an employer fails to raise an objection to the adjudicator's jurisdiction based on one of the foregoing requirements prior to the commencement of the adjudication hearing, it will be deemed to have waived its right to object and will be precluded from subsequently raising the objection during the hearing.[414]

The requirement that the claimant must be an employee brings into play the general definition of employee examined in Chapter 2. Even if the claimant is an employee, he or she will be ineligible if a manager as defined under the Code. The justifications for denying such persons protection are, first, that they will likely have adequate financial safeguards against wrongful dismissal at common law; second, that the common law reasonable notice period is relatively lengthy for managers; and third, that reinstatement would be inappropriate for senior level managers because of the unique trust relationship normally implicit in such positions. Clearly, these rationales are questionable in the case of low- and middle-level managers—often referred to as the "forgotten" level of industry.[415] Accordingly, courts have interpreted the manager exclusion in a "narrow and restrictive sense"[416] in order to limit it to high-echelon managerial positions. Thus, a manager must perform duties relating to the administration of the organization itself; it will not suffice if he or she performs only a core production or marketing function.[417] Administrative functions include personnel supervision (hiring, firing, and performance appraisal);[418] budget plan-

412 Ibid., s. 241(3).
413 Island Telegraph Co. v. Canada (Minister of Labour) (1991), 44 C.C.E.L. 168 at 183 (F.C.T.D.) [Island Telegraph], involving the "manager" exclusion.
414 Ennis v. King's Clear Indian Band (November 1994) (Bruce) at 1 and 12.
415 The Arthurs Report criticized this exclusion: above note 55 at 69–70.
416 Noel v. Sioux Valley Chief and Band Council (1 November 1987), Ont. Ref. No. 584 (Fox-Decent), at 3 of the award, following the remarks of Heald J. in Avalon Aviation Ltd. v. Desgagne (1981), 42 N.R. 337 (F.C.A.).
417 Lee-Shanok v. Banca Nazionale Del Lavoro of Canada Ltd., [1987] 3 F.C. 578 (C.A.), especially at 589–90, Stone J.; Canada (A.G.) v. Gauthier, [1980] 2 F.C. 393 (C.A.).
418 Control over hiring, firing, and performance appraisal by itself, however, will not establish status as a "manager" without authority over other key organizational matters: e.g., Walsh v. A.M.R. Ground Handling Services (January 1994)

ning; making contracts with suppliers and customers; allocating expenditures for the purchase, repair, and maintenance of the plant and equipment; allocating wage increases; making decisions about product and service design; and regulating the work process in general. In addition, a manager must have the responsibility to implement decisions in his or her own right; it will not suffice if he or she merely submits recommendations to a superior authority who makes the decision. As a federal trial judge put it, a manager must exercise "independent action, autonomy and discretion."[419] In addressing this question, adjudicators look at what the employee concerned actually does, not solely at a formal job description. Thus, if an employee does not have the *de jure* authority to implement decisions, but the person who does consistently rubber-stamps the employee's recommendations, then that employee will be a manager.[420] Conversely, an employee will not be a manager if his or her *de jure* decision-making authority in practice is subject to approval by a superior.[421]

The manager exclusion in respect to section 240 of the *Canada Labour Code* must not be confused with the exclusion from collective bargaining rights of employees who exercise "managerial functions." The latter category encompasses relatively low-echelon supervisors who have the power to make decisions in areas critical to an employee's career, such as discipline and dismissal, performance appraisal, promotion, and hiring. However, despite some earlier intimations to the contrary,[422] section 240 adjudicators now hold that the exercise of managerial functions in this sense is not a sufficient condition for manager status under section 240. This is because the policy reasons for the managerial functions exclusion from collective bargaining rights differ from the policy reasons for the manager exclusion from the unjust discharge scheme.

The requirement that a claimant must have twelve consecutive months of continuous employment with his or her employer is normally justified as providing the employer with a trial period to appraise the

---

(Musgrave) at 4. In contrast, effective control over these matters will suffice to establish that a person exercises "managerial functions" under collective bargaining legislation: e.g., *McIntyre Porcupine Mines Ltd. v. U.S.W.A.*, [1975] 2 C.L.R.B.R. 234 (O.L.R.B.).

419 Mackay J. in *Island Telegraph*, above note 413 at 184.

420 Example: *Khanbabi v. U.L.S. International Inc.* (29 August 1986), B.C. Ref. No. 676 (O'Shea).

421 Example: *Morris v. Moricetown Indian Band*, [1994] C.L.A.D. No. 669 at 24–25 (Gillis).

422 *Canadian Imperial Bank of Commerce v. Bateman*, [1991] 3 F.C. 586 (T.D.).

employee's performance and as reducing the costs to the public purse of processing an excessive number of complaints. However, in Nova Scotia the qualifying period is ten consecutive years of continuous employment with the same employer; in Quebec it is two years. Lengthy qualifying periods that have the effect of excluding short-term workers run the risk of being challenged under section 15 of the *Charter*[423] as indirectly discriminating against women and members of visible minorities since these groups occupy most short-term jobs. The critical questions are which interruptions of active work on the employee's part and which forms of corporate restructuring will rupture the accrual of continuous employment.

The starting point in determining the effect of an absence from active work on the accrual of continuous employment—for example, a temporary layoff, a disciplinary suspension, or a sabbatical leave—is to ascertain whether or not the parties expressly or impliedly intend their contract of employment to persist throughout the hiatus. Only if the contractual nexus is severed by the absence will continuous employment be interrupted and the employee have to requalify by working a further twelve-month period of continuous employment.[424] In the absence of express terms on the matter, the parties' intentions must be determined from all of the surrounding circumstances. For example, continuous employment was held not to have been ruptured where the employer approved a two-month leave of absence for the employee;[425] where casual workers were retained on the payroll on an "on call" basis, even though the workers were not assigned to perform any work for a substantial time;[426] and where seasonal workers are consistently recalled from layoff at the beginning of each new season,[427] especially if the employer records the off-season as a layoff—as opposed to a termination for unemployment insurance purposes,[428] or maintains the workers' eligibility for fringe benefit coverage during the off-season.[429] However, if either the employee or the employer takes "some affirma-

---

423 Above note 22.

424 *Larocque v. Louis Bull Tribe, Hobbema*, December 2003 (Dunlop) at 21, aff'd 2005 FC 1536 (T.D.).

425 *Harper v. MTF Transport Ltd.* (27 March 1991), B.C. Ref. No. 1392 (Taylor).

426 Example: *Fink v. International Carriers Ltd.* (26 April 1979) (Ianni) [*Fink*].

427 *Carew, Davis and Dean v. Beothuk Data Systems Ltd.* (26 April 1994) (Blanchard) at 25 [*Beothuk*].

428 Example: *Mongrain v. Pelee Island Transportation* (5 August 1986), Ont. Ref. No. 558 (Ambramowitz).

429 Example: *Priegnitz v. BeauDril Ltd.* (27 October 1986), Alta. Ref. No. 713 (Samuels).

tive action . . . to terminate the employment relationship"[430] during a leave of absence, continuity of employment will be severed.

The common law of the employment contract plays the dominant role in determining when a leave of absence will interrupt continuous employment, with the legislation itself having relatively little to say on the matter. The governor in council is empowered under section 245 of the *Canada Labour Code* to make regulations on interruptions in employment that will be deemed not to have interrupted continuity of employment. As yet, the regulations provide no comprehensive guidance on the matter. It is perhaps surprising that the legislators should have deferred to the intention of the parties on this matter when the expenditure of substantial public funds on processing claims is at stake.

Regarding the effect of corporate restructuring on the accrual of continuous employment, at common law any change in the corporate identity of the employer—for example, by way of a merger or amalgamation—operates as a dismissal, even if employees are kept on by the new employer; there is no automatic assignment of the employment contract at common law.[431] Therefore, unless the new employer agrees, expressly or impliedly, to recognize any previous seniority with the predecessor employer, the employee's continuous employment is ruptured. In order to protect the employee in this situation, the *Canada Labour Code* contains a "successor rights" provision, which states that where any "federal work, undertaking or business, or part thereof" is "transferred" from one employer to another in the federal jurisdiction by way of "sale, lease, merger or otherwise," the seniority of transferred employees is preserved *vis-à-vis* the new employer.[432] The successorship provision only applies in the default position where the parties have not agreed in their contract of employment that accrued seniority with the predecessor employer will carry over.[433]

Furthermore, section 255 of the *Canada Labour Code* grants the minister discretion to declare two or more employers to be a "single employer" for the purpose of, *inter alia*, section 240 provided that they

---

430 *Fink*, above note 426 at 4.

431 *Nokes v. Doncaster Amalgamated Collieries Ltd.*, [1940] A.C. 1014 (H.L.). This topic is examined in Chapter 2, Section B.

432 *CLC*, above note 28, ss. 189 and 246. For detailed elaboration of the interpretive difficulties arising under these sections, see *MacLachlan v. Pineridge Broadcasting* (9 April 1985), Ont. Ref. No. 483 (Emrich), and *Lafrenière v. Loomis Courier Service* (1 February 1991), Que. Ref. No. 1137 (Cossette). On the "successorship" provisions generally, see Chapter 2, Section B.

433 *Graham v. Laurentian Bank of Canada*, [1995] C.L.A.D. No. 946 (Stanley), especially at 8.

are operating "associated or related federal works, undertakings or businesses" under "common control or direction." This is usually referred to as a common employer declaration.[434]

Finally, the Nova Scotia courts have held that an employee's prior service in a position excluded from the *Labour Standards Code* can be counted towards the ten-year qualifying period if he or she is subsequently transferred into a position covered by the Code.[435] The ruling would presumably apply to the federal Code, too.

In order to be timely under section 240(2) of the *Canada Labour Code*, a complaint of unjust discharge must be filed with an inspector of the Canada Human Resources and Skills Development Department within ninety days of the date on which the employee was dismissed. The minister, however, has the discretion to extend this deadline where the complainant filed a complaint with a "government official" whom he or she erroneously "believed" to have authority to deal with it.[436] In determining whether or not to grant an extension, the minister must provide both protagonists with a summary of the information on which he or she is basing the judgment and allow each to make written representations prior to rendering a decision.

The employment relationship can end for various reasons, but adjudication under section 240 is only available if it ends as a result of a dismissal. The hallmark of a dismissal is that the employment contract must be terminated by the act of the employer, not by an act of the employee, such as a resignation, nor by operation of law, such as the doctrine of frustration of contract. It follows that if an employee is hired under a contract that is expressed to expire *automatically* after a fixed time or upon completion of a designated task, there is no dismissal if the contract expires in the specified way without being renewed.[437] Potentially, therefore, employers could circumvent section 240 simply by engaging their employees under a series of fixed term contracts of less than twelve months' duration. Article 2.3 of the ILO's *Termination of Employment Recommendation No. 119* requires governments to legislate safeguards against abuse of fixed term contracts,[438] but this has not yet happened in Canada.

---

434 See generally Chapter 2, Section B.

435 *Murphy v. Halifax (City of)* (1995), 9 C.C.E.L. (2d) 1 (N.S.C.A.).

436 *CLC*, above note 28, s. 240(3).

437 Example: *Eskasoni School Board v. MacIsaac* (1986), 86 C.L.L.C. ¶14,042 (F.C.A.).

438 In Britain, legislation states that if a fixed-term contract is renewed over a period of four or more years, employment is deemed to be continuous for the purpose of statutory entitlements: "Department of Trade and Industry Guidelines on Employment Legislation, Fixed Term Work," online: www.berr.gov.uk/employment/employment-legislation/employment-guidance/page18475.html.

Earlier in this chapter we saw that at common law, it is sometimes difficult to distinguish between a *bona fide* resignation on the employee's part and a disguised dismissal.[439] This difficulty also arises under section 240 of the *Canada Labour Code*. Echoing that of collective agreement arbitrators, the response of adjudicators is accurately stated as follows:

(1) A resignation has both a subjective element (the intention to resign) and an objective element (an act resulting from the intention to resign).

(2) Resignation is a right personal to the employee and not the employer; it should thus be voluntary.

(3) A resignation is perceived differently depending on whether or not the intention to resign has been expressed.

(4) The intention to resign is not presumed unless the employee's conduct is inconsistent with any other interpretation.

(5) The expression of an intention to resign is not necessarily conclusive as to the employee's real intention.

(6) In case of ambiguity, a resignation is generally not found.[440]

(7) The prior and subsequent conduct of the parties is an important element in determining whether there has been a resignation.[441]

The doctrine of constructive dismissal[442] has been incorporated by implication under section 240 by almost all adjudicators. The currently accepted test for the existence of a constructive dismissal is whether the employer's treatment of the employee is sufficiently unreasonable and unfair to warrant the average employee in the claimant's position quitting in response.[443] Unquestionably, it is essential to apply the constructive dismissal doctrine; otherwise, the employer could easily circumvent the section by deliberately making life so miserable for the employee that he or she resigns. However, in one key respect, constructive dismissal is given a different meaning under section 240 than

---

439 See Section D(1), above in this chapter.

440 See, for example, *Taylor v. RTL-Robinson Enterprises Ltd.*, [1995] C.L.A.D. No. 648 (Koshman) at 10.

441 *Gonzola v. Smith Rutherford Transport Inc.*, [2005] C.L.A.D. No. 441 (Yost) at para. 35; *Boyce v. Gershman Transport International Ltd.*, [1994] C.L.A.D. No. 1163 (Coke) at para. 41, citing an earlier award of adjudicator Cregan in *Overall v. Sybarite Investments Ltd.* (8 August 1985), B.C. Ref. No. 528.

442 The common law application of the doctrine is examined in Section D(3), above in this chapter.

443 Examples: *Stanger v. John Grant Haulage Ltd.*, May 2002 (Wacyk) at 10; *Hirst v. Canadian Imperial Bank of Commerce*, [1995] C.L.A.D. No. 623 (Wright) at 6–7 [*Hirst*].

at common law. Because an employee who is laid off because of "lack of work or the discontinuance of a function" is disqualified from bringing a section 240 complaint,[444] constructive dismissal cannot apply where the employer unilaterally changes terms and conditions of employment for legitimate economic reasons—at common law, such changes will ground constructive dismissal.[445]

Of all the eligibility prerequisities, none has generated as many difficulties of interpretation as the layoff exception. Section 242(3.1)(a) of the *Canada Labour Code* precludes a complaint of unjust dismissal if the employee "has been laid off because of lack of work or because of the discontinuance of a function." The main rationale for this exclusion is to avoid adjudicators having to pronounce upon the "justness" of an employer's business decisions in organizing the enterprise to maximize profits and efficiency.[446] If an adjudicator could review an employer's decisions to restructure its operations under the broad standard of just cause, the adjudicator could be led to a slippery slope of substituting his or her business judgments for those of the employer. For example, the adjudicator might be asked to pronounce upon the justness of the employer deciding to lay off the claimant in order to weather adverse economic conditions, instead of reducing dividends to shareholders. In addition, excluding layoffs from the unjust dismissal scheme avoids the difficulty of fashioning a remedy for a claimant whose layoff is ruled unjust, but whose position has nonetheless been abolished. Attempting to fashion a right to recall based on the claimant's seniority also raises almost intractable questions of how a seniority system would be structured: Would seniority accrue on a classification, departmental, or plant basis? Would seniority apply within a local, regional, or national level in multi-plant organizations? Would recall depend only on seniority or on sufficient or relative skill and ability? How long would a right to recall last? How would a "bumping" system operate? In the unionized sector, where seniority is widely recognized in layoffs, these (and other) questions are usually dealt with in the express terms of the collective agreement, but even then arbitrators have encountered enormous difficulties in applying such provisions. Rather than lead section 240 adjudicators into these murky waters, the legislators elected to exempt layoffs from the statutory scheme.

---

444 *CLC*, above note 28, s. 242(3.1)(a).
445 *Hewton v. Dickson's Transport and Coach Lines (Napanee) Ltd.*, November 2002 (Adell), especially at 8–11.
446 See the comments to this effect in *Bellamy v. CN North America*, [1996] C.L.A.D. No. 128 (Dorsey) at 6–7.

The adjudicative and court decisions on the layoff exemption are often replete with finely spun questions of interpretation of the statutory language. It is submitted that these interpretive niceties are best resolved by keeping in mind that the underlying purpose of the layoff exemption is to insulate from adjudicative review the employer's substantive business judgments about how its operations ought best to be structured in order to enhance efficiency and, therefore, profitability. It follows that adjudicators faced with the layoff defence should ensure that an employer's actions are a *bona fide* attempt to improve efficiency and not a veiled attempt to get rid of an unwanted employee for extraneous reasons. Indeed, in order to safeguard against the latter risk, adjudicators commonly ask two questions where the layoff defence is raised. The first is whether the alleged layoff is genuine, and the second is whether, notwithstanding the presence of a genuine layoff, the employer acted properly in selecting the claimant for release rather than someone else.[447] The onus of proving a valid layoff is on the employer, being in the best position to explain its own reasons for terminating the claimant.[448]

Regarding the first question of whether or not a genuine layoff exists, the statute defines a layoff somewhat ambiguously as a termination of employment caused by either a "lack of work" or a "discontinuance of a function." It has been argued that these words mean that an employee who is released following the employer's decision to reassign some or all of his or her former job duties to other positions, within or outside the organization, has not been laid off, since his or her "function" is still being performed. However, this interpretation of the word "function" has been rejected by most adjudicators, who have followed the Supreme Court of Canada's definition of that term in another statute.[449] The Supreme Court ruled that a function refers to "the 'office', that is to say the bundle of responsibilities, duties and activities that are carried out by a particular employee or group of employees" and held that a function will be "discontinued" where "that set of activities which forms an office is no longer carried out as a result of a decision

---

447 *Godfrey v. Brucelandair International* (27 October 1989), Ont. Ref. No. 1125 (Swan), especially at 9 [*Godfrey*]. This "two stage" approach has received judicial approval in *Sedpex, Inc. v. Canada (Labour Code Adjudicator)* (1988), [1989] 2 F.C. 289 (T.D.) [*Sedpex*].
448 *Sedpex, ibid.* at 300.
449 *Flieger v. New Brunswick*, [1993] 2 S.C.R. 651 [*Flieger*]. The Court was interpreting this phrase in the *Civil Service Act*, S.N.B. 1984, c. C-5.1, s. 26(1). Most adjudicators and trial judges have followed this test, e.g., *Badu v. Purolator Courier Ltd.*, [1995] C.L.A.D. No. 31 (Kaufman) at 35 [*Badu*].

374 INDIVIDUAL EMPLOYMENT LAW

of an employer acting in good faith."[450] Accordingly, there will be a discontinuance of a function so as to preclude an unjust dismissal complaint where the employer either transfers the claimant's job duties to one or more pre-existing positions within the organization[451] or creates a new position that combines the claimant's job duties with other duties.[452] The "bundle of responsibilities, duties and activities" carried out by the claimant in his or her *personal position* will have been discontinued within the meaning of the Supreme Court of Canada's test, even though the overall duties are still being performed by other persons elsewhere in the firm. Furthermore, even if this interpretation of the phrase "discontinuance of a function" is incorrect, there would appear to be a lack of work in such circumstances: the level of the claimant's job duties may not have declined, but the number of employees required to perform them would have.[453]

It would appear to follow from the foregoing reasoning that if an employer terminates employees and subcontracts to have an outsider perform the employees' job duties, there will be a discontinuance of a function because the employer's need for a particular *kind* of function—namely, work performed by its *own* employees—has been discontinued. Also, this interpretation would ensure that the employer, not an adjudicator, would make the sensitive business decision of whether or not subcontracting is economically justifiable. Most (but not all[454]) adjudicators have held that replacing employees with subcontracted labour constitutes a discontinuance of a function.[455] Nevertheless, some adjudicators seem reluctant to find a discontinuance of a function if there has been no change in how the work is performed by the subcontractor compared with how the employee performed it.[456] It is submitted that this factor should be irrelevant, since it has nothing

---

450   *Flieger, ibid.* at 664, Cory J.

451   Example: *Bull-Giroux v. Louis Bull Tribe, Hobbema,* June 2003 (Dunlop). The equivalent provision in the Nova Scotia unjust discharge scheme has also been applied in this sense: e.g., *Sutton v. Halifax Development Ltd.* (1995), 13 C.C.E.L. (2d) 112 at 119 (N.S.C.A.).

452   Example: *Singer v. Bell Canada,* [2006] C.L.A.D. No. 403 (O'Brien-Kelly).

453   Example: *Froner v. Bradley Air Services Ltd.* (September 1994) (Abbott) at 13–14.

454   Example: *Leta v. Pine Creek First Nation,* [1995] C.L.A.D. No. 256 (Gray) [*Leta*].

455   Examples: *Badu,* above note 449 at 42; *Meeches v. Long Plain First Nation* (May 2004) (Deeley) at 23; *Martins v. Tap-Air Portugal* (3 May 1991), Ont. Ref. No. 1380 (Franks); *Flieger,* above note 449.

456   For example, in *Leta,* above note 454 at 7, where the employer terminated the claimant and then contracted-out to him his old job exactly as before, the adjudicator regarded this feature as critical. This distinction was also regarded as crucial by Cory J. in *Flieger,* above note 449 at 666.

to do with the fundamental policy goal of the subsection—to insulate substantive business decisions from adjudicative review—and potentially leads adjudicators into a quagmire in determining exactly when the claimant's old job has been transformed into a different job.

The foregoing analysis presupposes that the reassignment of the claimant's job duties to other employees or to subcontractors is motivated by legitimate business purposes and is not a disguised method to get rid of unwelcome employees.[457] Adjudicators will scrutinize the evidence to ensure good faith on the employer's part. It must be re-emphasized, however, that the purpose of the inquiry is not to decide whether the reassignment is a sound business decision but to determine whether it is "made in good faith and is not motivated by ulterior or unlawful considerations."[458]

Adjudicators have held employers to an exacting standard of proof in *all* situations where the layoff defence is raised, not just in cases involving reassignment of duties. Whatever the alleged business justification may be for releasing an employee—technological change, financial exigency, overstaffing, redeployment of manpower, reclassification, decline in market demand for the product or service in question, closure or relocation of some or all of the enterprise, and so on—the employer must present comprehensive written evidence of the economic and organizational factors underpinning its decision.[459] For example, there was held not to be valid layoff where a replacement was hired shortly after the claimant was released to fill the claimant's position, the duties of which remained undiminished.[460] Similarly, where the existence of a layoff was not raised by the employer until after dismissal for another

---

457 See, for example, *Hamel v. Laidlaw Carriers Tank G.P. Inc.*, [2006] C.L.A.D. No. 495 (Dumoulin) at 10 [*Hamel*]. *Devereaux v. Sedpex Ltd.* (20 January 1987), Nfld. Ref. No. 721 (Browne), upheld *sub nom. Sedpex, Inc. v. Canada (Labour Code Adjudicator)*, above note 447; *Preston v. MacGregor the Mover* (3 November 1986), Ont. Ref. No. 718 (Willes); *Moreau v. Relay Systems* (21 April 1986), Que. Ref. No. 649 (Frumkin).

458 Per adjudicator Dissanayake in *Lauzon v. Atomic Energy of Canada Ltd.*, [1995] C.L.A.D. No. 914 at 10 of the award. In *Munak v. Canadian Broadcasting Corp.* (30 December 1987), Que. Ref. No. 872 at 10 of the award, Descoteaux said that adjudicators must ensure that an alleged layoff is not "a sham, a subterfuge, or done as a pretext for some other reason."

459 Thus, in *Horne v. Cerescorp Inc.* (9 July 1985), N.S. Ref. No. 504 (Outhouse) at 13 of the award, it was stated that "bald assertions" of valid business reasons, without supporting documentation of the relevant details, will not suffice. Furthermore, written documentation, not oral testimony is required: e.g., *Greaves v. Economy Carriers Ltd.*, [1995] C.L.A.D. No. 21 (Malone) at 11 [*Economy Carriers*].

460 Example: *Keller v. Lheit-Lit'en Nation*, [1996] C.L.A.D. No. 1009 (Hamilton) at 6.

cause was alleged, it was held not to be valid.[461] The layoff defence was rejected where the employer's past practice in similar economic circumstances was to share the working opportunities instead of implementing layoffs,[462] and where a vacancy arose in the claimant's old position within a reasonable time following the layoff and the claimant was not offered it.[463]

If the employer's motive for terminating a claimant is partially related to legitimate economic reasons, but is also tainted by an extraneous purpose, such as personal dislike of the employee or the perception that he or she is a poor performer, there will not be a valid layoff and dismissal will be ruled unjust.[464] Nevertheless, a "mixed motive" on the employer's part is relevant in determining the appropriate "make whole" remedy for a claimant whose dismissal is ruled unjust. For example, if the claimant's position is eliminated for legitimate economic reasons, he or she would not be reinstated, but would instead receive compensation up to the date of the position elimination, since he or she would not have remained employed beyond that date anyway.[465]

Even if valid business reasons exist to support an alleged layoff, the defence may fail if the adjudicator finds that the employer selected the claimant for termination — rather than somebody else to whom the layoff conditions also applied — for an extraneous reason, such as personal animosity. This does not mean that an adjudicator can review the fairness of an employer's procedures or criteria for selecting whom to release in a layoff situation — such matters are assumed to be within the domain of the employer's expertise, not within the competence of adjudicators.[466] Thus, the employer is free to choose whom to lay off on whatever basis it prefers — operational factors,[467] straight seniority,[468]

---

461 *Miller v. Neskainlith Indian Band* (10 November 1987), B.C. Ref. No. 835 (Fetterly) [*Neskainlith*].

462 Example: *Economy Carriers*, above note 459 at 10–11.

463 See the comments to this effect in *MacPhail v. Cape Breton Development Corporation* (29 February 1984), N.S. Ref. No. 311 (MacDonald).

464 Example: *Hamel*, above note 457 at 12.

465 *Graham v. Bison Diversified Inc.* (11 October 1991), Man. Ref. No. 1451 (Steel) at 17 of the award [*Bison Diversified*].

466 In some countries, however, the fairness of the employer's selection procedures and criteria are reviewable, e.g., *Employment Protection (Consolidation) Act, 1978* (U.K.), c. 44, ss. 54–80. See generally C. Grunfeld, *The Law of Redundancy*, 3d ed. (London: Sweet & Maxwell, 1989) at 302–24.

467 Example: *Godfrey*, above note 447.

468 Example: *Wilkie v. Toronto-Dominion Bank* (29 July 1986), Ont. Ref. No. 639 (Picher).

comparative skill and ability,[469] a mixture of both seniority and ability,[470] or even position on the pay scale.[471]

The rationale for the collective agreement exclusion[472] seems to be that the statutory protection would be superfluous in light of the protections that collective agreements normally contain against unjust discharge. But collective agreements do not always contain such a provision, and even if they do, a negotiated just cause clause may not match the statutory standard in terms of the breadth of protection and remedies available. It is surprising, therefore, that the *Canada Labour Code* does not expressly require that a collectively bargained just cause clause must guarantee equivalent protection to that provided by the legislative scheme before the latter can be excluded.

The rationale for excluding a complaint under section 240 when an alternative statutory procedure for redress is available[473] to the claimant also seems to be to avoid superfluity. Yet the courts have not required that the alternative statutory procedure be as favourable to the employee as section 240 would.[474] Most adjudicators have interpreted *Byers* as automatically barring an unjust dismissal complaint if the employee is entitled to commence proceedings under another statute; it does not matter whether such proceedings have commenced.[475] Some adjudicators, however, have taken a more generous view. They would bar an unjust dismissal complaint only where the alternative statutory procedure specifically remits for adjudication the question of just cause for dismissal—as opposed to remitting another question for adjudication, such as whether the employer's motive for dismissal was based on an impermissible ground under the human rights or collective bargaining legislation[476] (even though the justness of the dismissal is important evidence of such an illicit intent). The Arthurs Report recommended dealing with the problem of overlapping statutory forums by having

469 Example: *Ayotte v. Royal Bank of Canada*, [2005] C.L.A.D. No. 508 (Keast).
470 Example: *Marin v. Canadian Mortgage and Housing Corporation* (27 March 1987) (Casgrain). However, if the employer commits itself to take into account seniority along with merit, but subsequently ignores the claimant's seniority, this would show bad faith: e.g., *Kalisz v. Peterborough Freight Lines Ltd.* (8 August 1993) (Eaton).
471 *Usher v. Norcanair Airlines Inc.* (January 2005) (England) at 6.
472 *CLC*, above note 28, s. 240(1)(b).
473 *Ibid.*, s. 242(3.1)(b).
474 *Byers Transport Ltd. v. Kosanovich* (1995), 126 D.L.R. (4d) 679 at 686 (F.C.A.) [*Byers*].
475 Example: *Woods v. 2712270 Manitoba Ltd. o/a Pizzey's Milling and Baking Company*, [2005] C.L.A.D. No. 512 (Paterson) at 10.
476 Example: *Laronde v. Warren Gibson Ltd.*, August 1998 (MacLean) at 10–12 and 16.

the federal bureaucrats with Human Resources and Skills Development liaise with their counterparts under the alternative statutory regime in order to decide which forum would be the most suitable for handling a complaint: they would look at the complaint in light of its distinctive nature and available remedies.[477]

Compulsory conciliation is the centrepiece of the federal unjust discharge scheme. The Code requires an inspector from Human Resources and Skills Development to investigate complaints and attempt to conciliate a voluntary settlement between the parties before the complaint can proceed to adjudication.[478] Conciliation has been relatively successful in producing voluntary settlement, with about 70 percent of complaints resolved in this way each year. It is unknown, however, whether the settlements achieved in conciliation are roughly in line with those that an adjudicator would have awarded. A voluntary settlement of the complaint will bind the employee[479] unless the adjudicator avoids the settlement under the usual common law doctrines of duress and unconscionability.[480] If conciliation fails to resolve the complaint, the minister has the discretion to remit the case to adjudication or to reject it. The minister uses this discretion to weed out those relatively few cases that are frivolous or non-meritorious.

There is no express requirement in the Code that an adjudicator must hear and render a decision on the complaint within a designated time. Delay can be particularly prejudicial to the employee, of course, since he or she may have limited financial resources compared with the employer's and may have difficulty finding another job while carrying the taint of having been dismissed. Indeed, a hard-nosed employer might even try to deliberately engineer delays in order to intensify the pressure on a claimant to accept a less generous financial settlement than might otherwise appear warranted. Unfortunately, the system suffers from chronic delays. On average, six months elapse from the time a complaint is made until an adjudicator is appointed, a further delay of three months until the case is heard, and yet another delay of three months before a decision is rendered.[481] The Arthurs Report recommended that the system could be speeded up if the Human Resources

---

477 Arthurs Report, above note 55 at 95–98 and 184–85.
478 *CLC*, above note 28, s. 241(2).
479 It has been held that s. 168(1) of the *CLC*, *ibid.*, does not automatically avoid a voluntary settlement agreement, e.g., *Brine v. Canada Ports Corp. (Ports Canada Police)*, [1996] C.L.A.D. No. 1131 (Outhouse) at 4.
480 Example: *Cannon v. Purolator Courier Ltd.* (17 December 1991), Ont. Ref. No. 1495 (Sheppard) at 5.
481 Arthurs Report, above note 55 at 181.

and Skills Development established a standing panel of adjudicators, supported by its own administrators, to process and adjudicate complaints; under the current system, ad hoc adjudicators appointed by the Human Resources and Skills Development schedule their own hearings.[482] As yet this recommendation has not been implemented.

Next, we review the standards of just cause under the *Canada Labour Code*.

b) The Meaning of Just Cause

Statutory adjudicators have developed remarkably similar standards of just cause to those applied by collective agreement arbitrators.[483] Since the common law standards of just cause are also similar to the arbitral standard in most (but not all) respects, there is a relatively high degree of conformity among the three legal regimes governing just cause for dismissal. We examined the common law standards of just cause earlier in this chapter, and the reader is referred back to that material for a detailed analysis of the principles governing just cause for dismissal.[484] To summarize, the notion of just cause in adjudication encompasses the following requirements: the employer must prove that the worker's conduct has caused or is likely to cause substantial harm to the production process, the symbolic legitimacy of management's authority to issue orders, or public confidence in the employer's business; the penalty of dismissal must be proportional to the degree of harm suffered by the employer; appropriate corrective measures must have been followed in dismissals for misconduct and incompetence in order to give the employee a chance to rehabilitate; and any mitigating factors that reduce the severity of the employee's actions must be taken into account. Here, attention need only be focused on the seven main ways in which just cause differs from these common law standards and from the standards applied in collective agreement arbitration.

First, at common law an employer need not establish just cause if the employee is terminated with due notice or pay in lieu, but this is not the case under section 240; rather, the employer's substantive reasons for dismissal are always reviewable under the just cause test; otherwise, the employer could fire an employee for the most arbitrary and obnoxious of reasons by the simple expedient of giving due notice or pay in lieu.[485]

---

482 *Ibid.* at 185–86.

483 The leading authority is *Duhamel v. Bank of Montreal* (26 October 1981), B.C. Ref. No. 74 (Hickling).

484 See Section C, above in this chapter.

485 *Iron v. Kanaweyimik Child and Family Services Inc.*, October 2002 (England) at 5–6; *Goodwin v. Conair Aviation Ltd.* December 2002 (Gordon) at 16–18.

Second, if a contract of employment or a collective agreement expressly provides that certain conduct shall constitute cause for discharge, effect must be given to such express provisions in deference to freedom of contract, even though they might be harsher than the generally accepted standards of just cause. However, express contractual definitions of just cause do not automatically bind section 240 adjudicators, since the parties are not allowed to contract-out of the *Canada Labour Code*.[486] Consequently, contractual provisions stating that dismissal is automatically justifiable for designated offences,[487] providing that discharge is to be at the unfettered discretion of management,[488] or applying discharge automatically for specified offences without first allowing the employee to explain his or her actions[489] are overridden by the statutory standard of cause. This does not mean that express contractual definitions of just cause are irrelevant under section 240—such provisions may be highly relevant in demonstrating, for example, that an employee knows in advance how seriously an employer regards certain conduct for the purpose of satisfying the requirements of corrective discipline and procedural fairness.[490] Moreover, if the employer fails to follow its own dismissal procedures contained in the employment contract, this failure will likely result in the discharge being ruled unjust under section 240 on the basis of procedural unfairness.[491] However, if the employer complied with its procedures and the outcome of the case is not changed, that ruling would not be made.[492] As we shall see below, where a procedural flaw results in a dismissal being ruled unjust even though the employee is substantively at fault for committing acts of misconduct or incompetence, the adjudicator may reduce the compensation payable to the employee and/or refuse

---

486 *CLC*, above note 28, s. 168.

487 Examples: *Salata v. Challenger Motor Freight Inc.*, April 2004 (Dissanayake) at 8–9 [*Salata*]; *Loughride v. CHUM Ltd.* (30 March 1984), Ont. Ref. No. 265 (Devlin) at 17 of the award [*Loughride*].

488 Examples: *Hughes v. Stoney Education Authority*, October 2002 (Moreau) at 8; *Loughride, ibid.* at 15.

489 Example: *Roy v. Imperial Oil Ltd.*, [1995] C.L.A.D. No. 329 (Darby) at 37.

490 Example: *Ibid.* at 19; *Salata*, above note 487 at 8–9; *Gouthro v. Warren Gibson Ltd.*, December 2002 (Stevens), involving a "last chance" agreement.

491 Examples: *CanXpress Ltd. v. Reagan*, [2003] F.C.J. No. 963 (T.D.); *Bell Canada v. Hallé* (1989), 99 N.R. 149 (F.C.T.D.).

492 Example: *Yeung v. HSBC Bank of Canada*, [2006] C.L.A.D. No. 175 (Hickling) at 35 and 41 [*Yeung*], where a bank employee was dismissed for theft without being given an opportunity to explain, but nothing she could have told her employer would have altered the fact that she had committed the theft and that no mitigating circumstances applied.

to reinstate him or her in order to take account of such contributory blameworthiness.[493]

Third, section 241 of the *Canada Labour Code* obliges the employer to furnish a written statement of the reasons for discharge within fifteen days of receiving a request for such a statement from the claimant or a government inspector. Failure to provide such written reasons raises a strong presumption of unjust dismissal.[494] In addition, the employer may be criminally liable and face a maximum fine of $5,000 and/or imprisonment for up to one year.[495] These requirements are not present under collective agreement and employment contract law.

Fourth, section 240 adjudicators will depart from the arbitral norms in order to reflect the fact that complainants are non-unionized. For example, arbitral doctrines based on the ubiquity of seniority in the unionized sector would presumably be refashioned to take account of the minimal role seniority has in the non-unionized sector.

Fifth, where the reason for dismissal is disobedience to orders — in arbitral parlance, "insubordination" — section 240 adjudicators recognize a broader defence of "reasonable excuse" than is normally applied in arbitration.[496] The common law, too, recognizes an equally broad defence of reasonable excuse. The explanation for the difference is that the non-unionized employee does not have the opportunity to grieve and arbitrate the legality of an order after he or she has obeyed it, whereas unionized employees do.

Sixth, while section 240 adjudicators apply the arbitral doctrine of the culminating incident, which permits the employer to justify dismissal on a combination of the immediate offence and previous offences on the employee's work record, section 240 adjudicators (unlike arbitrators) afford the employee an opportunity to challenge the justness of any previous offences as part of the dismissal hearing.[497]

---

493 See Section E(1)(c), above in this chapter.

494 Example: *Wygant v. Regional Cablesystems Inc., Sudbury, Ontario (No. 1)* July 2000 (Kaufman) at 24 and *Wygant v. Regional Cablesystems Inc., Sudbury, Ontario (No. 2)* September 2001 (Kaufman), both aff'd [2003] F.C.J. No. 321 (T.D).

495 *CLC*, above note 28, s. 256.

496 Examples: *Penner v. Chinook Carriers Ltd.*, [1995] C.L.A.D. No. 1108 (Kubara); *Wolfe v. Pelmorex Broadcasting Ltd.* (August 1994) (Abbott), especially at 25–26 of the award. In arbitration, the generally recognized exceptions to the "work now, grieve later" principle are safeguarding health and safety, avoiding the commission of an illegality, and safeguarding the employee's right to determine personal appearance.

497 Examples: *Bank of Nova Scotia v. Webster*, [2006] C.L.A.D. No. 344 (Snow) at 23; *Benard v. Trans-Provincial Freight Carriers Ltd.*, [1997] C.L.A.D. No. 2 (Aggarwal) at 25.

The rationale is that non-unionized employees do not have access to a grievance and arbitration procedure to challenge disciplinary warnings and suspensions at the time they are applied. Accordingly, a *de facto* mini-hearing will take place on the justness of any previous offences for the purpose of determining whether the totality of a claimant's conduct grounds cause for discharge.[498] This usually occurs in common law actions where the employer relies on the employee's prior record to justify dismissal.

Seventh, unlike at common law, where previously condoned acts of misconduct or incompetence can be revived by a culminating incident to support cause for dismissal,[499] section 240 adjudicators treat such condoned acts as irrelevant to the determination of cause.[500] It is submitted that the adjudicative approach is preferable to the common law position.

Adjudicators have differed on whether section 240 imposes a duty of procedural fairness that requires the employer to warn employees of their wrongdoings, give them an opportunity of explanation, and conduct a fair and thorough investigation of alleged wrongdoings prior to invoking dismissals. Most adjudicators impose these requirements as components of the progressive discipline doctrine and the test of contextual proportionality,[501] but some have held that the duty of procedural fairness is an independent element under the statutory just cause standard.[502] A minority of adjudicators refuse to recognize any duty of procedural fairness,[503] but as we have already seen, the courts, too, have disagreed on this issue.[504] As submitted earlier, imposing a duty of procedural fairness makes sense because it avoids unnecessary litigation, and dismissals that are procedurally sullied, yet substantively fair can be handled by reducing the employee's compensation, possibly even to zero in appropriate circumstances.[505]

---

498 Example: *Nelson v. Dalor Management Services Ltd.* (20 October 1988), B.C. Ref. No. 974 (Chertkow).

499 Example: *Cook*, above note 262.

500 Example: *Cree v. Six Nations Traditional Hereditary Chiefs* (25 November 1988), Que. Ref. Nos. 864–67 (Lippé).

501 Examples: *Arkinson v. Sagkeeng Alcohol Rehabilitation Centre Inc.*, December 1994 (Brazeau) at 18; *Beaulieu v. Ted Josepfowich Ltd.*, February 1992 (Dumoulin) at 15.

502 Examples: *Fehr v. Canadian Pacific Railway Company*, February 2000 (Schwartz) at 16; *Yeung*, above note 492 at 32.

503 Example: *Paul v. St. Mary's First Nation*, [2005] C.L.A.D. No. 517 (Bruce) at 8.

504 See Section C(4), above in this chapter.

505 This has been done under the English unfair dismissal legislation in *Earle v. Slater and Wheeler (Airlyne) Ltd.*, [1972] I.C.R. 508 (N.I.R.C.).

The major difference between the common law regime of wrongful dismissal and the statutory unjust discharge schemes is in regard to remedies, as we shall see next.

c)   Remedies for "Unjust Discharge"

The remedies available to an unjustly dismissed employee under the statutory schemes in the federal jurisdiction, Quebec, and Nova Scotia differ dramatically from the common law position in two key respects. First, compulsory reinstatement is the preferred remedy for unjust dismissal under the statutory schemes, unlike at common law, where reinstatement is rarely available.[506] Second, under the statutory schemes, an unjustly dismissed employee is compensated for the real-world losses flowing from the fact of the dismissal,[507] unlike at common law, where damages are limited to contractual entitlements that the employee would have received during the notice period, but not thereafter. This "make whole" philosophy underlies, for example, section 242(4)(c) of the *Canada Labour Code*, which empowers an adjudicator to "do any other like thing that it is equitable to require the employer to do in order to remedy or counteract any consequence of the dismissal." It is clear from the history of the International Labor Organization's 1963 *Termination of Employment Recommendation* No. 119 that these remedies are intended to be pivotal features of the protection against unjust discharge. Indeed, were it not for these special remedies, there would appear to be little point to enacting the statutory schemes, since they would largely parallel the common law. Therefore, those adjudicative awards that have applied the common law measure of damages or suggested that reinstatement is an exceptional remedy should be regarded as palpably wrong.[508]

Regarding reinstatement, most adjudicators have recognized that such orders are the preferred remedy for unjust dismissal, not least because reinstatement is the obvious tool for restoring the psychological satisfaction that an employee derives from his or her job[509] and for

---

506   The common law position is analyzed in Section F(2), below in this chapter.

507   Judicial endorsements of the "make whole" approach include *Geauvreau-Turner Estate v. Ojibways of Onigaming First Nation*, [2006] F.C.J. No. 638 at paras. 10 and 14; *Slaight*, above note 332 (C.A.), Urie J.; *Banca Nazionale Del Lavoro of Canada Ltd. v. Lee-Shanok* (1988), 22 C.C.E.L. 59, especially at 74 (F.C.A.), Stone J. [*Banca Nazionale*].

508   Example: *Atkey v. Valley Reefer Services* (1994), 12 C.C.E.L. (2d) 61 (Blaxford). Such decisions are clearly irreconcilable with the judicial precedents cited in note 507, *ibid*.

509   *Turner v. NASC Child and Family Services Inc., Sturgeon Lake First Nation (No.1)*, [2006] C.L.A.D. No. 391 (England) at 23 [*Turner*]; *Collins v. Driftpile First Nation*

restoring the employee's professional reputation.[510] Accordingly, this reasoning has led many adjudicatiors to say that reinstatement should only be denied in exceptional circumstances.[511] The courts, nevertheless, have ruled that reinstatement is not automatic: it depends on the adjudicator's discretion in the circumstances of the case.[512]. In practice, reinstatement is awarded less regularly under section 240 than in arbitration, basically because the non-unionized employee does not have the trade union's protection to ensure proper treatment by the employer after the reinstatement takes effect. Thus, many employees do not ask for reinstatement, or if they do, they may trade it for a larger financial settlement from their employer.[513] Indeed, reinstatement, awarded in about one-third of the decisions in which dismissal is found to be unjust, appears likely to become a lost remedy.[514] Adjudicator Steele has summarized the following circumstances in which reinstatement will be denied to an employee who requests it:

1. The deterioration of personal relations between the complainant and management or other employees;
2. The disappearance of the relationship of trust which must exist in particular when the complainant is high up in the company hierarchy;
3. Contributory fault on the part of the complainant justifying the reduction of his dismissal to a lesser sanction;

Band, September 2002 (Dunlop) at 52; Yesno v. Eabametoong First Nation Education Authority, Eabamet Lake Ontario, [2006] C.L.A.D. No. 352 (Kaufman) at 68.
510 Johhny v. Tsewultan Police Service Board, July 2000 (Savage) at 18.
511 Example: Ella v. Trans-Northern Pipelines Inc. (23 March 1992), Ont. Ref. No. 1295 (Swan) [Ella] at 26 of the award, where adjudicator Swan said that "the presumptive remedy in a case of wrongful dismissal under this statute is reinstatement with full compensation"; Anthony v. Kamloops Indian Band, [1997] C.L.A.D. No. 49 (Chertkow) at 8 of the award, where reinstatement was described as the "primary" remedy that should only be denied in "exceptional" circumstances; and Shorting v. Anishinabe Child & Family Services, [1995] C.L.A.D. No. 1057 (Menzies) at 12, where it was stated that reinstatement should be denied only in "truly exceptional circumstances."
512 Chalifoux v. Driftpile First Nation, 2002 FCA 521 at paras. 11–14 and 28–30.
513 Refusing to request reinstatement without good reasons may breach the employee's duty to mitigate his or her losses and result in a reduction in compensation: e.g., McCluskie v. Cascade Aerospace Inc. (February 2005) (Gordon) at 14. This ruling is consistent with the Supreme Court of Canada's decision that refusing an employer's offer of ongoing employment following a wrongful dismissal at common law may breach the employee's duty to mitigate: Evans, above note 183.
514 G. England, "Unjust Dismissal and Other Termination-Related Provisions," Report to the Federal Labour Standards Review (Ottawa: Human Resources and Social Development Canada, 2006) at 51.

4. An attitude on the part of the complainant leading to the belief that reinstatement would bring no improvement;

5. The complainant's physical inability to start work again immediately;

6. The abolition of the post held by the complainant at the time of his dismissal;

7. Other events subsequent to the dismissal making reinstatement impossible, such as bankruptcy or layoffs.[515]

The onus of proving that reinstatement is inappropriate rests with the employer.

Where an employer argues that reinstatement should be refused due to an irretrievable breakdown of personal relations between the claimant and the claimant's superiors and/or colleagues, adjudicators will generally accede only where the claimant is largely responsible for the breakdown and holds a grudge against the employer[516] or where the enterprise is relatively small so that face-to-face contacts are inescapable.[517] Some adjudicators deny reinstatement almost automatically whenever the employer asserts that relationships have irretrievably soured, instead of verifying the assertion objectively. It is submitted that employers should carry most of the burden of ensuring that their own supervisors and other employees, whom, after all, they control, change their attitude towards a reinstated claimant. Most adjudicators, however, require stringent objective evidence of an irretrievable breakdown in personal relationships before reinstatement will be denied.[518] One alternative to denying reinstatement outright in this situation is to order the employer to re-engage the claimant in a position where he or she will be well away from the superiors and colleagues.[519]

The reinstatement remedy is applied flexibly. If the claimant's position has been eliminated for economic reasons, the adjudicator may

---

515 *Bison Diversified*, above note 465 at 15.

516 Examples: *Hardy v. CMI Joint Venture Terminal*, [2006] C.L.A.D. No. 82 (Denysiuk) at 17–18 [*Hardy*]; *Leung v. Sumitomo Matsui Banking Corp.* (September 2004) (Hartman) at 29.

517 Examples: *Hardy, ibid.* at 17–18; *McGunigle v. Transx Ltd.* (30 March 1994) (Renouf) at 21 of the award.

518 Examples: *Young v. Railtran Services Inc.* (August 2003) (Adell) at 20 [*Young*]; *Nason v. 3937844 Canada Inc. o/a CIQX FM Station "The Breeze" Newcap Broadcasting Ltd.* (November 2004) (O'Brien-Kelly) at 19.

519 Adjudicators have the jurisdiction to reinstate the employee in a different position in this and other situations where it would be appropriate: e.g., *Valentino Polochies v. Woodstock First Nation* (April 2002) (Kuttner); *Legault v. DHL Int'l Express Ltd.* (November 1998) (Dissanayake) at 31–32; *Gendron v. Kelowna Flightcraft Ltd.* (October 1999) (Love) at 22.

make reinstatement conditional upon the position subsequently being revived within a designated time,[520] or may reinstate the employee in a different vacant position that he or she is capable of fulfilling.[521] If the adjudicator doubts whether the claimant will successfully rehabilitate following reinstatement, the adjudicator may make reinstatement conditional on the claimant successfully completing a probationary period.[522] If it remains doubtful whether the employee will be medically fit to perform the duties of his or her position, reinstatement may be made conditional upon the claimant meeting designated attendance criteria and undertaking medical examinations. Thus, alcoholic or drug-dependent employees are often reinstated subject to successfully completing a rehabilitation program.[523] An employee will not be reinstated by "bumping" a less senior employee out of a job.[524] Where a replacement has been hired to fill the dismissed employee's position, reinstatement may not be ordered if doing this would impose an undue hardship on the replacement worker, for example, if he or she has occupied the job for a lengthy period and chances of finding alternative work are slim; however, such circumstances would be exceptional.[525]

Reinstatement may be denied in order to reflect the claimant's contributory blameworthiness where a dismissal is *technically* without cause — for example, if the employer failed to give a proper warning — but the claimant is substantively at fault.[526] Where the employee's misconduct or incompetence is serious, but does not quite cross the threshold of providing cause for dismissal and the employee does not appear receptive to rehabilitation, reinstatement may also be denied.[527] Alternatively, if the employee appears amenable to rehabilitation, the adjudicator may order reinstatement along with a lesser penalty, such as a formal warning or an unpaid suspension.[528]

---

520 Example: *Peckford v. Beothuk Trans. Ltd.* (July 1981) (Hattenhauer).

521 Example: *Bonnie Polochies v. Woodstock First Nation* (September 2002) (Kuttner) at 19.

522 *Giberson v. Kelowna Flight Craft Ltd.* (September 2004) (Stephens) at 39. But see the cautionary remarks of adjudicator Adell in *Young,* above note 518 at 21–22.

523 Example: *Bauer v. Seaspan Int'l Ltd.* (October 2003) (Hall) at 29, aff'd (2004), 40 C.C.E.L. (3d) 142 (F.C.T.D.).

524 Example: *Kane v. Brinks Canada Ltd.* (July 1989) (Steele) at 14.

525 *Turner,* above note 509 at 25; *Sprint Canada v. Lancaster* (2005), 38 C.C.E.L. (3d) 144 at 157 (F.C.T.D.).

526 *Perrault v. Purolator Courier Ltd.* (20 February 1989), Ont. Ref. No. 1039 (Pyle).

527 Example: *Ella,* above note 511; *Campbell v. Purolator Courier Ltd.* (24 April 1992), Ont. Ref. No. 1489 (Hinnegan) at 7.

528 Examples: *Vancol v. Royal Bank of Canada* (April 1993) (Satterfield) at 17; *Magas v. Westcom Radio Group Ltd.* (14 April 1993) (Schulman) at 17.

A major obstacle to the success of any legislated unjust discharge scheme featuring compulsory reinstatement for non-unionized workers is making the remedy workable in the absence of a trade union that will ensure the employee's fair treatment after reinstatement. A study of the post-reinstatement experience of non-unionized federal workers in Quebec reported that approximately two-thirds of such workers felt that they had been unjustly treated by their employer, and that 38.5 percent of those who had been reinstated previously pursuant to an adjudicative order had quit by the time the study was conducted.[529] Currently, adjudicators do not have jurisdiction to supervise a reinstatement order once it has been issued to ensure that the employer complies with it; rather, enforcement of such orders must proceed exclusively under section 244 of the *Canada Labour Code*.[530] Overcoming this obstacle will not be easy.[531]

Regarding monetary remedies, the "make whole" philosophy involves compensating the claimant for the loss of earnings that would have been obtained had he or she not been unjustly dismissed. The common law notice period is irrelevant to this question. Sometimes it will be easy to quantify loss of earnings — for instance, if by the adjudication hearing, the claimant has found replacement work at more or less the same compensation level as was enjoyed in the former job. However, that will often not have occurred, with the result that the adjudicator will have to make difficult predictions about the employee's future employment prospects.[532] For example, it will be necessary to predict how long it will likely take the claimant to find alternative work in his or her field of expertise, having regard to the state of the labour market and the personal attractiveness of the employee to potential employers; how long it will take for the claimant's compensation levels in the new job to catch up with what he or she would have earned with the previous employer; whether or not the claimant would have received general wage increases, personal merit bonuses, overtime opportunities, or promotions had he or she not been unjustly dismissed from the former position; and whether or not the claimant's former

---

529 See G. Trudeau, "Is Reinstatement a Suitable Remedy to At-Will Employees?" (1991) 30 R.I./I.R. 302 at 311.

530 *Slaight*, above note 332.

531 See the recommendations of G. England, "Unjust Dismissal and Other Termination-Related Provisions," above note 514 at 52–53.

532 Instructive examples of this "make whole" approach are *Larocque v. Louis Bull Tribe Hobbema (No.2)*, [2006] C.L.A.D. No. 111, March 2006 (Dunlop) at 14–22; *Wygant v. Regional Cablesystems Inc. Sudbury Ontario (No. 2)*, above note 494; *Willberg v. Jo-Anne Trucking Ltd.*, November 1982 (England).

position would have been abolished for economic reasons after the dismissal, so as to cut off compensation at the date of the layoff. Clearly, this process is not an exact science and adjudicators must resort to considerable "reasoned speculation."[533] Perhaps the unfamiliarity of making this kind of inquiry explains why some adjudicators have incorrectly persisted in applying the common law measure of damages.[534] Nonetheless, the "make whole" process is fairer to the employee than the common law approach. Nor must it be forgotten that the unjustly dismissed employee is under a duty to mitigate his or her losses, so that deductions are made for wages earned elsewhere after the dismissal and/or for failure to make reasonable efforts to secure suitable alternative employment.[535]

The "make whole" philosophy also entitles the employee to be compensated for the loss of employment-related benefits other than straight salary. Potential losses include the value of medical, dental, pension, and other fringe benefits up to the time when the claimant can reasonably be expected to gain similar benefits of an equivalent value in subsequent employment; the opportunity to work overtime and to achieve performance bonuses; *ex gratia* but reasonably expected gifts; the personal use of a company car; the opportunity to take training courses; a housing allowance; a meal allowance; the value of the employer's contributions to a stock purchase plan; and the value of the employer's contributions to the federal unemployment insurance fund and the Canada Pension Plan. Of course, any expenses incurred by the employee in attempting to secure replacement employment pursuant to the duty to mitigate are recoverable, as is the case at common law.

Significantly, the "make whole" philosophy under section 240 has been interpreted as allowing adjudicators to compensate the claimant for pyschological distress suffered as a result of the unjust dismissal.[536] As we shall see, at common law, damages for mental distress have often

---

533   *Scarfe v. Saskatchewan Indian Cultural Centre*, [1996] C.L.A.D. No. 1088 (Ball) at 27.

534   Labour relations boards under collective bargaining legislation and human rights tribunals under human rights statutes have applied the "make whole" philosophy to awarding compensation for many years, but strangely almost no s. 240 adjudicators have tapped this invaluable source of experience. On the experience of labour boards, see Adams, above note 397 at paras. 10.1670–10.1760, 10.1890, 10.1980–10.2040. The human rights statutes are considered in Chapter 7 of this book.

535   The duty to mitigate is examined in Section D(3)(c), above in this chapter.

536   Thus, damages for mental distress have been awarded in *Charles v. Lac La Ronge Indian Band* (November 1998) (Wallace) at 58–60, aff'd (*sub nom. Lac La Ronge Indian Band v. Laliberté*) [2000] F.C.J. No. 640 (T.D.); *Turner*, above note 509 at 27.

been ruled irrecoverable because the employee could not prove that symptoms were caused by the employer's failure to give the requisite notice of termination due under the employment contract.[537] However, the very purpose of the "make whole" philosophy is to make the contractual notice period irrelevant; what counts under section 240 is whether the psychological harm flowed from the *fact* of being unjustly dismissed. Adjudicators have also compensated the employee for the injury to his or her dignity that results from the employer having violated his or her statutory rights, adopting the practice of human rights tribunals and labour relations boards in this regard.[538] As well, and in contrast to the common law, the "make whole" philosophy encompasses an award of compensation for injury to reputation caused by the dismissal.[539]

In addition, adjudicators have compensated employees for a broad range of financial losses that can result from being unjustly dismissed. These include removal expenses incurred to take alternative employment; costs associated with retraining counselling; losses incurred in selling a residence; costs incurred in attending the hearing; and income tax losses resulting from receiving back pay from a past year in a different tax year. However, the courts have ruled that solicitor-client costs can be awarded to a successful claimant only "in circumstances that are clearly exceptional, as would be the case where an adjudicator wished thereby to mark his disapproval of a party's conduct in a proceeding."[540] In practice, though, many adjudicators have applied this test broadly—almost to the point of paying it mere lip service; the result is that such costs are often awarded almost as a matter of course.[541] In contrast, only one adjudicator has seen fit to award the successful employer its solicitor-client costs,[542] presumably because such a policy of making the loser pay would likely deter employees from claiming

---

537 See Section F(1)(c), below in this chapter.

538 Examples: *Greyeyes v. Ahtahakoop Cree Nation* (May 2003) (England) at 27–28; *Medynski v. Dene Tha' First Nation* (June 2004) (Gibson) at 24 [*Medynski*].

539 *Smith v. Rumble Transport Ltd.* (8 June 1989), Ont. Ref. No. 1084 (Kilgour) at 5. The common law is examined in Section F(1)(c), below in this chapter.

540 *Banca Nazionale*, above note 507 at 79.

541 Thus, costs were awarded without detailed examination of the "clearly exceptional" test in *Strawberry v. The O'Chiese Band* (May 1994) (McFetridge) at 5–6 of the award; *McGrath v. Newfoundland Telephone Company Ltd.* (3 January 1992), Nfld. Ref. No. 1266 (Clarke).

542 *Mitic v. Chatham Coach Ltd.* (6 March 1994) (Brandt). Compare the normal approach exemplified in *Persaud v. Royal Bank of Canada* (6 March 1984), Ont. Ref. No. 329 (Baum); *Kennedy v. U.S. Air* (26 May 1989), Ont. Ref. No. 936 (Kirkwood) at 18–19.

unjust dismissal. The latter approach is difficult to square with the remedial goal of the legislation.

Most adjudicators have refused to award punitive damages, reasoning—rightly, it is submitted—that the sole purpose of the "make whole" philosophy is to compensate, not to deter or exact vengeance.[543] It is strongly arguable that punitive measures should be available for use against employers who flagrantly violate the Code's standards of fairness, but this would require an express legislative amendment. Several adjudicators, however, have awarded extra damages to reflect bad faith on the employer's part in the manner of dismissal, following the *Wallace* decision at common law.[544] Furthermore, section 242(4) does not permit an adjudicator to compensate a claimant for benefits that he or she is entitled to by virtue of another protective statute or under his or her contract of employment.[545] Instead, the employee must commence proceedings in the appropriate forum in order to remedy violations of such rights. Interestingly, one adjudicator has issued an interim order to compensate an employee who was in dire financial distress after her dismissal and who would have been seriously prejudiced had she had to wait until the final hearing for redress.[546]

The "make whole" mandate has also been used to fashion various non-pecuniary remedies that would assist the unjustly dismissed employee in finding replacement work. For example, employers have been directed to remove from the employee's personnel record material pertaining to the unjust dismissal,[547] to issue a public apology,[548] and to provide reference letters to prospective employers.[549] The Supreme Court of Canada has held that ordering an employer to write a reference letter will not violate the employer's "freedom of expression"

---

543 *Hill v. Desolation Sound Tribal Council* (18 July 1988), B.C. Ref. No. 813 (Greyell).

544 Examples: *Valentino Polochies v. Woodstock First Nation* (April 2001) (Kuttner) at 14–16; *Day v. Sagashtawao Healing Lodge Inc.*, [2000] C.L.A.D. No. 499 (Kaufman). The *Wallace* doctrine is examined in Section B(3)(c)(vi), above in this chapter.

545 Examples: *Hunt v. Canadian Imperial Bank of Commerce* (7 March 1995), Ont. Ref. No. 430 (Adams), especially at 12; *Hanscome v. Loomis Armoured Car Service Ltd.* (12 December 1985), N.B. Ref. No. 599 (MacLean).

546 *Turner v. NASC Child and Family Services Inc., Sturgeon Lake First Nation (No.2)* (March 2007) (England).

547 Examples: *Morrisseau v. Tootinaowaziibeeng First Nation* (July 2004) (Peltz) at 23 [*Morrisseau*]; *Gulf Canada Products v. Griffiths* (1983), 3 C.C.E.L. 139 (Rose).

548 Example: *Morrisseau, ibid.* at 23. Compare *Medynksi*, above note 538 at 27, who argued that forced apologies are worthless.

549 Examples: *Munro v. Paul's Hauling Ltd.*, [1995] C.L.A.D. No. 1111 (Cooper) at 17; *Pilling*, above note 403 at 36.

under section 2(b) of the *Charter*, so long as the direction relates exclusively to recording factual information about the employee's career and job performance and does not force the employer to state opinions about the employee that are not genuinely held.[550] In contrast, at common law the courts do not recognize an implied obligation on the employer under the employment contract to provide an employee with a fair reference.[551]

The "make whole" approach does not countenance the employee's making an unjust enrichment out of his or her unlawful dismissal. Accordingly, if the employee is contributorily at fault in the events leading up to the dismissal, but the dismissal is nonetheless unjust — for example, the employer may have failed to give a proper warning as required under the principles of corrective discipline — the employee's damages may be reduced to reflect his or her degree of blame, possibly even to zero. As well, solicitor-client costs may be reduced or even denied for this reason. The duty to mitigate applies in the usual common law way, with the employer carrying the onus of proof. A deduction will be made for any amounts that the employee would have been required to pay to the Canada Pension Plan, Revenue Canada, or the Employment Insurance Commission had he or she not been discharged. Of course, the employer must remit these amounts to the appropriate state bureaucracies.[552]

Finally, in order to make whole the claimant's monetary losses, section 240 adjudicators follow the practice of including interest, at the prevailing prime rate, on compensation awards.[553]

In conclusion, the experience with statutory unjust discharge protections in the federal jurisdiction, Nova Scotia, and Quebec leaves several important questions unanswered: (1) Does such legislation have a disemployment effect, or otherwise undermine the economic efficiency of employers? (2) Can reinstatement ever be a practicable remedy in the non-unionized sector, and if not, what alternative remedies can be devised to fill the gap? (3) Does the enactment of statutory unjust discharge protection "chill" trade unions' organizing appeal to non-organized workers? (4) To what extent has the legislation stimulated employers to voluntarily reform their internal disciplinary procedures? (5) Are government investigators doing an adequate job in ensuring that claimants who are not represented by legal counsel get a fair deal in mediated settlements with their employer? (6) How can procedures be speeded up

---

550 *Slaight*, above note 332 (S.C.C.).
551 See Chapter 5.
552 Example: *Bison Diversified*, above note 465 at 18 of the award.
553 *Banca Nazionale*, above note 507 at 74.

so that the vulnerable employee is not kept waiting for justice? Further empirical studies of these and other issues are urgently needed.

2) Wrongful Dismissal of Statutorily Regulated Employees and Public Office Holders

Most employers in the public sector derive their authority to manage from a statute and regulations made thereunder. Frequently, this legislation will define the substantive grounds upon which dismissal can be invoked and the procedures that must be followed when invoking dismissal. If the employer violates such legislation, the dismissal is *ultra vires* for excess of jurisdiction, and an administrative law remedy can be obtained by the employee, as we shall see below.[554]

In addition, prior to 2008, the courts recognized that certain positions in the public sector constitute "public offices" that transcend the regular employment relationship and entitle the occupants to the protection of a duty of procedural fairness in the event of removal from office.[555] However, in 2008, the Supreme Court of Canada held that office holders will only be covered by a duty of procedural fairness in relatively narrow circumstances. These are as follows: (1) where the employee does not have a contract of employment, such as to entitle him or her to bring a common law action for wrongful dismissal—for example, a judge, a Crown minister, or a person holding an office purely at the pleasure of the Crown[556]—or (2) where the statutory power governing the employment relationship implies a duty of procedural fairness.[557] The outcome is that most office holders will now be treated the same as regular employees.

Where the employee is about to be dismissed for misconduct or incompetence, the duty of fairness entitles the employee to know in

---

554 Examples: *Hallyburton v. Markham (Town of)* (1988), 63 O.R. (2d) 449 (C.A.); *Placsko v. Humboldt School Board Unit No. 47* (1971), 18 D.L.R. (3d) 374 (Sask. Q.B.), aff'd (1971), 22 D.L.R. (3d) 663 (Sask. C.A.); *Abouna v. Foothills Provincial General Hospital Board (No. 2)*, [1977] 5 W.W.R. 75 (Alta. S.C.T.D.), rev'g in part [1978] 2 W.W.R. 130 (Alta. S.C.A.D.) [*Abouna*].

555 The leading cases were *Nicholson v. Haldimand-Norfolk (Regional Municipality) Commissioners of Police*, [1979] 1 S.C.R. 311 [*Nicholson*]. Nicholson's subsequent claim for wages succeeded: (1980), 31 O.R. (2d) 195 at 196 (Div. Ct.), var'd (1980), 31 O.R. (2d) 195 at 202 (C.A.), leave to appeal to S.C.C. refused, [1981] 1 S.C.R. 92; *Knight v. Indian Head School Division No. 19*, [1990] 1 S.C.R. 653 [*Knight*].

556 As a result of *Wells v. Newfoundland*, [1999] S.C.J. No. 50, most "at pleasure" employees will have a contractual relationship with the Crown.

557 *Dunsmuir*, above note 267 at paras. 115–16.

advance the reasons for dismissal and to have the opportunity of presenting his or her side of the story to the employer before dismissal is invoked.[558] The employer need not conduct a full-scale judicial hearing with all the trappings of natural justice; rather, the hearing's objective is to ensure that the employer will have the full facts before it, so as to improve the quality of its decision on whether or not to proceed with the dismissal. This requirement is dispensed with if giving the employee the right to know and to respond to the allegations would be superflous, for example, where the employee has had ample opportunity to explain his or her side of the story in earlier disciplinary hearings.[559]

Where dismissal is for economic reasons, the courts have held that the employee is not entitled to an opportunity to present information to the employer prior to dismissal because, it is assumed, the employee will have nothing of value to add to such decisions, which fall within the employer's expertise.[560] This assumption, however, is almost certainly incorrect, for the experience with employee involvement in joint layoff committees established under employment standards legislation is that individual employees often have valuable suggestions for handling layoffs.

If the employee is dismissed in breach of a statute or the duty of procedural fairness, the courts can issue a declaration that dismissal is void *ab initio*.[561] A declaration does not legally *compel* the employer to apply reinstatement, but most employers honour the spirit of the declaration and reinstate the employee. However, if necessary, a court can issue an injunction compelling reinstatement.[562] It is then incumbent on the employer, if it wishes to proceed with the dismissal, to do so properly. This may seem to be a waste of time, since the employer may simply dismiss the worker again, but at least the symbolic legitimacy of the dismissal procedure will be upheld. It must be emphasized that the declaration is a discretionary remedy. Indeed, courts usually do not grant a declaration where the employee has other adequate avenues of

---

558 Examples: *Kopij v. Metropolitan Toronto (Municipality of)* (1997), 21 C.C.E.L. (2d) 272 at 285 (Ont. Gen. Div.); *Broderick v. Kanata (City of)* (1995), 18 C.C.E.L. (2d) 193 (Ont. Div. Ct.).

559 As in *Lasch v. Miramachi Planning District* (1999), 47 C.C.E.L. (2d) 290 at 305–6 (N.B.C.A.); *Wong v. College of Traditional Chinese Medicine Practitioners* (2004), 35 C.C.E.L. (3d) 216 at 222 (B.C.S.C.); *Knight*, above note 555.

560 *Lethbridge v. Newfoundland (Minister of Health)* (1992), 47 C.C.E.L. 258 at 294 (Nfld. S.C.T.D.).

561 See, for example, *Nicholson*, above note 555; *Gerrard v. Sackville (Town of)* (1992), 39 C.C.E.L. 113 (N.B.C.A.).

562 Example: *Smith v. Nova Scotia (Attorney General)*, (2003), 26 C.C.E.L. (3d) 226 (N.S.T.D.).

relief available[563] or where reinstatement would be inappropriate because working relationships have irretrievably broken down, especially if the employee is wholly or partially to blame for the breakdown.[564]

If the court grants a declaration that the dismissal is null and void, the employee is entitled to recover full back wages and benefits up to the date of judgment by way of salary owed, not by way of damages, since his or her employment is deemed never to have ended. It follows that the employee would not be required to mitigate his or her losses by trying to find replacement work. The prospect of compensating an employee while he or she does nothing has proven so unpalatable to some judges that they have refused to exercise their discretion to grant such a declaration.[565] Another consequence of declaring dismissal a nullity is that the employee is entitled to recover the value of benefits that would have vested after the date of dismissal, and especially pension benefits that would have vested at that time. Moreover, damages for wrongful dismissal may be awarded on the basis that the statutory procedures and the requirements of natural justice and fairness have become incorporated, expressly or impliedly, into the employment contract,[566] in which case the duty to mitigate would apply because compensation would flow from the breach of contract.

F. COMMON LAW REMEDIES FOR WRONGFUL DISMISSAL

At common law, the remedies available to a wrongfully dismissed employee are less beneficial than those available to a unionized employee under a collective agreement or to a non-unionized employee under a statutory unjust discharge scheme, such as section 240 of the *Canada Labour Code*, in two critical respects. First, the measure of damages at common law is restricted to the value of contractual entitlements

---

563 Examples: *Harelkin v. University of Regina*, [1979] 2 S.C.R. 561, appeal available before the University Senate; *Hitchcock v. New Brunswick (Deputy Solicitor General)* (1988), 93 N.B.R. (2d) 294 (Q.B.T.D.), statutory grievance and arbitration procedure available.

564 Example: *Abouna*, above note 554.

565 See, for example, the judgments of Parker and Singleton L.JJ. in *Vine v. National Dock Labour Board* (1956), [1957] A.C. 488 (H.L.); *Francis v. Kuala Lumpur Municipal Councillors*, [1962] 1 W.L.R. 1411 at 1418 (P.C.).

566 This seems to be the theoretical basis for the damages award in *Cohnstaedt v. University of Regina* (1994), 2 C.C.E.L. (2d) 161 (Sask. C.A.); and in *Abouna*, above note 554.

that would have vested in the employee during the period required to terminate the contract of employment, and secondly, the remedy of compulsory reinstatement is normally unavailable at common law. Proponents of equality of treatment argue that this result is unjustifiable and recommend that courts be more willing than before to order reinstatement and compensate employees for their real-world losses on a "make whole" basis.

1) Financial Compensation

The objective of awarding compensation for wrongful dismissal is not to make whole the employee's losses flowing from the dismissal; rather, it is to compensate the employee for the employer's failure to comply with its contractual duty to give due notice of termination.[567] Several important consequences follow from this objective. First, the determination of the reasonable notice period assumes critical importance in calculating the employee's damages. We saw earlier that the dominant trend since the 1950s has been for courts to increase the length of the notice period in order to achieve various policy desiderata, notably cushioning the employee against the blow of unemployment and compensating him or her for mistreatment at the hands of the employer.[568] The breadth of the reasonable notice test has indirectly enabled courts to pursue the "make whole" philosophy by means of extending the period of reasonable notice where required in order to make whole the employee's real-world losses. Thus, most courts have increased the notice period where the employee's chances of finding replacement employment are slim because of age, firm-specific skills, or the general state of the labour market or because the manner of dismissal diminished the employee's reputation or personal health—such factors clearly have a make whole ring. Nevertheless, the courts' ability to make whole a wrongfully dismissed employee's losses by manipulating the reasonable notice period is limited. For example, the unofficial upper limit on reasonable notice is currently twenty-four months in most provinces, and if the employment contract contains a relatively short express notice period, the courts are bound to honour it, subject to any *contra proferentem* interpretations and the doctrine of unconscionability.[569]

---

567 *Vorvis*, above note 106 at 1096–97; *Wallace*, above note 93.

568 See Section B(3)(a) and (c), above in this chapter.

569 The twenty-four-month ceiling could be exceeded if the employer has handled the dismissal in bad faith or in an unprofessional manner, following the holding in *Wallace*, above note 93, considered in Chapter 5, Section A. The treatment of express termination clauses is examined in Section B(3)(a), above in this chapter.

Second, the unlawful element in wrongful dismissal is the violation of the notice requirement, not the fact of dismissal itself. This emphasis creates an obstacle to the recovery of damages for psychological harm, since such harm usually flows from the fact that the employee has been fired, not from the failure to give due notice or wages in lieu thereof. We shall see below how some courts, inspired by the "make whole" philosophy, have sought to circumvent this limitation.

Third, at common law the employee is only entitled to be compensated for wages and benefits that he or she would have been contractually entitled to during the notice period, not for *ex gratia* expectancies. The courts assume that the employer would have minimized its costs by performing the contract during the notice period in the manner most advantageous to it.[570]

The scope of the employer's contractual liability to a wrongfully dismissed employee is subject to the general contract law rules of remoteness of damages enunciated in the seminal case of *Hadley v. Baxendale* as follows:

> Where two parties have made a contract which one of them has broken, the damages which the other party ought to receive in respect of such breach of contract should be such as may fairly and reasonably be considered either arising naturally, i.e., according to the usual course of things, from such breach of contract itself, or such as may reasonably be supposed to have been in the contemplation of both parties, at the time they made the contract, as the probable result of the breach of it.[571]

On the other hand, greater scope for the "make whole" philosophy exists in the law of tort, and a wrongfully dismissed employee may often be able to launch a tort action concurrently with a wrongful dismissal suit. In the law of tort, the objective of awarding damages is to put the plaintiff in the same position he or she would have occupied had the tort not been committed.[572] Also, the rules of remoteness in tort are broader than in contract, and in tort foreseeability is ascertained when the tort is committed, not when the contract was made.[573] Therefore, a wrongfully dismissed worker may sue in the tort of defamation

---

570 *Monk v. Coca-Cola Bottling Ltd.* (1996), 20 C.C.E.L. (2d) 280 at 299 (N.S.S.C.) [*Monk*]; *Lavarack v. Woods of Colchester Ltd.* (1966), [1967] 1 Q.B. 278 (C.A.) [*Lavarack*].

571 (1854), 9 Ex. 341, 156 E.R. 145 at 354 [*Hadley*].

572 The most illuminating analysis of the tort principles is that of J.G. Fleming, *The Law of Torts*, 7th ed. (Sydney: Law Book Company, 1987) at 186–94.

573 *Ibid.*

for injury to reputation[574] or seek compensation for mental suffering in torts such as wilful and/or negligent infliction of "nervous shock,"[575] or wilful and/or negligent infliction of "harassment and oppression,"[576] (but not, after 1997, in the novel tort of "bad faith" or "retaliatory discharge"[577]). We shall examine these torts in greater detail below.

Despite the attempt by many courts to extend the "make whole" principle in wrongful dismissal actions by means of the reasonable notice test and tort innovations, it is clear that only limited success can be achieved, since the make whole philosophy is squarely at odds with the fundamental contract law principles governing wrongful dismissal. The reader is advised to compare the approach of courts at common law with the explicit "make whole" approach applied by statutory adjudicators under section 240 of the *Canada Labour Code* and by human rights tribunals under human rights legislation.[578]

Next, we examine the common law principles in greater detail in regard to wage increases, bonuses, and fringe benefits.

a) Wage Increases, Commissions, and Bonuses

Any wage increase, commission, or bonus that would have fallen due during the notice period is only compensable if the employee would have been contractually entitled to it.[579] Therefore, any increase or bonus that depends on the employer's discretion would be non-compensable, unless it is possible to fetter the exercise of such discretion by the express or implied terms of the contract. In order to protect the employee's real-world expectation that such discretionary increases, commissions, or bonuses would likely have been given to him or her had he or she remained employed during the notice period, many (but not all) courts have implied a term into the employment contract requiring the employer to assess the employee's performance in good faith and reasonably in determining whether or not the employee should receive a discretionary

---

574 Example: *Chahal*, above note 247.

575 *Clark v. Canada* (1994), 94 C.L.L.C. ¶14,028 at 12,148–49 (F.C.T.D.) [*Clark*]; *Boothman v. Canada*, [1993] 3 F.C. 381 (T.D.) [*Boothman*].

576 *Rahemtulla v. Vanfed Credit Union*, [1984] 3 W.W.R. 296 (B.C.S.C.) [*Rahemtulla*].

577 The existence of such a novel tort was rejected by the Supreme Court of Canada in *Wallace*, above note 93 at 735–36. Some previous trial judges appeared to favour such a tort: *Duplessis v. Walwyn Stodgell Cochran Murray Ltd.* (1988), 20 C.C.E.L. 245 (B.C.S.C.) [*Duplessis*].

578 See, respectively, Section E(1)(c), above in this chapter, and Chapter 7.

579 Increases and bonuses were ruled non-compensable for this reason in *Lavarack*, above note 570; and *Monk*, above note 570.

increase or bonus.[580] This enables a court to predict the probable quality of the employee's performance over the notice period—the employee's past performance over a representative period of time is usually taken as a proxy for future performance—in order to determine whether or not the employer, acting in good faith and reasonably, would have awarded the increase, commission, or bonus during the notice period. Of course, account will also be taken of other factors that would have affected the size of any increase, commission, or bonus during the period—for example, a sudden slump in demand for the firm's products or services,[581] or an increase in the firm's profitability.

However, this analysis cannot be applied where an increase or bonus is intended to operate on the basis of an "entire contract" whereunder payment is made subject to the condition precedent that the employee actually work until the end of a specified period, at which time the employee can receive the bonus, but not before.[582] Here, an employee who is dismissed before the designated date for payment of the increase or bonus would be disallowed from recovering compensation on a pro-rated basis for any service performed prior to the payment date.[583] It is a matter of construction of the terms of the bonus plan whether or not the parties intend the bonus to operate on an entire contract basis. Most courts are reluctant to find such an intention in the absence of clear evidence to that effect because of the potential prejudice to wrongfully dismissed employees.

The calculation of lost earnings is complicated where an employee is paid in whole or in part on a commission basis or some other form of profit-sharing. It is easy to state in the abstract that the common law entitles the employee to be compensated for losing the opportunity of earning a commission over the notice period,[584] but calculating how much money the employee has lost presents practical difficulties. The onus of proving such losses is on the employee. He or she must be

---

580 Examples: *Chann v. RBC Dominion Securities Inc.* (2004), 34 C.C.E.L. (3d) 244 at 256 (Ont. S.C.J.), involving a merit bonus; *Duprey v. Seanix Technology (Canada) Inc.*, [2003] C.L.L.C. ¶210-008 at 141,073–74 (B.C.S.C.), involving a commission.

581 Example: *Wiebe v. Central Transport Refrigeration (Manitoba) Ltd.* (1993), 45 C.C.E.L. 1 at 7 (Man. Q.B.), var'd on other grounds, above note 97 (C.A.), where the court estimated that a discretionary wage increase would have been granted during the notice period due to an industry recession.

582 *Cutter v. Powell* (1795), 6 Term 320, 101 E.R. 573 (K.B.). See S.J. Stoljar, "The Great Case of *Cutter v. Powell*" (1956) 34 Can. Bar Rev. 288.

583 Example: *Daniels v. Canadian Tire Corporation* (1991), 39 C.C.E.L. 107 at 108–9 (Ont. Gen. Div.).

584 Examples: *D.H. Howden & Co. v. Sparling*, [1970] S.C.R. 883; *Macdonald v. Richardson Greenshields of Canada Ltd.* (1985), 12 C.C.E.L. 22 (B.C.S.C.).

able to establish, on a balance of probabilities, that there is a "reasonable chance" or a "real possibility"[585] that the amount claimed would have been earned had he or she worked during the notice period. The employee's previous earnings during a representative sample of past service is usually taken as a proxy for future earnings, but the court must also factor in other contingencies that could occur during the notice period, such as the employee's personal health deteriorating or the firm going into a downswing.[586]

The law of unjust enrichment may entitle an employee to recover compensation for non–contractually binding expectancies if the following prerequisites are met: (1) the defendant must have requested the plaintiff, expressly or impliedly, to provide the benefit, or have acquiesced in the plaintiff receiving the benefit; (2) the benefit must be "ascertainable" and "incontrovertible";[587] (3) the benefit must be irrecoverable in a breach of contract action; and (4) it must be unjust to deny the plaintiff compensation for the benefit.[588] In one case, an insurance broker who was wrongfully fired before he could exercise an option under his employment contract to purchase from the employer his "business book," valued at a specific dollar amount, was awarded compensation in the law of restitution for the loss of the opportunity to purchase the book.[589] Accordingly, an employee whose wrongful dismissal prevents him or her from earning an increase, bonus, or other benefit could arguably be compensated for such a loss in the law of restitution. Furthermore, an employee can presumably recover under a *quantum meruit* in the law of restitution for the fair value of work performed in the expectation of receiving an increase or bonus. Courts have frequently compensated employees for the "fair" value of work performed in the absence of a contractual obligation on the employer's part.[590]

---

585 Goodman J.A. in *Prozak v. Bell Telephone Co. of Canada* (1984), 4 C.C.E.L. 202 at 227 (Ont. C.A.).

586 Examples: *Bragg*, above note 239; *Veach v. Diversey Inc.* (1993) 1 C.C.E.L. (2d) 242 at 247 (B.C.S.C.).

587 *Peel (Regional Municipality of) v. Canada*, [1992] 3 S.C.R. 762, McLachlin J.

588 Examples: *Nicholson v. St. Denis* (1975), 8 O.R. (2d) 315 (C.A.); *Duxbury v. Training Inc.* (2002), 16 C.C.E.L. (3d) 120 at 132–38 (Alta. Prov. Ct.) [*Duxbury*].

589 *Alyea v. South Waterloo Edgar Insurance Brokers Ltd.* (1994), 50 C.C.E.L. 266 at 277 (Ont. Gen. Div.).

590 Examples: *Duxbury*, above note 588; *Hill v. Develcon Electronics Ltd.* (1991), 37 C.C.E.L. 19, especially at 35 (Sask. Q.B.). The leading Canadian authority on *quantum meruit* is *Deglman v. Brunet Estate*, [1954] S.C.R. 725.

b) Fringe Benefits, Pension Rights, and Other Benefits

Strict contract law principles entitle a wrongfully dismissed employee to be compensated only in respect to lost fringe benefits that he or she would have been contractually entitled to during the notice period.

Regarding pensions, the employee's measure of damages in the case of pension benefits that have *not* vested[591] in him or her at the date of dismissal, but would have vested during the notice period, is the value of the vested benefits that he or she would have received had he or she remained in employment throughout the notice period.[592] One method is to award the employee an amount equal to the employer's contributions over the notice period.[593] Another method is to award an amount that would enable the employee to purchase an annuity of equal value to the value of the pension benefits that he or she would have been entitled to at the end of the notice period.[594] But if the notice period expires before vesting occurs, the wrongfully dismissed employee can recover only his or her own past contributions to the plan, not those of the employer.[595]

Regarding medical, dental, medical, life, and disability benefits provided under an employer's insurance plan, the courts generally reimburse the wrongfully dismissed employee for any out-of-pocket expenses incurred during the notice period that would otherwise have been covered by the plan.[596] Consequently, if the employee becomes disabled, dies, is sick, or requires expensive dental work during the no-

---

591 Pension benefits are said to "vest" when the employee becomes irrevocably entitled to retain the benefit of the employer's contributions to the plan. Pension plans normally state that vesting occurs after the worker reaches a specified age or has worked for the employer for a minimum period of time. Pension plan provisions on vesting, however, must comply with the minimum vesting rules established in pension benefits acts in all Canadian jurisdictions. Thus, under the Canada *Pension Benefits Standards Act, 1985*, R.S.C. 1985 (2d Supp.), c. 32, ss. 16(1), (3), 17, and 18, benefits must vest after two years of continuous service with an employer.

592 Examples: *White v. Woolworth Canada Inc.* (1996), 22 C.C.E.L. (2d) 110 at 144 (Nfld. C.A.) [*Woolworth*]; *Walsh v. Alberta and Southern Gas Co.* (1991), 41 C.C.E.L. 145 at 190 (Alta. Q.B.).

593 Examples: *Datardina v. Royal Trust Corporation of Canada* (1993), 49 C.C.E.L. 255 at 267 (B.C.S.C.); *Fleming*, above note 152 at 155.

594 Examples: *Boylan v. Canadian Broadcasting Corp.* (1994), 3 C.C.E.L. (2d) 64 (Alta. Q.B.); *Peet v. Babcock and Wilcox Industries Ltd.* (2001), 12 C.C.E.L (3d) 5 (Ont. C.A.) [*Peet*].

595 Examples: *Elliott v. Parksville (City of)* (1989), 89 C.L.L.C. ¶14,038 at 12,322–23, aff'd (1990), 29 C.C.E.L. 263 (B.C.C.A.); *Corab Services Ltd. v. Cramer* (1983), 26 Alta. L.R. (2d) 313 (C.A.).

596 *McKilligan v. Pacific Vocational Institute* (1981), 28 B.C.L.R. 324 at 340 (C.A.).

tice period, the employer is responsible for the full amount.[597] Employers wishing to avoid this peril should retain full insurance coverage for dismissed employees throughout their notice periods. Of course, if the employee has purchased replacement insurance coverage for the risks in question, it is the cost of maintaining such coverage during the notice period that will be compensated.[598] However, some courts in Ontario and Alberta have taken the tack of awarding the wrongfully dismissed employee an amount equivalent to the employer's contributions to the insurance plan over the notice period, notwithstanding that the employee may not have incurred financial loss.[599]

Regarding paid vacations that would have fallen due during the notice period, some courts refuse to award a wrongfully dismissed employee vacation pay for such a holiday on the basis that the employee is receiving pay in the form of damages without having to work; awarding additional vacation pay would, under this view, constitute "double compensation."[600] In contrast, other courts award an extra amount for vacation pay on the basis that a wrongfully dismissed employee cannot properly be regarded as being "on holiday" from employment.[601] There is no doctrinal obstacle against compensating the employee for the loss of personal satisfaction and pleasure that would have come from taking a vacation during the notice period.[602] Nevertheless, most (but not all[603]) courts have balked at taking this step, reasoning – rather ungenerously, it is submitted – that being unemployed after a wrongful dismissal is tantamount to being on vacation anyway.[604] There is no

---

597 Examples: *Gareau v. Oracle Corporation of Canada* (1992), 47 C.C.E.L. 202 at 209 (Ont. Gen. Div.); *Prince v. T. Eaton Co.* (1992), 41 C.C.E.L. 72 at 86 (B.C.C.A.).

598 Example: *Tull v. Norske Skog Canada Ltd.* (2004), 34 C.C.E.L. (3d) 225 at 233 (B.C.S.C.).

599 *Davidson v. Allelix Inc.* (1991), 7 O.R. (3d) 581 at 589–60 (C.A.); *Christianson v. North Hill News Inc.* (1993), 49 C.C.E.L. 182 (Alta. C.A.).

600 Examples: *Cronk*, above note 127 at 141,294; *Landry v. Canadian Forest Products Ltd.* (1992), 42 C.C.E.L. 59 at 65 (B.C.C.A.); *Driscoll v. Coseka Resources Ltd.* (1992), 4 Alta. L.R. (3d) 106 at 117 (Q.B.).

601 Examples: *Mitchell v. Lorell Furs Inc.* (1991), 36 C.C.E.L. 187 at 189 (N.S.S.C.T.D.); *Fitzgerald v. Waterford Hospital* (1995), 15 C.C.E.L. (2d) 143 at 158 (Nfld. S.C.T.D.).

602 This regularly happens, for example, in the famous "holiday" cases: e.g., *Jackson v. Horizon Holidays Ltd.*, [1975] 1 W.L.R. 1468 (C.A.).

603 Example: *Bavaro v. North America Tea, Coffee and Herbs Trading Co.* (2001), 8 C.C.E.L. (3d) 24 at 30–31 (B.C.C.A.).

604 Example: *Turner v. Westburne Electrical Inc.* (2004), 36 C.C.E.L. (3d) 227 at 252 (Alta. Q.B.).

doubt, however, that vacation pay accrued up to the date of dismissal is compensable.[605]

Other benefits that the employer would have been legally obliged to provide during the notice period are also compensable; these include: the employer's statutory contributions to the Canada Pension Plan and the Employment Insurance Commission, the opportunity to exercise stock options that the wrongfully dismissed employee has been denied, tips and gratuities, overtime opportunities, use of a company car for private purposes, club membership fees provided primarily for the employee's private (as opposed to business) use, discount schemes that enable the employee to buy the employer's products or services at reduced rates, meal and accommodation allowances, and accumulated sick leave.

c) Psychological Harm and Injury to Reputation

It is widely known that many employees suffer psychological harm, such as depression and stress, as a result of being dismissed, especially where the dismissal is handled in a callous or insensitive manner. Often, physical symptoms, such as high blood pressure, heart attacks, and eating disorders, become manifest. Even if such symptoms can be causally related to the dismissal as opposed to other circumstances in the employee's private life,[606] the law of wrongful dismissal still places major obstacles on the recovery of compensation for them. The fundamental principle is that a wrongful dismissal action compensates the employee for the employer's failure to give the proper notice of termination or pay in lieu thereof.[607] It will be relatively rare that a plaintiff's mental distress will flow from the failure to give notice. Instead, such distress usually flows from the fact of losing one's job, regardless of whether or not due notice was given, and from the fact that the employer may have treated the employee callously or insensitively over a period of time leading up to and following the dismissal. Accordingly, this principle has led courts to deny claims for mental distress where it has resulted from factors such as the difficulty of finding alternative employment in an unfavourable labour market[608] or the abusive treatment

---

605 *Orke v. Quintette Coal Ltd.* (1992), 39 C.C.E.L. 146 at 147 (B.C.S.C.), where the plaintiff's vacation fell due before his termination date.

606 Establishing such a causal connection on the basis of the medical evidence is no easy matter. See I.F. Ivankovich, "Mental Distress in Wrongful Dismissals: Towards a More Rationalized Approach" (1989) 18 Man. L.J. 277, especially at 282–83 for a synthesis of the caselaw on this point.

607 This principle has been reaffirmed by the Supreme Court of Canada in *Wallace*, above note 93; and in *Vorvis*, above note 106 at 1103–4, McIntyre J.

608 *Sheehy v. Wolf* (1984), 6 C.C.E.L. 101 (Ont. Co. Ct.).

of the employee by a manager prior to dismissal.[609] Furthermore, the common law rules of remoteness of damages require that the employer must be able to reasonably foresee the harm sustained by the employee in a wrongful dismissal situation at the date the contract is made, not at the date it is breached.[610] Clearly, an employer might know of circumstances at the date of wrongful dismissal that would reasonably lead it to suppose that the employee would likely suffer psychological harm—for example, the employer might have become aware that the employee has fallen into hard financial times or has developed a stress condition—but that were unknowable at the date of original hiring.

Nevertheless, many courts have balked at imposing such narrow limits on the employer's liability for damages for mental distress and have used various legal techniques in an attempt to make whole the wrongfully dismissed employee who suffers such harm at the employer's hands.

First, some courts have ruled that the plaintiff's mental suffering was caused by the employer's failure to give proper notice and was therefore compensable.[611] This analysis is somewhat unreal.

Second, some courts have held that where the employee's mental distress was caused by a combination of factors including the failure to give proper notice, the doctrine of "aggravated" damages can be used to compensate the employee fully for such distress.[612] According to this doctrine, the notice irregularity brings into play the other contributory factors, so that compensation can be awarded for the harm that results from all the operative factors. Moreover, aggravated damages are based on what the employer ought reasonably to have foreseen at the date of the dismissal.[613] The scope of the aggravated damages appears to have been narrowed significantly, however, by the Supreme Court of Canada's ruling in *Vorvis*[614] that such damages "generally" may be awarded only where the employee's psychological distress is caused by conduct on the employer's part that constitutes an "independently actionable" wrong, such as a tort or breach of a term in the employment contract other than the notice requirement. Although some trial courts seem to

---

609 Examples: *Vorvis*, above note 106; *McPhillips v. British Columbia Ferry Corporation* (1995), 15 C.C.E.L. (2d) 189 at 195 (B.C.S.C.).

610 *Hadley*, above note 571.

611 Example: *Russello v. Jannock Ltd.* (1987), 37 D.L.R. (4th) 372 at 374 (Ont. Div. Ct.).

612 Examples: *Prinzo v. Baycrest Centre for Geriatric Care* (2002), 17 C.C.E.L. (3d) 207 at 227 (Ont C.A.) [*Prinzo*]; *Bradbury v. Newfoundland (A.G.)* (2002), 13 C.C.E.L. (3d) 173 at 201–6 (Nfld. C.A.).

613 *Ibid.*

614 Above note 106.

have either overlooked or simply paid lip service to this ruling, in 1995 the Ontario Court of Appeal relied on it to quash an award of aggravated damages to a bank manager who had been wrongfully dismissed in a particularly egregious manner that gave the false impression that he was a thief.[615] Therefore, the aggravated damages doctrine must now be regarded as of relatively limited use in compensating mental distress unless the employee can establish an independently actionable wrong.

Third, some courts have been quite ingenious in linking the mental distress to an independently actionable wrong separate from the failure to give due notice. They have found the employer to have breached various independent terms in the employment contract, such as a disciplinary procedure expressly incorporated into the contract,[616] a verbal guaranty of job security,[617] a verbal promise of promotion,[618] an implied promise to safeguard the employee's personal health and safety,[619] an implied promise to safeguard the employee against bullying,[620] and even an implied promise to treat the employee decently in dismissal situations.[621] One might have thought that the courts would have taken the obvious step of implying into the employment contract a general duty on the employer to treat the employee fairly and in good faith in dismissal situations.[622] However, the Supreme Court of Canada in 1997 ruled that no such term can be implied into the employment contract as a matter of general law, since otherwise, the traditional principle that the employer need not provide just cause for dismissal so long as it honours the contractual notice requirement would potentially be eroded.[623] Instead, the Court ruled that if an employer handles dismissal in a callous, insensitive, or unprofessional manner such as to cause the employee psychological harm, this treatment can be reflected

615 *Francis v. Canadian Imperial Bank of Commerce* (1994), 7 C.C.E.L. (2d) 1 at 15 (Ont. C.A.), var'g (1992), 41 C.C.E.L. 37 (Ont. Gen. Div.) [*Francis*].
616 *Roddick*, above note 265.
617 *Lightburn v. Mid Island Consumer Services Co-operative* (1984), 4 C.C.E.L. 263 (B.C. Co. Ct.).
618 *Wuorinen v. British Columbia (Workers' Compensation Board)* (1983), 1 C.C.E.L. 29 (B.C.S.C.).
619 *Haggarty v. McCullough*, [2002] C.L.L.C. ¶210-022 at 141,265 (Alta. Prov. Ct.).
620 Example: *Stamos*, above note 369 at 141,404.
621 *Leonard v. Wilson* (1992), 41 C.C.E.L. 226 at 240 (Ont. Gen. Div.), where this was an alternative ground for the decision; *Carrick v. Cooper Canada Ltd.* (1983), 2 C.C.E.L. 87 at 106–7 (Ont. H.C.J.).
622 Indeed, Gomery J. took this step in *Bernardin v. Alitalia Air Lines* (1993), 50 C.C.E.L. 156 at 162 (Que. Sup. Ct.).
623 *Wallace*, above note 93. But compare the vigorous dissent of McLachlin J. on this point.

in a damages award by increasing the length of the reasonable notice period.[624]

Fourth, independently actionable wrongs may be found in the law of tort so as to compensate the employee for mental distress. For example, the manner of dismissal may amount to the tort of defamation of character,[625] dismissing an employee on deliberately fabricated grounds may constitute the tort of deceit[626] or the tort of inducing breach of contract,[627] and dismissing an employee in a brutally insensitive manner or for reasons in bad faith may constitute the tort of intentional infliction of nervous shock.[628] Some trial courts have also attempted to invent novel torts, such as "wilful or negligent infliction of harassment and oppression"[629] and "retaliatory discharge"[630] in order to safeguard employees who suffer emotional or other harm from unprofessionally handled dismissals, but in its 1997 *Wallace* decision, the Supreme Court of Canada held that no such tort as "bad faith discharge" exists,[631] thereby apparently blocking further innovations in the law of tort designed to regulate the employer's dismissal power.

Regarding the employer's liability for injury to reputation sustained by the employee as a result of wrongful dismissal, it is a well-established principle of law that such an action is unavailable as part of the wrongful dismissal claim and must be brought as a separate claim in the tort of defamation of character.[632] However, there are two exceptions. First, where the dominant purpose of the employment contract in question is to enhance the employee's reputation—for example, in the case of sports performers or entertainers—damages for injury to reputation have been awarded.[633] Second, where the manner of dismissal has damaged the employee's reputation, resulting in the person facing greater

---

624 See Section B(3)(c)(vi), above in this chapter.

625 *Larsen v. A & B Sound Ltd.* (1996), 18 C.C.E.L. (2d) 237 at 242–43 (B.C.S.C.).

626 *Dixon v. British Columbia Transit* (1995), 13 C.C.E.L. (2d) 272 at 309 (B.C.S.C.).

627 *Ribeiro*, below note 674 (Ont. C.A.).

628 *Prinzo*, above note 612 at 227; *Zorn-Smith*, above note 143 at 314; *Clark*, above note 575 at 12,148–49 The seminal authority on this tort is *Wilkinson v. Downton*, [1897] 2 Q.B. 57, especially at 58–59, commonly studied by first-year law students.

629 *Rahemtulla*, above note 576.

630 *Ruggeiro v. Emco Ltd.* (1993), 6 C.C.E.L. (2d) 57 (Ont. Gen. Div.); *Duplessis*, above note 577.

631 Above note 93.

632 Examples: *Peso Silver Mines Ltd. v. Cropper*, [1966] S.C.R. 673, Cartwright J.; *Abouna*, above note 554. These authorities are based on *Addis v. Gramophone Co.*, [1909] A.C. 488 (H.L.).

633 Example: *Marbé v. George Edwardes (Daly's Theatre) Ltd.*, [1928] 1 K.B. 269 (C.A.).

than usual difficulties in securing a replacement job, the courts can increase the reasonable notice period under the cushion rationale to take account of this fact.[634]

d) Deductions from Damages under the Duty to Mitigate

A wrongfully dismissed employee is required to take reasonable steps to minimize the extent of the losses sustained as a consequence of the dismissal. If the employer can prove that the employee has failed to mitigate his or her losses — the onus of proof resting with the employer — the employee's damages will be reduced commensurately.[635] If the employee allows reasonably avoidable losses to increase, such losses can rightly be said to have been caused by the employee's own actions (or lack thereof), not by the actions of the employer. Moreover, by providing an incentive to the employee to try to find alternative employment, the duty to mitigate fosters labour mobility, something that is in the general public interest. One effect of the duty to mitigate is that the employee's damages will be reduced by any replacement earnings obtained during the period of notice of termination, effective as of the date the replacement job commences.[636] This is only the case, however, if the employee would not have acquired the monies in question, but for the wrongful dismissal.[637]

The thorniest issue under the duty to mitigate is usually whether or not an employee has made reasonable efforts to find replacement work. It might seem odd that the burden of proving that the employee has failed to mitigate should be placed on the employer, given that the employee would appear to be in the best position to establish what he or she did in order to find alternative work. Moreover, it can be costly for employers to have to monitor all the available job postings within the purview of the employee's skills following a wrongful dismissal, so as to cross-examine the employee on whether he or she applied for them. Probably the practice reflects the courts' reluctance to assist the employer who is, after all, the wrongdoer. Be that as it may, expert evidence of professional recruiters is often adduced to help courts evaluate the state of the labour market and the level of demand for the plaintiff's

---

634 Example: *Hudson v. Giant Yellowknife Mines Ltd.* (1992), 44 C.C.E.L. 109 at 112 (N.W.T.S.C.). See generally on the determination of "reasonable notice" Section B(3)(c), above in this chapter.

635 *Red Deer College v. Michaels* (1975), [1976] 2 S.C.R. 324 [*Red Deer College*].

636 *Shaw Communications Inc. v. Lum*, [2005] C.L.L.C. ¶210-005, especially at 141,031 (N.B.C.A.).

637 This follows from the reasoning in *Ellis v. White Pass Transportation Ltd.* (1983), 42 B.C.L.R. 351 (C.A.).

services.[638] The courts generally determine what is reasonable for any given worker by his or her personal circumstances, not in relation to reducing the employer's costs.[639] Important considerations are the geographical location of the alternative work, the nature of the work[640] (including pay, status, and responsibility[641]), and the employee's individual situation. An example of the latter is not expecting elderly workers who have developed roots in their community to accept employment beyond daily commuting distance of their homes.[642] Normally, the court will allow the plaintiff a period of one or two months to recover from the trauma of wrongful dismissal before he or she starts a job search.[643] If an employee has failed to find replacement work despite making earnest efforts for a substantial time, the courts will permit relaxing the intensity of his or her efforts, recognizing that it would be pointless to expect the employee to continue to bang on doors that have already been closed in his or her face.[644] If the employee spends the time setting up his or her own business instead of searching for work as an employee, the courts have ruled that this endeavour will not breach the duty to mitigate if the plaintiff could not reasonably be expected to find a relatively secure replacement position as an employee due to age or an otherwise unfavourable labour market.[645] Indeed, some courts have even held that monies obtained by the employee from operating his or her own business will not be deducted from damages for wrongful

---

638 Example: *Valentini v. Monarch Broadcasting Ltd.* (1992), 41 C.C.E.L. 243 at 248 (B.C.S.C.).

639 *Coutts v. Brian Jessel Autosports Inc.*, [2005] C.L.L.C. ¶210-022 at 141,185 (B.C.C.A.).

640 Normally, the employee must seek out and accept "similar" work to his or her old job: *Thiessen v. Leduc*, [1975] 4 W.W.R. 387 at 401 (Alta. S.C.T.D.).

641 Example: *Allen v. Assaly Holdings Ltd.* (1991), 34 C.C.E.L. 81 at 90 (Ont. Gen. Div.). Thus, managers are normally not compelled to accept non-managerial positions: e.g., *Radley v. Sanden Machine Ltd.* (1992), 44 C.C.E.L. 250, especially at 253 (Ont. Gen. Div.) [*Radley*].

642 Example: *Peet*, above note 594 at 7.

643 *Christianson v. North Hill News Inc.* (1992), 39 C.C.E.L. 243 at 251 (Alta. Q.B.), where two months was held to suffice for a "reasonable person"; varied, but not on this point, by the Court of Appeal, above note 599; *Pauloski*, above note 130 at 225.

644 *MacBride v. ICG Liquid Gas Ltd.* (1992), 47 C.C.E.L. 309, especially at 311 (B.C.S.C.).

645 Examples: *Ward v. Royal Trust Corporation of Canada* (1994), 1 C.C.E.L. (2d) 153 at 158 (B.C.S.C.); *Waters v. MTI Canada Ltd.* (1996), 19 C.C.E.L. (2d) 24 at 69 (Ont. Gen. Div.).

dismissal, where such monies are ploughed back into the business in order to help it get established.[646]

Where wrongful dismissal takes the form of a constructive dismissal, special considerations come into play regarding the duty to mitigate. As of the late 1980s,[647] the courts began to require that a constructively dismissed employee, in order to mitigate his or her losses, must continue to work under the changed terms and conditions of employment implemented by the employer while conducting a search for replacement employment, but only provided that doing so would not cause the employee an undue hardship. The aim was indirectly to relieve employers from some of the burden of the extremely rigid constructive dismissal doctrine.[648] In 2008, the Supreme Court of Canada extended this principle to offers of continued employment made to a former employee following wrongful dismissal.[649] Again, it seems that indirectly the Court is aiming to relieve employers from some of the burden of extremely generous reasonable notice periods.

The duty to mitigate is inapplicable to severance payments that are expressed in the employment contract to be debts, rather than payments for breach of the promise to provide due notice of termination. In order for a severance payment to constitute a debt, the contract must specify an ascertainable amount of money and clearly state that the entitlement to it is not conditional on the employee working for the balance of the notice period.[650] Such clauses are usually found only in the contracts of high-echelon managers and professionals. The duty to mitigate also does not apply to compensation for psychological harm and a *Wallace* extension since such harm is unaffected by taking alternative employment.[651]

Finally, the employee is entitled to be compensated by the employer for any expenses incurred in complying with the duty to mitigate, such as the costs of conducting a job search or relocating to another city to accept work.

---

646 Example: *Foster v. MTI Canada Inc.* (1992), 42 C.C.E.L. 1 at 3 (Ont. C.A.).

647 The leading authority is *Mifsud v. MacMillan Bathurst Inc.* (1989), 28 C.C.E.L. 228 (Ont. C.A.).

648 See Section D(3), above in this chapter.

649 *Evans*, above note 183 at para. 33.

650 Examples: *Borkovich v. Canadian Membership Warehouse Ltd.* (1991), 34 C.C.E.L. 42 at 48 (B.C.S.C.); *Zielenski v. Saskatchewan Beef Stabilization Board* (1992), 42 C.C.E.L. 24 (Sask. Q.B.).

651 Example: *Bouma*, above note 252 at 4, citing *Prinzo*, above note 612 at 497.

e) Deductions from Damages under the Collateral Benefits Rule

An employee who has been wrongfully dismissed may receive income from various extraneous sources during the notice period. The most common of such "collateral benefits" are disability, illness, and pension benefits provided under private insurance plans; tax savings; and employment insurance, workers' compensation, and welfare payments. The question is whether the value of collateral benefits should be deducted from the employee's damages for wrongful dismissal. On the one hand, the objective of awarding damages for breach of contract is to protect the employee against the lost value of the broken promise, not to provide him or her with a windfall at the employer's expense. Moreover, increasing the employer's costs of terminating employees in this way could have a disemployment effect and other adverse economic effects.[652] On the other hand, to reduce the damages by taking the collateral benefit into account would provide the employer with a windfall[653] and may even provide an incentive for wrongful dismissal by making it cheaper to breach than to perform. Also, where the collateral benefit takes the form of insurance that the employee has had the foresight to arrange wholly or partially at his or her own expense, to offset it against damages is to allow the employer to take advantage of the employee's good judgment and might even discourage the practice of self-insuring. Perhaps the fairest solution would allow the courts to apportion the value of any given collateral benefit between the employer and the employee, having regard to their respective interests in the circumstances of each case. However, the law does not take this view.

Regarding any disability or illness benefits received by the employee during the notice period under a private insurance plan, the courts have traditionally held that such benefits will not be deducted from damages for wrongful dismissal provided that the employee has "paid" for the insurance coverage "in some manner."[654] The Supreme Court of Canada, in a case involving the law of tort, ruled that an employee would be regarded as having paid for insurance coverage if the employee contributes part of his or her wages to the plan by way of a periodic paycheque deduction, or in the case of a non-contributory plan, if the

---

652 The economic costs and benefits associated with high termination settlements are reviewed at above note 1 and accompanying text.

653 *Quaere* whether, in the case of benefits provided under a private insurance plan, such as disability coverage, the ideal resolution to the who-gets-an-unjustifiable-windfall debate would be to make the benefit non-deductible, but require the employee to pay it into the insurance fund so as to benefit all fund members.

654 *Cunningham v. Wheeler*, [1994] 1 S.C.R. 359.

employer takes into account the cost of the insurance coverage in determining the value of the employee's total compensation package.[655] The latter obstacle would appear to be relatively easy to surmount. However, in its 1997 decision in *Sylvester v. British Columbia*,[656] the Supreme Court of Canada appeared to reverse the traditional principles by offsetting the value of short-term disability benefits received by the plaintiff during the reasonable notice period from his damages for wrongful dismissal. The Court reasoned that, since the terms of the insurance plan prohibited a recipient of disability benefits from receiving regular wages at the same time, the employee would not have been entitled to receive both disability benefits and his regular wages had he worked out his notice period. Therefore, offsetting the value of any disability benefits from damages for wrongful dismissal was necessary to avoid unjustly enriching the employee. Justice Major put it as follows:

> The respondent's contractual right to damages for wrongful dismissal and his contractual right to disability benefits are based on opposite assumptions about his ability to work and it is incompatible with the contract of employment for the respondent to receive both amounts. The damages are based on the premise that he would have worked during the notice period. The disability payments are only payable because he could not work. It makes no sense to pay damages based on the assumption that he would have worked in addition to the disability benefits which arose solely because he could not work. This suggests that the parties did not intend the respondent to receive both damages and disability benefits.[657]

Although this logic may seem impeccable[658]—the courts have also applied it to maternity benefits received under an employer's insurance plan during the reasonable notice period[659]—rights-inspired judges seeking to preserve the wrongfully dismissed employee's financial

---

655 *Ibid.*

656 [1997] 2 S.C.R. 315, quashing (1995), 125 D.L.R. (4th) 541 (B.C.C.A.) [*Sylvester*]. See J.B. Payne, "Terminating the Disabled Employee in Ontario: Assessing the Impact of *Sylvester v. British Columbia*" (1998) 6 C.L.E.L.J. 99.

657 *Sylvester*, *ibid.* at 321.

658 The logic was endorsed in *Weber v. Capital Industrial Sale and Services Ltd.*, [2002] C.L.L.C. ¶210-002 at 141,023 (Alta. Prov. Ct.); *Swindley v. Saskatoon Tribal Council (STC) Urban First Nations Services* (July 2003) (Hood) at 29, unreported unjust discharge adjudication under the *CLC*, above note 28, s. 240.

659 Such benefits were ruled to be deductible in *Wilson v. UBS Securities Canada Inc.* (2005), 41 C.C.E.L. (3d) 131 at 156–58 (B.C.S.C.).

cushion have held that *Sylvester* only applies to insurance plans to which the employee has neither directly nor indirectly contributed.[660]

Regarding the income tax dimension of wrongful dismissal, Canadian courts have ruled that damages for wrongful dismissal are assessed on the basis of the employee's before-tax earnings.[661] However, the *Income Tax Act* treats compensation for wrongful dismissal as taxable income in the hands of the employee.[662] Section 153(1) of the Act requires employers to deduct income taxes from the monies handed over to the employee as damages for wrongful dismissal and to remit them to the receiver general.

Regarding unemployment insurance benefits, most courts now hold that damages for wrongful dismissal should be calculated without regard to such benefits.[663] Nevertheless, the employer does not obtain a windfall since the *Employment Insurance Act*[664] requires any employer who believes that an employee has received an unemployment insurance payment during the notice period to ascertain from the employee whether a payment has been received, and if so, to deduct such an amount from the employee's damages and remit it to the employment insurance administrators.

Regarding welfare payments received during the notice period, there have been no recent judicial pronouncements on the question of their deductibility from damages for wrongful dismissal. The employee cannot be said to have paid for such benefits, except in the indirect sense that he or she pays income tax. By analogy, in personal injury cases, welfare benefits are not offset from damages for lost earnings.[665] Presumably, the same outcome would prevail in the context of wrongful dismissal.

---

660 Example: *McNamara v. Alexander Centre Industries Ltd.* (2001), 8 C.C.E.L. (3d) 204 at 210 (Ont. C.A.).

661 *Harte v. Amfab Products Ltd.* (1970), 73 W.W.R. (N.S.) 561 (B.C.S.C.); *Ofstedahl v. Cam-Set Mechanical Contractors Ltd.* (1973), [1974] 1 W.W.R. 329 (Alta. S.C.A.D.).

662 See *Income Tax Act*, R.S.C. 1985 (5th Supp.), c. 1, ss. 56(1)(a)(ii), 60(j.1), 248(1) ("retiring allowance"); M.N.R., Interpretation Bulletin IT-337R2, "Income Tax Act Retiring Allowances" (22 May 1984), and Interpretation Bulletin IT-365R2, "Income Tax Act Damages, Settlements and Similar Receipts" (8 May 1987). See also G. St-Hilaire, "The Taxation of Damages for Wrongful Dismissal" (1999) 7 Can. Lab. & Emp. L.J. 135.

663 Examples: *Gaunt v. Consolidated Freightways Corporation of Delaware* (1990), 33 C.C.E.L. 255 at 263 (Man. Q.B.); *Radley*, above note 641 at 255. Many older authorities had taken the opposite view.

664 S.C. 1996, c. 23, 46(1) & (2).

665 *Boarelli v. Flannigan* (1973), 36 D.L.R. (3d) 4 at 9 (Ont. C.A.).

Regarding payments received under workers' compensation legislation, several recent decisions have deducted such monies from wrongful dismissal damages,[666] but there is earlier judicial authority to the opposite effect.[667]

Finally, the Ontario Court of Appeal settled a conflict between trial judges on the question of whether severance payments received under section 58 of the *Employment Standards Act* are deductible from damages for wrongful dismissal in the affirmative.[668] Severance payments under section 58 must not be confused with the minimum notice of termination or wages in lieu thereof that employees are entitled to under the employment standards statutes in all jurisdictions.[669] The latter have long been offset from damages for wrongful dismissal.

f)   Punitive Damages

Punitive, or exemplary, damages are not designed to compensate the employee who has been wrongfully dismissed, but to punish the employer in order to deter it and other employers from wrongfully dismissing their workers in the future. Traditionally, such damages have been awarded rarely—if at all—in breach of contract actions, including wrongful dismissal. Nevertheless, during the 1970s and 1980s several trial judges began to award such damages against employers who wrongfully dismissed their employees in a particularly egregious manner. The courts have ruled that punitive damages can be awarded only where they serve a "rationale" purpose. In the context of wrongful dismissal, this means that they can be awarded only where an additional financial penalty is needed due to the fact that compensatory damages, including a *Wallace* extension or aggravated damages, are not enough to deter and punish the employer.[670] In 1989, the Supreme Court of Canada affirmed the principle that punitive damages could be awarded in wrongful dismissal actions in exceptional circumstances where the

---

666   Examples: *Royster*, above note 103 at 267; *Antonacci v. Great Atlantic & Pacific Company of Canada* (1998), 98 C.L.L.C. ¶210–017 at 141,099 (Ont. Gen. Div.) [*Antonacci*]; *Salmi v. Greyfriar Developments Ltd.* (1985), 17 D.L.R. (4th) 186 at 189 (Alta. C.A.).

667   Example: *Dowsley v. Viceroy Fluid Power International Inc.* (1991), 91 C.L.L.C. ¶14,047 (Ont. Gen. Div.).

668   *Stevens*, above note 60, especially at 161–62.

669   See Section 2(A), above in this chapter.

670   The leading authority is *Whiton v. Pilot Insurance Co.*, [2002] S.C.J. No. 19, applied to wrongful dismissal in *Marshall*, above note 135 at 177; *Prinzo*, above note 612 at 230. See generally "Special Issues: the Future of Punitive Damages" (1998) 1 Wis. L. Rev., the entire volume dealing with the economic aspects of punitive damages.

employer's conduct is "deserving of punishment because of its shockingly harsh, vindictive, reprehensible and malicious nature."[671] It must be emphasized that punitive damages require more on the employer's part than mere unfair treatment of the employee; rather, the employer's actions must be flagrantly egregious in nature and the onus of proof is on the employee.[672] Examples of such conduct include fabricating allegations of serious misconduct or incompetence against an employee to support dismissal;[673] summarily firing an employee for serious misconduct, such as theft, without conducting a thorough and unbiased investigation, especially if the employer proceeds with the dismissal after it becomes clear that the employee is innocent;[674] implementing dismissal in a way that sets out to disparage the employee in the eyes of colleagues and potential employers;[675] resorting to hardball tactics so as to intimidate the employee into withdrawing or settling the wrongful dismissal claim (for example, withholding in bad faith monies owing to the employee under protective legislation);[676] harassing the employee by deliberately or recklessly giving a poor performance appraisal;[677] and violating the employee's statutory or common law human rights.[678] Most punitive damages awards are in the $5,000 range, but in egregious circumstances, amounts of $50,000[679] and even $175,000 have been awarded.[680] The largest award of punitive damages so far was $500,000, issued in 2005 against a company that engaged in a long and vicious campaign of unlawful harassment against an employee with a disabil-

---

671 *Vorvis*, above note 106 at 1130, Wilson J.

672 *Squires v. Corner Brook Pulp & Paper Ltd.* (1994), 5 C.C.E.L. (2d) 206 at 221 (Nfld. S.C.T.D.), where Woodridge J. stated that such awards "will rarely be made" and only within "narrow and stringent legal constraints."

673 Examples: *Mastrogiuseppe*, above note 107 at 141,055–56 (Ont. S.C.J.); *Fedele v. Windsor Teachers Credit Union* (2001), 10 C.C.E.L. (3d) 254 (Ont. C.A.).

674 Examples: *Bouma*, above note 252; *Ribeiro v. Canadian Imperial Bank of Commerce* (1989), 89 C.L.L.C. ¶14033 (Ont. H.C.J.), var'd (1992), 44 C.C.E.L. 165 (Ont. C.A.), leave to appeal to S.C.C. refused (1993), 65 O.A.C. 79n [*Ribeiro*]; *Francis*, above note 615.

675 Examples: *Mastrogiuseppe*, above note 107 at 141,055–56 (Ont. S.C.J.); *Ribeiro*, above note 674.

676 Examples: *Strangis v. Hub International Ltd.* (2005), 39 C.C.E.L. (3d) 303 at 319–320 (Ont. S.C.J.); *Mustaji v. Tjin* (1996), 96 C.L.L.C. ¶210-051 (B.C.C.A.) [*Mustaji*].

677 Example: *Marlowe v. Ashland Canada Inc.*, [2002] C.L.L.C. ¶210-004 at 141,052 (B.C.S.C.); *Hawley v. GMD Resource Corp* (2002), 16 C.C.E.L. (3d) 248 (B.C.S.C.).

678 Example: *Moffatt v. Canso Pharmacy Ltd.* (1990), 96 N.S.R. (2d) 399 at 404 (S.C.T.D.).

679 *Ribeiro*, above note 674.

680 *Mustaji*, above note 676.

ity who had requested a reasonable accommodation.[681] The anecdotal evidence is that this sent a tremor of fear among employers. However, the award was reduced on appeal to $100,000.[682] Typically, if punitive damages are warranted, the court will also award the employee his or her solicitor-client costs.

2) Reinstatement

The traditional practice of courts is not to award a discretionary remedy, such as specific performance or an injunction to reinstate a wrongfully dismissed employee, save where a public employee has been dismissed in breach of a statute or in breach of the administrative law duty of procedural fairness.[683] Several rationales have been suggested for the no-reinstatement rule.[684]

First, it is argued that reinstatement is unnecessary, since a damages award will adequately compensate the wrongfully dismissed employee until he or she finds another job. However, this argument fails to recognize that damages may not always provide adequate relief—for example, if the employee stands to lose the vocational satisfaction that comes with some jobs, such as teaching, or if the employee's professional reputation has been damaged by the dismissal. As well, reinstating an employee who has been dismissed in a procedurally unfair manner and requiring the employer to comply with the requisite standards of fairness if it wishes to reimpose the dismissal will outwardly affirm the symbolic importance of procedural justice to the workforce as a whole.

Second, it is argued that if an employer could be forced to reinstate a wrongfully dismissed employee, it would follow under the principle of "mutuality" that an employer could likewise force an employee who wrongfully resigns to maintain the employment relationship, with an effect tantamount to "slavery." However, it seems exaggerated to claim that compelling one party to maintain an employment relationship until it terminates that relationship in the correct legal manner is akin to slavery. Furthermore, courts regularly issue interlocutory injunctions to preserve franchise agreements pending final trial, even though

681 *Keays v. Honda Canada Inc.*, [2005] O.J. No. 1145 (S.C.J.).
682 *Keays* C.A., above note 175.
683 *Ridge*, above note 264; *Page One Records Ltd. v. Britton* (1967), [1968] 1 W.L.R. 157 (Ch.); *Red Deer College*, above note 635.
684 See generally G. de N. Clark, "Unfair Dismissal and Reinstatement" (1969) 32 Mod. L. Rev. 532.

many franchise agreements involve close personal relations between the parties akin to an employment relationship.[685]

Third, it is argued that compulsory reinstatement is inappropriate, since the employment relationship is essentially one of personal trust and confidence between the employer and its employees and cannot be restored once dismissal has been invoked. Historically, this argument rings hollow since the primary remedy for the employee's refusal to comply with the contract under the old English master and servant acts was compulsory reinstatement.[686] Be that as it may, in the modern world not all dismissals result in an irretrievable breakdown of personal relationships. Moreover, modern personnel management techniques in many cases could succeed in healing hostile personal relationships, and even where they do not, it may be possible to reinstate the employee in a different work area away from the people with whom he or she dealt in the past.

Fourth, it is argued that compulsory reinstatement is unworkable in the non-unionized sector, since the employer will make life so miserable for the reinstated employee that he or she will resign anyway. Unquestionably, this is a real risk, as we have seen in connection with reinstatement under section 240 of the *Canada Labour Code*.[687] Of course, it leaves a sour taste to provide employers with the benefit of a no-reinstatement rule on the basis of the very egregious conduct that gave rise to an unjust dismissal in the first place.

Nevertheless, the no-reinstatement policy is not ironclad. Recently some British and Canadian courts have departed from it where the above-mentioned rationales for the policy are clearly inapplicable. For example, Lord Denning granted specific performance to reinstate an employee in whom the employer retained full confidence, but whom it had been forced to dismiss by a threatened strike.[688] The usual rationales for the no-reinstatement policy were absent—here, the employer clearly preferred to keep the employee on the books. Other factors also militated in favour of reinstatement: the employee stood to lose valuable pension benefits if his dismissal stood, and the threatened strike would shortly be illegal under pending amendments to the British industrial relations legislation.

---

685 Example: *Struik v. Dixie Lee Food Systems Ltd.*, [2006] O.J. No. 3269 at para. 80 (S.C.J.).

686 D. Hay, "England 1562–1875: The Law and Its Uses" in D. Hay & P. Craven, eds., *Masters, Servants and Magistrates in Britain and the Empire, 1562–1955* (Chapel Hill, NC: University of North Carolina Press, 2004) at 59.

687 Section E, above in this chapter.

688 *Hill v. C.A. Parsons & Co.*, [1972] Ch. 305 (C.A.).

It might also be thought that the usual rationales for refusing to re-instate would be inapplicable where the employer wrongfully dismiss-es an employee in violation of a dismissal procedure that is expressly or impliedly incorporated into the contract of employment. After all, it would not appear to derogate from the reciprocal trust between em-ployer and employee to compel the employer to honour a dismissal procedure of its own making that it has consented to including in the contract of employment. Indeed, some British courts[689] have recognized that requiring the employer to comply with such procedures prior to in-voking dismissal would, if anything, help restore trust and confidence between the parties. In a similar vein, one Ontario trial judge granted an interlocutory injunction to prevent the discharge of a clergyman for sexual abuse pending full compliance with the employer's own proced-ure for handling such matters in order "to avoid serious procedural un-fairness."[690] Furthermore, a Nova Scotia trial judge has intimated that where an employer fires an employee for an alleged criminal offence, but promises reinstatement if the employee is acquitted, the employer's promise may be specifically enforced if it subsequently reneges on the promise, at least so long as the employee does not occupy a managerial position.[691]

In addition, some Canadian judges have granted interlocutory or-ders of specific performance to reinstate employees, pending final trial, who clearly have bargained for a vocational component or some other psychological satisfaction as part of their employment contract, which a damages award would not adequately compensate. For example, an orchestra conductor was granted reinstatment under an interim injunc-tion so that he could conduct a major scheduled performance before his employment status could be determined in a final trial;[692] an aging ballerina was reinstated under an interim injunction to enable her to appear in what was likely to be her final performance;[693] and an em-

---

689 Example: *Robb v. Hammersmith and Fulham London Borough Council*, [1991] I.C.R.514 (Q.B.).

690 *Frogley v. Ottawa Presbytery of the United Church of Canada* (1995), 16 C.C.E.L. (2d) 249 (Ont. Gen. Div.). Compare *Wigglesworth v. Phipps* (2001), 7 C.C.E.L. (3d) 37 at 51 (Alta. Q.B.), where an injunction was denied in similar circum-stances.

691 *Backman*, above note 290 at 308, but on the facts, the court found that no such promise had been made.

692 *Boivin v. Orchestre Symphonique de Laval 1984 Inc.* (1993), 43 C.C.E.L. 304 (Que. Sup. Ct.). In a similar vein, see *McCaw v. United Church of Canada* (1991), 37 C.C.E.L. 214, especially at 223 (Ont. C.A.).

693 *National Ballet of Canada v. Glasco* (2000), 3 C.C.E.L. (3d) 141 at 158–59 (Ont. S.C.J.).

ployee who started up and operated a company as its first president was reinstated pending final trial to protect the unique personal satisfaction he derived from working in his position.[694]

On the other hand, such is the strength of the traditional policy against reinstatement in Canada that one Saskatchewan trial judge[695] has refused to specifically enforce an order of an arbitrator under the provincial *Arbitration Act* directing a trade union to reinstate unjustly dismissed employees of the union, partially on the ground of a perceived breakdown in the trust relationship between the parties. Of course, had the arbitrator considered the parties' relationship to have soured beyond repair, he would not have awarded reinstatement in the first place. Therefore, the traditional policy against reinstatement remains strong in Canada, despite the inroads described above.[696] In Ontario, however, this policy may be on the cusp of changing as a result of amendments in 2006 to the *Human Rights Code*. The amendments empower the courts in common law wrongful dismissal actions involving violations of the Code to apply the full panoply of "make whole" remedies available under the Code, including compulsory reinstatement.[697] It is possible that the courts' experience with reinstating employees who are wrongfully dismissed on human rights grounds will spill over into the general law of wrongful dismissal.

G. TERMINATION BY REASON OF FRUSTRATION OF CONTRACT

A contract of employment will end by reason of frustration if the circumstances existing when the contract was formed subsequently change so dramatically that further performance of the contract would either be impossible, or if possible, radically different from those that the parties had originally contemplated.[698] Assuming that neither party can foresee the change in circumstances, the contract of employment will terminate automatically by operation of law. In contract law theory,

---

694 *Computertime Network Corp. v. Zucker*, [1994] J.Q. no 259 (C.A.).

695 *Simmons v. Longworth*, [1981] 6 W.W.R. 329 (Sask. Q.B.).

696 See, for example, *Philp v. Expo 86 Corp.* (1987), 19 B.C.L.R. (2d) 88 at 97 (C.A.), reversing the decision of the trial court to award a declaration that dismissal was a nullity (1986), 13 C.C.E.L. 147 (B.C. Co. Ct.).

697 See Chapter 7.

698 *Davis Contractors Ltd. v. Fareham Urban District Council*, [1956] A.C. 696 (H.L.). See generally G.H. Treitel, *The Law of Contract*, 8th ed. (London: Stevens, 1991) c. 20.

this is achieved by implying into the employment contract a condition subsequent, whereby the parties are deemed to intend that their contract will subsist only so long as performance of their main obligations under it remains possible.

In real-world terms, the doctrine of frustration is concerned with who should bear the risk of the unforeseen events in question. Thus, if the contract is held to have been frustrated, the employee will be precluded from recovering compensation for wrongful dismissal. Instead, he or she would have to rely on provisions in the frustrated contracts acts, in provinces having them, which give courts the discretion to order that either party to a frustrated contract can recover from the other fair value for any services previously rendered under the contract.[699] Of course, such an amount may not be equivalent to the employee's lost wages and benefits over the notice period. Furthermore, since the employee will not have been dismissed, he or she is generally disentitled to benefits that depend on dismissal under the employment standards legislation, such as the minimum period of notice of termination.[700] In order to safeguard employees against these dangers, courts are generally reluctant to find that an employment contract has been frustrated.[701]

Next, we analyze the situations in which the frustration doctrine most often arises in the employment relationship.

First, an employment contract will be frustrated by "supervening illegality" where further continuance of the employment relationship would violate a statutory prohibition. For example, a contract between the English comedian Charlie Chester and his agent was frustrated when the former was conscripted for military service, so that the performance of any further work on his part would have been illegal.[702] If the employee is incarcerated by the courts for committing a criminal offence, it would appear that the employment contract would be frustrated, at least if a lengthy sentence is imposed. However, it is an established principle of contract law that there can be no frustration if the alleged frustrating event was brought about by the conduct of

699 Example: Ontario *Frustrated Contracts Act*, R.S.O. 1990, c. F.34, s. 3(3).
700 Section 55(h) of the *Alta. ESC*, above note 21, is typical in disentitling the employee from minimum notice or wages in lieu when employment ends as a result of a frustrating event.
701 Courts are slow to find frustration in commercial cases too: e.g., *Lord Strathcona Steamship Co. Ltd. v. Dominion Coal Co.* (1925), [1926] A.C. 108 at 114 (P.C.).
702 *Morgan v. Manser* (1947), [1948] 1 K.B. 184. See also *Thomas v. Lafleche Union Hospital* (1989), 27 C.C.E.L. 156 (Sask. Q.B.), aff'd on other grounds (1991), 36 C.C.E.L. 251 (Sask. C.A.), where the employment contract of a director of nursing was frustrated when her nursing certificate was revoked by the statutory licensing authority.

one of the contracting parties. Arguably, therefore, in this situation the employee is the author of his or her own misfortune. Certainly, Canadian courts have held the incarceration to be self-induced,[703] but some English judges have held otherwise.[704]

Second, death of the employee obviously frustrates the employment contract; the personality of the employee is regarded as being fundamental to the employment relationship. The employee's estate is entitled to wages earned by the deceased until his or her demise, at least unless the employee is hired under an entire contract that makes payment of wages conditional upon the completion of a defined task, and the employee draws his or her terminal breath before that condition is satisfied. However, death of the employer will probably only frustrate the employment contract if the parties' relationship is especially personal.[705] Of course, this will not be the case with run-of-the-mill employment contracts between corporate employers and their workers.

Third, illness on the part of the employee may frustrate the employment contract, but only in limited circumstances.[706] The test for frustration was enunciated by an English judge, Sir John Donaldson (as he then was), as follows:

[W]as the employee's incapacity, looked at before the purported dismissal, of such a nature, or did it appear likely to continue for such a period, that further performance of his obligations in the future would either be impossible or would be a thing radically different from that undertaken by him and accepted by the employer under the agreed terms of his employment.[707]

Justice Wood of the British Columbia Supreme Court has stated that the chance of an illness frustrating the employment contract will be increased in the following circumstances: (1) if the notice period is relatively short; (2) if the worker's entitlement to sick pay has expired; (3) if the expected duration of the employment in question, in the absence of sickness, is relatively brief;[708] (4) if the worker occupies a key

---

703 Example: *Tolpa v. Flint Engineering & Construction Ltd.* (1996), 18 C.C.E.L. (2d) 286 at 295–97 (Sask. Q.B.).
704 *Hare v. Murphy Bros. Ltd.*, [1974] 3 All E.R. 940 (C.A.).
705 *Graves v. Cohen* (1929), 46 T.L.R. 121, especially at 123–24 (K.B.); *Grant v. Johnson* (1864), 5 N.S.R. 493 (C.A.).
706 The leading Canadian authority is *Marks Estate*, above note 279.
707 *Marshall v. Harland and Wolff Ltd.*, [1972] 2 All E.R. 715 at 718 (N.I.R.C.).
708 Examples: *Loates v. Maple* (1903), 88 L.T. 288 (K.B.); *Poussard v. Spiers and Pond* (1876), 1 Q.B.D. 410.

position in which he or she must be replaced on a permanent basis;[709] and (5) if the period of past employment is relatively short.[710] However, none of these factors is conclusive in and of itself; the question ultimately remains whether or not, in the particular circumstances of each case, the illness will prevent the employee from performing the core functions of his or her position for a substantial part of the contractual term. In the context of an employment contract for an indefinite term, this requires determining whether the employee's medical prognosis is such that he or she will be incapacitated for the reasonably foreseeable future from performing core contractual duties. The Newfoundland Court of Appeal has suggested as a rule of thumb that between eighteen months' and two years' absence due to sickness will be required in order to frustrate the employment contract of a worker with long seniority hired without definite term.[711] Most courts are sympathetic towards sick employees and will not readily find frustration. Nevertheless, if the medical prognosis is that the employee will clearly remain permanently incapacitated, even a short absence from work will amount to frustration.[712]

Most courts require that the employee's medical prognosis be completed at the date of the trial, not at the earlier date of dismissal.[713] This requirement benefits the employee by giving her the advantage of any improvement in health since the date of dismissal. However, an employer who has made a fair assessment of the employee's medical condition at the time of dismissal that subsequently turns out to have been wrong will be penalized by this practice. This perhaps explains why a minority of courts have taken the date of dismissal as the operative time for the medical prognosis.[714]

Traditionally, the courts have not required the employer to modify the employee's work schedule or duties in order to avoid the conclusion that his or her illness frustrates the employment contract.[715] This con-

---

709   Example: *Burgess v. Central Trust Co.* (1988), 19 C.C.E.L. 193 (N.B.Q.B.T.D.).

710   *Yeager*, above note 279.

711   *Woolworth*, above note 592, especially at 125–26, where an eleven-month absence due to disability was held not to amount to frustration.

712   Example: *Dodge City*, above note 280, where the absence was only for ten weeks.

713   *Yeager*, above note 279 at 291; *Marks Estate*, above note 279 at 375. Most collective agreement arbitrators have favoured this view: see I. Christie, "The Right to Dismiss for Innocent Absenteeism: An Arbitrator's Perspective" (1993) Lab. Arb. Y.B. 201 at 205–6. But compare *Antonacci*, above note 666 at 141,098, where the date of dismissal was taken as the relevant date. (On the facts, this favoured the employee.)

714   Example: *Woolworth*, above note 592 at 498.

715   Example: *Condor v. Barron Knights Ltd.*, [1966] 1 W.L.R. 87.

trasts starkly with the position under human rights legislation, which obliges the employer to implement such modifications in order to accommodate an employee's physical or mental disability as defined in the statute up to the point of causing the firm undue hardship.[716] If such a duty of reasonable accommodation formed part of the common law, the scope of the doctrine of frustration could be narrowed significantly. For example, under the current common law, a hospital orderly who is prevented by a permanently disabled back from lifting patients would have his or her contract frustrated so long as lifting is a core function of the job, even though the employer might readily be able to swap the lifting part of the job with non–physically demanding duties being performed by a fit employee in another position.[717] Under the human rights legislation, however, the employer would have to swap the duty of patient lifting between the two employees, at least unless the reassignment would cause undue hardship. In her 1998 decision in *Antonacci*, Swinton J. held that an employment contract cannot be frustrated for mental or physical disability at common law unless the employer can prove that it has reasonably accommodated the employee up to the point of undue hardship.[718] It is submitted that this decision is welcome as bringing the common law into line with modern standards of human rights.

If an employee absent because of sickness is entitled to and is in receipt of long-term disability benefits under an employment contract, the contract almost certainly cannot be regarded as frustrated, since the parties will have foreseen the alleged frustrating event and have expressly contracted for it. It would be repugnant to freedom of contract to allow the employer to release a sick employee on the ground of frustration and deprive him or her of these insurance benefits.

It must be emphasized that summary dismissal is not for just cause if the reason for the employee's absenteeism is sickness or disability.[719] However, if the employee lies to the employer about being absent because of sickness, summary dismissal may be warranted on the ground of misconduct.

If the workplace is destroyed by fire so as to make further work impossible or unnecessary, the employment contract will be frustrated.[720] However, if the fire is caused by the negligence of the employer, the

---

716 See Chapter 7.
717 *Antonacci*, above note 666.
718 This hypothetical case is based loosely on the facts of *Parks*, above note 279, where frustration was found.
719 See above Section C(6).
720 *Polyco*, above note 38; *Taylor v. Caldwell* (1863), 3 B. & S. 826, 122 E.R. 309 (Q.B.).

doctrine of frustration presumably would be inapplicable by virtue of the rule against self-induced frustration.[721]

On the other hand, the employment contract is not frustrated where the employer releases workers for economic reasons, such as an unexpected downturn in demand for the firm's services or products.[722] In such circumstances, the employer must terminate the contract of employment by giving due notice or wages in lieu thereof. Even if the employer temporarily lays off employees for unexpected economic reasons, the employment contract is not frustrated. Rather, layoff constitutes a breach of contract on the employer's part, entitling the employee to recover damages for failure to give due notice, unless the employment contract either expressly or impliedly permits the employer to impose a layoff. The courts do not presume that employers enjoy an implied right to layoff as a matter of general law; instead, the employer must prove the existence of a reliable past practice in the firm in order for right to layoff to be implied into the contract.[723] Furthermore, the employment contract will not be frustrated where employees are laid off, temporarily or permanently, as a result of a strike or lockout affecting their employer.[724] Finally, frustration does not occur where an employer's financial difficulties force it into bankruptcy; rather, the employment contract is deemed to have been terminated by the act of the employer, so that employees are entitled to due notice of termination or wages in lieu thereof.

FURTHER READINGS

BRIDGE, M., "Contractual Remedies for Intangible Loss: A Comparative Analysis" (1984) 62 Can. Bar Rev. 323

CANADA, COMMISSION ON THE REVIEW OF FEDERAL LABOUR STANDARDS, *Fairness at Work: Federal Labour Standards for the 21st Century* by H.W. Arthurs (Ottawa: Commission on the Review of Federal Labour Standards, 2006) c. 8

COLLINS, H., *Justice in Dismissal* (Oxford: Clarendon Press, 1992)

---

721 *Polyco, ibid.* at 103.
722 Examples: *Smith v. Tamblyn (Alberta) Ltd.* (1979), 9 Alta. L.R. (2d) 274 at 279 (S.C.T.D.); *St. John v. TNT Canada Inc.* (1991), 38 C.C.E.L. 55 at 68–69 (B.C.S.C.) [*St. John*].
723 Example: *Style v. Carlingview Airport Inn* (1996), 18 C.C.E.L. (2d) 163 at 166–67 (Ont. Div. Ct.).
724 *St. John*, above note 722.

ECHLIN, R.E., & J.M. FANTINI, *Quitting for Good Reason: The Law of Constructive Dismissal in Canada* (Aurora, ON: Canada Law Book, 2001)

ECHLIN, R., R. SCOTT, & M.L.O. CERTOSIMO, *Just Cause: The Law of Summary Dismissal in Canada*, looseleaf (Aurora, ON: Canada Law Book, 1998–)

ENGLAND, G., "Section 240 of the *Canada Labour Code*: Some Current Pitfalls" (1999) 27 Man. L.J. 17

ENGLAND, G., "Unjust Dismissal and Other Termination-Related Provisions," Report to the Federal Labour Standards Review (Ottawa: Human Resources and Social Development Canada, 2006)

ENGLAND, G., R. WOOD, & I. CHRISTIE, *Employment Law in Canada*, 4th ed., looseleaf (Markham, ON: LexisNexis Canada, 2005–) cc. 12–18

EPSTEIN, R.A., "In Defence of the Contract at Will" (1984) 51 U. Chi. L. Rev. 947

EWING, K., "Remedies for Breach of the Employment Contract" (1993) 52 Cambridge L.J. 405

FRIESEN, J., "The Response of Wages to Protective Labour Legislation: Evidence from Canada" (1996) 49 Indus. & Lab. Rel. Rev. 243

FUDGE, J., "The Limits of Good Faith in the Contract of Employment: From *Addis* to *Vorvis* to *Wallace* and Back Again?" (2007) 32 Queen's L.J. 529

HARRIS, D., *Wrongful Dismissal*, 3d ed., looseleaf (Don Mills, ON: De Boo, 1984–)

JACOBY, S.M., "The Duration of Indefinite Term Contracts in the U.S.A. and England: An Historical Analysis" (1982) 5 Comp. Lab. L.J. 85

LAZEAR, E.P., "Job Security Provisions and Employment" (1990) 105 Q. J. Econ. 699

LECKIE, N., *An International Review of Labour Adjustment Policies and Practices* (Kingston, ON: University Industrial Relations Centre, Queen's University, 1993)

LEVITT, HOWARD A., *Law of Dismissal in Canada*, 3d ed., looseleaf (Aurora, ON: Canada Law Book, 2003–)

MACKILLOP, M.J., *Damage Control: An Employer's Guide to Just Cause Termination* (Aurora, ON: Canada Law Book, 1997)

MOLE, ELLEN E., *Wrongful Dismissal Practice Manual*, 2d ed., looseleaf (Toronto: LexisNexis Canada, 2005–)

ST-HILAIRE, G., "The Taxation of Damages for Wrongful Dismissal" (1999) 7 C.L.E.L.J. 135

STEUSSER, L., "Wrongful Dismissal — Playing Hardball: *Wallace v. United Grain Growers*" (1998) 25 Man. L.J. 547

SWAN, J., "Extended Damages and *Vorvis v. Insurance Corporation of B.C.*" (1990) 16 Can. Bus. L.J. 213

VANBUSKIRK, K., ""Damages for Improvident Employer Behaviour" (2004) 83 Can. Bar Rev. 755

CHAPTER 10

CONCLUSION

One need not be a Marxist to agree with the fundamental tenet of Marxist doctrine that the economic conditions of a society exert a tremendously strong—if not irresistible—influence on its laws, political values, and commercial practices. This is certainly borne out by the example of Canadian employment law. The cornerstone of the employment relationship—the individual contract of employment—is governed by the general principles of contract law originally formulated in a commercial context to facilitate the operation of free markets in the production and distribution of goods and services. Unquestionably, the application of free market principles to the employment relationship provides many benefits to employers, employees, and society at large. Today, no serious analysis would argue for the complete eradication of these principles from the employment relationship. Nevertheless, this contractualist approach to the relationship creates serious problems from the perspectives of each of the affected parties.

The root of these problems is the imbalance of bargaining power that favours employers over employees in most employment relationships. For most employees, employment is offered on a "take it or leave it" basis, and even after the contract has been formed, the employer usually has its way in controlling the terms and conditions of the job. Although it is true that the principles of contract law permit the employee to decline an offer of employment on terms that he or she does not like or to quit and sue for "constructive dismissal" if the employer changes the terms of an existing contract, the pressures of needing a job mean that the employee frequently has no real-world choice but to acquiesce to the employer's actions. Furthermore, the costs of civil litigation put whatever legal rights the employment contract does offer beyond the pockets of most employees save those in relatively high-level managerial, technical, and professional positions. Consequently, there is a gap between the legal theory of the employment contract, which promises "freedom of contract," and the real-world experience of the employment contract, which delivers dominance on the part of the employer.

This imbalance of power creates the potential for economic and psychological abuse of the worker. Canadian labour history is replete with examples, which are sufficiently well known as to require no cor-roboration here. Since the Second World War, the dominant theme in Canadian employment law has been to minimize the scope for such abuse in two ways. First, the courts have manipulated the rules of em-ployment contract law—sometimes within and sometimes beyond the boundaries of established precedents—in order to safeguard employ-ees' rights. Second, and much more important, governments have en-acted a plethora of protections for employees under labour standards, pay equity, privacy, occupational health and safety, pension benefits, human rights, and other protective legislation that comprises Canada's currently generous statutory "floor of rights." These changes have been inspired by the general movement to advance individual rights in all walks of life: something that has dominated Canadian political culture during most of the post-war period. In turn, this political movement has been made possible by economic conditions that have favoured Canad-ian businesses in the key manufacturing and resource sectors; namely, the absence of competition from emerging countries with a compara-tive advantage in lower labour and other operating costs. Simply put, Canadian employers could afford to provide relatively generous terms and conditions of employment because their main competitors in Eur-ope and the United States were in roughly the same position. Moreover, during this period, federal and provincial governments could afford to borrow huge sums of money in international bond markets to meet their electorates' demands for greater employment and other social wel-fare rights, in the belief that Canada's future economic growth would be sufficient to pay back the debts. Again, the lack of robust foreign competition for Canada's leading businesses made that belief reason-ably plausible, if somewhat incautious.

Today, the economic map has been redrawn in ways that have de-stroyed the foregoing assumptions. Canada's traditional manufactur-ing and resource industries are facing increasingly intense competition

from emerging nations, facilitated by the ease of transferring production technology and investment capital across national boundaries, improved transnational communications, technological advances, and the
gradual movement towards international free trade. Faced with these
conditions, Canadian employers are increasingly being pressured to
reduce their unit labour costs. The relative weakness of the Canadian
dollar between 1990 and 2007 ameliorated some of this pressure; now
that our currency has strengthened, however, the pressure on Canadian
employers to reduce labour costs has increased significantly. Governments, too, have been forced to reduce the levels of public debt under
the pressure of increasing interest premiums demanded by purchasers
of their debt instruments, which has resulted in government employees
being laid off and having their wages and benefits reduced or frozen.

These economic changes seem to have occasioned a change in Canadian political culture. There has been a growing public dissatisfaction
with "government interference" in all forms—with politicians, administrative tribunals, and beneficiaries of government largesse, such as
welfare recipients; a growing preference for private solutions over state
solutions to social and economic problems; and a growing sympathy
with the call of employers to relax employment laws in order to facilitate their quest for enhanced economic efficiency.

The burning question in contemporary Canadian employment law
is how these new economic and social forces will affect the scope of
employee rights in the workplace. Counterbalancing the above-mentioned pressures for relaxing the current level of the employee's legal
protection is the strong possibility that employers may derive efficiency
gains from such protections. At the macro level, a relatively stable society is clearly more conducive to economic growth than a society in
turmoil due to economic hardship. At the micro level, individual firms
may recoup productivity gains by treating their employees fairly and
generously. Of course, the difficult question is to determine the opti-
mal point of balance at which legal protections will advance employee rights without diminishing the efficiency of the firm's operations.
Unfortunately, there have been remarkably few economic cost–benefit
analyses of many of the employment laws considered in this book, especially of important common law rules of the employment contract,
such as the obligation to give "reasonable" notice of termination and
the duty (such as it is) to treat employees fairly. Moreover, an even more
difficult question is to determine at what point an employer's economic
efficiency should be reduced in the name of securing the employee's
personal rights. The study of employment law is not for the intellec-
tually faint of heart!

428   INDIVIDUAL EMPLOYMENT LAW

In Chapter 2 of this book, we examined the threshold question of which working relationships qualify as "employment relationships" in order to fall within the protections of the floor of rights legislation and the common law of the employment contract. We saw that the hallmark of the employment relationship is a relatively high degree of economic subordination on the part of the worker to the employer, combined with a relatively high degree of control by the employer over the residual "where and when" of employment. This test complements on the legal plane the employer's real-world interest in having the employee obey its commands as to how the job should be carried on. It also complements the policy of the floor of rights legislation, which is to protect the economically disadvantaged. However, administrative tribunals and courts are careful to exclude from the definition of "employee" persons who are entrepreneurs running their own businesses: our system envisages such individuals as competing in a relatively free marketplace without the safety net of protective employment legislation. We also saw that many employers have attempted to rearrange the details of their relationships with their workers in order to prevent the relationships from meeting the definition of employee status—for example, by making earnings depend on the employee's personal accomplishments and by having work performed on an "on call" basis. The employers' purpose, of course, is to avoid what they perceive to be the exorbitant costs of hiring employees. We saw that the traditional tests for determining employee status will have to be modified, possibly by the enactment of special "dependent contractor" provisions, if it is thought desirable to encompass such relationships within the protective floor of rights. As well, employers are outsourcing their operations to non-employee contractors or utilizing various forms of short-term and casual labour, often hired through labour-supply agencies. The latter may necessitate using alternatives to the traditional employment contract, such as portable benefit banks, in order to safeguard the rights of those workers. These remedies may prove to be even more damaging than the disease, though, because if employers respond to the increasing costs by replacing human labour with technology, there will be fewer jobs for the self-employed, too.

Having defined the employment relationship and the role of the employee, we next asked, Who is the employer? The recent explosion in corporate amalgamation, mergers, and takeovers, along with the growth of conglomerates comprising many separate corporate employers, has brought to the fore the question of how an employee's accrued benefits under the employment contract and the protective legislation can be safeguarded in the face of such frequent changes in the legal

identity of his or her "employer." We saw that the courts have ameliorated the employee's position somewhat by adopting various novel techniques—for example, by counting seniority with previous employers as
part of determining reasonable notice of termination unless the parties
state otherwise—and that several provinces have introduced special
"successor employer" and "common employer" provisions into their
employment standards acts in order to protect the employee's statutory
(but not private) benefits.

In Chapter 3, we analyzed the formation and modification of employment contracts. We saw that they are governed by the general principles of contract law, but that the courts have had to finesse these
principles to fit the unique context of the employment relationship.
Thus, the indeterminate nature of the relationship results in relatively
few employment contracts with comprehensive express provisions—the
constantly changing business environment means that employers must
regularly readjust the terms and conditions of employment over an indefinite term hiring. Accordingly, the crucial "consideration" for which
any employer bargains is the right to have the employee obey its orders
relating to the operation of the labour process. Of course, this element
of subordination on the part of the employee to the employer's power
of command gives the employment contract an unavoidably political
dimension, which transcends the economics of the parties' bargain and
situates employment law squarely within the field of civil liberties and
fundamental human rights. To fill the gap left by the relative paucity of
express regulation, the courts have had to liberally apply the rules of
certainty in order to uphold employment contracts. Furthermore, great
reliance is placed on the implied term in formulating the parties' rights
and obligations.

The courts have always used the implied term as a vehicle for ef-
fecting their policy choices as to what an ideal employment relationship *ought* to resemble, and these policy choices change over time to
reflect the prevailing standards of personnel management practice and
society's vision of how work relations ought to be conducted. Although
courts often claim that they are implying terms to reflect the unstated
factual intentions of the parties—which is, of course, the established
basis for implying terms in a legal regime of freed contracting—it is
clear that this criterion is largely a fictive formality for the pursuit of
other judicial policy desiderata. (Nowhere is this process more evident than in the determination of reasonable notice of termination,
where a veritable ratatouille of policy considerations marks the field;
see Chapter 9.) Less obviously, perhaps, it explains the formulation of
the standardized obligations of the employee and the employer, which

are implied into all employment contracts. Occasionally, judges frankly acknowledge the true nature of the process of implication, thereby enabling the merits of the policy considerations to be dissected up front. The employment contract, despite being cloaked in the nomenclature of freedom of contract, nonetheless displays a substantial "status" component, in the sense that the parties' rights and obligations are in no small degree created for them by fiat of the judges rather than by true mutual consent. This does not, however, signal the demise of free contracting, for any express terms negotiated by the parties will always take precedence over judicially implied terms. It is almost certain that the dramatic economic and social changes now taking place in Canadian society under the conditions of the "new economy" will eventually be reflected in judicial reformulations of the implied terms and other malleable employment law doctrines.

The application of general contract law principles to the formation and modification of the employment relationship, while unquestionably giving employers the upper hand in setting the terms and conditions of employment at the original hiring, may nonetheless hamstring employers when it comes to making subsequent modifications. Employers have a critical interest in having the flexibility to change the terms and conditions of the employment relationship on an ongoing basis to meet the imperatives of a changing business environment. Yet general contract law principles disallow the employer from unilaterally amending the terms of the bargain without committing a breach of contract, which may entitle the employee to quit and sue for damages for constructive dismissal. (The latter doctrine was examined in Chapter 9.) Several courts have responded to the increasing competitive pressures on Canadian employers by enlarging their scope to change contractual terms without falling foul of the constructive dismissal doctrine and by requiring employees to work under the changed terms pursuant to their common law duty of mitigation unless doing so would cause the employee undue hardship. Moreover, even if the employee continues to work under the changes introduced by the employer, difficulties can arise in determining whether the employee truly agreed to a contractual modification and provided additional consideration to support it.

Other general contract law principles also apply to the employment relationship. These include misrepresentation, mistake, illegality, and the doctrines of duress, undue influence, and unconscionability. Among these, the doctrine of unconscionability would appear to have the greatest potential scope for application to the employment relationship. Nevertheless, we saw that the courts so far have proceeded cautiously in applying this doctrine, effectively limiting it to "procedural" abuses, such as failing to notify an employee of a harsh termination clause in his or her employment contract at the date of a promotion, rather than "substantive" abuses, such as paying an unfair wage. Of course, the justification for this approach is that in a predominantly free labour market such as Canada's, the substantive fairness of wages and benefits should be determined by market forces and by legislators through the medium of employment standards acts, not by judges. Courts are experienced at identifying procedural injustice, but not with instances where substantive injustice is claimed. Indeed, courts have applied the torts of fraudulent and negligent misstatement to the employment relationship to safeguard each party against the procedural injustices at the heart of those torts.

The implied obligations of the employee towards the employer were examined in detail in Chapter 4; the reciprocal implied obligations of the employer towards the employee were examined in Chapter 5. Together, these rights and duties represent the common law "status" of employer and employee. Each of the employee's implied duties—to obey orders, to work competently, to avoid wrongfully exploiting the employer's business opportunities, and to give due notice of termination—ultimately derives from the employee's fundamental obligation to conduct himself or herself in the best interests of the firm. The common law vision of the employment relationship, therefore, is essentially "unitary" in nature: the employee and the employer are assumed to be striving as a team towards the common goal of enhancing the firm's efficiency. Of course, this vision does not correspond with reality, for while the interests of employees and employers unquestionably converge in many respects, ultimately the employee's primary goal of achieving security of income and tenure will collide with the employer's primary goal of maximizing efficiency. The courts have nevertheless fashioned an extremely rigorous set of obligations on the employee, which accords paramountcy to the employer's interests in virtually all areas. Indeed, most of these duties have been transplanted from the law of the pre–Industrial Revolution employment contract, under which the "servant" was bound by a strict duty of loyalty to his or her "master." In contrast, the implied obligations of the employer towards the employee are considerably less extensive. Save for the duty to give reasonable notice of termination and to provide a reasonably safe working environment, the employer's implied obligations at common law have traditionally been minimal. Indeed, we saw that the Supreme Court of Canada in its 1997 decision in *Wallace* v. *United Grain Growers Ltd.*[1]

1   [1997] 3 S.C.R. 701 [*Wallace*].

refused to recognize a standardized implied term that would require employers to treat their employees fairly, despite considerable judicial and academic support for such a step.

The rigour of the employee's implied common law obligations to the employer has been tempered to take account of modern personnel practices under the rubric of the requirement that the employer must prove "just cause" for summarily dismissing an employee with less than the specified due notice or wages in lieu thereof. (The detailed requirements of just cause were examined in Chapter 9.) Just cause requires that the severity of the employee's conduct must be proportionate to the penalty of dismissal; that the employer must act in good faith, non-arbitrarily, and without discrimination; and that a fair attempt to rehabilitate the employee must have been made prior to invoking dismissal. Most modern courts have infused the components of a duty of procedural fairness in the determination of just cause—by means of doctrines, such as culminating incident, corrective discipline, condonation, and the requirement that work rules must be known and consistently enforced in order to ground insubordination. They have done so despite the traditional common law rule that there is no inherent obligation on the employer to observe natural justice in firing employees.

On the other side of the coin, the meagreness of the employer's implied common law obligations to the employee has been tempered by extensive statutory intervention in the form of floor of rights legislation granting employees a relatively comprehensive set of irreducible entitlements, which the parties are at liberty to expand in their employment contract, but not to abridge. In Chapter 6, we saw that the statutory "floor" currently includes minimum wages, maximum hours of work, overtime entitlements, holidays, annual vacations, severance benefits, leaves of absence for a wide variety of reasons, rest periods, wage protection, equal pay, privacy, occupational health and safety standards, workers' compensation, and, in some provinces, mandatory fringe benefit coverage of part-timers and adjudication of claims of "unjust discharge." These protections reflect the growing public concern during the post-war era with extending rights to those in a position of economic subordination. While most of the rights in question are substantive in nature, there has been a discernible trend towards conferring a right to participate on non-unionized workers, notably under joint labour adjustment and health and safety committees. Today, Canada's statutory floor of rights matches up to the standards recommended by the International Labour Organization in most respects, the main exception being that only the federal jurisdiction, Nova Scotia, and Quebec have enacted protections against unjust discharge.

Nevertheless, serious flaws remain with our floor of rights. First, it has proven extremely difficult to secure compliance on the part of employers with their statutory obligations. The *raison d'être* of the legislative protections is to provide employees with an affordable substitute for civil action to enforce their employment rights. It is clear that the most impressive body of substantive rights is only as good as its enforcement machinery, but nobody as yet has succeeded in discovering the secret to securing compliance with the legislation. Second (as we saw in Chapter 8), the absence of a unified labour court charged with enforcing claims under all protective statutes as well as under the common law causes unnecessary complications where an employee wishes to enforce his or her rights. Third, the future of the floor of rights is clouded by the increasing difficulties that Canadian firms are encountering in competing with overseas producers who have comparatively cheaper labour costs. There is increasing pressure on Canadian governments to refrain from legislating further rights and even to eliminate existing ones. Unfortunately, not enough studies of the precise economic costs to employers of many of the rights now legislated have been undertaken. Moreover, it remains unclear whether or to what extent the existing floor of rights contributes to Canada's "unemployment problem." Certainly, the moral force of the floor of rights legislation would be shaken if it were shown to be the case that the rights in question benefit those lucky enough to have jobs to the detriment of the unemployed. So far, no province has made significant reductions to its floor of rights in response to changing economic forces, but there has been a discernible lull in the momentum to legislate new rights. The pressure on Canadian firms to reduce their labour costs will likely continue to intensify, and it is possible that significant dismantling of the statutory floor may occur under such conditions. Of course, the juxtaposition of a continuing public demand for further rights with an economy that cannot afford to provide them could have serious repercussions for general social stability.

This impetus for increasing rights in employment has been spurred on by the general human rights legislation (along with the *Charter*), which we examined in Chapter 7. This legislation applies to all walks of life, but nowhere is it more important than in the field of employment. It is no exaggeration to say that human rights legislation has radically transformed Canadian employment law. The following key features of the legislation were identified.

First, the concept of "indirect" discrimination enshrined in the legislation is concerned with ameliorating the disadvantages that protected groups now suffer as a result of past discrimination. Accordingly, it is not a necessary condition of liability that a particular employer deliberately and wilfully intends to penalize protected group members today. For example, an under- representation of females in particular occupations may be attributed to cultural forces from an earlier age that have operated to exclude females from entering those occupations, and this alone may result in a finding of indirect discrimination, even though the employer may not have had a purposeful intent to exclude women. The human rights legislation, therefore, is concerned with achieving equality of results, not just equality of treatment. Clearly, this notion of discrimination invites considerable controversy about whether the current disadvantages suffered by protected groups are causally linked to historical discrimination or to other factors, such as personal choice, and about whether it is fair to make employers liable for the discriminatory attitudes of their predecessors.

Second, it follows from the definition of indirect discrimination that special affirmative action remedies that give preferential treatment to disadvantaged groups—for example, a hiring quota—may be necessary in order to redress the effects of historical discrimination. To many laypersons it appears wrong-headed that unequal treatment in favour of disadvantaged groups should appear in a statute designed to eliminate discrimination, but the inconsistency can be viewed as a necessary adjunct of a results-based definition of proscribed discrimination. Nevertheless, we saw that most human rights tribunals have proceeded cautiously in implementing hiring and promotion quotas as part of their remedial mandate and that only the federal jurisdiction has enacted a special statute to impose such measures, namely, the *Employment Equity Act*. In Ontario, the repeal of the highly unpopular *Employment Equity Act* by the Progressive Conservative government, which won the provincial election in 1995 by making this a cornerstone of its platform, appears to show that affirmative action measures, such as preferential treatment in hiring and promotion, are not supported by the general populace. Of course, employers are free to adopt such programs voluntarily. Furthermore, human rights tribunals are empowered to grant a broad range of monetary and other remedies, including reinstatement, to "make whole" the successful complainant of illegal discrimination. The make whole philosophy marks a dramatic departure from the usual method of remedying breach of the employment contract, which is to compensate the plaintiff for the value of the broken promise in question. In a wrongful dismissal action at common law, for instance, this involves giving the employee his or her lost wages and contractually grounded benefits over the notice period. In contrast, the make whole approach attempts, much more broadly, to put the claimant in the position he or she would have occupied had the unlawful discrimination not happened. For instance, an employee who is dismissed for a discriminatory reason, but who does not want the job back can recover compensation for lost wages and benefits beyond the notice period. This development will likely influence the courts in common law actions under the employment contract to infuse a greater make whole element into their awards. Indeed, the influence of the make whole philosophy is already evident in judicial determinations of reasonable notice of termination, where a broad range of policy factors—including make whole—are taken into account.

Third, if an employer's work rules or practices serve a legitimate business purpose, but adversely affect an employee because of his or her protected characteristics, the employer is required under human rights acts to provide reasonable accommodation up to the point of causing the firm undue hardship before the work rules or practices can be applied. For example, if a female is physically unable to drive a truck that does not have power steering, the employer must investigate whether it would impose an undue cost on the firm to install power steering before it can refuse to hire the female for the position. This duty of reasonable accommodation is of pivotal importance because it invites human rights tribunals to make substantive determinations at the very core of traditional managerial prerogatives. So far, tribunals have applied the duty relatively cautiously, recognizing (implicitly if not always explicitly) that the employer, not the human rights tribunal, has the superior expertise to make sensitive business decisions and must take ultimate responsibility for economic failure. The duty of reasonable accommodation is tantamount to a duty of substantive fairness, essentially encapsulating the notion of striking a balance of proportionality between the interests of the employee and the employer. Potentially, the recognition of this principle in the human rights context is already spreading into other areas of employment law. After all, it can be argued that if it is a fundamental human right to require employers to reasonably accommodate protected groups, the same treatment should be expected by non-protected employees. The duty of reasonable accommodation, therefore, could open a veritable Pandora's box of legal claims. In 1997, the Supreme Court of Canada refused to imply an independent duty of fairness on employers under the employment contract,[2] but one must question how long this position can hold under the pressure of the duty of reasonable accommodation. Subsequent to that ruling, many

---

2   *Wallace*, *ibid.*, examined in Chapter 5, Sections A and B(3)(c)(vi), as well as Chapter 9, Section F(1)(c).

courts have relied on an implied obligation to treat the employee fairly in order to ground constructive dismissal. Unquestionably, the main components of the human rights legislation—the duty of reasonable accommodation, the concepts of indirect discrimination and affirmative action, and other make whole remedies—are unprecedented in Canadian employment law in the scope and depth of their penetration into managerial prerogatives.

However, the human rights legislation, no less than the other floor of rights statutes, will almost certainly come under close scrutiny in regard to its impact on employers' profitability under increasing foreign competition. Any attempt to reduce the current legislated protections, however, will face scrutiny under the *Charter*, and in several important decisions; the *Charter* has already been used to strike down statutory provisions. The uncertainty of employers' legal obligations under human rights statutes is of particular concern in this regard, for concepts, such as indirect discrimination and reasonable accommodation, must necessarily be flexible; uncertainty, of course, represents a cost to employers in and of itself. There is a risk of social instability if society's expectations for greater recognition of rights cannot be matched by the economic performance of Canadian firms. However, not to take decisive measures now to integrate Canada's growing numbers of immigrant and other minority groups may also invite social disruption in the future. Furthermore, there is clearly an urgent need to speed up the enforcement of human rights complaints; nobody wins by atrocious delays, save the human rights bureaucrats who are shielded against possible redundancy by a full caseload.

In Chapter 8, we examined the difficulties that can arise where the same incident—say, a dismissal—entitles the employee to launch a complaint in several forums, such as a common law action for wrongful dismissal; a complaint under the human rights act for a racially- or gender-inspired dismissal; and a claim under the employment standards act for statutory pay in lieu of notice. If the employee launches a suit and obtains a decision in one forum, that decision may bind the decision-maker in the alternate forums by virtue of the doctrine of issue estoppel. Accordingly, the employee is well advised to commence his or action in the forum that is most favourable in terms of cost, speed, and available remedies. Eventually, the current patchwork quilt of overlapping forums may be simplified by having a single labour court with jurisdiction over *all* facets of employment law, but as yet no Canadian jurisdiction has this.

Last, but by no means least, we examined termination of employment in Chapter 9. This is the focal point of most of the other topics examined in the book, since employees generally will only sue their employer for benefits under the employment contract—or, for that matter, under the employment standards legislation—once it is clear that the employment relationship has terminated. Thus, questions over the existence of an employment relationship, the employee's entitlements under the contract of employment, the scope of the employee's express and implied obligations to the employer, and the employer's right to modify the terms of the contract and the application of doctrines, such as unconscionability, misrepresentation, and illegality, are frequently litigated in the context of wrongful dismissal. We saw that the dominant trend since the Second World War has been to extend protections to employees under employment standards statutes. Thus, all provinces' employment standards acts contain relatively generous minimum notice periods (or pay in lieu thereof) for workers who are dismissed for economic reasons. The period normally increases with the worker's seniority with his or her employer. Many provinces provide for additional notice periods and require employers to form labour readjustment committees with their employees in "mass" termination situations involving the simultaneous layoff of large numbers of employees. Furthermore, three jurisdictions—Quebec, Nova Scotia, and the federal jurisdiction—have enacted a right to neutral adjudication where an employee contests dismissal for misconduct or incompetence on the basis that it was not for just cause. Significantly, these schemes provide for compulsory reinstatement and the issuance of make whole remedies.

The common law, too, has been marked by a consistent expansion of the employee's protections in termination situations during this period. Thus, in economic dismissals the courts have gradually lengthened the period of reasonable notice to an unofficial upper limit of two years in most provinces, with the primary purpose of providing those employees who are likely to encounter difficulty in finding replacement work with a financial cushion to weather the storm of unemployment. Indeed, the determination of reasonable notice is a veritable catch-all for judicial policy-making, with the courts lengthening or shortening the notice period to reflect a wide variety of factors that the particular judge considers to be "fair." In particular, the courts have extended the reasonable notice period where the employer dismisses an employee in a bad-faith or otherwise unprofessional manner. In the area of dismissal for misconduct or incompetence, the courts have fashioned standards of just cause that closely approximate (with few exceptions) those fashioned by collective agreement arbitrators for unionized employees. Thus, the requirements of substantive proportionality between the offence and the penalty of dismissal, procedural fairness, and rehabilitative discipline feature prominently in the common law standards of just cause. Of course, the remedy of reinstatement remains unavailable at common law, unlike in arbitration, and the common law measure of damages is much more restrictive than the make whole approach applied by statutory adjudicators and human rights tribunals. The major limitation of the common law safeguards, however, is that the costs of financing civil litigation place this option beyond the reach of most low- to middle-level employees. For the latter groups, the employment standards acts remain their sole realistic source of employment protections.

Nevertheless, the above-mentioned protections will probably attract close scrutiny as employers strive to reduce their termination costs in the face of intensifying foreign competition. Indeed, this has already occurred at common law, where some judges have expressed concern with what they consider to be unduly long reasonable notice periods and have used various legal techniques to shorten them. As yet, they represent a minority approach, but this could change in the future. Unfortunately, there is almost no empirical research in Canada on the economic costs and benefits of the courts' practices with regard to determining reasonable notice. Nor, for that matter, is there much empirical evidence of the costs and benefits of the statutory minimum notice periods, the mass termination provisions, or the standards of just cause in Canada. Yet it is critical to know at what point, if any, the costs of complying with the legal safeguards of laying off and dismissing workers will have adverse economic effects, such as discouraging new hiring, encouraging employers to retain inefficient workers, and discouraging investment in Canada. It may well be that generous legal protections could increase efficiency—for example, by increasing worker job satisfaction and lubricating labour mobility—but more empirical work is necessary to test these possibilities.

It is an exciting time to study employment law. The law is clearly at a crossroads. The forces of the new economy are challenging the dominant paradigm since the Second World War, which has favoured the continuous expansion of employee rights. Today, it is clear that the courts and legislators must be concerned with ensuring that the level of employee rights is consistent with what Canadian employers can reasonably afford. Finding the appropriate point of balance promises to be most interesting.

TABLE OF CASES

INDEX

ABOUT THE AUTHOR

Geoffrey England is a Professor of Labour Law and Industrial Relations at the Edwards School of Business, and an Adjunct Professor at the College of Law at the University of Saskatchewan. He has an LL.B. from the London School of Economics; an LL.M. from Dalhousie University; and an M.A. in Industrial Relations from Warwick University. He taught previously at the law schools at Calgary, Queen's, and Cardiff. He also acts as an Appeals Adjudicator under the Saskatchewan *Labour Standards Act* and as a collective agreement arbitrator.